THE PIANO BOOK

Buying & Owning a New or Used Piano

Fourth Edition

Larry Fine

Illustrated by Douglas R. Gilbert

Foreword by Keith Jarrett

BROOKSIDE PRESS • BOSTON, MASSACHUSETTS

Brookside Press
P.O. Box 178, Jamaica Plain, Massachusetts 02130
(617) 522-7182
(800) 545-2022
(425) 795-2692 FAX
info@pianobook.com
www.pianobook.com

Distributed to the book trade by:
Independent Publishers Group, 814 N. Franklin St., Chicago,
Illinois 60610
(800) 888-4741
(312) 337-0747
(312) 337-5985 fax
frontdesk@ipgbook.com

In Europe, order from:
Pianos Online, Diamond Villa, 69 Highclere Road,
Knaphill, Woking, Surrey GU21 2PJ, United Kingdom
+44 (0)1483 475 750
+44 (0)1483 856 907 fax
info@pianosonline.co.uk

First printing, January 2001

See also the *Annual Supplement to The Piano Book.*

Printed in the United States of America

Cover design by Laurie Dolphin
Typesetting by Gallagher, Hopkinton, Massachusetts

Library of Congress Catalog Card Number 00-136088

ISBN 1-929145-02-0 (cloth)
ISBN 1-929145-01-2 (paper)

To three whose generosity and devotion
during my youth enriched my musical life:

Beatrice Fine, my mother
Lucille (Boyd) Spreen, my piano teacher
Anna Lenti, my friend

Contents

Foreword

Pianos are complicated instruments. Some have deep, dark secrets, some have sunny dispositions, some have no secrets at all. There are pianos with a grey, metallic "European" sound; some with a stringier but brilliant "American" sound; some with a laser-sharp, "straight" "Japanese" sound. There are pianos with a wealth of overtones, and some with very few; some thick-sounding instruments, some thin and weak but interesting. But if a dozen people were asked to draw pianos, they would almost all look the same.

There have been some extraordinary shapes of pianos in the past (square, left-handed, "giraffe"), but the important thing about a piano is what's inside the case. If we drew a portrait of a piano, we would have to deal with its moods, not just its clothes. So, obviously, the piano is not its case. But is this really so obvious? Certainly not to the people (too numerous to conceal themselves) who have their piano in a sunburnt area of their house with the top perpetually open (in case unexpected guests arrive? or so they can feel "artistic"?). To them a piano has to look the part, not demand proper treatment. These people don't need a piano, they just need something that looks like one.

I grew up with pianos; I've literally spent my life with them. I don't remember ever thinking, "Oh, this is a neat-looking piano. I bet it's really good." If I played it and it told me something, it was an interesting instrument. If I played it and it said little (although it might be noisy), I hoped I would never have to meet it under more crucial circumstances. In fact (and this is fortunate) there is no perfect piano. How good a piano is depends on what its use is to be. It could be the "perfect" piano for playing Debussy and a disaster for Stravinsky. But I think the best pianos can handle both with great success. Out of the hundreds or thousands of instruments I've played, I can recall perhaps five or six that could play almost any music equally well under a large variety of circumstances (different halls, for example).

I personally feel the piano to be far in advance of any of the more recent keyboard instruments in that it still demands that you use your whole body and all your muscles, whereas everything since has been denying that need. Artificially adding piano-like touch control to a synthesizer is about as much of an improvement as electrifying a pepper mill. So what?

The piano was a historic achievement in that it both incorporated the true innovations before it and answered the artists' need to be more involved, *not* to get more done with less effort. The "artistic need" that has generated instruments since the piano, on the other hand, is the need to find something that could be successfully played at Yankee Stadium or played by typists on a lunch break. One is a media need (although "need" isn't the right word); the other is the desire to be creative in one's "spare time." To me, leisure and creativity are as far apart as the *Reader's Digest* and the *Well-Tempered Clavier*.

Piano music is a kind of medium between our "progressive" age and the feelings that existed before this age. The piano may be relatively sophisticated, but it is by no means always civilized. In my opinion, a good piano can produce more variations in tone color than any other acoustic keyboard instrument, and more than *any* keyboard instrument can without flipping a switch or turning a knob.

When I consider, now, what I know about pianos, it's still not very much, but probably much more than most professional pianists. Since most pianists don't carry their instrument with them, they tend to let piano technicians take care of the instruments they encounter. By contrast, a clarinet player doesn't have a clarinet tuner backstage in case something goes wrong. After a while, ignorance becomes apathy. So pianos begin to get the reputation of being these amazingly stable pieces of furniture with strings and some mysterious workings inside that just last and last and are good investments and are always ready just in case some talented friend comes over to tickle the ivories.

It's all a bit more serious (and quite a bit more intriguing) than that. Pianos respond to care with amazing lifelikeness. I used to have to have my piano tuned several times a month if I was working on something, but after I decided to control the humidity and temperature year-round, magically, the piano didn't really need tuning more than twice or three times a year. In contrast, I played a beautiful German Steinway in San Francisco, and after it spent a few months as a rental in Jamaica, it came back a disaster. Oh, it *looked* the same, but when my technician asked me to play it and tell him what I thought, I not only didn't recognize anything about its sound, but immediately knew it was a terrible instrument. Only a few months before, it had been one of the pianos I might have purchased at almost any price. So pianos can die as suddenly as humans.

Speaking of technicians, there is a commonly held belief that, just as all pianos are shaped the same and go "bong . . . bong," all technicians are the same. Please do not make this mistake! Find the one good local technician you *might* have in your area, and if there isn't one, don't be afraid to spend a little more to get one from farther away. I once had a "legendary" technician (the few legendary technicians I've met should have stayed legends) come out to find a mysterious little buzzing noise in the second D above middle C. He came out month after month looking for that little devil. He even brought a second legend with him and they crawled around on the floor, inspected the windows for rattles, voiced (tone-regulated) and re-voiced the instrument until I'm sure it felt eighty years old in some places; but they did not remove the buzz. About six months later, I decided to ask my traveling technician to come down from Boston and check out this sound. He came, had dinner, went upstairs, and it took him about three minutes to adjust the string around its pin and eliminate the buzz . . . forever!

A young technician who used to work for me was very excited to be hired to tune the piano at a music festival in the Northeast. Just before a favorite pianist of his was to go on stage, the technician walked on to check the piano, which, he knew, was badly in need of tuning. The pianist asked him what he was doing, and the technician explained that he heard how badly the piano was holding pitch and that he was going out to tune it. But the pianist said, "No, it's okay. It doesn't matter." I think perhaps one could take this attitude to its logical conclusion by saying that, then, the music doesn't matter either.

I have been in countless situations where I've asserted myself regarding the poor condition of an instrument and it's been considered bad mannered. "But, Monsieur Jarrett, Mr. _____ and Mr. _____ played on this piano only a matter of months ago." (Months! A piano doesn't need more than a matter of days to be destroyed.) Or: "Mr. Jarrett, so-and-so played on this piano last week and he didn't complain." Or: "Oh, Mr. Jarrett, everyone complains about this piano. . . . I don't know what to do." "Have it voiced," I said to one club owner. "Really. What is voicing?" "Something not enough pianists know anything about." (The club owner said okay, not a word he used often.) In fact, numerous pianists had been playing on his instrument and complaining, but offering no insight as to whether there was anything that could be done. "These artists, they're so moody and temperamental." Well, pianos can get that way too, and we have to work together.

Actually, I have gotten a reputation for being a prima donna or a perfectionist based on only one thing: I know what I need to make the music I will be making. If I don't know this, only the music can suffer. If the music suffers, then what am I doing here halfway around the world from home? Jet lag doesn't help either, so why have more things wrong than just the unpredictable?

I could tell a lot more stories about my piano experiences, but what I'm getting at is this: We are not well enough informed about the nature of the piano to either know what we are missing or appreciate what we have. We can complain or we can hope for a chance love affair, but if we don't *know* something about our own instrument, our limits are the limits of our luck.

This certainly applies to purchasing a piano as well, and Larry Fine's book will make it harder to ignore many things about the piano that can either contribute to a successful purchase or lead to a rip-off. Don't think someone else will make the right choice for you. Not even pianists can choose pianos for other pianists. Attempts to do so have failed many times. Of course, if you end up after all this with an instrument you love or an instrument that satisfactorily fills your needs, you may not have to ever go piano shopping again. Pianos can easily outlive people.

As good as this book is, it has its limits. It cannot tell you how to hear or what sound to like (though it can tell you some things to listen for). It can't be responsible for the care of your instrument (but it provides lots of pointers). And it can't help you at all if you want a piano just to put a silk throw over it and some antique vases on it. But you already know that, or you probably would have spent your money on *The Silk-Throw Book* instead. (I wouldn't be surprised if that book has a chapter about just which pianos look better under the silk!)

So we're back in the solarium with a sunburnt, cracking finish on the wood (although this part faces the wall and the heat ducts, of course but *not* incoming guests), a soundboard that, every sunny morning, knows the real meaning of stress, not to mention a cast-iron frame that could fry an egg once a day. I have absolutely no tolerance for humans behaving in this way toward pianos because, as I said before, I've lived with pianos all my life and have learned to respect their needs. To me, they are often much more alive than the people I see every day.

However, for those of you who are truly interested in buying a piano to make music on it (or in learning about the piano you already have), *The Piano Book* is the most comprehensive and helpful guide to the mysteries of the piano, and how to buy one, yet published. It ought to be on your bookshelf.

KEITH JARRETT

Preface

For well over a century, the piano has been a mainstay of home entertainment, and of Western musical culture in general. It has been estimated that there are at least ten million pianos in the United States; each year about 100 thousand new ones are sold and, in addition, hundreds of thousands of older ones change hands. More than twenty million people in this country play the piano. Yet despite the piano's popularity, most people—piano owners included—know virtually nothing about how a piano works or how to go about buying one, and countless numbers of people continue to make blunders in purchasing a piano that only the most naïve would make in buying a car or appliance.

Why is this? To at least some degree, the fault lies in the nearly complete absence of consumer information about the piano. The crying need for such information becomes immediately obvious to almost anyone who attempts to buy a piano. The large variety of brands, models, and styles, strange terminology, competing claims by manufacturers and dealers, the relatively small number of piano experts and technicians, and the lack of criteria by which to evaluate pianos—all these factors and more make purchasing a piano like navigating through a foreign land without a map. This fact faces me almost daily as I field telephone calls from anxious customers begging for a few scraps of information to guide them in a bewildering endeavor.

But if all I intended to do was to tell you which brands are worth buying or how to find a used piano, a book of this size and scope would hardly be necessary. Indeed, I have two other motives for writing. One of the by-products of the scarcity of consumer information is a climate in which shoddy merchandise, unethical selling practices, and poor service can flourish. I'm sure that the vast majority of piano dealers, salespeople, and manufacturing personnel are honest people doing their best to make an honest living. Very few, if any, are consciously trying to defraud the public, and those few who from time to time do are pretty quickly put out of business. But as in any competitive business where the difference between competing products and services is often subtle or nonexistent, or even where the difference is large but

the public is uninformed, small acts of dishonesty gradually creep into the business in the form of distorted or outright false technical claims, phony sales, and less-than-satisfactory service. Because these practices evolve slowly and are so widespread, they are passed off as "business as usual," rather than the deception and disservice that they really are. The same phenomenon occurs in countless other fields of business, and I'm sure that the piano industry is no worse than any other. Ironically, when a person in one industry encounters these tactics in another industry, he or she complains loudly (for example when a piano dealer buys a car), without ever noticing the similarity—such is the capacity of the human mind to ignore what it doesn't want to see. Throughout this book I give examples of such products and behavior, which I can assure you are not just isolated or bizarre occurrences.

But, as I said, business people do not usually mean to be deceptive. Most businesses are simply doing what they perceive to be necessary for their survival in a highly competitive environment. Though I won't deny that each person in business must take ethical responsibility for the way he or she responds to business pressures, in truth, most businesses offer just about what the consuming public wants, which are usually the products advertised as having the most "features" and sold at the biggest "discount." To ask them to do otherwise would be to ask them to go out of business! All the moralizing in the world will not improve products and services as much as will changing consumers' desires and demands through education. This book is a modest attempt at such education.

My other motive for writing is simply to share with you my 35-year love for this incredible instrument. The piano is, I believe, unique in our culture in the way it weaves music, craft, history, business, science, and engineering—both low-tech and high-tech—into a remarkable tale worth telling. One very practical way to tell this tale is through a consumer guide such as this.

There has been no better time in the past twenty-five years to buy a piano than the present. The large influx of foreign imports and the growth of computerized manufacturing technologies have caused the prices of new pianos to plummet and the quality to rise. Also, the renewed interest in piano technology as a profession over the past fifteen years means that many competent piano technicians stand ready to sell you a used or restored instrument and to service it in the years ahead. I offer this volume with the hope that it will inspire you to take advantage of this opportunity to invest in a good piano and—whatever piano you buy—to appreciate what went into making it.

I would like to give special thanks to:

Kathleen Cushman, editorial and publishing consultant, of Harvard, Massachusetts, for so generously contributing her time, skills, and resources to this project, and whose enthusiasm, encouragement, and assistance were chiefly responsible for publication of *The Piano Book*;

Doug Gilbert, illustrator, whose quick grasp of the subject and insightful questions taught me to look at the piano in new ways, and whose friendship, support, and skillful, dependable work were indispensable parts of this project;

Linda Ziedrich, for meticulous copyediting and expert book design that made an otherwise complicated book easy and enjoyable to read and use;

Keith Jarrett, for writing the Foreword;

Fifty piano technicians who must remain anonymous, for examining pianos and making themselves available for consultation, and many piano dealers and manufacturers, for providing information and assistance;

My family and friends, for their patience and support during the long period of time in which this book was written and produced;

The staff of *Keyboard Magazine*, for giving me the opportunity to write a monthly column, in which parts of Chapters 3 and 7 first appeared in slightly different form, and to William McDonald, some of whose illustrations for those columns have been adapted for use in this book;

The following music industry publications, which were especially useful to me in my research: *The Music Trades*, *The Purchaser's Guide to the Music Industries*, *Musical Merchandise Review*, *Piano Technicians Journal*, and Ancott Associates' *Music Product Directory*.

Thanks also to the following people who read portions of the manuscript, offered constructive criticism and suggestions, and in other ways made significant contributions to this book: Donald Bancroft, Alan Bern, Del Fandrich, Alan Frank, Harriet Goldberg, Frank Hanson, Sally Jameson, Donald Jaynes, Roy Kehl, Jack Krefting, Robert Lane, Richard Lehnert, Robert Loomis, Christine Lovgren, Joseph Meehan, Robert Meyers, Robert Moog, Paul Murphy, Joseph Pagano, Anthony and Joseph Paratore, Arthur Reblitz, Robert Sparling, Walter Terzano, John von Rohr. It should not be assumed, however, that each of these people necessarily agrees with everything written herein; I, alone, am responsible for any errors.

PREFACE TO THE FOURTH EDITION

This revision of *The Piano Book* is more extensive than previous ones, and this edition is twenty-five percent longer than the last. Some of the highlights are:

• Updated reviews of new pianos based on a survey of more than fifty technicians who examined over thirteen hundred pianos made during the last five years and a database of the service records for more than four thousand additional new pianos. Stephen H. Brady, editor of the *Piano Technicians Journal*, assisted with the research and writing.
• Extensive rewriting of the section on shopping for a new piano, addressing such topics as the piano as an investment, questions of value for the money and long-term value, dealing with trade-ins, price vs. service, and shopping on the internet. Changes have also been made to reflect the latest tactics of both salespeople and customers in the battle for the best deal.
• An expanded rating system for new pianos to more closely reflect the subtle ways in which pianos differ in quality.
• Many changes to the technical information on how pianos differ in quality and the sales pitches used to exploit those differences.
• More extensive coverage of electronic player piano systems.
• Changes to the chapter on buying a used piano, addressing the question of how long pianos last, the controversy surrounding so-called "gray market" Japanese pianos, and shopping on the internet.

• A grand piano rebuilding checklist to help you plan the rebuilding of your piano or when considering the purchase of a rebuilt instrument.
• A checklist for examining a used piano prior to purchase.
• An expanded depreciation schedule for used pianos.
• A revised table of market values of used and rebuilt pianos.
• A discussion of some of the issues that may come up in relation to rebuilt pianos, particularly Steinways and Mason & Hamlins.
• A revision of Roy Kehl's celebrated list of old Steinway models, based on his ongoing historical research.

• A new list of Steinway serial numbers and dates, different from the list provided by the company.
• Information on room acoustics.
• Additional resources of interest to pianophiles, including mail-order sources for piano accessories.
• Many other small changes throughout the book to keep it current and useful, and in response to readers' comments over the years.

I enjoy hearing from readers about their experiences with pianos and piano buying. Please visit my web site at **www.pianobook.com**.

HOW TO USE THIS BOOK

Readers will undoubtedly come to this book from many different backgrounds and with many different questions. Some will have had considerable experience with pianos; others will be buying their first piano just so that their child can begin taking lessons. Some will want to buy a new piano, some a used piano, and still others won't be sure. Some will have only a few hundred dollars to spend; for others, money will be no object. In designing this book, I've done my best to make sure that these interests are addressed to some extent. But not all interests can be equally well served in the same volume. If your interest is in buying the least expensive instrument possible, exclusive of all other considerations, you probably don't need this book. Just look at the piano ads in the Sunday paper. Conversely, if your needs and resources are such that only the finest concert grands will do, you may find this book interesting, but of little practical help, as you are traveling in the rarefied air where the differences between pianos are more a matter of personal taste than quality, and by now you probably know your taste quite well. It is to the broad middle range of buyers—those who are interested in both quality and price, are relatively inexperienced with pianos, and are curious about them—that this book is largely directed.

It's tempting, when writing a consumer book on a technical subject, to aim it at the lowest technical level possible so it can be understood by everyone. I've avoided doing this, partly because it would render this project terribly boring and unsatisfying for me, and partly because the piano is an unavoidably complex instrument, and to pretend that it's not is to rob it of a great deal of its beauty and mystery. Nevertheless, like many complicated pieces of machinery the piano can be broken down into some rather simple

parts and concepts, and in describing these things, I've assumed no previous piano-related knowledge or technical expertise on the part of the reader. For those readers who have an aversion to anything more technical than a pencil, there is also plenty of completely nontechnical material here from which you can glean a great deal of useful information.

The following summary will help you locate the kind of information and level of complexity you seek. Chapter 1, "How the Piano Works," describes the piano's workings in the simplest possible terms. It also names and illustrates the most important parts. Everyone should read at least the first part of this chapter.

Chapter 2, "Buying a Piano: An Orientation," is a completely nontechnical introduction to the subject of buying a new or used piano. Every potential buyer should read this whole chapter.

Chapter 3, "Buying a New Piano," begins and ends with nontechnical information on the piano market and how to shop for a new piano. The large center section of this chapter consists of a mildly technical discussion of how pianos differ from one another in quality and features. It includes many "Buying Tips" —what to look or listen for or ask about. This section will also be useful in evaluating the quality and features of a used piano, especially one that is relatively young, to the degree that they have not yet been obscured by age and wear.

Chapter 4, "A Consumer Guide to New and Recently Made Pianos," is a reference section that lists and, where possible, describes and evaluates most brands of piano made or sold in the United States during the last twenty years. Be sure and read first the nontechnical "Overview" beginning on page 87— it will help you decide which brands to look up. A summary of brands and ratings begins on page 80.

Chapter 5, "Buying a Used Piano," begins and ends with nontechnical information on how to find a used piano and how much you can expect to pay for it. The middle of the chapter is mildly technical; it gives instructions on how to take off the outer cabinet parts to look inside and how to tentatively evaluate the piano's condition—how it has been affected by age and wear—pending a final inspection by a piano tech-nician before purchase. This chapter also contains a brief history of the piano. An addendum to this chapter gives special information that may be useful to those considering the purchase of a used Steinway or Mason & Hamlin.

Chapter 6, "Moving and Storage," and Chapter 7, "A Beginner's Guide to Piano Care," are mostly non-technical.

CHAPTER ONE

How the Piano Works

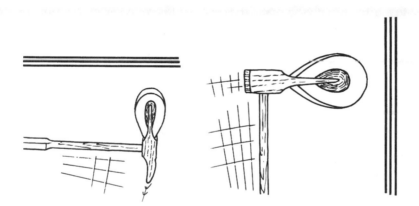

FIGURE 1-1.

Stripped down to its barest essentials, a piano consists of taut metal wires, called **strings,** that vibrate when struck by felt-covered wooden mallets, called **hammers.** A **grand** piano is one whose strings are stretched horizontally, parallel to the floor. A **vertical** piano, not surprisingly, is one whose strings are stretched on a vertical plane, perpendicular to the floor. The construction of a vertical piano is described below, in Figures 1-2 through 1-9. Note that the parts are presented in the order in which they are most easily understood, not necessarily the order in which the piano is constructed.

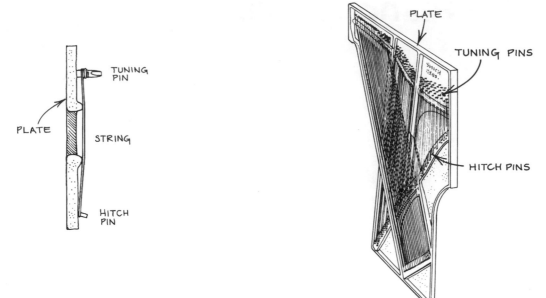

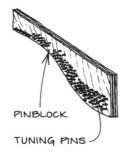

FIGURE 1-2.

The more than two hundred strings in a piano are stretched across a cast-iron frame called the **plate**. One end of each string is attached to a **hitch pin** on the plate; the other end is coiled around a **tuning pin**. Turning the tuning pin adjusts the tension at which the string is stretched.

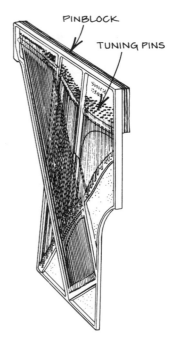

FIGURE 1-3.

The tuning pins pass through holes in the plate and are embedded in a laminated hardwood plank called the **pinblock**. The pinblock holds the tuning pins so as to prevent the stretched strings from unwinding, but the tuning pins can still be turned with a special wrench known as a "tuning hammer."

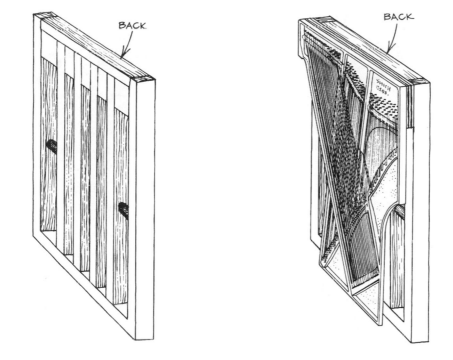

FIGURE 1-4.

The plate is bolted, and the pinblock glued and screwed, to a wooden structure called the **back**. The plate, pinblock, and back together form the structural framework of the vertical piano.

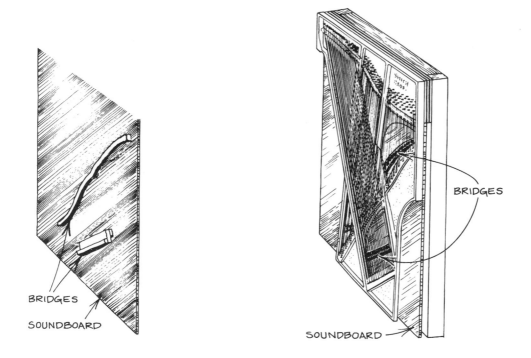

FIGURE 1-5.

The sound of piano strings vibrating is rather feeble, so the volume is increased by use of a **soundboard**, a large, thin wooden diaphragm glued around its perimeter to the piano back. Wooden **bridges**, against which the strings press, transfer the strings' vibrations to the soundboard. The soundboard increases the volume of sound because it moves more air than the strings could alone.

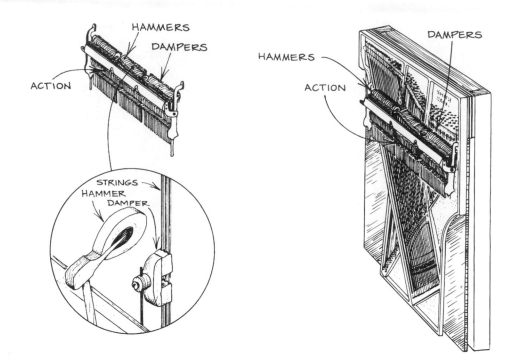

FIGURE 1-6.

The hammers, which strike the strings to make them vibrate, are part of a complicated contraption of levers and springs called the **action**. Another set of felt-covered action parts called **dampers**, located behind the hammers, stops the strings from vibrating.

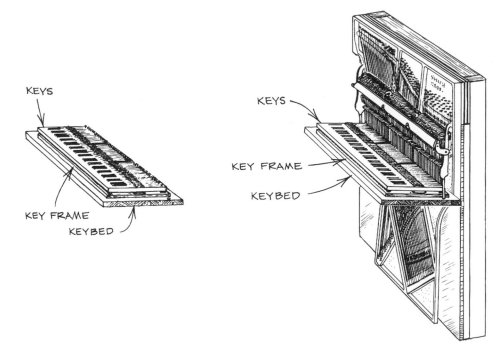

FIGURE 1-7.

The action parts are activated by eighty-eight wooden levers called **keys** (collectively known as the **keyboard**), covered with plastic, wood, or ivory at their playing end, which pivot like seesaws on a **key frame**. The keys, key frame, and action are supported by a structural member called the **keybed**.

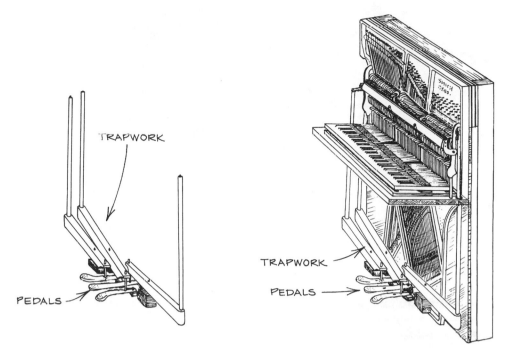

FIGURE 1-8.

The **pedals**, usually three of them, perform special operations like sustaining or softening the sound of the piano. They are connected to the action by a series of levers, dowels, and springs called the **trapwork**.

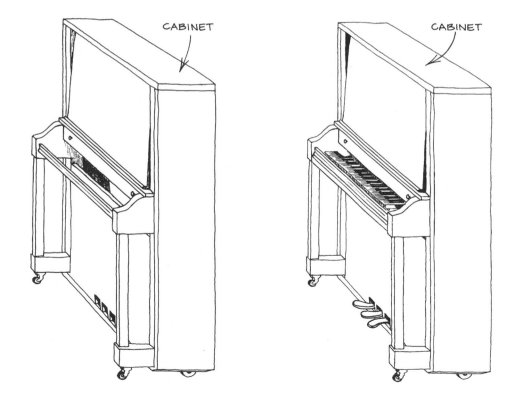

FIGURE 1-9.

The piano **cabinet** covers the internal parts, adds aesthetic beauty, and provides some additional structural support.

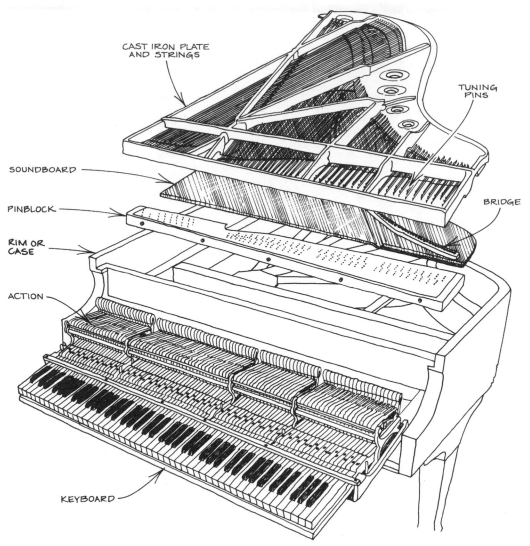

FIGURE 1-10. Exploded view of a grand piano. (Adapted from "The Coupled Motions of Piano Strings" by Gabriel Weinreich. Copyright © 1979 by Scientific American, Inc. All rights reserved.)

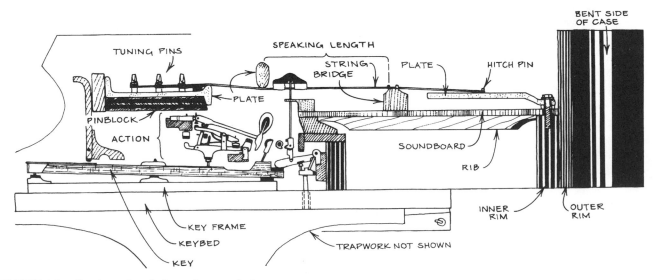

FIGURE 1-11. Cross-sectional view of a grand piano.

As shown in the exploded and cross-sectional views opposite, the grand piano resembles a vertical piano laid on its back and raised up on legs, except that the vertical's back is replaced by the grand's curved wooden **rim** or **case**, and the action, pedals, and trapwork are redesigned to accommodate the horizontal layout of the instrument. Otherwise, the basic principles of construction are similar.

Note, by the way, that only part of each string actually vibrates. This part, called the **speaking length**, is delineated by two *bearing points* that the string contacts. The "lower" bearing point is the point of first contact with the bridge; the "upper" bearing point is a portion of the plate, or hardware attached to the plate, that contacts the string near the tuning pins. ("Lower" and "upper" refer to the relative positions in a vertical piano; in a grand, "lower" translates as the end of the piano opposite the keyboard.) The portions of the string other than the speaking length—one near the hitch pin and the other near the tuning pins—are either muted with cloth or vibrate only sympathetically.

Here are a few other details to answer some questions that may have come to mind:

Q: What is meant by the terms *bass* and *treble*?

A: Bass refers to the lower-pitched notes, which are sounded by the keys toward the left end of the keyboard. *Treble* refers to the higher-pitched notes, sounded by the keys toward the right. Technically, the structure of the plate divides the strings into sections (Figure 1-12). The section that is arranged above and

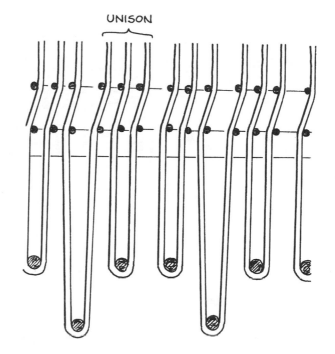

FIGURE 1-13. Loop stringing.

diagonally across the other sections is the bass. The remaining strings make up the treble, which may be further subdivided as shown in the drawing, or in other ways depending on the particular piano.

Q: If there are only eighty-eight keys, why are there more than two hundred strings?

A: With a few exceptions and variations, there are three strings for each treble note, two strings for each upper bass note, and one string for each lower bass note. This is because higher notes are made by thinner strings. If solitary, the thin treble strings would be overpowered by the thick bass strings. Each set of one, two, or three strings is called a *unison* because all the strings in a set must be tuned at exactly the same pitch (i.e., in unison) to sound as one note when struck by a hammer.

An interesting twist to this, however, is that in the treble section of most pianos, each length of wire serves as *two* strings, first passing over the bridge and around the hitch pin and then passing over the bridge again as a neighboring string, as shown in Figure 1-13. Because of the wire's tension, and its stiffness where it bends around the hitch pin, each string can retain its own pitch without affecting its neighbor. This scheme is known as *loop stringing*. Bass strings, and occasional odd treble strings, each have a hitch pin to themselves and serve as one string only.

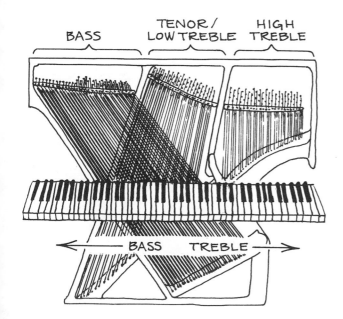

FIGURE 1-12. Bass and treble.

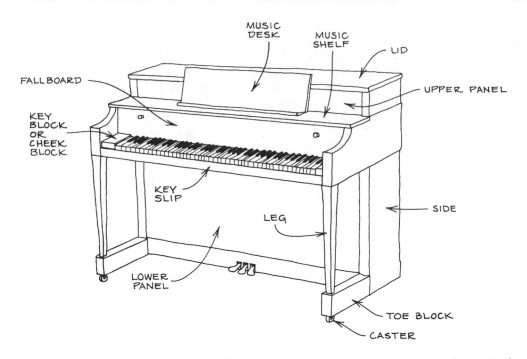

FIGURE 1-14. The cabinet parts of a vertical piano. Depending on the size and style, some parts may be omitted or may look slightly different.

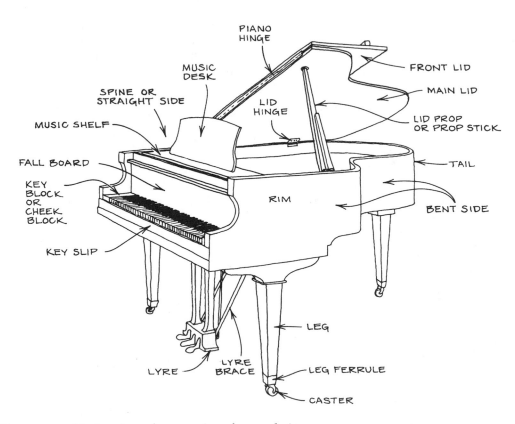

FIGURE 1-15. The case or cabinet parts, and accessories, of a grand piano.

THE ACTION

The piano action, with its five to ten thousand parts (depending on how you count them), is easily the most complicated part of the piano. An intimate knowledge of how it works is not really necessary in buying a piano, but certainly can't hurt, especially when trying to track down the reason why a note doesn't work on a used piano. Those readers who love Rube Goldberg–style mechanical contraptions will find a piano action absolutely captivating.

How the Action Works in a Vertical Piano

1. When the key is pressed down at the front, the back end rises and pushes up (sometimes via a **sticker**) on the escapement mechanism, consisting of the **wippen**, and hinged to it, the **jack**. The jack pushes against the hammer **butt**, causing it to pivot and move the hammer toward the string.

2. When the hammer is about halfway toward the string, the small metal **spoon** on the back of the wippen contacts the bottom of the **damper lever**, making the damper lever pivot and lift the damper off the string. This allows the string to vibrate freely when struck.

3. When the hammer is about 1/8 inch from the string, the "toe" of the jack (if you look at the jack as a boot) contacts the **letoff button**, causing the top of the jack to pivot out from under the hammer butt. This is called *escapement* or *letoff* (Figure 1-16 right). Without letoff, the hammer would jam against the string, causing parts to break and preventing the string from vibrating.

4. With the jack disengaged, the hammer goes the remaining small distance to the string on its own momentum, strikes the string, and rebounds. On rebound, the **catcher** on the hammer butt is caught by the **backcheck**.

5. When the key is released, everything begins to fall to its rest position. The spoon releases the damper lever, allowing the damper spring to push the damper back onto the string , stopping its vibration. The hammer **shank** returns to its rest position on the **hammer rail**. The coil spring under the toe of the jack causes the top of the jack to pivot back under the hammer butt, where it will be ready for the next stroke.

How the Action Works in a Grand Piano

1. When the key is pressed down at the front, the back end rises and pushes up on the escapement mechanism, consisting of the **wippen**, the **jack**, and the **repetition lever**. (Notice that the jack sticks up through a slot in the repetition lever.) The repetition lever and the jack jointly push up on the **knuckle** attached to the hammer **shank**, sending the hammer toward the string.

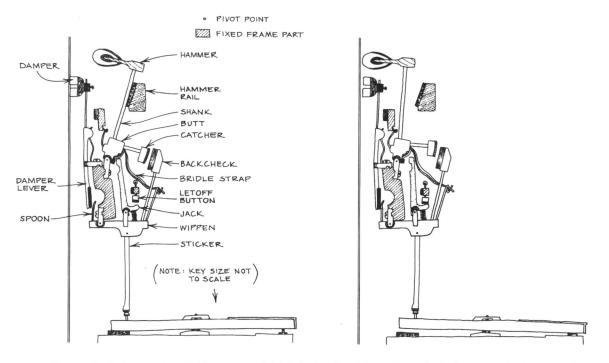

FIGURE 1-16. The vertical piano action (left) at rest and (right) after letoff (step 3), with the key near the bottom of its travel.

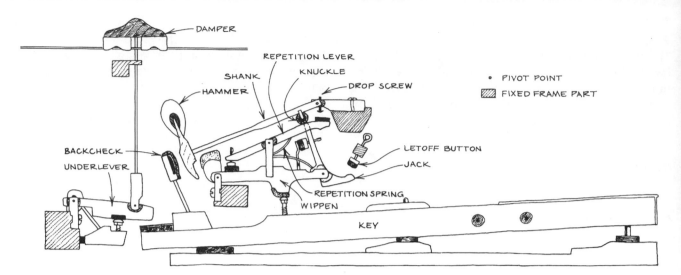

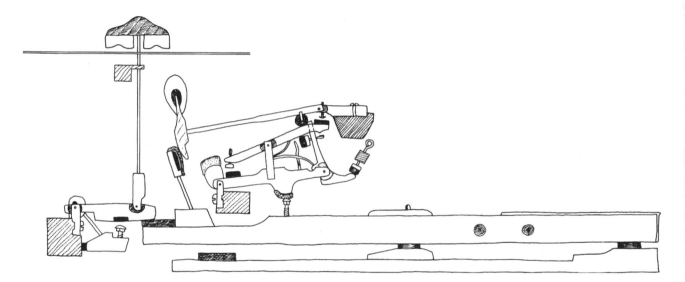

FIGURE 1-17. The grand piano action (top) at rest and (bottom) after the hammer has hit the string, rebounded, and been caught by the backcheck (step 4).

2. When the hammer is a third to half of the way toward the string, the back end of the key contacts the damper **underlever**, causing the damper to rise off the string. This allows the string to vibrate freely when struck.

3. When the hammer is about ⅛ inch from the string, the "toe" of the jack (if you look at the jack as a boot) contacts the **letoff button**, causing the top of the jack to pivot out from under the knuckle. Simultaneously, the end of the repetition lever contacts the **drop screw**, preventing the repetition lever from rising any further. These two actions constitute an event called *escapement* or *letoff*. Without letoff, the hammer

would jam against the string, causing parts to break and preventing the string from vibrating.

4. With both the jack and the repetition lever disengaged, the hammer goes the remaining small distance to the string on its own momentum, strikes the string, and rebounds. On the rebound, the hammer knuckle lands on the repetition lever, causing it to pivot and compress the **repetition spring**. At the same time, the tail of the hammer head is caught by the **backcheck**, which prevents the compressed repetition spring from pushing the hammer away (Figure 1-17 bottom).

5. When the key is released even a little bit, the backcheck releases the hammer tail just enough so that

the compressed repetition spring can now push the hammer (via the repetition lever and knuckle) toward the string again. The hammer doesn't actually strike the string a second time, however, because the drop screw is still limiting the upward movement of the repetition lever. But the upward movement of the hammer gives the jack, pulled by its spring, enough room to pivot back underneath the knuckle, ready for another stroke, even though the key has not yet returned to its rest position.

6. When the key is fully released, everything falls back to its rest position. The back end of the key releases the damper underlever, allowing the damper to drop back onto the string and stop its vibration. The hammer shank falls back to its rest position, just a little above the hammer rail or rest cushion.

The operation of the pedals in both grand and vertical pianos is described on page 53.

CHAPTER TWO

Buying A Piano: An Orientation

THE PURPOSE OF THIS CHAPTER IS TO PROVIDE a basic orientation toward the piano market for those people who have little or no experience in this field. We'll be considering some of the general factors that will influence your choice of a piano, and we'll be developing an attitude that will make shopping for a piano more enjoyable. This chapter gives only very general advice; more specific information on quality, price, warranty, condition, and so on, is presented in later chapters.

It's useful to have some knowledge of piano terminology and of how a piano works when looking to buy one. For this reason, I suggest that, if you haven't done so already, you should read through Chapter 1, "How The Piano Works."

INITIAL CONSIDERATIONS

There are a few basic points you need to consider before beginning that search for the right instrument. These considerations will assist you in determining your needs and in taking stock of what resources you have available to meet those needs.

Proficiency Level

If you (or whoever will be the primary user) are a beginner, you may not want to invest a lot of money in your first piano. But resist the temptation to pick up an old "klunker." It's difficult enough to learn to play

an instrument without having to deal with problems within the instrument itself, such as squeaks, rattles, and keys that stick or otherwise don't work properly. Children, especially, get discouraged easily by such annoyances and will be quick to comment on how different their piano at home is from their teacher's piano. In addition to sapping your motivation, this kind of piano may also sap your bank account with the necessity for extra tunings and frequent repairs. In my experience, in fact, some of the pianos that have been the most expensive in the long run were initially obtained for free or "just for the moving" because nobody would pay anything for them. Little did the recipients of these "gifts" know what they were in for! In general, it's a good idea to buy a piano of slightly higher quality than you think you deserve and then grow into it. If there are several pianists in the family, aim your purchase toward the most advanced. You'll be more motivated to learn because the piano will be more fun to play and also because you will have made more of an investment. Pianos tend to be excellent investments. If your attempts to learn to play don't work out, chances are good that you can sell the piano for close to what you paid for it, provided that you chose wisely to begin with and maintained it properly.

Space

A vertical piano is about 5 feet wide and about 2 to 2½ feet deep. Add to this about 2 more feet for the piano bench and room to sit at it. That makes a total of 5 feet wide by about 4¹/₂ feet deep that should be allowed for a vertical piano, not including any space on the sides that you may want to leave. *The height of a vertical piano makes no difference in the floor area needed.*

The width of a grand piano is also about 5 feet. The length will vary from 4¹/₂ to 9¹/₂ feet, depending on which you choose to buy (5 to 7 feet is best for most homes), and again, add 2 feet for pianist and bench. These dimensions indicate the least amount of floor space allowable. Grand pianos, especially, may need more space for aesthetic reasons; verticals can more easily be tucked into corners.

When planning the layout of your room, don't forget to take into account sources of heat and cold. Since they respond very readily to temperature and humidity changes and extremes, pianos should be placed well away from radiators, heating vents, direct sunlight, drafty windows and doors, woodstoves, fireplaces, and so on. Failure to heed this warning will, at the very least, make it difficult to keep the piano in tune. At worst, it could lead to premature structural damage to the instrument.

Money

Money is the biggest factor preventing people from getting the piano they want, and is the one about which potential buyers are the most naïve. Piano prices vary widely according to size, brand, condition, location, and so on, but very generally speaking, a used old upright in half decent shape purchased from a private owner might cost from $300 to $1,000, while a used grand in similar condition could run from $1,500 to $3,000. Used verticals of more recent origin, or older verticals that have had significant repairs, could be priced at $1,500 to $3,000, younger or better-quality grands from $3,000 to $8,000 (much more for a Steinway and certain other fine makes). New verticals of reasonably good quality begin at about $3,000, new grands at about $7,000 (and soar upward to astronomical figures). The days when a good old upright could be had just for moving it are largely gone. While it's true that people still do sometimes find spectacular bargains, it's also true that for every person who pays $200 for a Steinway grand, at least a dozen others pay $2,000 for a piece of junk.

I strongly suggest that if you can't afford to buy a reasonably good-quality piano now and can't arrange a loan or credit plan, then save up for the piano you want rather than temporarily settling for a poor one. A poor-quality piano will cost you more in the long run for maintenance and repairs and will rob you of your enthusiasm, as mentioned before. While you're saving,

see if you can arrange to use the piano at a friend's, a school, or a church, or rent a practice studio.

You might also consider renting a piano on a plan that permits you to apply some of the rental payments toward purchase later on. Renting has its drawbacks, however. Dealers tell me that with the pressure of ongoing monthly payments, parents tend to be too quick to cancel the rental contract and return the piano when their child temporarily loses interest in practicing, thus aborting, possibly forever, the child's musical experience. Also, when rental payments are to be applied toward purchase, you are less likely to get a good deal on the purchase price. Buying a good used piano is usually the smarter way to go and, unlike with renting, you are likely to be able to recoup your investment if the lessons don't work out.

Don't forget to set aside money for moving, tuning, and other maintenance. Generally a budget of about $200 to $500 a year will suffice for tuning and maintaining a piano in good condition in the home. Pianos in schools and other institutions may require two or three times this amount (though they rarely get it), depending on the extent of their use and abuse. If you buy a used piano, it may initially require a larger expenditure to bring it into normal operating condition before this budget can apply. *If you can't afford to maintain your piano, you really can't afford to buy one.*

Furniture

There's nothing wrong with wanting a good-quality instrument to look nice too, but if your major reason for buying a piano is for its value as furniture, let's be honest about it. There's definitely a portion of the piano industry that thrives on selling low-quality instruments inside of beautiful cases. You'll be an easy mark for them if your primary interest is in a piece of furniture. Of course, there are some legitimate questions to ask about the piano's cabinet; for instance, how solid is its construction? how durable is its finish? But some pianos that come in cute decorator styles score low on these points, so in those cases you may find it necessary to reconsider your priorities.

These four general considerations will lead naturally to three specific questions:

Should I Buy a Grand or a Vertical Piano?

The answer to this question will depend on the space and money you have available and on your playing requirements. The action of a grand piano generally allows for more reliable repetition of notes and for better, more subtle control of expression and tone than does a vertical action. Also, the horizontal construction of a grand allows the tone to develop in a more pleasing manner. In a vertical, the sound tends to bounce right back into the performer's face, or else remains boxed in. For these reasons, the grand is always the choice of concert artists. But for many other uses and levels of proficiency, a vertical piano may be more appropriate.

Space is an obvious consideration. A grand may need more space for aesthetic reasons than a mere measuring of the instrument would indicate.

Grands usually cost from three to six times as much as verticals of similar quality and condition. The imposing quality of a grand piano can bring prestige to your home, but be forewarned: To buy a cheap grand or one in poor condition just for prestige is to make a terrible investment. Your expectations will be higher, and therefore the piano's faults will be more noticeable. The results will be disappointing and expensive. If your playing truly requires a grand piano, save up and buy one of sufficient quality to be worth your while. If your playing doesn't justify a grand, or if you're not willing to spend the money for a good one, you'll probably be making a better investment, both musically and financially, if you buy a high-quality vertical piano.

What Size Piano Should I Buy?

Both grands and verticals come in a number of sizes. The height of a vertical piano is measured from the floor to the top of the piano. The length of a grand is measured from the very front of the keyboard end of the piano to the very back of the piano, with the lid closed (Figure 2-1).

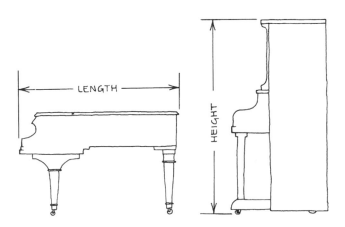

FIGURE 2-1. How a grand piano (left) and a vertical piano (right) are measured.

Vertical Pianos

Full-size or Professional Upright	47–60″
Studio	43–47″
Console	40–44″
Spinet	36–40″

Grand Pianos

Concert Grand	$7^1/_2$–$9^1/_2$′
Medium Grand	$5^1/_2$–$7^1/_2$′
Small (Baby) Grand	$4^1/_2$–$5^1/_2$′

The names and sizes listed above are quite general and there is some overlapping between them. Vertical piano types are defined not only by their height, as shown above, but also by the kinds of action they have (which tend to vary with the size). This is important—please read about different kinds of action in detail on page 44. Note that old pianos labeled "upright grand" or "cabinet grand" are really just uprights.

The size of a piano is probably the single most important factor influencing its tonal quality. The longer strings, particularly in the bass section of the larger sizes of grands and verticals, results in greater resonance of tone and in a harmonic content that is most pleasing to the listener. The smaller the piano, the worse the tonal quality, especially in the lower bass, and also in the tenor, just above the bass.

An additional factor, though, makes the question of size even more important: because the tonal quality of small pianos tends to be poor, the people who buy these pianos are usually more interested in the styling and looks of the case than in the quality of the instrument inside the case. Therefore, the manufacturers invest more of their money in the appearance of the instrument than in its quality. The result is that, quite apart from any effects of acoustical laws, smaller pianos are often more poorly built than larger ones.

If space and money were no obstacle, I would place the different types and sizes of piano in the following order of preference:

1. Concert Grand
2. Medium Grand
3. Full-size Upright
4. Studio   } Small Grand
5. Console
6. Spinet

The placement of a particular small grand in this list would depend on its size and quality. While most grands have longer strings than most verticals, some larger verticals may surpass some smaller grands in these respects and for this and other reasons may be better instruments.

Unless your ceilings are only four feet high, "lack of space" is not a valid reason for getting a small vertical, since the only difference in size between small and large verticals is their height, not the floor space they occupy.

Spinets have been placed at the bottom of the list, not only because of their small size and generally poor quality, but also because their action is inaccessible and hard to service. Please read page 45 for the many reasons to not buy a spinet.

If you can, buy a grand piano at least 6 feet long or a vertical at least 48 inches tall, but in no case should you buy a grand less than 5 feet or a vertical under 40 inches.

Should I Buy a New or a Used Piano?

Many people, when thinking of a "used" piano, conjure up images of a piano on its last legs, in terrible need of repair. This image is based in part on the incredibly large numbers of such pianos that actually exist. But "used" can also refer to several other classes of piano:

- The older piano that still has many years of life ahead;
- The piano that needs only minor repair to be in good shape;
- The piano that is only a couple of years old and practically like new that is being sold because the owner is moving or wants to buy a better instrument;
- The piano that has been reconditioned or rebuilt by a competent piano technician and is in excellent condition. Some pianos like this are actually better than new ones, carry a similar guarantee, and cost almost as much.

I find that people spend large sums of money on new pianos that are smaller or of lower quality than they would have liked, or that really don't suit their needs, because they aren't aware of the used-piano option. It's especially sad when someone buys one of those new, pitifully small grands when they could have spent no more on a used grand of decent size.

There are other good reasons to buy a used piano. Since the average life of a piano is around fifty years, and with proper restoration at least fifty more, recycling older pianos makes good ecological sense. Some used pianos have exquisite veneers, leg styles, carved cases, and ivory keys unavailable today on new pianos at reasonable prices. Many of the companies that produce new pianos today are huge conglomerates that turn out pianos by the thousands in far-away cities. How much more satisfying to contribute to your local small-scale economy by buying a used piano that has been restored to usefulness by local craftspeople.

Of course, there's a trade-off when buying a used piano—you may have to take more time and look harder to find what you want, you'll take a greater risk, and you may give up a warranty and some number of years of a piano's life in return for paying less money. This means that it's especially important to have a competent piano technician inspect the piano before you buy it. He or she can advise and teach you about pianos during your search, as well as inspect and maintain your piano after the search is over. There will be few others who will be able to help you, for while professional pianists and piano teachers may have opinions about the tone and touch of a piano, they usually know next to nothing about the technical aspects of their instrument.

LOOKING FOR A PIANO
(Or Zen and the Art of Piano Buying)

"Looking for a piano" is a process of developing a "piano awareness," and this begins by doing your homework—asking yourself some basic questions about your needs and resources and learning all you can about pianos before you start to look for one. The process continues as you shop for a piano and find out what's available, become more aware of the differences between pianos, and discover what it is that you like. It's been my experience that the attitude with which you approach the piano market may be just as important as any technical information or expertise you possess.

Two common pitfalls tend to trap prospective piano buyers. Those who have had some previous experience with pianos have often accumulated notions about them that may not be accurate—notions based on misconceptions, incomplete information, and isolated experiences with particular brands and models. "Brand X pianos are always too loud," they say, or "Grand pianos always have a hard touch," or "No used piano would ever look good in my living room." It's helpful to have some idea of what you want before starting to look, but unless your needs are very specific—say, you're a concert artist looking for a concert grand—it's best to remain as flexible and open as possible at the beginning of your search. Then if you discover that some of your original ideas were faulty, it will be easier to change your course of action.

Buyers with little or no experience with pianos, particularly people who tend to feel intimidated by mechanical devices, fall into the opposite category: they often feel swamped by the sea of options available to them, feel bewildered about how to begin looking, and resign themselves to getting less than they deserve. These people often settle for one of the first pianos to come along.

Know that it *is* possible to make a successful purchase without being a piano expert yourself. Actually, shopping for a piano is an important part of the process of learning about pianos. I would suggest that you begin your search by setting aside a certain amount of time (for instance, an hour or two a week for two months)—during which you forbid yourself to buy a piano—for examining the entire new and used piano markets. Bring along a trusted friend (preferably one who plays the piano, if you don't) and try out as many pianos as you can in the allotted time. Visit piano dealers and rebuilders; look in the want ads and make some inquiries; even try out pianos that aren't for sale, as in friends' homes or community buildings. Include in your sampling a few pianos you know you could never buy, such as a concert grand (or a spinet!). This approach will take the pressure off while you're developing piano awareness and discovering where your pianistic needs fit into the scheme of things. It will also be a lot of fun. Later, when you feel more confident, you can narrow your field with an intent to buy.

Trust your feelings about the pianos you meet—don't be intimidated by other people's opinions—but *analyze* your reactions. "I don't like the tone of this piano" is not a very useful statement. However, "The bass notes don't sound clear, and the treble is brilliant but lacks depth" gives you a basis for comparison with other pianos by turning a blanket judgment into a useful observation. The ability to analyze the tone, touch, and looks of a piano this way will come to you gradu-

ally as you meet more of them and learn to be specific about your feelings. Pianos that before had all seemed alike will then begin to assume personalities of their own, and you in turn will discover that you prefer some over others.

At some point you'll want to stop looking. Some people don't stop until they find a piano that is obviously the one they've been looking for, one that practically shouts "Take ME!" Others set a time limit, after which they make a choice from the pianos they've seen. Caution: Beware of the "buy of a lifetime"—the offer that can't be refused—when the major attraction is the price tag. Be sure you are completely satisfied with the instrument in *all* respects. After the money has been spent, the price will no longer be of interest to you and you'll have to live with what you bought.

How much time you spend looking for a piano will depend on your priorities, but be sure to allow enough time for things to happen in your life—for the feelers you've put out to produce some results—and for your piano awareness to develop. And again, when you find a piano you like, don't forget to have a professional piano technician inspect it before you buy it. The small fee you pay for this service (usually fifty to one hundred dollars)* may save you much grief later, for pianos can have expensive problems that are not obvious.

---

*When inspecting a piano, some technicians prefer to tune it as well, at an additional charge, because some piano problems that might not otherwise be apparent may show up during a tuning, and because it is impossible to accurately judge the tone of a piano unless it is in tune.

CHAPTER THREE
Buying a New Piano

IF YOU'VE EVER STOPPED BY A PIANO STORE with the thought of buying a new piano, you may well have been overwhelmed by the number of choices you would have to make to do so. It's not enough that there are a variety of brands, models, sizes, styles, and finishes to choose from. You also have to choose between particle-board and real wood case construction, laminated and solid spruce soundboard, and plastic and wood action parts, just to name a few. Then a perusal of the sales literature reveals such ponderous space-age terms as "Mezzo-Thermoneal Stabilizer," "Duraphonic Multi-Radial Soundboard™," and "Vacuum Shield Mold Process." About this time, you begin to wonder if it might not be simpler to take up the kazoo!

My purpose in this chapter is to guide you through this maze of choices and technical terms and to identify the real differences between brands and models, as opposed to those that are just advertising hype. This may aid you in your defense against high-pressure salespeople and misleading ad copy that make every piano, no matter how poor, sound like God's gift to humanity. Tips are also given on checking out a piano prior to purchase, negotiating the price, and other matters you should know about to conclude the deal successfully. Information in this chapter is of a general nature; specific brands are covered in Chapter 4.

MARKETING

When I first began to research the piano market, I was struck by the fact that some manufacturers produced several versions of the same size and type of piano. These versions differed in the sophistication of their cabinet styling, of course, and were priced hundreds of dollars apart. But the higher-priced models also contained different technical features which, I came to realize, were sometimes of minor importance and often involved little extra in production cost. What's more, the manufacturers were changing these technical features in a seemingly random manner every year or two.

For example, this year "Smith Bros." (a fictitious name) might produce an inexpensive console with blued tuning pins and "10-pound" hammers and a more expensive version with nickel-plated tuning pins and "12-pound" hammers—not much of a difference, I can assure you. Then next year might see the retirement of the bottom-of-the-line model and its replacement with a "deluxe" model which, in addition to the "better" hammers and tuning pins, has a solid spruce soundboard instead of a laminated one. Why (I thought naïvely), if the production cost is about the same, doesn't the manufacturer simply put all the best technical features into all the models and just build different cabinets around them? It wasn't long before I discovered the reason for this craziness: marketing.

Marketing is the process by which the need or desire for a product is measured and the manufactured product is advertised and sold. It includes everything except the actual design and manufacturing of the product. Marketing is a vital part of any business, for the best product in the world will come to naught if the buying public is unaware of its existence or does not sense a need for it. In the hands of some companies, though, marketing takes on a dimension of trickery.

In the world of pianos, this latter kind of marketing works something like this: A company produces (or the dealer stocks) a limited number of absolutely bottom-of-the-line pianos, verticals or grands, that it hopes few people will actually buy. Why? Because these pianos are to be used primarily as advertising bait to get you in the store. When you see an ad in the paper that says, "Sale—Pianos from $1,995," the $1,995 piano is the bait. The manufacturer and dealer make little profit on this piano, and the salesperson, if he or she actually sells the piano, will probably make little or no commission. Once you're in the store, therefore, the salesperson will do everything possible to try to get you to buy a more expensive piano, either of the same brand or of a different one. This tactic is called "bait and switch" and the stripped-down piano is known as a "leader" or "promotional model." Right now, Chinese pianos serve this purpose for many dealers. Said one dealer (as quoted in the trade magazine *The Music Trades*), "Being able to advertise an acoustic piano for under $2,000 brings people in the store. Most leave with a more expensive product, but the Chinese piano gives us a real lure."

In a typical scenario, Mr. Jones, the father of an eight-year-old girl who is about to start taking piano lessons, walks into our piano store and asks about the $1,995 wonder he has just seen advertised. Somewhat reluctantly, the salesperson guides him to it (it's probably in a dark corner at the back of the store), remarking that it hasn't been tuned since it arrived from the factory. Predictably, it sounds wretched.

"You know, Mr. Jones," says the salesperson, "for only a few more dollars a month, you could own our Deluxe Console, with its rust-resistant, nickel-plated tuning pins and its heavy-duty, reinforced, 12-pound hammers, and of course its more attractive custom styling." As our shopper fingers a few keys on the Deluxe Console, the salesperson, trying to sound sincere, asks, "Mr. Jones, have you ever considered a studio?" Without waiting for a response, the salesman continues his pitch: "Our Custom Studio features the more responsive full-size action, and with its diagonally-grained laminated spruce soundboard, guaranteed not to crack for sixty years, and its price hardly any higher than that of the Deluxe Console, it's a terrific bargain." And on and on this goes, each higher-priced model offering some wonderful new feature, until the bewildered father calls a halt when the prices being asked begin to exceed his budget.

Each of these technical characteristics is called a "step-up feature" and is designed to persuade you to buy a higher-priced piano. I'm not saying that these features don't have any technical value; some do and some don't. But often they aren't installed for their actual technical value, only for their perceived value. By organizing the piano market in this fashion (and incidentally, many other consumer goods markets operate similarly), a manufacturer is able to offer a piano with specific features and perceived advantages at each of many different price levels, *and thus to sell you something regardless of how much money you have to spend*. If the dealer didn't have a model whose price matched the amount of money in your pocket, he or she would have to suggest you buy a different brand of piano, or, worse yet, direct you to a competitor down the street.

Each of these price levels is called a "price point," and at each price point a manufacturer tries to provide a feature that no other manufacturer offers in a piano at the same price. ("Mr. Jones, did you know that this Deluxe Studio is the only studio at this price that offers a genuine, solid spruce soundboard?") To match changes made by the competitors, as well as to respond to other market factors, this game requires a periodic reshuffling of models, features, and styles, which accounts for the seemingly random changes in manufacturers' offerings.

Obviously, I've exaggerated this sales pitch to make a point. Although I *have* heard conversations like this, lest you be too concerned I should say that most salespeople have good manners and will give you the kind of personal service you deserve. But this brief example illustrates the way the piano market has traditionally been structured, and that structure determines to some extent what products you will find in the store and how they will be sold to you.

Actually, the use of this kind of marketing scheme has declined considerably since its heydey in the 1960s, '70s, and '80s, in part, I like to think, because of *The Piano Book*, first published in 1987. Most mid-priced brands today offer three or four grades of piano: promotional or entry-level, regular, premium, and sometimes a super-premium grade—the last usually made in a separate factory by an elite group of craftspeople. Some companies have relatively few models, with features that remain unchanged for many years at a stretch. A few companies build all their pianos to a single technical standard, varying them only in size and cabinet style. These firms are more interested in building a high-quality instrument than in trying to sell something to everybody. (Of course, they, too, have marketing departments eager to sell you on the features in their pianos.)

As you might expect, the quality-oriented companies are often small; many make a limited number of rather high-priced pianos using a great deal of human, rather than machine, labor. But this is by no means the whole story. Every piano manufacturer today uses a mixture of hand and machine labor, and the Japanese are known for turning out vast numbers of pianos in unbelievably automated factories while maintaining high levels of quality. The terms "hand-crafted" and "precision machine-made" are popular in piano advertising literature, but the truth is that both human labor and machines can be used for good or ill, depending on the philosophy and orientation of management and their relations with labor. Expensive machines can turn out sloppy parts by the thousands if designed only for speed and misused by their human operators. On the other hand, humans can do very careful work if well trained and well treated and if high standards are set, or they can turn out junk if treated like the machines just mentioned.

Another buzzword to be wary of is "tradition." This word is sometimes used in relation to the number of years a firm has been in business, a figure that might be thought to indicate a company's ability to produce good products. Rarely so in the piano world. Most companies that claim they date back to 1830 (or whenever) do so only through numerous sales, mergers, acquisitions, and changes in management and ownership, and have about as much relation to the original company as you and I do to Adam and Eve. In many cases, seeing the pianos now made in his name would make the old master roll over in his grave.

"Tradition" is also used with respect to materials and methods of manufacture. In some cases, the traditional methods and materials *are* better, or you may have an aesthetic or philosophical preference for them. Sometimes, though, the original reason for using a particular material or method has been forgotten, or a better one has become available. Yet some companies continue to follow the old way because their marketing departments are afraid the public won't accept a departure from tradition. This fear causes a certain amount of tension between the marketing and engineering ends of most companies; marketing, needless to say, almost always has the final say. So when companies resist the use of plastics, particle board, and other synthetics in piano manufacturing, it's often because they feel their image may be damaged by using these materials, rather than because the materials are inferior. You can bet that when the use of synthetics becomes widely accepted, the resisting companies will jump on the bandwagon and begin using the ones that have been proven superior.

Ironically, a marketing department sometimes boxes itself into a corner with its concerns. One company, for instance, after years of touting their scale design (tonal design) as a great one (which it wasn't) and using it as a major selling feature, decided to replace it with a better one. Because they feared that people would ask, "If that one was really so great, why are they replacing it?" they phased the new design in very slowly, one model at a time and didn't advertise it. Frankly, I sometimes think these marketing people take themselves a little too seriously: how many people do you imagine would really lie awake at night wondering why a mediocre piano company decided to change its scale design?

HOW PIANOS DIFFER IN QUALITY AND FEATURES

To the uninitiated, chances are that one piano in a piano store looks pretty much like another, except for the price tag and cabinet styling. And if the piano is being bought just so Junior can begin taking lessons, why pay more money than absolutely necessary? This is the question technicians and dealers hear every day. Sometimes, no doubt, these buyers simply can't afford a more expensive piano. But just as often they are moderately well-to-do people who have just spent thirty thousand dollars on an automobile, which will last less than one-tenth as long as the piano before being replaced. Why, then, the resistance to investing in a good instrument? In part, it's because a fancy car confers much more prestige than does a high-quality piano. But in addition, it's simply that most piano buyers don't understand what they are getting for their money. Technical information and brand comparisons abound for cars, but little or nothing of the kind exists for pianos. People therefore have very little incentive to purchase something whose value is not clear.

It's largely, though not entirely, true that the price of a piano is a fairly good indication of its quality. Just what makes a well-made piano more expensive? Briefly, good pianos require better raw materials, which are prepared to more exacting tolerances and subjected to stricter standards of quality than materials in lesser pianos. Sometimes a great deal of expensive material (such as wood, felt, or leather) that does not conform to these standards is rejected or discarded. In both design and workmanship, much more time and attention is paid to details that might otherwise plague the owner or technician later. In the best factories, workers are more apt to be treated as craftspeople and given considerable responsibility, while in lesser factories most jobs are broken down into tiny, easily learned tasks, rendering workers replaceable cogs in a machine. Workers on the high-quality pianos are therefore better trained, stay with the company longer, and receive higher pay and benefits. Where machinery is used, it is at least as much in the interest of quality as efficiency, which may entail greater expense in its design. The result is pianos that are more uniform from one to the next, perform better, last longer, and require less remedial maintenance than lesser instruments.

Of course, cost is not always related to product quality. The lower cost of foreign labor, or of non-union labor in this country; differences in rent and taxes in various locations; savings due to larger production runs and greater manufacturing efficiencies; international currency fluctuations and import duties; and the fanciness of the furniture all play an important part in the price of the instrument.

In the following pages, I'd like to discuss selected technical aspects of pianos and elaborate a bit on the ways pianos differ in quality and construction. Some of these differences can actually be seen, heard, and felt, whereas others, nonetheless important, can't be observed as separate entities in the final product. Some separate the shoddy from the average, others the average from the superior. Though I could cite hundreds of such details, I include here only those most important for the consumer to know, or most widely advertised but actually least important, or easiest for the purchaser to inspect.* "Buying Tips" scattered throughout identify those features that you can inspect yourself or ask about if you want to be especially thorough.

Several themes run through these descriptions: Which features are really just marketing gimmicks? (I'll detail some more marketing nonsense to entertain you.) What will I gain (or give up) if I buy a more (or less) expensive piano? How important is it to me to buy a piano with "traditional" as opposed to synthetic or nontraditional materials? How important is it to me to buy a piano that will last a lifetime (or longer)?

Before I begin, though, several cautions are in order. First of all, much about pianos is simply unknown or cannot be judged good or bad. This is because little basic research has been done, as piano manufacture has evolved along empirical, rather than experimental, lines, or because the choice among some features is simply a matter of taste. My intent here is to present a consensus of informed opinion where such a consensus exists, and to be honest about where it doesn't. Even knowing what *isn't* known can be useful when confronted with unwarranted claims.

Second, no piano is perfect. Every piano, no matter how expensive or well made, has limitations inherent in the physical laws governing the various aspects of design and construction, in which conflicting needs may necessitate compromise. Most piano designs require compromises simply to make the product affordable to the average person. And, too, some otherwise wonderful instruments may have a thing or two about them that is just plain faulty. Therefore it would be a

mistake to categorically dismiss a piano just because it contains some feature that I have labeled here as "incorrect." Each piano must be seen in its entirety and evaluated in terms of its intended use, longevity, and price.

Third, this book is written from the point of view of a consumer advocate and therefore necessarily focuses attention on the negative aspects of the piano industry—false technical claims, shoddy products, and poor service. After all, as a piano shopper you will soon enough hear from the dealers how wonderful their products and services are. Presumably you have bought this book to find out those things that the dealers won't tell you. The problem with this approach is that you may get the erroneous idea that all piano dealers, salespeople, and manufacturers are crooks. In fact, many conduct their businesses with great integrity and admirably support and service their products. You need fear being ripped off no more than with any other comparable consumer purchase.

Pianos have improved a lot during the last decade. Some of the grosser defects in piano design outlined in the following pages are rarely found in pianos being made today except, sometimes, in pianos from developing countries. However, they will be found in abundance in pianos made in the U.S. from about 1960 to the early 1980s, a period in the history of the American piano when a particularly large amount of junk was produced. So although this chapter is written mainly for those buying new pianos, most of it will also be useful in evaluating the quality of a relatively young used piano.

I wish to emphasize that it is not necessary to immerse yourself in technical details to successfully purchase a piano. I have included the technical information on the following pages for the benefit of those shoppers who want to be especially thorough or who enjoy learning how things work. Others may skip ahead. Non-technical information about piano cabinetry and finish can be found on pages 26 and 27, and general information about shopping for a new piano continues on page 60.

Case and Cabinet Construction, Styling, and Finish

I know that many of you reading this are concerned at least as much with the furniture aspect of the piano as

---

*For a more complete and detailed account of how a high-quality piano is manufactured, I highly recommend *The Wonders of the Piano: The Anatomy of the Instrument*, Second Edition, by Catherine C. Bielefeldt (William Anton Publishing, 1991).

with its musical aspects, so we'll begin there. A piano's furniture value is reflected in two ways : how it looks now and how it will hold up over the years. For a piano, "over the years" is a long time, for you should expect a well-made piano to last long enough to be enjoyed by your children and their children, too, and it takes very careful craftsmanship to accomplish that. Making a piano look good now, at least to the untrained eye, is a lot easier to do; every company allocates a large portion of its budget to this end, often at the expense of both the piano's musical value and its long-range furniture value. When you buy a very inexpensive piano, not only might you be getting a poor instrument, but its beauty may be only as deep as three coats of lacquer, its imitation Mediterranean styling notwithstanding.

Panel construction. A discussion of furniture begins with the subject of wood. Contrary to popular thought, most fine furniture is not made with planks or pieces of solid wood just as they are cut from the tree. For one thing, most trees that are cut down for furniture wood these days are too thin to provide large planks. Panels more than a few inches wide are usually made by gluing thinner strips of wood together edge to edge. For another thing, large panels of solid wood are not dimensionally stable; they tend to warp and change size from season to season. Thus, they are not suitable for furniture in most cases. Solid woods are used, though, for such parts as legs and moldings, which are not likely to be much affected by warping.

Most furniture these days is made of some kind of plywood, though not the cheap grade you use to board up windows or walk on over ditches. The word *plywood* refers to any wood product made of several layers glued together in a sandwich. Five-ply "lumber-core" plywood (Figure 3-1 top) is the most common type used in piano cabinetry. It consists of a core of "solid" wood (that is, thin pieces glued edge to edge), usually poplar or birch, covered on each side by two layers of veneer with grain running at right angles to each other. Wood expands and contracts more across the grain than along it, so this cross-banded veneer construction lessens warping and changes in size. Another kind of plywood used less often in pianos is "veneer-core" plywood, basically a sandwich of cross-banded veneers.

Plywood has many advantages over solid wood. In addition to minimizing warpage, plywood is equally strong in all dimensions and can be manufactured in a wide variety of sizes and thicknesses to suit specific purposes. Whereas solid wood made from edge-glued strips might have a chaotic grain pattern, the visual characteristics of a plywood panel can be controlled by the manufacturer through the choice of face veneer

(the outer veneer layer). Most well-constructed furniture today is made from a combination of solid wood and plywood, each used to its best advantage.

Particle board. As the wood supply dwindles and wood prices increase, greater and greater use is being made of *particle board*, a material made of compressed chips, flakes, particles, or fibers of wood or sawdust held together by glue. Although much of the public doesn't realize it, a lot of so-called fine furniture today is made of particle board, usually as a substitute for the solid lumber in lumber-core plywood. Its use in piano cabinets, somewhat controversial, is mostly limited to verticals, but at least one maker uses it even for grand piano lids. While no piano maker advertises that it uses particle board, many advertise that they *don't* use it. Its use, though, is easily disguised.

SALES PITCH: *"Mr. Jones, Smith Bros. pianos contain no particle board, unlike lesser pianos. As you can see from the edge of this panel, we use only real plywood construction."*

TRUTH: When the subject of particle board came up on one of my factory visits, the factory technician beckoned me to follow him and ushered me into a room whose walls were lined with his competitors' pianos. Approaching one well-known Japanese make, he pulled off the lower panel, a large piece measuring about two feet by four feet, and pointed to its edge. The familiar stripes of cross-grain layers indicated that the panel was made of seven-ply veneer-core plywood construction. Then he pointed to the center of the panel, where a large gouge had been made through the black finish and into the wood. Looking closely at the intentionally damaged spot, it was clear from the texture and appearance that the panel was actually made of particle board. Why was the edge different from the rest of the board?

Particle board is frequently "lumber-banded" along its perimeter with solid lumber or plywood (Figure 3-1 bottom) to increase the overall strength of the panel and to allow the edge to be shaped or contoured, an operation which is difficult to do successfully with most types of particle board. It also camouflages the particle board, allowing it to be used even by those who would rather not be known for it. The giveaway, by the way, is the weight of the case part. Particle board is very dense. If the part seems to weigh more than any wood you know, you can bet it's particle board.

Particle board has a number of advantages over wood. Having no grain or knots, it doesn't warp, can be easily cut and machined, and is very easily veneered. It uses materials that used to be considered waste and discarded, and thus makes good ecological and economic sense. By varying the density, type of "particle," and method of manufacture, it can be made to suit many construction needs, and the technology for this industry is rapidly expanding. It's even possible now to print a simulated wood grain on the faces and edges of particle board that looks so realistic it can't be told from the real thing. (Though I use the term *particle board* generically, the material in fact comes in many different forms, which vary in their strength and suitability for piano construction. The most popular type used in pianos is called MDF, or medium-density fiberboard.)

Particle board also has some drawbacks. Its screw-holding power is limited; each time a screw is removed it brings with it a trickle of sawdust, and within a short time the screw hole becomes stripped. This can be gotten around either by lumber-banding the piece and screwing into the wood, or by redesigning the cabinet so that removable screws are unnecessary. Particle board also tends toward brittleness, and

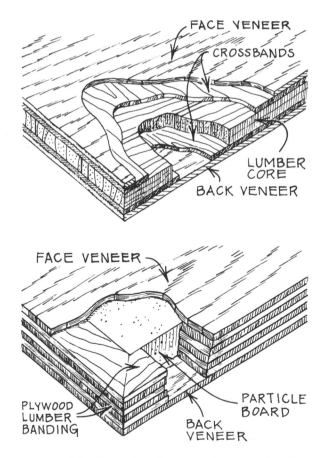

FIGURE 3-1. Most large furniture panels are made of some form of plywood. Top: Traditional five-ply lumber-core plywood. Bottom: Particle board-core plywood with plywood lumber-banding to strengthen and camouflage the particle board. Not all particle board-core plywood is lumber-banded.

when broken, is pretty much unrepairable. Breakage of this sort is not common in piano cabinetry, but sometimes occurs during shipment, and could result from vandalism or rough play. If you expect rough treatment, I'd recommend "the real thing,"—that is, plywood—not particle board.

There is also some indication that, because of its density, particle board may muffle the sound of a vertical piano somewhat. But the proof is in the sound: if a particle board piano sounds good, this argument becomes academic.

Particle board has a bad name in piano cabinetry mostly because of the poor quality of its early days and the inappropriate uses to which it was put. Today the production of particle board is more sophisticated. When it is used appropriately, particle board has huge technical advantages to the mass producer and only slight technical drawbacks, if any, to the consumer. The chief objection to it at this point seems to be a psychological one: it lacks aesthetic appeal. After all, part of the lure of the piano has always been its fine wooden cabinetry and all that that symbolizes: a connection with nature, with old-world craftsmanship, and with the skill it takes to make something out of wood that will weather the seasons and endure. But much of this, today, is pure fantasy, since plywood, with all its glue, is already halfway toward particle board, and, in most large piano factories, "old-world" craftsmanship is hard to find. Craftsmanship these days is often of the high-tech and impersonal kind, of which particle board is a natural extension.

It suffices to say, then, that when you shop for a piano, your choice of particle board–core or lumber-core plywood will be largely based on aesthetic and economic, rather than technical, considerations. Most of the large piano manufacturers are making increasing use of particle board, while the makers of more expensive pianos use it only sparingly or not at all.

Quality in woodworking. While the debate about particle board rages on, the more important differences between quality and mediocrity, as might be expected, are subtler. Regardless of whether a piano contains real wood or particle board in its large panels, it still uses real wood elsewhere—in structural and acoustical parts, veneers, action parts, and in smaller cabinet parts. Some manufacturers are fussier than others in the quality of wood they purchase, insisting on greater uniformity of grain pattern and absence of knots, voids (empty spaces), discoloration, or other imperfections, even in parts that don't show. They pay a premium for the highest-quality woods available. Where certain critical parts—soundboard, pinblock, bridges—are involved, the better piano makers use large amounts of quarter-sawn lumber, whose grain orientation ensures maximum dimensional stability (Figure 3-2a). But quarter-sawn lumber is many times more expensive than plain-sawn, so lesser makers use the cheaper material or let planks of plain-sawn lumber slip in when expedient. In the long run, this can have disastrous consequences.

Many kinds of wood are used in a piano. In deciding which kind to use for a particular purpose, piano designers have to take into account such factors as moisture content, strength, weight, stiffness, and how well the wood seasons, as well as its availability and cost. For makers of lower-quality pianos, availability and cost figure more prominently. Spruce is often used for structural parts like vertical back posts and grand braces because its long, uniform, close grain gives it stiffness with less weight. Other woods are also used. Spruce is used for soundboards because of its excellent acoustical properties. Where hardness is required, such as in pinblocks and action parts, maple or beech is used. Wood for grand piano cases, which are made of many thin layers bent and glued around a form, is best chosen for its acoustical, as well as its structural, properties (in verticals the structure affects the sound only minimally). The better makers of grand pianos usually choose the denser and more expensive maple (or beech) over the cheaper but less satisfactory mahogany or poplar. (Note: the outer veneer, being decorative, may be different).

Wood must go through an extensive drying process before it is usable for construction of any kind. First it must be air-dried for from six months to two years, and then the moisture content is usually further reduced by drying in automatic kilns. Attempts to hasten this process, or not drying the wood to a sufficiently low moisture content, can result in warped, cracked, or binding case or structural parts. Even after this dried wood is made into parts, some manufacturers are fastidious enough that they will cure these parts for long periods of time before using them. For instance, after gluing up a grand piano rim, most makers of fine pianos let it sit in a conditioning room for months before using it. Foreign manufacturers newly importing to North America have the most severe problems with improperly dried wood; they often underestimate the effect that our extremes of dryness and dampness will have on their pianos.

After the wood is selected and dried, there are literally dozens of examples of proper woodworking procedure in which a manufacturer can show its true colors. Most of these you will never see any sign of—if the job is done right (Figure 3-2). The manufacturer must take into account the species of the wood, the direction of the grain, the stress that will be applied, the type of wood joint to be used, the tolerances to which the wood will be machined, the kind of glue to be used, and many other factors.

In each case, the manufacturer must decide whether the piano will be built to last a lifetime or if portions of it will begin to disintegrate about the time the warranty runs out. And even if nothing disastrous occurs, there will be many problems to plague the person who owns or has to service a poorly made piano: a fallboard that binds in sticky weather and won't slide or fold down over the keys without scratching the finish, parts that warp and prevent the free movement of the keys, legs that are very unstable and come loose or break too easily, screw and knob holes that strip out, grand piano lids or other case parts that split where the hinges are attached, and music desks that split and come unhinged (these are a few of my fa-vor-ite things).

If you are not experienced in cabinetmaking, judging the quality of woodworking in a piano cabinet is not an easy thing to do. But by inspecting and comparing pianos you know to be of widely differing quality, you can begin to develop an eye for such things. The thickness (though not necessarily the weight) of cabinet sides, rims, panels, music desks, lids, and lyres; the extent to which particle board is used (though not necessarily important per se); the ease with which panels lift off for service; how well adjacent parts seem to fit together; the appearance of the finish (discussed later)—all these taken together give a good idea of the intentions of the manufacturer with respect to the model.

Sophistication in cabinetry. There are a number of differences in piano cabinetry that indicate not so much the quality of woodworking as its level of sophistication. That is, the absence of certain features would not make a piano potentially defective, it would just make the piano plainer. Some of the items shown in Figure 3-3 differ between manufacturers; others differ between the various offerings of a single manufacturer. Some companies make dozens of models and styles, all with more or less the same instrument inside of them, but they may be priced many hundreds of dollars apart because of these cabinetry differences. You pay through the nose for sophisticated cabinetry, not only because of the extra material cost, but also because of the additional costs of design, inventory, handling, cutting, scrap, fitting, and finishing involved, and the profit margin added on.

Furniture styles. Period furniture or decorator styling is very popular in the vertical piano market, and to a lesser extent in the grand market. With most brands, the styling differences are found only in the shape of the music desk and the legs. That is, a Smith Bros.

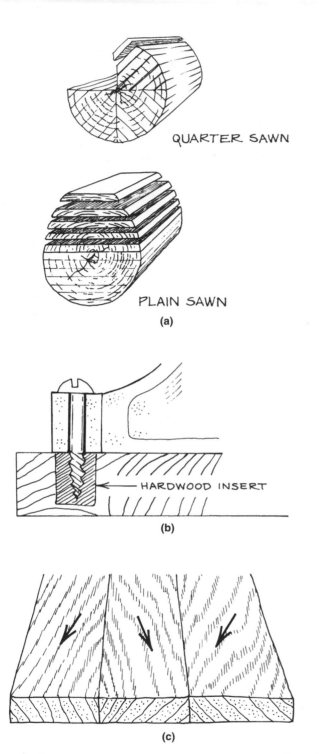

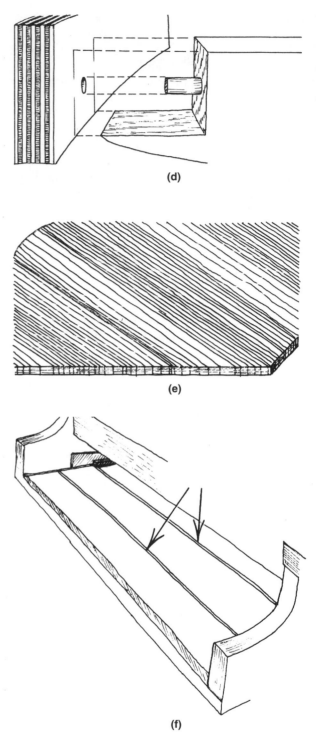

FIGURE 3-2. All piano manufacturers must pay close attention to proper woodworking principles to ensure that their instruments will perform well and hold up over time. Some manufacturers are more conscientious than others. Shown here in generalized form are several examples of steps some makers take in building a durable product: (a) quarter-sawn lumber for maximum dimensional stability versus the cheaper, but less satisfactory, plain-sawn lumber; (b) the use of hardwood or hardwood inserts where screws or other metal hardware would otherwise wear away the wood; (c) careful attention to grain direction where pieces are joined (to prevent warping), or where acoustical properties are involved (the latter not shown); (d) tight, carefully fitted doweled joints for structural integrity; (e) close-grained wood with uniform grain pattern for acoustical, structural, and aesthetic reasons; (f) expansion joints to prevent warping and consequent mechanical problems.

Deluxe Console in Mediterranean style could be changed to French Provincial by just switching the music desk and the two front legs. Some manufacturers, in some models, may alter other features or occasionally even completely redesign the cabinet from style to style. This is obviously much more expensive to do. In addition to period styling, there is also the "continental" (also known as "contemporary") or "European" style, popular in European and Asian vertical pianos and distinguished by its plain, nondescript lines and the absence of front legs; and the "professional" or "institutional" style with legs supported by "toe blocks" (Figure 3-5).

Finish. Most piano companies put their cabinets through a very elaborate finishing process—much more elaborate than the process that the musical portion of the instrument goes through—for they know this is what will sell the piano. The finishing process, with sometimes twenty or more steps, consists of staining, sanding, filling, shading, sealing, more sanding, lacquer, more sanding, more lacquer, hand rubbing, and polishing. Staining is done to make wood with a large natural variation in color look more uniform, or to change the color of the wood entirely, or to make a cheaper wood look like a more expensive variety. For instance, we usually think of mahogany as being dark reddish brown, but much mahogany actually starts out a honey-colored brown. Through staining, a cheaper wood like gum can be made to look like mahogany. Filling closes or fills the pores of open-grained woods to make them smoother and less porous. It also adds color. Some woods are intentionally left unfilled to let their open grain show. Hand rubbing and polishing with very fine sandpaper and pumice give the utmost in smoothness and elegance to the surface.

The top finish coat is either lacquer or polyester, lacquer being the favored finish among North American firms and polyester predominating among the imports. Polyester is usually applied in one or two thick coats and so is suitable primarily for pianos whose cabinets have little surface detail, which would otherwise get buried, such as the continental-style pianos. Lacquer is applied in many thin coats and so is used for period-style pianos with their sometimes elaborate ornamentation. Polyester is more durable and scratch-resistant, needs little maintenance, and can more easily be polished to create a high-gloss finish. Lacquer has

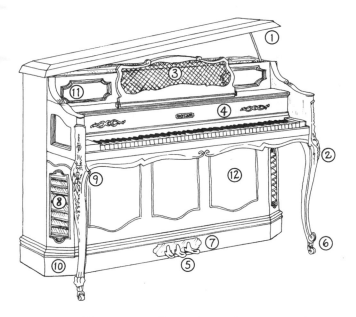
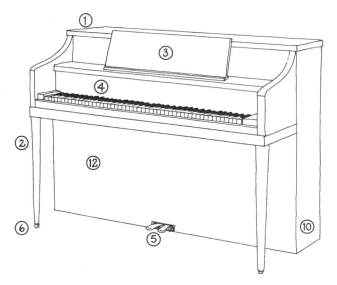

FIGURE 3-3. Pianos can differ in the sophistication of their cabinet design, which is not necessarily related to the quality of construction. Shown here are some of these differences: (1) grand-style lid with beveled edges versus regular lid with square edges; (2) fancy, curved legs doweled into case sides versus plain legs screwed into keybed; (3) fancy, carved music desk with metal grillwork hinged to music shelf versus plain, stationary music desk; (4) folding fallboard with brass appointments versus sliding fallboard or no fallboard at all; (5) three solid cast brass pedals with horns versus two simple stamped brass or brass-plated pedals; (6) casters on front legs versus no casters; (7) brass kick plate around pedals; (8) "tone louvers" and other special features; (9) carved features on legs and moldings; (10) angled sides versus straight sides; (11) relief features on panels; (12) well-matched or even book-matched veneers versus bland veneer patterns (detail not shown).

Buying Tips: Piano Cabinetry and Finish

The average piano purchaser pays an inordinate amount of attention to the way a piano looks, while often not seeing the real differences in cabinet construction at all, not to mention the musical differences. The serious musician is usually less concerned about appearances, but both groups miss a number of very mundane, yet highly practical, cabinet-related considerations.

Here are some buying tips relating to the cabinetry and accessory parts of pianos. Some of them are minor and shouldn't prevent you from buying an otherwise high-quality instrument, but they may prove useful to you in avoiding future problems.

Legs. Manufacturers say that broken spinet and console legs are among the most common warranty problems reported to them. Take a look at these legs yourself and you'll have to agree they look rather weak and unstable. They get broken in shipment or even just from repeated moving away from a wall for service or cleaning. There are two types of legs—those that are glued and doweled into the case sides and those that are screwed into the keybed at the front (see Figure 3-3). I'm not convinced that one is inherently better than the other, though the former is considered fancier. The best way to avoid the problem of broken legs is either to buy a studio or full-size upright piano with toe blocks that support the legs, or to buy a piano with continental styling that has no legs at all (see Figure 3-5). If you buy one without legs, be sure it's properly balanced. Some have a slight tendency to tip, especially when standing on thick carpeting (try giving it a gentle push).

One more thing about legs: If you buy a spinet or console with legs, make sure the legs reach the floor. You heard right! Sometimes, because of inaccurate case construction or maybe even twisting of the whole piano structure, one leg will not touch the floor.

Casters and Caster Cups. If you do buy a piano with unsupported legs, make sure the legs have casters, which may help slightly to prevent breakage. If you plan to move a piano like this around a lot, you should have it permanently mounted on a "piano truck" made for this purpose (see Chapter 6). Some continental-style pianos have no casters—don't plan on moving them much. A few cheap pianos have fake casters with wheels that neither turn nor touch the floor.

Caster Cups in wood or plastic are available to help protect your floor or carpet from the pressure of the casters. Caution: Caster cups with felt on the bottom may transfer the color of the felt to the floor or carpet after a while.

Finish. Some points to consider when evaluating the quality of the finish are:
- If the piano has a natural wood finish, do the legs and other cabinet parts match one another in coloration? (Note: The bench is made separately, so it may not match the piano perfectly.)
- Are the natural wood veneers the woods they purport to be (more expensive) or just stained to look like it (more common)?
- Have the edges been sanded through and then touched up with stain, or have the surfaces been so carefully sanded that no touch-up is necessary?

- Have the back sides of panels been thoroughly sanded and finished, or have they been left rough? Failure to finish both sides with the same amount and type of finish can cause warpage of even the sturdiest panels and trim parts.
- Has the finish been hand-rubbed, and, if so, have all exposed surfaces been rubbed, or just the ones that are most obvious?
- Does the natural wood finish look completely transparent, or does it appear like a cloudy protective guard?
- Are there any ripples or unevenness to the finish? This can be caused by slight movement of the veneer underneath if the woodworking was faulty. (I once saw a foreign-made piano with a high-gloss finish that looked like it was covered in crumpled plastic wrap. The veneer was buckling due to moisture problems.)

Fallboard. Technically, a fallboard (keyboard cover) isn't really necessary, but all good pianos have one. Only some of the cheapest promotional pianos have no fallboard at all. Vertical piano fallboards come in two varieties—one slides down over the keys, the other folds down. The folding kind is definitely superior. The sliding fallboard is a nuisance to remove for servicing the keys, and can even make tuning more difficult. Be sure that the fallboard, when fully open, doesn't stick out over the keys so your fingers would hit it as you played. Grand pianos always have a folding fallboard. Be sure it isn't prone to shutting on your fingers at the slightest opportunity. Many are now hydraulically damped and shut slowly, a definite advantage.

Lid. Some vertical pianos come with a "grand-style lid;" that is, a lid that hinges on the left side rather than at the back (see Figure 3-3). On the right side, inside the piano, is a propstick that props the lid open, just like on a grand. Advantages: It looks elegant and gives an outlet for the sound in a direction other than into the performer's face. Disadvantage: Where will you put your music, lamp, metronome, and knickknacks, if not on the piano lid? Some of these lids, especially on slightly older models, are difficult to remove, and keeping them open for servicing can be an exercise in resourcefulness. If you buy a piano with a grand-style lid, please be sure it is easy to remove.

Grand piano lids are in two parts, usually connected by a long "piano hinge." On some promotional models the hinge is missing, and the front part of the lid must be removed entirely. When it's removed, however, the music desk comes with it. It's probably best to avoid this kind of piano. Some grands also have only one propstick for the lid. You will probably find it most convenient if the lid comes with both a long and a short propstick. One more thing: make sure the lid isn't too heavy to lift!

Safety note: Be sure whichever propstick you use is in the correct position. Piano lids are very heavy and must be supported properly. To avoid accidents that can cause serious personal injury and/or damage to your piano, be absolutely sure the propstick and lid are always at right angles to one another.

Music desk. Many spinets and consoles employ a music desk that's hinged on its thin edges by two wood screws, which act as hinge pins (Figure 3-4). Here's what's likely to happen: In order to stop the desk from rattling, the screws will be overtightened. After a short time, one of the screws will strip out its hole and fall out, and the desk will collapse. If this doesn't happen, someone will lean on or tug on the desk, splitting out its fragile thin edge, and then it will collapse, requiring wood-working repair or replacement. These are both very common occurrences. Only if the desk is especially thick or reinforced with metal brackets should this design even be considered.

In fairness, I should say that it's next to impossible to find a really secure music desk hinge system, one that's reasonably immune to destruction. Music desks that employ regular desk hinges attached to the back will probably last a little longer, but some technicians report having to repair as many of one kind as of the other (as well as bent-beyond-recognition brass folding hinge supports, the operation of which was beyond the intelligence of a user).

Be sure that the music desk is capable of holding the amount and type of music you plan to use. Some desks may have trouble holding single sheets of paper upright, or large books, or may be too small for the large amounts of music used in teaching. The music desks I like best run the full width of the piano, and the horizontal portion is covered with cloth or a leather-like material that grips the bottom edge of the sheet music so it doesn't slip down.

One more minor note about music desks: There are reports that buzzing sounds occasionally emanate from the wire grill-work in some fancy music desks.

Lyre. The grand piano pedal lyre should be attached to the underside of the piano with a metal lyre plate or with bolts that screw into threaded metal holes. Even though it's partially reinforced by the diagonal braces behind it, the lyre takes an incredible beating by the feet over the years. Although it isn't done today, in the recent past some cheaper pianos used only wood screws to attach the lyre, and invariably these screws stripped out their holes (a familiar story?) and the lyre fell off. A permanent repair usually involves installing lyre plates anyway,

so you might as well have them from the beginning. (If you're buying a used grand piano, a technician can check this for you.)

If you compare lyres of pianos of widely differing quality, you can see how much more substantially and solidly constructed the better one is. Make sure that the lyre doesn't move or twist when the pedals are pressed.

Keybed. When you sit on the bench that usually comes with the piano, be sure that the keybed is at the right height for you. It should allow adequate room for your legs, and the keyboard should be at a comfortable level. This height is fairly standard, but there is some variation. Check to be sure that the bottom of the keybed isn't rough; there have been a number of reports of clothing being filled with splinters.

Bench. Some points to consider when evaluating benches:

• Wood-top benches vary considerably in the quality of woodworking, especially in the hardness of the woods used for the top and sides. Better-quality benches have sides and legs of hard maple, mahogany, or walnut, whereas lesser-quality benches use softer woods like gum or laminated stock that is less durable and therefore will not hold up under continuous usage. Under the veneer, high-quality wood tops use a lumber-core interior banded with hardwood maple; less expensive tops use particle board with softwood edges.

• Virtually all benches made today have legs that are bolted on. As they loosen, they can be tightened with an ordinary wrench. Glued-on legs inevitably loosen with time and climatic changes and are more difficult to repair.

• Make sure that benches with plain wood tops have beveled edges so that sharp corners don't cut into your legs. Benches with cushioned or upholstered tops may be both less expensive and more comfortable. Bench cushions can also be purchased separately.

• Beware of benches finished in high-gloss polyester that squeak. This means the polyester was incorrectly applied and will always squeak.

• Some benches open up to store music, some don't. Make sure a bench that stores music has a sturdy bottom that is set into the bench sides, not tacked on underneath. Otherwise, as soon as you overfill the storage compartment, the music will fall out the bottom onto the floor.

• The king of benches is the artist bench, adjustable in height and covered in vinyl or leather. It comes in three different sizes at a cost of $400 and up. Artist benches vary in (among other things) the quality of the adjustable mechanism and in its ability to be repaired as it wears. The "scissors" mechanism with replaceable bushings is said to be the best kind. Better benches also have thicker foam padding under the vinyl or leather. Leather ($300-plus additional) breathes better and is more comfortable if you will be spending long hours at the piano. Otherwise, the two materials wear about the same.

You may not have much choice in the matter of what bench you get with a particular piano, but most dealers will allow you to trade up to a better bench for an additional fee. My sources tell me that the best benches, both regular and adjustable, are manufactured by Jansen & Son. See Chapter 7 for a list of companies that sell benches and other accessories direct to consumers.

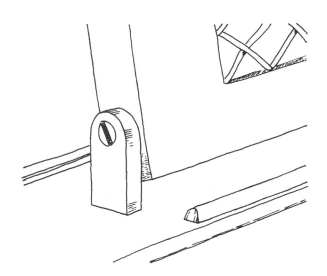

FIGURE 3-4. A music desk hinged on its thin edge with screws serving as hinge pins is likely to come apart or break unless it is especially thick or reinforced with metal brackets.

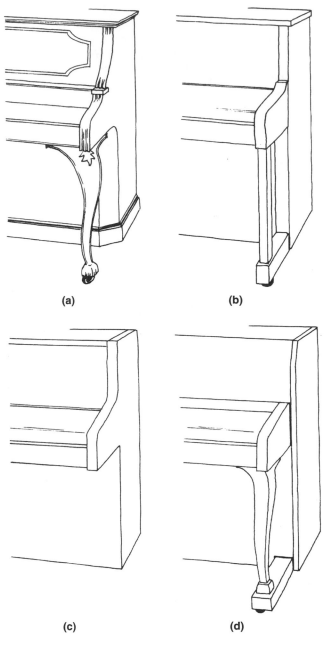

FIGURE 3-5. Four common vertical piano styles; (a) period or decorator style with free-standing front legs; (b) institutional or professional style with legs supported by toe blocks; (c) continental style without legs; (d) hybrid style combining (a) and (b), now sometimes called Chippendale.

been the traditional preference for many years and is usually quite satisfactory if well cared for.

Most finishes are either "satin," which reflects light but not images, or "high gloss" (also known as "polish"), which is mirror-like. Though all are applied in a similar fashion, finishes do differ in the number of steps involved (the number of sandings, the number of

coats of lacquer) and, certainly, in the care with which the process is carried out.

Note that most high-gloss finishes are polyester, but a few expensive pianos have high-gloss *lacquer* finishes. These are very time-consuming and expensive to produce, and show scratches very easily, but, in my opinion, look much less artificial than their polyester counterparts. Some manufacturers are now offering lacquer semi-gloss finishes, too, perhaps the loveliest finishes of all.

A black finish is known as an "ebonized" finish, an imitation of ebony wood. Generally a lower-quality veneer is used for this finish since it won't be seen, which accounts, in part, for the lower price of these pianos. The veneer is stained black and covered with a topcoat of lacquer or polyester containing a black pigment. Some manufacturers also make pianos with a white, ivory, or colored finish. Unusual artcase pianos, with traditional or avant-garde themes, are available from Steinway and the European makers.

Structural and Tuning Stability

Wooden structure. A piano has more than two hundred strings, and when they're all stretched to vibrate at their assigned pitches, they exert a combined pull of sixteen to twenty-three tons, depending on the size of the piano. To handle this kind of stress, the strings are stretched across a cast-iron frame called the **plate**. The plate, in turn, is usually bolted to a wooden framework. In a vertical piano, this wooden piano **back** generally consists of several vertical posts with connecting horizontal pieces (Figure 3-6); in a grand, the familiar curved **rim** and its connecting braces do the job (Figure 3-7).

PITCH: "Mr. Jones, this Smith Bros. Deluxe Console features six strong oak posts permanently attached with bolts that go all the way through the piano, while some lesser pianos have only five posts, and no bolts. This piano will stay in tune longer than others will."

TRUTH: Actually, there is no agreement among engineers on the amount of wooden framework needed in a piano, and anyway this amount undoubtedly varies from piano to piano depending on the design of the plate and the distribution of the string tension across it. Many foreign manufacturers make pianos with an extra-thick plate and sell them with only three posts, or sometimes with no posts, in their own countries, but market them here with five or six in order to satisfy customers who come into the store counting back posts. Some U.S. companies market their six-post pianos abroad with only three posts. Resulting changes in tuning stability have not been documented. If the posts run the full height of the piano, they are probably serving a useful purpose, but close inspection will often reveal shorter posts to be useless appendages tacked on for show.

Almost certainly, pianos with regular, thin plates need some kind of wooden back assembly to keep the plates from warping. Just how much is not clear. But to whatever degree the posts *are* necessary, it's their total size, not their number, that's important. Witness that the five back posts of some verticals may have nearly twice the total cross-sectional area of the six posts on some other pianos. Pianos go out of tune primarily because the seasonal swelling and shrinking of the soundboard alters the tension on the strings, and this happens regardless of how strong the structure is. A stronger *total* structure (plate and wooden framework) will accept these seasonal changes more gracefully than a weaker one and therefore will go out of tune less chaotically, if no less often. But counting and measuring wooden posts will not tell you how strong the piano is or how well it will hold its tune; only examining the piano's performance and service record over time will.

As far as back post material is concerned, spruce is often considered the optimum wood because of its high strength-to-weight ratio and stiffness. But commenting on the five woods most often used—spruce, maple, oak, beech, and poplar—one factory technician said that for most companies the choice is a matter of appearance, cost, weight, availability, and what the competition is using. Strength is taken for granted.

In grand pianos, the wooden structure is thought to have an additional function—to reflect sound back into the soundboard for a more resonant, singing tone. As mentioned before, better pianos usually have

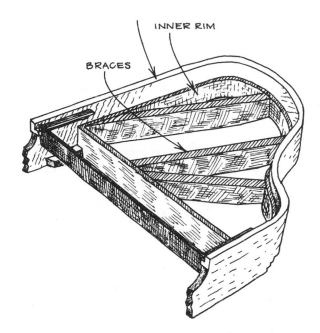

FIGURE 3-7. The rim of a grand piano is the wooden framework to which the cast-iron plate is bolted and the soundboard is glued. Notice that the rim is in two parts, an inner rim and an outer rim. The plate and soundboard are actually attached to the inner rim. On some of the best pianos, the inner and outer rim are made as one piece to provide a firmer foundation, both structurally and acoustically. On others, the outer rim is added later, and is mostly decorative.

denser woods, such as maple or beech, in their rims. They may also have thicker, sturdier rims and substantial amounts of wooden bracing underneath the piano, connecting parts of the rim. As with the verticals, however, the amount of wooden bracing needed depends on the particular piano design and the strength of the plate. Some grands, especially small ones, may have wooden braces for only marketing, not engineering, reasons. Although additional research needs to be done in this area, it is speculated that a grand piano will sound better, and sound better longer, if its wooden structural parts fit together tightly.

PITCH: "Mr. Jones, this Smith Bros. Parlor Grand has a rim made of genuine hardwoods. Those Asian pianos, on the other hand, have softwood rims that will soon fall apart."

TRUTH: The hardness or density of the inner rim determines how much of the strings' vibrational energy will be reflected back into the soundboard for a more sustained sound, instead of being absorbed by the rim. Although this is only one factor in choosing wood for grand piano rims, it is an important one to many makers of fine pianos. Maple and beech are today considered the premium woods for this purpose. The

FIGURE 3-6. The vertical piano back is the wooden framework to which the cast-iron plate is bolted and the soundboard is glued. Shown here is a traditional back with full-length back posts.

rim density affects the tonal quality, and may contribute somewhat to the piano's longevity, but is not solely responsible for it. Asian and other pianos with softer rims may have a tendency toward tone of shorter duration, but they are not about to "fall apart." In fact, one of the world's finest pianos, Bösendorfer, has a rim made of spruce, a softwood.

Furthermore, the term "hardwood" is much abused. "Hardwood" and "softwood" are botanical terms referring to the type of tree from which they come, hardwoods from deciduous trees and softwoods from conifers. Not all hardwoods are appropriate for use in piano rims, and some softwoods are actually denser than some hardwoods. "Hardwood," when used in piano advertising literature, is generally a code word meaning that the rims are *not* made of maple or beech, because if they were, the literature would have said so specifically.

Cast-Iron Plate. (See Figure 3-8.)

PITCH: "Mr. Jones, this piano has a full-perimeter plate. Many other pianos employ the traditional harp-style plate, which has large empty spaces around its perimeter and couldn't possibly be as strong. "

TRUTH: The traditional harp-style plate, used with a supporting wooden back structure, employs metal where it's needed to counteract the pull of the strings, which is not necessarily around the perimeter of the piano. Pianos without a wooden back require a "full-perimeter plate," a massive plate with a very thick ridge of iron all the way around it. Some pianos advertised as having full-perimeter plates, however, really have regular, thin plates with some additional metal pieces around the perimeter, but these add little strength to the plate and are mostly for show.

Perhaps the more important difference among plates is not so much their strength as it is the accuracy of the casting and the drilling of the holes for the tuning pins and other hardware. These are critical because a piano is virtually built around its plate. Irregularities in the casting or drilling can cause structural and cabinet parts to fit improperly, tuning pins and strings to be unevenly spaced, and strings to bear irregularly against the plate and bridges, creating tonal problems. Sometimes these imperfections can be great enough to create a really defective piano. With the advent of computer-controlled drilling, gross defects of this kind are usually limited to pianos from developing countries; a tell-tale sign is poorly-spaced strings. The better companies put a great deal of time and care into the preparation of the plate, especially those parts of the plate and associated hardware that serve as termination points for the vibrating strings.

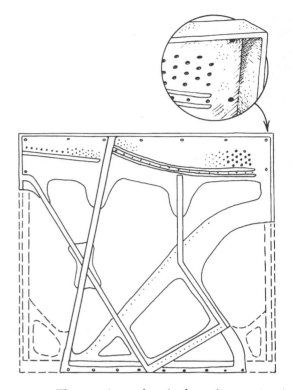

FIGURE 3-8. The cast-iron plate is the primary structural framework of the piano, withstanding the sixteen or more tons of tension exerted by the strings. The dotted lines show the additional metal pieces added around the perimeter of some vertical plates to imitate a "full-perimeter plate." The inset shows that a real full-perimeter plate (or any other plate intended for use in pianos with no wooden back posts), is very thick and massive. Compare this to the plate in Figure 3-9.

The plates for most U.S. makers come from The O.S. Kelly Co. in Springfield, Ohio. The company was recently purchased by Steinway. Baldwin, formerly O.S. Kelly's biggest customer, now makes most of its plates at a foundry in Brazil. The traditional casting method involves pouring molten iron into a mold of moist green sand. This process, though fraught with difficulty, has been pretty well mastered over the last hundred years. If manufacturers properly maintain their plate patterns (which they often do not), this process usually produces plates that are very acceptable, though perhaps not perfectly consistent from one to the next. A new vacuum system of plate casting ("V-process") is now being used by some Japanese and Korean makers, producing smoother, more uniform plates with finer decorative detail. These plates may be slightly faster and less expensive to produce because they require less finishing work, but other than the finer decorative detail, they are functionally about equivalent to well-made traditional castings. (Some say the two types of casting have different effects on the piano's tone, with the sand-cast plates producing a warmer tone, but the jury is still out on this.) In general, grand piano plates, being more visible, are given the royal treatment in sanding and finishing. Vertical piano plates are left in a rougher condition, except that "deluxe" models may have their upper halves finished smooth.

Pinblock and tuning pins. Also part of the piano structure is the **pinblock** (Figure 3-9), sometimes called the **wrestplank**, a laminated hardwood plank running the width of the piano and attached to the plate, the wooden framework, or both. Embedded in holes in the pinblock are steel **tuning pins**, around each of which is coiled one end of a piano string. Tuning pins undergo a "bluing" process—a controlled oxidation that makes them hold better in the wood. In addition, some tuning pins are nickel-plated, which may help them to look better longer.

The pinblock has to hold the tuning pins tightly enough, by friction alone, so that all the strings are maintained at the right tension without unwinding. The piano is tuned by turning the tuning pins slightly with a "tuning hammer," thereby increasing or decreasing the tension on the strings, as needed, to make them sound in harmony with one another. Alternate layers of the pinblock run cross-grain to each other to prevent warping and cracking and to aid in even gripping of the fine threads on the tuning pins.

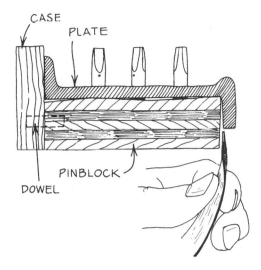

FIGURE 3-10. The pinblock must be perfectly fitted to the plate at the surfaces they share in common. Otherwise, when tension is applied to the strings, the pinblock may move (even though it's screwed to the plate), creating tremendous tuning and structural problems. One of the hidden differences between pianos of differing quality is in the care with which this fitting process is done. The fitting of the pinblock shown here is poor, both at the top and at the flange. (Sometimes technicians will test the fit at the flange by attempting to stuff a piece of paper between the pinblock and the plate. If they can, the fit could be better.) Makers of the finest pianos not only screw the pinblock to the plate but may dowel or mortise it into the case as well.

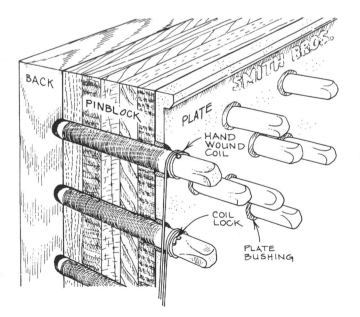

FIGURE 3-9. A laminated hardwood pinblock grips the tuning pins to keep the strings from slackening. On most pianos, a hardwood plate bushing surrounds each tuning pin where it passes through a hole in the plate. They are, however, not necessary, and not all pianos have them.

PITCH: "Mr. Jones, this Deluxe Console has a two-inch-thick, sixteen-ply pinblock, thicker and with more laminations than even some of the biggest-name pianos on the market. The tuning pins will never get loose, I guarantee."

TRUTH: There is no particular advantage to having a large number of pinblock laminations per se, so don't bother counting them. Pinblocks come in several varieties, which differ in the number of laminations they contain (from three to forty-one), the thickness of each layer, and their density. The denser pinblocks may perform better and last longer when subjected to extreme dryness and dampness, but all types are capable of good service under normal conditions. Pinblock failure resulting in loose tuning pins in poorly made pianos, when not due to abusive treatment, is caused by inferior wood that hasn't been seasoned long enough, or by inaccurate fitting of the pinblock to the plate (Figure 3-10), or by sloppy drilling of the holes for the tuning pins. In any case, this failure is unlikely to have anything to do with the number of laminations in the pinblock. Furthermore, the maximum penetration of a tuning pin in the wood is only about 1¼ inches, so some pinblocks are endowed with extra

Pinblock Quality

The issue of quality is probably more critical with respect to the pinblock than it is with respect to any other single part of the piano. Repair or replacement of the pinblock is so expensive that, for vertical pianos and many inexpensive grands, when the pinblock is shot the piano is dead. A defective pinblock might compare with, say, a badly cracked engine block in a car. We're not talking about just a tune-up job here—we're talking about junking the instrument or going through an expensive rebuilding process.

Most pinblocks fall into one of three categories (Figure 3-11). The type traditionally used in North American pianos consists of five or six laminations of hard rock maple, each layer about 1/4-inch thick. Provided that the wood is of good quality, dried properly, and so forth, this material is entirely satisfactory under most normal conditions. Steinway has always used this kind of pinblock, as have many other makers. Some manufacturers and rebuilders use a high-quality pinblock of this type that is sold under the brand name Bolduc, made in Canada.

A second type of pinblock material, known as "multi-laminated," is made of about nineteen to forty-one highly compressed veneers of beech or maple. This extremely dense, hard material is used in most Baldwin pianos, as well as in many expensive European and other foreign pianos, often under the brand name Delignit. This material is so dense and impervious to moisture that it's likely to perform well in any climate. Critics of this material point out that veneers, being rotary-cut (peeled off a log like paper towels off a roll), don't have the best grain orientation for supporting the tuning pins, and that there is almost as much glue as there is wood in this type of pinblock, making it more subject to wearing away. So far, however, experience has not proven out these fears.

Perhaps a more important criticism is that extreme densification results in wood that is almost completely lacking in resilience, therefore requiring extreme accuracy in drilling for the tuning pin holes. Since some variation in both drilling and pin size is inevitable, highly densified pinblocks are more likely to have tuning pins that are too tight for careful tuning as well as some tuning pins that are too loose. For that reason, probably the best form of multi-laminated pinblock is one that has not been too highly compressed, and it is best used by companies with high levels of quality control.

The third kind of material is also "multi-laminated" (sort of), with from nine to sixteen 1/8-inch plies, but is less dense than the second type. My sense is that this third type of pinblock material is used by those manufacturers who want to jump on the multi-laminate bandwagon, to satisfy customers who come into the store counting pinblock laminations, without actually using the denser material. As with the other types, the success of this one depends on the quality of wood used and the accuracy in drilling the tuning pin holes.

Drilling the tuning pin holes accurately is the most critical part of making a good pinblock. The tuning pins must be uniform in their angle and position in the holes and uniform in tightness, with a torque (resistance to turning) high enough to hold the strings in tune while allowing for some loosening with age, but not so high as to prevent fine tuning. The more conscientious makers use pinblock material that is more uniform in quality and density, and a drilling apparatus that controls for angle, speed of rotation, the speed with which the drill enters and leaves the wood, and the temperaure of the drill bit, producing very uniform holes.

Today, most established makers do a very credible job of manufacturing their pinblocks. But a look at some of the least advanced brands from developing countries—as well as some of the less expensive pianos produced in the U.S. between 1960 and 1985—will reveal the sloppiness with which the holes were drilled and the extreme variation in tuning pin torque. Pianos like these are likely to suffer a short life.

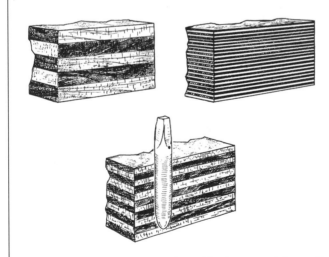

FIGURE 3-11. Three types of pinblock material: traditional five-ply, very dense multi-laminated, and a type in between.

laminations only because they are thicker than they need to be to hold the tuning pins. In some cases the extra thickness may help make the structure a little more stable, but it's not the number of laminations per se that accomplishes this.

PITCH: *"Unlike some other piano brands, all Smith Bros. vertical pianos have a strip of wood covering the top of the piano back structure, acting as a protective moisture barrier to assure the long life of the pinblock. Other pianos are exposed to the elements."*

TRUTH: It should probably be called a "sight barrier" rather than a "moisture barrier," as often, on cheaper pianos, its real purpose is to keep you from seeing rough workmanship underneath.

PITCH: *"Mr. Jones, let me demonstrate to you the superiority of the Japanese tuning pins that Smith Bros. uses in all their pianos. As you can see, when this tuning pin is twisted inside a hankerchief, it snags when turned counterclockwise, but moves smoothly when turned clockwise. This is because the process by which the threads are cut leaves microscopic teeth angled so that the pin can be easily turned in a direction of higher pitch, but encounters resistance when turned in a direction of lower pitch. This helps keep the piano in tune."*

TRUTH: This is absurd. For one thing, it assumes that pianos go out of tune because the tuning pins turn. In fact, as I said before, pianos go out of tune mostly because the seasonal swelling and shrinking of the soundboard alters the tension on the strings. If a piano goes out of tune because the tuning pins turn by themselves, then the tuning pins are loose and the piano is defective. Second, this sales ploy implies that tuners only turn the tuning pins in the direction of higher pitch when tuning the piano. In fact, we turn the pins just as often in one direction as the other. (What Smith Bros. doesn't tell us is why the teeth don't grind out the holes and ruin the pinblock.) This is a good example of how marketing will take a simple, neutral fact concerning the manufacturing process and turn it into a "feature" or "benefit."

Scale Design and Strings

Scale design. The musical design of a piano (as opposed to its cabinetry) is known as its *scale design*. In its everyday usage, this term usually refers just to the stringing scale—that is, the dimensions of the strings (length, thickness, tension) and their arrangement across the plate; but in formal usage, it also includes such factors as the point on the strings contacted by the hammers and dampers, the placement of the bridges, and

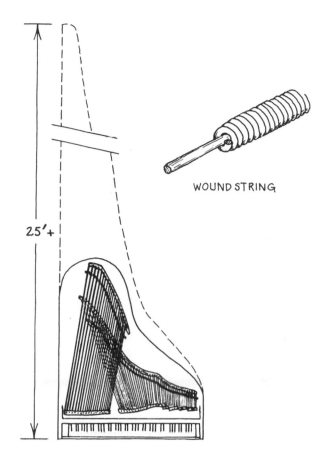

WOUND STRING

FIGURE 3-12. Foreshortening of the scale. If all piano strings were of the same thickness and tension, the piano would have to be more than twenty-five feet long to play all eighty-eight notes (the required string length doubles with each octave). Since this is impractical, the strings are made thicker as well as longer, and the tension varied as needed, to produce the lower notes. Where the steel strings would be too thick to vibrate well, the required mass is attained without reducing flexibility by instead winding copper onto thinner steel. These *wound strings* are used mostly in the bass section. The bass strings are also *overstrung* or *cross-strung* above the treble strings to achieve maximum length and optimum tonal quality in a case of a given size. The particular combination of all these factors varies from model to model and is known as the *stringing scale*, an important part of the *scale design*.

the construction of the soundboard, to name a few. The scale design is like the "genetic code" of a piano. It is a principal determinant of piano tone, and it differs from one piano brand and model to another.

Since there is a practical limit to the height of a vertical piano or the length of a grand we can fit in our homes, strings are made thicker, instead of just longer, to create lower-sounding notes (Figure 3-12). The smaller the piano, the more thickness must be substituted for length in producing sounds of lower pitch. When the steel strings would otherwise become too thick and stiff to produce a good tone, they are wound with

Buying Tip: Check for Inadequacies in Stringing Scale

1. On small pianos, it's common to find wound strings in the tenor section, but you should avoid pianos in which the wound strings extend farther up the scale than the note E32 (the E below middle C). This somewhat arbitrary limit is based on the fact that most tuners use a tuning procedure that begins on the note F33; the procedure is complicated by the presence of wound strings from that point upward in the scale. More important, only a piano that is just plain too small would require wound strings higher than E32.

2. Virtually all pianos made today have three strings per note throughout most of the treble, two strings per note in the upper bass, and one per note in the lower bass (see page 7). A few cheap models made in the last few decades have only two strings per note in the treble and one per note in the bass, and far fewer than eighty-eight notes total. Even if you are looking for a small piano, avoid the temptation to buy one of these. They are so poorly made in every respect that they would best be classified as junk.

copper to give the requisite mass without sacrificing flexibility too much. These *wound* strings are principally used in the bass section, but they may also be used judiciously in the area of the treble section just above the bass (often called the *tenor* section), especially in small pianos, where plain strings would otherwise have a poor tone.

This method of using thicker strings instead of longer strings to produce lower-pitched notes has its limitations. The smaller the piano, the harder it becomes to get a good tone out of the strings in the tenor and lower bass sections, regardless of the use of copper windings. All piano strings give off slightly distorted harmonics, a property known as *inharmonicity*, which contributes to the characteristic sound of the piano. But the relatively short, thick tenor and bass strings of small pianos have an excessive amount of inharmonicity, producing a nasal or hollow sound and making it impossible to tune the piano so that the various sections blend together in harmony. The tuners of these instruments must harden their sensibilities much as one might grimace when taking an unpleasant medicine. For this reason, other factors being equal, you should always buy the largest piano that you can afford and have space for.

PITCH: *"Mr. Jones, all Smith Bros. consoles are a full 42 inches tall. Most other consoles are only 40 or 41 inches."*

TRUTH: No single factor is more important to the scale design and tone of a piano than its size (meaning the height of a vertical piano or the length of a grand). But don't be fooled by the difference of an inch or two in height or length. For example, 40-, 41-, and 42-inch pianos may all have only a 40-inch scale design. In a vertical, the difference in height can easily be created by an extra-thick lid, larger casters, or a redesigned cabinet—in a grand, by a slightly longer case—and may not contribute one iota to the tone quality.

PITCH: *"Because the Smith Bros. console is taller, its longest bass string is a full two inches longer than that of its nearest competitor. This means that the tone will be superior."*

TRUTH: Because string length is so important and this idea is easily communicated to consumers, some manufacturers make a very big deal about the length of their longest strings. Usually they advertise the length of the string for A_1, the lowest note on the piano.

But scale design is too complex to characterize an entire piano by the length of one string. Under certain circumstances, a slightly shorter speaking length with a different combination of thickness and tension or a longer tail length might produce a better tone, and some pianos may be scaled well in one section and not in another. The maxim that longer strings make for a better tone, while essentially correct, is most useful when comparing pianos whose scale designs are substantially different in size—at least three to six inches—not for making nitpicking comparisons between similarly sized pianos.

Furthermore, there are trade-offs in scale designing; an insistence on the longest strings possible may create problems elsewhere in the piano. For instance, you'll notice that bass strings are always positioned above and diagonally across the treble strings, partly to achieve greater string length in a given size case. The bass hammers are mounted on their shanks to match, as closely as possible, the angle of the bass strings. But the maximum angle at which the hammers can be mounted is very limited, and when the bass strings are at too great an angle to the treble strings, it's impossible to align the hammers to match. Bass hammers in such pianos, mounted at the maximum possible angle, have a tendency to collide with each other during playing or to graze adjacent strings, causing discordant sounds. Therefore, excellence in scale design cannot be communicated through marketing gimmicry because such excellence depends on the masterful coordination of all tone-related factors, rather than on the single-minded pursuit of any particular factor.

Figure 3-13 shows some of the more common physical and service-related problems caused by sloppy

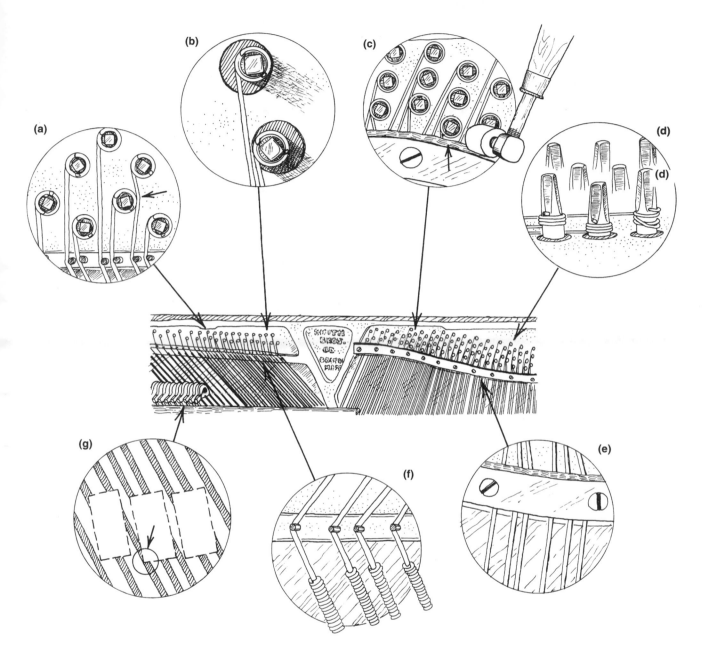

FIGURE 3-13. Some examples of sloppy workmanship and poor scale design. Only a few of these are found in pianos being made today, but most are common in cheaper pianos made from about 1960 to the early 1980s. Clockwise from top left: (a) strings bend around neighboring tuning pins, causing tuning problems; (b) tuning pin holes drilled off-center; (c) tuning pins too closely spaced or placed too close to the pressure bar so the tuning hammer won't fit over them; (d) sloppy string coils around tuning pins, or coils at uneven heights above plate, the latter indicating possible pinblock problems; (e) treble strings poorly spaced or shifting position, resulting in uneven wear to hammers and dampers; (f) bass strings haphazardly spaced and strung at too great an angle around the upper bearing point (the latter may result in premature breakage); (g) bass hammers at an angle to bass strings such that the hammers strike the strings of neighboring notes, producing discordant sounds.

Buying Tip: Check for Discordant Sounds

As mentioned above and shown in Figure 3-13g, the scale design of some pianos is such that the bass hammers tend to graze strings belonging to neighboring notes. If the dampers are sitting on those neighboring strings, you may not hear them. But if you are using the sustain pedal (the right-hand pedal)—which lifts all the dampers to allow the tone to sustain—this misalignment of hammers and strings will show up as an ugly dissonance. If this problem is inherent in the design of the piano, there is literally nothing you can do about it (except chop off part of the offending hammers). The smaller the piano, the more likely this problem will occur, although it happens even on some otherwise well-designed studio pianos.

When inspecting a piano you're thinking of buying, you can check aurally for this problem; a visual check alone may be misleading. First, look inside the piano to see on what note the overstrung section (angled bass strings) begins (on a vertical piano, have the salesperson remove the upper panel for you). On small and medium-size pianos the overstrung section usually begins about an octave or less below middle C. With the right-hand pedal depressed, play the note loudly and listen carefully. You will hear a general sympathetic reverberation of all the strings, but this is not what you're listening for. Listen for a dissonance—a sound as if you had also played the next lower note at the same time. (If you're unsure of what that would sound like, try actually playing both notes at the same time.) Next, release the pedal to stop the sound. Now, press the pedal again and play the next lower note loudly, listening again for the dissonance of two neighboring notes sounding simultaneously. Continue in this manner down the keyboard through most of the bass section. Where the hammers begin striking only one string per note (the lowest portion of the bass section), you can stop, as the problem won't exist there. If you have found only one or two dissonance problems, you can inquire as to whether they might be corrected by adjusting the spacing of the hammers. If you have found many such problems, think twice about buying that model.

workmanship and poor scale design in many pianos made during the past four decades.

PITCH: "The scales of Smith Bros. pianos were all designed with the help of the Tasmania State University computer. They are the best scales possible."

TRUTH: With the advent of the computer age, some piano makers are now claiming that their scales are designed by computer. In fact, some really poor scale designs have been dramatically improved with the help of computers. On the other hand, many of the world's best scale designs originated over a hundred years ago and have scarcely changed a bit since then.

Since scales derived from formula always need to be corrected, to some extent, by trial and error, computers can be an aid, but by no means do they assure success.

PITCH: "Smith Bros. now imports this new Bürgstein piano from Mongolia. Not only is it designed by a German scale designer, but it also has a German pinblock, German strings, German hammers, German action, German keys, and German pedals. It's virtually a German piano at one-tenth the price!"

TRUTH: An increasing number of companies—especially Korean and Chinese—hire "German" scale designers or engineers with German-sounding names to redesign their pianos. Some of these engineers are very good at what they do, but they are not necessarily free to do anything they like. They must work within parameters set by the company concerning materials and manufacturing processes, and must limit their work to changes that are economically viable and technologically possible. Although they may make improvements, the instruments will still retain many, if not most, of the limitations of the original, unimproved version.

In addition to imported scale designers, German-sounding piano names are also highly sought after by manufacturers, and German-made parts are frequently used in non-German pianos. Without a doubt, the pianos are better with the German parts than without, but how the parts are cut, fitted, glued, drilled, mounted, adjusted, and regulated probably counts for as much as, if not more than, where the parts came from. So the presence of many German parts in a piano from a developing country should be considered a plus, but not a cure-all.

As for the German name? It improves the piano two hundred percent, of course!

PITCH: "The Smith Bros. grand contains a duplex scale for added tonal color, just like the world's best pianos."

TRUTH: Usually the back end of each string, between the bridge and the hitch pin, and the front end, near the tuning pin, are muted with cloth so they don't vibrate sympathetically. On some grands and a few verticals, though, the back end of the string is further subdivided with a small metal bar or plate called an **aliquot**, and the section of string between the aliquot and the bridge is allowed to vibrate sympathetically at some higher frequency (Figure 3-14). The waste end of the string near the tuning pin may also be left unmuted for the same purpose. This *duplex scale* can add tonal color, brilliance, and sustain to the treble, and is usually an advantage. Sometimes, however, a duplex scale adds objectionable overtones and buzzes to the

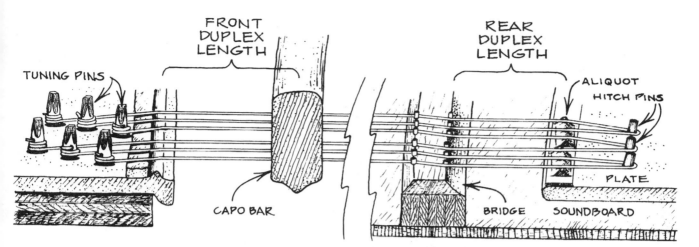

FIGURE 3-14. Duplex scale. The length of string between the bridge and the aliquot, and the length near the tuning pin, instead of being muted with cloth, vibrate sympathetically and add color to the tone.

Buying Tip: Check String Spacing

Strings should be perfectly and uniformly spaced in relation to each other, as in Figure 3-15. Poorly made pianos will frequently have strings spaced incorrectly (see Figure 3-13e). The spacing can be temporarily corrected by a technician, but the strings may gradually creep back as they are played. Defective design or construction can actually make correct alignment of the tuning pin, plate, string, and bridge impossible. Over time, the hammers hitting incorrectly spaced strings will wear unevenly, the dampers won't be able to seat properly to stop the sound, and, in extreme cases, tuning may be more difficult. Badly spaced strings are one of the most obvious signs of a badly constructed instrument.

One way the string spacing problem is solved on some pianos is with the use of small brass fittings called *agraffes* (pronounced *AY-grafs*), which are screwed into the plate. The agraffes have holes through which the strings pass, keeping them perfectly spaced regardless of whatever forces may be inducing them to shift. Generally considered an indication of good quality, agraffes seem to be most useful in the tenor and bass sections of the piano, where the string spacing is especially critical for the operation of the dampers. Some pianos have "full agraffes"—eighty-eight of them—but this is not necessarily good, even though it looks pretty. Some technicians feel that agraffes above the middle treble tend to diminish the tonal palette to a rather "woody," thin sound, and they consider full agraffes to be a disadvantage tonally in many pianos.

Also check that the coils around the tuning pins are neat and reasonably uniform in their distance from the plate.

When a piano is new, the tuning pins are installed so that the coils are $3/16$ inch (give or take a little) from the plate. This allows some room for tapping the tuning pins further into the pinblock if they should get loose with age. If the coils are uneven in height, or if many are already down against the plate, this may indicate that the tuning pins have already gotten loose and the pinblock may be faulty (see Figure 3-13d).

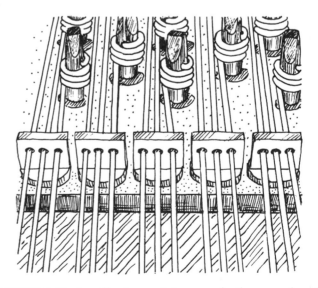

FIGURE 3-15. Agraffes keep strings perfectly spaced and provide a good upper bearing point for the speaking length (vibrating portion of the string).

Buying Tip: Check for Rattling Bass Strings and Buzzing Treble Strings

Play each bass note loudly and listen for a rattling or buzzing sound indicating a faulty bass string. This is a very common defect and dealers are accustomed to correcting it—you need only point it out to them. Also check for any buzzing treble strings, often caused by manufacturing debris lodged against a string at the bridge, or by poor contact between the string and its bearing points.

sound, or makes no difference at all. Because it's so visible, duplex scaling is frequently used as a selling feature, regardless of whether it actually improves the sound of the piano. Interestingly, although the portion of the duplex scale at the back end of the string is the most featured and celebrated, the portion near the tuning pin is often the most effective, or the most troublesome, as the case may be.

Strings. Bass strings are made with steel wire weighted down with a winding of solid copper to slow their vibration without impairing their flexibility. Really, they

could be wound with any material that produced the required mass—iron windings were used in the old days—but copper has been found to produce a nice tone, and it doesn't rust like iron.

PITCH: "The string coils around Smith Bros. tuning pins contain a patented coil lock that prevents the coils from ever slipping off the tuning pins."

TRUTH: A coil properly made by a piano technician will never in a hundred years slip off a tuning pin. Some factories, however, have automated their stringing process, the strings being wound around the tuning pins by machine in one department and much later installed in the piano by hand in another department. If not for the coil lock—which is just a bent piece of the wire (see Figure 3-9)—the string might indeed slip out of its hole in the tuning pin while waiting to be installed, making the installer's job more difficult. Many companies still perform the entire stringing process by hand in one operation, in which case the coil lock is not needed. The presence of the coil lock makes tuning pin and string repairs more difficult for the service technician.

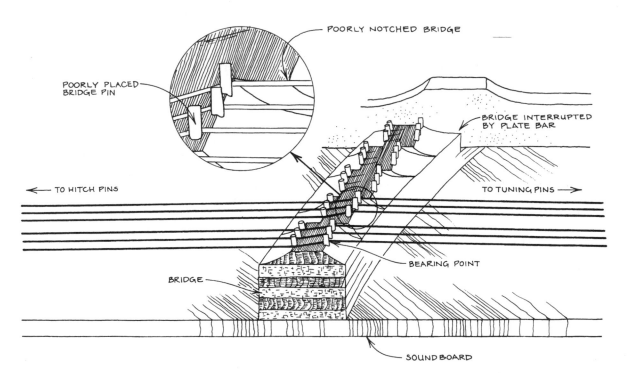

FIGURE 3-16. The point where the string first contacts the bridge is one of the string's bearing points (the ends of its speaking length). To avoid poor tone and wild strings, each string must contact the wooden bridge at the exact same point it contacts its bridge pin. That is, the beginning of the notch in the bridge must bisect the row of bridge pins. The inset in the drawing shows a poorly spaced bridge pin. The string that contacts it will be "confused" as to whether its bearing point is the edge of the notch or the pin, resulting in a "confused" sound. The inset also shows a notch that is not wide enough; the string may touch the side of the notch and cause a buzz. The main drawing shows a bridge interrupted by a part of the cast-iron plate. Often the tone of the notes immediately on either side of this interruption will be deficient. Better pianos avoid this kind of arrangement.

Bridges and Soundboard

Bridges. The strings pass over wooden **bridges**—a long, curved one for the treble and a shorter one for the bass strings—which transmit the vibrations of the strings to the soundboard. The transmission of energy is aided by the slight *downbearing* of the strings against the bridge and by the *sidebearing* of the strings against pairs of staggered metal bridge pins driven into the bridge. The bridge pins also delineate the end of the vibrating part of the string, just as a violinist's or guitarist's fingers "stop" a string by pressing it against the finger board or frets. So the strings don't touch the bridge before contacting the bridge pins, the bridge is *notched*—cut away—at its edges (Figure 3-16).

Bridges must be well constructed, both to transmit vibration properly and to avoid splitting under the pressure of the strings. Most bridges are made of maple or beech, either solid or vertically laminated, sometimes with a top layer or **cap**. Some are horizontally laminated (Figure 3-17). This last type is easiest to manufacture and often used on cheaper pianos. Because these pianos at times don't sound very good, it has long been thought that this type of bridge construction was faulty due to the horizontal grain orientation and glue lines. Some experts now believe that this type of construction can be as satisfactory as the others if good materials and design are utilized.

The accuracy of bridge notching is extremely important (see Figure 3-16). Inaccurate notching can result in "wild strings" (which produce permanently out-of-tune sounds known as *false beats*), buzzing sounds, and tinny tone. The traditional method of notching—still used on many of the finest brands of piano—is by hand; that is, by a woodworker with a chisel, working by eye. Other methods include using hand-held routing machines guided by a metal template or a beam of light, and using computer-controlled routing machines. Any of these methods, either by hand or by machine, can produce good or poor work depending on the standards set by company management. For instance, at one factory I visited I observed that a metal template set up to guide a router was moving every time the router hit it. This particular "machine" produced an inaccurate cut.

Traditionally, both the front and rear of the bridge are notched, even though the rear ends of the strings are usually muted with cloth. In theory, this is so the strings will contact only a minimal area of the bridge, allowing the bridge to vibrate more freely. On some of the cheaper verticals, to save money, only the front of the bridge is notched. The result of this shortcut may be a greater chance of problems with buzzing strings, hardly worth the miniscule savings realized on each piano. In any case, you can take the lack of rear notching

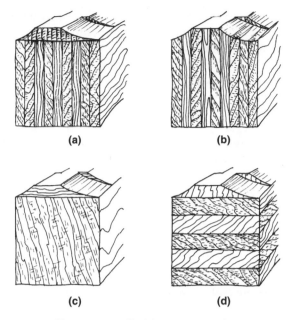

FIGURE 3-17. Four types of bridge construction commonly used: (a) vertical laminations with cap, used by Steinway; (b) vertical laminations without cap, used by Baldwin; (c) solid bridge with cap, used by many makers; (d) horizontal laminations, sometimes used on cheaper pianos.

as a signal that corners are being cut slightly on that model. (At one time there were also cheap pianos whose bridges were unnotched throughout, front *and* rear. The tone was so bad that they were virtually untunable.)

Soundboard. The bridges are glued to the **soundboard**, which changes the strings' vibrating energy into sound waves that we can hear. The soundboard has a slight curvature, or *crown*, built into it to help it resist the downpressure of the strings on the bridges; also, wood under tension transmits sound better. As mentioned before, the downbearing of the strings against the bridges is necessary for good transmission of tone, but the sum total of all this downbearing can be as much as a thousand pounds, and without the upward crown of the soundboard, the strings would simply push the bridges away until contact was negligible.

Soundboards are traditionally made of a solid sheet of quarter-sawn spruce, 1/4 to 3/8-inch thick, made by gluing narrower boards together edge to edge. Spruce is used because it has a fine, straight grain, is strong and resilient, and reproduces the sound of the strings better than any other material. It is also used in violins and other fine stringed instruments. The best-quality spruce has from eight to twenty annular rings (growth lines) per inch (the more the better), a very straight and uniform grain, and is quite light in color. Coarser and darker spruce is sometimes used in cheaper pianos, but not as successfully. However, top-quality spruce is getting more scarce and expensive all the time.

Over the past few decades, an increasing number of pianos have been made with laminated soundboards consisting of three layers of spruce or other woods, or spruce combined with other woods. Usually a thick layer in the middle is surrounded by two layers of veneer (Figure 3-18). Sometimes the three layers are of equal thickness. The advantage of a laminated soundboard is that it is virtually immune to cracking and loss of crown. Most laminated soundboards are in fact warranted against these problems for from fifty to eighty years!

PITCH: "Many of our Smith Bros. pianos contain laminated soundboards, guaranteed not to crack or lose their crown for sixty years."

TRUTH: Solid spruce soundboards are highly affected by changes in humidity, and if special care isn't taken in their manufacture and installation, or if they are subjected to extreme conditions, they can quickly develop cracks or lose their crown. Even the best solid spruce soundboards under normal conditions may develop cracks after a few decades in certain climates. Laminated boards, on the other hand, are virtually immune to these problems because the outer layers run crossgrain to the inner layer. Manufacturers can take less care with these boards and still guarantee them almost indefinitely.

Laminated soundboards still have a bad reputation because of poor quality in their early years (1960s and '70s). Either they were installed in the worst promotional pianos or were simply substituted for solid spruce soundboards without any regard for the special design requirements of laminated boards (such as ribbing and downbearing) due to their different stiffness and weight characteristics. Most pianos with laminated soundboards of this period (and still occasionally today) are judged to have a tone variously described as "muddy," "thumpy," or weak in the bass and tenor, and uniformly bright in the treble in a way that initially sounds interesting but eventually wears poorly on the ears. Sometimes the sound dies away too quickly, too, particularly in the middle area of the keyboard. The worst laminated soundboards are those made of basswood or mahogany, not spruce. Makers of these pianos have been concerned only with keeping down cost, or inducing you to buy their next more expensive model with a better soundboard.

During the last decade, though, laminated soundboards have greatly improved as they have graduated from the "lower class" to the "middle class" of pianos. As market acceptance increases, so will research into the best ways of designing this type of soundboard. Even if laminated soundboards never replace solid ones in the highest quality pianos, we can still expect

FIGURE 3-18. Top: Solid spruce soundboard. Bottom: Laminated soundboard. Right: It is usually difficult to tell whether the soundboard is solid or laminated by looking at the front or back since the outer veneers may be chosen to resemble a solid spruce board. If the wood is clearly not spruce or the grain runs horizontally, you can be sure the soundboard is laminated, because all non-spruce boards are laminated and all solid spruce boards are installed with the grain running diagonally for best tone. If there is a hole in the soundboard through which a plate bolt passes to a vertical back post or grand rim brace, careful inspection of the exposed edges may reveal the soundboard's true nature. But sometimes the veneers are too thin to be seen or the exposed edges are actually doctored to deceive the customer. Note: Turn the drawing to the right clockwise 90 degrees to picture a grand piano's soundboard viewed from below.

to see them more often in the years ahead in pianos of average and good quality.

My advice, however, is to pay attention only to how the piano sounds and not to buy a piano just because of claims that its laminated soundboard won't crack. These claims, though true, are only capitalizing on the great fear of the Cracked Soundboard. Contrary to popular myth, a cracked soundboard does not mean the death of the piano. It's true that cracks indicate that drying has occurred, with a possible loss of some crown and attendant tonal changes. But, in practice, most cracking does not seem to adversely affect the tone unless the cracking is extensive (and sometimes not even then), and many wonderful-sounding pianos have cracked soundboards. Anyway, if you buy a good piano and don't subject it to abusive conditions, it will be a long time before cracks appear. Laminated soundboards were invented as a way to cut costs in the manufacturing process and reduce warranty problems, and their sixty-year warranties are a way to promote them. If a piano with a laminated soundboard sounds good, fine; in the long run this soundboard may have some slight benefits. Otherwise avoid it.

PITCH: "All Smith Bros. pianos have full-length ribs to better support the crown of the soundboard."

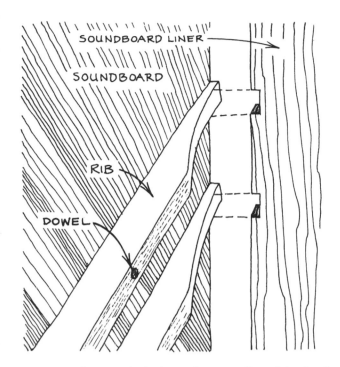

FIGURE 3-19. In a vertical piano, the soundboard is glued to a "liner," a simple frame attached to the wooden back. In a grand, the soundboard is glued directly to the inner rim, under the plate. In most pianos, the ribs extend all the way to the edge of the soundboard and are recessed into notches cut in the rim or liner. In some pianos, the ribs are cut short, usually to avoid the expense of cutting the notches, but possibly for other reasons. Also shown: On some of the finest pianos, the bridges are doweled to the soundboard—for extra holding power—in addition to being glued, and the dowels extend through the ribs. Note: To picture a grand, turn this drawing clockwise 90 degrees and substitute "inner rim" for "soundboard liner."

Buying Tip: Check for Crown

As already mentioned, a soundboard must have crown to ensure good tone. Some pianos—even some expensive, top-quality pianos—are reportedly coming out of the factory with no measurable crown, or with so little crown that it disappears entirely when the soundboard shrinks during the dry season. In theory, a piano with no measurable crown shouldn't sound good—at least not for very long. But in reality, plenty of fine pianos, both old and new, have no crown and sound great. Small, cheap pianos have so many other tonal limitations that I'm not sure you should fuss too much about soundboard crown. But if you are buying a top-quality instrument, you owe it to yourself to check for crown (or have your technician check for it), and to at least place a question mark next to any new piano with no measurable crown. See page 193 to learn how to check for crown.

Buying Tip: Look for a Strike-Point Adjuster

To a very large extent, the tone of each note is determined by the exact point along the length of the string at which the hammer strikes. The *strike point* is especially critical in the high treble section, where a variation of barely 1/16 inch can make the difference between a dull thud and a clear, ringing tone. The strike point is set in the factory, but sometimes needs to be changed later by a technician when servicing the hammers or when the factory setting appears to be wrong. For this reason most grand pianos have a "strike-point adjuster" mechanism, which can reposition the whole action relative to the strings. The mechanism is located inside of or near the treble keyblock (see Figure 1-15 for the location of the keyblocks). Some less expensive grands—the ones most likely to need this feature—don't have it. A grand piano is a long-term investment, and at some point in the life of your piano you are likely to need this adjustment. Verticals don't have a strike-point adjuster per se, but adjustment can usually be made by other means, and often needs to be. Some verticals, however, are mounted so as to make strike-point adjustment virtually impossible. A technician may be able to identify these models for you.

TRUTH: The **ribs** on the back of a soundboard help to maintain its crown (curvature), transmit vibration across the grain of the soundboard, and generally "tie" the soundboard together. On most pianos, the ribs extend all the way to the edge of the soundboard and fit into notches cut into the liner to which the soundboard is glued (Figure 3-19). These ribs are said to be "let in" or "full length." This construction practice was developed for the purely practical reason that the animal hide glues used during the first few decades of piano development were not always very reliable, and the ribs sometimes came loose if not tightly fit into these notches. In some of today's factories this practice may still be advisable, but if modern glues are used and the gluing process carefully monitored, it is no longer necessary. No test evidence I am aware of indicates that having the ribs set into notches helps to maintain crown. This practice seems to continue primarily for reasons of marketing and tradition. One way some companies save money is by cutting off the ribs just short of the liner. Usually this is an indication that the piano is cheaply made, but it's entirely possible that this type of construction could be called for as part of a well-thought-out scale design.

Listening to Tone

This is certainly no place to pay any attention to the promotional literature, as all the manufacturers will tell you how marvelous their piano's tone is. The only way to judge is to listen, take a lot of time, and make numerous comparisons between instruments. Compare pianos of the same brand and model and pianos of different models. (Nothing beats having two pianos sitting right next to each other for comparison.) Frankly, though, when shopping among today's pianos, especially at the low end of the market, it's easy to get lost in a sea of mediocrity and forget just what a good piano sounds like. When you do, the cure is always to go back and play some of the finest pianos money can buy—even if you have no intention of buying one—just to refresh your memory of what a great piano sounds like so you can place other pianos in comparison. (Warning:

This advice may be hazardous to your bank account.)

As your ear tries to make comparisons, however, two obstacles will stand in the way: (1) In order for you to judge its tone, a piano must be in very good tune. As I will explain later in this chapter, it may be hard to find many pianos that are in tune on the showroom floor. There's not much I can do to help you about this. (2) If you are inexperienced with pianos, you may not know just what to listen for. Writing about how to listen to tone is something like writing about how to look at art—only worse. Nevertheless, here's some information that may help.

What we call *tone* consists of several components (Figure 3-20): *volume* of sound—how loud or soft it is;

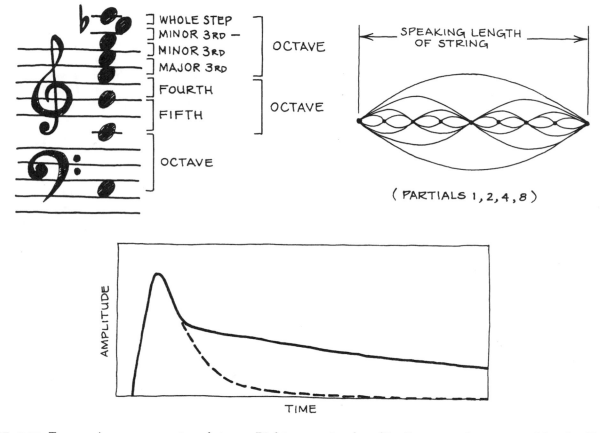

FIGURE 3-20. Two major components of tone. Right: Harmonic content. When a string vibrates, it subdivides into many smaller vibrating segments that simultaneously give off fainter, higher pitched tones called *partials* or *overtones*. These partials bear a definite harmonic relationship to one another called the *harmonic series*. Left: The first eight tones of the harmonic series for low C are shown here in their approximate relationship on the musical staff. The note actually played (in this case, low C) is called the *fundamental*, or first partial. Theoretically, there are an infinite number of partials. We can actually hear dozens of them, usually without knowing it. The relative strength of each of these partials and the degree to which they deviate from their theoretical frequency (this deviation is known as *inharmonicity*) make up what we interpret as *tonal quality*. For example, a tone said to be "bright" contains many loud higher partials; a "mellow" tone has fewer high partials. Bottom: Attack and decay. When we play a note on the piano, we first hear an initial burst of sound, called the *attack*, lasting milliseconds, followed by a rapid but incomplete *decay* lasting a fraction of a second, followed by a slower, more lingering decay, until the sound dies out completely. When the slow portion of the decay is relatively loud and long-lasting (as in the drawing), the tone could be said to be "singing." When the sound dies out quickly (shown by the dotted line), the tone might be called "dead" or "short." This is actually a gross simplification, as each individual partial has its own attack and decay rate. The possible varieties of tone are therefore virtually infinite.

Buying Tip: Put the Lid Down

Some dealers make a point of displaying all their grand pianos in cavernous rooms with hardwood floors, and with the lids up, because they know that in such a "live" acoustical environment *any* piano will sound "grand." A buyer of one of these pianos may be in for a rude awakening when the instrument is delivered to his or her home. You may not be able to change the dealer's showroom acoustics, but you can at least put the lid down, which will probably more closely simulate the way the piano will be played in your home.

harmonic content, which manifests itself as "bright," "mellow," "nasal," and so on; *attack*—the initial sound of the hammer striking the string, lasting only milliseconds; and *sustain time* or *decay*—how long the tone sustains when you hold a key down, and how it fades away. These should be fairly uniform from note to note and from one section of the piano to another, and different sections should blend in pleasing harmony with each other when played together. To accomplish this requires very careful design and coordination of scale design, strings, soundboard, bridges, and hammers.

When smaller pianos were first introduced, they suffered from the problem that their smaller soundboards produced a smaller sound. To compensate for this, their scales were redesigned to stretch their strings at a higher tension, which produced a louder, brighter tone. But this also made the strings stiffer and reduced the quality of tone even while increasing the volume. It's tempting for beginners to confuse loudness and brightness of tone with quality. Therefore, many of these pianos have done quite well in the marketplace even though they sound bad to experts. (There are, however, many pianos today with well-designed high-tension scales.)

The volume of sound and the harmonic content are often difficult to differentiate from each other; in fact, they are very closely related. They can also be changed to some extent through a process known as *voicing*; a loud or bright piano can be made softer or mellower, or vice versa. But keep in mind two things when listening to these aspects of tone: (1) room acoustics strongly affect the loudness or brightness you hear, and (2) pianos become brighter over time as the hammer felt packs down. If your home has carpeting, draperies, and upholstered furniture, then the piano will probably sound more subdued there than it will in the dealer's showroom because all these objects absorb sound, particularly high frequencies. However, the piano will get louder with time, so choose one that sounds now just about the way you'd like it to eventu-

ally. If your room acoustics are about the same as the dealer's, then choose a piano that is softer than you'd ultimately like; otherwise, it will become intolerably bright over time (though this can be adjusted—at some expense—when the time comes). It's usually better to err on the mellow side. Also check to see that the piano has an adequate dynamic range—that it can be played both soft and loud and many shades in between. Many pianos today can be played only loud and louder. (For more information on room acoustics, see page 229.)

Play notes in different areas of the keyboard and observe how long the tone sustains, especially in the mid-treble where most melodic lines are played. Consider only that portion of the tone loud enough to be useful in playing. Sustain time can be difficult to judge note by note. Try playing a piece of music in which a melody must be sustained against the background of an accompaniment. Does the melody "sing"? Or do the notes seem to disappear under your fingers, so to speak?

Listen to make sure that the tone is fairly uniform from section to section. There are a number of special problem areas to which you should pay particular attention. The transition from treble strings to bass strings is hard to scale smoothly on small and medium-size pianos. This transition usually occurs somewhere within the octave between middle C and the C below it. Often the bottom few notes in the treble string section will sound peculiar and the sustain will be deficient. Listen also to the highest notes in the treble. Do

Buying Tip: Listen to Differences in Tone and Form Your Own Opinion

Whether by cultural accident, successful marketing, or its inherent qualities, the kind of tone that has been most sought after in North America for the last hundred years is the "Steinway sound," best described as having a strong, singing treble and a powerful bass, rich in high harmonics. But the Steinway sound is not the only tone in town. Other manufacturers, by preference, tradition, or an inability to match the Steinway sound, offer other models of tone for you to choose from. Some European pianos, for instance, emphasize the fundamental tone rather than the harmonics, and probably because of their style of construction, have a tone that sustains at a lower volume. This results in a much less powerful sound that Steinway enthusiasts would likely find dull, but one which has been traditional in Europe since before Steinway was founded. Many Asian pianos have a bright, brittle tone, also short on sustain, which is often preferred by jazz pianists for its crispness. Listen for these differences and form your own opinion and tastes.

they sound clear like the other treble notes, or do they sound like wood hitting metal? Now listen to the bottom bass notes. Do they sound musical, or do they just go "thud"? How definite is their pitch? (This is largely a function of the piano's size.) The quality of sound from the little-used notes on either end may or may not be important to you.

Finally, listen for how the piano blends in harmony with itself. This is largely a function of the piano's size and the length of its bass strings, as well as the skill with which it has been designed. Play a chord in the middle of the piano and, while holding it, play a corresponding note in the low bass. Do they blend smoothly in harmony, or do they sound jarring, as if two different instruments were being played, one bass and one treble? (This can be partially remedied by clever tuning, but not entirely.)

I want to repeat that all of these listening tests depend on the piano being in very good tune. Out-of-tuneness, from slight to gross, can make a piano sound either better (occasionally) or worse (usually) than it really is.

The Action

Defining vertical piano types. Defining the different types of vertical piano may seem like a straightforward and objective task, but there is actually much confusion over it. Vertical pianos come in four basic types, depending partly on their height, and partly on the size of the **action**—the mechanical playing mechanism—and its position in the piano, which in turn de-

pend mostly on the piano's height. However, the popular definitions of these types take into account their height and furniture styling only, ignoring the action. These definitions are often reinforced by salespeople, who are instructed not to get "too technical" with their prospects. So, for example, there are pianos on the market which are of a size and style usually reserved for consoles, and which the dealers will call consoles, but which have studio actions in them. Whereas it may be useful for interior decorators to look at a piano in terms of its styling, musicians will find it more instructive to see these different types of piano in terms of their action.

As shown in Figure 3-21, vertical piano actions come in two different sizes—full-size and compressed (sometimes called "compact")—which can be connected to the keyboard in three different ways—direct blow, extended direct blow, and indirect blow—depending on the action's location in the piano. While the hammers must be positioned to strike the strings at a certain point along their length for good tone (and this position is obviously higher the taller the piano), the keys, in contrast, must always be at about the same height regardless of the size of the piano so that they can be comfortably played by the average person. Because the action must span this distance between the keyboard and the hammer striking point, its size and position depend on the height of the piano.

When most vertical pianos were *full-size uprights* (before about 1930), their actions were full-size and of the extended direct blow–type. The action, located to-

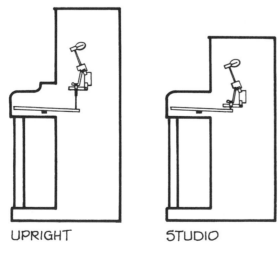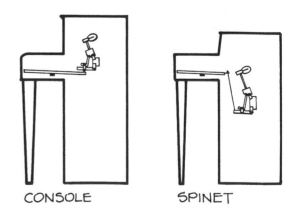

UPRIGHT   STUDIO   CONSOLE   SPINET

FIGURE 3-21. The key and action parts for one note show how the size and position of the action depend on the height of the piano. (a) Full-size upright (47 to 60 inches [currently made only to 52 inches])—full-size action, extended direct-blow type. (b) Studio (43 to 47 inches)—full-size action, direct-blow type. (c) Console (40 to 44 inches)—compressed action (notice the smaller action parts), direct-blow type. (d) Spinet (36 to 40 inches)—full-size action, *in*direct-blow type. Most domestic vertical actions made in the past hundred years fall into these general categories, but foreign-made pianos may have action parts whose size falls in between two types, and occasional hybrid or unusual actions may defy classification.

Buying Tip: Look For a Full-Size, Direct-Blow Action

When buying a vertical piano, choose one with a full-size, direct-blow (or extended direct-blow) action. This means either a studio or a full-size upright. Traditionally, these pianos have been 45 inches tall or taller and sometimes rather imposing. Some manufacturers, however, have been able to fit a full-size studio action into a piano as small as 42½ or 43 inches tall, styled as a console. This satisfies the need for both a more responsive action and, for those that require it, attractive low-profile styling. You may find these small studios variously called consoles, studios, and studio consoles, among other names. Only by inquiring as to both the size of the piano *and* the type of action can you determine just what kind of vertical piano you are really getting.

ward the upper end of the strings, was connected to the keyboard with stilt-like extensions called **stickers**, which were attached either to the action or to the back of the keys. With extended *direct-blow* action, when a key was depressed at the front, the back end would rise and push up on the action parts via the sticker, sending the hammer to strike the strings. In the first round of size-cutting, the *studio* piano was created by simply eliminating the extensions and placing the action right on the back end of the keys. With further reduction in the size of the piano, the full-size action wouldn't fit, so it was "compressed" by reducing the size of some of its parts, and the *console* piano was born. When the piano was made so small that no action would fit in the usual manner at all, the keys were shortened and a full-size, but *indirect-blow* or *drop*, action was installed behind and beneath them. This action gets its name because it is connected to the keys with metal or wooden stickers that extend *downward* and *pull* up on the action parts instead of extending upward and pushing up on the action as with the other types. Pianos with indirect blow actions are called *spinets*.

The advantages and disadvantages of the various sizes of piano have already been discussed in terms of their string length and tone—basically, the larger the piano, the better the tone. This is generally the case with the action as well: all other things being equal, the compressed actions found in consoles do not perform as well as the full-size actions found in studio or upright pianos. The smaller parts of the compressed action meet at greater angles, resulting in more friction and wear, poorer leverage, and lowered ability to repeat notes quickly.

Spinets, although they employ a full-size action, are very difficult to service because even the smallest repair requiring the removal of the action becomes a major ordeal. Each of the connecting stickers has to be disconnected and tied up to the action and all the keys have to be removed from the piano before the action can be lifted out. Then the process has to be reversed when the repair is completed. What would be a five-minute job on a piano with a direct-blow action could take a half hour or an hour on an indirect-blow spinet action. Because of the location of the action, even minor adjustments not requiring action removal can be hard to perform, and the connections between the keys and the stickers are often noisy and troublesome. The shortened keys offer very poor leverage. Add to this the short strings and resulting poor tone, and do you need any more reasons not to buy a spinet? Fortunately, during the past decade, spinets have largely disappeared from the new-piano market, presently being made by only one company.

Action design and manufacturing. Actions are made in several different designs by a number of manufacturers. Some firms, such as Baldwin (operating under the name "Pratt-Win") and the large Asian companies, make some or all of their own keys and actions. Other action suppliers include Langer, a British company (formerly called Herrburger Brooks) that makes the Langer action, and Renner, a German company reputed to make the finest actions in the world. Kluge, a German company now owned by Steinway, makes keys for a number of manufacturers. Sometimes an action made by one company will be of a *type* originally designed by another. For instance, some actions could be of a "Renner-type," although not actually made by Renner.

Both vertical and grand actions come in a number of different designs. Most of these designs differ in the location and type of various springs, the leverage

Buying Tip: Check for Buckskin

Traditionally, buckskin has been used for minimum friction and maximum durability on certain action parts that get a great deal of wear, such as the hammer butts in a vertical piano. At one time, when buckskin was scarce, cloth was substituted in some of the cheaper verticals. Those early cloth actions quickly led to disaster when the cloth compressed and wore right through, but the cloth has since been substantially improved and may now be preferred to some of the rough buckskin, cowhide, and other mediocre substitutes sometimes used. For pianos that get regular or strenuous use, though, fine-textured buckskin, or a high-quality synthetic alternative, is still suggested. In addition to wearing away faster, inferior materials may add unwanted noise and friction to the action. The dealer or technician may be able to provide you with information about the material used for a particular piano.

Buying Tip: Testing the Action

If you are an advanced pianist, test an action with your most technically demanding passages, especially those with trills and repeating notes. Also test to make sure you can play very soft passages without the action "missing." If you have problems, of course, the fault could lie in the "regulation," or adjustment, of the action. The dealer's technician may be able to cure the problem, but don't rely on a promise; make sure the action is fully capable of performing to your satisfaction before agreeing to buy the piano.

On vertical pianos, all pianists should make sure they can play lightly without the hammers double-striking (hitting the string several times on a single stroke of the key). This is especially a problem for people who have a naturally light touch, such as children, and occurs primarily in the center area of the keyboard of pianos with a Schwander-type action, most of which are of Asian or European origin. Sometimes this problem can be corrected, sometimes not. These Schwander-type vertical actions are very well designed and well made in many respects, but tend to be more sensitive to slight changes in adjustment that cause malfunction than the standard American action (Figure 3-22).

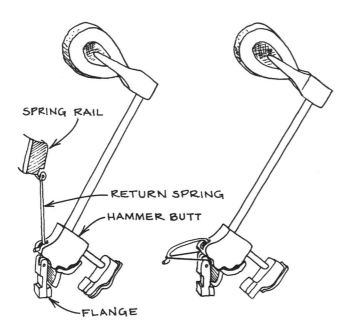

FIGURE 3-22. Left: An American-style vertical hammer assembly. The hammer return spring is attached to a separate rail and bears against a groove in the hammer butt. Right: A Schwander-type hammer assembly. The return spring for each hammer is part of the hammer butt itself and bears against a silk or nylon cord attached to the hammer flange (hinge). This kind of spring may be a little weaker and lead to the phenomenon of "double-striking" on some pianos.

between parts, and other engineering specifications. These variations translate into differences in the "feel" of the action, the speed with which notes can be repeated ("repetition"), and the accuracy and ease of adjustment. For most average pianists, some of these differences are probably academic. (After all, does it really matter whether an action is capable of repeating fourteen or sixteen times a second when most pianists can barely play at half those speeds?) However, for the more advanced pianist, and in some special situations, the design differences may be significant.

For instance, Pratt-Win ("American-style") vertical actions are, in my opinion, more coarsely designed than most of the foreign actions. That is, they will usually not respond as well to nuances of touch, making it more difficult to play at different dynamic levels. The other side of the coin, though, is that the American-style actions will tolerate going far out of adjustment before they will begin to malfunction, whereas the Schwander-type, for example, may fail to work properly if the regulation is off by even a little bit.

Actions also differ in the accuracy with which they're made. Cheaper actions have rougher, less uniform-looking parts, use lower-quality cloth and other material that will compress and wear away faster, are liable to be more sloppily assembled, and may not be capable of fine adjustment or regulation. Parts are more likely to get stuck, rub against one another, and otherwise make life miserable for the pianist (and for the technician). At times, actions in some of the cheapest promotional pianos have actually omitted parts that have traditionally been considered essential, such as bridle straps and key buttons. Companies can generally be expected to use an action whose quality is consistent with that of the rest of the piano, sometimes employing one style for their cheaper or smaller pianos and a better style for the larger, more expensive ones.

Many people expect a vertical piano action to perform as well as a grand. Actually, the two differ significantly. The grand action employs a special "repetition mechanism" (Figure 3-23; also see page 10) that allows it to reset itself for the next stroke of the key much sooner than a vertical action. Thus a grand action will usually repeat notes faster and more reliably than a vertical. The grand action uses gravity, rather than springs, to return the hammer to rest position after a note is played. Thus a grand action is likely to feel more even from note to note than a vertical. In general, a grand action can be played with greater control and expressiveness than a vertical. However, a well-made and properly adjusted vertical action may actually perform better than that of a mediocre grand.

During the past decade, several manufacturers have brought out new vertical action designs that attempt to mimic the workings of a grand action through the use of special springs, levers, or magnets. Best known of these is the Fandrich Vertical Action by Fandrich Design, Inc. This action is custom-installed in selected pianos by the Seattle-based inventor.

PITCH: "Mr. Jones, unlike some other brands, all the action parts in Smith Bros. pianos are made of solid maple—no plastic parts in our pianos!"

TRUTH: Some manufacturers use a high grade of plastic for certain action parts, both grand and vertical. Tooling up to produce these parts is too expensive for all but the largest firms, but in the long run saves money over the expensive hardwoods normally used in actions. Those companies that are *not* using plastic use *that* fact as a marketing weapon against those that do, telling customers that plastic action parts used in pianos during the 1940s and 1950s crumbled into a sticky mess after a few decades. This is true, but the plastic being used today bears no resemblance to the stuff used back then. As you are probably aware, the plastics industry has come a long way since 1940. Several plastics engineers I consulted assured me that modern plastic deteriorates only when regularly exposed to ultraviolet light, and that types of plastic similar to those in piano actions are now used in many kinds of industrial machinery. The new plastic has actually been in use in pianos since about 1970 and has undergone extensive testing over the years, showing no adverse results.

Plastic parts actually have a number of advantages over wooden ones. They can be made more uniform in shape and weight, are indifferent to temperature and humidity changes, and have no glue joints to come apart. The main disadvantage, as with many other synthetic materials, is aesthetic. Plastic is a sterile material, whereas the charm and spirit of a wooden mechanism is what draws many piano owners and craftspeople to the instrument in the first place. (But, as one technician quipped, "The spiritual quality of the run-of-the-mill upright is minimal anyway and the use of plastic would seem to have little effect on that. Why waste good wood?")

Although plastic action parts have some advantages, well-made wooden parts are quite uniform and relatively trouble-free, and have worked well for many, many years.

Keys

There is no part of the piano with which you will become more intimate than the keyboard. Keys are very innocent-looking sticks of wood, but their design is actually rather complex. What it boils down to, though, is this: If keys are too short, too angled, or not weighted properly, the action will feel uneven (requiring different pressure on the keys from note to note) and unresponsive (making it difficult to express yourself musically), parts of the keys will wear away quickly, and keys will get stuck easily. It will be impossible to develop any kind of decent playing technique.

Key length. A key is like a seesaw: it pivots on a fulcrum, or *balance point*, located behind the fallboard. And as with a seesaw, the closer you are to the balance point the more force (known as *down weight*) you have to apply to get the key to go down, and the shorter the distance (known as *key dip*) the key will travel downward. The shorter the overall length of the key (including the part behind the fallboard that you can't see), the shorter the distance will be between the pianist's fingers and the balance point of the key. And the shorter this distance, the greater variation there will be in down weight and key dip between the front and the rear of the playing portion of the key (Figure 3-24).

To see why all this matters, try the following exercise on a piano (Figure 3-25): Using either hand, place your thumb on a B-flat and your little finger on the B-flat an octave higher or lower (depending on which hand you use). Now play the D and F in between with your index and middle fingers. Notice that you were forced to play the white keys way back near the fallboard instead of at the front in order to play the black keys. This is a very common hand position.

Some variation in touch between the front and back of the key is inevitable, but the less variation the better if a pianist is to have proper control of his or her playing. When every movement of the fingers on the keys

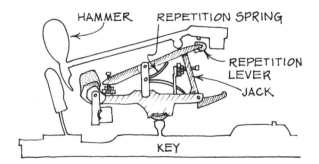

FIGURE 3-23. The repetition mechanism from one note of a grand piano, surrounded by its key and hammer. This complicated mechanism has an extra spring and lever that hold the hammer up in the air, after it rebounds from the string, so that the jack can reset itself for another stroke without the necessity of bringing the key all the way back to its starting position first. This allows notes to be repeated much faster and more reliably on grands than on most verticals. See Chapter 1 for details on this mechanism's operation.

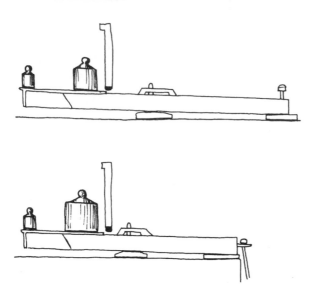

FIGURE 3-24. On short keys there is a greater variation in down weight between the front and back of the playing surface than on long keys. This makes it more difficult to develop control and good playing technique. Also see Figure 3-25.

FIGURE 3-25. A very common hand position shows why the touch at the rear of the playing surface is as important as at the front (from Figure 3-24).

requires a different amount of force, there is no way of accurately controlling how loud or soft the sound produced will be. This can foul up the playing of beginners and advanced alike. Short keys are typically found in a spinet, where the key length must be reduced to accommodate the indirect-blow action, and in any vertical piano where the designers and market-ing people have decided that the piano must be as slim as possible to attract buyers. Because the decision about key length tends to be made on the basis of cabinet styling, unfortunately, there may be little correlation between the length of the keys and the quality of the rest of the piano.

Buying Tip: Measure the Overall Key Length

The overall key length in a vertical piano should ideally be 14 to 16 inches or more. On some spinets or ultra-thin pianos, the keys may be as short as 11½ inches. If the total depth of the piano is less than about 23 inches, check the length of the keys to see if they're short. Key length is not generally a problem in grand pianos.

Buying Tip: Measure the Length of the Key Covering

In addition to varying in the overall length of their keys, pianos can also vary in the length of the *covered* portion of the keys—the part you can see and play. Some pianos feature *sharps*, or black keys, and *naturals*, or white keys, that are longer by a small fraction of an inch than those of other pianos. This extra length will be an advantage for more advanced players, players with long fingers, or those who for various reasons (like flamboyant playing) would otherwise hit their fingers against the fallboard while playing. When testing out pianos in the showroom, be sure to pay attention to this very small, but surprisingly important, difference between models.

Key angle. Another problem with short keys is that they often have too great a bend in them (Figure 3-26). Notice that behind the fallboard the keys fan out slightly to line up with their respective action parts. The shorter the key, the greater the bending angle necessary. On angled keys, most of the weight of the action parts is borne by the side of the key toward the inside of the bend, causing the metal guide pin at the balance point to wear away the cloth key bushing on the opposite side. Premature wearing away of the key bushing on one side causes the key to become lopsided and greatly increases its chance of becoming sluggish and failing to return properly. This is a major problem in pianos with highly angled keys, especially spinets.

Key weighting. The forces required to maintain key movement, collectively called *touch weight*, include *down weight*, the force required to make a key go down, and *up weight*, the force with which the returning key pushes up against the finger after being played. Down weight usually measures between 45 and 55 grams (with the damper system disengaged). Much more than this and the piano will be too tiring to play; much less and the pianist will not be able to maintain adequate control of his or her playing and the keys may be sluggish in returning. Don't make the mistake of choosing a piano with too light a touch.

An element of touch weight important to pianists but rarely addressed is *inertia*, a measure of which is the force required to accelerate a key in actual playing, which is a function of the total amount of mass in the key and action parts of each note. An action with too much inertia may be difficult and tiring to play even though the specifications for down weight and up weight are correct.*

To attain the proper touch weight and balance the weight of the action, most keys have lead weights

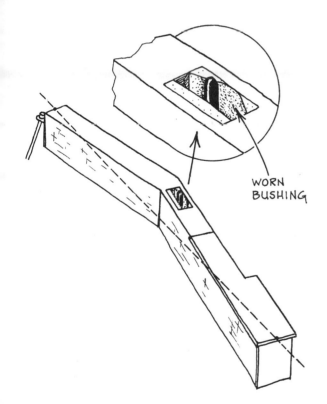

FIGURE 3-26. In theory, a straight line from the front to the back of the key should pass through the balance point. If the key is highly angled in such a way that this condition is not met, then it will lean slightly in one direction and prematurely wear away the cloth key bushing on the opposite side, resulting in sluggishness and noise. The possibility of this happening is much greater when the bend of the key begins behind the balance point instead of right behind the key covering material, and when the key has no key button for added support (see Figure 3-27). Angled keys may also have a greater chance of breaking because the grain of the wood may not always be oriented in the direction of maximum strength.

called **key leads** imbedded in them (see Figure 3-27). In grands, these are essential; the required touch weight couldn't be attained without them. Because of the different leverage of vertical piano keys, though, cost-conscious manufacturers of these pianos may be able to get away without using key leads. Most of their pianos will still be quite playable; some will tend toward a very light touch and will be prone to sticking.

PITCH: "The keys on Smith Bros. pianos are individually weighted for a more uniform touch."

TRUTH: There are two kinds of key weighting used. "Engineered weights" are installed according to an average—the same in every piano of that model regardless of slight variations in wood density, friction, and so on, that may exist from piano to piano or key to key. On most grands and some higher-quality verticals, to even out these differences, the touch weight of each key is individually measured and the key fitted with the appropriate key leads. Keys that undergo the latter process are said to be "individually weighed-off" or "individually weighted and balanced."

In theory, weighing off keys individually sounds like a good idea, and perhaps it works well in some factories. But most factories weigh off their keys before the final regulation, with key bushings of varying tightness, hammers not yet shaped, and many action adjustments not yet made. Once these are done, the weigh-off will no longer be accurate. Sometimes key leading is even used to compensate for gross errors in manufacturing. If quality control is reasonably good, it is not that difficult to predict the right amount of lead to use, and a well-engineered set of key weights will work quite well.

One particularly aggravating and pathetic problem sometimes occurs in verticals with unweighted or poorly weighted keys: under certain circumstances the weight of the action will actually be insufficient to hold the back end of the keys down. The pianist's complaint will be that some notes get "hung up;" that is, they don't repeat. When the technician makes the adjustment that normally cures that problem, the result is that the front of the offending key droops below the level of the surrounding keys—and the note still doesn't repeat. Short of adding extra weights, nothing can be done to remedy this condition. Notes will never repeat well, and the level of the keyboard will always be uneven.

*See page 233 for information on the Stanwood Precision TouchDesign™ System, a method for calibrating the weight and leverage characteristics of a piano action.

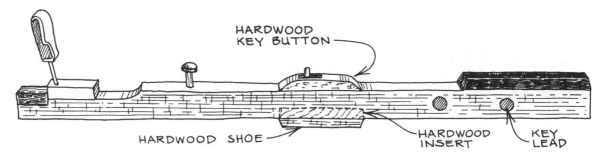

FIGURE 3-27. Some features in a high-quality key: It is long, thick, and straight-grained with a hardwood key button and a hardwood "shoe" or insert to protect against wear by the balance rail guide pin. Also shown are key leads. Sugar pine and spruce are preferred for key making over the cheaper basswood.

Buying Tip: Avoid Key Weighting Problems

You can avoid key weighting problems by, first of all, staying away from spinets and other verticals that have very short, unweighted keys. Second, when "test driving" a new piano, play for a while with the sustain (right-hand) pedal depressed. Although this will create quite a din and annoy the salesperson, it will quickly show up keys that are sluggish in returning, because the weight of the dampers will be disconnected from the keys. Often this sluggishness is caused by excess friction, in turn caused by tight key bushings, and can be eliminated by some simple adjustments. When that fails, however, poorly weighted and balanced keys are likely the culprit.

Buying Tip: Check for Warped Keys

Sometimes keys will warp if the wood has not been properly seasoned prior to making the keyboard. This is especially likely on pianos made in foreign countries with a humid climate, but is certainly not unknown on American-made pianos as well.

Kneel down so the keys are at eye-level. Notice whether any keys are unevenly spaced between their neighbors, or tilted (Figure 3-28). These may just need some minor adjustments—or they may have been purposely misadjusted in the factory or in the store. Why? If keys are warped, the easy (read *lazy*) way to keep them from rubbing against each other at the rear is to "fudge" them at the front. This is less work than sanding them down—or sending the piano back for a new keyboard.

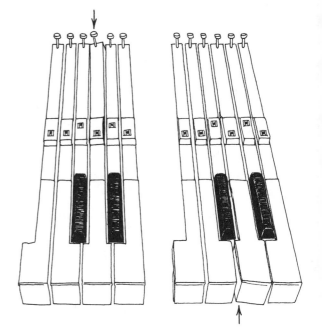

FIGURE 3-28. When a key is warped enough to be interfering with a neighboring one, the technician can correct the problem by slightly bending the guide pin at the balance point to tilt the key in the other direction. This is only permissible, though, if it does not cause the front of the key to be noticeably lopsided. If any keys appear to be tilted at the front, you should find out why. This is a common trick to avoid the more extensive woodworking that may be necessary to correct warpage.

Key quality. Believe it or not, keys actually flex slightly when played hard, robbing the hammer of some power, and can even break. Making keys as rigid and durable as possible is a high priority for makers of top-quality instruments. Measures taken include: using well-seasoned, straightgrained wood with the grain oriented in the direction of maximum resistance to breaking (which is hard to do if the key has a sharp angle bend in it); making the keys as thick as reasonably possible; and using hardwood key buttons and "shoes" at the balance point of the key, where it's weakest (Figure 3-27).

Buying Tip: Choosing Keytops

Practically all pianos made today have plastic key coverings for both the naturals and the sharps. Formerly the naturals were of ivory, the importation of which is now prohibited because it requires the killing of elephants for their tusks. Ivory is usually preferred by pianists because it absorbs sweat from the fingers and so doesn't get slippery like plastic does. It is also said to have a "warmer" or "softer" feel to it. Several piano manufacturers have developed synthetic materials that mimic the properties of ivory.

Sharps used to be made of ebony wood; the plastic sharps used today may be shiny or of a slightly dulled appearance. Personally, I would recommend the dulled sharps, which are often standard on the better pianos. Whether it's an illusion or not, I'm not sure, but my fingers seem to slip off the shiny ones more easily, and the reflection from them annoys me. See if you agree.

Also run your finger under the overhanging lip of plastic naturals to check for sharp edges or burrs that should be filed down.

Buying Tip: Check for Slapping Key Frame

On a grand piano, play each note several times with a hard blow, and listen for tapping or slapping sounds indicating that the key frame is not properly fitted to the keybed. Listen especially to the keys near the ends of the keyboard. This problem can be fixed by the technician, so bring it to the attention of the salesperson (Figure 3-29)

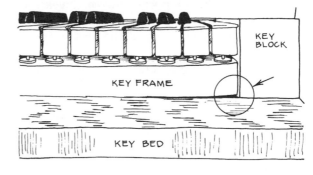

FIGURE 3-29.

Key frame. The keys pivot on a **key frame** and the key frame rests on the **keybed**. If either of these parts warps or changes dimension it will throw the action out of adjustment, so conscientious manufacturers take extra pains to use the best seasoned lumber and appropriate methods of joinery to prevent these occurrences. On a vertical piano, the key frame is permanently screwed to the keybed. Better verticals have a key frame with three horizontal rails; on cheaper verticals the back rail is omitted and the key frame cloth is glued directly to the keybed. On a grand, the key frame can be pulled out like a drawer for servicing, so measures have to be taken to ensure that it fits the keybed like a glove or it will slap against it under hard playing, making an unpleasant noise. The better companies also provide special hardwood inserts in those parts of the keys, key frame, and keybed where extra strength and durability are called for.

Hammers

Piano **hammers** are felt-covered wooden mallets that must be at once finely engineered, ruggedly constructed, and delicately balanced; capable of producing barely audible pianissimos and thundering fortissimos with equal ease; and able to endure literally millions of collisions with steel strings, with minimal wear. A tall order!

A **hammer head** consists of a wooden **molding** surrounded by dense **hammer felt** (Figure 3-30). The felt is applied to the molding under pressure in such a way that the outer layers are under great tension and the

inner layers under great compression. The balance between these two forces makes the hammer resilient so that it can strike the strings and immediately rebound, leaving the strings free to vibrate. Each hammer head is mounted on a thin dowel called a **hammer shank**. Some manufacturers make their own hammers; others buy from companies that specialize in hammer making.

Generally, one can't tell much about the quality of a hammer by simply looking at it. One has to listen to the tone produced and have experience servicing the

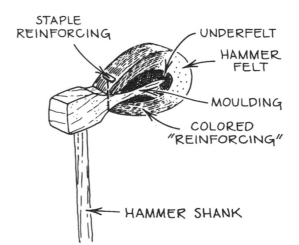

FIGURE 3-30. Parts of a typical hammer. Not all hammers have a staple or colored reinforcing or underfelt. Notice the dotted line under the staple. The best staples go all the way through the hammer in a specially drilled hole and are twisted or bent over on the other side.

hammers to make any judgment about them. Even then, a judgment must be qualified, as many other factors can also influence the tone. The better hammers use felt of higher-quality wool (such as with finer fibers) and more strictly controlled density and uniformity. They are more neatly trimmed and finished, and have fine wood moldings. One thing you *can* look at is how much felt is present at the striking point of the treble hammers. The felt packs down and wears away with repeated striking of the strings, and some treble hammers have too little felt at the striking point to enjoy a long life.

The felt in many hammers is artificially hardened by being doped with chemicals or overly compressed during the manufacturing process. Pianos with these hammers often sound quite good in the showroom, but become harsh after a couple of years of playing. The traditional style of tone regulating depends on the balance of tension and compression inside the hammer. Thus these hammers may be more difficult and unpredictable to service.

Buying Tip: Check for Shaping of Hammers

Hammers develop a concave surface during the manufacturing process. To "finish" them, the felt is sanded flat and smooth so the striking surface is parallel to the strings (Figure 3-31). On some of the cheapest pianos, this operation is omitted, and the hammers actually miss nearly one-third of the strings. With the front panel off a vertical piano, push some hammers toward the strings with your hand and check to see whether their striking surface is parallel to the line of the strings.

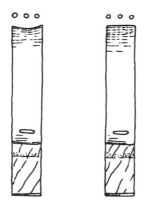

FIGURE 3-31. Two piano hammers seen from above. Because the one on the left remains in the concave shape formed in the manufacturing process, it will probably miss the center string of its unison (set of three strings). The one on the right has been sanded so its striking surface is parallel to the line of strings.

PITCH: "This Deluxe Console is the only one on the market to use 14-pound hammers; all the others use 12-pound hammers."

TRUTH: Hammers are the subject of several marketing gimmicks. One of them is the "weight" of the hammer. Usually ranging from "10 pounds" up to "18 pounds" or higher, this number expresses the weight of an entire sheet of felt, from which many sets of hammers are made. (The actual weight of the felt on an individual hammer head is only the barest fraction of an ounce.) Unfortunately, no industry standard specifies how many sets of hammers can be made from a sheet of felt, so this expression of "weight" is left without much meaning or usefulness. It is true that larger pianos require heavier hammers to set into motion the longer, heavier strings. But it is not necessarily true, as the marketing people would have you believe, that a console with "14-pound" hammers is always noticeably better than one with "12-pound" hammers. What is important is that the weight, shape, and density of the hammer be properly matched to the rest of the scale design, which you and I can tell only by listening (if then). Some pianos have hammers that are simply too small and light to elicit a strong sound from the strings, especially in the bass.

PITCH: "The hammers are also chemically reinforced (see this colored portion of the hammer?) and stapled so they'll never come apart."

TRUTH: Chemical reinforcing is one of the biggest jokes in the industry. Long ago, when weaker animal hide glues were used to attach the hammer felt to the molding, the felt was chemically treated to make it less absorbent so it would make a better glue bond with the moulding. With modern glues, it is no longer necessary to treat the felt. Although in a few cases an actual stiffening agent is still used on the felt in the belief that the stiffener helps the felt keep its shape longer, the vast majority of piano hammers contain only a colored dye, whose sole purpose is to fool you. Consumers are the only ones to be fooled; every manufacturer, technician, and salesperson knows that this is a hoax. The gimmick seems to have originated in an attempt to copy the looks of Steinway hammers, which do contain a real stiffening agent, colored grey. Other companies use yellow or green dye, and I expect a rainbow-colored hammer to appear on the market any day. Even when the reinforcing is real, there is no general agreement in the profession whether it's useful or desirable.

Stapled reinforcement is another gimmick. There are actually two kinds of staples, one worse than useless and the other probably useful, or at the very least harmless. The most common type of staple looks like the sort that comes out of an ordinary office stapler. During the manufacturing process, these staples are driven into the shoulder of the hammer. Often the staples never reach wood; they are imbedded in the felt only, where they perform no function whatsoever and can be easily picked out with your fingernail. Where they do reach the wooden hammer molding, they may occasionally split it. Better no staples should be used at all than this kind of staple! However, since stapled hammers are used as a selling feature, most hammers without staples are found in the cheapest pianos.

The other kind of staple is found in the better pianos. It is a long staple that goes all the way through the hammer in holes drilled especially for it, and is twisted or bent over on the other side. This kind of staple is thought to maintain the compression on the shoulder of the hammer so that the hammer will retain its resilience longer (Fig. 3-30).

The maple hammer shanks on which the hammer heads are mounted are prone to warping and, eventually, to breaking. Manufacturers of premium-quality pianos take special care in curing their shanks, and then hand-select only those that are absolutely straight. Furthermore, these companies also install each and every shank with the grain of the wood oriented in the direction of maximum strength to protect against breakage. Few manufacturers indulge in such expensive precautions, especially for vertical pianos.

Buying Tip: Check Hammer Spacing

On a vertical piano, with the front panel removed, notice whether the hammers are all evenly spaced and aligned, with none warped or crooked (Figure 3-32). Push groups of four or five treble hammers at a time toward the strings with the back of your hand, and observe whether they line up perfectly with the strings, each hammer centered on its group of three strings. On a grand, this is harder to do. You'll have to observe how the hammers line up with the strings as you look down from above the strings while pressing several keys at a time.

The angled bass hammers move in a compound arc to strike the strings. The more angled the hammers are, the harder it is to space them so they won't collide with each other when in motion. Check visually to make sure that, when played, none of the hammers are rubbing against each other and getting stuck. Point out any problems to the salesperson or technician. On some of the smaller, cheaper verticals, getting the hammers properly aligned with the strings and spaced in relation to each other can be an almost impossible challenge, and the spacing may be so critical that the slightest change in humidity can cause a malfunction again.

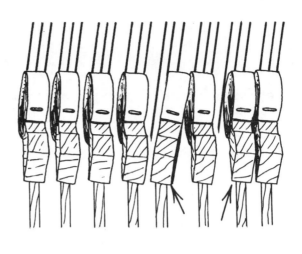

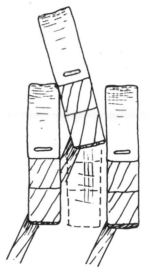

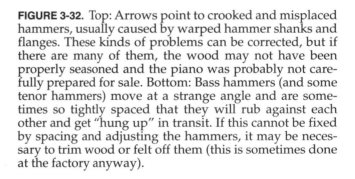

FIGURE 3-32. Top: Arrows point to crooked and misplaced hammers, usually caused by warped hammer shanks and flanges. These kinds of problems can be corrected, but if there are many of them, the wood may not have been properly seasoned and the piano was probably not carefully prepared for sale. Bottom: Bass hammers (and some tenor hammers) move at a strange angle and are sometimes so tightly spaced that they will rub against each other and get "hung up" in transit. If this cannot be fixed by spacing and adjusting the hammers, it may be necessary to trim wood or felt off them (this is sometimes done at the factory anyway).

Pedals and Trapwork

With all the variables involved in buying a piano, at least the pedals operate the same on all of them, don't they? Sorry to say you're only about two-thirds right. See Figure 3-33.

The right-hand pedal, or **sustain pedal**, does the same thing on all pianos, grand and vertical: it lifts all the dampers off the strings simultaneously so that any

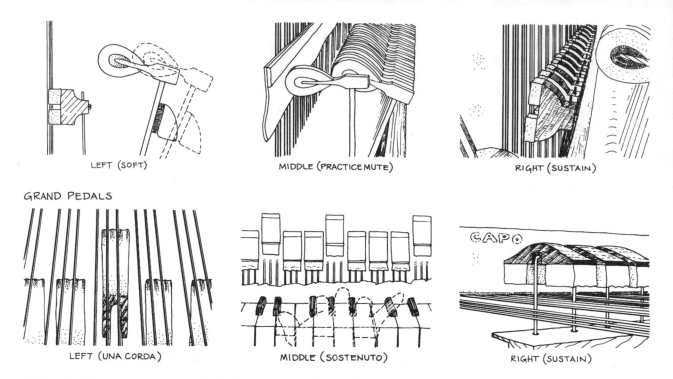

FIGURE 3-33. How the pedals work. Left, vertical: **Soft pedal**. The hammers move closer to the strings, softening the sound. Left, grand: **Una corda pedal**. The entire keyboard and hammers shift slightly to one side so that the treble hammers strike only two of their three strings per note, softening the sound. Middle, vertical: Varies. Shown here is the **practice pedal**. A piece of felt drops between the hammers and strings, muffling the sound. Middle, grand: Usually a **sostenuto pedal**. Selectively sustains only those notes whose dampers are in the up position at the moment this pedal is pressed. Right, vertical and grand: **Sustain pedal**. Lifts all the dampers off the strings simultaneously, sustaining all notes played thereafter.

notes played while the pedal is down will continue to sound. When the pedal is released, the dampers fall back against the strings and stop the sound. This is the pedal we all use the most, and, for many pianists, the only one they will ever need.

The left-hand pedal, or **soft pedal**, always makes the sound softer, but operates entirely differently on verticals and grands. On verticals, depressing the soft pedal moves the hammer rail so that all the hammers move closer to the strings. With the shortened blow distance, the hammers can't develop as much speed before they strike the strings; therefore they produce a quieter sound. Unfortunately, this rather hokey system changes the relationship between the various action parts, puts the action grossly out of regulation, and makes the touch very strange every time the soft pedal is pressed. When the pedal is released, of course, everything falls back immediately into proper adjustment. On grands, the soft pedal, also known as the **una corda pedal**, shifts the entire action and keyboard slightly to one side so that the treble hammers strike only two of their three strings per note. This creates no action regulation problems.

It's really only with the middle pedal that you have some choice when shopping for a piano. On all good grands and a few exceptional verticals, the middle pedal is a **sostenuto pedal**. Its use is a bit esoteric: Say you'd like to sustain a chord, but you need both hands to continue playing elsewhere on the keyboard. You know that if you simply pressed the sustain pedal, not only your chord would be sustained but also everything that followed, creating an unwanted blur. So how to do it? Play your chord, and, while holding it down, press the sostenuto pedal. With this pedal held down, you can now release your fingers and the chord will continue sounding. Keep holding that pedal down and you can now use both your hands to play elsewhere. Only those notes you played *prior* to depressing the sostenuto pedal will be affected by it; the new notes you play afterward will not be sustained unless you choose to sustain them with the sustain (right-hand pedal). The sostenuto pedal is used almost exclusively in some nineteenth- and twentieth-century "classical" music. If you are an aspiring concert pianist, or even a serious student of the classical repertoire, you really should have this pedal. Others will not need it.

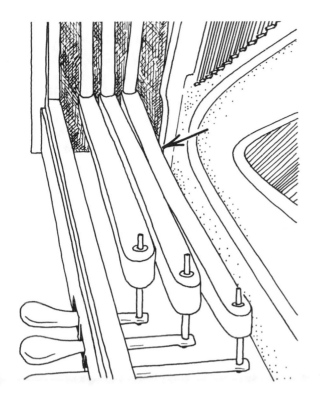

FIGURE 3-34. When the trap levers are made of wood and all three are on the same side of the piano, slight warpage or sloppy workmanship may cause them to rub against each other or against the cast-iron plate. Be sure this problem is corrected before the piano leaves the store.

Cheap modern grands and most American-made verticals have a middle pedal that operates a **bass sustain**. When pressed, this pedal lifts the bass dampers only. This seems to be an attempt to mimic the sostenuto pedal, but it works only if all the notes you want to sustain are in the bass and all the notes you don't want to sustain are in the treble. Most people never use this pedal and don't even know what it does. When it appears on a modern grand, it is a sign that the grand is a cheap one indeed. (Note: some good *old* grands also had this feature.)

A third kind of middle pedal, found only on verticals, and particularly foreign-made verticals, is the **practice pedal**. This is actually one of the better uses for the middle pedal. When it is pressed, a thin piece of felt is lowered between the hammers and the strings, muffling the sound to a whisper. The practice pedal is intended for those who live in apartment houses and want to practice at 3 A.M. (or in some similar situation). Sometimes the pedal can be locked into the "on" position, by sliding it to one side, so you don't have to hold it down. This may be a welcome feature if you've ever had to hold a pedal down for hours. If your piano does not come with a practice pedal, you may be able to buy an inexpensive add-on device called "Quiet Keys" to

accomplish the same thing. See page 232 for details.

The middle pedal on verticals can also be a duplicate soft pedal, a dummy pedal—just for show—or missing entirely. Interestingly, pianos with only two pedals include some of the very cheapest—the maker was apparently too cheap to bother—and some of the very best—perhaps the maker was too wise to bother.

Buying Tips: Check the Operation of Pedals and Dampers

1. **Check for smooth and noiseless operation of the pedals and trapwork, and make sure that the pedals are not too stiff.** (However, some pedals are intentionally made stiff for faster return, which may be an advantage to better pianists.) On cheaper verticals, there is sometimes insufficient clearance between the horizontal trap levers at the bottom of the piano. A little warpage results in their rubbing against each other or against the plate—a troublesome problem to correct (Figure 3-34).

2. **Depress the sustain (right-hand) pedal very slowly while observing the dampers.** The pedal should go down a fraction of an inch before the dampers start to lift. Then all the dampers should lift simultaneously, as if they were made of one single piece of wood and felt. Work the pedal up and down very slowly, watching for any early rising dampers or late stragglers.

3. On a grand, check the operation of the sostenuto pedal, using the example given earlier. Another way to check the sostenuto pedal: First, press and hold the sustain pedal. Then press and hold the sostenuto pedal. Last, release the sustain pedal. All the dampers are now being held off the strings if the sostenuto pedal is working correctly.

4. On a grand, check the operation of the una corda (soft) pedal, making sure that when pressed, the treble hammers shift over just far enough to miss one string of each unison (set of three strings), but not so far as to hit the strings of the adjacent note.

5. On a piano with a well-engineered pedal system, the sustain pedal can be operated with a surprising amount of control to produce special effects such as "half-pedaling," where the pedal is not quite "on" and not quite "off." For an accomplished pianist, this is a very important tool. Other pianos may require a player to "pump" the pedal up and down, producing a choppy, disconnected musical line. If you aspire to a high level of playing, be sure to check that the sustain pedal operates with the degree of musical control you need by playing a piece of music requiring a legato melodic line and complicated pedaling.

6. Play each note and make sure that upon release its damper cuts the sound off cleanly without buzzing or other stray sounds.

7. When depressing the sustain pedal, make sure the bass dampers do not strum the strings as they rise, sounding like a guitar. If they do, the dampers may need trimming or adjusting.

The various levers and dowels, wooden or metal, that connect the pedals with the action are collectively known as the **trapwork**. The springs and pivot systems used in the trapwork vary in quality. Some cheap verticals use crude "pelican" springs that can't provide precise control over the pedaling. The trap levers just kind of wobble around, eventually finding their way after bouncing off adjacent levers or nearby case parts. On inferior grands, the trapwork parts may not line up with each other perfectly, resulting in abnormal wear and squeaks and groans that become increasingly difficult to eliminate.

Final Preparation

One of the very biggest and most visible differences between pianos of differing quality is in the final preparation they receive in the factory prior to being shipped to the dealer. I'm always amazed at how so many Japanese pianos can be shipped ten thousand miles and arrive at the dealer barely needing tuning, whereas many of their American counterparts require hours of remedial work by the dealer's technician after being shipped across town.

In the factory, final preparation of the piano includes such things as chipping and tuning, action regulating, voicing, and cleanup. The more of this done in the factory, the less will have to be done by the dealer. Since many dealers are notorious for doing very little prep work on their pianos (more about that later), conscientiousness in the factory will mean less initial servicing that you have to pay for or suffer without.

Tuning. New piano strings require many tunings before they stop stretching and will hold a tuning for a reasonable length of time. The first few tunings in the

---

Buying Tip: Insist that the Piano Be Tuned

If a piano that you are seriously considering buying is wildly out of tune on the showroom floor, tell the salesperson that you are delaying your purchase decision until the piano has been tuned. Make sure it is tuned to the standard pitch of A-440 (A above middle C vibrates at 440 cycles per second). This is entirely justifiable since it's impossible to tell what a piano really sounds like when it is out of tune or not at standard pitch. This in-store tuning should be *in addition* to the in-home tuning that customarily comes with the piano, not instead of it. In this way, you will make sure that the piano gets the extra tuning it probably didn't get at the factory or from the dealer, and that it will therefore need fewer remedial tunings at your expense. If the dealer refuses, shop elsewhere.

Buying Tip: Check Action Regulation

Space doesn't permit fully describing here how to test the regulation of the action. A piano technician you hire to inspect the piano before purchase can test for that. However, instructions for checking certain aspects of the regulation, such as the hammer spacing and the pedal operation, have already been given. The alignment of the hammers and the adjustment of the dampers are two items that are frequently in disarray in lower-quality pianos unless a very conscientious dealer has corrected them. Two other problems to check for are hammers that bounce or hit the strings twice when you play softly up and down the keyboard and hammers that block against the strings.

---

factory are done before the action is installed; the tuner plucks the strings with a wooden chip in a process called "chipping." Vertical pianos normally receive two chippings followed by one to four tunings, depending on the quality and price of the piano. Grands receive two chippings and from four to seven tunings. There may be a settling-in period of days or weeks between successive tunings. Even with all this tuning, most pianos require at least four tunings in the home during the first year of ownership. An inexpensive piano that is not tuned enough in the factory, even if tuned by the dealer, may go disastrously out of tune in your home and need several remedial tunings (paid for by you) before it will even begin to hold its tune.

Action regulating. Regulating refers to the fine adjustment of the thousands of action parts so that they perform the way they were designed to. These adjustments may take the form of turning adjusting screws, making minute bends in wires, and placing small shims of paper and cardboard under keys. There are many adjustments that have to be made to each note, some of them to tolerances of just a few thousandths of an inch, plus several adjustments for the action as a whole. The action must be regulated when the piano is new, of course, but it also requires regulating after an initial period of use has caused the cloth and felt parts to compact, and thereafter to compensate for wear.

Actions are regulated in the factory, at least enough to make them work, but sometimes not much better than that. Higher-quality pianos usually undergo a second, or even a third, regulation before being shipped off to the dealer. In a few factories, machines with eighty-eight rubber plungers pound on the keys thousands of times to simulate hours of playing, after which the pianos are regulated again (boy, do those machines make a racket!). This process of breaking in a piano is highly desirable, but it is time consuming and thus too expensive for most mass producers. Action regulating in the home is expensive too, so the more breaking in and regulating done in the factory, the longer it will be before you have to foot the bill.

Voicing. *Voicing*, or tone regulating, mostly involves adjusting the shape and density of the hammer felt to control the tonal quality of the piano. If the piano sounds too bright, the hammers are pricked with needles to soften them; if too mellow or dull, chemical hardeners are usually applied. If the shape of the hammer is wrong, too, the tonal quality will be affected; the hammer felt is sanded to restore the proper shape. There are also more sophisticated aspects of voicing, such as mating the hammers and strings so that the hammer contacts all three strings of a unison at the same time (see Figure 3-31).

As I mentioned under the subject of hammers, the least expensive pianos receive no hammer preparation at all and therefore start out with three strikes against them. Most vertical pianos have their hammers sanded to at least a reasonable shape, but aside from getting a few squirts of hammer hardener on the top six hammers to make them sound presentable, they receive no other voicing. Top-of-the-line verticals and most grands get more hammer voicing, though few get much attention paid to string and hammer mating. A knowledgeable technician you hire to inspect the piano should check for this.

Cleanup. During the manufacturing process, small chips of wood and sawdust collect in the piano, settling on the soundboard and bridges, against the strings, and in the bottom of verticals. Often chips of wood that have lodged against the strings on the bridges are responsible for buzzing sounds. Manufac-

turers are supposed to blow or vacuum this stuff out, but many pianos arrive at the dealer full of debris. I've also seen new pianos in the home in which dripping glue from action assembly work had immobilized a hammer. Isn't it remarkable that neither the manufacturer nor the dealer noticed it?

Serviceability

Whether a piano is more or less serviceable depends mainly on how easily the case parts can be removed and how accessible the action is. Some examples of designs that hinder serviceability have already been given: grand-style lids with nonremovable hinge pins on verticals, sliding fallboards, spinet actions, and so on. You may wonder what this has to do with you, however. After all, isn't poor serviceability the technician's headache? Maybe. But if your grand piano requires removing fourteen screws (instead of two) to pull out the action, don't expect your technician to conscientiously make those small adjustments to the action that he or she might otherwise do for free after tuning the piano. Fortunately, in response to technicians' requests, most manufacturers now pay more attention to streamlining access for servicing than they did in the past.

Warranty

RULE OF THUMB: The longer and more extravagant-sounding the warranty, the worse the piano.

Sound incredible? The reason is that the warranty, like many "features," is used as a marketing tool. When the product has less in the way of quality or reputation to recommend it, the manufacturer hopes that

Buying Tip: Voicing in the Home

Because room acoustics profoundly affect a piano's tonal quality, final voicing (tone regulating) should ideally be done after the piano is delivered to the home and tuned. Inquire of the dealer whether this is possible. Also, after the piano has been played for six months or a year, its sound will probably be much brighter, and it may need voicing again. The voicing will continue to change, slowly, over time.

It's important to realize, however, that there is always some risk the piano will not sound just as you'd hoped it would, even after voicing in the home. Ignore promises from the dealer that the technician can coax any sort of tone you want from any piano in any acoustical environment. It's just not that simple

"Look on the bright side, Mr. Jones, the laminated soundboard is still under warranty for another 59 years!"

a long warranty will provide an additional inducement to buy. Although this rule of thumb is obviously an exaggeration, witness that Steinway's warranty is for only five years, the shortest in the business.

In 1975, the U.S. Congress enacted the Magnuson-Moss Warranty Act, which set federal standards for warranties on consumer products costing more than ten dollars. One requirement of the Act is that every warranty must be conspicuously labeled "full" or "limited." A full warranty is one that meets every one of the following five conditions. A limited warranty is one that does not meet one or more of these conditions. If a warranty is full for some parts of a product and limited for other parts, it is called a "multiple" warranty.

1. The manufacturer will provide warranty service to anyone who owns the product during the period covered by the warranty. (In other words, the warranty is transferable to future owners if you should sell the piano during the warranty period.)

2. The manufacturer will provide warranty service free of charge, including such costs as returning the product or removing and reinstalling the product when necessary. (In other words, you will not be charged for the labor necessary to replace a defective part, or for transporting the piano to the dealer or manufacturer, should this be necessary.)

3. The manufacturer will provide, at the consumer's choice, either a replacement or a full refund if it is unable, after a reasonable number of tries, to repair the product. (In other words, you will not be required to take a replacement if you prefer a refund.)

4. The manufacturer will provide warranty service without requiring that consumers return a warranty registration card. (Your warranty will not be invalidated just because you failed to mail in the registration card.)

5. The warranty will not limit the duration of implied warranties. (See Chapter 5, "Buying A Used Piano," for a discussion of implied warranties.)

A warranty must be clearly labeled on its face as full or limited. Beware of confusing phrases like "Full Ten-Year Limited Warranty," as one piano ad read. Please also note that the word *limited* does *not* refer to a limitation on the duration of the warranty; it simply means that at least one of the above federal standards for a full warranty has not been met.

Fine print in most warranties contains exclusions that may severely limit coverage. Some of these exclusions relate to the federal standards, and some don't. Some are reasonable and justified, and some, in my opinion, are not. For instance, accidental damage and normal changes in tuning, regulation, and voicing obviously should not be covered. Nor should damage to the piano caused by placing it next to a radiator. But why should warranty coverage cease when you sell the piano? Many piano warranties cover the original purchaser only, an unfair restriction, in my opinion.

Sometimes dealers buy inexpensive, entry-level pianos at a discount from the manufacturer in return for relieving the manufacturer of the obligation of providing a warranty. The dealers then resell the pianos to the public with only the dealer's warranty. Some of these warranties may cover only the cost of replacement *parts*, not the labor to install them, and may also require that the customer pay the cost of shipping the piano back to the dealer if it cannot be repaired in the home. Such warranties are virtually worthless. Even with relatively minor defects, the cost of labor is almost always much greater than the cost of parts, and shipping can be a significant expense.

Some other possible limitations you should know about are —

- Some warranties become void if any rust appears on the strings or tuning pins, as this is considered evidence that the owner has not properly protected the piano from abnormally humid conditions. However, rust will sometimes appear for reasons unrelated to neglect, perhaps because of faulty manufacturing of the music wire. This leads to a "Catch-22" situation: the warranty becomes void the moment a defect is found.

- Some warranties do not cover the piano finish. I see no reason why a good finish should not be expected to last for at least ten years, subject to normal wear.

- Some warranties require that to collect on the warranty you furnish proof that you have had the piano regularly maintained by a qualified technician. This sounds reasonable, but, in fact, most piano defects are completely unrelated to whether or not the piano has ever been tuned. This is an easy out for the manufacturer, who knows that the vast majority of piano owners fail to maintain their pianos.

- Some warranties do not allow a refund, no matter what happens.

- Most piano warranties do not cover pianos used in commercial or institutional settings, such as in schools, hospitals, clubs, or restaurants.

All warranties cover only defects in material and workmanship. Most such defects show up in the first five to ten years of a piano's life. Any defects that appear later will probably be construed by the manufacturer as having been caused by wear and tear, dryness, and so on, and, therefore, will not be covered by the warranty. So, in practice, a very long warranty probably offers no more protection than one of normal duration.

Even if a long warranty covered every possible thing that might go wrong with a piano, the warranty has value only as long as the company offering it remains in business and cares about protecting its good name. Some piano companies these days do not actually manufacture pianos; they merely distribute and put their name on pianos made by other, mostly foreign, firms, and the warranty is issued in the name of the distributor, not the manufacturer. In fact, the consumer may not know who the manufacturer is. Of the three kinds of businesses — manufacturer, distributor, and dealer — the distributor, in my opinion, is the least likely to be around to honor the warranty in five, ten, or twenty years.

Cautions about fine print notwithstanding, the best manufacturers and dealers will go to considerable lengths to satisfy a customer when a bona fide defect is reported, even, at times, when they could conceivably avoid doing so. For instance, one customer of mine owns a vertical piano that had tuning pins made of an experimental material one company used very briefly in the mid-1950s. The experiment was apparently unsuccessful, as the tuning pins became extremely loose with time and the piano would not hold a tuning. The piano was not played or tuned for many years, and, following the death of the original owner, it was shipped to her daughter, at which time I was called to service it. Realizing that trying to tune the piano was a hopeless task and that there was something odd about the tuning pins, I contacted the maker's dealer in my area, who called the factory. Even though the warranty had been expired for twenty years, the factory authorized the dealer to install, at no charge to the customer, a completely new set of tuning pins and strings, which would otherwise have cost her more than five hundred dollars. No arm-twisting whatsoever was required on my part to get the dealer and factory to do this. It's interesting to note, however, that before authorizing this work the factory ascertained that the piano was still in the same family. Apparently companies with nontransferable warranties — even generous ones—balk at waiving that particular restriction.

Not all companies are so willing to cooperate. Naturally, the ones that produce the most lemons are the most difficult to deal with. One disreputable company, for example, initially refused to take back a piano whose strings had all rusted for no apparent reason within a few years of purchase. Then they agreed to take it back if the customer would foot the bill for shipping it to the factory (the dealer from whom it was bought had gone out of business). When the customer refused and her technician interceded on her behalf, the factory agreed to pay the technician to restring the piano, but at only one-third the commercial rate for the job.

The better companies produce very few really defective pianos. Most defects are extremely minor, such

Buying Tips: Warranty Pointers

1. You are much less likely to have a serious warranty problem with a piano than you are with, say, a car. The exact terms of the warranty need not be an overriding concern if you buy a piano that comes otherwise well recommended.

2. Parts-only warranties are rare these days, but possible on some entry-level pianos. Think twice about buying a piano that has a warranty like this. Such warranties are next to worthless. Even with minor defects, the cost of labor is almost always much greater than the cost of parts. If you must buy such a piano, ask the dealer to give you, in writing, a labor warranty that runs for as long as the parts warranty. Also beware of warranties that require the customer to pay the freight when the piano must be returned to the dealer for repair.

3. If you are buying a piano with the idea you might sell it if Junior decides to stop taking lessons, the resale value may be enhanced if the warranty is transferable to future owners.

4. Be sure you take a copy of the warranty home with you when you buy the piano, and take careful note of what servicing is required to comply with its terms.

5. Mail in the warranty registration card. It will make any warranty claim easier.

6. If you buy a piano from a dealer who is not authorized by that brand's manufacturer to sell its products, your warranty may be void. Beware of dealers who tell you they can get any brand of piano you want; they will buy those brands they are not authorized to sell from other dealers at prices slightly above wholesale—an unethical transaction called "transshipping"—and then resell to you. It's also possible they may be used pianos. If in doubt, ask to see the dealer agreement, which authorizes the dealer to sell the brand in question, or call the manufacturer.

7. All other things being equal, it is better to buy a piano that is warranted by a manufacturer—preferably one with a strong presence in this country—than by a distributor. If that isn't possible, then be sure to get a warranty from the dealer as well. In any case, a good dealer can be a big asset when trying to get warranty service from a manufacturer or distributor. Buy from someone who seems likely to stay in business and will honor the warranty without hassles (more on choosing a dealer coming up).

as rattling bass strings, and are taken care of by the dealer before the piano is sold or at the time of the first home tuning. If you or your technician should discover a defect you think may be covered by the warranty, the technician should contact the dealer from whom the piano was purchased (the technician can probably describe the problem more precisely than you can). The dealer will either send a technician to inspect the piano or will simply authorize your technician to make the repair and send a bill. If the defect is likely to be expensive to repair, or if a question arises about who is liable, the dealer will call the factory for instructions, since the factory will share the repair bill with the dealer.

If you are unable to get satisfaction from the dealer, or if either the dealer has gone out of business or you have moved out of the dealer's area, your technician should call the Technical Services department of the manufacturer or importer. Someone there will refer you to a local dealer (if you have moved), authorize your technician to do the work, or turn your request down (at which point you can become an irate consumer).

If your request is turned down, be sure you are on solid ground before appealing further. Remember that a warranty is a contract between you and the dealer or manufacturer, and that by buying the product you indicate acceptance of its terms. If the terms provide for a replacement in the case of a defective piano, then don't expect to get a refund. If the manufacturer had wanted to provide for a refund, the piano would have had to cost more to cover that possibility. This may seem obvious, but consumers these days have come to expect so much protection (sometimes from their own mistakes) that they often demand things to which they are simply not entitled. That having been said, dealers' warranties and state laws will sometimes provide protection exceeding that of the manufacturer's warranty, so in the case of a problem, it doesn't hurt to check.

SHOPPING FOR A NEW PIANO
The Approach

This section is about the actual mechanics of shopping for a new piano. An eight-step outline includes references to other sections of the book, and to other resources, that have more detailed information on certain topics. In this section, as in previous ones, I mention some potential problems and hazards to look out for. If some of you get the idea from this that buying a piano is likely to be a dreadful experience, unfortunately, some of you may be right. Faced with a shrinking piano market and increasing competition, some salespeople resort to tactics that are quite irritat-

ing, if not downright unethical. There are also some *great* piano stores around; the difference between the two types can be breathtaking. In any case, it is my job as your advocate to warn you of the *worst* that can happen and the simple steps you can take to avoid problems.

Understand the piano market. The first step in buying a new piano is to understand the piano market, and the best way to start doing that is to think about buying a car. A car, you say? Yes, a car. Because the market for automobiles is quite similar to that for pianos. Both are expensive, highly technical items that are purchased infrequently. They come from similar manufacturing locations (the U.S., Germany, Japan, Korea). For both, negotiating for price is considered normal, and both have a large market for used goods. But there is one big difference between them: Most people know next to nothing about pianos, but by the time a person has reached adulthood in our society, he or she knows a lot about cars. You can leverage this knowledge in several ways into an understanding of the piano market.

You see, pianos are not made in a vacuum. Piano makers are part of the world manufacturing community and share with their counterparts in other industries similar advantages and problems in such areas as raw materials, labor, and technology. By now, most of you probably have an intuitive understanding of how cars from different regions of the world differ from one another in quality and price even if you don't know the exact technical reasons for those differences.

For example, cars from Western Europe tend to be of very high quality, expensive, and last a long time. They fetch a premium on the used market and are often rebuilt. Japanese cars are more moderately priced, intelligently designed, and have excellent quality control, but the materials and finish are not quite as durable as on the European cars. They are great to own and trouble-free for many years, but are not expected to last as long or to be as thoroughly rebuilt. Korean cars are a good value for the money at this point, but have a troublesome recent past, are still not as trouble-free to own as Japanese cars, and their longevity is perhaps not as great. America led the world in automobile design and production for most of a century. Some of the old designs are classic, but quality control has suffered during the past few decades, perhaps only now experiencing a comeback. Some "foreign" cars are now made in the U.S.

If you had substituted "pianos" for "cars" in the above paragraph, you would have come close to a reasonable description of much of the piano market. Of course, the parallels can only be drawn so far. Pianos last longer, are found here from a larger variety of countries than are cars, are not subject to safety and regulatory controls, and are described in terms of "tone" and "touch," whereas quality in cars takes other names and forms. Nevertheless, comparing what you know about cars to what you are learning about pianos is an excellent way to prepare yourself for the piano-shopping experience.

At this point, I recommend skipping ahead to page 87 in Chapter 4 and reading the section entitled "The Piano Industry Today: An Overview." It's about the global piano market you will encounter when you shop. When finished, please return here.

Decide on your needs, desires, and resources. If you haven't already done so, read Chapter 2, "Buying A Piano: An Orientation." That chapter deals with the following basic questions you need to answer: What type of piano, grand or vertical, do you require? What size piano is called for by your tastes, technical requirements, or the space available? How much money do you have to spend? Should you buy new or used? What type of furniture styling seems preferable, and what types are clearly not appropriate?

Notice that I mentioned both needs and *desires* above. This is to acknowledge that there may be a difference between the minimum technical requirements for your level of playing, on the one hand, and your desires, on the other. This is another place where an examination of how you would buy a car can be of assistance in buying a piano. After all, if you own a BMW, did you really think that a lesser brand would not get you to the grocery store or the kids' soccer practice? Of course not. You bought it because you appreciate goods of high quality and have the means to purchase them. (Nothing wrong with that!) Likewise, many who don't play a note buy grand pianos costing thirty thousand dollars or more. Of course, there are other possibilities: You may be well off, but don't value a piano right now as much as a car; or you may be a person of average means, with a beat-up car like mine, who just wants a piano that will get them by for a while. If you are a person of limited means whose technical requirements are high (a starving concert artist), you should probably consider a used piano, rather than a new one that won't meet your musical needs. My point is that, whatever your situation, buying a piano, like buying a car, is as much a lifestyle decision (i.e., what you value and how you choose to spend your money) as a technical one. A little soul-searching now about what you need, desire, and can afford will save you time later.

Make a preliminary selection. While you're searching your soul, you may also want to search ahead to page 84, where you'll find a Summary of Brands and

Ratings. Here piano brands are divided into five basic categories according to quality, price, and intended use. Once you decide approximately where you fit into this system, look up the reviews for those brands in Chapter 4. Remember to read pages 76–81 first, which explains how the reviews were arrived at and how to interpret them. There is also an Index to Trade Names on page 90, which may be of help in locating reviews or mentions of some of the more obscure new piano brands.

This might also be a good time to obtain a copy of the *Annual Supplement to The Piano Book* for the current year, which you can get from the publisher (see last page for details) or from your local bookstore, internet bookstore, or library. It has updated manufacturer and product information since this fourth edition of *The Piano Book* was written in the summer of 2000. Also, most importantly, it contains a list of virtually every brand, model, style, and finish of new piano available in the U.S. and Canada (over 2,500 models), along with "list" prices and advice on figuring "street" prices.

If you enjoy surfing the internet, you can also glean additional information from manufacturers' web sites (web addresses are listed at the beginning of each review) or from various newsgroups and message boards. A note of caution, however: Don't believe everything you read. Manufacturers will obviously shine their best light on their own products. Message writers, with the best of intentions, often pass on inaccurate information or uninformed personal opinions that will only confuse you. Still, provided you maintain a healthy sense of skepticism, you may pick up a useful bit or two of information or get a question answered. See "Shopping for a New Piano on the Internet," later, for more information.

Plan Your Strategy. Let's face it: Even if you become golf buddies with your piano dealer, eventually there will come a point when your interests will diverge, and that will be over price. Although a low price should not be your only objective, it will naturally be one of them, just as a high price will naturally be one of the dealer's objectives. Therefore, it would be advisable to think ahead a little bit about how you will approach the negotiating table. Read "Choosing a Piano Dealer," "Prices, Sales, and Merchandising," "How To Save Money," "Price and Service," and "Dealing With Trade-Ins," coming up in this chapter. Do this before you set foot in a store or call a dealer.

The most common strategies revolve around finding several sources for the same piano model, or for different models that will fulfill your needs about equally, and then letting the dealers of those models bid for your business. ("You know, Mr. Salespitch, Plastic

Piano Co. across town will sell me a Hammerschlager console from Slovenia for only $2,800. Do you think you could meet that price on the Smith Bros. console?") But in practice, your personal strategy will depend on how specific your needs or desires are for a particular brand, tone, or touch; how many sources of supply you can find, how far you are willing to travel to find them, how much time you want to spend looking, how aggressive a negotiator you are, and whether you have an older piano to trade in. Don't get so caught up in your strategizing about price that you fail to take into account other factors that may matter to you, such as your musical preferences, the quality of the instrument, the dealer's reputation for pre- and post-sale service, and the convenience of doing business with someone nearby.

Go shopping. Before you go, check the Yellow Pages and the newspaper ads for dealers in your area. Be aware that some of the brands mentioned in dealers' ads may be used pianos, not new, and other brands offered may not be listed at all, so call ahead if you're looking for a particular brand. Also check the *Piano Book* web site (www.pianobook.com), which from time to time may have resources to help piano buyers like yourself find dealers and technicians in their area.

Also, before leaving, I suggest you become acquainted with the basic technical features of the piano, especially those mentioned in Chapter 1. You certainly don't have to learn and memorize every detail. If you've read and understood the foregoing part of this chapter, you already know more than many of the salespeople you are going to meet. Having a little technical knowledge in advance will help you avoid confusion and information overload later, and may help you judge the competence and veracity of the salespeople.

Spend plenty of time browsing in piano showrooms. Make several trips over a period of several weeks if necessary. Try to become attuned to the differences between pianos that have been pointed out in this chapter. As described in Chapter 2, play as many pianos as possible, from the best to the worst, including ones that you have no intention of buying. Take written notes if you feel so inclined. This is the fun part of buying a new piano.

Make a deal. At some point you will begin to narrow your choice to a few instruments whose appearance, tone, touch, and features appeal to you. They may be ones that were on your preliminary list, or some others. Don't be surprised if you end up buying a piano costing several times what you had planned. It happens all the time!

Using the information in the *Annual Supplement*, make a note of the approximate price range in which your models are likely to trade, and compare that to the dealer's asking price. This will give you some idea of how much room there could be for negotiating. Indeed, one of the values of this information is that if the dealer's asking price is already close to the low end of the range, you will know that it is a waste of time to negotiate further.

Keep in mind, though, that the information in the *Annual Supplement* about typical discounts from list price is not precise and is based on anecdotal reports from across the country. There is considerable variation from one locale to another, one dealership to another, and one situation to another. Don't get upset or abusive if the salesperson is unwilling to negotiate as low as you would like. He or she wants to make a deal as much as you do—after all, they're in business to sell pianos—but has to make a business decision, just as you do, as to how to maximize the value of their assets. On the other hand, don't give in too soon, either; a lot of bluffing goes on, and it's not unusual for an offer at first refused to eventually be accepted. Note that a few dealers (very few, actually) have non-negotiable prices.

Get a second opinion (optional). While you were trying out pianos, you pointed out to the salesperson any obvious defects or problems that needed correcting, didn't you? (The Buying Tips throughout this chapter list trouble spots you can look for if you want to be extra conscientious.) If you have any doubts about the piano, now is the time to have a professional piano technician check the piano over for those items that are beyond your ability to inspect, such as the regulation of the action and the tightness of the tuning pins. The dealer may need a few days to give the piano its final make-ready, if this has not already been done, and if you say your technician will be around later in the week, it will give the dealer an incentive to do a good job of it. If you are buying a brand with a reputation for arriving at the dealer in perfect condition, such as some of the Japanese and European brands, and if you have superb confidence in the dealer, you may be able to omit this step.

If you do get the piano inspected, be sure you choose a technician who is not connected with the store and owes it no favors. In fact, be sure you choose a technician who is not connected with the store's competitors, either. Hiring a technician to inspect a new piano can sometimes be awkward for all concerned. There is a lot of pressure on technicians (and teachers) to approve pianos, especially in areas where they depend on dealers for referrals. Some technicians, wishing to stay on good terms with local dealers, prefer not to enter a store to inspect a piano for a customer. Others will do so, but will take commissions and fees from both sides—highly unethical (teachers are sometimes even worse in this regard). A technician associated with a competitor might unjustly find fault with a piano to discourage the sale. You should question closely any technician you are considering hiring about their ability to work for you and you only.

If you or your technician have found any serious problems with the piano, you may want to make another trip to inspect it before agreeing to have it shipped. *Don't let the dealer tell you that the store's technician will fix everything after the piano is delivered to your home.* This promise is permissible for minor adjustments only. Once the piano is delivered, you will have little leverage over the dealer to get things done. If the piano needs a lot of action regulating or if it is grossly out of tune or far from standard pitch, this should be corrected *before* the piano leaves the store. (The reasons for this are given on page 56 in relation to tuning and pitch and on pages 56 and 73 in relation to regulating and other work.)

If a piano of the particular style or finish you desire is not in stock, it's probably best not to accept the salesperson's offer to order one and have it sent directly to your home. Rather, have it sent to the store first. Each piano is individual, even if of the same brand and model, and ought to go through the same inspection and approval procedure outlined here before you accept it. It's true that some brands are so uniform in quality, tone, and action that you could probably get away with buying one sight unseen, but you're spending a lot of money here, so a little caution is advisable.

Before leaving the store, copy down the serial number of the piano, and then make sure the same piano is delivered to your home. Mistakes are rare, but possible. Also take a copy of the warranty and service recommendations home with you.

Arrange for servicing after delivery. When the piano is delivered, make sure it is placed in a spot where the temperature and humidity will remain as constant as possible, and away from radiators, heating vents, fireplaces, and direct sunlight. See Chapter 7 for details on where, and where not, to put the piano. Within the first month or so, be sure to contact the dealer for your free home tuning. If possible, though, as long as the piano is not unpleasant to play, try to wait until near the end of the free-tuning period (usually about a month) before doing so. This will allow the piano the maximum amount of time to acclimate to its new environment and go out of tune and regulation.

Choosing a Piano Dealer

Most of the information on new pianos in this book concerns the differences between *manufacturers*. Almost as important to you—indeed, sometimes *more* important—is your choice of *dealer* from which to buy the piano. The principal reason for this is that most pianos, as we've seen, arrive from the factory needing a considerable amount of adjusting and tuning before they are ready for you to inspect, much less to buy. Dealers vary greatly in their willingness to provide this necessary pre-sale service, as well as in other ways.

Magazine articles on piano purchasing invariably advise the reader to find a "reputable" dealer. Just exactly what that means, or how to find such a business, the writers rarely say. (And do they think that without that advice you are going to look for a *disreputable* dealer?) Let's take a look at what you want from a dealer and how to find one to match your needs.

You want a dealer that maintains high service standards. As a technician from Colorado wrote me—

I would expect, if I were buying a piano, that everything would be in order with it when new; that is, it would be completely regulated, up to pitch, and voiced to some degree of evenness of tone across the keyboard. Of course, most pianos are not. The best makes come in with keys badly out of square, unlevel, with too much lost motion, with uneven letoff, with too much lost motion in the pedals, and so on. Why don't they regulate them at the factory? Wouldn't the customers be more satisfied if they didn't have to pay a technician to regulate a brand new piano? "Dealer preps" are essentially nonexistent at our store. They want to pay technicians only for tuning—"Don't spend more than about an hour on a piano," the dealers instruct—and pretend that regulating is just sugar on top.

Most dealers realize they can get away without servicing their pianos at all, and hardly anybody will know the difference. Many take advantage of the cost savings, figuring that if you can't tell the difference, then you probably don't need—or deserve—the extra service. Some dealers, though, will service their pianos anyway, and to standards considerably higher than those of both the manufacturer and their unknowledgeable customers. They permit their technicians to do whatever is best for the pianos.

At the very least, a store that expects to service its pianos properly should have the facilities and personnel—either on staff or independent—to perform basic pre-sale service on the premises. Don't buy from dealers who don't service their pianos before they're sold, but who assure you the independent technician they hire will do all the servicing that's needed after the piano is moved to your home. Ask several independent technicians which stores have good service departments. If the salesperson has to take packing materials out of the piano before it can be played, you know it has not been serviced.

Many piano rebuilding shops carry new instruments as a sideline. Although I am, of course, biased, it seems to me that, all other things being equal, a dealership owned and run by piano technicians is likely to be more conscientious than one owned by businesspeople with little technical background. Technicians are more likely to be devoted to their craft, and so to carry better-quality instruments and service them more carefully than non-technicians. They are also perhaps more likely to be straightforward in their business dealings and rely less on deceptive sales techniques. But since there are always exceptions to generalizations such as this, this rule should not be followed religiously.

You want a dealer who keeps the pianos on the sales floor in tune. Nothing can be more frustrating than shopping for a piano when half of those you look at are out of tune. There's no way you can adequately judge the tone of a piano in this situation. Of course, it's unreasonable to expect that each of two hundred pianos in a store be in concert-perfect tune at all times, but most should be quite playable and musical. You can expect that some of the cheapest promotional pianos may be left untuned, at least partly to discourage anyone from buying them.

You want a dealer whose salespeople are knowledgeable, courteous, and helpful. Many salespeople know very little about pianos and could just as well be selling shoes or appliances. What little they do know has been fed them in special seminars sponsored by manufacturers' marketing departments, where they learn to promote the various gimmicks described throughout this chapter. But others have prior technical experience with pianos, are doubling as both technician and salesperson, or have taken the time and trouble to find out what this field is really all about. Even if they aren't technicians, they won't have to bluff their way through a sales presentation.

Even more than knowledge, courtesy is a trait you will appreciate in a salesperson. A good salesperson will be present when you have questions and scarce when you just want to browse. Many shoppers tell me the salespeople in certain piano stores in my area pester them and push them toward a sale until they are ready to scream and walk out. Some salespeople will also help you more than others in narrowing your choices to the piano that best meets your needs and re-

sources. It helps to remember, though, that the primary job of salespeople is to sell you a piano they have in stock. You are responsible for looking out for your needs, just as they are responsible for looking out for theirs.

Lately, an increasing number of salespeople are engaging in the practice of "negative selling"—selling their pianos primarily by disparaging competing brands and dealers. By the time the customer has visited all the dealers in the area, all he or she knows is how bad all the pianos are. This is a recipe for confusion and despair; many customers simply give up at this point. You will do yourself a great service by ignoring such tactics—which are often laced with lies and distortions—and, where possible, favoring more honest and helpful salespeople. (A variant of negative selling is to place on the sales floor an instrument of a competing brand for comparison purposes. Sometimes this can be a legitimate and useful comparison, but usually the competing piano is deliberately kept in poor condition to look bad.)

You want a real—not a hit-and-run—piano dealer. My point here is to warn you against buying from companies (not real piano dealers) that specialize in liquidating discontinued or damaged merchandise or from trucking companies that sell "repossessed" pianos out of the backs of their trucks, never to be seen again. You may have no way of checking on the true status and condition of these pianos and, in the case of truck sales, too little time to make an informed decision. Some of these pianos may not come with a manufacturer's warranty. Also, contrary to these companies' sales pitches, identical pianos may be less expensive at regular piano stores. (I understand there may be a few legitimate companies that carry on these activities, but it could be difficult to distinguish these from the other kind.)

Although no prescription can guarantee you'll find a "reputable" dealer, keeping these guidelines in mind and asking local independent piano technicians for their recommendations will most likely lead you to a dealer you can trust and enjoy doing business with.

Prices, Sales, and Merchandising

Most piano dealers aim for a gross profit margin on their pianos of about 40 percent. This means 40 percent of the retail price is profit above cost; the other 60 percent is the wholesale cost to the dealer. Depending on local economic conditions, competition, and the dealer's overhead, a slightly higher or lower profit margin may be desirable or acceptable, but 40 percent is considered about average. However, the price quoted to you or written on the price tag as the "list price" or "manufacturer's suggested retail price" is usually figured on a profit margin of 50 percent—that is, double the wholesale price—to allow for "negotiating" with you or for offering you a "discount." Indeed, sometimes the "list price" may reflect an even higher profit margin, as we shall see in a moment. (Customers frequently complain about these bogus discounts and the difficulty of finding out the "real" prices of products.)

You might think that piano dealers must get rich on such a large profit margin on such a high-ticket item. After all, automobile dealers often make only a few hundred dollars on each sale. But, in fact, during periods of recession, many piano dealerships go bankrupt. For one thing, pianos are very much a "luxury" item, the first to be crossed off the shopping list when times are hard. Second, dealers usually have to borrow money to buy their instruments, often at outrageously high commercial interest rates. Since a piano may sit around on the sales floor for months (or even years) before being sold, much of the dealer's profit is eaten up by interest charges. In addition, a dealer often has to rent a rather large space in a busy downtown location, pay salespeople and technicians, keep hundreds of pianos tuned, maintain a repair and rebuilding shop, and pay for advertising. Unless business is quite brisk, there may be little (net) profit left over for the owner. Though I'm a consumer advocate, I realize that a large gross profit margin (profit over the cost of goods) is absolutely necessary if a piano dealer is to pay for overhead, remain in business, and give good service.

In addition to the marketing gimmicks perpetrated by the manufacturer, which were described in the first part of this chapter, a number of sales gimmicks are also used by the dealer. I'm sure that piano dealers are no worse in this regard—and probably better—than other retailers; nevertheless, you should know about these ploys.

Not long ago, I received a call from a woman who had just visited a dealer who was having a spectacular "sale"—$1,000 off the "regular" price of their console. The sale was to end the next day, so she was soliciting my advice to help her make a decision in a hurry. I asked her what the sale price was for the model, and comparing it with the regular price from another dealer of the same brand, found them to be almost identical. The woman was taken aback by this news and was quite angry that the dealer had so brazenly lied about the "sale."

Unfortunately, this tactic is extremely common in the piano world, even among otherwise reputable dealers. The dealer will simply put an artificially high "list price" on each piano and then advertise a sale.

Real sales of any consequence are rare. Even where prices are actually reduced by as much as 10 percent, most of the time the buyer could have achieved the same price simply through negotiation.

Some stores go so far as to use a similar tactic every day, without even advertising a sale. During my travels, I stopped at a store selling high-quality pianos in the Midwest. After playing a few, I examined some price tags and was surprised to find a price of $20,000 on a piano I knew to sell for about $14,000 back home. At first I thought that the tag must have gotten switched with that of the next larger model, but all the tags turned out to be too high by almost 50 percent. In response to my questioning, the salesman replied that any interested customers are immediately told that they will receive a 30 percent discount. He explained that all the piano stores in the area do this, and that his store would be at a competitive disadvantage if it didn't follow this practice.

A variation on this is the "piano warehouse." One famous piano store regularly takes out large advertisements in the local papers representing itself as a "piano warehouse" and "discount factory outlet." When customers enter the store, they actually have to pass through a warehouse piled high with piano crates with Japanese and Korean names on them before entering the showroom. Only very savvy customers can avoid the feeling that here they are *really* going to get a bargain. In reality, the "list prices" on the pianos at this store sometimes approach *two-and-a-half times* the wholesale prices, and even after striking a generous "bargain," the average customer will still pay more than twice the wholesale price.

Because manufacturers' and dealers' list prices can be based on any arbitrary markup above wholesale, shopping by comparing discounts from these prices is futile. The *Annual Supplement to The Piano Book* solves this problem by giving its own "list" prices based on a standardized, uniform markup. Discounts from these "list" prices can be reliably compared. Typical discounts will vary depending in part on a brand's position in the market. For example, Japanese and Korean pianos are typically discounted (from the "list" prices in the *Annual Supplement*) from fifteen to twenty percent; Steinways from zero to ten percent; expensive European pianos from twenty to twenty-five percent. In highly competitive situations, or when the dealer is very motivated to sell, however, discounts from five to ten percentage points greater than those mentioned above are sometimes possible. See the *Annual Supplement* for more information.

Other tricks are used to draw customers into the store. At the beginning of this chapter I mentioned "leaders," or "promotional" pianos—bottom-of-the-line

But Is It a Good Value?

I do hundreds of telephone consultations a year with readers of *The Piano Book*. Some of them are considering buying very expensive pianos. These people usually begin the conversation by asking if the brand in question is of high "quality," to which I invariably reply "yes." Then, somewhat shyly, they ask if it's a good "value," to which I generally reply "no." This answer always catches them by surprise and is followed by an awkward silence until I explain myself. The explanation may seem obvious to you, but I encounter such fuzziness about the concept of "value" that I thought best to digress here.

Earlier in this chapter I said that many brands offer three or four levels of quality to choose from. Generally, these levels can be labeled "price," "value," and "performance," and the same terms could be applied to the piano market as a whole. The lowest level is (besides to get people in the door) for those who need a piano at the lowest possible price, within reason regardless of quality. The middle level, sometimes further subdivided into two levels, balances concerns of price and quality about equally. The highest level is for those who want a piano that performs the best, regardless of price. Since the definition of "value" in this context is quality per unit price, the highest level is, virtually by definition, not a good value.

The reason these pianos are not, strictly speaking, a good value is that a graph of quality vs. price is a curved line, not a straight one. In the marketplace, as a general rule, goods that are a little better cost a lot more, and goods that are a lot better cost a *whole* lot more. In addition to using more expensive materials, better goods are made in smaller quantities, so the overhead costs must be borne by a smaller number of units. Also, quite simply, the market will bear the higher price because the people who are looking for the best performance typically are less sensitive to price considerations. Since quality is subjective and not often quantifiable, it's impossible to prove or disprove this, but it generally agrees with experience: You pay through the nose for each extra increment of quality. *I don't mean for a moment to suggest that one not buy an expensive piano*, only that one should be clear that one is buying it for its superior *performance*, not for its being "a good value."

All this having been said, within their own quality class, some pianos may be a better value than others, although the market tends to compensate for this by giving bigger discounts for the disadvantaged brands. And certainly there are ways that consumers can get more value for their money. See the section "How To Save Money" for some of these ways.

pianos advertised at rock-bottom prices to serve as bait. Once you are in the store, the salesperson will attempt to sell you up to a higher-priced piano.

A variation on the "leader" is the "factory second." At another Midwestern dealership—this one selling low-quality pianos—a newspaper advertisement taped to the door announced that a limited number of "factory seconds"—pianos with slight cosmetic defects—were being sold at "half price." This piqued my curiosity, since it was my impression that most factories either touched up such defects and sold the pianos at full price or didn't sell them at all. A thorough inspection of several of these "seconds" failed to reveal anything that could be classified as a "defect" (except that the pianos were very sloppily made, but that was typical for the brand). After introducing myself as a technician, I asked the salesman to show me where the defects were. "Well . . . there really aren't any defects," he hesitantly replied. "That's just a way of getting people into the store." And as he turned to greet a customer walking in the door, he whispered, "It's what we call merchandising."

Sometimes a "second" is actually created on purpose by a salesperson, who makes a small, but repairable, scratch or gouge in the finish. Then he or she can create a sense of urgency in the customer, who now believes she has a rare chance to save money on a piano with a slight "defect"!

Some of the gimmicks described above are a bit crass, but there are also more subtle forms of creative selling that appeal to a more sophisticated crowd. For example, some dealers claim that their pianos make good "investments." They make no specific promises of returns, but they imply that their pianos are collectibles that will rise in value over time. Pianos are wonderful investments in a lifetime of pleasure or a child's educational development, and they depreciate more slowly than many other expensive items, but most make lousy financial investments if making money is your goal.

As an example, my parents bought a new grand piano in 1967 for around $3,800. I inherited the piano, and today it might bring as much as $15,000 on the used market, or about four times what my parents paid for it. This may at first seem like a great return, but in fact, it represents a very poor return, even a loss from a certain perspective. If the $3,800 had been put into even a mediocre investment in 1967 and had grown at a rate of only five percent per year, compounded, it would be worth nearly $20,000 today. More importantly, the same model that cost $3,800 in 1967 costs nearly $38,000 today (in 2000), so my $15,000 piano has actually lost about sixty percent of its inflation-adjusted value over the years if you use the current price of that model as a measure of inflation (only twenty-five percent if you use the Consumer Price Index). Of course, we're thrilled to have "lost" that money; it represents a tremendous amount of pleasure gained through the years. My point is only that as a purely financial investment, it doesn't fly. (Artcase and limited-edition pianos, pianos with exotic veneers, intricate carvings, fancy legs, inlays, and so forth, which are valued as art objects as much as they are valued as pianos, are definite exceptions to the discussion above and may increase in real value.) ·

Another sales ploy that may not be worth as much as it seems is the trade-up guarantee. This is a guarantee that if you decide to trade up to a more expensive model within a certain number of years, the dealer will apply the full original purchase price of the older piano toward the purchase price of the new one. If you are seriously considering trading up within a short time, this offer may be worthwhile. However, you should get this guarantee in writing and read the fine print. Sometimes the deal requires that the second piano you buy cost at least twice as much as the first; or that the price of the first piano is deducted from the "tag price" of the second, which, as we've seen, can be any amount the dealer chooses it to be. At the very least, you're unlikely to get much of a discount off the price of the second piano. Only a small percentage of people who buy a new piano ever actually trade up, which is one reason why the dealer can afford to make this offer. Certainly the offer doesn't hurt, but most people shouldn't give it much weight.

During the past few years, there has been a great increase in the number of large-scale piano sales events, variously called "armory sales," "warehouse sales," "university sales," or named after a local concert festival. Typically, nearly-new pianos on loan or lease to the festival or university are sold off, presumably at a "discount," and hundreds of brand new ones are trucked in by the manufacturer especially for the occasion. Sometimes a team of professional high-pressure salespeople is hired to stage the event.

The advantage of shopping at such events is that the selection may be much greater than you will ever find at your local dealer, which is handy if you've been looking for some unusual furniture style or finish (although most of the pianos may be in crates, with only samples available to be seen). Also, sometimes you can really get a good deal on a piano that is only one or two years old, or even on a new one. The disadvantages are that often the "bargains" will be no bargain at all despite the claims of "30 percent off;" the pianos brought in from the factory will probably have received little or no preparation before being delivered to your home (and, as I said, may be crated so you can't try them out); and the pressure to "buy today" will likely be enormous. Dealers that don't participate in these mega-sales can often offer you a better deal, and virtually always, a more pleasant shopping experience.

Does It Hold Its Value?

I am frequently asked whether a given piano "holds its value" or has a "good resale value." I find I get slightly irritated by this query, in part because I feel frustrated at not being able to give a definitive answer to what, after all, is a reasonable question, and in part because it isn't always clear what the questioner means. Are they asking about the financial return? Or whether the piano will physically hold up? Or whether the name will carry as much prestige later as it does now? Usually I answer the question from the financial point of view. Of course, many who ask this question have no intention of ever selling the instrument, but nobody likes the idea that they might take a bath if they do.

A depreciation schedule for used pianos can be found on page 203. From this, one can see that, on average, a piano will lose about fifteen percent of its value immediately upon delivery to your home, and thirty-eight percent of its inflation-adjusted value within the first ten years. But the story is actually more complicated than that. If you bought the piano at an especially low price, you might actually make a profit if you sold within the first few years. On the other hand, if you overpaid for it, then a quick sale might produce a large loss. The resale value of foreign-made pianos will also be affected, sometimes sharply, by changes in the currency exchange rate because the value of a used piano is, in large part, pegged to the price of a new one. Also for this reason, the value of a used piano of a brand in current manufacture will be affected by local competitive conditions for that brand. A lot of competition usually means a lower price for the new piano and, therefore, for the used one, too.

Resale value also depends on how popular the brand is and how long you are willing to wait to get your price. Brands like Steinway, Yamaha, and Baldwin tend to sell fairly quickly. Steinways usually sell at a premium to what a depreciation schedule would show because demand outstrips supply. With Yamaha and Baldwin, both demand and supply are great, so the pianos usually sell quickly at an average price, neither especially high nor low. On the other hand, if you're trying to sell a little-known European seven-foot grand in French Provincial mahogany, you might have to wait quite a while to get your price. If you're not willing to wait, you might have to sacrifice.

Most people mistakenly figure depreciation by comparing the selling price of the used piano with their original purchase price. This method can result in vastly underestimating actual depreciation—or even turning depreciation into an imaginary profit—because it doesn't take into account the change in the value of the money (inflation). The proper method is to compare the selling price of the used piano with the selling price of a new piano of the same or comparable brand and model, as in the depreciation schedule in this book. Over short periods of time (a few years), the difference doesn't matter much, but for longer periods it can be substantial. (See page 66 for a real-life example of this.)

University sales, in particular, have a certain unethical quality inherent in them because educational institutions are seen by the public as making decisions based on quality and merit and not on purely commercial grounds. But schools are strapped for money with which to buy instruments and so will frequently trade the use of their good name for a new crop of free pianos every year or so. They will probably not associate themselves with junk, but the association should not be considered an artistic endorsement, either. In any case, be aware that many of the new pianos brought in for the event may not even be of the same brand or model used by the school. (Note: Most of the pianos that have actually been used at the school will still be in excellent condition, but occasionally one will have been abused. Used pianos should always be inspected by a piano technician before purchase.)

I recommend that you not use one of these mega-sales as your first piano-shopping experience. You'll be easy prey for fast-talking sales people. Spend plenty of time shopping among the dealers in your area well in advance of a sale, decide what you want and what you're willing to pay, and then wait for a sale and bargain like crazy. You'll be in a much stronger position to judge the truth of what the salesperson says and you may get a really good deal. Also, because the piano will probably have received no pre-sale servicing by the dealer, be prepared to hire your own technician later on to make it right. If you do find yourself a novice at one of these events, try to negotiate some time to think about it by asking that the piano be moved to the dealer's regular location after the sale, but be prepared to be refused. Remember that Federal law usually allows you three days to rescind the agreement and get your money back, but only if the sale is not at the dealer's regular place of business and you did not previously negotiate with the dealer there.

Finally, a claim that you should "buy now because the manufacturer is raising the price next week" is usually a lie; you can call the manufacturer to check if you want. But even if true, prices are so adjustable at the retail level that any impending wholesale price increase should have absolutely no effect on you. Besides, the dealer bought the piano at the old price, not the new one.

How To Save Money

Given that promotions are so often phony, how, then, can a buyer save money?

Although dealers have protected sales territories for most of the brands they sell, these territories are sometimes small. It's not unusual for several dealers to sell the same brand in a large metropolitan area. Even though sales and discounts are usually phony, prices are far from uniform, and it's worth your while to shop around and negotiate. In fact, it would be foolish not to negotiate, because most price tags are inflated in anticipation that you will. Sometimes it's possible to negotiate a very good deal, as the following example will illustrate:

Two friends of mine went shopping for a piano on which their young son was to begin taking lessons. After some looking around, they settled on a medium-quality console piano sold through an American manufacturer. The piano was actually manufactured by a Korean company (as indicated by a tag on the back of the piano), but was being marketed by the American company with its own name on the piano. The couple offered the dealer several hundred dollars less than the $2,600 price on the price tag, expecting him to negotiate. To their surprise, he refused to budge. "I think it's a fair price," he said, and that was that.

My friends next went to another dealer, where they saw a piano of the exact same model, style, and finish as the one described above, except that it had the *Korean* company's name on it instead of the American. It was selling for only $2,300, or $300 less than the identical piano with the American name on it. They were tempted to buy this piano, but decided that they would prefer a piano with an American name on it, even if not actually made here, so they continued looking.

Finally, my friends went to a store in another town, in which they found the same model with the American name, but, alas, not with the finish they liked. So they made the salesman an offer: If he could get them the piano with the finish they wanted and deliver it to their home with bench and tuning included, they would be willing to pay $2,100—and no sales tax. This might seem like an outrageous offer, but the salesman picked up the phone, called the first store the couple had visited to ascertain that they had the correct piano, and then accepted the offer. My friends now have in their home the same instrument they had refused to buy at $2,600—for 25 percent less.

Just what the relationship was between the first and last stores, and why the last store was willing to negotiate the low price, I don't know. Perhaps the dealer was tight for cash and was willing to forgo some profit to make a sale. My point is that opportunities for negotiating a lower price are there to be had.

You may not have to be so bold as to ask for a low price, either. These days piano prices are very adjustable. Most dealers would rather make a very small profit than not make the sale at all. If a salesperson senses you're shopping around, he or she may very quickly offer you an attractive price. You can be in the best negotiating position if there are at least two pianos of similar quality you are interested in at two different dealerships and you let them bid for your business. You may be surprised at how low a price you can get if the salesperson knows that you're really willing to walk out the door.

Here are some more points to consider when trying to save money:

- If you have decided on a brand of vertical piano, and are choosing a particular model, the best value will almost always be found with the school or institutional model. This will be ruggedly built, of adequate size, and much less expensive because of its plain furniture styling. The American decorator-style pianos offer you the least value for the money as far as the musical instrument is concerned.

- Sometimes a salesperson will offer to "throw in" a lamp or some piano lessons instead of dropping the inflated price on the tag. If these items don't interest you, say so and ask for a lower price instead.

- Although your local dealer will hate it and manufacturers strongly discourage this practice, you may get a better price from a dealer in another city. If that city is across state lines, you might avoid paying sales tax, too. At the very least, you can use the threat of this option as a bargaining chip with your local dealer. Because obtaining warranty service from a distant dealer may be more problematical, though, this option works best with piano brands that maintain a high level of quality control. See also "Shopping For a New Piano On the Internet."

  Be aware that if you don't pay sales tax in the other state, you are supposed to pay it as a "use tax" to your own state. Of course, few people ever do. Warning: Although rare, some dealers, upon learning that prospective customers have gone across state lines to buy a piano elsewhere, regularly report these customers to their state tax authorities to get even. (Yuk! Why would anyone ever want to do business with someone like that?)

- If you are fortunate enough to know exactly what piano you want and have not yet entered the store that sells it, try calling the store's owner or manager directly. By bypassing the salespeople and their commissions, the owner or manager may be able to give you a special price. Once you've entered the store and been greeted by a salesperson, however, the owner is ethically obliged to credit him or her with the sale. (This tactic may work best when contacting a store in another city.)

- If you are considering the purchase of a piano with a small dealer network, such as one of the expensive European pianos, you might try calling the manufacturer or its U.S. distributor (phone numbers are given in the reviews in Chapter 4). If there is no authorized dealer in your area, a manufacturer or distributor may be willing to sell you a piano directly, possibly at a large discount. Of course, you will have to work out the details of moving and warranty service, as you would with any long-distance purchase.

- Salespeople sometimes offer commissions to piano teachers and technicians for referring customers to them. But the salesperson cannot afford to both pay a big commission and offer you a big discount. If the salesperson must pay a commission, this may limit his or her ability to negotiate with you. Commissions make sense from a business point of view, but they present some ethical problems. How unbiased can such a referral be? If you are referred by a teacher or technician, you may want to ask that person whether he or she will be receiving a commission and, if the answer is yes, whether the commission could be waived or split with you.

- Sometimes piano technicians and rebuilders sell new pianos out of their home or shop. Their profit margin may be much less than that of a regular piano dealer because they may not be dependent on these sales as their principal source of income, they may be using extra space in their home or shop which would otherwise go unused, and they may not be located in a prime business location with a high overhead. The brands they sell may be less well known, because once a brand has achieved acceptance in the marketplace the manufacturer prefers to give a franchise to a large dealer in a good location who will sell many pianos. But some little-known brands are, in fact, excellent and worth your consideration. One drawback to shopping at a technician's home or shop is that the selection of models, styles, and finishes may be smaller because of limited space.

- The more expensive and little-known the piano and the longer it has been sitting around on the sales floor, the more irrelevant is the "suggested retail price" and the more room there is for bargaining. For this reason, it's not uncommon for very large discounts to be given on expensive European grand pianos.

- If, after careful research, you have offered the salesperson a price you consider to be reasonable, and the salesperson has refused your offer, I suggest you wait at least forty-eight hours before consenting to a higher price. It's not uncommon for a salesperson to call a customer about twenty-four hours later to say that "in the interim I have spoken to the manufacturer and they have agreed to give me a special price on the piano"—or some such story—and to make you a better offer. Of course, you run a small risk the piano will be sold while you are waiting, so this tactic shouldn't be used if losing the piano would be a serious setback.

- Traditionally, spring and early summer have been the slow times in the piano business, and therefore the times when you could strike the best bargain. With the current year-round barrage of mega-sales, however, I'm not certain there are any slow times anymore. Still, if it's convenient, try shopping from April to July. (However, rumors that you may be able to get a better price by shopping at the end of the month/quarter/year because the salesperson needs to meet a quota are rarely true.)

- Whether you pay cash or buy on time is unlikely to affect the price you pay for the piano. Likewise, finance rates will probably be comparable whether you finance through the dealer or on the outside, though a bank will probably finance for a longer term. Still, you should shop around for financing. If you're buying a very expensive piano, you may save a bundle over the long run by borrowing at a lower rate on the equity in your home.

- Be sure, when negotiating, that a piano bench, moving, and tuning in your home are all included in the price. Almost every piano on the market comes with a bench (except some European pianos). It's not an "extra."

Price and Service

When you buy from a store that habitually sells its merchandise at absurdly low prices, there is a good chance that the pianos are not being serviced properly and that you may have trouble getting good warranty service should you need it. Many of a dealer's costs are fixed; there are a limited number of ways to reduce costs to lower prices, and service is usually the first to go. This may not matter much if you are buying a piano that needs little preparation for sale, but if it does need work, you could end up sorry that you "saved money."

Even as I write this, though, I know that sometimes the concept of service is blown out of proportion to its real value. A very reliable piano may be sold unserviced at such a low price that even after you hire your own technician to service it completely, you still come out far ahead. In such a case, only the crazy or the very timid would pass up the chance to pocket the savings. Also, price is not always related to service. Some dealerships that operate on a high profit margin and talk a good line on service actually give only lip service, whereas there are dealers that are able to give great service at a low price because they have lower over-head costs of other kinds (commissions, rent, advertising, etc.) or because they are owned and operated by piano technicians and rebuilders who double as salespeople. Inquiring among piano technicians in your area may reveal some of these differences between dealers.

Service becomes an issue especially when a piano is being delivered to the home right out of the crate with no pre-sale preparation, or when doing business with a dealer in another part of the country and no after-sale service (and sometimes no pre-sale preparation) is expected. The problem for the piano shopper is figuring out just how much these differences in service are worth. Sometimes salespeople speak of "service" in hushed terms that are intentionally vague, as if to imply that the concept cannot be reduced to mere numbers and therefore that superior service can justify any price quoted. But between dealers and their accountants, it's a different story: service occupies specific line items in the profit-and-loss statement. It may not be possible to state with pinpoint accuracy how much of the price is attributable to service, but it is possible to estimate it.

There are several different service-related activities whose provision may vary between dealers or from one situation to another: pre-sale servicing of the piano in the store, delivering the piano to your home, servicing the piano in your home soon after delivery, and minor warranty service for which the dealer will not be reimbursed by the manufacturer. Dealers generally pay technicians from $50 to $200 to do pre-sale service on a new vertical piano, and from $100 to $500 on a new grand (possibly more for Steinways and other professional instruments). The higher amounts listed are actually uncommon, but possible for a dealer who is being thorough. Of course, the dealer usually pays the technician at a wholesale rate. If you had to hire a technician to do this work, you might pay a rate about fifty percent higher. If delivery to your home is not included in the price of the piano, the dealership will usually charge its wholesale cost of from $100 to $350 for this service (if you're moving the piano cross-country, you'll have to add in the additional cost). The dealership will pay its technician something like $35 to $75 to service the piano in your home soon after delivery, more if much travel is required. If you had to hire the technician independently, the cost would be about double. Finally, dealers usually include in their budget from one to two percent of the retail price of the piano as a reserve to cover future warranty work. The price ranges given above represent differences in the service needs of different brands, in the fussiness of the customers, and in the cost of living in different regions of the country.

Let's look now at a worse-case scenario, where one dealer is selling a piano with absolutely no service of any kind and another is providing complete service. Applying the above figures in a reasonable fashion to a typical $5,000 vertical and a $15,000 grand, the difference in service would be worth in round figures from about $300 to $750 for the vertical and from $600 to $1,500 for the grand. Of course, this stark contrast in service is unusual and was chosen for illustrative purposes only. More likely, both dealers would offer some service, but the quality or level of service would differ. Nevertheless, this example gives you some idea of what order of magnitude the concept of service actually occupies in the price calculation.

There are also some other factors to consider that are harder to quantify or that vary from person to person. If you are other than a beginner at the piano, you will probably want to choose a piano that has had good pre-sale service because that is the only way you can make an informed decision about how the piano sounds and plays. A technician who services the same brand and model of piano over and over may know how to solve its little problems better than another technician you hire on your own, even if your own technician is very competent. Your tolerance for risk will also play a part in your decision about service. Knowing that you can call an agreeable local dealer if you encounter problems provides peace of mind. Also, frankly, you'll probably find it more pleasant and interesting to do business with someone who seems to care about their product and service than with someone who treats the piano as if it were no more than a washing machine or a refrigerator. How much, if anything, these factors are worth, however, is a highly personal decision. For some, a price that's low enough will trump all other considerations.

Dealing With Trade-Ins

If you already own a piano, the dealer may offer you an unreasonably generous trade-in allowance on a new piano, at least as much as you would get if you sold it privately. But in this case, you are less likely to get much of a discount off the "list price" of the new piano. You will usually come out ahead if you sell your present piano privately and use the money toward a negotiated price on the new piano.

If you prefer not to go through the hassle of selling your old piano privately, however, you should at least find out what it's really worth to the dealer so you can tell whether the dealer's offer on the new piano is any good. Here's how to do it: Before you enter any store for the first time, call several dealers at whose stores you are thinking of shopping, and ask how much they would pay you for your old piano. Try not to give your name, and don't mention you are planning to buy a new piano. (If you've already shopped at the store, they may have both your name and phone number in their database, so, in that case, try not to give your phone number, either, when you call.) Describe your old piano as best you can: brand, size, age, furniture style and finish, condition, and when it was last serviced. If several dealers tell you they are not interested in buying it, there's a good chance it's not worth anything, at least not at the wholesale level. If they balk at giving you a figure without seeing it first, try at least to get a "ballpark" figure. Dealers get calls like this every day and are used to answering them. This will tell you what the piano is really worth to the dealer.

When you enter the store a few days later, the salesperson, while "qualifying" you (finding out about your piano-related needs and resources), will ask you about any piano you currently own. For example, he or she may ask, "And what is little Johnny playing on now?" If the salesperson believes you are going to trade in a piano, he or she will be on notice to inflate the asking price of the new one to allow for a generous trade-in. Obviously, if you are planning to sell the old piano privately, you should make that clear at the outset. If you have elected to trade in your old piano, however, having already inquired as to the true value of the piano, you will now have a way to judge both the salesperson's offer and his or her veracity.

For example, you are offered a trade-in credit of $2,000 against the $7,000 tag price of a new piano. Another dealer asks $5,000 for a similar piano less a $1,000 trade-in. Is the first piano really worth more than the second, and if so, by how much? Is the second dealer being stingy about the trade-in value? The *Annual Supplement* will help answer the first question. Inquiring in advance what the dealers would pay for the old piano will answer the second. If, for instance, the first dealer originally told you over the phone that the trade-in was worth $1,000, then the offer of a $2,000 credit against a $7,000 tag price is really an offer of a $1,000 credit against a $6,000 price (and the salesperson is engaging in a little "creative selling"). You can now compare the $6,000 price of the first piano with the $5,000 price of the second in the *Annual Supplement* to see which really represents the better deal. You also now know that the second dealer was more honest about the trade-in value. By finding out in advance the true value of the trade-in, as well as by using the *Annual Supplement*, you will be able to compare the various prices and figure out which actually represents the best value.

Note that digital pianos and electronic keyboards have little or no trade-in value, whereas used pianos generally do. Therefore, if you're thinking of trying out an inexpensive alternative before committing to the purchase of a new piano, a good used piano may be a better value than a digital in the long run.

Shopping For a New Piano On the Internet

A perusal of manufacturers' and dealers' web sites (and there are many) will reveal a curious phenomenon: Almost nobody is mentioning prices of new pianos. Some dealers' sites don't even say which brands they carry. Considering the mania taking place on such sites as eBay and Priceline.com, why is the world of new pianos so restrained?

"Restrained" is probably the right word. Virtually all manufacturers' dealer agreements contain terms that prevent a dealership from advertising outside its market area, which is defined in the agreement. Recently, manufacturers have been applying this provision to advertising on the internet. Of course, a manufacturer can't prevent a dealer from having a web site, but it can demand that the site not contain any price information, brand names, or anything else that might be construed as a solicitation to buyers outside the local area.

The reasoning for this restriction goes something like this: Suppose Yamaha dealers were allowed to sell new Yamahas online. A price war would soon break out, with some dealers offering extremely low prices with cross-country moving, after-sale service, etc. included, until the competition drove the price of Yamaha pianos down to the point where most dealers could no longer afford to carry them. They would abandon the brand in favor of other brands with higher profit margins, and Yamaha would be left without a dealer network.

That's the reasoning, but I have some doubts about whether it would actually turn out that way. A milder version of this already goes on in metropolitan areas with several dealers carrying the same or similar brands, but somehow an accommodation occurs in the marketplace and they do not all go out of business. In addition, pianos are not completely uniform, interchangeable commodities that can be purchased sight unseen (although some brands come close). Most buyers want to try out the actual piano they are going to buy. Still, for those who have no particular preferences in tone and touch and just want a dependable piano at the lowest price, shopping on the internet could offer big advantages. The same is true for those who are willing to travel a long distance to try out the piano, especially for expensive pianos where the potential savings is large. In practice, allowing the advertising and sale of new pianos on the internet would probably result in some dealers doing a high-volume, low-margin, long-distance business, and others, stressing service to the customer, doing a more traditional business—in other words, just like it is now, except over a larger geographical area.

Dealers themselves have mixed feelings about the internet, and about doing business outside their market territory in general. They can become very sanctimonious when they discover that another dealer has "stolen" a customer from their area, getting on the phone with the manufacturer and demanding that something be done about "that renegade dealer." In private, though, many dealers will admit that they are chomping at the bit to be able to advertise and sell new pianos on the internet—as long as nobody else is allowed to do the same! (And some already do it if they think they can get away with it.) Of course, I'm writing this in the spring of 2000. With the speed at which law and commerce are evolving to adapt to the internet, it's possible that all will have changed by the time you read this.

In the meantime, here are a couple of small ways you can use the internet to shop for a new piano (see Chapter 5 for using the internet to buy a used piano). You will find a very nice list of manufacturers' and dealers' web sites (and much other good information) on The Piano Page, the web site of the Piano Technicians Guild (www.ptg.org). As I mentioned earlier, manufacturers' web sites are full of information about their products, including detailed specifications, historical information, and virtual factory tours. Some manufacturers also make available a list of their dealers, but to inhibit shopping around, they dispense them one at a time in response to your typing in your zip code. Of course, there's nothing to stop you from typing in the zip code of locations other than your home, say a place you visit often or wouldn't mind visiting. Also, although most manufacturers will not permit their dealers to advertise on the internet, there may still be some manufacturers that look the other way, particularly ones that have very small dealer networks and feel that the benefit of advertising outweighs the risks. Don't forget to consult the *Piano Book* web site (www.pianobook.com), which may from time to time have resources to help you find a dealer or technician.

Having found several dealers that sell the brand in which you are interested, you can look up their web sites, e-mail them, or phone them. Don't expect to talk price much over the phone or by e-mail with far-away dealers. They can get in trouble for doing that for the reasons discussed earlier. The most they might do is vaguely allude to the fact that they're willing to deal. You'll generally have to visit their store to do more. Be sure to ascertain that they carry the particular model you're looking for before making the trip.

If you do decide to buy a new piano from far away, make sure the dealer is actually authorized to sell the brand in question (or the manufacturer's warranty will be void), and be sure you and the dealer have a firm understanding of how warranty service will be handled. The dealer may handle moving arrangements; if not, some piano movers that do cross-country moving are listed in Chapter 6. If, by some remote chance, you make a deal over the phone or by e-mail and decide to buy the piano sight unseen (not recommended), you should hire a technician in that city to inspect the piano on your behalf. The Piano Page (www.ptg.org) has a list of Registered Piano Technicians nationwide listed by state and province, or call the Piano Technicians Guild at 816-753-7747. Also see the *Piano Book* web site.

I've noticed that a few dealers sneak around their restrictions by advertising brand new pianos in classified ads on sites intended primarily for the sale of used pianos, such as www.pianomart.com, at least for as long as they can get away with it (until another dealer complains). Dealers also advertise used pianos in these classifieds, but keep them listed long after they've sold. When you call to inquire about the used piano, a dealer may try to sell you on a new one.

If you are interested in reading opinions about the various brands of pianos, other than the opinions in this book, there are several internet message boards on which such discussions take place. One is a newsgroup known as "rec.music.makers.piano". You can also access it via the web at www.deja.com. Click on "discussion groups" and type in or search for the name. There is also a message board at www.pianoworld.com. As far as I can tell, these boards tend to be populated by three types of people: innocent newcomers with sincere questions, people with bizarre opinions loaded with misinformation, and a variety of piano salespeople and technicians who patiently try to answer the newcomers' questions while correcting the misinformation and keeping the discussion from becoming overheated. Although these boards can be mildly interesting to read for a while, I think there is relatively little useful information about the quality of new pianos to be gained from them for the time spent.

Servicing After Delivery

After your new piano has been in your home for a few weeks, be sure to get in touch with the dealer to arrange for your free in-home tuning. At this time, the technician will also take care of any minor problems not corrected at the store and any others you have noticed since the piano arrived at your home. If you had the piano inspected by an independent technician before it left the store, there should be little for the store technician to do now besides tuning, and everything should go smoothly.

If you failed to have the piano inspected, and if the dealer did little to prepare the piano for sale, you may now be faced with a problem. You see, the dealer and the store technician usually have an arrangement whereby the dealer pays the technician a flat fee for servicing a new piano in the home, regardless of how much work is involved. Furthermore, the fee is usually very, very low because there is an implicit understanding that the technician will be compensated by retaining the customer as a tuning client in the future. Unfortunately, this arrangement offers little incentive for the technician to do a conscientious job, and results in little more than a quick tuning and a brief attempt to correct whatever problems the customer actually notices, which may be far less than what the piano truly needs. Some dealers pay a higher fee and are willing to pay extra when more work is required, but many dealers, especially those who sell the cheaper pianos, do not. This is the cause of disharmony between many a technician and dealer.

If you failed to see that the piano was prepared and inspected in the store and are now faced with the sorry situation of not knowing what work the piano needs and how to get it done, you should speak to the store technician frankly about it when he or she arrives to tune your piano. Say you understand that the technician's fee doesn't come close to paying the true cost of doing the adjustments that may be needed, but that you would like a candid assessment of the piano and are willing to pay the difference between what the technician is paid by the dealer and what the job is worth. In fact, this is a good tack even if the piano needs only tuning. You will make a good friend and receive the most thorough job possible. Naturally, if the piano cost $2,000 and you are told that it will cost $500 to put it in the kind of condition it should have been in the first place, you will be understandably upset. But before you complain to the dealer, remember that doing so will get the honest technician who gave you the bad news in trouble. (This advice assumes the technician is, in fact, honest. If he or she is not, you may get ripped off.)

I would also advise that even if you plan to use another technician in the future, you use the store technician for the initial tuning in your home. This technician has undoubtedly serviced scores of pianos of the same make and model and is acutely aware of all their idiosyncrasies and their remedies, where these exist. He or she also has easiest access to spare parts and advice from the factory when necessary. Another technician, even if extremely competent, may lack this specific experience and support and so may be less effective or efficient. You should be aware, however, that not all store technicians are equally qualified; many are beginners who stay with the store only until they build up a clientele sufficient to support themselves independently. If you don't have full confidence in the store technician, you may want to immediately follow up the free initial tuning with a service call by a technician of your choice.

Pianos often need more servicing during the first few years of their life than they need for many years afterward. Because the strings will be new and still stretching, you should have the piano tuned four times the first year. After that, the frequency of tuning will depend on humidity, usage, your ear, and your budget. See Chapter 7 for details on how often, and when, to have your piano tuned. During the first year or two, the cloth and felt parts in the action will compact, so you can expect to need some action and tone regulating during this time, too. Sometimes dealers offer additional service during the first six months or year of ownership. Be sure to keep track of what service you are due and make sure you receive it.

Buying a School or Institutional Piano

Pianos in schools and other institutions take a terrible beating, and are usually appallingly neglected by the administrators charged with their care—even at some prestigious music schools and universities where one would expect people to know better. Sometimes one technician is supposed to maintain hundreds of pianos, but, due to the demand for service to recital and faculty instruments, can barely give the practice room pianos a quick tuning once or twice a year, though most of them are in dire need of regulating or even rebuilding. One might think that this neglect must be caused by a lack of funds, but at the same time, school administrators may budget tens of thousands of dollars for the purchase of new pianos, often citing the state of disrepair of the present crop as justification for buying new ones. "And if these don't hold up, we'll try a different brand next time," they all too often say.*

If you are an administrator charged with buying new pianos for your school or other institution, please stop or a moment and reconsider whether new instruments are really needed. Do you realize you could have *dozens* of pianos completely regulated, or at least

Adapted from Jack Krefting, "The Technical Forum," *Piano Technicians Journal*, March 1983, p. 8.

several pianos completely restored or rebuilt, for the price of a single high-quality new piano? Or that by diverting some of the money budgeted for new instruments toward the hiring of another piano technician, you could save thousands of dollars each year that would otherwise have to be spent replacing neglected instruments? I realize that restrictions inherent in the budgetary process sometimes dictate how certain funds are to be used, particularly when the funds come from foundation grants or charitable donations. But you should make every effort to see that, wherever possible, the money is directed where it makes most sense. Seventy-five percent of the time, in my estimate, that means in piano maintenance and repair, not purchase. Guidelines for the maintenance of institutional pianos are available from the Piano Technicians Guild. See page 231.

Pianos in institutions suffer not only from lack of service, of course, but from overuse, occasional vandalism, and—perhaps more than anything else—lack of climate control. Throughout most of the country, overheating during the winter days, freezing at night and on weekends and holidays, and then unremitting humidity in the summer ages school pianos long before their time. Under these conditions, my contacts at schools and universities tell me, virtually all brands of piano hold up equally poorly. Spending some money on climate control would probably be of greater benefit than buying new pianos. But where this is not possible, purchasing pianos with plastic action parts, laminated soundboards, laminated bridges, multilaminated pinblocks, and other indestructible features might actually be a good idea, especially for practice-room pianos, which are almost never in tune anyway and rarely expected to have a great tone.

In a slightly less cynical vein, as both a pianist and a piano technician I would recommend that you pay special attention to the quality of keys and action in practice pianos. Most of these instruments are being used by students to develop technical facility more than tone production, the latter being almost impossible given the weird acoustics of the cubicles in which the pianos are placed, not to mention the state of their tuning. Students can put up with a good deal of variance in tuning and tone, but are completely stymied when a key is stuck or the action is grossly uneven. Long, properly weighted keys and trouble-free actions that repeat well and are in good regulation will probably be appreciated more than most other features.

The bidding process for school pianos tends to be a rerun of the marketing gimmicks described earlier in this chapter. Typically, a school purchasing agent will decide what brand and model of piano he or she would like to purchase, but, because it's not considered proper to actually name the piano in the bidding specs, the agent will instead describe the piano in terms of its features—the number of back posts, the number of laminations in the pinblock, and so on. Of course, only one or two brands will actually fit the description. Dealers are allowed to enter alternate bids for slightly different pianos, and purchasing agents are usually given some latitude in awarding contracts for reasons other than a piano's fitting the exact description and bearing the lowest price; still, the agent usually ends up purchasing the piano that he or she had in mind at the start.

This bidding procedure is designed to protect the school district by setting minimum quality standards for its pianos, and probably to protect the purchasing agent from accusations of prejudice for or against certain brands or dealers. My guess is that this process was most useful in the sixties and seventies, when so many truly awful pianos were being built. But nowadays it simply adds red tape, requiring people to write, read, decipher, and match a list of specifications that may or may not be related to quality and that are simply a ruse anyway. One manufacturing executive told me his company could make a better school piano

for less money if it didn't have to pattern its specifications after certain Japanese pianos that so many purchasing agents were using to write bids.

When buying a school piano, keep in mind a few additional considerations:

- Heavy-duty casters and locks for the fallboard and lid are standard features on many, but not all, institutional models. If any of these are not standard, you can specify that they should be added.
- You should specify exactly what pre-sale and post-sale service you expect to be included. A dealer's reputation for providing this service should be taken into account when awarding contracts.
- Be sure to check the manufacturer's warranty policy. Some consumer warranties do not extend to institutional or commercial use.

Player Pianos

See page 160 in Chapter 4 for information on electronic player piano systems. See page 178 in Chapter 5 for information on traditional, pneumatically-driven player pianos.

CHAPTER FOUR

A Consumer Guide to New and Recently Made Pianos

THE NEW PIANO SURVEY

TO THE BEST OF MY KNOWLEDGE, A GOOD, detailed brand-by-brand review of new pianos has never before been written, even by consumer magazines that tackle everything from dog food to hair spray. There are some good reasons why this is so. For one thing, it's very hard to design "tests" for a piano. Sure, we could test how fast a note is able to repeat, or electronically analyze the scale design—and these tests could be useful to a degree—but, in the end, there are too few such tests that can be done, and they fail to tell us enough about the piano. Sometimes sketchy magazine articles substitute "features" for tests. If the piano has enough of the "right" features, it's recommended. But, as we've seen in the last chapter, many features are just marketing gimmicks with no real value, and despite having all the right features, some pianos still don't sound good.

There are other impediments to reviewing pianos. The number of different piano brands and models is probably comparable to that of automobiles, but the number of piano experts and technicians is much smaller. Furthermore, piano repair records are not generally kept in sufficient detail to provide long-term information on the incidence of repair. And, although given enough resources these obstacles could be overcome, the relatively small size of the piano market doesn't justify the expenditure of money that would be required to collect this data. Of course, that doesn't help *you*, one of those who need this information.

The Myth of Objectivity

One of the reasons often cited for not even attempting to review pianos is that the critique would be just a "bunch of opinions." It would certainly be hard to deny that evaluating a piano involves a lot of judgments; opinions about tone, touch, design, looks, and so on, are all central to such an evaluation. But a close look at many consumer product evaluations reveals that they, too, are much more subjective than the magazines in which they appear would care to admit. When a car is said to "handle well," "comfortably seat four," or "have a lot of engine noise," are these not matters of opinion? Subjectivity is present in more subtle ways as well: in simply deciding what information is desirable about a product and designing tests for it, one brand may be favored over another, even though the piece of information being sought may not be particularly useful to the buyer of the product. A good example of this is the amazingly complicated technical data that often accompanies reviews of stereos and speakers. "But does it sound good?" you ask. "Well, that's just somebody's opinion."

The fact is, though, we seek other people's opinions all the time in our daily lives, even on matters we know must be judged subjectively. One of the ways we determine whose opinion to trust is by the amount of experience they have with the subject and by the amount of detail they can offer to back up their opinion. We do this with the assumption that their experience has enabled them to develop more finely honed senses than ours (such as with music or art), and we do so at least as much for our peace of mind—to validate our own opinions—as to gather new information. Of course, sometimes we *do* receive new information, such as when an auto mechanic warns us of a problem common to a particular brand of automobile we are considering buying.

Thus, when someone calls and asks me for advice on buying a piano, it is precisely my *opinion* that they desire (as subjective as it might be), plus any facts that might support it or that might be useful or interesting to them. In designing a survey appropriate to the task of evaluating pianos, then, it was important not to shy away from subjective opinions, but also, to the extent possible, to survey as much useful objective information as possible.

The Survey and Its Limitations

To assist me in advising readers, about fifty piano technicians from across the United States were recruited to participate in a written survey of the condition of new and almost-new pianos. The technicians were chosen on the basis of their experience (both in general and with specific brands), their interest in my work, and my perception of their ability to be articulate and fair-minded. Most of the technicians had between ten and thirty years of experience servicing pianos, with an average of eighteen years, and nearly all were Registered Piano Technician (RPT) members of the Piano Technicians Guild (although the Guild itself played no part in this survey).

Most of the survey research for this edition was conducted under my supervision by Stephen H. Brady, RPT, one of the most widely respected piano technicians in the United States and, since 1995, editor of the *Piano Technicians Journal*. Steve, who has done graduate work in musicology, is also head piano technician at the University of Washington. He resides with his wife Judith Cohen, a concert pianist, in Seattle. After Steve conducted the survey as described below, he and I together analyzed and discussed the results. Steve wrote initial drafts of some of the reviews, after which I did further writing and editing. I, alone, am responsible for the published material.

Pads of survey forms were distributed to the technicians, with instructions that they fill out one form for each piano five years old or younger that they serviced during the following several months. The forms had space for brand, model, age, place of service, and other identifying information; had a checklist of sixty-nine possible problems a piano might have; and asked that any additional information be provided in the margins or on the back of the form. The age of the piano was determined from the time of sale, not manufacture, and sometimes had to be estimated. Actual age may differ by several years. The period of time during which the survey was taken was primarily during the last three months of 1999.

We included pianos that were as much as five years old, rather than only brand-new pianos, because we believe a piano must demonstrate its ability to hold up with time and use before being considered acceptable. Some pianos that seem flawless when new may not pass muster a few years down the road. Other pianos may arrive from the factory needing much work, but once the work is done they may hold up beautifully. The written survey was an attempt to take a "snapshot" in time to discover how the pianos hold up and what problems seem to occur most often.

More than thirteen hundred forms were returned by the technicians. (Similar surveys were conducted in 1983, 1989, and 1994 for the first three editions of this book.) Many forms contained additional comments that explained problems in more detail and effectively expanded the sample by indicating which problems were common to other pianos of the same model and which were just quirks.

We want to emphasize that this survey was not intended as a precise scientific instrument, and its results cannot be considered statistically valid. Rather we considered it a fact-finding tool from which a limited amount of useful information might be extracted. It was also a way of encouraging technicians to look more closely at the pianos they were servicing, and a way of opening up conversation with the technicians that would lead to the development of an accurate picture of each brand.

After reviewing the results, we interviewed most of the technicians (plus a few others not involved in the written survey) to glean additional information and to find out how the written results actually corresponded to their experience and opinions. We also "shopped" at piano stores, inspected new pianos, and spoke to dealers, salespeople, manufacturers, and other technicians whenever the opportunity arose. To ensure maximum objectivity and prevent harassment by dealers or manufacturers, all technicians participating in this study were guaranteed anonymity. Most interviews were conducted in the winter and spring of 2000, with some follow-up interviews in the summer.

In addition to the survey described above, for this edition we were also able to obtain access to a service database maintained by an organization that has a contract to provide piano service for several piano dealers in a large metropolitan area. This database contains detailed service records for over 4,000 pianos sold by these stores from mid-1994 to mid-1999. A total of nearly 7,500 service calls were performed by over one hundred technicians, about 5,500 service calls for tuning only and nearly 2,000 for repairs or adjustments. Information from this database is integrated into the reviews.

To make the most appropriate use of a survey of this kind, you need to understand its limitations. It was our intention to write fair and balanced, but candid, reviews that could serve as a guide to consumers, who otherwise have nowhere else to turn for advice. But this is not the last word on pianos. These are reviews of pianos as seen by a few members of a particular segment of the population—piano technicians—whose concerns may not always be the same as yours. We chose piano technicians, rather than musicians or dealers, because they have the widest exposure, the most technical knowledge, and the least bias of all those connected with the piano industry. But they are not entirely without prejudice. They often tend to see pianos more in terms of their serviceability than their playability. Many technicians, in fact, do not play the piano. In some cases, their assessment of tone may be based on how the piano sounds when it is being tuned rather than when it is played. (Some pianos are very difficult to tune, but when all closed up sound just fine—and vice versa.) So some pianos that technicians don't like may still be acceptable, especially for use by beginners.

The technicians differed in how closely they examined pianos, perhaps finding more fault with pianos they were predisposed not to like than with others. They also differed in their standards of quality. By keeping close tabs on the survey forms returned by each participant, and through interviews that revealed each participant's quality standards and degree of exposure to particular brands, we were able to compensate for these differences somewhat in the final results. But although we have been as objective as reasonably possible given the subject matter and the resources available, it would be a mistake to consider this to be a scientific endeavor; a more apt analogy would be "investigative reporting," with all the potential for human error that implies.

There are also limitations you should know about that apply to the service database information in particular. The database only contained service records for pianos sold by the client stores. Though these stores sell quite a few brands, they do not sell every brand. Therefore, several major brands and many smaller ones are conspicuously absent from the data set. Unlike the technician survey, the database contains records only for *post-sale* service—service in the home (including warranty service) during the months and years following the sale. Since many piano owners eventually go on to use a technician of their own

choosing not connected with the store, the data probably underestimates the actually amount of service required by the pianos. Therefore, it would be more appropriate to use the data as a *relative* indicator of a brand's service needs, rather than as an absolute one. Although the same organization also provided much of the pre-sale service on these pianos, that information was not recorded. Depending on the thoroughness of pre-sale service provided, consumers in other areas may experience a different level of post-sale problems than that reported here. Last, most of the data was collected from 1994 to 1997. The contract between the service organization and its client stores changed in 1998, so the data is more sparse for the last couple of years.

This brings us to our own roles in this study, which were far from those of neutral observers. In addition to designing the survey and doing the interviews, we had to evaluate the credibility of our sources, make decisions on how to handle conflicting information, and in other ways process the information we received. Not to do so would have been unfair to everyone involved. Steve and I also had to inspect pianos personally in some cases. (We believe we were aided in this by our combined eighty-four years as pianists and fifty-three years in the field of piano technology.) We have done our best to state when opinions are strictly our own, but even those opinions attributed to other technicians ultimately represent only our own best assessment of their views, based on our research. Despite these limitations and the subjective nature of the reviews, we believe that when used with discretion, good judgment, and common sense, this guide will result in a better purchase and a little more peace of mind.

How to Use This Guide

Information of many different kinds is contained in these reviews, whose thoroughness varies, depending on the amount of information available, what information seemed most useful for the consumer, and other considerations.

Each review begins with the name, address, phone number, and e-mail address of the company or its U.S. distributor so you can contact the company to find out if there is a dealer near you, or to settle a warranty claim that cannot be satisfactorily settled with the dealer. The manufacturer's or distributor's web site address is also given, where applicable.

This is followed by the name of the actual owner of the company (or in the case of a distributor, the maker of the piano) and by the trade names the company has used during the past few decades in those cases where the name as listed is different from the actual owner, maker, or trade name. (Some of these companies own many more trade names than are listed, but have not recently used them.) Although a certain amount of cross-referencing is contained within the alphabetical listings, a list of all trade names mentioned in this guide and the names of the companies under which they are reviewed can be found on pages 90–91. Trade names that belong to dealers and distributors, not manufacturers, are known as "stencil pianos," explained on page 92.

A little bit of the history of some companies, especially their recent history, is included, partly for interest, partly to warn you when recent changes of ownership, management, location, and so on, may affect the products' quality.

A listing and evaluation of pianos follows. In the evaluations, emphasis was placed on information obtained from the interviews, with data from the written survey and the service database included where we felt it would be illuminating. Some information and evaluations from previous surveys are also included to provide some continuity and context and to assist those considering a slightly used piano.

It's important not to be too alarmed by problems listed in the reviews. No piano is perfect and many problems are minor and easily corrected. Since companies are continually solving old problems and discovering new ones, and because of differences between one instrument and another or between one production run and another, there is no guarantee that any of the problems listed would appear in your piano if you bought one of that brand.

Problems and defects are listed not to scare you away, but rather to help provide a more accurate picture of each brand. The lists, taken in context with the rest of the review and in conjunction with the technical material presented in chapter 3, can be useful to you as you shop for a piano or when you or your technician examines the piano before you purchase it. It may point out potential problems that could make the piano unsuitable for you or may help you in making a list of problems that need to be corrected before you will accept delivery. And even though the manufacturer may have corrected some of the specific defects listed, or changed models, by the time you get around to shopping for a piano, the type and number of such defects or problems may give you a better general idea of what to expect from that brand of piano. Because of the large time span covered in these reviews, this guide is also intended for those who are buying a used piano of recent origin.

Most major manufacturers and distributors were sent or read a draft of their review prior to publication so they could correct factual errors and provide updated information. It is inevitable, though, that reviews of this kind are to some extent out of date by the time they are published. My apologies to those manufacturers whose products are inaccurately described as a result.

Note: In this edition, a greater number of specific technical items and problems are mentioned than in past editions, in part to satisfy the informational needs of piano technicians. To save space, technical terms mentioned in the reviews may not be explained where they appear. Most can be looked up in the Glossary/Index, but in some cases you may want to ask a technician for an explanation.

NEED MORE HELP?

Making decisions about the purchase of a piano can sometimes be difficult and confusing. Sorting out the conflicting claims of dealers and manufacturers and deciding which piano represents the best value for you can often be aided by speaking to a sympathetic and knowledgeable person who is not trying to sell you something. In response to many requests for additional information and advice, I have developed a telephone consulting service to assist people shopping for a new piano.

For a fee of fifty dollars (subject to change) charged to your credit card, I will spend up to a half hour on the phone advising you on which piano brands and models best fit your particular needs, preferences, and budget (longer calls are prorated at the same rate). I can also tell you the approximate prices I consider typical in the marketplace, and how to bargain for the lowest price. Finally, I can supply you with names of qualified piano technicians in your area and other information about piano maintenance. Many customers have reported that the advice they received saved them hundreds or even thousands of dollars on their purchase, as well as giving them greater peace of mind.

To make the best use of this service, I suggest you first read this book, as many of your questions may be answered here, and that you do some shopping to acquaint yourself with the various brands, dealers, and prices in your area. Then, to make an appointment, call the publisher, Brookside Press, at 800-545-2022 (617-522-7182 from outside the U.S.) and leave your name, phone number, credit card information, and the best times to reach you. I will return your call collect, usually within a day or two.

Note: The purchase of a *used* piano requires detailed, on-site inspection and evaluation. Telephone advice about such pianos, therefore, can only be of a very general nature.

Models and Prices. Toward the end of each review, for general reference purposes, is a list of the models currently offered by the company. This is a generic listing and does not include the actual furniture styles and finishes available. Also given is a general price range into which the majority of the company's products fall. This range reflects only the lowest-priced style and finish of each model, and does not include concert grands. Prices represent typical asking or "tag" prices, not actual selling prices, which can vary widely (see page 64 in Chapter 3). See the latest edition of the *Annual Supplement to The Piano Book* for a current listing of all models, styles, and finishes, list prices, and suggestions for estimating actual selling prices.

Ratings

In this edition, by popular demand, I have expanded the rating of pianos, albeit reluctantly. The rating of pianos is risky business, highly subjective, and subject to abuse by dealers and customers alike. Despite all the disclaimers, customers tend to rely too heavily on anything that has numbers associated with it, as if it represents the word of God, while dealers will attempt to split hairs in order to convince you that their brand—with a half-point higher rating—is superior to the competition. However, I also realize that people absorb information in different ways, and that there is a legitimate need for a simple, visual summary display of information to supplement the written word.

Ratings have been made in several categories of quality, explained below, and expressed with stars, from one to five in half-step increments. Depending on how fussy you are about your pianos, you may wish to use one or the other of the following two keys for relating the symbol to the quality level:

Fussy		Normal	
✻ ✻ ✻ ✻ ✻	= Excellent	✻ ✻ ✻ ✻ ✻	= Excellent
✻ ✻ ✻ ✻	= Good	✻ ✻ ✻ ✻	= Very Good
✻ ✻ ✻	= Fair	✻ ✻ ✻	= Good
✻ ✻	= Poor	✻ ✻	= Fair
✻	= Unacceptable	✻	= Poor

Brands are obviously rated in comparison to one another. However, due to the sheer volume of judgments to be made, don't expect perfect consistency or perfect correlation with the reviews. I would consider about half a point to be the "margin of error" in any particular rating category. That is, this is the amount by which I might differ if I were to do these ratings again from scratch, and the amount by which I believe informed but unbiased members of my profession might differ from one another in their opinions. I have purposely painted with rather broad strokes, rather than subdi-

viding and rating to a finer level of detail, choosing to take the middle road of providing consumers with an "at-a-glance" presentation of informed opinion without trying to micromanage their opinion. Where a manufacturer has several markedly different levels of quality, I have sometimes rated these levels separately, but in most cases I have chosen not to rate super-premium-level pianos, such as concert grands, that are issued in very limited quantities. Where I simply don't have enough information to evaluate, I have indicated this. A summary of all brands and ratings follows this explanation.

Although the ratings are obviously informed by my research, ultimately they should be considered to be my own subjective opinion, not necessarily the opinions of the technicians we interviewed. The ratings are offered as an aid to piano shoppers, but should not be considered authoritative or scientific.

Performance: This is a measure, *relative to other pianos of the same or similar size*, of how well a piano plays, sounds, and looks when new, after reasonably thorough preparation by the dealer *commensurate with the price of the piano*. It is a function of the piano's design, materials, and workmanship, as well as the biases and customs in today's musical world. My intention here is to let you know how I believe members of my profession regard this piano's performance under fairly optimal conditions, not to enshrine my own personal preferences. Some pianos, therefore, may receive a high rating on the basis of their reputation, even though, personally, they may not be "my cup of tea." I have chosen not to further subdivide this category into ratings for tone, touch, looks, and so forth, because it would require a mind-numbing quantity of highly subjective decisions on my part. I suggest you learn to make these evaluations yourself.

Confidence: In a world of perfect information, this would be a measure of the piano's longevity or durability. But since the length of a piano's life depends on many factors (not the least of which is how one defines the death of a piano), this rating instead expresses my subjective confidence in the piano's durability. My confidence is a function of what I know about the piano's design, materials, and workmanship; the reports I have received from technicians; my confidence in the people who run the company; how long the piano has been sold in the United States; the political and economic conditions for manufacturing in the country of origin; and other factors. Because my confidence depends on how much I know, it's possible that a perfectly good piano could receive a somewhat lower rating than it deserves if I have little information about it.

Quality Control: This is a combined estimate of how much one instrument of this brand is likely to differ from another of the same model, how much preparation is likely to be required by the dealer, and how troublesome the piano is likely to be to the customer in the short run (until the bugs are worked out), especially if the dealer does not prep it adequately. Most of the time, these qualities run together. A caution, however: Some otherwise excellent instruments rate rather poorly in these regards, but perform and function well in the long run. Therefore, don't dismiss a piano purely because of a low rating in this category. Instead, I suggest that any piano rating much less than four stars be inspected by a piano technician prior to purchase.

Warranty: This expresses my best guess as to how generous a manufacturer or distributor is likely to be in resolving customer complaints and warranty claims. Although the length and terms of the warranty sometimes factor into this rating, the manufacturer's or distributor's reputation concerning the liberality with which it interprets the warranty, and the length it is willing to go to satisfy a customer, factor more strongly. This is the weakest of the ratings; there is relatively little objective information to go on because most warranty issues are small and resolved at the dealer level. I have based the ratings largely on information and anecdotal reports from technicians about warranty service. Since piano owners will most often receive their warranty service through technicians, this feedback is relevant. Sometimes, however, it may more acccurately reflect a manufacturer's or distributor's relations with technicians than with consumers.

In truth, most manufacturers and distributors today are quite responsive to warranty claims from dissatisfied customers. Therefore, this rating should be considered much less important than the others. A rating of four stars should be considered normal; this is the default rating unless I have information that suggests otherwise. If a brand receives a much lower rating than that, I recommend not rejecting the piano, but rather asking for a written warranty from the dealer. Note that the warranty rating may also be affected very negatively where the piano is from a foreign country such as China or Russia in which it would be difficult or impossible for an American to pursue a warranty claim if a small distributor went out of business or stopped carrying the brand. In such cases, a warranty from the dealer is much advised. The rating is also downgraded a little if the length of the warranty is less than ten years or is for parts only.

Information: This is a measure of how much information the above ratings are based on, so you know how much to rely on them. A rating of one star here means that the ratings are an educated guess, based as much on what I know about other pianos from that region of the world with similar materials and in a similar price range as on the rated pianos themselves. (But if I really don't know enough about a brand to rate it responsibly, I haven't.) A rating above three stars means that I have an abundance of information and feel quite confident about the ratings.

SUMMARY OF BRANDS and RATINGS
in alphabetical order

BRAND	Performance	Confidence	Quality Control	Warranty	Information*
	INS = Insufficient information to rate				
Albrecht, Charles	INS				
Altenburg, F.E.	INS				
Altenburg, Otto	See "Samick" and "Samick/World" — also see text				
Astin-Weight	✶ ✶ ✶ ✶ 1/2	✶ ✶ ✶ ✶ 1/2	✶ ✶ ✶ ✶ 1/2	✶ ✶ ✶ ✶	✶ ✶ 1/2
Baldwin Verticals: 248A	✶ ✶ ✶ ✶	✶ ✶ ✶ ✶	✶ ✶ ✶	✶ ✶ ✶ 1/2	✶ ✶ 1/2
Baldwin Verticals (except 248A)	✶ ✶ ✶ 1/2	✶ ✶ ✶ ✶	✶ ✶ ✶	✶ ✶ ✶ 1/2	✶ ✶ ✶ ✶ 1/2
Baldwin Grands: M1, R1, L1	✶ ✶ ✶ ✶ 1/2	✶ ✶ ✶ ✶ ✶	✶ ✶ ✶	✶ ✶ ✶ 1/2	✶ ✶ ✶ ✶ 1/2
Baldwin Grands: SF-10	✶ ✶ ✶ ✶ ✶	✶ ✶ ✶ ✶ ✶	✶ ✶ ✶ 1/2	✶ ✶ ✶ 1/2	✶ ✶ ✶ 1/2
Bechstein, C.	✶ ✶ ✶ ✶ ✶	✶ ✶ ✶ ✶ ✶	✶ ✶ ✶ ✶ ✶	✶ ✶ ✶ 1/2	✶ ✶ 1/2
Becker, J.	✶ ✶	✶ 1/2	✶ 1/2	✶ ✶	✶
Bentley	INS				
Bergmann	✶ ✶	✶ 1/2	✶ 1/2	✶ ✶ ✶ ✶ 1/2	✶ ✶ 1/2
Blondel	INS				

*Differences in information between grands and verticals not always shown in this chart.

BRAND	Performance	Confidence	Quality Control	Warranty	Information*
Blüthner	* * * * *	* * * * *	* * * * *	* * * *	* * 1/2
Bösendorfer	* * * * *	* * * * *	* * * * *	* * * *	* * *
Boston Grands	* * * *	* * * *	* * * * 1/2	* * * 1/2	* * * 1/2
Boston Verticals/Amer.	* * * *	* * * *	* * * *	* * * 1/2	* * *
Boston Verticals/Japanese	* * * *	* * * *	* * * * 1/2	* * * 1/2	* * *
Brentwood	INS				
Broadwood Grands	* * * * 1/2	* * * * *	* * * * *	* * * *	* *
Broadwood Verticals	INS				
Chickering	* * 1/2	* * *	* * 1/2	* * * 1/2	* * 1/2
Cline	See "Young Chang: G (Gold)"				
Conn	See "Krakauer"				
Conover-Cable	See "Samick/Korean"				
Dietmann	INS				
Essex	INS				
Estonia	* * * * 1/2	* * * *	* * * 1/2	* * * *	* * 1/2
Eterna	* *	* * 1/2	* * *	* * * * *	* *
Everett	INS				
Fandrich & Sons	INS				
Fazioli	* * * * *	* * * * *	* * * * *	* * * 1/2	* * 1/2
Förster, August	* * * * *	* * * * *	* * * * *	* * * *	* *
Grotrian	* * * * *	* * * * *	* * * * *	* * * 1/2	* * 1/2
Haessler	* * * * 1/2	* * * * *	* * * * *	* * * *	* *
Hallet & Davis	various — see text				
Hoffmann, W.	* * * * 1/2	* * * * *	* * * * *	* * * *	* 1/2
Hofmann & Scholz	INS				
Hyundai	See "Samick/Korean"				
Irmler	INS				
Kawai: CX-5H and 504	* * *	* * *	* * * *	* * * * *	* * * *
Kawai Consoles & Studios (except CX-5H and 504)	* * * *	* * * *	* * * *	* * * * *	* * * *
Kawai Uprights	* * * *	* * * *	* * * * 1/2	* * * * *	* * * 1/2
Kawai Grands: GM, GE	* * * 1/2	* * * 1/2	* * * *	* * * * *	* * * *
Kawai Grands: RX	* * * *	* * * *	* * * * 1/2	* * * * *	* * * *
Kawai, Shigeru Grands	* * * * 1/2	* * * * 1/2	* * * * *	* * * * *	* *
Kemble	* * * * 1/2	* * * *	* * * * 1/2	* * * *	* * 1/2
Kingsburg	* *	* *	* *	* * 1/2	* 1/2
Knabe	See "Bergmann"				
Knabe, Wm.	See "Young Chang"				
Knight	INS				
Kohler & Campbell	See "Samick"				
Krakauer	* *	* 1/2	* 1/2	* * 1/2	* 1/2
Maeari	See "Samick"				
Mason & Hamlin	* * * * *	* * * * *	* * * *	* * * *	* * *
Mecklenburg	INS				
Muzelle	INS				
Niemeyer	* *	* 1/2	* 1/2	* 1/2	*
Niendorf	INS				
Nordiska	* *	* *	* *	* * 1/2	* * 1/2
Pearl River	* *	* *	* *	* * *	* *
Petrof Grands	* * * * 1/2	* * * * 1/2	* * * 1/2	* * * 1/2	* * * *
Petrof Verticals/Detoa	* * * *	* * * 1/2	* * * 1/2	* * * 1/2	* * * *
Petrof Verticals/Renner	* * * * 1/2	* * * * 1/2	* * * *	* * * 1/2	* * * *
Pleyel	INS				
Ridgewood	various — see text				
Rieger-Kloss	INS				

BRAND	Performance	Confidence	Quality Control	Warranty	Information*
Ritmüller Grands	** 1/2	** 1/2	** 1/2	***	*
Ritmüller Verticals	See "Pearl River"				
Sagenhaft	INS				
Samick Grands/Indonesian	** 1/2	** 1/2	** 1/2	*** 1/2	***
Samick Grands/Korean	***	***	***	*** 1/2	*****
Samick Grands/World	****	****	****	*** 1/2	**
Samick Verticals/Indonesian	** 1/2	** 1/2	** 1/2	*** 1/2	***
Samick Verticals/Korean	***	***	***	*** 1/2	****
Samick Verticals/World	****	*** 1/2	*** 1/2	*** 1/2	* 1/2
Sängler & Söhne	various — see text				
Sauter	**** 1/2	*****	*****	****	**
Schafer & Sons	See "Young Chang: G (Gold)"				
Schimmel	**** 1/2	**** 1/2	*****	****	*** 1/2
Schirmer & Son	INS				
Schubert	**	* 1/2	* 1/2	* 1/2	**
Schultz & Sons	INS				
Schulze Pollmann	****	**** 1/2	**** 1/2	****	**
Seidl & Sohn	INS				
Seiler	**** 1/2	**** 1/2	*****	****	**
Steck, George	See "Pearl River"				
Steinberg, Wilh.	INS				
Steiner, Bernhard	See "Samick/Korean"				
Steingraeber & Sohne	*****	*****	*****	****	* 1/2
Steinway & Sons	*****	*****	*** 1/2	***	*****
Story & Clark Grands/American	INS				
Story & Clark Verticals/American	***	*** 1/2	***	****	**
Strauss	*	*	*	*	**
Walter, Charles Grand	**** 1/2	*****	**** 1/2	****	**
Walter, Charles Verticals	**** 1/2	**** 1/2	**** 1/2	****	****
Weber/Chinese	**	* 1/2	* 1/2	****	**
Weber/Korean	***	*** 1/2	***	****	****
Weinbach	See "Petrof"				
Welmar	INS				
Westbrook	INS				
Whelpdale Maxwell & Codd	See "Bentley," "Broadwood," "Knight," and "Welmar"				
Wieler	See "Sängler & Söhne"				
Woodchester	INS				
Wurlitzer Grands	***	***	***	*** 1/2	***
Wurlitzer Verticals/American	** 1/2	*** 1/2	** 1/2	*** 1/2	***
Wurlitzer Verticals/Chinese	**	* 1/2	* 1/2	***	*
Yamaha Consoles & Studios	****	****	****	*****	*****
Yamaha Uprights	****	****	**** 1/2	*****	*****
Yamaha Grands: GA1	*** 1/2	*** 1/2	**** 1/2	*****	***
Yamaha Grands: GP1, GH1	** 1/2	*** 1/2	**** 1/2	*****	*****
Yamaha Grands: C	****	****	*****	*****	*****
Yamaha Grands: S	**** 1/2	**** 1/2	*****	*****	**
Young Chang Grands: G (Gold)	***	*** 1/2	***	**** 1/2	****
Young Chang Grands: PG	****	*** 1/2	***	**** 1/2	*** 1/2
Young Chang Grands: JP	INS				
Young Chang Verticals	***	*** 1/2	***	**** 1/2	*** 1/2

SUMMARY OF BRANDS and RATINGS
in approximate descending order of quality

- Read the explanation and key on pages 80–81.
- Remember that these ratings represent my opinion; they're not scientific.
- Quality order was determined by averaging the ratings for Performance and Confidence. All brands with the same average rating were listed together, in order first by Quality Control, then by Warranty, then by Information, and finally, where necessary, alphabetically.
- The order in which the brands are listed by quality should not be taken too literally. In some cases the order is influenced by the amount of information I had available or by alphabetical order, neither of which has anything to do with quality. With appropriate pre-sale service and assurances from the dealer, warranty and quality-control concerns may be reduced to near zero. Therefore, brands listed close to one another may, for all practical purposes, be considered to be of similar quality.
- Performance and Confidence were considered equally in determining quality order, with the other concerns definitely secondary. Depending on your particular needs and values, you may weight the quality characteristics differently, resulting in a very different quality order.
- Except where more narrowly described, a brand listing refers to most of the brand's models, grand or vertical as the case may be, excluding concert grands. However, even where broadly described, there still may be some variation in quality within a particular product line.
- Remember that verticals should be compared only with other verticals, grands with other grands, and both should be compared *only with similarly-sized instruments.*
- Quality ratings cannot possibly reflect subtle differences between brands. Be sure to read the brand reviews in this book and obtain information from other sources before buying.
- Prices given represent an approximate range of non-discounted list prices for the lowest-priced style and finish of the smallest and largest models, *excluding concert grands.* Actual selling prices, and prices for other styles and finishes, may vary.
- For brands not listed, see alphabetical listing, page 81, for reason or for comparable brand.

Group 1: Highest quality performance pianos. These instruments use the best materials, and the manufacturing process emphasizes much hand labor and refinement of details. Advanced designs painstakingly executed, putting quality considerations far ahead of cost and production output. Suitable for the most advanced and demanding professional and artistic uses. Pianos in this group are typically American and European. **Cost: Verticals $13,000-38,000; Grands $27,300-104,000.**

BRAND	Performance	Confidence	Quality Control	Warranty	Information
Grands					
Bösendorfer	* * * * *	* * * * *	* * * * *	* * * *	* * *
Blüthner	* * * * *	* * * * *	* * * * *	* * * *	* * 1/2
Förster, August	* * * * *	* * * * *	* * * * *	* * * *	* *
Steingraeber & Sohne	* * * * *	* * * * *	* * * * *	* * * *	* 1/2
Bechstein, C.	* * * * *	* * * * *	* * * * *	* * * 1/2	* * 1/2
Fazioli	* * * * *	* * * * *	* * * * *	* * * 1/2	* * 1/2
Grotrian	* * * * *	* * * * *	* * * * *	* * * 1/2	* * 1/2
Mason & Hamlin	* * * * *	* * * * *	* * * *	* * * *	* * *
Steinway & Sons	* * * * *	* * * * *	* * * 1/2	* * *	* * * * *
Baldwin: SF-10	* * * * *	* * * * *	* * *	* * * 1/2	* * * 1/2
Verticals					
Blüthner	* * * * *	* * * * *	* * * * *	* * * *	* *
Bösendorfer	* * * * *	* * * * *	* * * * *	* * * *	* *
Förster, August	* * * * *	* * * * *	* * * * *	* * * *	* 1/2
Steingraeber & Sohne	* * * * *	* * * * *	* * * * *	* * * *	*
Bechstein, C.	* * * * *	* * * * *	* * * * *	* * * 1/2	* *
Grotrian	* * * * *	* * * * *	* * * * *	* * * 1/2	* *
Mason & Hamlin	* * * * *	* * * * *	* * * *	* * * *	* *
Steinway & Sons	* * * * *	* * * * *	* * * 1/2	* * *	* * * *

Group 2: High-performance pianos. These instruments are built to a standard favoring high-performance design features, materials, and workmanship. Most are consistent, predictably uniform instruments with few defects. Greater hand labor put into refining touch and tone during manufacture. Probably more durable over the long term than those in lower categories. Suitable for home, institutional, and some professional and artistic uses. Most pianos in this group are American and European; a few are upper-level Japanese pianos.
Cost: Verticals $6,500-24,500; Grands $18,600-70,000.

BRAND	Performance	Confidence	Quality Control	Warranty	Information
Grands					
Broadwood	★★★★½	★★★★★	★★★★★	★★★★	★★
Haessler	★★★★½	★★★★★	★★★★★	★★★★	★★
Sauter	★★★★½	★★★★★	★★★★★	★★★★	★★
Hoffmann, W.	★★★★½	★★★★★	★★★★★	★★★★	★½
Walter, Charles R.	★★★★½	★★★★★	★★★★½	★★★★	★★
Baldwin: M1, R1, L1	★★★★½	★★★★★	★★★	★★★½	★★★★½
Kawai, Shigeru	★★★★½	★★★★½	★★★★★	★★★★★	★★
Yamaha: S	★★★★½	★★★★½	★★★★★	★★★★★	★★
Schimmel	★★★★½	★★★★½	★★★★★	★★★★	★★★½
Seiler	★★★★½	★★★★½	★★★★★	★★★★	★★
Petrof	★★★★½	★★★★½	★★★½	★★★½	★★★★
Schulze Pollmann	★★★★	★★★★½	★★★★½	★★★★	★★
Estonia	★★★★½	★★★★	★★★½	★★★★	★★½
Verticals					
Sauter	★★★★½	★★★★★	★★★★★	★★★★	★★
Haessler	★★★★½	★★★★★	★★★★★	★★★★	★½
Hoffmann, W.	★★★★½	★★★★★	★★★★★	★★★★	★½
Schimmel	★★★★½	★★★★½	★★★★★	★★★★	★★★
Seiler	★★★★½	★★★★½	★★★★★	★★★★	★★
Walter, Charles R.	★★★★½	★★★★½	★★★★½	★★★★	★★★★
Astin-Weight	★★★★½	★★★★½	★★★★½	★★★★	★★½
Petrof w/Renner parts	★★★★½	★★★★½	★★★★	★★★½	★★★★
Kemble	★★★★½	★★★★	★★★★½	★★★★	★★½
Schulze Pollmann	★★★★	★★★★½	★★★★½	★★★★	★★

Group 3: Better quality consumer-grade pianos. These instruments give roughly equal weight to economy and performance. Most are mass produced but with attention to detail, and are consistent, predictably uniform instruments with few defects, suitable for both home and institutional use. The better pianos in this group are made by Japanese companies; the others are Korean, American, and Czech.
Cost: Verticals $4,700-12,600; Grands $10,000-39,800.

BRAND	Performance	Confidence	Quality Control	Warranty	Information
Grands					
Yamaha: C	★★★★	★★★★	★★★★★	★★★★★	★★★★★
Kawai: RX	★★★★	★★★★	★★★★½	★★★★★	★★★★
Boston	★★★★	★★★★	★★★★½	★★★½	★★★½
Samick: World/Millen.	★★★★	★★★★	★★★★	★★★½	★★
Young Chang: PG	★★★★	★★★½	★★★	★★★★½	★★★½
Yamaha: GA1	★★★½	★★★½	★★★★½	★★★★★	★★★
Kawai: GM, GE	★★★½	★★★½	★★★★	★★★★★	★★★★
Verticals					
Yamaha Uprights	★★★★	★★★★	★★★★½	★★★★★	★★★★★
Kawai Uprights	★★★★	★★★★	★★★★½	★★★★★	★★★½
Boston/Japanese	★★★★	★★★★	★★★★½	★★★½	★★★
Yamaha Consoles & Studios	★★★★	★★★★	★★★★	★★★★★	★★★★★
Kawai Consoles & Studios (except CX-5H and 504)	★★★★	★★★★	★★★★	★★★★★	★★★★
Boston/American	★★★★	★★★★	★★★★	★★★½	★★★
Baldwin: 248A	★★★★	★★★★	★★★	★★★½	★★½
Petrof w/Detoa action	★★★★	★★★½	★★★½	★★★½	★★★★
Samick: World/Millen.	★★★★	★★★½	★★★½	★★★½	★½
Baldwin (except 248A)	★★★½	★★★★	★★★	★★★½	★★★★½

Group 4: Medium quality consumer-grade pianos. These instruments are somewhat more oriented toward economy than performance. They may have some problems requiring technician attention before and after sale, but are generally reliable and suitable for average home or lighter institutional use. Students with smaller models of some of these brands may wish to upgrade to a larger or better instrument after a number of years. Pianos in this group are usually Korean or American, but a few are lower-grade Japanese or better-grade Chinese instruments. **Cost: Verticals $2,800-6,000; Grands $7,500-16,000.**

BRAND	Performance	Confidence	Quality Control	Warranty	Information
Grands					
Young Chang: G (Gold)	* * *	* * * 1/2	* * *	* * * * 1/2	* * * *
Weber/Korean	* * *	* * * 1/2	* * *	* * * *	* * * *
Yamaha: GP1, GH1	* * 1/2	* * * 1/2	* * * * 1/2	* * * * *	* * * * *
Samick/Korean	* * *	* * *	* * *	* * * 1/2	* * * * *
Wurlitzer	* * *	* * *	* * *	* * * 1/2	* * *
Chickering	* * 1/2	* * *	* * 1/2	* * * 1/2	* * 1/2
Samick/Indonesian	* * 1/2	* * 1/2	* * 1/2	* * * 1/2	* * *
Ritmüller	* * 1/2	* * 1/2	* * 1/2	* * *	*
Verticals					
Young Chang	* * *	* * * 1/2	* * *	* * * * 1/2	* * * 1/2
Weber/Korean	* * *	* * * 1/2	* * *	* * * *	* * * 1/2
Story & Clark/American	* * *	* * * 1/2	* * *	* * * *	* *
Kawai: CX-5H and 504	* * *	* * *	* * * *	* * * * *	* * * *
Samick/Korean	* * *	* * *	* * *	* * * 1/2	* * * *
Wurlitzer/American	* * 1/2	* * * 1/2	* * 1/2	* * * 1/2	* * *
Kingsburg	* * *	* * 1/2	* * *	* * 1/2	* 1/2
Samick/Indonesian	* * 1/2	* * 1/2	* * 1/2	* * * 1/2	* * *
Eterna	* *	* * 1/2	* * *	* * * * *	* *

Group 5: Economy pianos. These pianos are priced for the economy-conscious buyer, with minimal refinement of touch and tone. Some appear to have higher service needs before and after sale. Sometimes these pianos are billed as an alternative to a used piano for those on a restricted budget, and perhaps they could be, at least temporarily, if meticulously serviced by the dealer. But they might be limiting to a player's advancement, and I would recommend a good used piano over some of the models toward the bottom of this group. Most brands in this group are from China and countries of the former Soviet Union. **Cost: Verticals $1,900-5,100; Grands $7,600-17,500.**

BRAND	Performance	Confidence	Quality Control	Warranty	Information
Grands					
Pearl River	* *	* *	* *	* * *	* *
Nordiska	* *	* *	* *	* * 1/2	* 1/2
Kingsburg	* *	* *	* *	* * 1/2	*
Bergmann	* *	* 1/2	* 1/2	* * * * 1/2	* * 1/2
Weber/Chinese	* *	* 1/2	* 1/2	* * * *	* *
Becker, J.	* *	* 1/2	* 1/2	* *	*
Verticals					
Pearl River	* *	* *	* *	* * *	* *
Nordiska	* *	* *	* *	* * 1/2	* 1/2
Bergmann	* *	* 1/2	* 1/2	* * * * 1/2	* * 1/2
Weber/Chinese	* *	* 1/2	* 1/2	* * * *	* *
Wurlitzer/Chinese	* *	* 1/2	* 1/2	* * *	*
Krakauer	* *	* 1/2	* 1/2	* * 1/2	* 1/2
Becker, J.	* *	* 1/2	* 1/2	* *	*
Niemeyer	* *	* 1/2	* 1/2	* 1/2	*
Schubert	* *	* 1/2	* 1/2	* 1/2	* *
Strauss	*	*	*	*	* *

THE PIANO INDUSTRY TODAY: AN OVERVIEW

Sales of new pianos in the United States in the post-World War II era, including imports, peaked in 1978 at over 282 thousand per year. By 1996, however, fewer than 100 thousand were being sold each year, and that number had increased only slightly to just over 100 thousand by 1999. Although the trend seems, once again, to be slightly on the upswing, new piano sales are clearly only a shadow of what they once were. The culprits appear to be electronic musical instruments and used pianos.

Over the last two decades there has been an explosion in the digital keyboard and synthesizer market. Some of these instruments are now able to produce a sound and feel that is virtually indistinguishable from that of a real piano. When encased in piano-like cabinets and priced right, they may make a real piano a questionable purchase for some buyers, especially those who would otherwise buy an inexpensive vertical piano or a used piano. Interestingly, some industry experts now feel that hybrid digital/acoustic pianos may actually save the piano industry from extinction, especially the growing interest by non-pianists in acoustic pianos outfitted with electronic player-piano systems as entertainment devices (see listings beginning on page 160 for the Yamaha Disklavier, PianoDisc, QRS Pianomation, Baldwin ConcertMaster, and Young Chang/Kurzweil Player System). In addition, there is a small but steady stream of converts back to the acoustic piano as electronic keyboard players seek a more traditional musical experience or their teachers tell them it is time to "graduate" to a real piano.

From the decline in new piano sales, one might come to the conclusion that due to demographic and cultural changes, nobody is playing the piano anymore. Certainly it's true that the piano no longer occupies the place in the home it did when many of us were growing up. But surveys sponsored by the American Music Conference and carried out by the Gallup Organization report that amateur piano playing is still very widespread, and suggest that one to two million families may be purchasing a piano each year. Clearly the vast majority of these sales are of used pianos, and most of these are private transactions that therefore go unreported.

The used-piano boom frankly took the piano industry by surprise. It wasn't until the 1990s that industry experts realized that in the mid- to late-1970s, when the baby boomers started to leave home and their parents retired and moved to smaller quarters, the older generation began to get rid of all those pianos they had purchased following World War II. At the same time, the growing pool of skilled piano technicians who entered the profession in the 1970s and '80s developed the capability to rebuild and recondition these and older used pianos to higher standards than were previously achievable. The glut of used pianos is now beginning to dry up, and the low-end of the new piano market is reviving, just as barely-acceptable new pianos from China are arriving.

The decline in new-piano sales over the last twenty years has been especially devastating to the piano industry in the United States. Seventy-five years ago there were literally hundreds of piano makers in this country, and even two decades ago there were at least a dozen firms. Now only a few remain. Recent *additions* to U.S. piano making, however, have included some large foreign firms that have set up shop here, as well as a few small American companies that cater to niche markets.

For much of the last half century, some of the world's best raw materials for piano manufacture have been assembled in the United States using a combination of imprecise machinery, inefficient factory methods, and poorly managed human labor. Although some blame the American worker for the shoddy results, responsibility really lies with poor factory management, and with a culture that accepts inferior merchandise as a matter of course. From a business standpoint, everything worked just fine as long as there was no competition from abroad. But since the 1960s and '70s, American piano firms have increasingly been forced to compete with the efficient methods and low prices of foreign producers. These foreign companies—mostly Asian—have also been aided by (until recently) lower labor costs, greater technical sophistication and automation, favorable tariffs, and the ability to more rapidly assess and meet changing consumer desires. At the same time, declining sales of U.S. pianos have precluded all but the strongest U.S. firms from making the investments necessary for effective competition.

Changing consumer buying patterns and tastes have encouraged the internationalization of the U.S. piano market. Many adults of the baby-boom generation, having played piano as children, are returning to the instrument now that their families and careers are more settled. Although they may be buying pianos partly for their children to learn on, they are looking for good quality more than for low price, especially when their professions (such as computers, business, and medicine) make a better piano affordable. Asian manufacturers were supplying these buyers with good large uprights and grands at very reasonable prices while American manufacturers were still busy trying to sell spinets and consoles—until it was too late. So while the total number of new pianos sold has dropped precipitously, most of the drop has been among the cheaper American-made verticals, whose potential buyers now favor digital pianos, while the proportion of imported grands sold each year has increased dramatically. There has also been a turn away from decorator-style pianos toward simpler styles, leaving behind those manufacturers whose pianos were primarily fancy furniture.

When you enter a piano store, you are going to find a greater international mix of piano brands than ever before, including pianos from the United States, Germany, Japan, Korea, China, Indonesia, Belarus, Russia, the Czech Republic, England, France, Italy, Estonia, Austria, Poland, and occasional other countries. Furthermore, some foreign manufacturers also own factories in the United States and some U.S. companies sell foreign-made pianos under their own (American) label. This makes the piano shopper's job more difficult and confusing than ever before, and some kind of guidance more essential. The following summary of the more detailed listings and recommendations contained in this chapter may help orient you at the start of your search. Be sure, however, to read the detailed listings before making a purchase.

During the past three or four decades, U.S.-made pianos have ranged from the sublime to the ridiculous. On the low end, and usually to be avoided, are several makers who passed away in the 1980s and '90s, but whose pianos may occasionally be for sale, usually on the used market, such as Aeolian (under numerous trade names—see listing), Kohler & Campbell, Story & Clark, Currier, Marantz (also under the names Grand, Kincaid, and Jesse French), and earlier Kimball pianos. (Note, however, that a few of these companies' names, such as Kohler & Campbell and Story & Clark, are again being used, but by companies unrelated to the original.) Baldwin, the country's largest piano manufacturer, now also owns the Wurlitzer and Chickering trade names. Baldwin pianos range in quality from medium-quality beginner pianos to state-of-the-art grands, an amazing array from a single company. In recent times, Baldwin's piano sales have declined and its quality control has been criticized, as with some other American companies. All pianos sold under the Baldwin name are made in the U.S. in Arkansas, although some components may originate elsewhere. Vertical pianos sold under the Wurlitzer name are low-end pianos from the U.S. and China, including the world's sole remaining spinet models. Wurlitzer grands are made by Samick in Korea. Baldwin uses the Chickering name on a series of less-expensive American-made grands.

Carrying on an American tradition of craftsmanship that never entirely disappeared are Steinway in New York and Mason & Hamlin in Massachusetts, as well as the lesser-known makers Astin-Weight, which manufactures unusual pianos in Utah, and Charles R. Walter, which makes verticals and grands in Indiana. Story & Clark makes entry-level pianos and player pianos in Pennsylvania, and imports pianos from Korea and China as well. Though it is perhaps dangerous to make generalizations about such a broad range of makes, American-made pianos, not including those made here by foreign firms, have traditionally tended toward a powerful, but complex, "stringy" tone, full of the higher harmonics. Some, particularly those of Steinway and Baldwin, also tend to need a lot of servicing by the dealer to bring out their full potential.

Japan has been making pianos since about 1900, but began exporting them to the United States only about 1960. At first the pianos fell apart because the wood was not dried to meet the demands of our climatic extremes, but within a few years the quality improved and the price gave U.S. makers a run for their money. For a variety of reasons, including currency fluctuations and higher wages, Japanese pianos have over time become much more expensive in this country. At the same time, sales of these pianos have been severely undercut by the Korean piano industry as well as by diminishing worldwide demand, forcing the Japanese to tighten their belt and to market a more professional image to compete. The two major Japanese companies, Yamaha and Kawai, have also set up shop in the United States, both to take advantage of favorable labor conditions here and to sidestep the punitive tariffs occasionally threatened against Japanese imports. Both brands are often recommended by piano technicians for general home and institutional use. Despite some cheapening of the smaller vertical pianos, which constitute the majority of their U.S. production, the U.S.-made pianos are considered nearly as well made as those from Japan. Kawai also makes the Boston piano, a line designed by Steinway & Sons and sold through Steinway dealers.

In Japan, industrial engineering is a highly respected profession and factory management is elevated to a high art. The Japanese factories are among the most automated anywhere, and Japanese pianos are among the most uniformly made. This precision, and the intelligence with which the pianos are designed, especially for servicing, are the chief assets of Japanese pianos. But due to Japan's high volume of production, and the relative scarcity and higher cost of fine woods, Japanese pianos usually contain less expensive woods than the higher-priced American and European pianos. This and the pianos' designs are thought to affect the tone of the pianos, and possibly their longevity as well. Japanese pianos, especially Yamahas, tend to have a crisp, bright, brittle tone that is a little short on sustaining qualities and other tonal nuances. Jazz pianists tend to seek out this kind of tone and so may be drawn to Yamaha pianos. Kawai (and Boston) pianos tend to be a little more versatile tonally, and so may draw both classical and jazz pianists. Both Yamaha and Kawai pianos hold up well in our climate and piano technicians love to service them, but it would be unreasonable to expect them to sound as good after decades of use as some of the more expensive American and European pianos would under similar conditions.

Western European pianos are sold in the United States in relatively small quantities due to their high price and low name recognition, but there is quite a list of them, and most are of very high quality. They tend to lap at our shores like the tide, coming and going as the currency values fluctuate. Best known here are Bösendorfer (Austria), owned by Kimball; Bechstein (Germany); and the popular Schimmel (Germany). Other Western European names include Grotrian, Seiler, Blüthner, August Förster, W. Hoffmann, Wilh. Steinberg, Sauter, and Steingraeber (all German); Kemble, Woodchester, Knight, and Broadwood (England); Pleyel (France); and Fazioli and Schulze Pollmann (Italy), among others.

Most Western European piano makers are very small compared to an American company like Baldwin, and like a fly on an elephant compared to a giant like Yamaha. Interestingly, despite their size and contrary to their image, a few of them are also extremely automated and computerized. Many also have access to the best woods and carry forth a tradition of impeccable craftsmanship and exquisite cabinetmaking. Given this combination of talent and resources, it would appear that European piano makers are the ideal source of quality instruments, and their reputation—and, yes, their prices, too—reflects this. Be aware, though, that for reasons of both tradition and design, many European pianos emphasize the fundamental part of the tone rather than the higher harmonics, particularly in the bass, and so have a purer, clearer (some say "warmer") tone than American pianos, one that may not always be suitable when a more powerful sound is desired.

Eastern European pianos are also sold here. They often have great scale designs, exquisite cabinets, and a beautiful sound. Due to the legacy of the Communist system, however, quality control is not as good as with the Western European pianos and they tend to need more preparation and troubleshooting by the dealer. This situation is rapidly changing for the better as Eastern Europe adopts the ways of the free market and as business partnerships develop between Eastern and Western European companies. Prices are usually much lower than those of their Western counterparts, making them quite a good value for the money where the

quality is acceptable. Best known are Petrof and Weinbach from the Czech Republic and the Estonia brand from the country of the same name. Other names include Rieger-Kloss and Seidl from the Czech Republic and Schirmer & Son from Poland.

Regarding pianos from countries of the former Soviet Union, Russia and Belarus in particular, a leading trade magazine writes, "While Russian pianos are undeniably cheap, they are generally of such shoddy quality as to be virtually unsalable at any price" (*The Music Trades*, June 1994). This is an exaggeration, since many have been sold, and because there has been some improvement since that quote was written. But until these countries adopt real market and legal reforms that are inviting to foreign capital, pianos from this region of the world will never be acceptable by our standards. It's possible that if meticulously prepared by the dealer they may be acceptable for a while, but I have serious doubts about their ability to hold up over time and generally do not recommend them. (Note: Some "Soviet" pianos come here through European distributors who may also provide technical assistance to the factories. Dealers sometimes claim these are "European" pianos, obscuring their Soviet origin.)

The Korean piano industry is less than fifty years old, and growing up as it did in an impoverished and war-torn economy, it has had to borrow all its technical know-how from Japan and West Germany. Like Japan, Korea has little in the way of natural resources, so the raw materials have to be imported, too. When Korean pianos first entered the United States in the late 1970s, like the Japanese before them they experienced great humidity-related problems. By the mid-1980s, though, they were improving so rapidly that it appeared as if any day they would overtake the Japanese in quality. This prediction turned out to be premature, and the pianos continued to be only barely satisfactory throughout most of the 1980s, improving during the 1990s.

During the 1980s and '90s, the Korean piano industry went through the same transition that the Japanese industry had gone through several decades earlier: as domestic wages rose, automation was rapidly introduced. Also, in the late 1990s, low-wage offshore production facilities were developed in China by Young Chang and in Indonesia by Samick so the industry could remain competitive in the world market. As world-wide demand for pianos slackens and competition heats up, the Koreans, like the Japanese, are paying more attention to quality control and to marketing a more professional image. Today, the two major brands, Young Chang and Samick, have improved to the point where their Korean-made pianos are certainly suitable for most purposes. (Their Chinese and Indonesian pianos are not yet at that point.) Remaining competitive in the U.S. market has been helped by the devaluation of the Korean currency a few years ago. Though still lagging behind the Japanese in quality control, Korean pianos are definitely a good value for the money for most buyers. It would be difficult, however, to describe the tone of a Korean piano, as they have not yet developed an identity or "voice" of their own. As musical machines, they usually work quite well after conscientious dealer prep, but their tone tends to mimic a variety of American, Japanese, and European tonal elements.

Young Chang and Samick pianos are available here under a variety of labels besides their own. Young Chang pianos are sold under the names Pramberger, Weber, Wm. Knabe, Cline, and Schafer & Sons; the Chinese pianos go by the names Bergmann, Knabe, and Weber. Steinway has announced that it will design a piano called Essex to be produced by Young Chang. Samick pianos are sold under the names Kohler & Campbell, Conover-Cable, Bernhard Steiner, Hyundai, Maeari, Hallet & Davis, Wurlitzer, and miscellaneous smaller labels. Although several brands are made by the same company, their specifications may differ; see the reviews for details. Note that Daewoo, a large Korean trading company, until a few years ago made pianos under the Sojin name. These should be avoided.

As mentioned above, the past few years have seen Chinese and Indonesian pianos join the mainstream piano community for the first time. Several years of investment in infrastructure and training by piano manufacturers in joint venture with the Chinese government, and in Indonesia, have just started to bear fruit. Prior to three years ago, many pianos from this part of the world had too many obvious gross defects to be taken seriously. Most of the new manufacturing capacity in China is devoted to the market created by the rapidly growing Chinese middle class.

A smaller portion is being diverted to the U.S. and other markets, aimed at consumers who would otherwise purchase an inexpensive used piano.

For some, these new Chinese and Indonesian pianos may indeed be a viable alternative to a used one, especially in areas where good used pianos are hard to come by or when shopping time is limited. But while many of these instruments are now acceptable, the quality is far from uniform or consistent, and the majority require extensive adjusting by the importer or dealer. Occasionally, large numbers of instruments have had to be returned for repair. Prospective customers should be reminded that these are, at best, entry-level pianos and that they have little or no track record. In addition, brand names and distributorships are in flux as the players position themselves in the market, so some warranties may offer less security than others. I would recommend, therefore, for the time being, that purchase be limited to those brands whose warranties are backed by major manufacturers or distributors. Additionally, a warranty from the dealer might be advisable.

In addition to the Young Chang factory, the other Chinese piano manufacturers producing for the U.S. market (and some of the brand names they produce) include Guangzhou Pearl River (Pearl River, Ritmüller, George Steck, Hallet & Davis, Ridgewood, Sängler & Söhne, Wieler, Eterna [with Yamaha]), Beijing (Hallet & Davis, Wurlitzer [certain models only]), Dongbei (Story & Clark/Prelude, Everett, Niemeyer, Nordiska, Ridgewood, Sagenhaft), Shanghai (Strauss), Yantai Longfeng (Kingsburg), and Artfield (Krakauer, Conn). The quality of these pianos is improving quite rapidly. At the time of this writing (summer 2000), the best Chinese pianos are those from the Pearl River and Yantai Longfeng factories, followed by those made in Dongbei's Nordiska facility. The others are quickly catching up.

INDEX TO TRADE NAMES

For explanation of survey and review procedures, model listings, and price ranges, please see pages 76–81.

Trade Name	See Under
Conn	Krakauer; Kimball
Conover-Cable	Samick
Currier	Currier
Daesung	Muzelle; Lyon & Healy
Daewoo	Sojin; Ibach
Daytron	Sojin
DeVoe & Sons	Kimball
Diapason	Kawai
Dietmann	Dietmann
Disklavier	Yamaha; also page 161
Dongbei	Nordiska; Sagenhaft; Ridgewood; Everett; Story & Clark
Duo/Art	Aeolian
Ellington	Baldwin
Entertainer	Aeolian
Essex	Essex
Estonia	Estonia
Eterna	Yamaha
Everett	Everett; Yamaha
Falcone	Falcone; Mason & Hamlin
Fandrich	Fandrich
Fandrich & Sons	Fandrich & Sons
Fazer	Fazer
Fazioli	Fazioli
Feurich	Feurich
Fischer, J.& C.	Wurlitzer; Aeolian
Förster, August	Förster, August
French, Jesse	Marantz/Pianocorder
Gaveau	Pleyel
George Steck	Steck, George
Grand	Marantz/Pianocorder
Grinnell Bros.	Grinnell Bros.; Samick
Grotrian (-Steinweg)	Grotrian
Guangzhou	Pearl River
Haessler	Blüthner
Hallet & Davis	Hallet & Davis
Hamilton	Baldwin
Hampton	Story & Clark
Hardman (Duo)	Aeolian
Hardman, Peck	Aeolian
Harrison	Kimball
Hastings	Hastings
Heintzman	Heintzman
Helios	Strauss
Hinze	Kimball
Hoffmann, W.	Bechstein, C.
Hofmann & Scholz	Hofmann & Scholz
Hohner	Hohner
Horugel	Samick
Howard	Baldwin
Hyundai	Hyundai; Samick
Ibach	Ibach
Irmler	Irmler
Ivers & Pond	Aeolian
Janssen	Walter, Charles R.
Jasper (-American)	Kimball
Jonas Chickering	Wurlitzer
Kawai	Kawai
Kemble	Kemble
Kimball (W.W.)	Kimball
Kincaid	Marantz/Pianocorder
Kingsburg	Kingsburg
Knabe, Wm.	Knabe, Wm.; Aeolian; Mason & Hamlin
Knight	Whelpdale Maxwell & Codd
Kohler (& Campbell)	Kohler & Campbell; Samick
Krakauer	Krakauer
Kranich & Bach	Baldwin; Aeolian
La Petite	Kimball
Legnica	Schirmer & Son
Lesage	Lesage
Lowrey	Story & Clark
Lyon & Healy	Lyon & Healy
Maddison	Maddison
Maeari	Hyundai
Marantz	Marantz/Pianocorder
Mason & Hamlin	Mason & Hamlin; Aeolian
Mason & Risch	Aeolian
Mecklenburg	Hofmann & Scholz

Trade Name	See Under
Melodigrand	Aeolian
Miller, Henry F.	Aeolian
Monarch	Baldwin
Musette	Aeolian
Muzelle	Muzelle
Nakamichi	Nakamichi/Nakamura
Nakamura	Nakamichi/Nakamura
Nieer	Strauss
Niemeyer	Niemeyer
Niendorf	Niendorf
Nordiska	Nordiska
Otto Bach	Dietmann
Pearl River	Pearl River
Petrof	Petrof
Pianocorder	Marantz/Pianocorder
PianoDisc	Knabe, Wm.; also page 165
Pianola	Aeolian
Pianomation	QRS Pianomation MIDI, page 166
Pleyel	Pleyel
QRS	QRS Pianomation MIDI, page 166
Rameau	Pleyel
Ridgewood	Ridgewood
Rieger-Kloss	Rieger-Kloss
Rippen	Lyon & Healy
Ritmüller	Pearl River
Rösler	Petrof
Royale	Sojin
Rudolf Wurlitzer	Wurlitzer
Sagenhaft	Sagenhaft
Samick	Samick
Sängler & Söhne	Sängler & Söhne
Sauter	Sauter
Schafer & Sons	Schafer & Sons; Young Chang
Schiedmayer	Kawai
Schimmel	Schimmel
Schirmer & Son	Schirmer & Son
Schubert	Schubert; Lyon & Healy
Schuerman	Kimball
Schultz & Sons	Schultz & Sons
Schulze Pollmann	Schulze Pollmann
Schumann	Schumann
Seidl & Sohn	Seidl & Sohn
Seiler	Seiler
Sherlock-Manning	Sherlock-Manning
Sherman Clay	Sherman Clay
Sohmer	Sohmer; Mason & Hamlin
Sojin	Sojin
Steck, George	Steck, George; Aeolian
Stegler	Samick
Steigerman	Steigerman
Steinberg, Wilh.	Steinberg, Wilh.
Steiner, Bernhard	Steiner, Bernhard; Dietmann; Samick
Steingraeber & Sohne	Steingraeber & Sohne
Steinway & Sons	Steinway & Sons
Sting II	Aeolian
Story & Clark	Story & Clark
Strauss	Strauss
Tadashi	Tadashi
Tokai	Tokai
Toyo	Toyo
Vose	Aeolian
Walter, Charles R.	Walter, Charles R.
Weber	Weber; Young Chang
Weinbach	Petrof
Wellington	Aeolian
Welmar	Whelpdale Maxwell & Codd
Westbrook	Westbrook
Whelpdale Maxwell & Codd	Whelpdale Maxwell & Codd
Whitney	Kimball
Whittaker	Kimball
Wieler	Sängler & Söhne
Winter	Aeolian
Woodchester	Woodchester
Wurlitzer	Wurlitzer; Baldwin
Yamaha	Yamaha
Yantai Longfeng	Kingsburg
Young Chang	Young Chang
Zimmermann	Zimmermann; Bechstein, C.; Niendorf

Stencil Pianos

Stencil pianos are those bearing the name of a dealer or distributor, rather than the name of a manufacturer. The practice of selling stencil pianos, also known as "private-label" or "house" brands, must be at least a century old. The term comes from the stenciled name on the fallboard of a piano. This is usually the name of the manufacturer, but a buyer who purchases a certain minimum number of pianos can often request that a different stencil be applied instead. Historically this practice has been carried on by dealers, but during the past decade many importer-distributors have sprung up to import look-alike Asian pianos. I believe that the various names used by these firms can rightly be called stencil names as well, despite the fact that some may have technical specifications slightly different from the manufacturer's own brand. In recent years, large dealers and distributors have succeeded in even having their chosen name cast into or attached to the iron plate.

Why would a manufacturer and dealer want to do this? For a manufacturer, it means selling more pianos to more dealers ("increasing market share") without having to worry about breaking franchise agreements. One dealer can sell "Jones Bros." pianos and the dealer next door can sell "Smith Bros." pianos, and the customer who is trying to decide which to buy doesn't realize they're the same. For the dealer, a private-label brand can be prestigious, has no competition, appears to offer the customer a larger choice, and can fill a low price point without forcing the dealer to promote a brand name that may be associated with poor quality or sold by a competitor.

Some manufacturers own a variety of trade names that they will put on pianos at the request of dealers. On one of my factory visits, I was shown a large drawer full of stencils with various names I had never heard of that were being applied to pianos according to dealer's requests. This and similar tricks are used extensively in marketing all kinds of goods, from electronics to laundry detergents. Although not illegal, it can be extremely confusing to the consumer.

The stencil pianos most widely distributed in the United States are included in this book, but stencil names generally confined to one or a few stores are too numerous to list (an exception being those few pianos that are distinctly different from pianos sold under the manufacturer's name). If while shopping for a piano you find one with the name of the dealer or a name that you don't recognize or that is not listed in this book, ask whether it is a stencil piano and, if so, who makes it. Many salespeople will not want to tell you. If they claim ignorance or say the dealer manufacturers it, they are probably lying. Usually they will admit it is made by someone else (they may not say by whom), but they'll add that it is made to the dealer's "specifications," implying it is somehow better than the manufacturer's regular model. The truth is that, with only a few exceptions, it's probably the same as the regular model, except possibly for the particular style and finish and the name on it, and it may well be an inferior model. Stencil pianos usually carry a warranty from the dealer or distributor, not from the manufacturer. If the real manufacturer is a recommended one and you trust the dealer's warranty, there is no particular reason not to buy a stencil piano.

BRAND-BY-BRAND LISTINGS AND REVIEWS

ACROSONIC

See "Baldwin"

AEOLIAN

No longer in business

Names used: Aeolian, Bradbury, Cabaret, Cable, Cambridge, Chickering, Duo/Art, Entertainer, J.& C. Fischer, Hallet & Davis, Hardman, Hardman Duo; Hardman, Peck; Ivers & Pond, Knabe, Kranich & Bach, Mason & Hamlin, Mason & Risch, Melodigrand, Henry F. Miller, Musette, Pianola, Geo. Steck, The Sting II, Vose, Wellington, Winter, possibly others.

Aeolian Pianos is no longer in business, but its history, and the trade names it owned, will continue to be important to the piano industry for many years. Although Aeolian shut down operations in 1985, some of the pianos it manufactured may still be found on showroom floors, though usually as used pianos taken in on trade for new ones.

Aeolian Pianos was established in 1887 and became a major manufacturer of player pianos. In 1903, it joined with a number of other companies to form the Aeolian, Weber Piano & Pianola Co., Inc. In 1932, in the midst of the Depression, Aeolian merged with the American Piano Co., creating the Aeolian-American Corp. American itself had been created in 1908 as a combination of many brands, and controlled such illustrious names as Chickering & Sons, Wm. Knabe & Co., and Mason & Hamlin. In 1959, Winter & Co. acquired Aeolian-American, changing its name in 1964 to Aeolian Corp. and in 1981 to Aeolian Pianos, Inc. Winter was originally established in 1899 by Gottlieb Heller as Heller & Co., changing its name in 1903 to Winter & Co., and acquiring through purchase and merger many brand names over the years. By the 1980s, then, Aeolian held the title to dozens of trade names, each with their own colorful history, some dating back to the early 1800s. In 1983 Aeolian was sold by the Heller family to Peter Perez, a former president of Steinway & Sons.

Aeolian owned a piano factory in Memphis, Tennessee, where its cheaper verticals were made; a Canadian subsidiary, Mason & Risch, in Scarborough, Ontario; the company's Aeolian-American Division in East Rochester, New

For explanation of survey and review procedures, model listings, and price ranges, please see pages 76–81.

York, which manufactured most of its grands and better verticals; and a plate foundry in Randolph, New York.

The Memphis plant was known throughout the trade for making some of the worst pianos in the United States. In my first survey, taken at about the time Aeolian was sold to Perez, almost every one of the sixty Aeolian verticals examined was found to have from thirty to fifty of the sixty-nine possible problems listed on the survey form, and nearly all were rated "terrible" or "unsatisfactory" by the reviewers. Believe it or not, this was considered by many to be an *improvement* over previous years. (Aeolian also made player pianos, but according to informed sources, the player action was put together even more poorly than the piano was!) In addition, virtually identical pianos were being sold under a vast number of different trade names controlled by the company to give consumers the illusion of choice and to maximize market penetration by avoiding real franchise agreements, a tactic not uncommon among many large businesses today. (See "Stencil Pianos," page 92, for further information.)

While all this was going on in Memphis, the Rochester plant, long esteemed for its high level of craftsmanship, was turning out disappointing products. Finally, in the midst of the recession of the early 1980s, this plant was shut down entirely, putting hundreds of loyal and talented craftspeople out of work.

When Perez bought Aeolian, he immediately undertook to reform the company's marketing strategy and image, using the company's illustrious trade names to greatest advantage—for example, producing a line of low-priced Chickering consoles in Memphis. Another part of Perez's strategy was a promise to improve product quality, but this was never realized. Perez was not a piano engineer, and even had he been, it's possible that the Memphis factory was, technologically, too backward for the kind of reform that would have been necessary. Whatever brief success Perez had at Aeolian was due more to a change in marketing strategy and public relations than to anything else.

Perez also reopened the East Rochester factory under capable management. This factory had been making pianos under the illustrious names of Mason & Hamlin, Knabe, and Chickering in the same factory buildings since the 1930s. Each brand was originally made in a different building to different quality specifications, but for many years their production had been combined in a single building with the same quality standards for all. Generally, the Mason & Hamlin design was considered to be superior to the other two, but through most of the production process all three were given about equal treatment. The Mason & Hamlin instruments were singled out for special care principally in the final stages of action and tone regulating. All were available in both grand and vertical styles. The Mason & Hamlin 50" upright was, for about fifty years, the only tall upright being manufactured in the United States. The Knabe console had also been popular for many years. Since Aeolian-American had been acquired by Winter, however, this factory had been neglected and quality had suffered. The new management at Rochester had plans to upgrade and modernize equipment and raise quality as resources would allow.

Unfortunately for Perez and company, the activity in Memphis and Rochester was cut short by cash-flow problems, made worse by the decline in demand for low-priced vertical pianos. In 1985 Citicorp, Perez's primary lender, called in its loan, took over Aeolian, and closed the factories when Perez was unable to meet his financial obligations to their satisfaction. The Chickering name, patterns, equipment, and unfinished pianos, plus all other assets of the Memphis factory (including most of the trade names Aeolian owned), were sold to The Wurlitzer Co., now part of Baldwin. The Mason & Hamlin and Knabe names, patterns, equipment, and unfinished pianos were sold to Sohmer & Co., now part of Mason & Hamlin. (See "Wurlitzer," "Baldwin," "Sohmer," "Knabe," and "Mason & Hamlin.")

You may run across Aeolian pianos, both pre- and post-Perez, when looking for a used piano. Avoid like the plague the Aeolian pianos made in Memphis—they're junk. Most of the verticals made in Rochester were reasonably good. Grands made at the Rochester plant toward the end had improved, but probably not enough to warrant your purchase.

[Important note: Aeolian made a grand about 4'10" in size, sold under a variety of names, such as J.& C Fischer and Geo. Steck. Those made in earlier years were not bad, but ones made from the mid-1960s onward had a weak cast-iron plate, prone to breakage. Avoid them! Other sizes, even with the same names, did not have that problem.]

ALBRECHT, CHARLES

Charles Albrecht Piano Corporation
68 Chestnut Lane
Woodbury, New York 11797
(800) 572-4858
(631) 752-8611
sales@charlesalbrecht.com
service@charlesalbrecht.com
www.charlesalbrecht.com

Owned by: Global "88" Ltd.

Pianos made by: Samick Musical Instrument Mfg. Co. Ltd., Inchon, South Korea; Guangzhou Pearl River Piano Group, Guangzhou, China; formerly made in Belarus.

Charles Albrecht pianos are distributed by the same company that distributes Schultz & Sons pianos (see "Schultz & Sons"). The distributor says that the Albrecht pianos are joint ventures with established manufacturers with an emphasis on minor modifications, meticulous preparation, and low prices, and are suitable for the beginner- and intermediate-level student. They come with a lifetime trade-up option to the Schultz & Sons piano. At present, the Charles Albrecht name is being used on pianos by Samick, made in Korea and Indonesia, and by Pearl River in China. In the past, the Charles Albrecht name was used on pianos from Belarus.

Warranty: Twelve years, parts and labor, to original purchaser.

Price range: (Verticals) $3,600–6,200; (Grands) $9,100–11,600

Verticals	Grands
43" contemporary console (4300)	4'7" (G4701)
44" designer console (4400)	5' (G5001)
45" institutional studio (4500)	5'1" (G5101)

47" designer studio (4700)   5'2½" (G5209)
48" upright (4800)
49" upright (4900)
52" upright (5200)

Consumer Ratings: Insufficient information to rate, but see ratings for respective manufacturers for approximate ratings.

ALTENBURG

Altenburg Piano House, Inc.
1150 E. Jersey St.
Elizabeth, New Jersey 07201

(908) 351-2000
(800) 526-6979
www.altenburgpianos.com

Pianos made by: Samick, Inchon, South Korea; Niendorf, Luckenwalde, Germany

Names used: Otto Altenburg, F.E. Altenburg

This is the house brand of Altenburg Piano House. The Altenburg family name has been in the piano business for over 150 years, at one time as a manufacturer as well as a dealer. The pianos are sold primarily in the New York-New Jersey area.

Most Otto Altenburg pianos are made by Samick, though they are not necessarily identical to pianos bearing the Samick brand name. Some have different scale designs, as well as different cabinet designs. The smaller verticals are similar to the Samick verticals; the 48" and 52" verticals are like Samick's World Piano series, with a slow-close fallboard, sostenuto pedal, and Renner hammers. The Otto Altenburg grands include a 4'7" Indonesian-made model, 5'2", 5'10", and 6'3" models with individually-hitched stringing, and 7' and 9'2" models. The 5'2" and 5'10" models are optionally available with Kluge keys and Renner actions; the models over 6' have these features as standard.

New in 2000 is the F.E. Altenburg piano, a 6' grand made by the Niendorf piano company of Luckenwalde, Germany (see "Niendorf").

Altenburg actively sells his pianos via the internet for those who are comfortable buying through that medium.

Warranty: Twelve years, parts and labor, transferable, on the smaller Otto Altenburg verticals and the 4'7" grand, and on the F.E. Altenburg grand. Lifetime, parts and labor, on the larger Otto Altenburg verticals and all Otto Altenburg grands except the 4'7" model.

Consumer ratings: See ratings for respective manufacturers.

ASTIN-WEIGHT

Astin-Weight Piano Makers
120 West 3300 South
Salt Lake City, Utah 84115

(801) 487-0641
(801) 487-0468
astinwei@stinger.net
www.astinweightpianos.com

The Astin-Weight piano, manufactured in a small plant in

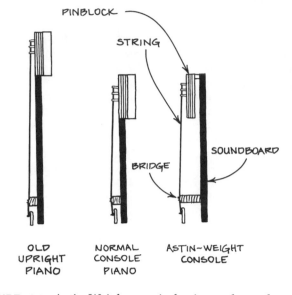

FIGURE 4-1. Astin-Weight vertical pianos have larger soundboards than do other pianos of similar size because the Astin-Weight soundboard is mounted behind the pinblock instead of under it. This arrangement requires the use of a very thick bridge to connect the soundboard with the strings.

Salt Lake City, Utah since 1959, is one of the oddest pianos made in this country. Even the owners of the company, Ray Astin and Don Weight, recognize that their piano is a bit strange, for they call it a "cult" piano, by which they mean that most purchasers of their piano had seen it before and specifically asked for it, whereas those who see it in a store for the first time may be somewhat intimidated by it.

Several things make the Astin-Weight a unique piano. First, both vertical models—a 41" console and a 50" upright—have no wooden back posts. Instead they use a massive full-perimeter cast-iron plate to support the string tension. According to the company, this eliminates the destabilizing effect of wooden posts expanding and contracting with changes in humidity. Note that this is a true full-perimeter plate, not the imitation sometimes used by other companies.

This alone would not be so strange, for some foreign-made pianos are constructed this way. What really sets these pianos apart, however, is the way the soundboard is attached. On most vertical pianos, the soundboard extends only part way up the piano back, because room must be left for the pinblock. On Astin-Weight pianos, the soundboard takes up the entire back of the piano, behind the pinblock; therefore, the vibrating area is much larger, resulting (says the company) in a much larger volume of sound (Figure 4-1). The company claims that its 41" console has a soundboard the same size as that of a conventional 54" piano, and its 50" upright the same as that of a 60" piano. Of course, the quality of sound also depends on the length of the bass and tenor strings and on the overall scale design. Astin-Weight verticals have bass strings that are about as long, or in some cases longer, than other pianos of comparable size, but the console still has a distinctly console-like sound.

For explanation of survey and review procedures, model listings, and price ranges, please see pages 76–81.

Astin-Weights are also unusual in their cabinet designs and finishes. Some of the designs are extremely simple, with cabinets finished in hand-rubbed oil finishes. Dealers report that some customers find this a refreshing alternative to the shiny lacquer and polyester finishes of every other brand. Some Astin-Weight models are available in lacquer finishes, too.

Astin-Weight pianos are made with solid spruce soundboards, Langer keys and actions from England, and Abel hammers from Germany.

Relatively few piano technicians are acquainted with Astin-Weight pianos, but those who are usually speak highly of the instruments. However, the pianos do produce a very rich spectrum of overtones that some technicians find odd-sounding or challenging to tune. Of course, this richness is precisely what many Astin-Weight owners love about their pianos. If, after careful comparison with other brands, you find you prefer the tone, touch, and other features of an Astin-Weight piano, I would definitely recommend buying one.

If you thought the verticals were strange, wait till you see the 5'9" grand, which has been produced in very limited numbers for quite a few years. Instead of having a straight side on the left and a curved side on the right as all other grands do, it's shaped almost symmetrically. This allows the bass bridge to be repositioned so that the bass strings are eighteen inches longer than normal for a piano that size, and increases the soundboard by forty-five percent, so the company says, resulting in the tonal equivalent of a 7'6" piano. Furthermore, the lid is hinged on the right (treble) size, instead of on the left (bass), a feature that Astin-Weight calls "Grand, American Style."

Warranty: Twenty-five years, parts and labor.

Price range: (Verticals) $7,800–12,000. Customers living in areas without an Astin-Weight dealer can buy an Astin-Weight piano direct from the factory at a savings of about forty percent.

Verticals
    41" console (375)
    50" upright (U-500)

Consumer Ratings:

Performance: * * * * 1/2
Confidence: * * * * 1/2
Quality Control: * * * * 1/2
Warranty: * * * *
Information: * * 1/2

AUGUST FÖRSTER

See "Förster, August"

BALDWIN
Including Chickering and Wurlitzer

Baldwin Piano & Organ Co.
4680 Parkway Drive
Mason, Ohio 45040

(513) 754-4500
(800) 876-2976
www.baldwinpiano.com

Owned by: Publicly owned (NASDAQ: BPAO)

Names used: Baldwin, Acrosonic, Hamilton, Classic, Chickering, Wurlitzer, ConcertMaster. No longer used: D.H. Baldwin, Kranich & Bach, Howard, Ellington, Monarch.

The Company: Baldwin Piano & Organ Co. was established in 1862 by Dwight Hamilton Baldwin, a music teacher in the Cincinnati area. Originally Baldwin was a retail enterprise, selling Steinway and Chickering pianos. Baldwin began manufacturing its own line of pianos in 1890 when it lost the Steinway franchise. Within ten years, the instruments attained such a level of excellence that they were awarded the Grand Prize at the 1900 International Exposition in Paris, and four years later they received the same recognition at the International Exposition in St. Louis. Lucien Wulsin, hired by the firm as a bookkeeper in 1866, became a partner in 1873, and purchased a controlling interest in the business after Baldwin died in 1899. Wulsin, and later Wulsin's heirs, pioneered methods of business organization and merchandising, still used today, that made Baldwin into one of the most successful and financially stable piano companies in the United States for many years. Recent times, though, have been more challenging for Baldwin. In 1999 Baldwin sold off its profitable financing divisions, and is concentrating on its core businesses of piano building and contract electronics.

Baldwin briefly became part of a publicly-owned insurance company in the early 1980s, became a private company again upon being sold to its top executives, and then went public in 1985. From 1962 to 1986, Baldwin owned the C. Bechstein company of Berlin, Germany, a major European piano manufacturer. In 1988, Baldwin purchased the piano and electronic keyboard business of The Wurlitzer Co., which had previously acquired the Chickering brand name, and now Baldwin makes or sells pianos under the Wurlitzer and Chickering names as well as under its own name. In 1997, the company introduced its ConcertMaster electronic player piano system, which is reviewed separately beginning on page 164.

Baldwin manufactures and distributes a full line of grand and vertical pianos, digital pianos, and electronic player pianos. The company's main piano assembly plant for both verticals and grands is in Trumann, Arkansas. Grand piano rims are also pressed there, then shipped to the company's factory in Conway, Arkansas for finishing. The Conway plant was outfitted with new polyester finishing equipment in 1998. Baldwin's rough-mill operation, where many of the wood parts are produced, such as keybeds and pinblocks, is in Greenwood, Mississippi. A Baldwin facility in Juarez, Mexico produces keys and actions for Baldwin and a few other keyboard manufacturers. Piano plates are made at a new foundry in Brazil that started production in 1999 with state-of-the-art equipment. Baldwin also operates a contract electronics manufacturing business at a plant in Fayetteville, Arkansas, which also makes some of the components for ConcertMaster. Baldwin is the largest-selling manufacturer of acoustic pianos in the United states, producing around twenty thousand pianos annually. It is headquartered in the Cincinnati area.

Vertical Pianos

The company's vertical piano line includes entry-priced Wurlitzer spinets and consoles and mid- to higher-priced Baldwin consoles, studios, and uprights. All are sold by the same dealer network.

Baldwin verticals: The Baldwin line of vertical pianos includes four sizes: 43½", 45" 48", and 52". The console, 43½" in height, comes in three basic model types. The three differ in cabinetry, but use the same back and action, including Baldwin's 19-ply hard rock maple pinblock, a solid spruce soundboard, and a "Full Blow" (full-size, direct blow) action. (According to my definition, this is actually a small studio due to the full-size action, but Baldwin, like most manufacturers, defines it as a console based on its case size.) The model E100 is the console with a continental-style cabinet. The model 660 series console is a furniture-style model known as the "Classic." The upper-level console, the model 2090 series, is called the "Acrosonic," a name Baldwin has traditionally used for its upper-level consoles and spinets. This model series has fancier cabinet features and hardware than the Classic, but is the same instrument inside. [Baldwin reports that in early 2001 it will introduce replacement models of the E100 series in continental style (E101) and "Classic" style with front legs and toe blocks (E102). They will be classified as studios, measuring approximately 45" in height.]

The Baldwin 45" studio vertical, still known as the "Hamilton," comes in three model types. The model 243HPA is the school studio. Its functional-looking cabinet was redesigned a few years ago to provide easier access for servicing. This model is one of the most popular school pianos ever made and, according to Baldwin, the largest-selling piano in the history of the industry, with sales of almost one-half million. Despite its simpler cabinetry, it may go well in a den, finished basement, or other place where furniture styling isn't a top priority. The model 5050 series studio, known as the "Limited Edition," is the furniture-style studio. It is made in only three styles, each limited to a production run of one thousand instruments, after which the style is changed. The model E250 is the studio in a contemporary cabinet style. All lacquer-finished Hamilton model cabinets use solid lumber-core construction. [Baldwin says it is replacing the model E250 with two new E260 designs in polyester finishes.]

The model 248A, a 48" Professional Upright, introduced in 1997, contains many interesting new technical features aimed primarily at enhancing tuning stability and evenness of tone. Baldwin's largest and most expensive vertical is the 52" model 6000 upright, also known as the Concert Vertical. It sports some unusual features, such as having some plain (instead of all wound) strings in the bass section and a "tone expander," a small brass weight attached to the soundboard to smooth out the break between the treble and bass bridges. The 48" and 52" models finished in satin lacquer also use lumber-core construction.

Among the general public, Baldwin has long been one of the best known and most respected names in music. Among piano technicians I've spoken with, however, Baldwin's rep-

For explanation of survey and review procedures, model listings, and price ranges, please see pages 76–81.

utation, at least with regard to its vertical pianos, has varied considerably over the decades. For most of the mid-twentieth century, at least through the 1960s, Baldwin was the unchallenged leader in vertical piano manufacturing in the United States. Many of us grew up with a high-quality Baldwin Acrosonic in our homes. In the 1970s and '80s, though, quality declined as the company attempted to compete with a flood of low-priced Japanese and Korean imports. During the early 1980s, much of Baldwin's competition turned out pretty poor products, so Baldwin's instruments still remained a good value in comparison. But by the middle to late 1980s, most of the inferior brands had either gone out of business or had improved their offerings. Against this backdrop, Baldwin verticals had less appeal. This perception was reinforced when, in 1986, Baldwin purchased the key and action business of Pratt-Read and began manufacturing these components in their facilities in Juarez, Mexico. Action quality plummeted and, though improved since then, to some extent still remains problematic today.

During the 1990s, reversing direction, Baldwin has been investing millions of dollars in equipment and processes to improve the quality of its products. Technicians say that quality is slowly, but erratically, improving. The technician survey for the last edition, about six years ago, still found numerous problems, especially in woodworking, gluing, and action making, and technicians were not particularly enthusiastic about the product. In the service database inspected for this edition, about one-third of the 562 Baldwin verticals sold, most of which were sold three to five years ago, were provided some kind of post-sale service other than tuning, usually for problems related to sluggish action (sticking keys, tight action centers, etc.); action, damper, and trapwork regulation; and smaller amounts of warped, broken, or unglued action parts. This percentage of pianos receiving post-sale service was comparable to the percentage received, for instance, by one of the Korean companies in the database during the time period covered (three to five years ago).

The current technician survey, conducted in the fall of 1999 and supplemented by interviews in the spring of 2000, found quite a bit of improvement, just in the last couple of years. Many technicians were still not crazy about the pianos, and many of the same problems were present, but to a much smaller extent. Although some pianos were in pretty good shape right from the factory, others depended heavily for their success on good preparation by the dealer. The general feeling seems to be that once you get rid of the annoying little problems, like action parts that make noise by rubbing against one another, misaligned hammers, and the occasional sticking key, they are reasonably good home and school pianos, sound good, and hold up well. "They are real survivors," said one technician.

The following are some specific observations and problems mentioned by technicians in the interviews and written survey:

- Some technicians said that Baldwins, like many other brands, are not tuned enough at the factory and need a few more tunings before the tuning becomes stable. They also may need other kinds of servicing, such as regulating, hammer spacing, and miscellaneous adjustments and repairs. Pianos delivered to the home unserviced are probably more likely to require service calls within a short time to correct problems. As with all pianos, Baldwins should be tuned a number of times during the first year in the home. Technicians say, though, that after the required number of tunings, Baldwin verticals exhibit above-average tuning stability (subject, of course, to local climatic conditions).

- As in previous surveys, a number of technicians reported difficulty in tuning Baldwin verticals due to tuning pins being too tight. The tight tuning pins, long a Baldwin trademark, are viewed as a problem by many technicians, especially those with less experience in tuning Baldwins. Other technicians, however, especially in colder, harsher climates, appreciate the long-term dependability of these tight tuning pins because they don't become loose in dry weather. "They mean more work for the technician, but the consumer inevitably gains," concluded one technician in an interview. Paradoxically, many technicians in the survey for the third edition said they found a number of isolated loose tuning pins in an otherwise sound pinblock. Baldwin seems to have substantially reduced the incidence of this problem, but it still exists occasionally, according to some technicians in the current survey.

- Technicians report that stringing needs some improvement. Strings are sometimes not spaced correctly at the strike point or in the tuning pin area, and the tuning pin coils are sometimes not well made. In addition, many technicians reported very prominent false beats (tonal irregularities that give a tinny or out-of-tune sound) in the treble. The false beats can be partially, but not completely, eliminated by seating the strings at the bridge.

- Baldwin vertical actions sometime begin to squeak at the balance rail and at the hammer butt (hammer return spring) or the damper lever (damper spring) after a year or two. A little lubricating by the technician will keep this under control. Some technicians said that Baldwin actions were a little noisier than those of other brands.

- Quality control in the action department could still use some improvement. Action parts tend to look rough, and a fair number of warped or twisted hammer shanks were reported in the survey. If the piano is serviced in the store, most of these and other woodworking problems will be caught there and corrected, but sometimes they turn up later on in the piano's life. This is not usually a big problem, but the buyer should be prepared for the possibility that the piano may occasionally need small repairs, usually covered under Baldwin's warranty.

- Comments about the new 48" upright (model 248A) have been few in number because the model is relatively new, but those comments I've received have generally been quite positive. Concerning the 52" upright, in my experience technicians seem to be quite divided over whether they like this model and both sides seem to have strong feelings about it.

Wurlitzer verticals: The Wurlitzer vertical piano line is now limited to a 37" spinet with a full-size but indirect blow ac-

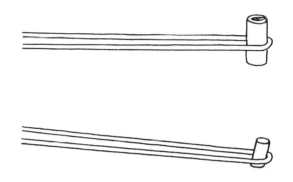

FIGURE 4-2. (Top) The Baldwin Accu-just hitch pins stand vertically, allowing the tail end of each string to be moved up or down to adjust its downbearing pressure on the bridge. (Bottom) Regular hitch pins are at a slant; the strings, under tension, always slide to the bottom and so cannot be adjusted up or down.

tion, and an entry-level 42" console with a compressed, direct blow action, all with a laminated spruce soundboard. Most of these are made in the U.S., but the 42" console from Baldwin's discontinued Kranich & Bach line of Chinese-made pianos (model WP50) is now offered with the Wurlitzer name on it as well. The Korean-made line of Wurlitzer verticals that Baldwin used to sell has been discontinued.

American-made Wurlitzer verticals, being made in the same factories as Baldwin verticals, not surprisingly share similar problems, except that the Wurlitzers are of a little lower quality. In the present survey, action regulation, especially key level, was rougher on new pianos, tone was poorer, especially in the bass, and key weighting was said to be poor. With proper servicing, these pianos could be satisfactory entry-level instruments and attractive pieces of furniture. I have no current reports specifically on Wurlitzer Chinese-made pianos, but based on reports of other companies' Chinese pianos, I would not yet recommend them due to lack of a track record. However, Chinese pianos are improving rapidly.

Grand Pianos

Baldwin sells grand pianos in three different levels of quality: the entry-priced Wurlitzer, the mid-priced Chickering, and the higher-priced Baldwin Artist grands.

Baldwin grands: Baldwin grands, known as the "Artist Series," include the model M1 (5'2"), R1 (5'8"), and L1 (6'3"), formerly called models M, R, and L, best for homes; the model SF-10 (7') for the more serious musician; and the model SD-10 (9') for the concert stage. Model 226E and 227E are versions of the model R1 in French Provincial cherry and Louis XVI styling, respectively.

All Baldwin Artist grands use the patented Accu-just hitch pin system (Figure 4-2), in which the downbearing pressure of each string on the bridge can be individually adjusted. This mainly allows for more efficient and uniform construction of grand bridges, but may also occasionally be useful in servicing the piano. The 7' and 9' models use special treble termination pieces to provide more precise termination of each treble string. The two largest models also use a Renner action rather than the regular Baldwin action. Baldwins use a strong, one-piece rim construction made entirely of maple (just switching over this year from a maple inner rim and poplar outer rim), soundboards are of tapered solid spruce, and pinblocks consist of forty-one highly densified laminations of maple. Baldwin maintains a long roster of well-known concert artists, musicians, and composers who endorse and use its concert grand, such as Dave Brubeck, Marian McPartland, Seiji Ozawa, and Earl Wild. These are non-paid artistic endorsements.

The year 2000 saw the completion of several years of upgrading to the new Artist grand series. All Baldwin Artist grands are now being shipped with Renner hammers and new action specifications to reduce friction and control intertia, resulting in an improved touch. Each piano now comes with an adjustable artist bench, and the sharps are now made of solid ebony wood instead of phenolic resin. During the past few years, Baldwin has invested heavily in new computer-controlled woodworking machinery for greater precision in manufacturing lids and other parts, and in new polyester finishing equipment. All high-gloss finishes for Baldwin Artist grands are now produced in polyester. In 1999, Baldwin began manufacturing plates in a joint-venture, state-of-the-art foundry in Brazil, producing sand-cast plates from high-grade Brazilian iron. The new one-piece maple rim mentioned above, upgraded soundboard specifications, a slow-close fallboard, and cosmetic enhancements are other features found in the upgraded Artist grand piano line.

In interviews with the survey technicians in the spring of 2000, I was struck by the amazing spread of opinion about Baldwin grands, with about half the technicians who were knowledgeable about Baldwins quite bullish about the pianos and the other half quite negative, almost as if the two groups were talking about different brands. A clue to the reason for this difference came from several technicians who remarked that the quality had slipped just recently, in the last year or so. Investigating the situation, I discovered that in 1999, Baldwin downsized a bit and consolidated all its piano assembly in its Trumann, Arkansas plant, moving grand piano assembly there from Conway, Arkansas. In the process, workers had to be retrained and new workers hired. In such a situation, it's reasonable to believe there may have been a temporary drop in quality, though in the long run the consolidation will probably benefit the quality. This situation may have affected vertical piano manufacturing, too, but for some reason the alleged lapse in quality showed up primarily in relation to the grands in this survey. Hopefully, by the time you read this, quality control will be back to normal. In the meantime, I would suggest having Baldwin grands inspected carefully before purchase.

Of course, I don't know for sure that all the problems found were caused by a scenario such as that described above, but their unusual nature suggests that some of them might have been. For example, a couple of pianos were reported to have had keyframes that were too short for the action cavity, meaning that stable positioning of the action in relation to the strings was difficult, if not impossible. In others, hammer tails on the bass hammers were shaped at the wrong angle, and in still others the pianos were regulated with so little key dip as to be completely unplayable. Each of these problems occurred in more than one piano. These, and other odd defects found, are problems of the sort that would not normally be encountered, even in factories with moderate quality control problems, suggesting that inexperienced new workers were to blame.

On the other hand, comments from technicians and reports from the company also suggest that aside from this temporary lapse, quality in Baldwin grands is on the upswing, and can probably be expected to resume that trend in the near future. Said one technician, "I think they're really close to making a great instrument, but the commitment to craftsmanship or the skill level isn't quite there." And another, who has serviced Baldwins for a dealer for twenty-six years: "Generally we've found things far more consistent than they were three to five years ago. We're still running into little problems like sticking flanges, and too much glue on damper guide rails. Some pianos suffer from insufficient or poor factory setup, but it's inconsistent—not all pianos and not always the same problems. For example, two pianos with very close serial numbers had coils crossed on a couple of tuning pins, indicative of one person in the factory not having quite got it down yet." [One technician, interviewed again just before this book went to press, reported a increase in the landed quality of Baldwin grands since the factory consolidation was completed.]

Here are a few other observations about Baldwin Artist grands:

- Baldwins are very sturdy pianos, and after a year or two of settling, hold their tune well. They also hold up well in institutional settings. As in previous surveys, a few technicians in the most recent survey found the Baldwin Artist grands difficult to tune because of the excessively tight, jumpy tuning pins. However, the pinblocks are extremely durable and unlikely to fail during the normal life of the piano. See the discussion about this in the section on Baldwin verticals.

- In the service database, the most common post-sale problems found among the 136 Artist grands sold, most of which were sold three to five years ago, were adjustments needed to dampers, trapwork, and the damper guide rail; the action needing regulating, and sticking keys or flanges. Voicing, and the fit and finish of cabinet parts, especially the fallboard, also figured prominently. The current technician survey turned up approximately the same issues.

- Several technicians in the most recent survey complained of poor tone in the treble. Much of this was due to voicing not having been done properly at the factory, but in a smaller number of cases it may have been due to problems in manufacture or design. Most of the tonal problems in the current survey were in model L grands, and that is the model about which I've received the most complaints in the past. Sometimes the tone in the mid-treble sounds brash or dead, or there are buzzing sounds or other noises from the front duplex area. One model L grand I played this summer had a wonderful feel to the action, but an unacceptable tone in the treble. Not all examples of this model are like this, but I would suggest listening carefully before purchase, as it may not be easy to cure this problem when present.

- As the above discussion suggests, servicing of the piano by the dealer is of paramount importance if it is to reach its potential as a musical instrument. Once serviced, most can be made into very good instruments. "When they're nice, or after problems have been ironed out," concluded one technician in an interview, "they're far more solidly built and would hold up better in the long run than Japanese pianos." But, he added, "There is just way more prep work to do than there should be."

- The seven-foot and nine-foot grands are definitely a notch above the other three models in performance quality, in part because they have Renner actions. Many consider them to be world-class pianos.

Technicians who recall older Baldwins that were difficult to access for servicing should take note that a number of years ago Baldwin made major improvements in this department. Keyslip, key blocks, and fallboard have been redesigned so as to attach to the case with a minimum of screws for easy removal and replacement. Lyre braces are now hand-adjustable; accurate adjustment takes less than a minute.

It's hard to have a conversation about Baldwin grands with a prospective piano buyer for more than a few minutes without the inevitable comparison with Steinway being brought up. For those readers who have always equated Baldwin and Steinway, you might want to know that in my opinion, Baldwin grands, when properly serviced, are good, solid instruments that approach the Steinway in quality, but only the 7' and 9' models could be considered Steinway's equal. The tone of the Baldwin grand is a little more percussive and less sustained than that of the Steinway, but not unpleasant when voiced. Baldwin grands are about one-third less expensive than comparably sized Steinways, however, and are considered by many technicians to be a good value as well as a good product.

Chickering grands: The Chickering line of American-made grands consists of two models, the 4'10" model 410 and the 5'7" model 507. They are adapted from the Classic line of Baldwin grands (no relation to Baldwin's Classic line of verticals) that was discontinued at the end of 1994. Readers may recall that the Classic line received one of the worst reviews ever to grace the pages of *The Piano Book*. Baldwin redesigned and structurally improved these pianos and then reissued them under the Chickering label. In 1998, several period-style furniture models were added to the Chickering line.

Although the Chickering grands contain some features, such as Accu-just hitch pins, solid spruce soundboard, and maple key buttons, used in the Baldwin Artist grands, they are far inferior to their upscale cousins. They are lighter structurally, with only two braces stabilizing the rim, as opposed to three or four on the Artist series, and their rims are made in two pieces of poplar, as opposed to the one-piece maple rim of the Artist grands. Unlike the Artist grands, the soundboards are not tapered and the bridges are not beveled, both of which could restrain somewhat the vibration of the soundboard. They use Baldwin hammers instead of Renner hammers, and the middle pedal operates a bass sustain mechanism instead of a sostenuto.

Although only a few Chickering grands appeared in the most recent survey, every one of them received poor marks for tone quality, with technicians calling the tone "hollow," "woody," "brassy," and "not very pleasant." Other complaints included very prominent false beats in the bass, sloppy bridge notching and pinning, problems with dampers and trapwork, the finish chipping off, and tight or jumpy tuning pins. In fairness, I should say that all the Chickerings in this survey were of the 4'10" model, which might be expected to have a poor bass tone because of its small size. I've played several examples of the 5'7" model, however and, as with the smaller model, found them to have a rather dull treble tone, lacking in resonance.

Some of these Chickering grand models are pretty pieces of furniture, and it's possible that the 5'7" model, after servicing, would be satisfactory as an entry-level grand. Musically speaking, however, and in terms of their design and workmanship, I believe they are a poor value for the money. Said one technician in an interview: "They're inexpensive pianos, but not exactly cheap. I would steer a customer to a Young Chang or a Samick over the Chickerings." Ironically, Baldwin's Wurlitzer line of grands, made by Samick, is priced lower than the Chickerings. [Baldwin reports that it intends to launch a new line of Chickering scales and designs in early 2001.]

Wurlitzer grands: Baldwin's Wurlitzer line of grands consists of 4'7", 5'1", and 5'8" models. These are made in Korea by Samick, with whom Baldwin has had a strategic alliance for nearly thirty years. The 4'7" and 5'1" models are technically similar to pianos sold under the Samick brand name, except for the soundboard, which has been changed from laminated to solid spruce. The 5'8" model is based on the scale design of Baldwin's model R in its Artist series of grands, but otherwise with construction features similar to the Samick, plus a solid spruce soundboard.

In the current survey, there was relatively little information specifically about Wurlitzer grands. The newer ones, all of which had previously been serviced by the dealer before sale, were described as "fair" and not too problematical. See "Samick" for more details. Wurlitzer grands are warranted by Baldwin, not Samick. For some Wurlitzer history and information on earlier Wurlitzer models, see "Wurlitzer."

Warranty: (Labor) Ten years on all Baldwin pianos except the Chinese imports, which have a five-year warranty. Warranty is to original owner only. (Parts) Twenty-five years on Baldwin Artist series grands, and on Baldwin studio and upright pianos; fifteen years on Acrosonic consoles; ten years on Classic and continental-style consoles, Chickering grands, and Wurlitzer grands.

While most warranty problems are dealt with promptly and fairly, a number of technicians complained of difficulty in getting calls returned, or of receiving defective replacement parts. The technical services department has recently been reorganized.

Price range: (Baldwin consoles and studios) $4,200–6,800; (Baldwin uprights) $7,400–9,600; (Wurlitzer spinets and consoles) $2,700–3,800; (Baldwin Artist grands) $23,900–43,400; (Chickering grands) $13,200–16,000; (Wurlitzer grands) $9,700–12,300.

Verticals—Baldwin	Grands—Baldwin (Artist)
43½" Classic console (600/E100)	5'2" (M1)
43½" Acrosonic console (2090)	5'8" (R1/226E/227E)
45" Hamilton studio (243HPA/5050A/E250)	6'3" (L1)
48" Professional Upright (248A)	7' (SF-10)
52" Concert Vertical (6000)	9' (SD-10)
Verticals—Wurlitzer	Grands—Chickering
37" Spinet (1175)	4'10" (410)
42" Console (2270)	5'7" (507)
42" Console (Chinese) (WP50)	Grands—Wurlitzer
	4'7" (C143)
	5'1" (C153)
	5'8" (C173)

Consumer Ratings:

Baldwin Verticals

Performance
  Model 248A: * * * *
  All other models: * * * ½
Confidence: * * * *
Quality Control: * * *
Warranty: * * * ½
Information
  Model 248A: * * ½
  All other models: * * * * ½

Wurlitzer Verticals

Performance
  American: * * ½
  Chinese: * *
Confidence
  American: * * * ½
  Chinese: * ½
Quality Control
  American: * * ½
  Chinese: * ½
Warranty
  American: * * * ½
  Chinese: * * *
Information
  American: * * *
  Chinese: *

Baldwin Artist Grands

Performance
  M1, R1, L1: * * * * ½
  SF-10: * * * * *
Confidence: * * * * *
Quality Control
  M1, R1, L1: * * *
  SF-10: * * * ½
Warranty: * * * ½

Information
  M1, R1, L1: * * * * ½
  SF-10: * * * ½

Chickering Grands

Performance: * * ½
Confidence: * * *
Quality Control: * * ½
Warranty: * * * ½
Information: * * ½

Wurlitzer Grands

Performance: * * *
Confidence: * * *
Quality Control: * * *
Warranty: * * * ½
Information: * * *

BECHSTEIN, C.

Including W. Hoffmann

Premier Piano Co., Inc.
P.O. Box 430
Dundee, Illinois 60118

(800) 531-0133

Pianos made by: C. Bechstein Pianoforte Fabrik GmbH, Berlin, Germany

Owned by: Karl Schulze

Names used: C. Bechstein, W. Hoffmann, Zimmermann

Bechstein was founded in 1853 by Carl Bechstein, a young German piano maker who, in the exploding world of piano technology of his day, had visions of building an instrument that the tradition-bound piano-making shops of Berlin were not interested in. Through fine workmanship and the endorsement of famous pianists, Bechstein soon became one of the leading piano makers in Europe, producing over five thousand pianos annually by 1900. The two world wars and the Depression virtually destroyed the company, but it rebuilt successfully, and in 1963 it was acquired by Baldwin. This sale supplied Bechstein with a source of capital and supplied Baldwin with a source of piano service internationally for concert artists who play Baldwin pianos. However, Bechstein kept operating as an autonomous unit, continuing its tradition of impeccable craftsmanship.

In 1986, Baldwin sold Bechstein to Karl Schulze, a leading West German piano retailer and master piano technician who, with a team of experts, undertook a complete technical and financial reorganization of the company. The three factories in Berlin, Karlsruhe, and Eschelbronn were closed and combined into one new state-of-the-art factory in Berlin, opened in 1989. The entire product line, scale designs, and manufacturing techniques were re-evaluated with an eye to restoring the original scales and techniques of the founder, serving the market, and combining efficient factory methods with traditional craftsmanship.

In the early 1990s, Bechstein acquired the names and factories of W. Hoffmann and Zimmermann, incorporating them into the Bechstein Gruppe-Berlin. The Euterpe factory, which made W. Hoffmann, was closed, and Zimmermann

For explanation of survey and review procedures, model listings, and price ranges, please see pages 76–81.

and W. Hoffmann are now being manufactured at the former Zimmermann factory in Seifhennersdorf, (East) Germany. Most basic manufacturing of Bechstein, W. Hoffmann, and Zimmermann pianos takes place at the Seifhennersdorf plant; final finishing work on the grands is done in Berlin. Zimmermann pianos are not currently being sold in the U.S. See "Zimmermann" for more information.

Bechstein makes verticals in 47", 49", 50", and 52" sizes, and grands in 5'2", 5'11", 6'2", 6'10", 7'6", and 9'2" sizes. In addition, a slightly lower-priced "Academy Series" comes in 6'2" and 6'10" sizes. All Bechstein pianos have Renner actions, solid European spruce soundboards, beech rims (grands), and Delignit pinblocks. The agraffes in Bechstein pianos incorporate a rounded bearing surface with a traditional agraffe in an effort to overcome some of the limitations of the traditional kind. Three pedals are standard on all pianos, the grands with sostenuto and the verticals with a practice pedal (sostenuto optional). All piano models are available in a variety of custom finishes. The lower-priced Academy Series differs from the regular series in only two ways—the pianos are available only in a satin ebony finish and the plate finish is less expensive.

Although the W. Hoffmann verticals are made by Bechstein, basic manufacturing of the grands is done by another European company to Bechstein's specifications. After completion, the pianos are sent to Bechstein for additional work, including regulating, voicing, and other final preparation.

I must say that the Bechstein verticals I've played have consistently been the most beautiful sounding vertical pianos I've ever encountered. The tone of Bechstein grands is what one might call "classically European." It is very clean and thin in the treble and emphasizes the fundamental rather than harmonics in the bass. Those of us who grew up on the sound of American pianos may find the Bechstein sound somewhat alien, though interesting. I personally find it to be quite lovely at low volumes, the clearly articulated attack giving it a delicate character, but sometimes find it too bright for my taste at higher volumes. I also prefer a more pronounced singing quality and a heavier action than the Bechstein provides. These are, of course, a matter of personal preference; many pianists revere the Bechstein, and it is considered to be one of the world's pre-eminent pianos.

Warranty: Five years, parts and labor, to original purchaser.

Price range: (Bechstein verticals) $18,000–33,500; (Bechstein grands, regular series) $53,500–89,600; (Bechstein grands, Academy series) $45,300–64,800; (W. Hoffmann verticals) $14,000–15,100; (W. Hoffmann grands) $24,700–30,800

Verticals—Bechstein	Grands—Bechstein
47" (118)	5'2" (K-158)
49" (124)	5'11" (M-180)
50" (11)	6'2" (A-189)
52" (8)	6'10" (B-208)
	7'6" (C-232)
	9'2" (D-280)

Verticals—W. Hoffmann	Grands—W. Hoffmann
47" (H-120)	5'2" (H-158)
49" (H-124)	5'7" (H-170)
50" (H-125)	6'3" (H-190)

Consumer Ratings:

Performance
  Bechstein: * * * * *
  W. Hoffmann: * * * * 1/2
Confidence: * * * * *
Quality Control: * * * * *
Warranty: * * * 1/2
Information
  Bechstein Grands: * * 1/2
  Bechstein Verticals: * *
  W. Hoffmann: * 1/2

BECKER, J.

The Piano Group
P.O. Box 14128
Bradenton, Florida 34280

(800) 336-9164

Pianos made by: J. Becker Piano Co., St. Petersburg, Russia; Belarus Piano Co., Belarus

J. Becker Piano Co. was established in 1841, was state-owned during the Communist era, and has since been privatized. The 46" model sold under this name is actually from the Belarus Piano Co. (see "Schubert"); the others are from J. Becker. The grands currently have a Czech (Detoa) action.

Pianos from this part of the world have had a rough history. I would use caution, especially with the grands.

Warranty: Twelve years, parts and labor, to original purchaser.

Price range: (verticals) $2,000-2,500; (grand) $7,900

Verticals	Grand
46" studio (B-120)	5'2" (GP-155M)
47" studio (E-120/J-120/A-120C)	

Consumer Ratings (Russian models):

Performance: * *
Confidence: * 1/2
Quality Control: * 1/2
Warranty: * *
Information: *

BELARUS

Pianos from the Belarus Piano Co. are sold in the U.S. under the names "Schubert" and "Sängler & Söhne" or "Wieler." See under those names.

BENTLEY

See "Whelpdale Maxwell & Codd"

BERGMANN

See "Young Chang"

BETTING, TH.

This name is no longer being used. Identical pianos are being made under the name "Schirmer & Son." See under that name.

BLONDEL, G.

A-440 Pianos
4100 Steve Reynolds Blvd., Suite F
Norcross, Georgia 30093

(770) 717-8047
(888) 565-5648
keys4mom@ix.netcom.com
www.A-440pianos.com

Georges Blondel was a French piano technician who worked for many years for the former Belgian piano manufacturer A. Hanlet. Now located in Paris, Pianos Hanlet S.A. is the largest piano dealer and distributor in France. After Blondel's death, Hanlet commemorated his years of service by using his name on a line of pianos distributed throughout Europe. The pianos are manufactured for Hanlet by the Bohemia Piano Co., makers of Rieger-Kloss pianos, in the Czech Republic, and are similar to the Rieger-Kloss models of similar size. All models have Renner actions, Delignit pinblocks, and agraffes throughout the scale.

Price range: (Verticals) $6,700–7,700; (Grands) $23,700

Verticals	Grands
43" console (Bolero)	6'1" (Tocata)
47" studio (Sarabande)	

Consumer Ratings: Insufficient information to rate

BLÜTHNER

Including Haessler
German Piano Imports LLC
5660 W. Grand River
Lansing, Michigan 48906

(517) 886-6000
(800) 954-3200
info@bluthnerpiano.com
www.bluthnerpiano.com

Pianos made by: Julius Blüthner Pianofortefabrik GmbH, Leipzig, Germany

Names used: Blüthner, Haessler

This firm has been making highest quality pianos in Leipzig, (East) Germany since 1853 and, though nationalized in 1972, has remained under the management of the Blüthner family to this day. Until 1900, Blüthner was Europe's largest piano factory. During World War II, the factory was bombed, but after the war the East German government allowed the Blüthner family and workers to rebuild it because the Blüthner piano was considered a national treasure (and because the Soviet Union needed quality pianos). With the liberation of Eastern Europe, Blüthner is again privately owned.

Blüthner pianos have beech rims (grands), solid spruce

For explanation of survey and review procedures, model listings, and price ranges, please see pages 76–81.

soundboards, Delignit pinblocks, Renner actions, and polyester finishes. Pianos for export have three pedals, including sostenuto on the grands and celeste (practice) on the verticals. Blüthner builds about 150 verticals a year in three sizes and 450 grands in six sizes.

A unique technical feature for which Blüthner pianos are famous is known as "aliquot stringing." In this scheme, each of the notes in the highest treble section (about the top two octaves) has four strings instead of three, the extra string being raised slightly above the others and not struck by the hammer. The effect is similar to that of a duplex scale—sympathetically vibrating strings adding tone color and brilliance to the treble—except that the fourth string is tuned in unison with the other strings, not to a higher harmonic. In the past, aliquot stringing was accomplished with a complicated system of agraffes and special bridge construction. A number of years ago the system was simplified, the aliquot strings terminating on the bridge and in special notches in the capo bar. The company says that the effect of aliquot stringing can be heard mainly on hard blows, not at softer levels of playing.

Blüthners also incorporate a few other uncommon construction features. The soundboard is crowned with the highest portion directly under the treble bridge, rather than being crowned spherically as is usual. This is thought to provide the most support where the downbearing force is greatest, aiding tonal transmission and reducing distortion of the crown. Looking down through the strings at the action, an observer may notice that the hammers look odd, though the reason may not be immediately apparent. It turns out that the angled hammers are actually cut at an angle and mounted straight on the shanks, instead of being cut straight and mounted at an angle. The company says that the effect is to more evenly distribute the force of the blow across both the strings and the hammer. Visually, the effect is an even, rather than a staggered, hammer line.

Blüthner pianos have a very full sound that is warm, romantic, and lyrical, generally deeper and darker than some of its West German counterparts. The sustain is good, but at a low level of volume, giving the tone a refined, delicate character. The action is a little light, but responsive. The pianos are built of superb materials. Their pricing—thirty percent less than the cost of new Bösendorfers or Faziolis of similar size—makes the Blüthners an attractive choice for pianists in the market for a fine, hand-fit instrument.

A few years ago, a new "Haessler" line of pianos was added to the Blüthner product line. (Haessler is a Blüthner family name.) Created to compete better in the American market, Haessler pianos have more conventional technical and cosmetic features than the regular models and cost about twenty-five percent less. For example, the grands are loop-strung instead of single-strung; omit the "aliquot" strings (fourth string per note); and have normal, straightcut angle-mounted hammers. Case and plate cosmetics are simpler. The Haessler line now contains several vertical models and 5'8" and 6'1" grands.

Warranty: Ten years, parts and labor, to original purchaser.

Price range: (Blüthner verticals) $17,000–25,000; (Blüthner grands) $44,000–70,000; (Haessler verticals) $12,000–20,000; (Haessler grands) $36,900–41,500

Blüthner—Verticals	Blüthner—Grands
45" studio (I)	5'1" (11)
46" studio (C)	5'5" (10)
49" upright (A)	6'3" (6)
52" upright (B)	6'10" (4)
	7'8" (2)
	9'2" (1)

Haessler—Verticals	Haessler—Grands
45" studio (115K)	5'8" (175)
46" studio (118K/118KM/118CH)	6'1" (186)
49" upright (124K/124KM)	
52" upright (132)	

Consumer Ratings:
Performance
    Blüthner: * * * * *
    Haessler: * * * * 1/2
Confidence: * * * * *
Quality Control: * * * * *
Warranty: * * * *
Information
    Blüthner Grands: * * 1/2
    Blüthner Verticals: * *
    Haessler Grands: * *
    Haessler Verticals: * 1/2

BOHEMIA

See under "Rieger-Kloss"

BÖSENDORFER

Bösendorfer Pianos
8331 W. State Rd. #56
West Baden Springs, Indiana 47469

(888) 936-2516
(812) 936-4522
rweisen@kimball.com
www.bosendorfer.com

Pianos made by: L. Bösendorfer Klavierfabrik AG, Vienna, Austria

Owned by: Kimball International

Bösendorfer was founded in 1828 in Vienna, Austria by Ignaz Bösendorfer. The young piano maker rose to fame when Franz Liszt endorsed his concert grand after being unable to destroy it in playing as he did every other piano set before him. Ignaz died in 1858 and the company was taken over by his son Ludwig. Under Ludwig's direction, the firm greatly prospered and the pianos became even more famous throughout Europe and the world. Ludwig, having no direct descendents, sold the firm to his friend Carl Hutterstrasser in 1909. Carl's sons Wolfgang and Alexander became partners in 1931.

Until the Depression, Bösendorfer made about two to four hundred pianos a year, after the Depression only about a hundred a year, except during the final years of World War II, when production ceased during and after the bombing of Vienna. Bösendorfer was sold to Kimball, a U.S. manufacturer of low- and medium-priced pianos, in 1966. Since then, production has been gradually increased to about 300 to 500 pianos annually, made by about 200 employees.

Bösendorfer makes one vertical piano—a 52" upright—and six models of grand piano, from 5'8" to the 9'6" Imperial Concert Grand, one of the world's largest pianos. In addition, Bösendorfer has added a line of slightly lower-priced grands known as the Conservatory Series (CS). Available in the 5'8", 6'7", and 7' sizes, Conservatory Series grands are just like the regular models except that the case and plate have a satin finish instead of high-polish, and the pianos are loop-strung instead of individually hitched (single-strung). All Bösendorfer pianos have three pedals, the middle pedal being a sostenuto.

One of the most distinctive features of the grands is that the largest four models have more than eighty-eight notes. The 7', 7'4", and 9' grands each have four extra notes in the bass, and the 9'6" grand has nine extra notes. The lowest strings vibrate so slowly that it's actually possible to hear the individual "ticks" of the vibration, and it's next to impossible to tune these strings accurately. They are also, of course, almost never used, except when playing some new music written expressly for them, but their presence, and the presence of the extra long bridge and larger soundboard to accommodate them, adds extra power, resonance, and clarity to the lowest regular notes of the piano. In order not to confuse pianists, who rely on the normal keyboard configuration for spatial orientation while playing, the keys for these extra notes are usually covered with a black ivorine material.

The rim of the Bösendorfer grand is built quite differently from that of all other grands. Instead of being made of veneers bent around a form as one continuous rim, the rim is made in solid sections and jointed together. It is also made of spruce instead of the maple, beech, or other hardwoods usually used. Spruce transmits sound well, making the Bösendorfer case an extension of the soundboard, but is sometimes said not to be as good at reflecting sound back to the soundboard as those other woods. These factors, as well as the scale design, are probably responsible for a sweeter, less powerful treble and a bass that features the fundamental tone more than the higher harmonics. It is an interesting and beautiful sound, but some think it may be better suited to Mozart than Rachmaninoff. To some extent, the largest grands make up for this difference simply by virtue of their size. In the current survey, one technician called the tone of the Bösendorfer "clean and sweet-sounding," but noted that it was not a particularly powerful piano. Another noted that the factory voicing has been mellower the last few years.

There are a few other Bösendorfer features that are either unique to it or are shared with only a few other brands. One is the removable capo d'astro bar in the treble. This facilitates rebuilding of the instrument and, Bösendorfer says, provides greater acoustic separation from the plate, thus less tonal absorption. Another is single-stringing, in which each string has its own individual hitch pin on the plate instead of being connected to a neighboring string. This may slightly improve tuning stability, and is an advantage in case of string breakage.

When Kimball was still in the piano business, it made extensive use of its ownership of Bösendorfer, both to promote Kimball pianos and to improve Kimball quality. Given this fact, potential buyers sometimes question whether Bösendorfers are still as good as their reputation and price suggest. Apparently they are. Although Bösendorfer pianos showed up infrequently in the present survey, the opinions of the technicians interviewed were unanimously favorable. They consider the Bösendorfer grand to be one of the finest pianos in the world. Perhaps the world's most expensive piano inch for inch, the Bösendorfer grands make an eloquent case for their prices, arriving from the factory needing little work but tuning and very minor regulation and voicing. As one technician said, "They come in from the factory astoundingly good. Literally, it's been difficult to find much else to do than tune them."

Distinctive in both appearance and sound, Bösendorfers are a joy for pianists to play and technicians to service.

Warranty: Ten years, parts and labor, to original purchaser.

Price range: (Vertical) $38,000; (Grands, regular series) $72,000–104,000; (Grands, Conservatory Series) $52,000–62,000

Vertical	Grands
52" upright (130CL)	5'8" (170/170CS)
	6'7" (200/200CS)
	7' (214/214CS)
	7'4" (225)
	9' (275)
	9'6" (290)

Consumer Ratings:

Performance: * * * * *
Confidence: * * * * *
Quality Control: * * * * *
Warranty: * * * *
Information
  Grands: * * *
  Verticals: * *

BOSTON

Boston Piano Co.
37-11 19th Ave.
Long Island City, New York 11105

(718) 721-7711
(800) 842-5397
bostoninfo@steinway.com
www.steinway.com

Owned by: Steinway Musical Instruments, Inc. (parent corporation of Steinway & Sons)

Pianos made by: Kawai Musical Instrument Mfg Co., Ltd., Hamamatsu, Japan and Lincolnton, North Carolina

In 1992, Steinway launched its Boston line of pianos, designed by Steinway & Sons and built by Kawai. Steinway's stated purpose in creating this line was to supply Steinway dealers with a quality, mid-priced piano for those customers "who were not yet ready for a Steinway." Sold only through select Steinway dealers, Boston pianos are currently available in five vertical and five grand models. As a general rule, satin-finished studio models are made in Kawai's factory in Lincolnton, North Carolina; high-polished studio models and all upright models are made in Japan.

In choosing to have the Boston piano line made in Japan, Steinway sought to take advantage of the efficient high-technology manufacturing methods of the Japanese. But by utilizing special design features of its own creation, Steinway may have managed to elicit from Japanese pianos more musicality than is normally found in them.

The most obvious grand piano design feature, visually, is the wide tail. Steinway says this allows the bridges to be positioned closer to the more lively central part of the soundboard, smoothing out the break between bass and treble. This, plus a thinner tapered soundboard and other scaling differences, may give the Boston grands a longer sustain, though less initial power. The verticals are said to have a greater overstringing angle for the same purpose.

Quite a few features in the Boston piano are similar to those in the Steinway. Like the Steinway, Boston pianos use vertically laminated bridges for best tonal transmission and duplex scaling for additional tonal color. Also, similar to the Steinway, hammer flanges are rosette-shaped to match the action rails, which Steinway says helps to preserve hammer spacing (see Figure 4-5 on page 145). The Boston grand action design is said to incorporate some of the latest refinements to the Steinway action. The grands have radial bracing, which Steinway says adds strength to the rim and contributes to the longevity of the soundboard crown. Cabinet detailing on the grands is similar to that on the Steinway. The Boston hammers are made differently from both Kawai and Steinway hammers, and voicers in the Kawai factory receive special instructions on voicing them. All Boston grand models come with a sostenuto pedal; the verticals have a practice pedal.

Boston grands also have certain things in common with Kawai RX series grands: the composition of their rims, pinblocks, and bridges; tuning pins, hardware, and grand leg and lyre assemblies; and the quality control apparent in their manufacture. Both have duplex scaling, radial bracing of their rims, and a sostenuto pedal. The same workers build the two brands in the same factory. One important way they differ is that Kawai uses ABS plastic for most of its action parts, whereas Boston uses only traditional wooden parts. (The differences between Boston and Kawai grands were originally greater than they are today. When Kawai created its RX series, it incorporated certain design elements that happened to be identical to those of the Boston piano, such as radial bracing and vertically laminated bridges with maple cap.)

Steinway officials say that the Boston piano represents an entirely new concept in piano design and should be considered on its own merits, rather than in comparison to the Kawai. Kawai is simply the current designated original equipment manufacturer for the Boston. Steinway could have selected another manufacturer and could do so in the

For explanation of survey and review procedures, model listings, and price ranges, please see pages 76–81.

future. The reality of the marketplace, however, is that consumers, knowing that the Boston is made by Kawai, will naturally compare the two brands, especially since the Boston is usually more expensive at the retail level. (They're generally much closer in price at the wholesale level, but Steinway/Boston dealers are usually able to command a higher profit margin than Kawai dealers at the retail level.) Kawai dealers, understandably, tend to play down the differences between the two brands, while Boston dealers play them up. Most of the important differences between the two brands are evident in their looks, tone, and touch, so interested shoppers can compare them and reach their own conclusions.

The survey for this edition included 52 Boston grands and 16 verticals. In comparing the survey results for the two brands, there was only one striking difference. The Boston grands, when new, needed more action regulating and hammer spacing than the Kawai RX grands, particularly in dry areas of the country. One technician who frequently services both brands, lives in a dry area, and pays attention to the way different brands react to his climate, said that in his opinion the difference is due to the material used for the action parts—ABS plastic for Kawai and wood for Boston. He feels that the plastic is more stable and recommends taking care to tighten action screws on new Boston pianos, both grand and vertical (which is good advice for any brand). The amount of regulating needed, however, is said to be within the normal expected range for a new piano and remains stable once performed. Few other differences stood out as being significant, and the technicians generally liked the Boston grands very much.

When asked about their preference in tone, relatively few technicians were familiar enough with both brands to make a judgment, but among those who were, they were about equally split. The tone of the Boston was sometimes said to be "warmer." Others preferred the Kawai for a variety of different reasons. In the survey for the previous edition of this book, some technicians described the Boston tone as having a little less attack sound and a bit more color than other Asian pianos, resulting in greater warmth to the tone.

As for the verticals in the survey, most were of the school studio model UP-118S, which is very similar to the Kawai model UST-8C. The problems noted were relatively minor and similar to those noted for the Kawais: insufficient tuning at the factory, some doubts about the long-term durability of the institutional cabinets, and a few comments about the trapwork design and about the tone in the upper treble (see "Kawai" for more information). As with the Kawais, the survey suggests that the verticals are relatively trouble-free.

Boston guarantees full trade-in value for a Boston piano at any time a purchaser wishes to upgrade to a Steinway grand.

Warranty: Ten years, parts and labor, to original purchaser.

Price range: (Verticals) $6,400–11,000; (Grands) $15,000–33,400

Verticals	Grands
45" continental-style studio (UP-118C)	5'1" (GP-156)
46" traditional-style studio (UP-118E)	5'4" (GP-163)
46" school studio (UP-118S)	5'10" (GP-178)
49" upright (UP-125E)	6'4" (GP-193)
49½" upright (UP-126)	7'2" (GP-218)
52" upright (UP-132E)	

Consumer Ratings:

Performance: * * * *
Confidence: * * * *
Quality Control
    Japanese-made: * * * * ½
    American-made: * * * *
Warranty: * * * ½
Information
    Grands: * * * ½
    Verticals: * * *

BRENTWOOD

See "Westbrook"

BROADWOOD, JOHN, & SONS

See "Whelpdale Maxwell & Codd"

CHARLES R. WALTER

See "Walter, Charles R."

CHICKERING

See "Baldwin," "Wurlitzer," and "Aeolian"

CLASSIC

See "Story & Clark"

CLINE

Cline Piano Co.
810 George Street
Santa Clara, California 95054
cline@coltonpiano.com
www.coltonpiano.com

Pianos made by: Young Chang Co., Ltd., Inchon, South Korea

Chester L. Cline began selling pianos in Tacoma, Washington in the 1880s, eventually expanding his chain of stores throughout the Northwest and then into California in the 1920s. Cline was a major Wurlitzer dealer during that company's heyday, and one of the largest piano dealers in the West.

During the 1980s, pianos bearing the Cline name were made by Kimball and Daewoo. Since 1992, Cline pianos have been manufactured by Young Chang. Most Cline models are identical to the "Gold series" Young Chang models of the same size, except possibly for some cabinetry differences. Clines are distributed through retail dealers, discount clubs, and special promotions, primarily in northern California, and occasionally elsewhere. See "Young Chang" for more information.

Warranty: Fifteen-year full (transferable) warranty; lifetime limited warranty to original purchaser on case, action parts, and iron frame. Warranty is underwritten by Young Chang America, but warranty service must be authorized by Cline Piano Co.

CONN

See "Krakauer"

CONOVER-CABLE

See "Samick"

CURRIER

Currier Piano Co.
Marion, North Carolina

No longer in business

Currier was founded in 1958 under the name of Westbrook Piano Co. Westbrook sold the company in 1970 and the name was changed to Currier. In April 1970 the Currier factory was struck by lightning and burned down (on Friday the 13th), but production continued in a nearby facility. In 1972 Currier was purchased by the Kaman Corporation, whose music division also makes Ovation guitars and other music products. In 1982, citing a depressed domestic piano market, Kaman closed Currier.

Currier's chief claim to fame occurred in 1981, when it introduced the "Strataphonic String Panel," a laminated panel of steel and medium-density fiberboard that replaced the traditional cast-iron plate in Currier pianos. The idea, though interesting, apparently didn't go over well enough to prevent Currier's continued decline.

Currier made spinets, consoles, and a studio piano. The spinets and consoles were very inconsistent in quality, but generally a little to one side or the other of satisfactory. The studio with the new Strataphonic String Panel was said to have "possibilities," though the tone was a bit loud and metallic.

DIAPASON

See "Kawai"

DIETMANN

Dietmann Pianos Ltd.
5840 Alpha Road
Dallas, Texas 75240

(972) 233-1967

Pianos made by: Dietmann Klavier, Hamburg, Germany (but assembled in South Africa)

Names used: Dietmann, Otto Bach, Bernhard Steiner

For explanation of survey and review procedures, model listings, and price ranges, please see pages 76–81.

The Dietmann piano company dates from 1903, but was purchased in 1985 by the Kahn family, owners of Bernhard Steiner pianos, which had been closely associated with Dietmann for many years. These two companies have, over the years, played an important "behind the scenes" role in the world piano industry, says Kahn, making pianos for a number of established manufacturers, mostly for sale outside the United States.

The pianos for sale in the U.S. bearing the above names use Ibach scales, the company says, and are manufactured in South Africa by a German subsidiary. They are sold around the world under various brand names. They are available in 42½", 46½", 48", and 50" sizes, use solid spruce soundboards, and are available with either Renner or Langer actions. No information is currently available about their quality. The names Dietmann, Otto Bach, and Bernhard Steiner are applied according to dealer request; they are the same piano.

Note that the Bernhard Steiner name is also used on a line of pianos made by Samick. See "Steiner, Bernhard" and "Samick."

Warranty: Twelve-year full warranty.

Consumer Ratings: Insufficient information to rate

DISKLAVIER

See "Electronic Player Piano Systems and Hybrid Acoustic/ Digital Pianos," page 160.

ESSEX

Boston Piano Co.
37-11 19th Ave.
Long Island City, New York 11105

(718) 721-7711
(800) 842-5397
bostoninfo@steinway.com
www.steinway.com

Owned by: Steinway Musical Instruments, Inc. (parent corporation of Steinway & Sons)

Pianos made by: Young Chang Co., Ltd., Inchon, South Korea

Essex is the name designated by Steinway to be used on pianos of its design to be produced by Young Chang. Steinway emphasizes that these are completely new piano designs, not copies of Young Chang pianos, and the only similarity between the two brands may be in some cabinet parts, such as legs and lyre, where using the Young Chang parts makes sense from a manufacturing perspective. Two vertical models and two grand models are scheduled to be introduced in early 2001. At press time, no further information was available about these models. As with Boston pianos, Essex dealers offer their customers a full trade-in value toward the purchase of a Steinway grand at any time.

Warranty: Ten years, parts and labor, to original purchaser.

Consumer Ratings: Insufficient information to rate

ESTONIA

Estonia Piano Factory U.S.
48 Avalon Gardens Drive
Nanuet, New York 10954

(888) 4ESTONIA (437-8664)
epfactory@aol.com
www.estoniapiano.com

Pianos made by: Estonia Piano Factory, Tallinn, Estonia

Estonia is a small republic in northern Europe on the Baltic sea, near Scandinavia. For centuries it was under Danish, Swedish, and Russian domination, finally gaining its independence in 1918, only to lose it again to the Soviet Union in 1940. It became free again in 1991 with the collapse of the Soviet Union.

Piano making in Estonia goes back over two hundred years, and from 1850 to 1940 there were nearly twenty piano manufacturers operating in the country. The most famous among them was Ernst Hiis, who studied piano making in the Steinway Hamburg and Blüthner factories and then established his own company in 1893. In 1950 the Communist-dominated Estonian government consolidated many smaller Estonian piano makers into the Hiis factory under the name Tallinn Piano Factory (Tallinn is the capital of Estonia). In 1994 the company was privatized and now operates under the Estonia name. Ownership remains with the factory employees, with the majority share owned by an Estonian who is a Juilliard-trained pianist and recording artist with a doctorate in music, who represents the company in the United States. The factory makes only grand pianos—over three hundred per year—made by more than one hundred employees.

Estonia pianos have rims of birch, sand-cast plates, Renner actions, Delignit pinblocks, Siberian solid spruce soundboards, and Abel hammers. They come in 5'6", 6'3", and 9' sizes. All have three pedals, including sostenuto.

Estonia pianos have been famous in Europe and used on the concert stage there for decades. They were first imported into the U.S. in 1994 by a Duluth importer of ski equipment who is active in the Estonian-American community. The first pianos, reviewed for the third edition of this book, appeared to be reasonable instruments, but lacked the finesse of western European pianos. At that time, I compared them to pianos from Korea. In the intervening years, Estonia pianos have become much more finished in their presentation and the company has made improvements to action geometry, pedal mechanisms, and scaling, among other things.

The present survey turned up only three Estonia grands. All three were considered very nice, well-built pianos, though one was said to have tuning pins which were only marginally tight for a new piano, a condition I have also heard in relation to other Estonias a couple of times. The survey sample for this brand was too small to know if this is much of a problem; most of the technicians said they had never experienced it. [The Estonia factory says it has recently changed the tuning pin torque specifications to tighten the tuning pins.]

Estonia pianos are often compared to Petrof pianos from the Czech Republic (see "Petrof"). Both companies' instruments have wonderful scale designs and have enjoyed success in Europe for years. Both are companies whose quality control suffered during the Communist era, now rapidly improving as they learn to compete in the world market. Both basically come from the factory in good condition, needing complete, but normal, regulating and voicing, as well as minor troubleshooting to correct small, quirky problems typical of mid-priced, "hand-made" pianos. And both are priced very low in comparison to the musical value they offer. One way the two brands differ, according to some technicians, is that Estonia pianos tend to have a very sweet, but less powerful sound, whereas Petrofs project more powerfully. Some technicians prefer Estonia, some prefer Petrof, but neither by a wide margin. In its short time in this country, Estonia has been very successful in garnering positive reviews and endorsements from customers and concert artists.

Estonia pianos are clearly well constructed, very musical, and a very good value. My exposure to them in the survey and elsewhere has been relatively small, but I would recommend them with only the caution that the tuning pins be checked by a technician for proper torque (tightness) before purchase and that appropriate measures be taken to keep an adequate and stable humidity level where the piano is located.

Warranty: Ten years, parts and labor, to original purchaser.

Price range: (Grands) $19,800–24,900

Grands
    5'6" (168)
    6'3" (190)
    9' (273)

Consumer Ratings:

Performance: * * * * 1/2
Confidence: * * * *
Quality Control: * * * 1/2
Warranty: * * * *
Information: * * 1/2

ETERNA

See "Yamaha"

EVERETT

Wrightwood Enterprises, Inc.
717 St. Joseph Drive
St. Joseph, Michigan 49085

(646) 383-1918
www.everettpiano.com

Pianos made by: Dongbei Piano Co., Dongbei, China; Artfield Piano Ltd., Qing Pu, China; Macao Piano Co., Macao; formerly made by Yamaha in South Haven, Michigan.

The Everett Piano Co. originated in Boston in 1883 and moved to South Haven, Michigan in 1926. It was acquired by Yamaha in 1973. Until mid-1986, Yamaha made a line of Everett vertical pianos in this factory alongside its U.S.-made Yamaha pianos. The Everett line consisted of a 41" console in several levels of quality and cabinetry, a 45" studio that was for years very popular in institutions, and very briefly a 48" upright similar to the Yamaha U1. There was also for a short time a 6' Everett grand, made in Japan, that was basically a copy of a Yamaha G3 (a forerunner of the C3). The Everett verticals, like the U.S.-made Yamaha verticals of the time, were considered reasonably good, but by no means outstanding. In the first edition of this book (1987), I list a variety of silly, nuisance problems found in these pianos that could easily have been solved if anybody had cared enough to spend a little time on it.

When Yamaha moved its U.S. piano manufacturing to Thomaston, Georgia, Everett did not go with it. Pianos bearing the name Everett thereafter were built by Baldwin using Yamaha scale designs, plates, and actions and Baldwin backs. These new models, distributed through the old Everett dealer network, could be identified by the letter C at the end of the model number. In 1988 the models were changed back again to the old Everett designs and built entirely by Baldwin (and the letter C designation dropped), and distributed through the regular Yamaha dealer network.

The first of the two Baldwin-made Everett models was not bad, but according to some dealers and technicians, the second left something to be desired. The contract under which Baldwin was manufacturing these pianos for Yamaha ended in 1989 and the Everett name and piano line was dropped by Yamaha permanently.

The Everett name has been used on pianos by Wrightwood Enterprises, Inc. since 1995. The line consists of 5', 5'5", and 6'1" grands and 44", 46", and 48" verticals. Most of Wrightwood's current Everett pianos are imported from, and made by, the Donbei Piano Co. in China. (See also "Nordiska" for more information.) Some furniture-style vertical pianos are made by Artfield (see "Krakauer") and by Macao. The grands have duplex scaling and a bass scale that is custom-made for the Everett brand, the company says.

Warranty: Ten years, parts and labor, to original purchaser.

Verticals	Grands
44" (112/113)	5'
46" (116)	5'5"
48" (122)	6'1"

Consumer Ratings: Insufficient information to rate. Though some Everett models may be built to different specifications, I suggest seeing under "Nordiska" and "Krakauer" for approximate ratings.

FALCONE

No longer being made

Name owned by: Mason & Hamlin Piano Co.

Falcone Piano Co. was founded by Santi Falcone (pronounced Fahl-KON-eh), a piano technician, rebuilder, and retailer in the Boston area who, in the early 1980s, began to build his own grand pianos. Originally from Sicily, Falcone came to the United States at the age of fourteen and began tuning pianos at sixteen, eventually owning a chain of seven

stores that sold and leased new pianos and rebuilt older ones (he was also the U.S. importer of Barock pianos from Japan). Troubled both by the inferior, mass-produced character of most pianos today and by the incredibly high price of the high-quality pianos, he set out to build an instrument that was at once of the highest caliber and affordable.

To do this, he gradually sold all of his stores and set up a workshop adjacent to one of them in Woburn, Massachusetts. In 1984, after several years of research and development, he began production, and in 1985 he and the eleven craftsmen he employed made about thirty pianos. With a large backlog of orders, Falcone moved to a much larger factory space in Haverhill, Massachusetts in the spring of 1986 with the intention of sharply increasing production over the next several years.

Although production did increase somewhat, raising capital, increasing production, and maintaining quality were not as easy as anticipated. Falcone eventually decided to sell a substantial amount of stock in the company to outside investors to raise needed capital, and hired Lloyd Meyer, a former president of Steinway & Sons, as a consultant. The major investor was Bernard Greer, a wealthy Seattle businessman who became interested in the company after purchasing a Falcone piano for himself. In 1989 Greer purchased the remaining shares in the company when Falcone ran into financial difficulty, and named Meyer chief executive officer. Falcone was offered a post in the company, but declined. Shortly thereafter, Greer also purchased all the rights and designs to the Sohmer, Mason & Hamlin, Knabe, and George Steck pianos, most left over from the bankrupt Aeolian company (see "Aeolian" and "Sohmer"), and renamed the company The Mason & Hamlin Companies. Eventually the new company also ran into financial difficulty, filing for bankruptcy in 1995, and was purchased from bankruptcy in 1996 by the Burgett brothers, owners of PianoDisc. At this point, the Burgetts have no plans to reissue the Falcone pianos or to use that name on another piano. Please see "Mason & Hamlin" for more information.

Three models of Falcone grand pianos were made from 1984 to 1994: 6'1", 7'4", and 9'. All three were loosely based on the scale designs of the three corresponding models of Steinway—A, C, and D—but with many refinements borrowed from European designs, as well as some of Falcone's own. One of Santi Falcone's inventions was a device that regulates the tension in the treble part of the soundboard, though there is some question about its actual effectiveness in enhancing the tone. All Falcone pianos had a maple rim, solid spruce soundboard, action parts made by Renner, and a sostenuto pedal.

Santi Falcone personally supervised the construction of about two hundred pianos (to about serial number 1200). Some Falcones from this period have had problems with veneer coming loose, pinblock problems, and other problems related to inadequate moisture control due to a lack of capital for expensive factory climate control equipment and facilities. After Greer took over the company, investments were made in the proper equipment and moisture-related problems were eliminated. The pianos were considered very well built, with the 7'4" instrument considered the most successful

For explanation of survey and review procedures, model listings, and price ranges, please see pages 76–81.

tonally, followed by the 9', and the 6'1" model being considered good but not superlative.

After leaving the piano business, Santi Falcone went on to establish a successful business making gourmet chocolates in the Boston area.

FANDRICH

Fandrich Piano Co., Inc.
113 E. 6th Street
Aberdeen, Washington 98520

(360) 532-2563
(360) 532-6688
pianobuilders@olynet.com
www.fandrichpiano.com

In 1989 Delwin Fandrich left his job as head of Research & Development at Baldwin and, after a short period of free-lance piano designing, started his own piano company. Del had in mind to try out a number of design features too unusual to be attempted by any established piano manufacturer, but his initial thoughts were to build a grand. Meanwhile, Del's brother Darrell Fandrich had invented a vertical action that played like a grand, and was looking for a piano in which to put it. When Del saw how well the action worked and was convinced it could be successfully manufactured, he decided to design and build an upright that sounded like a grand to complement the action that played like one. Darrell's company, Fandrich Design, Inc., initially licensed Del's company, Fandrich Piano Co., to assemble the action from special parts custom-made by Renner and others. The pianos were sold direct from the factory, as well as by a few dealers.

The unusual 48" Fandrich upright had a visually-striking back sculpted out of a single thick sheet of laminated maple and alder. The one-piece back, Fandrich said, performed the same function as the heavy bent rim of the best grand pianos, providing a firm foundation for the soundboard that both conserves tonal energy and prevents a relaxation of the soundboard crown with time. The patented Fandrich soundboard was designed to function like a modern audio speaker, directing various frequencies to the correct area of the soundboard based upon frequency/impedance matching. Special agraffes, an extra-heavy pressure bar, a multi-laminated maple pinblock, a newly designed scale, a five-ply lumber-core cabinet, and the Fandrich action outfitted with Abel hammers all served to create a truly impressive instrument. For a more complete technical description of the Fandrich upright, see the third edition of this book.

All told, about one hundred pianos were built and sold before a combination of various business, technical, and personal problems brought about the demise of the company. Many Fandrich owners were (and still are) very satisfied with their instruments. However, some early Fandrichs had tuning stability problems, finish problems, and a variety of action problems, since solved. All these pianos were repaired under warranty. After the company was dissolved, Del opened a piano rebuilding shop and is currently designing and building a new 6'7" grand piano, among other projects.

He is also exploring the possibility of bringing his upright back into production, but at the time of this writing, no firm plans had been made. Darrell Fandrich and his wife Heather have been outfitting pianos from various parts of the world with their Fandrich action and selling them under the name Fandrich & Sons (see below).

FANDRICH & SONS

Fandrich & Sons Pianos
7411 Silvana Terrace Road
Stanwood, Washington 98292

(360) 652-8980
(877) 737-1422
fandrich@fandrich.com
www.fandrich.com

Owned by: Darrell and Heather Fandrich

Pianos made by: various makers—see text

In the late 1980s, Darrell Fandrich, an engineer and piano technician, developed a vertical piano action designed to play like a grand. Darrell's brother Del, for his innovative upright (see "Fandrich," above), was the first piano manufacturer to use the action under license. When that collaboration ended, Darrell and his wife Heather decided to set up shop installing Fandrich actions in selected new pianos, selling them under the name Fandrich & Sons. In addition they continue to seek out established manufacturers who might be willing to make their pianos available with a Fandrich action as an option.

The Fandrich Vertical Action is designed to overcome the limitations inherent in the traditional vertical action. In the traditional action, the several parts of each note are in contact with one another when they are at rest, but alternately lose contact and bump into one another, in rapid succession, when the note is being repeated, a property known as "dynamic lost motion." This property gives a vertical piano its characteristic sloppy, out-of-control feel. Also, when a key is released on a vertical piano, the parts usually cannot reset themselves for a new stroke of the key until the key is nearly all the way up. The speed at which notes can be repeated is therefore limited. In a grand action, on the other hand, gravity acting on the horizontally positioned hammer and the front-weighted keys keeps the associated parts in contact with each other most of the time, and a repetition spring enables the parts to reset themselves without waiting for the key to be fully released.

Emulating the grand, the Fandrich action has front-weighted keys and individually adjustable hammer return springs that duplicate the force of gravity responsible for returning the hammer to rest in a grand, which enables the parts to stay tightly connected during most of the stroke. A repetition spring connecting the jack and hammer butt quickly brings them back together after they separate at letoff (Figure 4-3). As a result, the player of a Fandrich action has an exceptional amount of control over dynamics—including the ability to play softly (unusual for a vertical piano)—and the rapidity and evenness of touch of a good grand piano . . . on an upright.

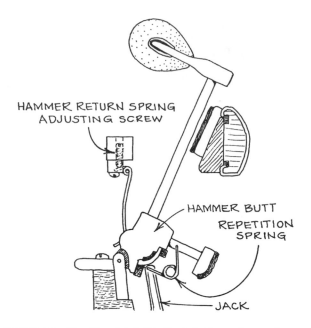

HAMMER RETURN SPRING
ADJUSTING SCREW

HAMMER BUTT

REPETITION
SPRING

JACK

FIGURE 4-3. The Fandrich Vertical Action, shown in part, contains repetition springs and individually-adjustable hammer return springs to simulate the performance characteristics of a grand piano action.

In the early Fandrich (not Fandrich & Sons) pianos in which the Fandrich action was first installed, there were a variety of action troubles, including repetition springs coming loose, excessive touch weight, and improperly regulated actions. The company says that all of these problems have long since been corrected.

Until recently, most Fandrich actions have been installed in Chinese pianos from the Guangzhou Pearl River factory. The Fandrichs have taken the pianos apart and rebuilt them as necessary to their standards before installing the Fandrich action. Some have also been sold without the Fandrich action. Recently, the Fandrichs announced that their Fandrich & Sons upright pianos are now being made by the Czech maker Klima and will feature the Fandrich action entirely built by Renner. Also, the German maker Wilh. Steinberg will offer the Fandrich action as an option in its pianos. The Fandrichs have licensed Renner to build Fandrich actions for Steinberg and others.

The Fandrichs sell their Fandrich & Sons pianos directly from their home workshop; there is no dealer network. Although most sales have thus far been in the Seattle area, there have also been a fair number of buyers from other parts of the world. A detailed regulation manual accompanies each piano so that technicians in other places will know how to properly regulate the action.

Warranty: Twelve years, parts and labor, to original purchaser.

Price range: Prices start at $8,900.

FAZER

Oy Musiikki Fazer Musik AB
Halkia, Finland

For explanation of survey and review procedures, model listings, and price ranges, please see pages 76–81.

No longer imported into the U.S.

Owned by: Hellas Piano, Finland

This marvelous 43″ studio piano was imported into the U.S. by Coast Wholesale Music Co. for several years in the mid-1980s. It had a four-ply laminated soundboard made of woods I've never heard of, a particle board cabinet, and sold for $3,000 or so. But despite this unflattering description, the piano was beautifully made, worked perfectly, and sounded great! Here are several comments about the piano from technicians: "Best bass sound on a piano this size with a laminated soundboard I've seen." "Beautiful piano—once again Fazer impresses! Smooth sound and action, gorgeous case." The piano also used a Langer action, and was considered a real bargain. Unfortunately, Fazer pianos are no longer available. In 1989 the wholesale price of the piano abruptly rose by forty percent, making it no longer worthwhile to import it.

FAZIOLI

International Brokers, Inc.
5827 A Crystal Hill Rd.
North Little Rock, Arkansas 72118
(501) 753-8616
piano@ipa.net
www.internationalbrokersinc.com

Pianos made by: Fazioli Pianoforti S.R.L., Sacile (Pordenone), Italy

In 1978, musician and engineer Paolo Fazioli of Rome, Italy began designing and building pianos under his own name with the object of making the finest quality pianos possible. Now even the most accomplished piano makers of Western Europe are praising them and artists throughout the world are using them successfully on the concert stage and elsewhere.

The roots of the Fazioli piano date back seventy years to Fazioli's father, Romano Fazioli. A carpenter with a background in piano playing, the elder Fazioli sought to expand his business into other areas of interest that would make use of his woodworking skills, and so decided to build pianos. Between 1930 and 1934, he and his associates built a number of experimental models, but turmoil in Europe prevented the continuation of the piano business.

Paolo, the youngest of Romano's six sons, studied music and engineering, receiving advanced degrees in both subjects. He briefly attempted to make a living as a concert pianist but decided he didn't have the talent to succeed and instead joined his family's furniture company, rising to the position of factory manager in the Rome and Turin factories. But his creative ambitions, combined with his personal search for the perfect piano, finally led him to conclude that he needed to build his own piano.

With advice and financial backing from his family, in 1977 Fazioli assembled a group of experts in woodworking, acoustics, and piano technology to study and scientifically analyze every aspect of piano design and construction. The following year, prototypes of his new instruments in hand, Fazioli began building pianos commercially. The piano factory is housed at one end of the family's Sacile furniture factory and shares some of its woodworking and finishing equipment. Fazioli Furniture is a top supplier of high-end office furniture in Italy. At the time of this writing, Fazioli is building a new piano factory which will allow the company to modestly increase production, efficiency, and quality control, and which will house a research area with testing equipment and a concert hall.

Fazioli builds grands only, in six sizes from 5'2" to 10'2", the largest piano in the world today. This model also has the distinction of having four pedals. Three are the usual sustain, sostenuto, and una corda. The fourth is a "soft" pedal that brings the hammers closer to the strings—just like on verticals, and some older grands—to soften the sound without altering the tonal quality as the una corda pedal often does. The fourth pedal is available as an option on the other models. The lid on the 10'2" model is so heavy that it must be divided into three parts, each part individually adjustable and containing its own propstick.

Fazioli now offers two actions and two pedal lyres as options on all its grand pianos. Having two actions allows for more voicing options without having to constantly revoice the hammers. This could be useful when several players with different requirements must regularly share the same instrument, or for a single player who prefers a radically different sound for certain pieces of music. The second pedal lyre is an option for those pianos outfitted with the fourth pedal, mentioned above. Because some pianists may not need the fourth pedal and may be confused by its presence, the optional second lyre contains only the standard three pedals.

Another option that has just become available on Fazioli pianos—and Fazioli is the first manufacturer to offer this—is the Magnetic Balanced Action, a device that enables the pianist, in less than a minute, to alter the piano's touch weight to suit his or her preference. The device is also available as a retrofit into older pianos or other brands. See page 233 for details.

All Fazioli pianos have inner rims of beech and ash, outer rims of mahogany, beech Delignit pinblocks, solid redspruce soundboards, and Renner actions, Kluge keyboards, Abel hammers, and front and rear duplex scales. The company says that a critical factor in the sound of its pianos is the scientific selection of its woods, such as the "resonant spruce" obtained from the Val di Fiemme, where Stradivarius reportedly sought woods for his violins. Each piece of wood is said to be carefully tested for certain resonant properties before being used in the pianos. An incredible level of detail has gone into the design and construction of these pianos. For instance, in one small portion of the soundboard where additional stiffness is required, the grain of the wood runs perpendicular to that of the rest of the soundboard, cleverly disguised so as to be almost unnoticeable.

Only two of the technicians interviewed for this edition had experience with Fazioli pianos, but both had high praise for the instruments. Said one, "The voicing was just incredible right out of the box."

Fazioli only makes about a hundred pianos a year so distribution in the United States is very limited.

Warranty: Five years, parts and labor, transferable.

Price range: $69,800–98,400 (fourth pedal, add'l $5,000)

Grands
  5'2" (F156)
  6' (F183)
  6'11" (F212)
  7'6" (F228)
  9'2" (F278)
  10'2" (F308)

Consumer Ratings:

Performance: * * * * *
Confidence: * * * * *
Quality Control: * * * * *
Warranty: * * * 1/2
Information: * * 1/2

FEURICH

Julius Feurich Pianofortefabrik GmbH
Gunzenhausen, Germany

Not currently being made

This German piano manufacturer was founded in Leipzig in 1851 by Julius Feurich. At its height in the early part of this century, the company employed 360 people, producing 1,200 upright and 600 grand pianos annually. Like many German manufacturers, however, Feurich lost its factory during the second World War. Following the war, the fourth generation of the Feurich family rebuilt in Langlau in what became West Germany.

In 1991, Bechstein purchased Feurich and closed the Langlau factory, but in 1993 the name was sold back to the Feurich family. Production was contracted out to other German manufacturers, while the Feurich family marketed and distributed the pianos. For several years, Feurich grands were manufactured for the Feurich family by Schimmel. They were identical in most respects to Schimmel grands of the same size, except that the Feurichs benefited from the use of Kluge keys with artificial-ivory keytops as well as some cosmetic changes to the cabinet. The arrangement with Schimmel was discontinued in 1998. Since that time, the Feurich family has been seeking another satisfactory arrangement for the production of pianos bearing its name, but by press time no such arrangement had been made.

FÖRSTER, AUGUST

German American Trading Co., Inc.
P.O. Box 17789
Tampa, Florida 33682
(813) 961-8405
germanamer@aol.com

Pianos made by: August Förster GmbH, Löbau, Germany

The Förster factory was founded by Friedrich August Förster in 1859 in Löbau, Germany, after Förster studied the art of piano building with others. During the years of control by the government of East Germany, the factory was managed by the fourth generation pianomaker, Wolfgang Förster. Since the reunification of Germany and privatization, Wolfgang and his family are once again the owners of the company.

Förster makes about 220 grands and 400 verticals a year, using a great deal of hand labor. At one time these high-quality pianos were very inexpensive, but with the reintroduction of capitalism have come competitive wages and much higher prices.

Förster manufactures four sizes of grand piano: 5'8", 6'4", 7'2", and 9'1". In addition to the conventional furniture style, the pianos are also available in Chippendale, Rococo, and Antique in satin or high polish finishes of black, walnut, or mahogany. Other veneers and finishes may be ordered. The pianos are extremely well built structurally and the cabinetry elegant. Rims and pinblocks are of beech, soundboards of Siberian spruce, bridges of hardrock maple (without graphite). Each string is individually terminated (single strung). The actions are made by Renner with Renner hammers. The keys feature leather key bushings instead of the usual cloth. A sostenuto pedal is standard on all grand models.

The tone of August Förster grands is quite unique, with a remarkable bass, dark and deep, yet clear. The treble is often quite bright, sometimes thin, and for some American tastes might be considered too much so, though it can be modified somewhat with voicing. The instruments are quite versatile, at home with Mozart or Prokofieff, classical or jazz. Some pianists consider the 6'4" to possess the best scale, and to be a better choice than the 5'8", which has a more discernible break between the bass and treble. The concert-quality 7'2" and 9'1" models are well balanced tonally and, over the years, have been endorsed by many famous artists. The Renner actions are very responsive and arrive in exacting regulation.

Förster verticals come in two sizes: 46" and 49". Most of the comments regarding quality of materials and workmanship of the grands also applies to the verticals, since the same workforce builds the verticals with the same materials and hand work.

The cabinet of the Förster vertical is of exceptional width, with extra-thick side panels of solid-core stock. Counter bridges are used on the outside of the soundboard to increase its mass. The verticals have a full set of agraffes and all the hardware and handmade wood parts are of elegant quality. The actions are built by Renner.

August Förster makes an excellent vertical that possesses the same warm, rich, deep bass tone of the Förster grands. Unfortunately, like other high quality German verticals, its cost makes it an impractical, if not impossible, choice, since the market is essentially reduced to customers with unlimited funds but limited space, a rare combination.

Please note that there is a piano sold under the August Förster name in Canada and several European countries which is made by Petrof and is similar to the Petrof piano (see "Petrof"). Except for the name, it has no connection to the August Förster pianos made in Germany. I'm told that this situation came about because of a legal conflict many years ago over the rights to the August Förster name, which resulted in an agreement specifying in which countries each

For explanation of survey and review procedures, model listings, and price ranges, please see pages 76–81.

manufacturer could market pianos under this name.

Warranty: Ten years, parts and labor.

Price range: (Verticals) $13,000–14,000; (Grands) $27,300–34,200

Verticals	Grands
46" (C/E)	5'8" (170)
49" (125G)	6'4" (190)
	7'2" (215)
	9'1" (275)

Consumer Ratings:

Performance: * * * * *
Confidence: * * * * *
Quality Control: * * * * *
Warranty: * * * *
Information
    Grands: * *
    Verticals: * ¹/₂

GAVEAU

See "Pleyel"

GEORGE STECK

See "Steck, George"

GRINNELL BROS.

Grinnell Bros. manufactured pianos in the midwest from 1902 to about 1960. The name is now owned by a Detroit-area piano dealer, Hammell Music. Pianos bearing this name were most recently made by Samick and were similar in features to pianos in the Kohler & Campbell line. See "Samick" for more information.

GROTRIAN

Strings Limited
314 S. Milwaukee Ave., Ste. B
Libertyville, Illinois 60048

(847) 367-5224
stringsltd@aol.com
www.grotrian.de

Pianos made by: Pianofortefabrikanten Grotrian-Steinweg, Braunschweig, Germany

Friedrich Grotrian was born in Schöningen, Germany in 1803, and as a young man lived in Moscow, where he ran a music business and was associated with piano manufacturing. Later in his life, he teamed up with Heinrich Steinweg and Heinrich's son Theodore to build pianos in Germany. Heinrich emigrated to the United States about 1850, soon to establish the firm of Steinway & Sons. Theodore followed in 1865, selling his share in the partnership to Wilhelm Grotrian, Wilhelm's father Friedrich having died in 1860. Thereafter, the firm became known as Grotrian-Steinweg. (In a legal settlement with Steinway & Sons, Grotrian-Steinweg agreed to use only the name Grotrian on pianos sold in North America.)

Even as early as the 1860s, Grotrian pianos were well known and highly respected throughout Europe. Each successive generation of the Grotrian family maintained the company's high standards and furthered the technical development of the instrument. Today the company is managed by the fifth generation of Grotrians. Housed in an up-to-date factory, and using a combination of modern technology and traditional craftsmanship, Grotrian makes about 1200 verticals and 300 grands a year.

Grotrian grands have beech rims, solid spruce soundboards, laminated beech pinblocks, and Renner actions. The instruments are single-strung (each length of wire has its own hitch pin), which may slightly aid tuning stability. Grotrian prides itself on what it calls its "homogeneous soundboard," in which each piece of wood is specially chosen for proper "balance" of sound. The cast-iron plate is attached with screws along the outer edges of the rim, instead of on top of the rim, which, the company says, allows the soundboard to vibrate more freely.

My experience with Grotrian pianos has been that the treble has extraordinary sustaining characteristics. It also has a definite sound of attack, more pronounced than, say, a Steinway, but subtle and delicate, almost but not quite "wooden." The tenor area has a darker sound than many other brands. The bass can be very powerful, but its power does not seem to come from the higher harmonics, so it has power without any stridency. Overall, I find Grotrians to have a quite unique, expressive sound and to be very pleasurable to play.

Warranty: Five-year full warranty

Price range: (Verticals) $19,000–27,200; (Grands) $44,600–65,000

Verticals	Grands
44" (Caret)	5'5" (165)
49" (Classic)	6'3" (192)
52" (Concertino)	7'4" (225)
	9'2" (277)

Consumer Ratings:

Performance: * * * * *
Confidence: * * * * *
Quality Control: * * * * *
Warranty: * * * 1/2
Information
    Grands: * * 1/2
    Verticals: * *

HAESSLER

See "Blüthner"

HAMILTON

See "Baldwin"

HALLET & DAVIS

North American Music, Inc.
126 Route 303
W. Nyack, New York 10994

(800) 541-2331
(845) 353-3520
www.namusic.com

Pianos made by: Samick Musical Instrument Mfg. Co., Ltd., Inchon, South Korea; Guangzhou Pearl River Piano Co., Guangzhou, China; Beijing Piano Co., Beijing, China.

This famous old American piano brand name dates back to at least 1843 and changed hands many times over the years. It eventually became part of the Aeolian group of piano brands, and instruments bearing the name were manufactured at Aeolian's Memphis plant before that company went out of business in 1985 (see "Aeolian"). For the past couple of years the name has been applied to pianos made by Samick in Korea and distributed by Hyundai, and have been nearly identical to those sold under Hyundai's Maeari label. This year the company has switched manufacturers and the pianos are now being made in China by Guangzhou Pearl River and Beijing.

At this point, Chinese pianos are only marginally recommended. If well prepared by the dealer, some are acceptable, but they do not have much of a track record to provide assurance of satisfaction over the long term. See "Samick" and "Pearl River" for more information about these pianos.

Price range: (Verticals) $2,500–5,700; (Grands) $8,600–9,600

Verticals	Grands
42" (UP-108)	4'11" (HDG-1480/1481)
45" (HS-450/452)	5'3" (GP-159)
46" (UP-115)	5'3" (HDG-1580)
46" (HB-115)	5'7" (HDG-1680)
48" (HB/HU-120)	
52" (HU-131/132)	

Models beginning with "UP" and "GP" are from the Guangzhou factory. Models beginning with "H" are from Beijing.

Consumer Ratings: See "Samick" for ratings of (former) Samick-made models. See "Pearl River" for ratings of pianos from the Guangzhou factory.

HASTINGS

Name no longer in use.

The Hastings piano, formerly distributed by Coast Wholesale Music, was made by Macao Piano Factory Ltd. of Macao, a subsidiary of the Guangzhou Pearl River factory in Guangzhou, China. Macao is a Portuguese colony off the coast of Hong Kong. The pianos were partly manufactured in the Guangzhou factory and completed in Macao.

HEINTZMAN

No longer being made in Canada.

Many technicians recall the old Heintzman piano, a high-quality upright made in Canada in the early part of this century. In the decades that followed, the Heintzman, like so many other brands, was gradually cheapened in quality. In 1978, the Heintzman company was sold to Sherlock-Manning, another Canadian piano manufacturer, which was controlled by a member of a different branch of the Heintzman family. Sherlock-Manning was renamed Heintzman Limited. In 1981 Sklar-Peppler, a large Canadian furniture maker, bought Heintzman Limited, and made very good quality Heintzman pianos for several years at the original Heintzman factory in Hanover, Ontario. In 1986, Sklar-Peppler decided to close the factory, and sold its remaining inventory of pianos to The Music Stand, a piano dealer in Oakville, Ontario and leased the trademarked Heintzman name to them. For a time, The Music Stand applied the Heintzman and Gerhard Heintzman names to inexpensive pianos from several U.S. and Korean makers. A member of the Heintzman family brought suit, and the Federal Court of Canada ruled that the use of the Heintzman name on pianos so different in origin from the original Canadian-made Heintzman without proper notification to the public caused the trademark to lose its "distinctiveness" and ordered the name stricken from the trademark register.

I am not aware of who, if anyone, owns the Heintzman name anymore, but it has apparently been seen on pianos from a variety of countries, including China and the Czech Republic. No further information is available.

HOFFMANN, W.

See "Bechstein, C."

HOFMANN & SCHOLZ

Hofmann & Scholz Piano Co.
1000 Lake Street, Building D
Ramsey, New Jersey 07446

(201) 825-7676
(888) 857-8100
info@klavierfabrik.de
www.klavierfabrik.de

Pianos made by: Klavierfabrik Nordpiano GmbH, Ducherow, Germany

Names used: Hofmann & Scholz, Mecklenburg

Hofmann & Scholz is the brand name of Klavierfabrik Nordpiano GmbH, established in 1996 in the German state of Mecklenburg with support and subsidies from the German government. At present, the company offers only one piano model, a 48" upright. The piano is sold with two upper panels, one in traditional styling and one in contemporary; the customer can choose which one to use and can change it at any time.

Although the piano is built in Germany, the plate casting and some of the spraying of lacquer are done in Russia. The instruments have Delignit pinblocks, Renner actions, and Abel hammers. The company provides free preparation of

For explanation of survey and review procedures, model listings, and price ranges, please see pages 76–81.

the pianos at the dealer's location when a dealer purchases at least three instruments. A version of the piano with a less expensive cabinet is available under the brand name "Mecklenburg."

Warranty: Full ten-year warranty

Price range: $8,000

Vertical
    48" upright (NP-121)

Consumer Ratings: Insufficient information to rate

HOHNER

No longer selling pianos in the U.S.

Hohner, a German company, is the world's largest maker of harmonicas. They also sell accordians, recorders, and a large assortment of other musical instruments and accessories. For a few years in the late 1980s, Hohner tried selling pianos, but this venture was apparently not successful in the U.S. Hohner pianos were made by Hellas, a Finnish company, which later became affiliated with Fazer. The wood used for the consoles was fairly ordinary, but the pianos were assembled well, looked and sounded quite good, and needed little preparation by the dealer. The weak point of the piano reportedly was the soundboard, which sometimes cracked in the New England climate, but otherwise there were no particular problems. The studios and uprights were of a little higher quality than the consoles.

HYUNDAI
Including Maeari

North American Music, Inc.
126 Route 303
W. Nyack, New York 10994

(800) 541-2331
(845) 353-3520
www.namusic.com

Pianos made by: Samick Musical Instrument Mfg. Co., Ltd., Inchon, South Korea

Names used: Hyundai, Maeari

Best known in the United States for its automobiles, Hyundai Corp. is one of Korea's largest industrial conglomerates, and makes or distributes many kinds of consumer goods. Just as Yamaha once relied on name recognition from its motorcycles, Hyundai is counting on name recognition from its automobile advertising to separate its pianos from those of its Korean competitors.

All Hyundai pianos are made by Samick. Some models are pretty much the same as those sold under the Samick brand name and some are of different scale designs. All use Samick's veneer-laminated spruce soundboard.

Hyundai also sells pianos under the name Maeari, which means "echo"—the name is well chosen because the Maeari pianos are the same as the Hyundai pianos—and, until recently, under the name Hallet & Davis (see "Hallet & Davis"), also, more or less, the same piano.

Warranty: Twelve-year full warranty; lifetime warranty on soundboard.

Price range: (Verticals) $3,750-5,600; (Grands) $9,900–17,400

Verticals	Grands
42" console (U-800)	4'7" (G-50A)
43" console (U-824)	5'1" (G-80A)
45" studio (U-822)	5'9" (G-81/G-82)
46" studio (U-842/U-852)	6'1" (G-84)
48" upright (U-832)	6'10" (G-85)
52" upright (U-837)	

For Maeari, vertical piano model numbers begin with "MU" instead of "U."

Consumer Ratings: See "Samick"

IBACH

Rud. Ibach Sohn
Schwelm, Germany

No longer being sold in the U.S.

Established by Johannes Adolf Ibach in 1794, Ibach has the distinction of being the oldest existing manufacturer of fine pianos in the world. (For perspective, in 1794, Haydn was writing his last works while Beethoven was writing his Opus 1 piano trios.) Ibach is still owned and managed by the original family, Messers. Christian and Rolf Ibach, the sixth generation.

Ibach has been notable in the development of both piano construction and the piano industry in general. One of the smaller piano builders of the world, until the recent economic crisis in Germany, Ibach manufactured approximately 1,000 vertical pianos and 250 grands a year for world consumption. Although not as well known in North America as some other European manufacturers, Ibach has quietly built a solid reputation in Europe over the last two centuries through fine craftsmanship and by supplying pianos to a long list of famous composers and artists, such as Wagner, R. Strauss, Liszt, Bartok, Schoenberg, and others.

Economic conditions in Germany during the last decade have hit all the small piano makers very hard, forcing Ibach to take a new direction in order to survive. In 1991, Daewoo, the Korean former manufacturer of Sojin pianos, purchased a thirty-three percent interest in Ibach, with Ibach to sell Korean-made Ibachs worldwide in addition to a small number of German-made Ibachs. Daewoo said it was going to duplicate Ibach factory equipment and production methods in its Korean facilities. At the last minute, a decision was made to distribute in Canada but not in the United States. Over the last few years, the Canadian distributor has not returned my phone calls, so I don't know the current status of production and distribution.

IRMLER

German Piano Imports LLC
5660 W. Grand River
Lansing, Michigan 48906

(517) 886-6000
(800) 954-3200

Irmler is a brand sold in Europe, now being imported into the U.S.. The importer is associated with Blüthner. Most of the models (the "standard edition") are made in China. At this time, one of the grands is also available as a collaboration between Czech and Polish firms (the "European edition"). All models have Renner actions and German pinblocks.

Price range: (Verticals) $2,800–4,300; (Grands—Standard) $9,800–17,500; (Grands—European) $23,000

Verticals	Grands
47" (P118)	5'3" (F16) (Standard)
48" (P120)	5'11" (F18 E) (European)
50" (P125)	7' (F21) (Standard)
52" (P130)	

Consumer Ratings: Insufficient information to rate

JASPER (-AMERICAN)

See "Kimball"

KAWAI

Kawai America Corporation
2055 E. University Drive
P.O. Box 9045
Compton, California 90224

(310) 631-1771
(800) 421-2177
acoustic@kawaius.com
www.kawaius.com

Owned and made by: Kawai Musical Instrument Mfg. Co., Ltd., Hamamatsu, Japan (publicly owned in Japan); also made in Lincolnton, North Carolina.

Names used: Kawai, K. Kawai, Shigeru Kawai. No longer used in U.S.: Diapason, Schiedmayer.

Kawai, Japan's second largest piano manufacturer, was founded in 1927 by Koichi Kawai, an inventor and former Yamaha employee who was the first Japanese to design and build a piano action. When Kawai first began exporting pianos to the United States in the 1960s, they were a relative unknown, and many dealers took them on only if they couldn't get the Yamaha dealership. While Kawai is still second to Yamaha in size, it has a well-deserved reputation all its own for quality and innovation.

Kawai makes a complete line of console, studio, and upright pianos from 43" to 52" in height, and grand pianos from 5' to 9'1" in length. All Kawai grand pianos and taller uprights are made in Japan, while the consoles and wood-finish studio pianos are assembled in Kawai's plant in Lincolnton, North Carolina.

Verticals: Kawai offers an array of vertical pianos that is sometimes confusing because the model letter and number designations and the sizes do not make clear what the differences are between one model and the next. Even some Kawai dealers admit this to be so, and add that constantly changing models and specifications, and the difficulty of getting up-to-date model information from the manufacturer, can sometimes make it hard for them to give proper guidance to the customer.

At the present time, Kawai offers a furniture-style console, the 43" model 505, and a fancier and better-scaled version, the 44" model 605. These models are assembled in the U.S. from a Japanese-made strung back and action and a U.S.-made cabinet.

The 45" model CX-5H is Kawai's least expensive and most popular vertical piano. The low cost, however, is clearly reflected in its construction. This model, according to my definition, is not a true studio upright, as its size and Kawai's marketing team would indicate, but actually a console in studio's clothing. (Like most manufacturers, Kawai uses the terms "studio" and "console" to indicate the furniture styling, rather than the size or technical features.) Using a scale design similar to the discontinued 41" model CX-5, the CX-5H has been made taller by the use of casters and an extended back. Although the extra height may be appealing to some customers, it confers no technical or musical advantage (nor disadvantage). This model contains a compressed action typical of a console (see page 44 for further explanation), a very insubstantial back structure with no wooden posts, a laminated mahogany-core, spruce-veneered soundboard, and uses lower-grade woods in a number of places. A variant, model 504, is the same piano in a furniture-style cabinet, but with a shorter, 43" back. These inexpensive models are satisfactory entry-level pianos, but for the reasons mentioned, they may not be quite the bargain they seem initially and are not appropriate for demanding applications, particularly if the piano needs to be moved much. The CX-5H may be assembled in North Carolina or in Japan, as production needs dictate.

Kawai's 46" institutional studio line consists of its traditional school model, the UST-7, and a less expensive version, the UST-8, both now made in the U.S. The UST-8 was designed to be more competitive in school bidding situations. Although it fulfills school requirements, its back is not as substantial as that of the UST-7, which has long been considered a school workhorse. Also, the UST-8 keybed is a steel frame structure, in contrast to the thick wood keybed of the UST-7. These models now have all their action parts made of Kawai's ABS plastic. The 46" model 902, although listed by Kawai as a console, is actually a furniture-style version of the UST-8 studio.

Last year, Kawai changed its upright line completely. It now consists of the 48" model K30, the 49" model K50 with NEOTEX™ (Kawai's brand of synthetic ivory) keytops on both the black and white keys, the 52" model K60 with duplex scale and agraffes, and the 52" model K80, which is the same as the K60, but with a true sostenuto and some cabinetry upgrades, including a grand-style music desk and a soft-close fallboard.

Kawai's quality control is very good. In the service database examined, of 289 Kawai verticals, most of which were sold from three to five years ago, post-sale service other than tuning was provided to about a quarter of the pianos, and most complaints were very minor. This is a moderate to moderately low percentage compared with other brands.

Probably the single biggest category of complaints was that of miscellaneous mechanical and acoustical noises—clicks, vibrations, squeaks, and echos—that had to be tracked down and eliminated, as well as tonal complaints that could be solved by voicing. Generally, the noise problems were solved by (as needed) tightening screws, adjusting dampers, softening damper felts, epoxying the occasional loose bridge pin, damping off the occasional sympathetically vibrating segment of string, adjusting pedals and trapwork, and regulating. About ten percent of the pianos sold required at least some small amount of post-sale work of this nature, usually very minor. A smaller number of pianos also had some sticking keys or tight action centers.

In the written survey, technicians inspected seventy-seven Kawai verticals sold during the last five years. Among the 500-series consoles and the CX-5H pianos, there was very little "wrong" with the pianos, but the tone was often said to be too thin, bright, or mediocre, and some new ones were said to show excessive seasonal pitch change or insufficient tuning at the factory (the CX-5H has a relatively weak back structure, which could account for some of this problem). With tuning and voicing, most were made okay, but few received compliments. The tuning pins were sometimes described as "spongy" or odd-feeling to turn, which can bother piano tuners, but should not affect the tuning stability.

The Kawai studio pianos (school models UST-7 and UST-8, and the furniture-style version 902) were generally liked, but there were a number of fairly consistent comments and mild complaints:

- As with the consoles, several technicians said they always seem to be pitch-raising the pianos, implying that the pianos aren't tuned enough at the factory or undergo excessive seasonal change. Eventually the tuning stabilizes, but it takes longer than it should. Also, five pianos, all about four years old, were found to have one or a few loose tuning pins each. [Kawai says it has recently revised the design of the studio pianos to address the issue of excessive seasonal pitch change.]

- Several technicians who service pianos for schools and universities commented that in their opinion, the cabinets of the American-made school studio are not as well made as when these models were manufactured in Japan, and they had some doubts about the ability of these cabinets to hold up well in the long run in institutional settings. Thin finishes and corners that rub off too easily were cited. The front panels were also said to be cumbersome in design for the frequent removal and replacement needed in an institutional setting, and the screws holding the front panel clasps were said to be too small and to strip out easily.

- The trapwork for the bass and treble dampers is linked together in a way that makes damper adjustment unnecessarily complicated. Also, the tubular trapwork "clicks" intermittently. Of perhaps greater interest to the player, the spring tension of the bass dampers sometimes is so great that it noticeably affects the touch. More specifically, the spring tension causes the touch to be substantially different depending on whether or not the sustain pedal is

For explanation of survey and review procedures, model listings, and price ranges, please see pages 76–81.

depressed. This difference is perceptible on many brands of vertical piano, but apparently more on this model than others. It may not be correctable because reducing the tension on the damper springs may create problems with damping of sound. However, this touch difference may not be a problem for everyone.

- Scaling in the low tenor was said to be particularly poor, and the tone in the upper treble was often said to be "woody." (Virtually all the pianos with poor tone in the low tenor were four years old. It's my understanding that there was a temporary production error at that time that caused this condition. Kawai has been very proactive in replacing the strings of any affected pianos.)

Other than the observation that the pianos were not tuned enough at the factory, the upright models were very well liked and no significant problems were found. Most of the pianos inspected were not of the current models, the models having changed last year, but Kawai's track record on its larger verticals has been very good over the years, so it's reasonable to assume the new models will be well received.

My impression is that as far as the consoles and the less expensive studios go, the technicians in this survey consider Kawai pianos to be a close second—but definitely a second—to Yamahas, with which they are frequently compared. Kawai pianos seem to have a few more fussy little things to take care of when new, and the problems tend to be less predictable. Yamaha pianos are just a little better thought out for servicing and a bit more uniformly made. It's true that Yamaha verticals are more likely to be unpleasantly bright sounding than Kawai verticals, but the scaling of Yamahas is more even and there are fewer tonal trouble spots. Both could use more tuning at the factory. Although the evidence is not conclusive, it seems possible that the tuning on new Yamaha verticals may stabilize a little sooner than on Kawais, but Yamaha tuning and regulation may be affected a bit more by humidity changes later on. (I believe Kawai's ABS plastic action parts contribute to the stability of the action regulation.) In general, Yamaha seems to have been more successful than Kawai at reducing the price of its consoles and studios without sacrificing quality too much. At the upright level, though, and probably with the UST-7 studio, too, the Kawai product is similar to the Yamaha in quality and, in fact, is preferred by some. Kawai's UST-7 studio appears to be more substantially built than the Yamaha studio models.

(Note: Many other Kawai vertical piano models have come and gone over the last fifteen years. I suggest you consult past editions of this book, available at libraries, for reviews or mentions of these models.)

[True to its reputation, as this book goes to press, Kawai has just announced yet another change to its console piano line. The models 504, 505, 605, and 902 will be phased out. The new consoles will be a 44" model 506S in a studio-style cabinet and a 44" model 606 in two levels of furniture-style cabinets, both based on the scale of the current model 605. A 46" model 906, based on the revised UST-8 studio, will replace the model 902. The model CX-5H will continue to be produced.]

Grands: Kawai consolidated its grand piano lines about four years ago, replacing the old KG series, the somewhat newer GS series, and the R (Artisan Select) series with the RX line. In doing this, Kawai engineers designed completely new instruments, according to the company. Also known as the "Artist Series," this RX series of six models ranging from 5'5" to 7'6" is accompanied by the entry-level "Performance Series" (GM and GE models).

Finally, a special execution of the five largest RX pianos, the Shigeru Kawai line, represents Kawai's ultimate effort in producing world-class mid-sized grands. Named after Kawai's chairman (and son of company founder Koichi Kawai), the limited edition Shigeru Kawai grands are made at the separate facility where Kawai's EX concert grands are made, and have upgraded hammers and soundboards. Each buyer of a Shigeru Kawai piano will receive a visit within the first year by a Kawai master technician from Japan, who will perform concert-level voicing and regulating of the piano. Speaking of the EX concert grand, it has been getting great press, having been chosen by top prize winners at a number of prestigious piano competitions.

Kawai's "Performance Series," consisting of the entry-level models GM-2 (5') and GE-1A (5'1"), is somewhat of a misnomer. Unlike the RX series, this entry-level series is designed more for efficiency in manufacturing than for performance. The RX pianos have better structural joinery and a tone collector coupling the beams with the plate, and their soundboards are tapered to improve tonal response. RX pianos also have lighter hammers made of lower-density felt (read: mellower sound). RX keys are made of spruce instead of basswood, but otherwise the actions are the same in all Kawai grands. Other features found in the RX line are duplex scaling and NEOTEX™ white and black keytops, although some of the GE-1A models have these, too. (A GE-1AS model has duplex scaling, a slow-close fallboard, and NEOTEX™ keytops.) Finally, the RX grands receive more tuning and regulating in the factory, and have nicer-looking, better-quality cabinets than the lower-priced models, which have lids made of MDF.

The difference between the GM and GE pianos is primarily in cabinetry. The GM pianos have bottom-of-the-line cabinet features, such as a non-movable music desk. The original GM-1 had a music desk that was screwed down; the GM-2 is a revised version in which the music desk is simply held in place with plastic fasteners and can be easily removed. In other features, the GM model uses a capo bar throughout the piano to save on cost, whereas the GE model has agraffes.

The quality control on Kawai grands is even better than on the verticals. In the service database, less than twenty percent of the 215 Kawai grands sold required post-sale service other than tuning. Most of the service provided consisted of voicing, minor action and pedal adjustments, and tracking down the occasional stray buzzing sound or squeak. In addition, fifty-six Kawai grands were examined by the survey technicians. As with the verticals, some technicians felt the grands were not receiving enough tuning at the factory. As a result, some of the newer pianos took a while to stabilize. Once the pianos had been tuned a few times, though, they were generally very stable. There were some complaints that the small, entry-level pianos were somewhat difficult to tune because of scaling problems and false beats, and that their tone was too bright because of overly hard hammers. Even these problems, however, were noted in a relatively small number of the instruments surveyed. Other problems occurred so rarely as to be insignificant. Comments about the tone and action of the RX pianos, especially the larger ones, were usually very positive.

As with the verticals, Kawai grands are often compared with Yamaha grands. While the majority of technicians, when pressed to express a preference between the two brands, chose Yamaha, most felt it was an extremely close call, and some admitted it was because of Yamaha's slightly better quality control and ease of servicing, rather than the pianos' musical qualities. One technician called Yamaha grands "the classic technician's dream." Another explained, "The Yamaha has an edge on being more trouble-free. Some Kawais have had little squeaks and voicing issues that had to be dealt with before the customer was satisfied. Kawais are 'less friendly' unless they've had attention."

Musically, most technicians seem to consider Kawai's entry-level grands to be more successful than Yamaha's. Despite their shortcomings, the GM and GE models were said to be pretty good for an entry-level instrument, and they even come with a sostenuto pedal, whereas the comparable Yamaha models GP1 and GH1 had more severe tonal and scaling problems reported and have fewer "features" (see the Yamaha review for more information). As for the regular grands, however, it's really just a matter of musical taste. Some prefer the bright, clear tone and lighter, smoother action of the Yamaha C series pianos. Others find the action too light and the tone too bright and one-dimensional, especially for classical music, and go for the Kawai. Said one technician, "I like the Kawai hammers better than Yamaha—more range, color, easier voicing, more tonal possibilities." The Kawai is also said to have a slightly firmer action, which some pianists, particularly the more advanced, may prefer.

One technician with long and extensive experience with both brands gave his perspective on the subject: ". . . Kawais are engineered more intelligently at this point, and they've made more of an effort to push the envelope. About thirty to forty percent of Yamaha grand sales in this area are Disklaviers, and Yamaha seems to be concentrating their R&D work on Disklaviers. I used to recommend Yamaha over Kawai because Kawai always seemed to be waiting to copy what Yamaha was doing. In the late '80s and early '90s, something started to change. Kawai built some really high-end instruments and started exploring some innovative engineering and construction features. With the introduction of the RX line, I think Kawai became a better piano than Yamaha, especially in terms of sound. Yamaha and Kawai are both wonderful instruments, so it's a subtle distinction, dependent on taste and repertoire. But I give Kawai an edge now in the grand pianos. In verticals, I often prefer the Yamahas, but it depends on the model."

The Shigeru Kawai line of top-level grands was too new to appear in the survey for this edition, but I played several of them at the trade show at which they were introduced and thought they were some of the best-sounding pianos yet to come from Japan.

Kawai uses a high grade of ABS plastic and related artificial materials in the fabrication of some of its action parts in both grands and verticals. This practice is often the subject of criticism by competing dealers. You should know that this criticism is unjustified and its object is simply to place doubt in your mind about Kawai pianos. Kawai's plastic parts work beautifully and are very durable, and have been shown in scientific tests to be stronger than analogous wooden parts; there is nothing wrong with them.

Kawai has a combination acoustic/digital piano called the "AnyTime" piano. Currently available in a CX-5H vertical (designated AT-105) and in the RX-2 grand (RX-2AT), it operates as a regular acoustic piano in every way, but turns into a digital piano when a lever located beneath the keybed is moved. See the section on electronic player pianos and hybrid acoustic/digital pianos, page 160, for more information on this type of instrument.

In the past, Kawai has sold pianos in the U.S. under the names Diapason and Schiedmayer. The Diapason is a line of pianos Kawai has sold in Japan for many years. Its scale design is said to be a little "warmer" than that of the Kawai. Schiedmayer is a German company, owned by Ibach, that makes celestes and pianos. Ibach licensed Kawai to produce and market pianos of Ibach design under the Schiedmayer label. Both the Diapason and Schiedmayer product lines have been discontinued in the U.S.

Kawai also makes pianos under the Boston label that were designed by Steinway and are sold by Steinway dealers. See "Boston" for more information.

Warranty: Kawai has a ten-year full warranty on all its pianos. The warranty is transferable to future owners within the warranty period. Kawai's service department is very competent and helpful, and considered to be among the best in the industry.

Price range: (consoles) $4,300–5,400; (studios) $5,600–6,700; (uprights) $6,400–12,600; (GM, GE grands) $11,900–14,000; (RX grands) $18,600–39,800; (Shigeru Kawai grands) approx. $35,000–75,000

Verticals	Grands
43" furniture-style console (504/505/605)	5' (GM-2A)
	5'1" (GE-1A)
45" studio-style console (CX-5H)	5'5" (RX-1)
46" studio (UST-7, UST-8)	5'10" (RX-2)
46" furniture-style studio (902)	6'1" (RX-3)
48" upright (K30)	6'6" (RX-5)
49" upright (K50)	7' (RX-6)
52" upright (K60, K80)	7'6" (RX-7)
	9'1" (GS-100/EX)

Consumer Ratings:

Verticals

Performance
  CX-5H: * * *
  All other verticals: * * * *

For explanation of survey and review procedures, model listings, and price ranges, please see pages 76–81.

Confidence
   CX-5H: * * *
   All other verticals: * * * *
Quality Control
   Consoles and Studios: * * * *
   Uprights: * * * * ¹/₂
Warranty: * * * * *
Information
   Consoles and Studios: * * * *
   Uprights: * * * ¹/₂

Grands

Performance
   GM, GE series: * * * ¹/₂
   RX series: * * * *
   Shigeru Kawai: * * * * ¹/₂
Confidence
   GM, GE series: * * * ¹/₂
   RX series: * * * *
   Shigeru Kawai: * * * * ¹/₂
Quality Control
   GM, GE series: * * * *
   RX series: * * * * ¹/₂
   Shigeru Kawai: * * * * *
Warranty: * * * * *
Information
   GM, GE, RX: * * * *
   Shigeru Kawai: * *

KEMBLE

Kemble & Company Ltd.
251 Memorial Road
Lititz, Pennsylvania 17543
(888) 3-KEMBLE
www.uk-piano.org/kemble/

Pianos made by: Kemble & Company Ltd., Bletchley, Milton Keynes, England

The Kemble family has been manufacturing pianos since 1911. In 1985, Kemble started making pianos for Yamaha for the European market, and in 1988 Yamaha bought a majority interest in the company and expanded and modernized the factory. Kemble is both England's and Western Europe's largest piano manufacturer, accounting for ninety percent of British piano production. Kemble pianos are sold primarily in Europe and the Far East; distribution in the U.S. started in 1994. Dealers can usually be found in the major metropolitan areas.

Kemble makes verticals only, in 43", 45", 48", and 52" sizes. The pianos contain spruce backposts, a Delignit pinblock, a solid spruce soundboard, a Japanese action, and spruce keys. The cabinets are a mixture of veneer-core plywood (where strength is needed) and laminate-covered fiberboard. The quality of the materials used in the Kemble is comparable to that in the Yamaha pianos Kemble makes, except that the soundboard of the Kemble is of German spruce, which gives it more of a "European" tone, the company says, and the cabinets tend to be fancier than Yamaha's. In addi-

tion to the polyester and open-pore finishes, Kemble has recently developed a beautiful satin lustre finish it uses on the mahogany version of its 48" upright. The 52" upright, new in 2000, is designed by noted furniture designer Terence Conran and features a slow open/close fallboard and sostenuto. Kemble pianos are positioned in price somewhere between the Yamaha and the Schimmel.

Warranty: Ten years, parts and labor, from the manufacturer.

Price range: $6,500–13,400

Verticals
   43" console (Cambridge 10/Oxford)
   45" studio (Cambridge 15/Traditional/Empire/Prestige)
   48" upright (K121Z)
   52" upright (K131Q)

Consumer Ratings:

Performance: * * * * ¹/₂
Confidence: * * * *
Quality Control: * * * * ¹/₂
Warranty: * * * *
Information: * * ¹/₂

KIMBALL

Kimball Piano Group
8331 W. State Road #56
West Baden Springs, Indiana 47469
(812) 936-4522
(888) 936-2516
rweisen@kimball.com

No longer making pianos

Names used: Kimball, Conn, Jasper-American, W.W. Kimball, Hinze, Harrison, Schuerman, DeVoe & Sons, Whittaker, Becker, La Petite, Krakauer, Whitney, possibly others; private-label brands also made.

Kimball Piano & Organ Co. was founded in 1857 under the name W.W. Kimball & Co. when Kimball, a poor Maine farmboy who had set up a business selling real estate and insurance in Iowa, moved to Chicago and opened up a piano store, convinced that there was money to be made supplying goods to "Western" pioneers. He soon became one of the largest merchants of keyboard instruments in the country. The 1880s saw a critical shortage of merchandise for Midwestern merchants, so in 1886 Kimball began to manufacture his own pianos, becoming a leading manufacturer within a short time. Kimball's company reached its peak in the early 1900s, but a combination of changing comsumer desires, the Depression, and poor managerial decisions on the part of Kimball's heirs and successors caused the company's decline toward insolvency. It was finally sold to the Jasper Corporation, an Indiana plywood and cabinet manufacturer, in 1959, and piano production was moved to Indiana.

During the next two decades, Jasper, now called Kimball International, purchased the renowned Austrian piano manufacturer Bösendorfer in 1966 (see "Bösendorfer"); the highly respected U.S. piano maker Krakauer in 1980 (see

"Krakauer"); supplier companies such as the English maker of the Schwander and Langer actions, Herrburger Brooks; and timber lands, lumber mills, and firms in other industries necessary to its operations. Kimball International is now a Fortune 500 company with involvements in furniture making, contract cabinetry, electronic subassembly, and plastics.

Throughout the 1960s, '70s, and early '80s, Kimball produced mostly low-priced pianos. Details about pianos from this period can be found in earlier editions of this book. Although these pianos may have filled a valid need in the market of their day, I would suggest not purchasing a used Kimball from this period, especially the spinet and the tiny 4'5" La Petite grand. Beginning in the mid-1980s, Kimball upgraded its factory equipment and operations in response to changing consumer desires in the piano market and consequently, the workmanship of Kimball pianos improved considerably. A used piano from this period could be an acceptable choice for a beginner on a limited budget.

In 1995, citing a depressed market for pianos in general and for low-priced furniture-style pianos in particular, Kimball decided to stop building pianos. First it stopped making grands, and for a year or so Kimball verticals were largely built by Baldwin, with only cabinets and final assembly by Kimball. In 1996, Kimball stopped all production of vertical pianos, too. Kimball will continue to honor its warranties, and continues to make piano cabinets for other makers, such as Kawai. The company sold most of its piano-making equipment to a Chinese piano manufacturer. It also sold its Herrburger Brooks division to a Chinese firm, but Herrburger Brooks is now back in British hands operating under the name Langer. The Bösendorfer division in Austria is still owned by Kimball International; it has been unaffected by these changes.

KINGSBURG

Poppenberg & Associates
966 South Pearl Street
Denver, Colorado 80209

(303) 765-5775
www.kingsburgpianos.com

Pianos made by: Yantai Longfeng Piano Co., Ltd., Yantai, China

Yantai Longfeng is a relatively small company established in 1991, and is outfitted with automated production equipment from Japan and Germany. Scales for the pianos were developed by German scale designer Klaus Fenner. Some of the piano components come from Japan and Germany. Among other things, the pianos feature Delignit pinblocks and solid spruce soundboards.

As mentioned elsewhere in this book, Chinese pianos are very inconsistent in quality and usually only marginally acceptable at the time of this writing. However, the Yantai Longfeng vertical pianos I've inspected seemed somewhat better made than many of the other Chinese pianos I've seen. No long-term information is yet available.

Pianos from Yantai Longfeng were previously marketed in the U.S. by a different distributor under the name Steigerman.

For explanation of survey and review procedures, model listings, and price ranges, please see pages 76–81.

Warranty: Ten years, parts and labor, to original owner
Price range: (Verticals) $3,900–5,100; (Grands) $14,000–16,500

Verticals	Grands
43" console (109)	5'2" (F158)
44" console (113)	6'1" (F185)
45" studio (115)	
46" studio (116/117)	
48" upright (122)	

Consumer Ratings:

Performance: * * *
Confidence: * * 1/2
Quality Control: * * *
Warranty: * * 1/2
Information
    Grands: *
    Verticals: * 1/2

KNABE, WM.

PianoDisc
4111-A North Freeway Blvd.
Sacramento, California 95834

(800) 566-3472
(916) 567-9999
www.pianodisc.com

Owned by: PianoDisc, Sacramento, California

Pianos made by: Young Chang Co. Ltd., Inchon, South Korea and Tianjin, China

Names used: Wm. Knabe, Knabe

The "PianoDisc" line of pianos previously offered by this company (not to be confused with the PianoDisc player piano system made by the same company) has been discontinued and replaced by two new lines of piano resurrecting the Knabe name. Knabe is an old American brand name that eventually became part of the Aeolian family of brands and then, following the demise of Aeolian in 1985, the Mason & Hamlin family of brands (see "Mason & Hamlin" and "Aeolian"). Pianos bearing the name "Wm. Knabe," like the discontinued PianoDisc line, are made by Young Chang in Korea. The piano's cabinet design and appearance have been altered, and the hammers have been changed, resulting in different touch characteristics, the company says. Pianos bearing only the name "Knabe" are made in Young Chang's facility in Tianjin, China. (Wm. Knabe model designations begin with KN; Knabe models begin with KB.) The pianos are extensively serviced at PianoDisc's California facility, and the PianoDisc player piano system installed, before being shipped to dealers.

At one time, the pianos could be ordered as regular acoustic pianos without a player piano system, but at the present time they are available only with a PianoDisc system installed. See the section on electronic player piano systems, page 165, for more information.

Warranty: Limited lifetime warranty on action and case parts to original purchaser, 15-year full warranty on everything else.

Price range: (with PDS 128 Plus system installed): (Wm. Knabe Verticals) $10,600–12,400; (Knabe Verticals) $8,900–9,600; (Wm. Knabe Grands) $20,500–29,200; (Knabe Grands) $16,300–16,700

Verticals	Grands
42" console (KN-420/KB-420)	4'11" (KN-500/KB-500)
43" console (KN-43/KB-43)	5'2" (KN-520/KB-520)
48" upright (KN-480/KB-480)	5'9" (KN-590)
	6'1" (KN-610)
	6'10" (KN-700)

"KN" models are from Korea, "KB" models are from China.

Consumer Ratings: See "Young Chang"

KNIGHT

See "Whelpdale Maxwell & Codd"

KOHLER & CAMPBELL

Pianos currently bearing the name Kohler & Campbell are made by Samick. See "Samick" for reviews of these instruments.

Kohler & Campbell, Inc.
Granite Falls, North Carolina

Out of business

Names used: Kohler & Campbell, Kohler, Brambach

Founded in 1896 in New York City as a partnership between Charles Kohler and J.C. Campbell, Kohler & Campbell was for many years a leading piano and player piano manufacturer. The company moved to Granite Falls, North Carolina in 1954, and went out of business in 1985.

Kohler & Campbell made verticals and grands in various sizes. The spinet and the console were actually of identical scale designs, with the console plate simply positioned in its cabinet to accept a console action. Most of the pianos had laminated soundboards. The pianos came in a wide variety of furniture styles and levels of sophistication in cabinetry.

In the survey for the first edition of this book, technicians found that the verticals were mechanically fairly well made and came out of the factory in decent regulation. The big complaint, especially about the spinets and consoles, was that the tone, and the ability of the pianos to be accurately tuned, was very bad, due to deficiencies in the scale design. In addition, technicians found the case parts to be very poorly designed for servicing. Technicians were very consistent and specific in their opinions about these pianos and found the majority of them to be unacceptable. The grands, not included in the written survey, seemed to be very average instruments, with a poor bass tone.

In 1984 Kohler & Campbell changed the name on its pianos, for marketing purposes, to Kohler. The name Brambach was put on its "budget" line of spinets and consoles. The company also made pianos for Universal Player Piano Co., which installed its own player mechanism in them.

KRAKAUER

Including Conn

Krakauer Pianos
22591 Weatherby Lane
Elkhart, Indiana 46514

(219) 262-9952
guill@fullnet.com
www.krakauer.net
www.connpianos.com

Pianos made by: Artfield Piano Ltd., Qing Pu, China

Names used: Krakauer, Conn

Founded in 1869 by Simon Krakauer, this company was controlled by the Krakauer family all the way to 1977. In that year, Howard Graves, a successful engineer who had always dreamed of owning a piano company, bought Krakauer and moved it from New York City to the small Amish town of Berlin, Ohio, where labor was cheaper and of high quality. But the costs of starting a new company, combined with a national economic recession, were too much, and Krakauer was acquired by Kimball in 1980. The manufacturing facilities remained separate from Kimball's and the standards much higher, and Graves was retained as manager. Kimball closed the Krakauer factory in 1985, citing market factors as the reason.

Concerning these older, American-made Krakauers, the old Krakauer upright made in the early part of this century was a highly esteemed instrument. In keeping with the times, the company switched to a mediocre console in its later years. After buying the company in 1977, Howard Graves changed to a different console design. This 41" instrument, made in a variety of furniture styles, was about as handcrafted as a piano can be, with especially meticulous care taken in the cabinetry and finish. Piano technicians tend to be oblivious to the furniture aspects of pianos, but the Krakauer, alone in my first survey, received rave reviews for its finish.

Krakauer made fewer than a thousand pianos a year. They had a variety of minor problems, such as not being tuned and regulated enough at the factory and poor tone in the bass, as consoles often do, but the treble tone was lovely and once the minor problems were fixed and adjustments made, the Krakauer was considered to be quite a good piano. After Krakauer went out of business in 1985, Kimball sometimes used the Krakauer name on its own pianos at the request of a dealer.

When Kimball ceased piano manufacturing in 1996, it sold the Krakauer name and Kimball's piano production equipment to Artfield Piano Ltd., a young Chinese firm. Today, Artfield makes pianos in American furniture-style and European-style cabinets under the names Krakauer and Conn (another name formerly owned by Kimball). Conn is an entry-level piano with a maple pinblock, Chinese hammers, and a three-ply laminated spruce soundboard. Krakauer pianos have better cabinets, a Delignit pinblock, Abel hammers, and a separate tenor bridge. Artfield also makes private-label pianos. Some former and present Kimball executives are assisting Artfield in presenting its pianos to the U.S. market.

At the time of this writing, Chinese pianos in general are of mediocre quality and very inconsistent, but rapidly improving. The Krakauer pianos I examined appeared to be average for a Chinese piano, with nice-looking cabinets. No long-term information is yet available.

Warranty: Ten years, parts and labor, transferable.

Price range: (Krakauer) $3,000–3,600; (Conn) $2,800

Verticals
    43" furniture-style console (K430/C430 series)
    43" continental-style console (K110)
    48" upright (K120)
    48 3/4" upright (K122)
    50" upright (K125)
Krakauer models begin with "K"; Conn models begin with "C".

Consumer Ratings:

Performance: * *
Confidence: * 1/2
Quality Control: * 1/2
Warranty: * * 1/2
Information: * 1/2

KRANICH & BACH

See "Baldwin" and "Aeolian"

LOWREY

See "Story & Clark"

LESAGE

This hundred-year-old Canadian piano maker was bought by the former owner of Sherlock-Manning, another Canadian piano company, in 1986, then closed soon after. A Canadian piano rebuilder by the name of Rosch then built pianos under the name Rosch-Lesage for another year or so, the last ones made in 1988.

LYON & HEALY

Lyon & Healy
Chicago, Illinois

No longer making or distributing pianos in the U.S.

Pianos made by: Rippen, The Netherlands; Daesung, South Korea

Names used: Lyon & Healy, Schubert

The original Lyon & Healy company, established in 1864, is best known for its harps, still the best in their field today. Lyon & Healy also made pianos from 1880 to 1930, as well as other musical instruments. The company eventually became part of the CBS Musical Instrument Divison in the 1970s, was sold in 1985 along with Steinway and others to Steinway Musical Properties, Inc., and then was sold again in 1987 to a

Swiss maker of harps and other musical instruments. From 1989 to 1992, Lyon & Healy distributed vertical pianos made by the Dutch piano maker Rippen with the Lyon & Healy name on them. Rippen pianos are considered medium-quality by European standards. Lyon & Healy also briefly distributed pianos made by the relatively unknown Korean piano maker Daesung under the name Schubert, and the well-known German maker Grotrian (see "Grotrian").

MADDISON

Name no longer in use.

This name is no longer in use. The verticals and 5'2" grand used a strung back and action from the Guangzhou Pearl River factory in Guangzhou, China. The strung back for the 5'6" grand came from the Beijing Piano Co. The piano was assembled in Macao using a Macao-made cabinet.

MAEARI

See "Hyundai"

MARANTZ/PIANOCORDER

Marantz Piano Co., Inc.
Morganton, North Carolina

Out of business

Names used: Marantz, Grand, Kincaid, Jesse French, Pianocorder

Marantz Piano Co. was a division of the same Marantz that makes stereo equipment. In fact, a small portion of the piano factory in Morganton, North Carolina was used for making stereo speakers. Marantz bought this factory from the Grand Piano Co. in the late 1970s. Although Marantz stopped making pianos in 1984, it continued making the Pianocorder Reproducing System for a few more years, until the rights to the Pianocorder were finally sold to Yamaha and the product was discontinued in 1987. (Yamaha introduced its own Disklavier system shortly thereafter.)

The Pianocorder was an electronic player piano mechanism that, by means of a cassette tape, could record or play a "live" performance on any piano in which it was installed. Marantz used to make some of its pianos with the Pianocorder already installed, some without, and separate Pianocorder kits that could be installed in any piano. Although the pianos and the kits have been discontinued, a few technicians and dealers may still have kits to install. More advanced digital player piano systems have supplanted the Pianocorder.

Until 1984, Marantz made a 39" spinet and a 42" console. The names Marantz, Grand, Kincaid, and Jesse French were used on them interchangeably, depending on the preference of the dealer to whom they were being sold. These pianos were quite possibly the worst pianos ever made in the United States. See previous editions of this book for details. The Pianocorder System, however, was reasonably well made. It came in two forms—a kit installed in the piano, operating through a slot cut in the keybed, and a separate unit that

For explanation of survey and review procedures, model listings, and price ranges, please see pages 76–81.

wheeled up to the piano, its eighty-eight rubber plungers positioned over the keys to play the piano. The latter kind was known as a "Vorsetzer." The Pianocorder System was run by cassette tapes with computer signals on them. The system reportedly worked well if properly installed and adjusted in a good piano (these are big "ifs"). The Pianocorder also came with an optional record system that didn't work so well.

MASON & HAMLIN

Mason & Hamlin Piano Co.
4111 North Freeway Blvd.
Sacramento, California 95834

(800) 566-3472
(916) 567-9999
www.masonhamlin.com

Owned by: Burgett Inc., Haverhill, Massachusetts

Pianos made by: Mason & Hamlin Piano Co., Haverhill, Massachusetts and Sacramento, California

Mason & Hamlin was founded in 1854 by Henry Mason and Emmons Hamlin. Mason was a musician and businessman and Hamlin was an inventor working with reed organs. Within a few years, Mason & Hamlin was one of the largest reed organ manufacturers in the country. The company began making pianos in 1881 in Boston, and soon became, along with Chickering, among the most prestigious of the Boston piano makers. By 1910, Mason & Hamlin was considered Steinway's chief competitor.

In 1912, Mason & Hamlin merged with the Cable Piano Co. The operations continued as before, but with an infusion of capital. In 1922, Cable sold Mason & Hamlin to the giant American Piano Co., which had earlier bought up Chickering & Sons and Wm. Knabe & Co., among others. With the rise of the radio and phonograph as the dominant forms of entertainment in the late 1920s, and then the Depression, the piano market declined. American ran into financial trouble and sold Mason & Hamlin to Aeolian in 1930. Aeolian also had troubles and merged with American in 1932 to form the Aeolian-American Corp. Aeolian-American closed the Mason & Hamlin, Chickering, and Knabe factories and consolidated them all into one factory in East Rochester, New York.

In 1959, Winter & Co. acquired Aeolian-American, changing its name in 1964 to Aeolian Corp. and in 1981 to Aeolian Pianos, Inc. (See "Aeolian" for details of this company's history.) In 1982, citing financial difficulties, Aeolian decided to shut down the operations in East Rochester. In 1983 Aeolian was sold to Peter Perez, a former president of Steinway & Sons, who reopened the factory with a promise to modernize equipment and upgrade quality. Unfortunately, this promise was never realized to any great extent, and the company went out of business in 1985.

Until 1932, Mason & Hamlin was considered one of America's pre-eminent pianos. After 1932, its reputation declined somewhat, but it was still considered a good, solid piano until the early 1960s, when Winter (and then Aeolian) allowed the quality to deteriorate, emphasizing instead the production of its cheaper pianos.

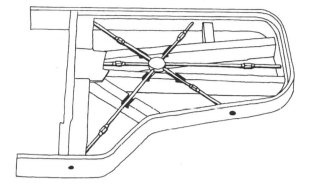

FIGURE 4-4. The Mason & Hamlin *tension resonator* is a series of turnbuckles connecting parts of the inner rim. In theory, this prevents the rim from expanding with age and therefore preserves the crown of the soundboard.

When Aeolian Pianos went out of business in 1985, the Mason & Hamlin, Knabe, and George Steck brand names and scale designs were sold to Sohmer, by then owned by Pratt, Read and operating in Ivoryton, Connecticut (see "Sohmer"). Pratt, Read left the piano business shortly thereafter, selling Sohmer to an investor. Sohmer tried to revive Mason & Hamlin, but due to a lack of skilled labor and other problems, very few Mason & Hamlin pianos were built in Ivoryton. In 1988, Sohmer moved its manufacturing facilities to Elysburg, Pennsylvania in a final attempt to continue manufacturing.

In 1989 Sohmer and the Mason & Hamlin, Knabe, and George Steck names and scales were sold to Seattle businessman and philanthropist Bernard Greer, who had just purchased the Falcone Piano Co. (see "Falcone") in Haverhill, Massachusetts. The name of the combined concern was changed to The Mason & Hamlin Companies. Under the new management, the Haverhill factory was reorganized for greater efficiency, and investments were made in new machinery, climate control, and conditioning rooms for wooden parts.

From 1989 to 1994, the 50" Mason & Hamlin upright, for many years the only tall upright being produced in the United States, was made in the Elysburg plant, along with Sohmer verticals. Also during that time period, two sizes of Mason & Hamlin grand, the model A (5'8") and the model BB (7') were made at the Haverhill factory, along with Falcone pianos. The pianos made during this time were of excellent quality, as the company did not just exploit the names, as is so common, but used the original scale designs, tooling, and patterns, as well as excellent materials and workmanship. Computer-aided design techniques were used to assure exact duplication of the original designs. In 1994, the company closed the Elysburg plant and consolidated all piano production in Haverhill.

Although the pianos were of excellent quality, apparently marketing efforts fell short of expectations. The company ran into financial difficulty and ceased production in mid-1994, and in 1995 filed for Chapter 7 (liquidation) bankruptcy. A Boston-based piano rebuilding firm, Premier Pianos, obtained the controlling interest in the company from its former owner and persuaded the Bankruptcy Court to change the bankruptcy filing to Chapter 11 (reorganization). From early 1995 to early 1996, the new owners completed the manufacture of pianos left unfinished when the plant closed, made some new pianos from scratch, and attempted to fight off legal attempts by creditors to force liquidation of the company or its sale to another party. (Many creditors did not have faith in the new owners' ability to put the company back on its feet.) In April 1996, the Court sided with the creditors and approved the sale of Mason & Hamlin to Kirk and Gary Burgett, owners of PianoDisc, makers of electronic player piano systems. The Mason & Hamlin assets also included the Falcone, Sohmer, Knabe, and George Steck brand names and designs (see under each of those names for their current use or status). (For those who have a need to know, the serial numbers of the Mason & Hamlin pianos built or completed by the interim [Premier] ownership were from 90590 to 90613, inclusive.)

For several years now, the Burgett brothers have been manufacturing Mason & Hamlin pianos once again at the Haverhill, Massachusetts factory, with the design plans used during the company's Boston era (1881-1932). The model A and BB grands are being made, as well as parts for the 50" upright. The upright parts are assembled into an imported cabinet at the PianoDisc factory in Sacramento, California. Some of the Mason & Hamlins are being sold with PianoDisc units installed.

Mason & Hamlin grands have maple rims bent on rim presses dating back to the 1800s; solid spruce soundboards; five-ply, quarter-sawn maple pinblocks; and Mason & Hamlin-designed actions using action parts and hammers made by Renner. The 50" uprights also have Renner actions. A model CC (9') concert grand is scheduled for production in the near future. Currently about 250 grand pianos are produced each year.

The grands are available in both ebony and mahogany, and in satin and polished finishes. All satin finishes are now being done in lacquer. These models are also available in a new stylized case design called Monticello, which has fluted, conical legs, similar to a Hepplewhite style, with matching lyre and bench.

Mason & Hamlin grands have a unique construction feature called a *tension resonator*, invented by Richard Gertz in 1900, which consists of a series of turnbuckles that connect various parts of the inner rim (Figure 4-4). In theory this web of turnbuckles, nicknamed "the spider," locks the rim in place so that it cannot expand with stress and age, thereby preserving the crown of the soundboard. (The soundboard is glued to the inner rim and would collapse if the rim expanded.) There is no modern-day experimental evidence to confirm or deny this theory, but many technicians believe in its validity nevertheless because unlike most older pianos, the soundboards of old Mason & Hamlins almost always have plenty of crown.

Eight Mason & Hamlin grands appeared in the written survey and several technicians were intimately familiar with them. Mason & Hamlins, like most brands, arrive at the dealer needing tuning and thorough, but normal, regulating. Voicing, in particular, is not yet at a high professional level at the factory, and the factory voicing is inconsistent and usu-

ally needs attention for the pianos to sound good. Some report no difficulty voicing the Renner hammers, but others, equally qualified, have been dissatisfied with the results, or have resorted to unusual voicing techniques to obtain good results. A possible reason, according to my most knowledgeable sources, is that a softer hammer may work better with this particular piano design. [Mason & Hamlin says it has recently provided its factory voicers with additional training on how to properly prep and voice the Renner hammers to achieve the "Mason & Hamlin sound."]

Soundboard, bridge work, and stringing at the factory are excellent. Cabinet work and finishing are competent, but as one technician said, "It's not Bechstein-quality finish work." Additional hand rubbing by the dealer's finish expert can do wonders for the appearance. [Mason & Hamlin says that pianos shipped since January 2000 have not needed additional hand rubbing.] The touch at the keyboard, made by Kluge, can be improved by lubricating the key bushings to reduce friction, normally done as part of the preparation of the piano by the dealer. Some technicians said that spring tension at the sustain pedal is quite strong and that the feel of the pedal may be improved by removing the spring entirely. [Mason & Hamlin says it uses the same trapwork design as Steinway and that in their experience customers are satisfied with it.]

Overall, technicians are impressed with the pianos and feel they have great potential: "I think they're moving in the right direction. I'm impressed with their commitment to taking the piano back to what it was. The newer ones (last one to two years) have been great pianos. There are many small things that need attention, but it's little stuff. With a little regulation, voicing, and string fitting, they sound great. Wonderful tonal palette." "Can be in serious competition with any of the other big names." The 7' model BB has the potential for a very full, even powerful, sound. The 5'8" model A is generally considered a warm, but less powerful, instrument.

Warranty: Lifetime on the case and action parts, twelve years on the soundboard.

Price range: (Vertical) $16,000; (Grands) $43,200–53,800.

Vertical	Grands
50" upright (50)	5'8" (A)
	7' (BB)

Consumer Ratings:

Performance: * * * * *
Confidence: * * * * *
Quality Control: * * * *
Warranty: * * * *
Information
   Grands: * * *
   Verticals: * *

For explanation of survey and review procedures, model listings, and price ranges, please see pages 76–81.

MECKLENBURG

See "Hofmann & Scholz"

MUZELLE

Resource West, Inc.
2295 E. Sahara Avenue
Las Vegas, Nevada 89104

(702) 457-7919
(800) 777-6874
info@resourcewest.com
www.resourcewest.com
www.muzelle.com

Pianos made by: Daesung Pianos, Inchon, Korea; Guangzhou Pearl River Piano Group, Guangzhou, China

The Muzelle name is put on regular pianos, traditional player pianos, and nickelodeons. The verticals are made by Daesung, a smaller Korean piano maker. The importer orders the pianos with Delignit pinblocks and German wire, among other superior technical features, and says it has its own quality control personnel at the factory to inspect the pianos before shipment. Plans are underway to introduce a line of grands made by Guangzhou in China. Resource West manufactures and installs the player mechanisms. It also rebuilds older pianos and turns them into player pianos with customized cabinets.

Warranty: Five years, parts and labor; second five years, parts only. Warranty is transferable.

Price range: (Verticals) $2,600–5,400; (Grands) $8,000–16,000

Consumer Ratings: See "Pearl River" for Guangzhou models. Insufficient information to rate Daesung models.

NAKAMICHI/NAKAMURA

Syckes Piano Imports
129 E. Hartford Ave.
Phoenix, Arizona 85022

(800) 942-5801

No longer being made

This was a hybrid Korean/Japanese piano. The entire piano was actually made in Korea by Young Chang, and was identical to the Young Chang piano. It was then sent to a private Japanese piano shop in Hamamatsu dedicated to this brand, where Abel hammers from Germany were installed, the piano regulated and voiced, and small modifications made in stringing and touchweight, among other changes. The object was to combine the low prices of Korean pianos with the greater attention to detail of Japanese pianos. For all this fussing, the customer paid only five to ten percent more than for the equivalent Young Chang piano, according to the company.

Due to a trademark conflict with the Nakamichi company that sells audio equipment, the name was later changed to "Nakamura." However, distribution was discontinued in 1998.

NIEMEYER

North American Music
126 Route 303
West Nyack, New York 10994

(845) 353-3520
(800) 541-2331
www.namusic.com

Pianos made by: Dongbei Piano Co., Dongbei, China

These pianos are made in China by the Dongbei Piano Co. According to Dongbei, the Niemeyer brand name is put on pianos from the "Prince" and "Princess" piano lines, which are Dongbei's lower-priced pianos.

As mentioned elsewhere, Chinese pianos are generally mediocre and inconsistent in quality at this point, but improving rapidly. No further information is available specifically about this brand name, but other brand names made by this company are Everett, Nordiska, and Sagenhaft.

Warranty: Ten years, parts only, transferable.

Price range: $2,700–3,100

Verticals
44" console (NI112)
45" studio (NI114)
48" upright (NI121)

Consumer Ratings:

Performance: * *
Confidence: * 1/2
Quality Control: * 1/2
Warranty: * 1/2
Information: *

NIENDORF

German American Trading Co., Inc.
P.O. Box 17789
Tampa, Florida 33682

(813) 961-8405
germanamer@aol.com

Pianos made by: Niendorf Regina Rotsch Flügel-und-Klavierbaufabrik, Luckenwalde, Germany

This hundred-year-old firm closed for a few years following the unification of Germany in the early 1990s, then reopened when management bought the company from the government. The company makes only grands in two sizes, 4'9" and 6'. The 4'9" grand is similar to the one that was made under the name Zimmermann in the 1980s (see "Zimmermann"). Niendorf grands have Renner actions and Renner hammers.

Warranty: Ten years, parts and labor, to original purchaser

Price range: (Grands) $19,400–22,600

Grands
    4'9" (145)
    6' (182)

Consumer Ratings: Insufficient information to rate

NORDISKA

Geneva International Corporation
29 East Hintz Road
Wheeling, Illinois 60090

(800) 533-2388
(847) 520-9970
geneva-intl@msn.com

Pianos made by: Dongbei Piano Co., Dongbei, China

Nordiska was a one-hundred-year-old Swedish piano manufacturer that, upon going out of business in 1988, sold all its designs, equipment, and technology to the Chinese company Dongbei. The Swedish-designed model, the model 116 studio, appeared to be strikingly more advanced than the other models Dongbei manufactured at that time. Beginning in 1998, this model and others by Dongbei are sold in the U.S. under the Nordiska name by Geneva International Corp., the distributor of Petrof pianos from the Czech Republic.

The Dongbei Piano Co. has two factories. An older factory manufactures Dongbei's original piano lines, known as "Prince" and "Princess." A newer factory, known by Dongbei as the "Nordiska" factory, manufactures vertical pianos to higher standards than the Prince and Princess lines, and also manufactures Dongbei grand pianos. Dongbei's most experienced workers are assigned to this factory. An on-going technical association with the German company Ibach has resulted in new computer-controlled production machinery, tooling, and designs. Although Dongbei calls this the Nordiska factory, actually the pianos can be manufactured under different names for different distributors. What remains constant is the higher standards to which the pianos are made. The Nordiska-brand pianos feature solid spruce soundboards, hard rock maple pinblocks, wet sand-cast full perimeter plates, and on the grands, Abel hammers.

Geneva (the importer) says it has the exclusive right to sell in the United States the pianos made in the Nordiska factory, as well as the exclusive right to use the Nordiska brand name in the United States. A letter I received from Dongbei confirms this agreement. However, several other U.S. distributors have told me that they can purchase pianos made in this factory, to the same specifications but under different brand names, at any time they wish, and in fact have done so. This apparent conflict need not concern the prospective purchaser; I mention it only to explain why there may be competing claims on this subject in the marketplace. (This also demonstrates some of the problems doing business with China.)

Although no Nordiska pianos showed up in the written survey, interviews indicate that like other Chinese pianos, until recently Nordiska and other Dongbei pianos have been rather mediocre in quality compared to the standards to which we are accustomed. Also, like other Chinese pianos,

they are rapidly improving. One brand-new Nordiska grand I played just prior to writing this appeared to be relatively free of problems and quite playable. However, no U.S. long-term information is yet available about them, so I would use caution, especially with grand pianos, which are more complicated to manufacture than verticals, or in areas with a dry indoor climate.

Warranty: Ten years, parts and labor, to the original purchaser.

Price range: (Verticals) $2,800–3,800; (Grands) $7,600–10,000

Verticals	Grands
44" console (112)	5' (152)
46"/47" studio (116/118)	5'5" (165)
48" upright (120/122)	6'1" (185)

Consumer Ratings:

Performance: * *
Confidence: * *
Quality Control: * *
Warranty: * * 1/2
Information: * 1/2

PEARL RIVER

Pearl River Piano Group America Ltd.
1216 S. Stoneman Ave.
Alhambra, California 91801

(626) 457-6398
prpg@msn.com
www.pearlriverpiano.com

Pianos made by: Guangzhou Pearl River Piano Group Ltd., Guangzhou, China

Names used: Pearl River, Ritmüller. This factory also makes pianos under the names George Steck, Hallet & Davis, Ridgewood, Sängler & Söhne, Wieler, and possibly other names, sold by other distributors.

Originally established in 1954 through the consolidation of several piano-making facilities, the Guangzhou Pearl River piano factory is now China's largest piano manufacturer and one of the largest in the world, with production of over 100,000 pianos annually by 4,500 workers. This is a return of the Pearl River name, which was present in the U.S. market several years ago, but discontinued because the quality at that time was not good enough to allow the brand to survive in the marketplace. With the influx of investment by the Chinese government and foreign businesses, the quality has greatly improved and continues to improve rapidly. Although Chinese pianos in general have been quite mediocre and often unacceptable, the Pearl River pianos seem to be a step ahead of the other Chinese brands in their evolution.

Guangzhou makes both verticals and grands under the Pearl River name, as well as making pianos under other names for other distributors (see list above). Note that the 49" model UP-125 M1 is a joint venture between Yamaha and Guangzhou. The parts are made by Guangzhou and assem-

For explanation of survey and review procedures, model listings, and price ranges, please see pages 76–81.

bled by Yamaha in a nearby factory. This model is distributed and warranted by Guangzhou, not Yamaha. Pearl River grands use a Czech Detoa-brand action, a wet sand-cast plate, and a veneer-laminated soundboard, among other features. Guangzhou also makes pianos under the name Ritmüller, which use the same strung back as the Pearl River, but have upgraded cabinets and finishes. The Ritmüller grands also have Renner actions and receive special preparation in a climate-controlled room, the company says.

Only four Pearl River pianos—two 47" verticals and two 5'3" grands—appeared in the written survey for this edition, all brand new at the dealer. One of the verticals had many loose tuning pins, the other was problem-free. One of the grands needed a great deal of action regulating, the other was nicely prepared at the factory and the tone was said to be even, but of poor quality. The technician who serviced these pianos and has had much experience with the Pearl River brand said that the company has improved its product markedly, obviously responding to feedback from the field. As recently as a year ago, action regulation and the alignment of action parts was poor. More recent pianos have been "pretty clean," with few or no recurring problems, just random things to take care of. The most marked improvement has been in the grands, but the verticals are better, too. Obviously, this is a small sample, and there is no really long-term information on how these pianos will behave in the various climates of the U.S., but based on current information, this is probably the most promising of the Chinese brands.

Warranty: Ten years, parts and labor, transferable.

Price range: (Pearl River Verticals) $2,600–4,900; (Pearl River Grands) $7,900–17,500; (Ritmüller Verticals) $3,000–5,300; (Ritmüller Grands) $8,400–14,000

Verticals	Grands
42¹/₂" console (UP108)	4'7" (GP142)
43" console (UP110)	5'3" (GP159)
47" upright (UP118)	6' (GP183)
48" upright (UP120)	7' (GP213)
49" upright (joint venture with Yamaha) (UP125M1)	9' (GP275)
51" upright (UP130)	

Ritmüller models have an "R" after the model number.

Consumer Ratings:

Performance
    Pearl River: * *
    Ritmüller verticals: * *
    Ritmüller grands: * * ¹/₂
Confidence
    Pearl River: * *
    Ritmüller verticals: * *
    Ritmüller grands: * * ¹/₂
Quality Control
    Pearl River: * *
    Ritmüller verticals: * *
    Ritmüller grands: * * ¹/₂
Warranty: * * *

Information
    Pearl River: * *
    Ritmüller: *

PETROF
Including Weinbach

Geneva International Corporation
29 East Hintz Road
Wheeling, Illinois 60090

(800) 533-2388
(847) 520-9970
geneva-intl@msn.com

Pianos made by: Petrof Pianos, Hradec Kralove, Czech Republic

Names used: Petrof, Weinbach. Used briefly in U.S.: Rösler. Used in Canada: August Förster (see important note at end of review).

The Petrof piano factory was founded in 1864 by Antonin Petrof in Hradec Kralove, an industrial town located 100 kilometers east of Prague in Czechoslovakia (now the Czech Republic). Three generations of the Petrof family owned and managed the business, during which time the company kept pace with technical developments and earned prizes for their pianos at international exhibitions. The Czech Republic has long been known for its vibrant musical instrument industry, which also includes makers of brass, woodwind, and stringed instruments.

In 1965, Petrof, along with other piano manufacturers, was forced to join Musicexport, the state-controlled import-export company for musical instruments. Over the last five years, the various factories that were part of this company have been spun off as private businesses, including Petrof, which is once again owned and controlled by the Petrof family. Currently Petrof manufactures 10,000 vertical pianos and 1,500 grands annually. Although the company controls a variety of piano names, only pianos made under the Petrof and Weinbach names are currently being exported to the United States. These two brands are identical in quality, but the Weinbach line is more limited in the variety of sizes, styles, and finishes available, and there may be some differences between the two brands in the cosmetic appearance of the cast-iron plate.

Petrof manufactures five sizes of grand piano—5'3", 5'8", 6'4", 7'9", and 9'3" (Weinbach only to 6'4")—and four sizes of vertical—42", 45", 50", and 52" (Weinbach only 45" and 50"). The majority of components are produced in Petrof or other Czech factories, including hardware, plates, and cabinetry. However, action parts for many models are now from Renner in Germany and mounted by Petrof on Petrof-made action frames (known as "Petrof/Renner actions"). The 7'9" and 9'3" grands have full Renner actions assembled in Germany, as does a special version of the 6'4" grand, model III-M, which is made in the same factory as the two larger models and shares some of their refinements. All other Petrof and Weinbach grands have the Petrof/Renner action. The Petrof 52" upright, not available under the Weinbach label, has a full Renner action and Renner hammers. All

Petrof and Weinbach 50″ uprights have Petrof/Renner actions with Renner hammers. The 42″ and 45″ verticals still use a Czech-made Detoa action, although the 45″ model is available with a Petrof/Renner action for about four hundred dollars additional.

All Petrof and Weinbach pianos use solid Bohemian spruce soundboards, wet sand-cast plates, and grand rims largely of beech. The grands and largest Petrof verticals use seven-ply beech pinblocks, the other verticals use Delignit pinblocks. Keys are of solid spruce, individually weighted. All grands have a sostenuto pedal; verticals have a practice pedal.

Petrofs and Weinbachs are known for their warm, rich, singing tone, full of color. Workmanship is quite good these days, but can vary. However, after careful preparation, the pianos can sound and feel quite beautiful and hold their own against some of the better-known European pianos. Best of all, due to much lower labor costs and no duty, the prices of these pianos are only a fraction of that of many other European instruments and sometimes even less expensive than pianos from Japan. When properly prepared, they are a very good value.

There have been many technical changes and improvements to Petrof pianos during the last few years, so it's worth reviewing some of the criticisms from the previous (third) edition to see what has changed. In the third edition I reported that Petrofs arrived at the dealer in somewhat rough condition, needing a lot of servicing, but sounded very good after preparation. The touch was often too heavy from excess friction, as well as from other causes that were harder to fix. Heavy action is no longer reported to be a problem. There is still, sometimes, too much friction, but fairly routine servicing cures this. In addition, the action has been lightened through a combination of switching to Renner action parts, lubrication, more consistent weigh-off in the factory, and removal of excess mass from some of the parts. In my opinion, the change to Renner action parts in most of the models has improved the pianos more than any other single factor.

In the previous edition, it was noted that sometimes legs did not fit correctly. This problem was solved quite early on. Petrof now uses a leg mounting system similar to that of some other major manufacturers, and there have been no reports of any problems. Also in the third edition, there were frequent reports of dead or buzzing bass strings and polyester squeaks in the verticals, and some reports of loose tuning pins. All of these are still reported, but only occasionally. Petrof has installed updated bass string winding equipment in the factory, and dead or buzzing bass strings are much less common. As mentioned earlier, Petrof now uses a seven-ply beech pinblock in the grands and high-end vertical model. The beech pinblock may be a little more tolerant of manufacturing anomalies than the Delignit block, and so less likely to produce random loose tuning pins, though the few loose tuning pins that showed up in the present survey occurred in both types of pinblock. Finally, the Czech-made action parts were said to be satisfactory but lack the refinement of Renner parts. This is still true, but there are fewer complaints about these parts than in the last survey, especially in brand-new verticals. There were some complaints about them in pi-

anos a few years old, however, including tight action centers and some parts that were coming unglued or looked sloppily made.

The service database examined for this (fourth) edition contained reports on 103 Petrof verticals and 66 grands, most of them sold three to five years ago. About a third of the verticals and forty-five percent of the grands were provided postsale service other than tuning. These percentages are not unlike those reported for Korean pianos at that time. For both verticals and grands, the most common complaints were for sticking keys and tight action centers, minor action regulating, and adjustment to dampers or trapwork. Note: Concerning tight action centers, this appears to have been a problem primarily in the Czech-made action parts in use at that time, not ones by Renner, but in any case, is a rare occurrence today.

Twenty-nine Petrof and Weinbach verticals appeared in the current written survey. Most arrive at the dealer free of major problems. Usually they need key easing, hammer spacing, and some regulating and minor troubleshooting. Sometimes excessive false beating in the treble and in bass strings was noted. Occasionally, a cabinet part fit too tightly, or there were loose screws that buzzed, or a lid button fell off—small stuff. The pianos were frequently complimented for their finish. The tone was sometimes too bright in the treble, but responded well to hammer fitting and voicing, and the larger verticals in particular received compliments for their sound. A few pianos three to five years old were said to be plagued with problems and not recommended for heavy use, but I believe that today's Petrofs are sufficiently improved that that is unlikely to be their fate. None of the newer Petrof verticals had severe problems. Technicians should take note that in the Czech-made vertical actions, butt plates connect the hammer butts with their flanges. Butt plate screws (not just hammer flange screws) must be tightened regularly to prevent center pins from walking out.

Twenty-one Petrof and Weinbach grands were examined as part of the written survey. Like the verticals, the grands, when new, also need key easing, hammer spacing, regulating, and voicing. Although action regulation is often fairly good right from the factory, a few pianos in the survey were said to be unexpectedly far out of regulation. There were reports of tight action centers and sticking dampers in pianos from a couple of years ago, but these problems were almost totally absent in the newest ones, probably because of the switch to Renner parts. Tonally, the grands are capable of a gorgeous sound, but this sometimes has to be coaxed out of extremely hard hammers. Until that's done, the pianos can be unpleasantly bright sounding.

In addition to the above, all of which could be said to be within the normal range of expected work on a new piano, there were also a number of "one of a kind" problems reported with the grands, suggesting a little less attention to detail in the grands than the verticals. Not to make too much of these, because they were, indeed, rarely repeated, but they included: a damaged keytop, a buzzing plate ornament, a keyframe guide pin falling out, unidentifiable dried substances (glue, finishing material?) on the keys, severe string cuts in brass duplex bars, severely bent action bracket screws (this was reported several times), unglued action parts, and

For explanation of survey and review procedures, model listings, and price ranges, please see pages 76–81.

stripped plate bolts. At least a third of the grands examined had something small of this sort to be fixed.

Despite this long list, comparing Petrof pianos of today with those of five years ago, there's no doubt that today's are better. The pianos of five years ago, though they sounded and looked good, had a number of systemic problems, such as action parts of dubious quality and heavy touch that could not easily be lightened, that cast some doubt upon their durability and their use as professional instruments. Today, in contrast, most of the problems are normal (regulating, voicing) or trivial, even if annoying, and even the trivial problems are less numerous. Once the pianos are properly serviced, they are usually very fine, solidly built, goodlooking, lovely sounding instruments. I still do have more confidence in the Renner action parts than the Czech, and suggest you choose a model that has them if possible. However, as far as I can tell, there is little effective difference between the full Renner and the Petrof/Renner actions.

Petrof also makes pianos under the name Rösler, which are distributed extensively in Europe. This line was briefly introduced into the U.S. in 1999, but discontinued shortly thereafter.

Note: The Petrof factory also makes a piano under the August Förster name, similar to the Petrof but different from the August Förster made in Germany. This Czech August Förster is available in Canada and several European countries, but not in the U.S. See under "Förster, August" for more information.

Warranty: Ten years, parts and labor—the first five from Petrof, the second five from the importer.

Price range: (Petrof Verticals) $5,600–10,000; (Petrof Grands) $18,600–35,800; Weinbach prices are about five percent lower on average.

Verticals	Grands
42" console (100)	5'3" (155/V)
45" studio (114/115)	5'8" (170/IV)
50" upright (124/125/126)	6'4" (192/III)
52" upright (131)	6'4" (III-M)
	7'9" (II)
	9'3" (I)

Model numbers above are given as Weinbach/Petrof or Petrof only.

Consumer Ratings:

Performance:
  With Renner action parts: * * * * 1/2
  With Detoa (Czech) action parts: * * * *
Confidence
  With Renner action parts: * * * * 1/2
  With Detoa (Czech) action parts: * * * 1/2
Quality Control
  Verticals with Renner action parts: * * * *
  Verticals with Detoa (Czech) action parts: * * * 1/2
  Grands: * * * 1/2
Warranty: * * * 1/2
Information: * * * *

PIANOCORDER

See "Marantz/Pianocorder"

PIANODISC

For PianoDisc electronic player piano systems, see "Electronic Player Piano Systems and Hybrid Acoustic/ Digital Pianos," page 160. For PianoDisc pianos, see "Knabe."

PLEYEL

Geneva International Corporation
29 East Hintz Road
Wheeling, Illinois 60090

(800) 533-2388
(847) 520-9970
geneva-intl@msn.com

Pianos made by: Manufacture Francaise de Pianos, Alès, France

Ignace Pleyel, an accomplished musician and composer, patron of music, and publisher, began manufacturing pianos in 1807 with the aim of adapting instruments to the new requirements of the composers and musicians of his day. By the time of his death in 1831, Pleyel pianos were known and exported throughout the world. His son, Camille, an accomplished pianist, continued the family business and brought it to new heights of success. As part of his work, Camille established the "Salle Pleyel," a music salon that served as a focus for the Parisian music scene of his time and where many famous musicians and composers were heard for the first time. It was at one of these concerts, in 1832, that Frederic Chopin made his Paris debut, and he played his final concert there in 1848. In addition to Chopin, who is closely associated with Pleyel pianos, other notable users included Claude Debussy, Cesar Franck, Edward Grieg, and Maurice Ravel.

Pleyel was also responsible for some of the technical innovations of his day. The company first introduced iron bracing into a piano in 1826, was the first to bring the upright piano to France, and is credited with inventing the sostenuto in 1860.

Today, Manufacture Francaise de Pianos makes Pleyel, Rameau, Gaveau, and Erard pianos in Provence in the south of France. The company employs 120 workers and builds about 100 grands and 2,000 verticals annually. Although pianos have been made under these names for nearly two hundred years, Pleyel and Gaveau were made by Schimmel, and were pretty much identical to Schimmel pianos, from 1971 to 1994. In that year the contract with Schimmel was terminated and the pianos were once again returned to France, where they are now made to different designs. Only the Pleyel brand is currently being imported into the United States.

At the present time, the models available in the U.S. are 47", 49", and 52" uprights and a 6'3" grand. Plans are in the works for 5'7" and 7'4" grands in the near future. All models feature Renner hammers and action, Delignit pinblock, and solid spruce soundboard from the famous Val de Fiemme. The grand comes with a Kluge keyboard. The grand's square-nose (tail) construction, the company says, increases soundboard area and bass string length. A Kluge keyboard and sostenuto pedal are offered as options on the 52" upright. A number of models are available with elaborate inlay work.

No information is available from my survey on these pianos because they are too new to the U.S. market. However, typically European, they appear to be of high quality. A few Pleyels I've played have had a bright, singing treble, a light touch, and an unusually deep, dark-sounding bass.

Warranty: Ten years, parts and labor, to the orignal purchaser.

Price range: (Verticals) $12,400–15,700; (Grands) $40,000

Verticals	Grands
47" upright (118)	6'3" grand (190)
49" upright (124)	
52" upright (131)	

Consumer Ratings: Insufficient information to rate, but probably in Group 2 (see "Summary of Brands and Ratings," page 84).

QRS/PIANOMATION

See "Electronic Player Piano Systems and Hybrid Acoustic/Digital Pianos," page 160.

RIDGEWOOD

Weber Piano Co.
40 Seaview Drive
Secaucus, New Jersey 07094

(800) 346-5351
(201) 902-0920
www.weberpiano.com

Pianos made by: Guangzhou Pearl River Piano Group Ltd., Guangzhou, China; Dongbei Piano Co., Dongbei, China

The Ridgewood name is being applied to verticals and to 5'2" and 7' grands made by the Guangzhou Pearl River company in Guangzhou, China, and most recently, by the Dongbei Piano Co. See "Pearl River" for more information on the Guangzhou pianos. See "Nordiska" and "Sagenhaft" for more information on the Dongbei pianos.

Warranty: Ten years, parts and labor, to original purchaser. The warranty is backed by Samsung.

Price range: (Verticals) $3,000–3,700; (Grands) $9,600–17,800

Verticals	Grands
43" console (108/110)	5'2" (159)
45½" studio (118)	7" (213)

Consumer Ratings: See "Pearl River" for pianos from the Guangzhou factory and "Nordiska" for pianos from the Dongbei factory.

RIEGER-KLOSS

Weber Piano Co.
40 Seaview Drive
Secaucus, New Jersey 07094

(800) 346-5351
(201) 902-0920
www.weberpiano.com

Pianos made by: Bohemia Piano s.r.o., Prague, Czech Republic

Names used: Rieger-Kloss, Bohemia

Rieger-Kloss is one of the piano brands that used to be part of the Czech state-owned enterprise that included Petrof. The factory that makes Rieger-Kloss was privatized in 1993. Rieger-Kloss makes about 3,000 verticals a year, mostly for export. Most of the components for the verticals are Czech, except for the Renner action used in the 50" upright. Note that the 44" model R-111 is less expensive because the cabinet is finished in a simulated wood finish. The factory is not equipped to fully produce grands itself, so it imports the strung backs for grands from Young Chang in Korea and the actions from Renner in Germany and then completes the assembly in the Czech Republic. The strung backs are identical to those of similarly-sized Young Chang pianos.

The Bohemia name is not currently being used on pianos imported into the U.S.

No information is available on Rieger-Kloss quality, but perhaps some conjecture could be made from reading the reviews of Petrof and Young Chang.

Warranty: Ten years, parts and labor, from Bohemia Piano Co.

Price range: (Verticals) $4,300–7,800; (Grands) $19,400–22,500

Verticals	Grands
43" console (R-109)	5'2" (RG-158)
44" console (R-111)	6'1" (RG-185)
47" upright (R-118)	
48" upright (R-121/122/123)	
50" upright (R-125/126)	

Consumer Ratings: Insufficient information to rate

RITMÜLLER

See "Pearl River"

RÖSLER

See "Petrof"

SAGENHAFT

Weber Piano Co.
40 Seaview Drive
Secaucus, New Jersey 07094

(800) 346-5351
(201) 902-0920
www.weberpiano.com

Pianos made by: Dongbei Piano Co., Dongbei, China

Sagenhaft pianos are made by the Dongbei Piano Co. in China. The S-116 models are Nordiska designs, which Dongbei purchased from the Swedish company of that name. A similar piano is sold under the Nordiska name by another distributor (see "Nordiska"). The other models are Dongbei's own designs. The model S-112 is a "deluxe" version of Dongbei's S-111 designed especially for Sagenhaft. It contains tone escapements, and end panels redesigned for greater physical stability.

Little information is available about quality, but see "Nordiska."

Warranty: Ten years, parts and labor, to original purchaser. The warranty is backed by Samsung.

Price range: (Verticals) $2,400–3,600; (Grands) $9,200

Verticals	Grands
44½" console (S-111/112)	5'5" (SG-165)
45½" studio (S-116)	
48" upright (S-121)	
50" upright (S-126)	

Consumer Ratings: Insufficient information to rate

SAMICK

Samick Music Corporation
18521 Railroad St.
City of Industry, California 91748
(626) 964-4700
(800) 592-9393
www.samickpiano.com

Owned by: Samick Musical Instrument Mfg. Co. Ltd., Inchon, South Korea (publicly owned in South Korea)

Names used: Samick, Kohler & Campbell, Conover Cable, Bernhard Steiner. No longer used: Horugel, Stegler, Schumann, Hazelton. Also makes pianos for other distributors under the names Hyundai, Wurlitzer (formerly D.H. Baldwin), Otto Altenburg, Charles Albrecht, Schultz & Sons, possibly others.

The Company: Samick was founded by Hyo Ick Lee in 1958 as a Baldwin distributor. Facing an immense challenge in impoverished and war-torn South Korea, Lee began to build and sell a very limited quantity of vertical pianos using largely imported parts in the early 1960s. As the Korean economy improved, Lee expanded his operation, and Samick is today one of the world's largest piano manufacturers (as well as the largest maker of fretted instruments), making most of the parts in house. In 1995, Samick opened a factory in Indonesia for the production of guitars and pianos, and as Korean wages rise, the company is gradually shifting much of its production there. For a time in the early 1990s, Samick assembled a few models of vertical piano in California, but ceased production there when the Indonesian facility came on line.

The Pianos: Samick manufactures and distributes four lines of pianos in the United States: Samick, Kohler & Campbell, Conover Cable, and Bernhard Steiner. The Samick brand consists of a lower-priced line made in Indonesia, a regular line made in Korea, and a higher-priced Korean line called the "World Piano" series. The Kohler & Campbell brand also consists of a lower-priced line made in Indonesia, a regular line made in Korea, and a higher-priced Korean line called the "Millennium Piano" series. The Conover Cable and Bernhard Steiner lines are available primarily in areas where additional lines are needed to avoid conflict with another Samick dealer's territory. They have very limited distribution and are similar to the models from the Samick and Kohler & Campbell lines. The pianos in the survey were primarily from the Samick and Kohler & Campbell lines, so only those two lines will be reviewed here. Samick also makes pianos that are distributed by other organizations, sold under other names (see list at beginning of review).

All of these differently-named pianos differ in at least two major respects: scale design and soundboard. In the mid-1980s, Samick hired German scale designer Klaus Fenner to redesign its scales, partly to improve them and partly to differentiate them from Samick pianos sold under other names. Samick then said these new pianos had "Imperial German Scale Designs." The Fenner scales are found primarily in the pianos sold under the Samick brand name, although they are also found in certain sizes of the other brands.

The Samick-brand pianos, in the Korean-made and some of the Indonesian-made regular models, use a three-ply laminated spruce soundboard, consisting of an inner core of solid spruce and two very thin outer veneers of spruce. Samick says that this type of soundboard, though technically laminated, behaves acoustically just like a solid spruce soundboard, except that it won't crack. Accordingly, Samick gives this soundboard a lifetime warranty. This soundboard is also used in some of the other-named pianos, most notably Hyundai. (Occasional Samick-brand models use a solid spruce soundboard. They are indicated by an S at the end of the model number. Also, the Samick "World" pianos use a solid spruce soundboard because their design calls for a tapered soundboard for better tonal response, and a laminated soundboard cannot be tapered.) Kohler & Campbell pianos, and those of some other brand names, use a soundboard of solid spruce.

Actually, most of this doesn't matter much because when it comes to scale design and soundboard, the only thing that's really important is how the piano sounds, which you can determine for yourself. I have gone to some lengths to discuss this confusing situation only because dealers will be using these features to convince you to buy their brand over the competition. To be honest, though, for most buyers the technical differences between these brands in scale design and soundboard are probably, for all practical purposes, insignificant. If you buy a piano made by Samick, you should make your choice between brands based on price, personal tonal preference, how well the piano has been serviced by the dealer, and if all else fails, which name you prefer. An exception would be the World and Millennium series pianos, or other Samick-made pianos with Renner action and other superior features, which could significantly add to the value.

Samick has gradually been shifting production of its less-expensive verticals and grands to its Indonesian factory. These models can be identified by their model numbers beginning with JS (Samick verticals), SIG (Samick grands), KC (Kohler & Campbell verticals), and KIG (Kohler & Campbell grands). These Indonesian-assembled pianos contain keys, actions, hammers, and plates from Korea, and cabinets and soundboards from Indonesia. Currently, the vertical soundboards are spruce-veneer laminated, and the grand soundboards are solid spruce. During 1996–97, the name "Hazelton" was briefly used on a 43" console assembled in Korea using materials from the Indonesian factory.

Samick's World Piano series and Kohler & Campbell's Millennium Piano series, developed a few years ago and revised in 1999, represent the company's best instruments. They are built in a separate facility reserved only for the premium pianos, using better materials, technicians, and processes. World and Millennium verticals have spruce back posts, a slow-close fallboard, agraffes, and in the 48" and 52" sizes, a sostenuto pedal. World and Millennium grands have rims made mostly of maple, Kluge keys, Renner actions, Abel hammers, and a whole assortment of features similar to those in some high-end pianos, such as a seven-ply maple pinblock fitted to the flange, high quality soundboard material from the Canadian maker Bolduc, vertically laminated maple bridges with maple cap, solid maple legs with leg plates, and a triangle shoe "tone collector" joining the beams and plate. The pianos are given final action and tone regulating in Samick's California facility before being shipped to the dealers. The only difference between the World and Millennium pianos is that the World pianos have duplex scaling, whereas the Millennium pianos have individual hitch pin stringing. The World and Millennium pianos I've played have sounded lovely. Because they are relatively new, only a couple of them appeared in the survey for this edition. World verticals are model numbers beginning with WSU; World grands, WFG. Millennium verticals are model numbers beginning with KMV; Millennium grands, KFM.

At the time of this writing, all Samick and Kohler & Campbell consoles are made in Indonesia. The studios and uprights are available in both Indonesian and Korean-made models. The grands are still mostly Korean-made at this point; each of the lines has only one small grand model from Indonesia. However, this may change over time.

Samick entered the U.S. market in the late 1970s under a variety of trade names, including Horugel and Stegler. These first pianos reacted very poorly to the climatic extremes of North America, as have the first imported pianos of every other Asian manufacturer, with wooden parts warping, cracking, and binding. Many of them had to be sent back to Korea.

Throughout most of the 1980s, Samick pianos were very erratic in quality. Many were plagued with problems, requiring hours of repair and adjustment by the dealer. To make matters worse, Korean labor unrest in 1987 culminating in strikes resulted in some highly defective pianos being shipped to the United States. On the other hand, not all had problems; some seemed to come through in relatively good shape. Although most technicians who were interviewed at that time disliked these pianos, some who were given latitude in servicing them and who were very experienced with them said they could be made into satisfactory instruments. Toward the end of the 1980s, Samicks improved a lot, especially after the opening of the company's new grand piano factory in 1989.

In the survey for the previous (third) edition (1994), the verticals were considered a little more consistent than the grands. When new, the verticals primarily needed extra tuning, key easing, and hammer spacing. Some hammer heads

were said to come unglued in dry weather and the pedal hardware needed some realignment. In the service database examined for this (fourth) edition, about a third of the twenty-four Korean Samick-made verticals, most sold three to five years ago, were provided some post-sale service other than tuning. The problems corrected were similar to those found in the previous survey: ease sticking keys, repin tight action centers, and occasionally reglue or repair action parts. The written survey for this (fourth) edition included twenty Korean-made Samick and Kohler & Campbell verticals. The most common complaints were overly tight tuning pins, making tuning difficult; poor or uneven action regulation, squeaking trapwork, hammers poorly spaced to strings, and some complaints that the tone was too bright. There were also a few broken cabinet parts on three- or four-year-old pianos. In general, the verticals were considered acceptable. One technician said the verticals were "as close to getting value for the dollar as you're going to get."

Technicians should take note that Samick verticals use butt plates to connect the hammer butts to their flanges. Butt plates (and not just hammer flanges) must be tightened regularly to prevent center pins from walking out.

As for the grands, the survey for the previous (third) edition found the following common problems: tight action centers, particularly in the damper system and hammer flanges, and tight key bushings and damper guide rail bushings; the need for thorough action regulating; initial tuning instability; and a great deal of action and pedal noise and squeaks in pianos three to five years old.

The service database examined for this (fourth) edition included 329 Korean Samick-made grands, of which about forty percent were provided post-sale service other than tuning, a moderately high percentage. The service provided was for virtually the same set of key, action, and damper problems mentioned above. There were also some, but fewer, complaints about action and pedal squeaks and noises.

The written survey for the fourth edition included fifty-four Samick and Kohler & Campbell grands. The most common complaints by far were noises and squeaks in the action and pedals, sometimes on new pianos, but especially on slightly older ones; tight action centers, but usually on slightly older pianos, not new ones; generally poor action regulation, including dampers and trapwork; excessive false beating in the treble; and various tonal complaints, usually that the tone was too bright and strident, but occasionally that the pianos sounded muffled. Also mentioned occasionally were case parts that did not fit properly and other sloppiness in woodworking, and initial tuning instability. It was very obvious from the written reports that the pianos made within the last year or so were arriving at the dealer in much better condition than they have in the past. [Samick says that proper pre-sale preparation of the pianos, especially including seating the strings at the bridge, will cure most of the false beating and will quickly stabilize the tuning.]

Reviewing Korean pianos has always been difficult because they are so inconsistent in how they present themselves when new. Interpreting the data is made even harder by the fact that some pianos may not be put into service until several years after they're manufactured, conditions of use

For explanation of survey and review procedures, model listings, and price ranges, please see pages 76–81.

and humidity differ, and different technicians are bothered by different kinds of problems. Nevertheless, after reviewing written and verbal reports on hundreds of Korean-made pianos over the years, I've come to some conclusions:

At this point, Samick pianos are arriving at the dealer in pretty good shape, perhaps even a little better prepared than Young Changs, and most problems are easily taken care of during normal pre-sale preparation. This reversal may have occurred only within the past year or two. However, judging from the reports I've received, the tuning of Samick pianos may take awhile to stabilize; installing a climate control system might help them adapt. After a few years, the actions of many Samick grands start showing signs of wear, with increasing squeaks and noises. It's always hard to know whether conditions like this in older pianos are due to age and wear, or are symptoms of problems that have since been solved, and this is no exception. But in the survey for the third edition, many Samick pianos three to five years old had a lot of action and pedal noise, and the same seems to be true again in the current survey. This leads me to speculate that either the action materials (felt, leather, etc.) are not of the best quality, or that there is some roughness to the wooden parts, or that the action geometry and leverage promote premature wear of the components. Similarly, the pedals and trapwork may have some material, alignment, or leverage problem. [Samick says that its World and Millenium pianos, which use high quality Renner actions, Kluge keys, better grades of wood, and more attention to detail, have been designed in part to address these issues, but at a considerable price difference. The company also says it has research and development in progress to improve the action geometry in its less-expensive grand pianos.]

In the survey for the third edition, I came to the tentative conclusion that Samick pianos sounded a little better than Young Changs, or at least certain models did. But in the current survey, the Samick pianos were often criticized for being either too strident or too muffled, and I was struck by how few were said to sound really good. Perhaps better voicing would have brought out some of the warmth that had previously been said to be possible from these pianos, especially the 5'9" Kohler & Campbell model.

In the follow-up interviews for the current survey, the technicians were asked to share their observations and opinions about Samick pianos, competitor Young Chang, and Korean pianos in general. The technicians expressed a slight preference for Young Chang over Samick, but not by much. (Note, however, that the World and Millenium series pianos were too new to the marketplace to be considered by the technicians.) Here is a sampling of their comments:

"Between the two, I think the Samicks tend to be a little more solid in terms of the finished product. They look more professional than the Young Changs, which seem to appear plasticky. . . . The Kohler & Campbells are acceptable pianos for the price they are sold for. Korean cabinetry starts to look old fairly fast. Stringing will hold up okay, but actions tend to become clacky (noisy)."

"I've experienced regulating problems with Korean pianos. . . . I find the two brands very similar, but if I had to make a choice, I'd say Samick."

"I prefer the Young Chang in terms of technical issues and tone. I don't see a huge difference, though. [My impression is that] most musicians tend to favor the Young Chang tone."

"[Comparing Young Chang and Samick] They're pretty equivalent; nothing really stands out consistently. They satisfy a real good price point in the market and give good value for the dollar."

"[About some Kohler & Campbells] The first thing I noticed overall is the lack of tone in the hammers. Small dynamic range, little power, short sustain. Extremely muted sound, which I'm finding pleases the customers because they were prepared for a harsh, overly bright sound. The ones that are a couple of years old seem to be wearing prematurely. Clicking noises, squeaky front rail [key] bushings, key end felts wearing out, backcheck leather wearing out, knuckle problems. The odd one will sound nice and seem to be a decent piano for the money. They need regulation. On some pianos a few action centers have gotten extremely tight after a couple of years of playing."

"[About Samicks] Tends to be some consistency when they are brand new. Some of the action components seem to wear out prematurely, though, especially backcheck leathers. Hammers are usually very hard and very tinny and thin-sounding. . . . I'd take the Young Chang over the Samick. . . ."

"I've always felt that Young Changs were the better of the two. Samicks are tolerable in the home, but less stability all the way around than Young Chang."

"I've heard some Samicks come in out of the crate sounding like the pianos had socks on the hammers. The pianos are pretty mediocre, but darn good for under $10,000. . . . After key easing and making friction problems go away, they're pretty decent. . . . [About servicing] You can't skip any steps."

"[About Samick] Better now than five years ago in just about every way. Their cases were always good, in my opinion. I think there is less work that needs to be done and less follow-up work that needs to be done. I would frequently have tight keys, but don't see that much anymore. I think less work has been needed on the dealer's floor to put them in the condition they would like before selling them. The dealer carried Young Chang for a short time, but dropped them. He felt the Samicks were less troublesome. . . . I feel that the Samicks are a great piano for the dollar."

Concerning Samick's Indonesian pianos, twenty-four verticals appeared in the written survey for this edition. Their problems were similar to those of their Korean counterparts, but a little more numerous: tuning pins too tight, regulation poor, tight key bushings, excessive false beating in the treble, and noisy or squeaky action. In addition, several pianos had loose tuning pins, a problem not normally seen in the Korean pianos. The Indonesian grands featured poor tone (these are the smallest of grand pianos, only 4'7"), poor action and damper regulation, manufacturing debris in the piano, excessive false beating in the treble, and noisy or squeaky action. They also have rather shaky legs and weak lyre systems. The 4'7" Kohler & Campbell, in particular, should probably be avoided (the Korean model, too). The 4'11½" Samick model is a more acceptable size.

Samick's Indonesian pianos are sometimes lumped together (in conversation) with the Chinese pianos of various makers. Although Samick had some problems early on in these pianos with warped keys and other moisture-related issues, those problems have been solved or minimized, and the pianos are better than much of what's coming out of China at this point (although the Chinese are fast catching up). One technician went so far as to say that inspecting the pianos, it would be hard to differentiate between the Korean and Indonesian models. I wouldn't go that far: In my view, the quality control is not as good as in the Korean-made pianos, but there are certainly fewer outrageous problems than found in some of the Chinese product. I find it hard to get excited about pianos like this, but I can imagine they might be an acceptable alternative to a used piano when a low price is a top priority. Obviously, even more than with the Korean pianos, good servicing of these instruments is extremely important if they are not to be utterly unplayable in a short time.

Summary: Samick pianos are good for average home use. I would not recommend them for heavy or institutional use at this time. There is still some inconsistency in how they present themselves when new, but there are few serious problems. The Korean models are made with better quality control than the Indonesian ones, but the latter are probably acceptable if serviced well. Buyers would probably be wise to avoid the smallest models, both vertical and grand. Special attention should be paid to pre-sale inspection and preparation, regular post-sale servicing, and climate control. The World and Millennium series pianos, although far more expensive, have features more like high-end instruments and show great promise, but because of their newness to the market, there was insufficient information available for this survey to make a definitive judgment about them.

See also separate listings for Hyundai, Baldwin (Wurlitzer), Otto Altenburg, Bernhard Steiner, Charles Albrecht, and Schultz & Sons.

Samick and Kohler & Campbell pianos have an unusual serial numbering system, beginning with several letters. The first two letters indicate the year of manufacture, according to the following key for recent years: IO=1995, IP=1996, IQ=1997, IR=1998, IS=1999, IT=2000.

Warranty: Plate, pinblock, rim, laminated soundboard—lifetime, parts and labor; solid spruce soundboard and rest of piano—twelve years, parts and labor. Note that Samick, Kohler & Campbell, Conover Cable, and Bernhard Steiner warranty requests are handled by Samick Music Corp. Warranty requests for all other names are handled by their respective distributors.

Samick warranty service is considered to be reasonably good, but not as generous as some of the other companies.

Price range: (verticals, Indonesian) $2,800–4,000; (verticals, regular Korean) $4,400–5,400; (verticals, World/Millennium) $4,800–6,000; (grands, Indonesian) $7,500–7,800; (grands, regular Korean) $9,200–12,500; (grands, World/Millennium) $18,000–27,000

Samick—Verticals	Grands
42 1/2" console (JS 042)	4'11 1/2" (SIG-50)
44" console (JS 044)	4'11 1/2" (SG-150)

45 1/2" studio (JS 115)	5'3 1/2" (SG-161)
46 1/2" studio (JS 118)	5'7" (SG-172)
46 1/2" studio (SU-118/147S)	5'7" (WFG-172)
46 1/2" studio (WSU-118)	6'1" (SG-185)
48" upright (JS 121)	6'1" (WFG-185)
48" upright (SU-121)	6'8" (WFG-205)
48" upright (WSU-121SD)	7' (WFG-215)
52" upright (SU-131)	7'4" (WFG-225)
52" upright (WSU-131MD)	9'1" (WFG-275)

Kohler & Campbell—Verticals	Grands
42 1/2" console (KC 142)	4'7" (KIG 47)
44" console (KC 144)	4'7" (SKG-400S)
45 1/2" studio (KC 145)	5'1" (SKG-500S)
46 1/2" studio (KC 118)	5'9" (SKG-600S)
46 1/2" studio (SKV 118/465S)	5'9" (KFM-600S)
46 1/2" studio (KMV-47)	6'1" (SKG-650S)
48" upright (KC 121)	6'1" (KFM-650S)
48" upright (SKV-48S)	6'8" (KFM-700S)
48" upright (KMV-48SD)	7' (KFM-800S)
52" upright (SKV-52S)	7'4" (KFM-850S)
52" upright (KMV-52MD)	9'1" (KFM-900S)

JS, KC, SIG, KIG = Indonesian models;
SU, SKV, SG, SKG = Korean regular models;
WSU, KMV, WFG, KFM = Korean "World" and "Millennium" models

Consumer Ratings:

Verticals

Performance
    Indonesian: * * 1/2
    Korean: * * *
    World/Millennium: * * * *
Confidence
    Indonesian: * * 1/2
    Korean: * * *
    World/Millennium: * * * 1/2
Quality Control
    Indonesian: * * 1/2
    Korean: * * *
    World/Millennium: * * * 1/2
Warranty: * * * 1/2
Information
    Indonesian: * * *
    Korean: * * * *
    World/Millennium: * 1/2

Grands

Performance
    Indonesian: * * 1/2
    Korean: * * *
    World/Millennium: * * * *
Confidence
    Indonesian: * * 1/2
    Korean: * * *
    World/Millennium: * * * *
Quality Control
    Indonesian: * * 1/2
    Korean: * * *
    World/Millennium: * * * *

Warranty: * * * 1/2
Information
    Indonesian: * * *
    Korean: * * * * *
    World/Millennium: * *

SÄNGLER & SÖHNE
Including Wieler

North American Music
126 Route 303
West Nyack, New York 10994

(845) 353-3520
(800) 541-2331
www.namusic.com

Pianos made by: Guangzhou Pearl River Piano Group Ltd., Guangzhou, China; Belarus Piano Co., Belarus

Names used: Sängler & Söhne, Wieler, various private label names

The console and studio pianos and the 5'3" grand made under these names are made in China by the Guangzhou Pearl River Piano Group and are similar to those made under the Pearl River name (see "Pearl River"). The 47" upright is made in Belarus (see also "Schubert"). These pianos are also available to dealers with a name of their choice. Some sample names are Ackermann, Langston, Steiff & Sohne, and Rohrbach.

Warranty: Ten years, parts only, transferable.

Price range: (Verticals) $2,000–3,000; (Grand) $8,600

Verticals	Grands
43" console (UP-108)	5'3" (GP-159)
44" console (UP-110)	
45" studio (UP-115)	
47" upright (BLR-120)	

Consumer Ratings: See ratings for "Pearl River" and "Schubert."

SAUTER

Unique Pianos, Inc.
223 E. New Haven Avenue
Melbourne, Florida 32901

(888) 725-6633
(321) 725-5690
www.uniquepianos.com

Pianos made by: Carl Sauter Pianofortefabrik, Spaichingen, Germany

The Sauter piano firm was founded by Johann Grimm, stepfather to Carl Sauter I, in 1819, and has been owned and managed by members of the Sauter family for six generations, currently by Ulrich Sauter. The factory currently produces about 2,000 pianos a year in its factory in the extreme south of Germany, at the foot of the Alps. Structural and acoustical parts are made of high-quality woods, including solid Bavarian spruce soundboards and beech pinblocks. Actions are made by Renner and Sauter makes its own keys. The keybed is reinforced with steel to prevent warping and all pianos carry the label "fully tropicalized." The larger verticals use an action, designed and patented by Sauter, that contains an auxiliary jack spring to aid in faster repetition. Sauter calls this the "R2 Double Escapement" action. (Although the term "Double Escapement" does not apply here as it has historically been used, the mechanism has some of the same effect.)

Grands and verticals are available in a variety of finishes and styles, many with intricate detail and inlay work. It is common to find such rare woods as Yew, Burl Walnut, Pyramid Mahogany, and genuine Ebony in the cabinets of Sauter pianos, as well as special engravings, which can be customized to any customer's desires. Sauter has a line of vertical pianos designated the "M line" which feature exclusive cabinet detailing and built-in features such as a hygrometer to measure relative humidity. The company also has introduced versions of its 48" upright and 6'1" grand with cabinets designed by the famous European designer Peter Maly, available by special order only.

The 7'3" model 220 grand has some unusual features that at first glance seem to be only decorative, but turn out to be functional. Colored lines painted on the soundboard and white inlays on the tops of the dampers act as guides to musicians performing music for "prepared piano"—that is, ultra-modern music requiring the insertion of foreign objects between the strings or the plucking or striking of strings directly by the performer. The colored lines indicate to the performer where to touch the strings to produce certain harmonics. The white inlays on certain dampers indicate the location of the black keys for easier navigation around the "keyboard" when accessing the strings directly. This model reportedly had its origin as a custom-made instrument for the Paris Conservatory. When it met with approval, it was integrated into the Sauter line.

Another unusual Sauter instrument—perhaps the most unusual piano I have ever encountered—is the Sauter 1/16 tone microtonal piano. At first glance, the piano appears to be a normal upright—that is, the black and white keys are arranged in their usual spatial relationship, and nothing seems amiss. A look inside, however, reveals hammers that are all the same size, strings that are all treble wire and all straight strung and all nearly the same thickness and length, and only one long, straight bridge, leaving one scratching one's head with the thought "What's wrong with this picture?" It turns out that this 97-key upright piano has a total pitch range from the lowest to the highest note of exactly one octave, with the pitch difference from key to key being only 1/16 of a tone (1/8 of a semitone). The sound, of course, is bizarre. I'm told this piano is sometimes used in concert with the "prepared piano" instrument described earlier—not a concert I'd care to attend!

The Sauter grands I've played have had a lush, full, singing tone, more like an "American" sound than most other European pianos. Sauter is considered in Europe to be a medium-high quality piano.

Warranty: Ten years, parts and labor, to original purchaser.

Price range: (Verticals) $13,500–24,500; (Grands) $38,000–54,900

Verticals	Grands
48" (122)	5'3" (160)
50" (128)	6'1" (185)
51" (130)	7'2" (220)
	9' (275)

Consumer Ratings:

Performance: * * * * 1/2
Confidence: * * * * *
Quality Control: * * * * *
Warranty: * * * *
Information: * *

SCHAFER & SONS

Schafer & Sons
810 George Street
Santa Clara, California 95054

schafer@coltonpiano.com
www.coltonpiano.com

Pianos made by: Young Chang Co., Ltd., Inchon, South Korea

Founded by Vern Schafer, Schafer & Sons was developed for a southern California retail chain, Colton Piano & Organ. After selling the Schafer & Sons brand successfully for a number of years, distribution was expanded by Mr. Schafer throughout the United States. Sales of current Schafer & Sons pianos are now being handled by others unrelated to the original distributor.

During the 1980s, pianos bearing the Schafer & Sons name were made by Samick, Wurlitzer, Kimball, and Daewoo. Since 1992, Schafer & Sons pianos have been manufactured by Young Chang. Most models are identical to the "Gold series" Young Chang models of the same size, except possibly for some cabinetry differences. Young Chang-made Schafer & Sons pianos are sold through retail dealers, discount clubs, and special promotions, primarily in northern California. See "Young Chang" for more information.

Warranty: Fifteen-year full (transferable) warranty; lifetime limited warranty to original purchaser on case, action parts, and iron frame. Warranty is underwritten by Young Chang America, but warranty service must be authorized by Schafer & Sons.

SCHIEDMAYER

See "Kawai"

SCHIMMEL

Schimmel Piano Corporation
251 Memorial Road
Lititz, Pennsylvania 17543

(800) 426-3205
schimmel@ptd.net
www.schimmel-piano.de

For explanation of survey and review procedures, model listings, and price ranges, please see pages 76–81.

Pianos made by: Wilhelm Schimmel Pianofortefabrik GmbH, Braunschweig, Germany

Wilhelm Schimmel began making pianos in 1885, and his company enjoyed steady growth through the late nineteenth and early twentieth centuries. The two world wars and the Depression disrupted production several times, but the company has gradually rebuilt itself over the past forty years with a strong reputation for quality. Today, Schimmel is owned and managed by Nikolaus Schimmel, the grandson of the founder. Schimmel makes about 4,500 verticals and 900 grands a year, and is one of the largest piano makers in Western Europe. Yamaha owns a 24.9 percent share of Schimmel[1].

The Schimmel piano line includes five sizes of studio and upright piano and three sizes of grand. The smaller verticals have a very big bass for their size, with a tone that emphasizes the fundamental. The 51" upright also has a very large sound, and listening to it, it would be easy to think you were in the presence of a grand. During the last few years, a number of changes have been made to the grands. The 5'1" grand was discontinued, the 5'10" grand was lengthened to 6' to—among other things—improve the feel by accommodating the longer keys and action also used in its larger grand, and in 1999 a new 7' grand model replaced the 6'10". The new 7' grand has a lighter action and better sustain than the one it replaced. All Schimmel grands now have duplex scaling. A 5'7" grand is scheduled to be introduced in early 2001.

In 1999, Schimmel introduced its "Diamond" series of grands and uprights. The Diamond grands, in both the 6' and 7' sizes, are technically the same as the regular series, but have fancier cabinet and plate features and detailing, and are available in a variety of exotic woods. The 49" Diamond upright is a completely new design, both technically and aesthetically. For greater sound volume and longer sustain, the soundboard shape, bridge positions, and pinblock arrangement have been designed more like those in a grand piano, according to Schimmel. In the Diamond Noblesse model, the decorative center panel in the bottom door can be exchanged, with a variety of exotic woods to choose from. In the Diamond Prestige model, all the panels in both the bottom and top doors can be exchanged, with striking results.

Schimmels have a very clean, bright sound. Although they have their own loyal following, players looking for a complex Steinway kind of sound may find the Schimmel sound to be less interesting.

Schimmels made a very small showing in the present survey—only two verticals and six grands—but a number of technicians were familiar enough with the brand to comment on them. Basically, Schimmels are terrific pianos with great sound and workmanship. But, typically European, the manufacturing tolerances are tight, and when the pianos first arrive at the dealer, or soon after, most have tight key balance holes, sometimes severely so, that need easing, and tight key bushings. Sometimes, too, humidity changes will have caused some case parts to bind or a few action centers to tighten. But the technicians said these problems are not serious, and once taken care of at the dealer they usually don't return. Furthermore, the technicians say that other than a little regulating, tuning, and some voicing, not much other servicing is required. My sense is that Schimmels, like many foreign-made pianos, may be a little more sensitive to humidity conditions than, say, a Steinway or Baldwin. It is not usually a problem, but special attention to climate control would be advisable in unusually dry climates.

Each time I do a survey for a new edition of the book, Schimmel pianos draw rave reviews from technicians. "One of the finest verticals I've ever tuned," wrote one technician. "Very meticulous work—clean and neat. Excellent tone and touch all the way up to note 88." Another technician, after servicing a grand, wrote: "In present-day piano manufacturing, Schimmel wins my award for MVP (Most Valuable Piano). It is as flawless as they come!" Schimmel dealers usually bill Schimmel pianos as exotic, "handcrafted" instruments, and the quotes above would seem to support that. Indeed, compared to most pianos for sale in this country, Schimmels are exquisite. But readers may be interested in knowing that, in fact, the Schimmel factory combines computer-controlled machinery with its handcraftsmanship, and my European contacts tell me that in Europe, where superbly crafted pianos are commonplace, Schimmels are considered good, but average, pianos. Competing dealers like to say that Schimmel is the "Kimball" of Europe, but with all due respect to Kimball, I think a more apt analogy might be to consider Schimmel as Europe's answer to Yamaha.

Anyway, at this level of quality, the difference between a piano like Schimmel and the very best pianos on the market becomes rather subtle, each slight quality increase raising the price substantially. For instance, a more expensive piano such as Bechstein would probably use more finely grained soundboard wood and slightly higher quality woods elsewhere, too. The pinblock would be fit more closely to the plate and more handwork would be done in the final preparation of the piano. But through the use of high technology, Schimmel is able to reduce the amount of expensive handwork while maintaining superb quality control. It can afford to do this because of the relatively high production levels it maintains compared to a company like Bechstein. This led one technician to write some years ago that "Schimmel has been my favorite grand for the past ten years, beating out Bechstein, Grotrian, Ibach, and the rest by virtue of its value [for the money]."

Warranty: Ten years, parts and labor, to original purchaser.

Price range: (Verticals) $12,000–15,400; (Grands) $34,600–40,200

Verticals	Grands
45" studio (112/114)	6' (182)
46" studio (116)	7' (213)
48" upright (120)	8'4" (256)
49" upright (122/125)	
51" upright (130)	

Consumer Ratings:

Performance: * * * * 1/2
Confidence: * * * * 1/2
Quality Control: * * * * *
Warranty: * * * *

Information
    Grands: * * * 1/2
    Verticals: * * *

SCHIRMER & SON

Syckes Piano Imports
129 E. Hartford Ave.
Phoenix, Arizona 85022
(800) 942-5801

Pianos made by: Legnicka Fabryka Fortepianow i Pianin, Legnica, Poland and other Polish piano factories

Names used: Schirmer & Son; formerly used: Th. Betting

Theodor Betting, an apprentice of Julius Blüthner, began making pianos in Kalisz, Poland in 1887. Theodor's son Julius continued the business, moving it to Leszno in 1921 when the Kalisz factory burned down. The founder's grandson Theodor, Jr. took over in 1935, managing it until World War II began, at which time piano production ceased. After the war, Janusz Betting, fourth owner of the company, began production again in the former Seiler factory in Legnica (formerly Liegnitz, Germany). Seiler had been one of Europe's largest piano manufacturers prior to the war, but had to disband and move when Poland took over part of Germany. Today, the Legnica factory manufactures over 4,000 pianos a year.

Four vertical piano models are imported into the United States, from a 42" console to a 50" upright. Identical pianos used to be available under both the Th. Betting and Schirmer & Son names, but only the Schirmer & Son name is imported today. Private-label (stencil) names are also possible. The pianos use solid spruce soundboards, quarter-sawn beech bridges, 17-ply beech pinblocks, and laminated spruce/beech back posts. Renner actions are available as an option.

Only one vertical piano from this company appeared in the current survey—a Th. Betting upright with a Renner action. The examining technician, who has serviced the instrument for several years, said it appeared to have reasonably good workmanship, not unlike, for example, Petrof pianos, and that it sounded good, but that it was quite sensitive to humidity conditions in terms of tuning stability, tight key bushings, and so forth. Climate control was recommended.

In 1997, the importer added three grands to its Schirmer & Son line. They were made by Estonia and were similar to the Estonia-brand grands, except that the two smaller grands used Czech actions instead of Renner actions. In 2000, the importer switched manufacturers of the Schirmer & Son grands from Estonia to a company in Kalisz, Poland. 5'3" and 5'11" sizes are being imported, with Detoa (Czech) actions. No quality-related information is available about these new grands at this time.

Warranty: Lifetime limited warranty from the importer.

Price range: (Verticals) $5,200–7,000; (Grands) $19,000–20,000

Verticals	Grands
42" console (M-105)	5'3" (M-160)
47" upright (M-118)	5'11" (M-180)
48" upright (M-120)	
51" upright (M-126)	

Consumer Ratings: Insufficient information to rate

SCHUBERT

The Piano Group
P.O. Box 14128
Bradenton, Florida 34280

(800) 336-9164

Pianos made by: Belarus Piano Co., Belarus; J. Becker Piano Co., St. Petersburg, Russia

Names used: Schubert; private-label brands

All the verticals except the model A-120 are from the Belarus Piano Co., a state-owned enterprise. The model A-120 and the 5'2" grand are from the J. Becker Piano Co. in St. Petersburg, Russia (see "Becker, J."). The Belarus pianos feature an all-spruce back, Delignit pinblock, and solid spruce soundboard.

Pianos from this part of the world have had a rough history. The service database examined for this edition contained 139 pianos sold under the name Belarus, the name formerly used for vertical pianos from the Belarus manufacturer, most sold three to five years ago. Nearly half of them received post-sale service other than tuning, much of it for serious problems, such as loose tuning pins and warped action parts. Customers were unhappy and some pianos had to be returned.

The pianos appear to have improved a lot over the last couple of years, based on the small amount of information available, including two private-label studio pianos that appeared in the current survey. Poor tone throughout the scale was noted for both. Other items noted included strings poorly spaced at the striking point, action parts looking sloppy, and excessive false beating strings in the treble. The examining technician said he felt the pianos exhibited somewhat poor construction and preparation. However, from the survey reports, the pianos do not seem to have problems as severe as they did five years ago.

Warranty: Twelve years, parts only, to original purchaser.

Price range: (Verticals) $1,900–2,600; (Grands) $7,100

Verticals	Grands
43" console (B-21)	5'2" (B-155)
44" studio (B-20/22/23)	
46" studio (B-7-R)	
47" studio (A-120)	
47" studio (B-15-A)	

Consumer Ratings (models from the Belarus factory):

Performance: * *
Confidence: * 1/2
Quality Control: * 1/2
Warranty: * 1/2
Information: * *

See "Becker, J." for ratings of pianos from Russia.

For explanation of survey and review procedures, model listings, and price ranges, please see pages 76–81.

SCHULTZ & SONS

Schultz & Sons Manufacturing Corporation
68 Chestnut Lane
Woodbury, New York 11797

(800) 572-4858
(631) 752-8611
sales@schultzpianos.com
service@schultzpianos.com
www.schultzpianos.com

Owned by: Schultz & Sons Musical Enterprises Ltd.

Pianos made by: John Broadwood & Sons, London, England (grand made in Germany); Samick Musical Instrument Mfg. Co. Ltd., Inchon, South Korea; formerly made by Kawai, Nakamichi, Kimball, and Sohmer.

Schultz & Sons pianos are joint ventures with established manufacturers in which Schultz designs and incorporates technical improvements of its own in the manufacturers' regular models. Some of these modifications are done by the original manufacturer, some by Schultz & Sons at its facility. Schultz pioneered this concept of co-produced pianos, a concept now widely used by others in the industry.

Schultz & Sons began its joint ventures with Sohmer and Kimball, then Nakamichi and Kawai (see previous editions for details). The most recent additions to the Schultz & Sons line are manufactured by Samick in Korea and by Broadwood in England (the grand is made in Germany). Schultz says the Samick pianos are ordered with an assortment of specifications from the upscale World and Millenium series in the Samick and Kohler & Campbell lines, for example, with Renner actions, Renner or Abel hammers, Kluge keys, maple rims, and higher quality soundboard material, as well as with some additional modifications unique to the Schultz & Sons line that vary from model to model. Then, Schultz says, for both the Samick and Broadwood pianos, in its own facility it makes scaling and damper refinements to improve tone, adds reinforcement to the vertical backposts and grand beam structures to enhance tuning stability, and calibrates the touch weight to make the action more even and responsive. Schultz & Sons also offers a limited number of custom-built art case pianos.

Schultz takes a novel approach to distribution and pricing. It says that its line of pianos will be sold only at nationally-known department stores, through universities and concert venues, and through a limited number of piano professionals (technicians, teachers, and rebuilders), but not through traditional piano retail outlets. Prices will be pre-negotiated at a discount of at least 27 percent from the standard list price given in the *Annual Supplement to The Piano Book* and will not be further negotiable, thus eliminating the haggling over price that customers are subjected to at most traditional retail outlets.

Warranty: Both the original manufacturer's warranty plus Schultz & Sons' warranty (varies by manufacturer)

Price range: (Verticals, Broadwood) $16,700–21,800; (Grands, Broadwood) $60,000; (Verticals, Samick) $9,700–11,100; (Grands, Samick) $16,600–40,000

Verticals—from Broadwood	Grands—from Broadwood
47"	6'
50"	

Verticals—from Samick	Grands—from Samick
47 1/2"	5'3 1/2"
48 1/2"	5'9 1/2"
52"	6'1"
	6'9"
	7'1"

Consumer Ratings: Insufficient information to rate

SCHULZE POLLMANN

North American Music Inc.
126 Route 203
West Nyack, New York 10994

(800) 541-2331
(845) 353-3520
www.schulzepollmann.com

Pianos made by: Schulze Pollmann, Fermingnano, Italy

Schulze Pollmann was formed in 1928 by the merger of two German piano builders who had moved to Italy, where the company still resides today. Since 1973 the firm has been owned by Generalmusic, which is best known for its digital pianos and organs and other musical electronics. Schulze Pollmann utilizes both sophisticated technology and hand work in its manufacturing, producing about 1,500 verticals and 150 grand pianos a year. The pianos contain Delignit pinblocks and Renner actions, except for the 45" vertical, which has a Detoa (Czech) action. Interesting features include a heavy, one-piece laminated vertical back, and finger-jointed construction on all soundboards to discourage future cracking. Many of the cabinets have beautiful designs and inlays.

The survey technicians had relatively little experience with Schulze Pollmann pianos. The comments I received were that the cabinets looked beautiful, and other workmanship was, for the most part, very good, too. The pianos arrive at the dealer in good shape and appear to be quality, crafted instruments. Several technicians placed the overall quality somewhere between Yamaha and Schimmel.

Warranty: Ten years, parts and labor, transferable.

Price range: (Verticals) $6,600–9,600; (Grands) $29,400–35,000

Verticals	Grands
45" (113E)	6'2" (190F)
46" (117E)	6'7" (197A)
50" (126E)	

Consumer Ratings:

Performance: * * * *
Confidence: * * * * 1/2
Quality Control: * * * * 1/2
Warranty: * * * *
Information: * *

SCHUMANN

Name not in use

Pianos bearing this name were made by Samick, except for the least expensive console and grand models, which were made by Kimball. The Schumann brand name is not presently being used.

SEIDL & SOHN

German American Trading Co., Inc.
P.O. Box 17789
Tampa, Florida 33682

(813) 961-8405
germanamer@aol.com

Pianos made by: Seidl Piano a.s., Jirikov, Czech Republic

Several generations of the Seidl family have been involved in piano-making for a hundred years as employees and directors of various Czech piano manufacturing firms. A few years ago, when the Czech government-run Musicexport company was split up, one of the factories was privatized to the Seidl family.

Seidl produces vertical pianos only, in 43", 46", 47", 48", and 51" sizes. A Czech-made action is standard in the pianos, though a Renner action is available at an additional cost of about $800.

Warranty: Ten years, parts and labor, to original purchaser

Price range: (Verticals) $4,800–6,800

Verticals
    43" (SL 109)
    46" (SL 113)
    47" (SL 117)
    48" (SL 120)
    51" (SL 127)

Consumer Ratings: Insufficient information to rate, but possibly similar to Petrof pianos with Detoa (Czech) action.

SEILER

Woods Piano International, Inc.
14929 Harrison Street
Brighton, Colorado 80602

(303) 457-2361
seilerpno@aol.com
info@seiler-pianos.de
www.seiler-pianos.de

Pianos made by: Ed. Seiler Pianofortefabrik, Kitzingen, Germany

Eduard Seiler, the company's founder, began making pianos in Liegnitz, Silesia, Germany in 1849. The company grew to over 435 employees, producing up to 3,000 pianos per year in 1923. Seiler was the largest piano manufacturer in Eastern Europe at that time. In 1945 and after World War II, the plant was occupied by Poland and the Seiler family left their native homeland with millions of other refugees. In 1951 Steffan Seiler re-established the company in Copenhagen under the fourth generation of family ownership, and in 1962 moved it to Kitzingen, Germany, where it resides today. Seiler is Germany's second largest piano manufacturer. It has over 200 employees and produces approximately 5,000 pianos annually.

Seiler makes high quality pianos using a combination of traditional methods and modern technology. The scale designs are of relatively high tension, producing a brilliant, balanced tone that is quite consistent from one Seiler to the next. The grands have wide tails for greater soundboard area and string length. Although brilliant, the tone also sings well due to, the company says, a unique soundboard feature called a Membrator—a tapered groove running around the perimeter of the board—that gives the soundboard flexibility without losing necessary stiffness. The pianos feature Bavarian spruce soundboards, multilaminated beech pinblocks, quarter-sawn beech bridges, Renner actions, and slow-close fallboards. Both the verticals and the 5'11" grand are available in dozens of models with beautiful wood inlays and brass ornamentation.

Seiler's 48" and 52" uprights are now available with the optional "Super Magnet Repetition" (SMR) action, a patented feature that uses magnets to increase repetition speed. Tiny magnets are attached to certain action parts of each note. During playing, the magnets repel each other, forcing the parts to return to their rest position faster, ready for a new key stroke.

Optional on all Seiler pianos is the patented "Duo Vox" system that can turn a regular piano into a hybrid acoustic/digital instrument (similar to the Yamaha MIDIPiano or "Silent Series" pianos). A key sensor system interfaces with a sound module to provide the digitized sound of a concert grand at the touch of a button. A lever-actuated "acoustic mute" rail completely silences the piano by preventing the hammers from hitting the strings, or the regular muffler (practice) rail can be used for quiet acoustic piano playing, if desired. Headphone jacks for private listening and MIDI ports for interfacing with peripherals are also provided.

No Seiler pianos appeared in the current survey, but when they have in the past, the comments have always been very positive. It's difficult to make such distinctions, but Seilers are generally considered similar in quality to, or perhaps slightly better than, Schimmel pianos.

Warranty: Ten years, parts and labor, to original purchaser.

Price range: (Verticals) $13,100–18,100; (Grands) $34,300–40,600

Verticals	Grands
46" studio (116)	5'11" (180)
48" upright (122)	6'9" (206)
52" upright (132)	8' (240)

Consumer Ratings:

Performance: * * * * 1/2
Confidence: * * * * 1/2
Quality Control: * * * * *
Warranty: * * * *
Information: * *

For explanation of survey and review procedures, model listings, and price ranges, please see pages 76–81.

SHERLOCK-MANNING

This hundred-year-old Canadian piano company stopped making pianos around 1988.

SHERMAN CLAY

Sherman Clay
851 Traeger Ave., Suite 200
San Bruno, California 94066
(650) 952-2300

This is the name of a national chain of piano stores. Until about 1987, pianos bearing the name Sherman Clay were made by Daewoo (Sojin); from 1987 to 1990, they were made by Kimball. Since 1990, the Sherman Clay name has not been used on any piano.

SOHMER

Name Owned by: Mason & Hamlin Piano Co.

Pianos not currently being made under this name.

Founded by German immigrant Hugo Sohmer in 1872, Sohmer & Co. was owned and managed by the Sohmer family in New York City for 110 years, most recently by the founder's grandsons Harry and Robert Sohmer. Getting old and having no descendents willing to take over the business, the Sohmer brothers sold the company in 1982 to Pratt, Read & Co., a leading manufacturer of piano keys and actions. Due to the decline of the U.S. piano industry and foreign competition, Pratt, Read had excess manufacturing capacity and a skilled work force, so the match seemed like a good one, and Sohmer & Co. was moved to Ivoryton, Connecticut. The Sohmer brothers moved, too, and for a while continued to play a part in managing the company, but most of the labor force and the rest of the management stayed behind in New York.

In 1986, continuing its withdrawal from the piano business, Pratt, Read sold Sohmer to a group of investors headed by Robert McNeil, former chief of McNeil Laboratories (creators of Tylenol). At the same time, McNeil purchased the Mason & Hamlin and Knabe names and assets from Citicorp, the owner of the bankrupt Aeolian Pianos (see "Aeolian" and "Mason & Hamlin" for more information). In 1989, McNeil sold Sohmer (and Mason & Hamlin/Knabe) to Bernard Greer, owner of Falcone Piano Co., and Greer renamed the combined firm The Mason & Hamlin Companies. Mason & Hamlin filed for bankruptcy in 1995 and was purchased out of bankruptcy in 1996 by Kirk and Gary Burgett, owners of PianoDisc, makers of electronic player piano systems. The current owners of the Sohmer name have no immediate plans for using it.

During its many years in New York, the Sohmer piano was known as a fine handcrafted instrument. Sohmer had a close informal association with the other major New York piano maker, Steinway, and many of Sohmer's manufacturing methods were similar to Steinway's. After the sale of the company by the Sohmer family, the new management in

Connecticut was technically knowledgeable and sought to maintain and even improve the product, which was generally considered to be one of the finest pianos made in the United States. After a few years, though, the Connecticut labor market became so tight that it was almost impossible to find the skilled labor necessary to build the pianos, which by this time also included the Mason & Hamlin line. Sohmer officials sometimes said they were competing with McDonald's for help.

Finally, in 1988, Sohmer moved its manufacturing facilities to Elysburg, Pennsylvania, an area with a large pool of skilled but unemployed woodworkers and craftspeople. In Elysburg, production of Sohmer pianos was gradually increased back to normal levels as the new workers were trained. Advances were made in the structure, cabinetry, and finish of the instruments. Unfortunately, due to the rising cost of doing business in Pennsylvania and the slow market for vertical pianos, the Elysburg plant was closed in 1994.

Sohmer made a 42" console, a 45" or 46" studio, and 5' and 5'7" grands. The company was best known for the studio model, which had about as solid a structure as a piano can have, and the furniture and cabinetry were well executed, too. The tone, action, and trapwork were satisfactory, but unexceptional. One reason is that the scale design of the studio was almost identical to that of the console, so the studio did not take full advantage of its larger size, and the tonal transition from treble to bass was similar to that of the console. Nevertheless, the studio was quite suitable for average home and institutional use.

About their grands, Sohmer was always very low-key, perhaps because in New York they were overshadowed by the pianos of neighbor Steinway. Or perhaps because the grands weren't particularly noteworthy. Basically, Sohmer grands were adequate instruments for casual use inside of nicely made cabinets.

SOJIN

Pianos no longer being made.

Pianos were made by: Daewoo Precision Industries Ltd., Yeoju, South Korea

Names used: Sojin; also, at times in the past, Royale, Daytron, Daewoo, Schafer & Sons, Sherman Clay, Cline, and other private-label names.

Sojin was founded in 1964 as a family firm, but sold out to Daewoo, one of Korea's largest industrial conglomerates, in 1977 and began exporting to the United States about 1980. Although each of the Daewoo units operates somewhat autonomously, Sojin was able to take advantage of the manufacturing and engineering expertise of companies engaged in such activities as auto making, shipbuilding, and the manufacture of heavy machinery.

Despite all this potential expertise, Sojin pianos were very inconsistent in quality, like the other Korean brands but worse. Some were terrible, some were not bad. Sometimes the grands were acceptable if prepared by the dealer, but I would not trust these pianos to hold up well with time and use.

In 1991 Daewoo completely changed direction and purchased a 33 percent interest in the prominent German piano manufacturer Ibach. The production of Sojin pianos was discontinued, to be replaced by the manufacture of Ibach pianos in Korea. According to Daewoo, most Sojin production equipment was sold to a Chinese company and replaced by copies of Ibach equipment. See "Ibach" for more information.

STECK, GEORGE

PianoDisc
4111-A North Freeway Blvd.
Sacramento, California 95834

(800) 566-3472
(916) 567-9999
www.pianodisc.com

Owned by: PianoDisc, Sacramento, California

Pianos made by: Guangzhou Pearl River Piano Group Ltd., Guangzhou, China

George Steck was an old American brand name that eventually became part of the Mason & Hamlin family of brands, along with Knabe and others (see "Mason & Hamlin"). The name is now being applied to a line of Chinese pianos from the Guangzhou Pearl River factory. The pianos are said to be similar to those sold under the Pearl River name. All are sold with a PianoDisc unit installed, and are serviced in PianoDisc's Sacramento, California facility prior to being shipped to dealers. See "Pearl River" for more information.

Warranty: Ten-year limited warranty to original purchaser.

Price range (includes PianoDisc PDS 128 Plus system installed): (Verticals) $7,900; (Grands) $14,000

Verticals	Grands
43" console (GSV43)	5'3" (GS530)

Consumer Ratings: See "Pearl River"

STEIGERMAN

Steigerman Music Corporation
2318 Kings Avenue
West Vancouver, British Columbia
Canada

(604) 921-6217

Name no longer being used in the U.S.

The Steigerman name is owned by Robert Loewen, a Canadian distributor. Over the last several decades, Loewen has used the Steigerman name on pianos from several manufacturers, including Yamaha and, more recently, Samick, imported into Canada. He also imports pianos from a variety of Chinese companies onto which dealers can place their own house-brand names. For a couple of years, Steigerman pianos were made by the Yantai Longfeng Piano Co. of Yantai City, China, but Steigerman discontinued importing these pianos in 1998. (Pianos from this manufacturer are now being imported under the name "Kingsburg." See under that name for more information.)

STEINBERG, WILH.

Poppenberg & Associates
966 South Pearl Street
Denver, Colorado 80209

(303) 765-5775

Pianos made by: Wilhelm Steinberg Pianofortefabrik GmbH,
Eisenberg-Thuringen, Germany

Wilhelm Steinberg Pianofortefabrik was formed from the merger of several East German piano companies following the unification of Germany. These companies collectively trace their origin back to 1877. Steinberg also purchased the Thuringen Key Co., which makes keys for several German piano manufacturers. Production is about 1,200 pianos per year. Steinberg also makes cabinets for other German companies.

Steinberg makes 46", 49", and 52" verticals, all with Renner actions. The 49" vertical will also be available with a Fandrich action, made by Renner (see "Fandrich & Sons" for more information). Steinberg also makes a 5'9" grand with a Renner action. This grand is actually designed by Steingraeber & Sohne, and pretty much identical to the Steingraeber piano, except for cabinet details, the company says.

Warranty: Ten years, parts and labor, to original purchaser.

Price range: (Verticals) $7,900–11,400; (Grands) $27,800

Verticals	Grands
46" (IQ 16)	5'9" (IQ 77)
49" (IQ 22)	
52" (IQ 28)	

Consumer Ratings: Insufficient information to rate, but the verticals are probably in Group 2 (see "Summary of Brands and Ratings," page 84).

STEINER, BERNHARD

Bernhard Steiner Pianos USA, Inc.
5840 Alpha Road
Dallas, Texas 75240

(972) 233-1967

Pianos made by: Samick Musical Instrument Mfg. Co. Ltd.,
Inchon, South Korea

In collaboration with the Kahn family, owners of Bernhard Steiner Pianos USA, Samick manufactures a full line of pianos under the Bernhard Steiner label. The company says this line is intended to service the upper level of the market for Korean pianos. The models are a selected mixture of Samick's old and new scales, some with Samick's three-ply laminated spruce soundboard and some with solid spruce soundboard. For more information, see "Samick."

A separate line of Bernhard Steiner pianos is also manufactured in South Africa by Dietmann-Bernhard Steiner. See "Dietmann."

Warranty: Bernhard Steiner pianos are warranted by Samick.

Consumer Ratings: See "Samick"

STEINGRAEBER & SOHNE

Unique Pianos, Inc.
223 E. New Haven Avenue
Melbourne, Florida 32901

(888) 725-6633
(321) 725-5690
www.uniquepianos.com

Pianos made by: Steingraeber & Sohne, Bayreuth, Germany

This small German piano maker (about 250 pianos per year) is once again actively marketing in the U.S. after an absence of a few years. Steingraeber sells three sizes of vertical piano in the U.S. The largest is 54" tall, one of the largest uprights made today. The 51" upright features a special action with a patented repetition mechanism. The company also makes two sizes of grand piano, 5'6" and 6'9". The 5'6" model has an unusually wide tail, allowing for a larger soundboard and longer bass strings than is customary for an instrument of its size, the company says.

Steingraeber is willing to make custom cabinets and finishes. One interesting option on the vertical pianos, available by special order, is "twist and change" panels. These are two-sided top and bottom panels, one side finished in polished ebony and the other a two-toned combination of a wood veneer and ebony. The panels can be reversed as desired by the piano owner to match room décor or just for a change of scenery. Steingraeber also specializes in so-called ecological or biological finishes, available as an option on most models. This involves the use of only organic materials in the piano, such as natural paints and glues in the case, and white keytops made from cattle bone.

In addition to its regular line of pianos, Steingraeber makes a piano that can be used by physically handicapped players who don't have the use of their legs. A switch in a backrest cushion operates the sustain pedal and a switch under the keybed operates the soft pedal. This mechanism can be installed in pianos of other makers if certain technical requirements are met.

Warranty: Ten years, parts and labor, to original purchaser

Price range: (Verticals) $21,800–31,800; (Grands) $47,700–64,500

Verticals	Grands
48" (122)	5'6" (168)
51" (130)	6'9" (205)
54" (138)	

Consumer Ratings:

Performance: * * * * *
Confidence: * * * * *
Quality Control: * * * * *
Warranty: * * * *
Information
    Grands: * 1/2
    Verticals: *

For explanation of survey and review procedures, model listings, and price ranges, please see pages 76–81.

STEINWAY & SONS

Steinway & Sons, Inc.
Steinway Place
Long Island City, New York 11105

(718) 721-2600
(800) 366-1853
www.steinway.com

Owned by: Steinway Musical Instruments, Inc., a public company (NYSE: LVB)

The Company: A Steinway family legend has it that Heinrich Engelhard Steinweg, a cabinetmaker and piano maker in Seesen, Germany, built his first piano in the kitchen of his house. He began building pianos in 1835 and exhibited three instruments at the state fair in Braunschweig in 1839, establishing a fair reputation as a piano builder before he emigrated to the United States in 1850 with his family. After first taking jobs with other piano manufacturers to learn the American way of doing business, he and his sons established Steinway & Sons in 1853. This came at a time when interest in the piano, already well established in Europe, was undergoing explosive growth in America, and the Steinways, with nearly twenty years of piano making already under their belt, were in a prime position to exploit the commercial, artistic, and technological potential of the piano in their adopted country.

Within a short time, the Steinways were granted patents that revolutionized the piano, and which were eventually adopted or imitated by other makers. Most of these patents concerned the quest for a stronger frame, a richer, more powerful sound, and a more sensitive action. Heinrich's son Theodore Steinway, a scientist and engineer, was assisted in his acoustical research by association and correspondence with prominent scientists of the day, including the noted German physicist Hermann von Helmholtz. The business grew rapidly due to good management, to high-quality products, to technical innovations, and to artist endorsements, which were actively used to promote the pianos, a practice still employed today with great success. By the 1880s, the Steinway piano was in most ways the modern piano we have today.

In the late 1800s, Steinway gradually moved its manufacturing facilities from Manhattan to Queens, and built a company village there for its employees, who were largely German immigrants. The Steinway family was very active in New York civic affairs, and their role is still remembered through the businesses, streets, and even a subway station named after them. In 1880, Steinway & Sons opened a branch factory in Hamburg, Germany to provide Steinway pianos for the European market.

In the early 1900s, there were fewer technical changes to the instruments, and the quality standards set by the previous generations were strictly adhered to. As Steinway's worldwide dealer network became established, its concert and repair services became widely accessible. The fame of the Steinway continued to spread, and ownership of Steinways with elaborately carved cases became a symbol of wealth and culture. The Depression and the rise of the radio

and phonograph both caused sweeping changes to the piano industry. Steinway survived this period by cutting back production, by selling pianos to radio (and later television) stations, and by producing smaller grands and verticals that would appeal to smaller homes and budgets. During World War II, Steinway, like most other piano manufacturers, was commandeered to produce materials for the war machine, but was also one of the few companies allowed to manufacture pianos used by the Army for the entertainment of G.I.s abroad.

In the 1960s, the fourth generation of Steinways found themselves without any heirs willing or able to take over the business, and with a lack of capital with which to finance much needed equipment modernization, so in 1972 the Steinways sold their company to CBS. CBS eventually discovered that it was out of its depth trying to run a musical instrument manufacturing company, so in 1985 it sold Steinway to an investment group consisting of several men with backgrounds in law, finance, marketing, and management. Ten years later, in April 1995, this group sold the company to Selmer Industries, Inc., parent company of the Selmer Company, a major manufacturer of brass and woodwind instruments. The combined company, now known as Steinway Musical Instruments, is listed on the New York Stock Exchange. Management at Steinway & Sons remained the same despite the change of ownership.

Since the mid-1980s, many factory processes have been reviewed and reorganized and new machinery designed, with an eye toward greater precision and efficiency. Steinway's ongoing challenge is to find the right balance between modern engineering and old-world craftsmanship that will preserve the integrity of its construction process. In line with this mandate, Steinway has made many changes to its pianos during the past fifteen years, particularly in the design and manufacturing of action parts. These changes have come about in response to the serious problem the company had for some time with the quality of the action parts and their assembly. From 1984 to 1992, while this work was going on, Steinway imported many of its action parts from Europe, especially for the larger grand models B and D. These parts were made for Steinway by Renner, the German firm that makes parts for Steinway's branch factory in Hamburg, Germany, and for most other makers of high-end pianos. Since 1992, all action parts for New York Steinway grands are now, once again, made in New York. Technicians say the new parts are a vast improvement over the old, though not as consistent as the Renner parts.

Since the most recent change in ownership, Steinway has made a number of bold moves to help ensure its long-term success. In 1999, the company purchased two of its most important suppliers: the Herman Kluge company, Europe's largest manufacturer of piano keys, and the O.S. Kelly company, the only remaining piano plate foundry in the U.S. The acquisition of these companies was vital to Steinway's long-term security, since suppliers of both keyboards and plates have become increasingly rare over the past twenty years.

By way of providing its dealers with a mid-priced product line, Steinway entered into an agreement with Kawai in 1991 to build Steinway-designed grands and verticals under the Boston name (see "Boston" for more information). Apparently the arrangement has been successful because Steinway recently announced that a similar deal is in the works with Young Chang to build a lower-priced, third line of pianos under the "Essex" name. This line is expected to debut in 2001.

Verticals: Steinway currently makes two kinds of vertical piano in three sizes—a 45" studio (model 4510), a 46½" studio (model 1098), and a 52" upright (model K-52). The model 45 and model 1098 have identical scale designs—only the cabinet is different—the former being in a period style for home use, and the latter for school use or less furniture-conscious home use. The model K-52 is a reissue (in 1981) of the model K piano that Steinway discontinued in 1929. Until 1986, Steinway also made a 40" console (model F). The studio and upright models all have three pedals, the middle one a true sostenuto. The console had only two, sustain and soft. All Steinway verticals use a solid spruce soundboard, have no particle board, and in many other ways are similar in design, materials, and quality of workmanship to Steinway grands. Actions are made by Renner.

Technicians generally like Steinway verticals, but usually complain that the pianos are extremely difficult to tune, especially in the treble section. There seem to be several reasons for this. First, the tuning pins are quite tight, although this alone could be an asset, not a drawback. Second, unlike most other brands of piano, Steinways do not have plate bushings surrounding each tuning pin where it passes through a hole in the plate. These bushings normally support the pin, preventing it from bending as it is turned during tuning. On pianos without plate bushings, it is more difficult to control and set the pins. Third, the strings do not move smoothly over their bearing (friction) points when the tuning pins are turned; as a result some strings may suddenly jump out of tune at some point after being tuned. Estimates reported to me of the extra time needed to tune a Steinway vertical ranged from three-quarters of an hour to two hours longer than other brands. Some technicians charge extra to tune a Steinway vertical for this reason. However, technicians report that once the pins are properly set and any initial jumping out of tune has been corrected, Steinway verticals hold their tune very well. As one technician wrote on a survey form: "I trust that this will also be like other [model] 1098s in that after a few years of string settling and solid tunings, the tuning will be more stable than other pianos."

A surprising number of technicians in the current survey also noted problems with very prominent false beats in the treble of the Steinway verticals they worked on, particularly the studio model. Also a form of tuning challenge, false beats can make it difficult for the tuner to make the unisons sound sharp and clear.

[Steinway says it recognizes that its vertical pianos can be difficult to tune and has taken steps to lessen this problem, including reducing friction across the string bearing surfaces and shortening the tuning pin length for better control.]

Despite the tuning difficulty, in my experience most technicians like how Steinway verticals perform, especially the model K-52, but consider the pianos expensive.

For explanation of survey and review procedures, model listings, and price ranges, please see pages 76–81.

Grands: Steinway makes five sizes of grand piano in its New York factory: 5'1" (model S), 5'7" (model M), 5'10½" (model L), 6'10½" (model B), and 8'11½" (model D).

The model S is billed as being "for the home where space is at a premium." Though very good for a small grand, it has the usual limitations of any small piano and so is not really recommended unless space considerations are paramount. Steinway introduced this model in 1935, when all the manufacturers were building smaller pianos in the hopes of reviving the depressed piano industry.

The model M is a full six inches longer, but costs little more than the S. Historically, this has been the most common model of Steinway grand—the one found in living rooms across the country—though more recently, larger models have surpassed it in sales. Its medium size makes the tone in certain areas slightly less than perfect, but it's an excellent home instrument.

The model L is only 3½" longer than the M, but the scale design and tone are far superior. This instrument is suitable for the more advanced player, larger living room, and many school and teaching situations.

The model B is my favorite of the New York-made Steinways, and the best choice for the serious pianist, recording or teaching studio, or small recital hall. The model D, the concert grand, is the flagship of the Steinway line and the piano of choice for the overwhelming majority of concert pianists. It's too large for most places other than the concert stage.

Steinway grand rims, both inner and outer, are made in one continuous bend from layers of maple, and the beams are of solid spruce. The keybed is of quartersawn spruce planks freely mortised together, and the keys are of Bavarian spruce. The pinblock consists of seven laminations of maple with successive grain orientations of 45 and 90 degrees. The soundboard is of solid Sitka spruce, the bridges are vertically laminated of maple with a solid maple cap, and all models have duplex scaling.

The present survey looked at 115 Steinway grands. As in past surveys, technicians indicated that Steinway grands are inconsistent in how they arrive from the factory. Many are quite free of problems, needing only normal servicing, but quite a few pianos in the current survey initially had small, and sometimes unusual, problems to be corrected. A comparison with the survey taken six years prior suggests that there may have been certain specific quality-control issues in the period between the two surveys. However, interviews and personal experience give some indication that factory preparation may have improved during the early months of the year 2000.

Typically, the pianos almost always need voicing—the treble tends to be too soft or weak—and thorough regulating, especially dampers. Since the early years, Steinway has produced relatively soft hammers for its New York instruments, contravening an industry trend toward harder hammers. This means that the new hammers, especially in the treble, must be brought up to the desired brightness and volume by treating them with a hardening solution. With the harder hammers used by other makers, the tone usually must be brought down to the desired volume and warmth by needling the felt. Some technicians would prefer that

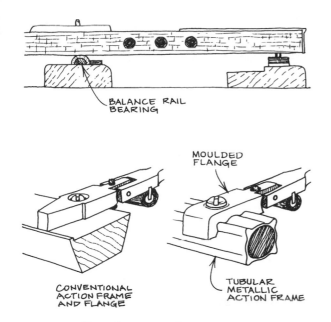

BALANCE RAIL
BEARING

MOULDED
FLANGE

CONVENTIONAL
ACTION FRAME
AND FLANGE

TUBULAR
METALLIC
ACTION FRAME

FIGURE 4-5. Two features of Steinway pianos: (Top) Accelerated action. The key balances on a half-round bearing instead of a flat surface, which, Steinway says, increases the speed of repetition. (Bottom) Tubular metallic action frame. The unique shape of the flange and rail virtually prevent movement of the flange, thus helping maintain proper alignment of action parts.

Steinway use harder hammers and skip the hardening solution, but Steinway says its method is the only way to achieve the "Steinway tone" without the hammers sounding too bright later on.

Although Steinway engineers have worked at making more consistent hammers that need less initial work, many technicians continue to report that new Steinways can sound muffled in the treble because the hammers are not hard enough. Salespeople often tell customers that after playing the piano for a while, the hammer felt will pack down and the piano will sound brighter. This is true, of course, but depending on how much the piano is used, this could take a long time to happen. Hardening the hammers to brighten the tone is a relatively simple operation; the customer shouldn't hesitate to request it, if necessary.

In addition to voicing and action regulating, the damper wires tend to bind in their guide-rail bushings, causing the occasional damper to stay up and the note to continue ringing after the key has been released—a problem we've seen in Steinway grands for many years. A Steinway factory criterion for damper installation requires that the damper wires must exert some side pressure on their guide-rail bushings. While this practice definitely reduces rattling noises from damper heads flopping around during playing, it may lead to a higher incidence of sticking dampers as well, since it's difficult to get exactly the right amount of side pressure on every bushing. As with voicing and action regulating, damper regulating is part of the normal preparation of the piano. When the piano is new, the customer may occasionally experience sticking dampers, but after a break-in period and some minor adjustments, the problem will go away.

Other normal prep work on Steinway grands might include eliminating noises caused by the occasional bad bass string, buzzing treble string, or noisy action part; taking care of friction problems by lubricating keyframe pins and knuckles, and fixing the occasional loose or tight action center; and correcting some just plain sloppy workmanship, such as poorly shaped hammers, rubber lid buttons that have fallen off, and random other small problems that may appear from time to time. These all fall within the realm of normal pre-sale servicing of Steinway grands, and if the piano is properly serviced, these conditions should not be problems for the purchaser.

In additional to the normal or typical pre-sale servicing mentioned above, several special or unusual problems of a temporary nature surfaced in the written survey or interviews:

Some technicians complained that their Steinway Bs and Ds in the survey were difficult to regulate correctly because the action stack (the unit containing the hammers and other action parts) had been installed too low relative to the strings. The traditional method for locating Steinway action stacks was to set them at a uniform height from the keybed. Unfortunately, the string height, as measured from the keybed, can vary significantly in larger pianos because of anomalies in the plate castings. Steinway says that new factory methods for establishing the height of the action stack relative to the strings, rather than to the keybed, should help reduce the incidence of this problem. In the meantime, Steinway advises technicians in the field to raise the stack if necessary and re-regulate the action to cure the problem. One symptom of this problem could be a wooden clicking sound on a hard blow. This noise is caused by the jack contacting the hammer flange tongue when the key is depressed fully.

A couple of university technicians reported that the large batches of new Steinway grands they received in 1997 and 1998 as part of purchases made by the university had nearly the same problems in many of the pianos. The problems included nicked front-rail key pins and loose or missing lead weights in keys and underlevers, among other things. Steinway supplied replacements for the missing or defective parts for the technicians to install. There were also some reports of poorly shaped keytops, which sometimes required sending the keyboard back to the factory for repair.

Some technicians noted that certain model S grands sold in the mid- to late-1990s had a string breakage problem in the extreme treble. This problem was thought by the technicians to be due to overly long string speaking lengths which resulted in the tension on those strings being too high. However, Steinway says that this infrequent occurrence can be alleviated in the field by reducing the angle at which the string approaches the capo bar. Technicians needing advice about this problem should contact the factory.

Many of the problems reported with Steinway grands in the current survey were related to the finish. Quite a few technicians complained that the lacquer finish on Steinway pianos tended to be too soft, almost always becoming deeply imprinted by the rubber lid buttons, and often wearing away at corners and edges or having factory veneer repairs "telegraph" through. An official at Steinway said that the company has honored all warranty claims stemming from "soft" finishes, and stated that the problems were due to a number of factors, including lacquer formulations with a slow curing rate and unheated shipping trucks. "The formulations have been tweaked and other issues have been rectified," he said.

Despite initial problems, the underlying excellence of the Steinway design and overall integrity of its construction process make it very likely that most Steinway grands, after thorough servicing, will be quite beautiful nonetheless. Although the reviews in this book tend, by their nature, to highlight the problem areas, my sense is that most technicians feel that Steinway grands, properly serviced, are among the best-performing pianos—if not *the* best—made. In the interviews and written survey, technicians spoke glowingly of the tone and playing characteristics of the instruments: "Beautiful, vibrant tone." "Tone is very rich and substantial." "This is one of the most perfect pianos in my customer base." "This piano has tons of power, and a depth of tone characteristic of healthy Steinways."

At the same time, as mentioned, the survey technicians initially found many, mostly small, flaws in the pianos, and some technicians, even as they extolled the brand's virtues, expressed dismay that such an expensive and prestigious brand would be so poorly or inconsistently prepared at the factory. Remarked one technician: "I'm probably more critical of Steinway than other instruments because they are so expensive and because they claim to be the best. Two Bs bought by [the school] had [gold lacquer] overspray on the strings, cosmetic imperfections all over the place, some trapwork put on so cockeyed I had to take it off and plug holes and redrill to mount it correctly. [However,] the thing I like about Steinway is that the pianos really repay the work you put into them, whereas a Yamaha is about as nice as it's going to get right out of the box." Another technician made the point more gently: "Steinways in general don't come out of the crate as eager to please their prospective owners as Yamahas do. They like to get a thorough working over by very skilled technicians, and then expect to be admired by everyone around them."

According to the company, the landed quality of the pianos has been continually improving because of the company's ongoing investment in plant and equipment, and a training program where new employees learn essential skills "before they get near the assembly process." Usually a day or two of work by the dealer's technician has been necessary to make a new instrument worthy of the Steinway name, but with very recent pianos it seems that less time may be needed. The best dealerships allow their technicians to give complete pre-sale service to the pianos. I am aware, however, that sometimes dealerships skimp on pre-sale service and then provide service in the home primarily in response to customer complaints.

My impression is that it takes quite a bit of servicing to uncover the potential of the Steinway, and that the expertise needed is very specific to the brand. When shopping for one, therefore, I suggest hiring a piano technician who is experienced in servicing modern Steinways. Very careful inspection and selection with the help of such a technician should help you sidestep most problems. Sometimes the store's technician may be the appropriate person to ask, sometimes not. (If able to speak candidly, the store's technician may be willing to tell you how much service the dealer authorizes for its Steinways. He or she also might be able to direct you to an instrument appropriate to your needs.) In addition, you may wish to hire this person to do further preparation of the piano after purchase, customizing it to your preferences. Although you should be reasonably happy with the piano when you buy it, bear in mind that it may have to be played for several years before it reaches its peak.

Customers seeking to purchase a model B or D Steinway who have not found the piano they are looking for at their local dealer can make arrangements with that dealer to visit the Steinway factory in New York, where a selection of the larger models is kept on hand for this purpose.

Steinway owns a branch factory in Hamburg, Germany. This factory makes most of the same models as the New York factory, plus a few additional ones (models O, A, and C) not found here. Quality control is reputed to be better in the Hamburg pianos. Historically, some of the materials used in manufacture and the musical qualities of the instruments have also differed, though in recent years Steinway has taken steps to reduce those differences. A limited edition model A grand, built to commemorate the 300th anniversary of the invention of the piano, is one example of Steinway's efforts to unify the products of its two factories. The piano's rim and belly (soundboard, bridges, strings) are made in Hamburg, while the action is made in New York; the cabinet is designed by noted furniture designer Dakota Jackson. Other than this special model, U.S. Steinway dealers do not stock the Hamburg pianos; they are made for markets in other parts of the world. However, you can order one through your local dealer if you wish, or you can go to Europe to buy one.

It is well known that Steinway's principal competition comes from used and rebuilt Steinways, many of which come in exotic veneers or have elaborately carved or custom-designed "art cases." The company has responded by expanding its product line to include modern-day versions of these collector's items: the Crown Jewel Collection, Limited Editions, and custom-designed artcase pianos.

The Crown Jewel Collection, unveiled in 1994, consists of the regular models in natural wood (non-ebonized) veneers, including such exotic ones as Cherry, Quartered Mahogany, Figured Makore, Teak, Figured Sapelle, Kewazinga Bubinga, Birds Eye Maple, Macassar Ebony, East Indian Rosewood, and Santos Rosewood. All Crown Jewel Collection models are being produced with Steinway's new Satin Lustre finish, which is half way between a satin and a high-polish finish. These new options represent a natural extension of Steinway's prodigious veneering talents, and will appeal to the company's upscale clientele. Crown Jewel Collection veneers are available on any model of grand or vertical, and add anywhere from $2,000 to $25,000 to the price of the instrument, depending on model and veneer.

Limited Edition models are reproductions of turn-of-the-century designs, available only in models L and B. The Limited Edition model issued in 1995, known as "Instrument of the Immortals," was actually an amalgam of several different Victorian-era features, such as round, "ice cream cone" legs; an elaborately carved music desk; and raised

For explanation of survey and review procedures, model listings, and price ranges, please see pages 76–81.

beads on the case and around the plate holes. In 1997, Steinway released a Limited Edition model, based on a 1903 design by J.B. Tiffany, to commemorate the 200th anniversary of the birth of Steinway founder Heinrich Engelhard Steinway. This design features over forty feet of hand-carved moldings on the lid, case edges, and legs in "Tulip" and "Egg & Dart" patterns.

In 1998, Steinway resumed its long tradition of building custom artcase pianos with the commissioning of noted furniture designer Frank Pollaro to create an art case in French art deco style for a model B grand. In 1999, Pollaro designed an artcase piano called "Rhapsody" to commemorate the 100th anniversary of the birth of George Gershwin. The piano featured a blue-dyed maple veneer adorned with more than 400 hand-cut mother-of-pearl stars, and a gilded silver plate. Several other artcase pianos were also built in 1999. Steinway says it would like to cultivate collaborations between itself, its clients, and furniture designers in the creation of custom artcase instruments.

As another way of capitalizing on the popularity of older Steinways, the company also operates the world's largest Steinway piano rebuilding facility at the factory for the restoration of older Steinways.

Information pertaining to the purchase of a used or rebuilt Steinway can be found in Chapter 5 on page 175 and pages 206 to 213. A more extended discussion of the company and its instruments, some of it no longer relevant to a purchaser but still of interest to Steinway aficionados, will be found in the first edition of this book (1987), available in many libraries.

Warranty: Five years, parts and labor, to original owner only. This is one of the shorter new-piano warranties in the industry, although informally Steinway may continue to honor the warranty when ownership is transferred between private parties. Steinway is pretty good about honoring its warranty when the defect is clearly identifiable or of a routine nature. Some technicians find Steinway difficult to deal with over technical and warranty issues, but the company says that a survey conducted by an independent research firm reported a Steinway customer satisfaction rating of 98 percent.

Price range: (Verticals) $16,400–21,400; (Grands) $35,200–53,900

Verticals	Grands
45" studio (4510)	5'1" (S)
46½" studio (1098)	5'7" (M)
52" upright (K-52)	5'10½" (L)
	6'10½" (B)
	8'11½" (D)

Consumer Ratings:

Performance: * * * * *
Confidence: * * * * *
Quality Control: * * * ½
Warranty: * * *
Information
    Verticals: * * * *
    Grands: * * * * *

STORY & CLARK

Story & Clark Piano Co.
Quaker Drive
Seneca, Pennsylvania 16346

(814) 676-6683

Owned by: QRS Music Technologies, Inc.

Names used: Story & Clark, Hobart M. Cable; no longer used: Classic, Lowrey, Hampton

Hampton Story began making pianos in 1857 and was joined by Melville Clark in 1884. The business settled in Grand Haven, Michigan in 1901, where it remained until about 1986. After a number of confusing business transactions, both Story & Clark and Lowrey Organ Co. ended up belonging to Norlin Industries, a large manufacturer of diverse products. In 1984 Norlin sold the organ and electronic keyboard division to two former piano company executives, who formed a company called Lowrey Industries. The Story & Clark Piano Co. was sold to the Bergsma Furniture Co. of Grand Rapids, Michigan, which had all along been making cabinet parts for Story & Clark. Bergsma consolidated the Story & Clark operation into its own factory and contracted with Lowrey Industries to market the pianos, but the newly organized piano business apparently never got off the ground, and piano manufacturing ceased about 1986.

Lowrey and Story & Clark vertical pianos made under Norlin's ownership in Grand Haven were made in the same factory. The Lowrey had fancier cabinetry, and the two had some relatively insignificant technical differences to differentiate them for marketing purposes, but they had the same scale design and were essentially the same piano. As one technician summed up the difference: "Lowrey pianos are sold by businessmen in suburban mall stores, and Story & Clark pianos are sold by technician-owned businesses."

Hampton was the name of the "budget"-model Lowrey, Hobart M. Cable the "budget"-model Story & Clark. These models had basswood laminated soundboards, instead of the spruce laminated "Storytone" soundboard of the regular models, cabinets of particle board instead of lumber-core plywood, and cheaper construction in many other parts, too.

The survey at that time (mid-1980s) found that Lowrey and Story & Clark verticals had many problems with cabinetry, hardware, pinblock, stringing, action regulation, and tone, and the pianos could not be recommended. A year later, the pianos were rescaled and reportedly had an improved tone. Lowrey and Story & Clark grands were also made at the Grand Haven factory until about 1984, when they were discontinued. The two differently-named grands were otherwise identical. They were apparently satisfactory instruments, with a sprinkling of minor problems, but nothing serious.

In 1990, Classic Player Piano Corporation purchased the Story & Clark and Hobart M. Cable names and designs from the Bergsma Furniture Co. For several years, the company manufactured player pianos under the name Classic, as well as regular pianos under the names Story & Clark and Hobart M. Cable. The Classic was built around a Baldwin-made back, plate, and pinblock (the same one used in the Baldwin

Hamilton), while the company built its own backs for the Story & Clark and Hobart M. Cable pianos. Both used Pratt-Win (Baldwin) actions.

In 1993, QRS Piano Rolls, Inc., now QRS Music Technologies, Inc., purchased Classic/Story & Clark. (Ironically, QRS was founded in 1901 by Melville Clark of the Story & Clark Piano Co. of old.) QRS, the nation's major source of music rolls for player pianos, has developed an electronic player piano system called Pianomation that can be retrofitted into any normal piano (see the section on electronic player piano systems at the end of this chapter).

With the change of ownership, the Classic name was dropped. All the pianos now bear the name Story & Clark, though the Hobart M. Cable name may be used when requested by a dealer. The company makes its own backs for these pianos using a modified version of the old Story & Clark plate designs. The action is from Pratt-Win (Baldwin). Both the 42" console and 46" studio have solid spruce soundboards.

The company also now makes a 5'5" grand, called the "Hampton," in the U.S. This piano is unusual in that unlike most grand rims, which are made as one continuous piece bent around a form, its maple rim is made in four pieces, glued and doweled together. The piano has German Abel hammers with a Czech- and Renner-made action, and comes in several different furniture styles.

Story & Clark also imports several models from China. The 44" console and 5'6" grand, both called "Prelude," are made by the Dongbei Piano Co. Some other Chinese pianos, made by the Beijing Piano Co. and called "Cambridge," have been discontinued. There are also 4'7" and 5'1" grands (models 47 and 51) made in Korea by Samick, similar to those sold under the Hyundai label.

Little information about the Story & Clark pianos surfaced in the present survey, but in a past survey, one technician, reviewing a new American-made Story & Clark console after being prepared for sale, described it as "ordinary but trouble-free." He said that both American-made vertical models represented reasonable values in entry-level pianos. The few Hampton grands I've played I've found unimpressive. About the foreign-made pianos, see under "Nordiska" (among others) for information about Dongbei and under "Samick" for the Korean-made models.

Both the console and the studio are available in a highly stylized cabinet with an old-style pneumatic player piano mechanism of the type formerly made by Universal. In the past Universal had installed its mechanism in pianos made by Lowrey/Story & Clark and by Kohler & Campbell. When those companies ceased production, Classic obtained the rights to update and manufacture the Universal mechanism.

Of the Universal player mechanism, one expert writes, "Indeed, all of the modern players with the exception of the Universal have the earmark of something engineered by bullheaded people who think they can invent something better than a product of the late 1920s that already had twenty-five years of experience behind it! The Universal was an exception, being engineered by people well-experienced in the strong and weak points of all the old brands of player actions."

All Story & Clark models are also available with modern-day Pianomation electronic player piano systems installed.

For explanation of survey and review procedures, model listings, and price ranges, please see pages 76–81.

The studio is also made in a 48" coin-operated Nickelodeon/Orchestrion version.

Price range: (Verticals) $2,800–5,000; (Grands) $9,900–23,600

Verticals	Grands
42" console	5'5" (Hampton)
44" console (Prelude)	5'6" (Prelude)
46" studio	

Consumer ratings (American-made verticals only):

Performance: * * *
Confidence: * * * 1/2
Quality Control: * * *
Warranty: * * * *
Information: * *

"Hampton" grands: Insufficient information to rate.

Foreign-made pianos: See ratings for them under other listings, as mentioned above.

STRAUSS

L & M International, Inc.
6452 Bresslyn Road
Nashville, Tennessee 37205

(615) 356-3686

Pianos made by: Shanghai Piano Co., Shanghai, China
Names used: Strauss; formerly used: Helios, Nieer.

The oldest piano manufacturer in China, Shanghai is said to have been founded over a hundred years ago by the British. The name was changed to Shanghai when the Communists took over China around 1950.

Shanghai makes pianos under a number of different names. The name currently used on pianos for export to the U.S. is Strauss. In the recent past, the names Helios and Nieer have sometimes been used.

A couple of Strauss verticals appeared in the survey. One technician who prepares new ones for a dealer said they were "worse than Pearl River" and had terrible tone and other problems. Ones I have inspected at trade shows for the past few years have had very unevenly spaced strings at the strike point—one sign of a poorly engineered piano—and generally looked shoddy inside. This appears to be one of the least advanced Chinese pianos to be marketed in the U.S. Like other Chinese pianos, however, they are improving a little each year.

Warranty: Ten years, parts only, to the dealer. The distributor says it does not give a written warranty to the consumer.

Consumer Ratings:

Performance: *
Confidence: *
Quality control: *
Warranty: *
Information: * *

TADASHI

No longer in business

Pianos made by: Atlas Piano Manufacturing Co., Hamamatsu, Japan; others

Names used: Tadashi, Atlas

Despite the Japanese name, Tadashi was a North American company, headquartered in the Toronto area, that imported Atlas pianos from Japan. Atlas was started in 1955 by Tadashi Yorikane as a technical joint venture with Kunitachi College of Music in Tokyo, which has a Musical Instrument Research Institute. The pianos were initially marketed in North America in the late 1970s under the tradename Atlas as was used in Japan, but American rights to this name turned out to be already owned by another music-related company, so the piano's name was changed here to Tadashi. (It's ironic that in Japan the piano went by an English name and in the United States by a Japanese name, but I'll bet it sold better that way.)

Tadashi pianos were an interesting blend of European-style design and Japanese precision, and quite nicely made for the most part. But the vertical pianos varied a lot in quality. On some the tone in the upper treble was quite dead and the action parts were not as perfectly aligned as is expected in a Japanese piano. Other pianos were free of these problems. The grands were more consistent and had a lovely singing treble and an even tone across the scale. Like other Japanese pianos, though, they could become quite bright with time.

In 1986, due to the sudden change in international currency values, importers of Japanese products scurried to find less expensive alternatives that would be more competitive in the U.S. market. Rather than go the Korean route like everyone else, Tadashi briefly tried importing pianos from Taiwan and from Canada, but was not able to survive and went out of business in 1987.

Several years later, the Tadashi name was revived by an American importer who, using the Tadashi name and piano design under license, had the piano made partly in Japan (but not by Atlas) and partly in Korea. The idea didn't exactly catch on, and the name is not presently being used.

TOKAI

No longer available

Pianos made by: Tokai Gakki Co., Ltd., Hamamatsu, Japan

We often assume that everything made in Japan is well made, but in the case of Tokai this is not so. Tokai pianos needed a lot of servicing by the dealer before being presentable, and the tonal quality, cabinet finish, workmanship, and materials in their pianos seemed closer to Korean quality of the 1980s than to Japanese. Distribution of Tokai pianos in the United States was dropped in 1989.

TOYO

No longer imported into the U.S.

This is a Japanese piano no longer imported into the U.S. It was considered a good piano, especially in the larger models.

WALTER, CHARLES R.

Walter Piano Company, Inc.
25416 CR 6
Elkhart, Indiana 46514
(219) 266-0615

Names used: Charles R. Walter; formerly used: Janssen

Charles Walter, an engineer, was head of Piano Design and Developmental Engineering at C. G. Conn in the 1960s, when Conn was doing important research in musical acoustics. In 1969 Walter bought the Janssen piano name from Conn, and continued to make Janssen pianos until 1981. In 1975, he brought out the Charles R. Walter line of consoles and studios, based on his continuing research in piano design. Fewer than two thousand of these pianos are made each year.

The Walter Piano Co. is fairly unique among U.S. piano manufacturers in that it is a family business, staffed by Charles and his wife, several of their grownup children and various in-laws, in addition to unrelated production employees. The Walters say that each piano is inspected by a member of their family before being shipped, and that person's signature can be found on the top of the piano back, underneath the lid. Dealers and technicians report that doing business with the Walters is a pleasure in itself.

The Charles R. Walter line consists of 43" and 45" studio pianos in various decorator and institutional styles, and a 6'4" grand. The 43" pianos are called "consoles" for marketing purposes because of their styling, but both the 43" and 45" pianos are really studios (as I define the term) by virtue of their studio-size actions, and are actually identical pianos in different sized cabinets. Because of the larger action, the "console" will outperform many real consoles on the market.

Although Mr. Walter is not oblivious to marketing concerns, his vertical piano bears the mark of being designed by an engineer who understands pianos and strives for quality. Exceptionally long, thick keys that are individually lead-weighted provide a very even feel across the keyboard. The scale design seems well thought out and the bass sounds good most of the way to the bottom. When at its best, the treble sings beautifully. The piano has a solid spruce soundboard, Delignit pinblock, a Langer action, and uses no particle board in the cabinetry, which is very substantial and beautifully finished. (Check out some of the fancy consoles, such as the Queen Anne models—they're strikingly beautiful.) Perhaps most appreciated by technicians and dealers is that most Walter pianos arrive at the dealer meticulously tuned and adjusted.

Most technicians have a great deal of respect for the Walter pianos. Phrases like "well constructed" and "good solid piano" come up frequently in conversations about these instruments. One technician said, "I haven't come across a Walter piano I didn't like," and another one commented that "generally they've fulfilled my expectations or exceeded them."

Nineteen Walter verticals appeared in the current survey. A few pianos were said to have minor finish problems— "spotty," one technician called the finish. As with many pianos, some tuners are uncomfortable with the extremely tight tuning pin feel of the Walters. (One technician suggested Walter change from a Delignit pinblock, known to produce super-tight tuning pins, to a maple block for a better feel.) Many pianos were said to have very prominent false beats in the treble, and a few technicians complained of some bass and tenor dampers not damping well. Surprisingly, there were also a few complaints about stability of tuning and regulation when new, though in my experience this is not a complaint often heard about Walters.

Some variability is found in the bass section of these pianos. According to one technician, the Walter vertical has "the best-tuning bass of any piano its size," a testament to Mr. Walter's careful scale design. Other technicians, though, found the implementation of that design to be sometimes problematic. Rattling bass strings were found in a couple of pianos, as were bass strings with mismatched windings, making for difficult tuning.

Tonally, the Walter verticals have proven to be generally satisfying to technicians and players. While some technicians in the survey called the tone "thin" or "whiny," most of the relatively few complaints about tone had to do with tonal transitions from section to section—especially at the bass/tenor break—not unusual in pianos of this size.

I recommend checking out the Walter verticals if you're shopping for a vertical piano in the middle to upper price range. Be sure to check several instruments to find the ones with the best tone. The Walter is one of the best American-made verticals on the market, and is a good value for the money.

In 1997 Walter finally came out with the 6'4" grand that had been in the development stage for many years. The piano features a Delignit pinblock, maple rim, Kluge keys, Renner action, Abel hammers, tapered solid spruce soundboard, and other features generally found in the finest pianos. Only one turned up in the present survey. It was said to have a "light, responsive action" and "very clean tone [which] could probably use a little more power, a little more body." The examining technician went on to call the Walter grand "one of the great American pianos, right up there with Steinway and Mason & Hamlin." Personally, I think this is a bit of an overstatement. Clearly, the piano is competently built and I would recommend it. But in my opinion, it does not have the kind of distinctive and expressive sound that would qualify it as one of the "great" pianos. Obviously, this is the kind of subjective judgment that each prospective buyer will have to make for him or herself.

Warranty: Twelve-year full warranty.

Price range: (Verticals) Approximately $6,800–7,800 depending on furniture style; (Grands) $30,000

Verticals	Grands
43" console-style studio (1520)	6'4" (W-190)
45" studio (1500)	

Consumer Ratings:

Performance: * * * * 1/2
Confidence
    Grands: * * * * *
    Verticals: * * * * 1/2
Quality Control: * * * * 1/2

For explanation of survey and review procedures, model listings, and price ranges, please see pages 76–81.

Warranty: * * * *
Information
    Grands: * *
    Verticals: * * * *

WEBER

Weber Piano Company
40 Seaview Drive
Secaucus, New Jersey 07094
(201) 902-0920
(800) 346-5351
www.weberpiano.com

Owned by: Samsung America Inc.

Pianos made by: Young Chang Co., Ltd., Inchon, South Korea

The present-day Weber Piano Co. was started by Young Chang, a Korean piano manufacturer, in 1986, at a time when protectionist sentiment was growing in the United States and there was a possibility that quotas might be placed on imported pianos. By spawning a second piano line, Young Chang hoped to garner a larger market share and therefore increase whatever quota might later be imposed on its products. (This tactic is used by many foreign companies.) About a year later, Young Chang sold the Weber name to Samsung, a large Korean industrial conglomerate. Young Chang continues, however, to manufacture all pianos sold under the Weber name.

The original Weber Piano Co. was founded by Albert Weber in 1852. The name later became part of the Aeolian group and was eventually purchased by Young Chang when Aeolian went out of business. Today's Weber pianos have no connection or resemblance to the original Weber pianos except for the name.

At the beginning, all Weber pianos were identical to the Young Changs except for slightly cheaper cabinets. Later, however, the two brands were generally considered to be of the same quality and sold for about the same price. Weber officials said that, as a rough rule of thumb, Weber piano models that were of the same size as Young Chang models were probably of identical scale design, though there were cosmetic differences that might attract buyers to one brand or the other. Two Weber grand models made in sizes not available in the Young Chang line, 5'1" and 5'7", were designed for Weber by Ibach, the company says. The Weber 7' grand utilizes a Renner action. Recently, Young Chang has been replacing its regular, or "Gold," series of pianos with ones redesigned by engineer Joseph Pramberger (see "Young Chang" for more information). Weber, however, continues to sell only the "Gold" series.

Weber has added several models made in Young Chang's new factory in Tianjin, China. In the model listing, these are the models with three-digit numbers (denoting centimeters). Models with two-digit numbers are still made in Young Chang's factory in Korea.

See "Young Chang" for information about the quality of Weber pianos.

Weber also imports and markets pianos from the Czech Republic (see "Rieger-Kloss") and from China (see "Sagenhaft" and "Ridgewood").

Warranty: Fifteen-year full warranty; lifetime warranty on action and case parts. Twelve-year full warranty on Chinese pianos; lifetime on action and case parts. The warranty is backed by Samsung.

Price range: (Verticals) $3,400–5,800; (Grands) $9,500–23,500

Verticals	Grands
43″ console (W-109)	4′11″ (WG-50)
43″ console (W-41A/WF-41)	4′11½″ (WG-150)
43½″ console (WF-108)	5′1″ (WG-51)
44½″ console (WFD-44)	5′7″ (WG-57)
46″ studio (WC-46/WS-46)	6′1″ (WG-60)
48″ upright (W-121)	6′10″ (WG-68)
48″ upright (W-48)	7′ (WG-70)
52″ upright (W-131)	9″ (WG-90)

Consumer Ratings:

Performance
   Korean: * * *
   Chinese: * *
Confidence
   Korean: * * * ½
   Chinese: * ½
Quality Control
   Korean: * * *
   Chinese: * ½
Warranty: * * * *
Information
   Korean Grands: * * * *
   Korean Verticals: * * * ½
   Chinese: * *

WEINBACH

See "Petrof"

WELMAR

See "Whelpdale Maxwell & Codd"

WESTBROOK
Including Brentwood

Westbrook Piano Company, Inc.
600 Rivermont Drive
Columbia, South Carolina 29210

(803) 799-4664
(800) 354-6188
swestbrk@aol.com

Pianos made by: Artfield Piano Ltd., Qing Pu, China; a piano factory in Shanghai, China.

Pianos bearing the Westbrook name are made in China by Artfield Piano Ltd. See "Krakauer" for more information on this manufacturer. Pianos bearing the Brentwood name are currently being made in a piano factory in Shanghai, China in which, the importer says, he has his own personnel supervising production of these pianos.

Warranty: Twelve years, parts and labor, to original purchaser.
Price range: (Verticals) $2,700–3,100

Verticals
   43″ console (CFR006/MP005/TR006)
   48″ upright (MP012)

Consumer Ratings: Insufficient information to rate Brentwood. See "Krakauer" for ratings of Westbrook.

WHELPDALE MAXWELL & CODD

Whelpdale Maxwell & Codd
154 Clapham Park Road
London SW4 7DE England

(44) 20-7978-2444
www.pianoforte.co.uk

Names used: Bentley, Broadwood, Knight, Welmar

This firm is the manufacturer and distributor of Knight, Broadwood, Bentley, and Welmar pianos. Founded in 1876 as a Blüthner distributor, Whelpdale has been making pianos since the 1930s. Over the years, it has purchased most of the British piano names. After an absence of a few years, Whelpdale is once again actively distributing in the U.S.

The Knight piano company was founded by Alfred Knight in 1936, and for many years was managed by Knight's daughter and her family. In 1990, Knight was sold to the Bentley Piano Co. and production was moved to the Bentley factories. Due to a worldwide decline in piano sales, Bentley was sold in 1993 to Whelpdale Maxwell & Codd, a competitor.

The Knight was a remarkable English vertical piano not well known in this country, but very highly regarded in Europe and among piano designers. In addition to impeccable workmanship throughout, Knight pianos had a few technical features that were fairly unique for a vertical piano, such as the mounting of the pinblock in a pocket cast in the plate, and the use of exceptionally hard phenolic tuning pin plate bushings, both of which enhanced tuning stability; and the absence of plate struts interrupting the treble bridge, which enhanced the treble tone. Whelpdale says it has retained some of these features in its version of the Knight piano.

Originally established in 1728, John Broadwood & Sons is one of the oldest and best-known piano brand names, having played an important part in the early history of the piano. The current Broadwoods are of modern design, of course, including four vertical models and one grand. The Welmar and Bentley names are less well known than the other brands in the U.S., but are built to similar standards and are available to dealers who wish to carry additional piano lines. Broadwood and Welmar grands are made in Germany by a leading German piano maker.

Warranty: Seven years, parts and labor, to original purchaser
Price range: (Verticals) $7,000–13,500; (Grands) $40,000–45,000

Verticals—Broadwood
    44" (St. James)
    47" (Berwick/Imperial)
    50" (Stratford)

Grands—Broadwood
    6'1" (Boudoir)

Verticals—Welmar
    44" (112/114)
    46" (118)
    48" (122)
    50" (126)

Grands—Welmar
    6'1" (186)

Verticals—Knight
    44" (K10)
    48" (Savoy)

Verticals—Bentley
    43" (Concord/Heritage)
    46" (Wessex/Berkeley)
    47" (Exeter/Berlin/London/Belgrave/Chelsea/
       Salisbury/Esher)

Consumer Ratings: Insufficient information to rate, except Broadwood Grand:

Performance: * * * * 1/2
Confidence: * * * * *
Quality Control: * * * * *
Warranty: * * * *
Information: * *

WIELER

See "Sängler & Söhne"

WOODCHESTER

Unique Pianos, Inc.
223 E. New Haven Avenue
Melbourne, Florida 32901

(888) 725-6633
(321) 725-5690
www.uniquepianos.com

Pianos made by: Woodchester Piano Co., Stroud, England

This English company was founded in 1994 on the site of the old Bentley piano factory, which was abandoned when Bentley was purchased by another company. Some of the old Bentley workforce continues to work for Woodchester. In 2000, Woodchester became part of the Whelpdale Maxwell & Codd piano group (see "Whelpdale Maxwell & Codd").

Woodchester manufactures 44" and 47½" vertical pianos. The larger model has a Renner action, Abel hammers, Delignit pinblock, and a back based on a Rippen design. Components for the smaller model are from Poland and the Czech Republic.

Warranty: Ten years, parts and labor, to original purchaser

Price range: (Verticals) $8,000–12,600

Verticals
    44" (Arlingham Tudor)
    47½" (Concerto)

For explanation of survey and review procedures, model listings, and price ranges, please see pages 76–81.

Consumer Ratings: Insufficient information to rate

WURLITZER

Baldwin Piano & Organ Co.
4680 Parkway Drive
Mason, Ohio 45040

(513) 754-4500
(800) 876-2976
www.baldwinpiano.com

Pianos made by: Baldwin Piano & Organ Co., Trumann, Arkansas

Names formerly used: J.& C. Fischer, Rudolph Wurlitzer, Chickering, Jonas Chickering, Cabaret, Casino

After coming to the United States from Germany in 1854, Rudolf Wurlitzer established himself as an importer of German pianos in 1856. In 1881 he commenced manufacturing his own pianos. For the past hundred years, Wurlitzer has been a major name in the music business, developing one of the first spinet pianos and the first electronic piano. But the company is perhaps best known among the public for organs ("The Mighty Wurlitzer") and jukeboxes.

As for other American piano manufacturers, the 1980s were very difficult for Wurlitzer due to foreign competition, a recession, and a declining market for pianos in general and for less expensive verticals in particular. Wurlitzer managed to keep its head above water by making its operation more efficient, selling a majority share of the business to investors, and taking in contract woodworking (including manufacturing Brunswick billiard tables) and electronic assembly jobs. Finally, in 1988 Wurlitzer was sold to Baldwin, and Wurlitzer manufacturing was moved to Baldwin plants. Baldwin now uses the Wurlitzer name on a line of entry-level vertical and grand pianos.

In 1985 Wurlitzer purchased the Chickering name and all the assets of Aeolian Pianos' Memphis factory when that company went out of business (see "Aeolian"). For several years Wurlitzer produced a line of Chickering consoles and studios and a "budget" line of Jonas Chickering spinets and consoles. The Jonas Chickerings were basically no-frills, entry-level pianos with laminated maple soundboards. The regular Chickering line approached a more reasonable quality. These models have been discontinued. Baldwin now uses the Chickering name on a line of less expensive grand pianos.

For a time, Wurlitzer sold under its own name verticals and grands made by Young Chang, a Korean manufacturer, identical to the models sold under the Young Chang name. These have been discontinued. Baldwin now puts the Wurlitzer name on a line of grand pianos made by Samick, another Korean manufacturer, as well as on a line of U.S.-made verticals.

U.S.-made Wurlitzers manufactured from the mid-1970s until the mid-1980s had, for the most part, trouble-free actions but poor tone. Overall, the workmanship was reasonable for a mass-produced piano in its time. The transition period from Wurlitzer to Baldwin ownership, roughly 1988 to 1990, saw much less consistency in the instruments. Many were quite troublesome, or at least needed much work by the dealer to set them right; others were praiseworthy. Under Baldwin ownership, Wurlitzer also made a 5' grand in the U.S. The several examples of this instrument that appeared in a previous survey were all either seriously flawed and returned to the factory or showed a good deal of carelessness in their construction. This model was discontinued.

Player pianos Wurlitzer used to market under the name Casino were made by Story & Clark (see "Story & Clark").

Baldwin marketed, under the Wurlitzer division, a Chinese vertical piano under the name J. & C. Fischer. This was made by the Beijing Piano Co. Eventually the name was changed to Kranich & Bach. Now a piano from this company is marketed by Baldwin under the Wurlitzer name.

See "Baldwin" and "Samick" for reviews of pianos currently made under the Wurlitzer name; see "Baldwin" for ratings.

YAMAHA

Yamaha Corporation of America
P.O. Box 6600
Buena Park, California 90622

(714) 522-9011
(800) 854-1569
infostation@yamaha.com
www.yamaha.com

Owned and made by: Yamaha Corporation, Hamamatsu, Japan and Thomaston, Georgia (publicly owned in Japan)

Names used: Yamaha, Eterna, Disklavier, MIDIPiano, Cable-Nelson; no longer used: Everett

The Company: Torakusu Yamaha, a watchmaker, developed Japan's first reed organ, founding Yamaha Reed Organ Manufacturing in 1887. In 1899, Yamaha visited the United States to learn to build pianos. Within a couple of years, he began making grand and vertical pianos under the name Nippon Gakki, Ltd. Beginning in the 1930s, Yamaha expanded its operations, first into other musical instruments, then into other goods and services (such as sporting goods, furniture, and other consumer products), and finally internationally.

Yamaha is probably the most international of the piano manufacturers. In addition to its factories in Japan, Yamaha has manufacturing plants and partnerships with other companies all over the world, including the United States, Germany (with Schimmel), England (with Kemble), Mexico, China, Indonesia, and Taiwan. Currently, only pianos assembled in Japan and the U.S. are sold here under the Yamaha name, but some of the parts used in these pianos are made elsewhere. At its height, Yamaha produced about 250 thousand pianos annually. Currently, with worldwide demand for pianos declining, increased competition, and an unfavorable currency exchange rate in relation to the dollar, annual production is much lower.

Export of pianos to the United States began about 1960. The first ones had severe moisture-related problems, but within a few years, the problems were rectified. In 1973 Yamaha acquired the Everett Piano Co. in South Haven, Michigan. From 1973 until mid-1986, Yamaha manufactured a complete line of verticals and grands in Japan and a completely different line of verticals at the Everett factory in Michigan, where it also made a line of Everett pianos. (See "Everett" for more information. Detailed information about Yamaha and Everett models from this period can also be found in the first edition of this book, available at many libraries.)

In mid-1986, Yamaha ceased making pianos at the Everett factory and moved all of its U.S. piano manufacturing to a plant in Thomaston, Georgia where some of its electronic musical instruments had been made. The decline of the U.S. organ industry had left this factory with excess capacity at the same time that sales of decorator-style verticals, Everett's primary focus, had also declined. At first the Georgia plant simply put Japanese parts inside of U.S.-made cabinets, but now the wooden back, soundboard, and pinblock are also made in Georgia, while the plate, action, keys, and other parts come from Japan and elsewhere. This plant also now has polyester finishing capabilities. This allows the company to manufacture and finish cabinet styles there that previously could only be made in Japan. At the time of this writing, the consoles and studios are made in the U.S., while the uprights are still made in Japan, as are the grands. In preparation for the start of grand piano manufacturing in Georgia, however, the 5'3" models GH1FP (the GH1B in French Provincial style) and the GH1G (in Georgian mahogany) are being imported from Japan manufactured but unassembled, and then finished and assembled at the Georgia plant. Cabinet parts such as lyres and legs are now being made there, too.

Yamaha now has a number of manufacturing relationships with China. First, the company operates a joint-venture factory in Guangzhou, China in which it assembles pianos using parts from the nearby Guangzhou Pearl River piano factory, maker of Pearl River pianos, as well as parts of its own from Japan and China. These pianos are sold in China under the Yamaha name, but in the U.S. and other parts of the world they appear only under the name "Eterna." Currently, this name is being applied by Yamaha only to a 44" console patterned after its model M1F. This model is backed by a Yamaha warranty. In addition, Yamaha has recently opened a solely funded factory in China, but this factory produces only action parts. Finally, Yamaha is building cabinet parts for two vertical models, the T116 and the T121, in Taiwan for final assembly in Japan (T121) or the U.S. (T116).

Yamaha also makes electronic player pianos called Disklaviers, as well as hybrid acoustic/digital pianos called MIDIPianos, that account for a substantial percentage of the company's sales. These products are reviewed separately beginning on page 160.

Verticals: Yamaha's console line consists of the M112 in continental style (a new model), the M450 series in plain cabinets, and the M500 series available in a variety of fancier furniture cabinets. All the consoles are 44" tall and have a compressed action. Note that the model M1F has been discontinued. The model M450 is occasionally made under the name Cable-Nelson.

The studio piano line consists of the very popular 45" P22, which is the school studio model, and the aforementioned model T116, which has traditional styling. The model P2F has been discontinued. The school model P22 is one of the best bargains in the Yamaha line because the furniture isn't fancy, but the piano is sturdily constructed for school use (or abuse) and priced low to compete for bids from school systems.

The upright line consists of the 48" model U1; the 48" model T121, which is like the U1 inside, but with a less expensive cabinet; the 52" model U3; and the 52" model U5, which contains more advanced features such as agraffes, duplex scaling, and a true sostenuto pedal. Most of the uprights now have Yamaha's "Soft-Close" fallboard. The WX series, with its radial back design, has been discontinued, though some of the same features (minus the radial back) are now embodied in the U series.

Yamaha has always had a reputation for superb quality control. Although the factory preparation of Yamaha pianos may have declined somewhat in recent years, they still arrive at the stores needing less work than practically any other make except some high-end, "handmade" pianos like Bösendorfers and Faziolis. For this edition, we examined a service database of 816 Yamaha verticals, most of which were sold three to five years ago. Less than fifteen percent of those pianos were provided any service other than tuning in the post-sale period, the lowest of any major brand. (Note: In the service database, we examined only non-Disklavier and non-MIDI Yamaha pianos for the purposes of this report.) In addition, in our own technician survey, thirty-eight technicians examined a total of 348 Yamaha verticals. Although a fair number of small problems were noted (partly a result of the abundance of information available), the technicians made it clear that these were, at most, minor inconveniences in what they considered to be very well-made pianos. Here are some of the observations gleaned from the database, survey, and interviews:

- Many of the problems that do exist in new Yamahas seem to be found much more often in the American-made instruments (the consoles and studios) than in those from Japan (the uprights). And among the American-made instruments, the consoles are more likely to have problems than the studios.

- Problems with cabinetry were found in a number of verticals, especially consoles and studios, that had poorly fit fallboards or front panels, usually too tight. More significantly, technicians hated the awkward design of the upper front panel/fallboard assembly on the models T116 and T121, both of which have their cabinets made in Taiwan. This assembly, in our experience, is just too heavy and cumbersome for comfortable removal from the instrument, something that needs to be done in order to tune the piano or service its action.

- Surprisingly, quite a few technicians made pointed remarks about the plainness of the model M450 cabinetry, and the cheap look of its bench. It was pointed out that the bench does not have a storage compartment for music. [Yamaha reports that it has just upgraded the bench and has included a storage compartment.]

- Many technicians noted problems with the stringing of some Yamaha verticals. Coils often were poorly made, or too high off the plate, and tuning pins were sometimes too tight. The combination of tight tuning pins and high coils often resulted in "flagpoling," or bending, of tuning pins during tuning, which makes it more difficult to do a stable tuning. Another common complaint was very prominent false beats in the treble. Again, these complaints were more frequent about the American-made pianos.

- Although many Yamaha verticals arrive from the factory in good tune and up to pitch, quite a few others were said to be "green," i.e., insufficiently tuned at the factory. In addition, some were said to vary in pitch excessively from season to season, and possibly in regulation as well, a criticism of Yamahas I've been hearing for many years. In my experience, Yamaha verticals will benefit more than many brands from installation of a climate control system in the piano (see Chapter 7 for details about these systems).

- I would suggest having all the action screws tightened in Yamaha verticals after six months or so of use to avoid the clicking sounds caused by loose flanges and, sometimes, by a loose letoff rail. This is considered part of normal service on any relatively new piano and is included free as part of the Yamaha Servicebond program if your dealer participates in it.

- As in previous surveys, technicians said that when Yamaha verticals are new, they need very little preparation by the dealer, at most tuning and minor amounts of key easing, hammer spacing, and regulating. The key easing is usually to ease tight balance holes, which can cause keys to hang up above the level of the other keys.

- Occasionally a technician will need to track down a squeak or other noise. Common sources of noise in Yamaha verticals are squeaks in the pedal system; case parts rubbing against each other, especially when the pedal is pressed hard; loose action flange screws; and a loose letoff rail.

- Double-striking of the hammer in the low tenor on a soft or incomplete stroke of the key is a common problem mentioned in regard to Yamaha verticals and should be taken seriously by those who play with an especially soft touch. This tendency of double-striking in soft playing is a characteristic of the action design, the trade-off being better-than-normal repetition for a vertical piano.

- A small number of Yamaha consoles and studios had keys that were so severely warped as to make leveling and regulation impossible. Reportedly, these keys came from Yamaha's factory in China, where they are still tweaking production methods to eliminate problems like this. True to its reputation for excellent service, Yamaha promptly replaces affected keyboards.

- Yamaha verticals tend to be bright sounding, sometimes even brash, and they get even brighter with use.

Technicians continue to be enthusiastic about servicing Yamaha verticals, especially the uprights, which are considered to be rather spectacular pianos. The 48" model U1 is still considered by many to be one of the best values among

For explanation of survey and review procedures, model listings, and price ranges, please see pages 76–81.

pianos. ". . . an absolutely gorgeous piano to tune, play and listen to," wrote one technician in the current survey about the U1. "Flawless!" wrote another, "Easy tuning—still my pick of the litter!"

As mentioned earlier, Yamaha also sells a Chinese-made console called "Eterna," which is patterned after the Yamaha model M1F. Chinese pianos are improving, but are still only barely satisfactory and have little in the way of a track record. Several Eternas that appeared in the current survey were not too bad mechanically and structurally, squeaking pedals and some regulation problems being the chief complaints, but the tone was deficient. "They tend to have a fairly cheap sound, lacking in the fundamental," said one technician in interview. "They tune okay, but it's not a satisfying musical experience."

Grands: There are three basic types of Yamaha grands—the G series, the C series, and the S series. The G series consists of the GA1 (4'11"), GP1 (5'3"), and the GH1 (5'3"). The C series consists of the C1 (5'3"), C2 (5'8"), C3 (6'1"), C5 (6'7"), C6 (6'11"), C7 (7'6"), and CFIIIS (9'). The S series consists of the S4 (6'3") and the S6 (6'11").

When Yamaha consolidated its grand piano lines a few years ago, it seemed that the idea was to eliminate the confusion of having the same size of grand appear in too many different lines. In some ways, however, the new lineup is even more confusing than before. Reflecting a strong market for smaller grands, the Yamaha lineup now includes three different models measuring 5'3". The model GH1 (usually expressed as GH1B) is the basic version, with a less-expensive version available in a cheaper cabinet (model GP1). The best of the three 5'3" grands, the model C1 features improved scaling across the bass/tenor break and, like the other C series grands, duplex scaling, a new plate-mounting system, improved structural integrity with the pinblock mortised into the stretcher, a new humidity-resistant keyframe, and a true sostenuto pedal. The models GH1, GP1, and the tiny GA1 lack all these features, and their middle pedal operates a bass-sustain function.

The smaller C series grands differ from the larger ones in that the C1 and C2 models have solid maple bridges with maple caps, whereas the models C3 through C7 have vertically laminated bridges with maple (and sometimes boxwood) caps. The vertically laminated design is similar to that found in Steinways and other fine pianos, and is considered to give the bridges greater strength and resistance to cracking and better transmission of vibrational energy. In addition, the larger C series grands have keytops made of Ivorite™.

The S series grands are made in Yamaha's concert grand factory along with the model CFIIIS concert grand. There is no assembly line to be found in this plant; all manufacturing is done by traditional techniques, such as one might find in a large rebuilding shop. Among the material differences in the S series are: a rim made of maple and mahogany; a "bell" in the treble (as in the larger Steinways) to enhance the treble tone; German strings instead of Japanese; and the use of a new wood product composite in place of ebony for the black keys. The CFIIIS concert grand made in this factory is endorsed and used by a number of notable concert artists, including André Watts, Sviatoslav Richter, and Michael Tilson Thomas.

One of the criticisms of Yamaha and some other Asian pianos is that they are substantially made of softer and less expensive woods. Conventional thinking on the subject is that grand piano rims must be made of very dense woods, such as the maple and beech used on most of the best American and European grands, in order to reflect sound energy back to the soundboard for a more sustained tone. Although Yamaha does use some maple and beech in their grand rims, they alternate them with layers of softer woods. As a result, so the theory goes, the Yamaha grand tone tends to be "brittle" and lack sustaining qualities. Other factors, such as the scale design and hammers also contribute to these tonal characteristics. Many jazz pianists, desiring a crisp, clear sound for runs up and down the keyboard, actually prefer this kind of tone. But players of other kinds of music requiring a singing melodic line above an accompaniment may be frustrated by the piano's apparent inability to produce it. Because the Yamaha has a tone that is rather pleasing in its own way, the problem may not be entirely obvious until one places a Yamaha and a higher quality piano side by side and plays the same music on both. The refinements in the larger C series grands and the S series grands may be an attempt to overcome these tonal limitations by making a harder rim and a less energy-absorbent plate, among other features.

A related problem with tone concerns the dampers and sustain pedal which (leave it to the Japanese!) work too efficiently. Possibly because the sound energy seems to dissipate too quickly, and perhaps because this tendency is exacerbated by the pedal leverage, I find that the dampers cause the sound to cut off too abruptly, making the music sound choppy, and making me work harder to play legato.

Yamaha grands have a well-deserved reputation for excellent quality control and ease of servicing. In the service database examined for this edition, of 374 Yamaha grands, most sold from three to five years ago, only ten percent were provided any post-sale service other than tuning, the lowest percentage of any major brand. (Note: In the service database, we examined only non-Disklavier and non-MIDI Yamaha pianos for the purposes of this report.) Voicing and minor pedal and action adjustments were practically the only post-sale service given. The 243 Yamaha grands examined in the written survey confirmed technicians' enthusiastic praise of the brand. The two most common problems found were tight key balance holes and overly strong repetition springs, the latter sometimes causing double striking in soft playing. Both of these problems are minor and usually corrected in the store (although Yamahas need so little dealer prep that many dealers have taken to simply shipping the piano to the customer right out of the crate and having the technician do the "dealer prep" in the home). A fair number of pianos exhibited very prominent false beats in the treble. A small but surprising number of Yamaha grands (surprising only because of Yamaha's reputation for superb quality control) were reported to have compression ridges in their soundboards.

Finally, many technicians complained about the tone quality of some Yamaha grands. The 5'3" models GH1 and

GP1 were both heavily criticized for poor tone and for tuning difficulties due to poor scaling. These two models also don't come with a sostenuto pedal, duplex scaling, and several other features found in the larger pianos, prompting some technicians to say they would recommend a Korean piano or a Kawai over these two models. Interestingly, the model GA1, though smaller than the other two, was said to be more successfully scaled in the critical tenor area and to be a better sounding piano in general, though the low bass in such a small piano was understandably quite limited. As in previous surveys, the grands were often said to be too bright sounding upon arrival from the factory, their hammers "hard as rocks." As one technician remarked, "The biggest comment from all my Yamaha clients is 'Can you make the thing quieter?'" With voicing, however, the C series pianos often sounded quite nice, the larger instruments, especially, garnering considerable praise. (No S series pianos appeared in the survey, but they, presumably, would sound even better.) Yamaha grands hold up well structurally and mechanically with use, but need frequent voicing, and probably sound better when relatively new than they will a number of years down the road.

In closing, it's my impression that for general home and school use, piano technicians recommend Yamaha pianos more often than any other brand. The precision and intelligence with which they're made, the lack of service problems, and their good performance make them an extremely good value for a consumer product. Said one technician, "I'm very impressed with Yamaha. I tell my clients that you can't get a better piano for the dollar. They're not the best piano in the world, but they are the best value." At the same time, the Yamaha tone, pleasing to some, may be too bright and limited in its tonal palette for those looking for a highly nuanced, classical kind of sound. (See also the Kawai review for some comparisons between the two brands.)

The Yamaha Servicebond program encourages Yamaha dealers to provide customers with follow-up service during the first six months of ownership by reimbursing the dealers for part of the cost of providing that service. Yamaha strongly urges its dealers to participate in this program. The program is voluntary, however, and it's possible that a dealer that sells a piano at a large discount might choose to save money by not promising or providing service under the Servicebond program. When negotiating the sale, a customer should inquire as to whether the dealer participates in the program. If so, the customer should make sure the service is actually provided. Service for which the dealer can be reimbursed includes a tuning and a general maintenance check (tightening action, trapwork, and plate screws, among other things). (Note: The Eterna piano does not come with the Servicebond.)

Warranty: Yamaha has a limited ten-year warranty on all its pianos, including the Eterna piano made in China. It covers parts and labor and is not transferable to future owners. However, when a problem is clearly due to a defect in design or manufacturing, Yamaha has frequently been known to provide warranty service long after the warranty has expired.

Be aware that Yamaha Corporation of America only provides parts and service for Yamaha pianos originally made for, and purchased in, North America. Yamaha pianos made for Japan and purchased in the U.S. on the "gray market"—new or used—are explicitly excluded from the warranty. See page 176 for more information on gray market pianos.

Yamaha's service department and warranty support are considered unsurpassed in the piano business. The speed, generosity, competence, and friendliness of the Yamaha technical support crew are the source of constant praise from piano technicians. Some technicians say that lately it's been a little harder to order parts because of Yamaha's "paranoia" (as they call it) about gray market pianos.

Price range: (Consoles and Studios) $3,800–5,200; (Uprights) $6,400–12,600; ("Eterna" console) $3,700; (G series grands) $10,000–14,500; (C series grands) $18,700–39,700; (S series grands) $52,500–59,400.

Verticals	Grands
44" console (M112, M450, M500)	4'11" (GA1)
45" studio (T116, P22)	5'3" (GP1, GH1)
48" upright (T121, U1)	5'3" (C1)
52" upright (U3, U5)	5'8" (C2)
	6'1" (C3)
44" "Eterna" console (ERC10)	6'3" (S4)
	6'7" (C5)
	6'11" (C6)
	6'11" (S6)
	7'6" (C7)
	9' (CFIIIS)

Consumer Ratings:

Yamaha Verticals

Performance: * * * *
Confidence: * * * *
Quality Control
    Consoles and Studios: * * * *
    Uprights: * * * * 1/2
Warranty: * * * * *
Information: * * * * *

Eterna Console

Performance: * *
Confidence: * *
Quality Control: * * *
Warranty: * * * * *
Information: * *

Yamaha Grands

Performance
    GA1: * * * 1/2
    GP1, GH1: * * 1/2
    C Series: * * * *
    S Series: * * * * 1/2
Confidence
    GA1, GP1, GH1: * * * 1/2
    C Series: * * * *
    S Series: * * * * 1/2
Quality Control
    GA1, GP1, GH1: * * * * 1/2
    C, S Series: * * * * *

For explanation of survey and review procedures, model listings, and price ranges, please see pages 76–81.

Warranty: * * * * *
Information
  GA1: * * *
  GP1, GH1, and C Series: * * * * *
  S Series: * *

YOUNG CHANG

Young Chang America, Inc.
9501 Lakewood Drive, S.W. #D
P.O. Box 99995
Lakewood, Washington 98499-0995

(253) 589-3200
www.youngchang.com

Owned by: Young Chang Co., Ltd., Inchon, South Korea (publicly owned in South Korea)

Names used: Young Chang, Pramberger, and Bergmann are distributed in the U.S. and Canada by Young Chang America. Pianos distributed in North America by other parties include Weber, Cline, Schafer & Sons, Knabe, and Essex. Young Chang Europe also distributes the Weber, Astor, and Bergmann names.

The Company: In 1956, three brothers, Young-Sup, Chang-Sup, and Jai-Sup Kim founded Young Chang and began selling Yamaha pianos in Korea under an agreement with that Japanese firm. Korea was recovering from a devastating war, and only the wealthy could afford pianos. But the prospects were bright for economic development, and as a symbol of cultural refinement the piano was much coveted. In 1962, the brothers incorporated as Young Chang Akki Co., Ltd. In 1964, due to competition and an extremely stiff tariff on Japanese goods (resulting from an age-old animosity between the two nations), Young Chang began importing partially completed instruments from Yamaha, doing final assembly work itself, to reduce import duties. This led to an agreement with Yamaha by which Yamaha helped Young Chang set up a full-fledged manufacturing operation. Doing so was no easy task, as restrictions and tariffs made it almost impossible to import basic industrial equipment, so Young Chang began making its own equipment and, thereafter, most of its own piano parts. In 1975, Yamaha and Young Chang parted company when the latter decided to expand to serve the world market, thus becoming a potential competitor.

In 1995, Young Chang built a new $40 million piano factory in Tianjin, China. With Korean wages on the rise, this new source of supply will enable the company to keep its prices competitive, as well as cater to the growing Chinese middle class. Unlike most other Chinese joint ventures, Young Chang chose to design and build the factory from scratch rather than try to reform an existing manufacturing facility. Young Chang says it uses the same machinery and piano designs for the Chinese pianos as for the ones made in Korea. At first, some of the Chinese pianos bore the Young Chang name, but as of January 2000, all pianos from the Tianjin factory distributed by Young Chang America bear the name "Bergmann."

Young Chang is now one of the world's largest piano manufacturers. In addition to making pianos, Young Chang also manufactures industrial woodworking machinery for worldwide distribution. In 1990 the company purchased Kurzweil Music Systems, a maker of high end digital and electronic musical instruments. Young Chang recently introduced the Kurzweil Player System, an electronic player piano. See Electronic Player Pianos and Hybrid Acoustic/Digital Pianos, page 160.

The Pianos: Young Chang's vertical piano line consists of 43" and 43$\frac{1}{2}$" continental-style and furniture-style consoles; 46" and 47" traditional, school, and furniture-style studios; and 48" and 52" uprights. The Young Chang grand piano line consists of models from 4'11$\frac{1}{2}$" to 9'. Under the Bergmann label, Young Chang sells Chinese-made verticals in sizes similar to those in the Korean line, but with fewer choices of style and finish. The Bergmann grand piano line so far consists of 4'11$\frac{1}{2}$" and 5'2" grands, with larger sizes on the way. The Bergmann pianos are assembled from a Chinese back, plate, and cabinet, and a Korean-made action. Current models, known as the Heritage Series, have an all-spruce laminated soundboard.

The first Young Chang pianos to enter this country, in 1978, had severe moisture-related problems, as did all other Asian pianos before them, due to inadequate seasoning of the wood for our climatic extremes. Many of these pianos were sent back to Korea. Throughout the 1980s, Young Changs continually improved and by mid-decade, some technicians considered them to be satisfactory for casual or less serious use. However, the quality control was still quite inconsistent and some pianos had problems that required a great deal of repair and adjustment by the dealer. Technicians sometimes reported being dissatisfied with the tone of the instruments, and the pianos were said to go out of adjustment in a relatively short amount of time. By the end of the '80s and into the '90s, the pianos were still quite inconsistent, with the particular problems varying by instrument and by shipment, but they generally needed much less work to set them right than in previous years. Among the many miscellaneous, occasional problems that showed up in the survey for the previous (third) edition of this book were tight action centers causing actions to seize up under continuous, hard playing; harsh, unpleasant tone unless extensively voiced; tight damper guide rail bushings in the grands, affecting damper operation; squeaky grand trapwork; and noisy grand action caused by squeaky knuckles.

In the service database examined for this (fourth) edition, about two-thirds of the 148 Korean-made Young Chang verticals and about forty percent of the 343 Korean-made Young Chang grands, most of them sold about three to five years ago, were provided post-sale service other than tuning. These are fairly high percentages compared to other brands in the database, suggesting rough quality control at that time. In the verticals, the most common post-sale problems encountered were sticking keys and tight action centers; adjustments to pedals and trapwork, among other things to eliminate squeaks; and the need for fairly extensive amounts of action regulating. In the grands, the same problems presented themselves as in the verticals, plus tight damper guide rail bushings, misaligned hammers, squeaky knuckles, the need for voicing, and tracking down and eliminating miscellaneous action noises.

The written survey for this edition looked at nineteen Korean-made Young Chang and Weber verticals and forty-six Korean-made Young Chang and Weber grands sold during the last five years. (Weber and Young Chang pianos, though made by the same company, are not necessarily identical, but the differences are unlikely to manifest as differences in quality control or mechanical defects.) The results of the written survey, supplemented by technician interviews, suggest that some of the same problems still exist in both grands and verticals, but to a slightly lesser extent as each year goes by. Information on the verticals was a bit sparse, but some technicians, working on very new instruments, reported cabinet parts that were ill-fitting, hammers and strings not spaced correctly, the need for a lot of action regulating, some bad bridge work; and poor-quality trapwork. Also, technicians are reminded that Young Chang verticals use metal butt plates to attach the hammer butts to their flanges. Butt plate screws (not just hammer flange screws) must be tightened regularly to prevent center pins from walking out.

New grands still had some tight action centers, but much less than before; hammers not aligned with the strings, possibly due to warping of hammershanks, but less than in the past; tight damper guide rail bushings causing dampers not to damp properly; occasional bad bridge work; an occasional warped keyslip binding on the keys; key bushings too tight or too loose; complaints that the trapwork and lyre were not installed securely; poor regulation; excessively false beating strings; and string noises in the duplex scale area, among other things. Many of the instruments with these problems were being serviced for the first time, either at the dealer or in the home. There were also some pianos being serviced for the first time that were relatively free of problems and sounded quite good. There were many that had been serviced properly in the past that were also relatively free of problems, and some that were not.

I have always found Young Chang pianos—and to some extent all Korean pianos—difficult to review because they are so inconsistent in how they present themselves when new. The list of problems that occur with some frequency is quite long, but perhaps it makes the pianos seem worse than they really are, especially since most of the problems are fixable and only a few of them may be present in any particular instrument. In the follow-up interviews, most technicians were cautiously optimistic about Young Chang pianos. They said that once the problems are taken care of, the pianos hold up reasonably well, including in institutional settings. Said one technician in interview: "My overall history with Young Chang is that they're okay, but require more prep work. More tweaking of regulation over the first year or two before they settle down and become decent pianos. Most of them I work on that are older seem to hold up pretty well. Once you get them in good condition they tend to stay."

Over the past five years or so, Young Chang has employed the services of Joseph Pramberger, once an engineer and manufacturing executive at Steinway & Sons, to evaluate its piano designs and make improvements. In most cases, the new "Pramberger Signature Series" models utilize the same scale designs as the older models, but Mr. Pramberger told me that his work has led to changes in soundboard design and construction, bridge placement, hammer construction, and action geometry. Cosmetic changes have also been made to the cabinet and plate. Pramberger is systematically working his way through the entire Young Chang line, and the models that incorporate his changes are designated by a "P" at the beginning of the model number.

Young Chang also recently announced a new line of "Pramberger Platinum Edition" pianos, available in 48" upright and 5'9", 6'1", and 6'10" grand models. The grands feature a maple inner rim, upgraded hammers and soundboard material, and exotic, matched veneers similar to those in Steinway's Crown Jewel Collection. The Pramberger Platinum grands have the name "Pramberger" on the fallboard instead of "Young Chang." I wasn't able to see finished versions of these models by press time.

Since Joseph Pramberger began to redesign the pianos, Young Chang has gradually been retiring the original models, known as the "Gold Series," from its line and relegating them to the pianos the company makes for other distributors, such as Weber. A question that frequently arises is whether the new Pramberger Signature Series models sound better than the others. The first time I heard one, specially prepared for a trade show, I thought so. It had better sustain and more color, and was more pleasing to listen to. Since then, I have heard examples of both types that sounded good, and ones that did not. I believe that the amount of prep work that is put into the piano probably affects the outcome more than whether or not the piano is a Pramberger model. However, I understand that Pramberger hammers are easier to voice, so it may be possible to get a better sound from them with less work.

In interview, a few technicians felt that the heavily-promoted Pramberger Signature Series was not as much of an improvement over the older series as the company claimed. For example, one technician, while complimenting Young Chang for its recent improvements, also commented: "The Pramberger designs are cosmetically attractive, cleaner-looking, but I don't think they sound any better. They have the same problems . . . they take very thorough prep work."

However, most of the technicians who were familiar with the issue weighed in on the side of the Pramberger designs. "The Pramberger PG-185 seems to be a real improvement," said one technician. "When you finish prepping that instrument, it's really pleasant to play and listen to. You can really do a lot with these pianos." "With the new Pramberger series, Young Chang has jumped ahead of the competition. . . . I compare the Pramberger line favorably with the Yamaha C series. They need more work out of the box than the Yamahas, but the quality is consistent. The touch maybe isn't quite as refined yet, but they're moving in the right direction. At a thirty to forty percent cost difference, it's a really good value." Finally, "Recently tuned and prepped a Pramberger grand, and it seemed like a pretty nice piano. It still had a few odd things about it, but they're definitely coming up in

For explanation of survey and review procedures, model listings, and price ranges, please see pages 76–81.

quality. I think the scale design is pretty good. The action needed a lot of regulation but responded well. The hammers were workable. In some respects, I'd rather prep one of those than [an American brand]."

At the other end of the spectrum, the technicians, in interview, were very nearly unanimous that Young Chang's Chinese-made pianos, like those of other manufacturers operating in China, still had a ways to go to be acceptable. They reported a variety of problems suggestive of inadequately seasoned wood, such as warped keys, misalignment of action parts, warping and cracking of case parts, cracking of the finish, and poor and unstable regulation, to name a few. Many of these pianos have been returned to the manufacturer. [Young Chang says that it has limited production from this factory for the last couple of years to address these manufacturing problems, and that the pianos coming out of there today, while perhaps not perfect, are largely free of major problems and are at least as good as those of other Chinese makers.] "The Chinese Young Changs have made leaps and bounds of progress in the last year and a half," says an experienced Young Chang dealer technician, "but they're still at the bottom of the food chain." Because Chinese pianos have not yet established an acceptable track record, I do not yet recommend them, especially for use in areas of this country with a dry indoor climate.

Steinway and Young Chang recently announced that Young Chang would manufacture a Steinway-designed piano under the name "Essex," to be sold by Steinway dealers. It will be priced below Steinway's Boston line of pianos. The new line will be introducd in early 2001.

Warranty: Fifteen-year full (transferable) warranty on Young Chang and Pramberger brand names; lifetime limited warranty to original purchaser on case, action parts, and iron frame. Ten-year limited warranty on the Bergmann brand name. Warranty also covers institutional and commercial applications. Young Chang's warranty service is considered excellent, even for its Chinese pianos.

Note that Young Chang also makes pianos under a variety of other names for other distributors (see names at beginning of review). However, only pianos sold under the Young Chang, Pramberger, and Bergmann labels are warranted by the manufacturer. The others are warranted by their respective distributors. Note that the Cline and Schafer & Sons warranties are underwritten by Young Chang America, but warranty service must be authorized through the distributors for those brands.

Price range: (Young Chang consoles and studios) $3,400–4,800; (Young Chang uprights) $4,700–6,000; (Young Chang grands) $10,800–27,200; (Pramberger "Platinum Edition" verticals) $7,400; (Pramberger "Platinum Edition" grands) $17,400–26,000; (Bergmann verticals) $2,700–3,600; (Bergmann grands) $8,400–9,400

Young Chang Verticals	Young Chang Grands
43" console (PE-102)	4'11½" (G-150, PG-150)
43½" console (PF-110)	5'2" (G-157, PG-157)
46½" studio (PE-116, PE-116S)	5'9" (G-175, PG-175)
47" studio (PE-118)	6'1" (PG-185)

48" upright (PE-121)	6'10" (PG-208)
52" upright (PE-131)	7' (PG-213)
	9' (G-275)

Pramberger ("Platinum Edition") Verticals	Pramberger ("Platinum Edition") Grands
48" upright (JP-48)	5'9" (JP-175)
	6'1" (JP-185)
	6'10" (JP-208)

Bergmann Verticals	Bergmann Grands
43" console (E-109, AF-108)	4'11" (TG-150)
47" studio (E-118, E-118S)	5'2" (TG-157)
48" upright (E-121)	
52" upright (E-131)	

Consumer Ratings:

Young Chang Verticals

Performance: * * *
Confidence: * * * ½
Quality Control: * * *
Warranty: * * * * ½
Information: * * * ½

Young Chang Grands

Performance
    G (Gold) series: * * *
    PG (Pramberger) series: * * * *
Confidence: * * * ½
Quality Control: * * *
Warranty: * * * * ½
Information
    G (Gold) series: * * * *
    PG (Pramberger) series: * * * ½

Pramberger (Platinum) Grands

Insufficient information to rate, but should be at least as good as Young Chang PG grands, above.

Bergmann Verticals and Grands

Performance: * *
Confidence: * ½
Quality Control: * ½
Warranty: * * * * ½
Information: * * ½

ZIMMERMANN

Premier Piano Co., Inc.
P.O. Box 430
Dundee, Illinois 60118

(800) 531-0133

Not sold in the U.S. at this time.

Pianos made by: C. Bechstein Pianoforte Fabrik GmbH, Berlin, Germany and Seifhennersdorf, Germany

Owned by: Karl Schulze

One of the Leipzig area piano builders, Zimmermann was started by two brothers, Max and Richard Zimmermann, under the name of Leipsiger Pianofortefabrik in the town of

Moelkin, Germany in 1884. By 1895, the enterprise had grown to 120 skilled workers, and future years brought branches in nearby towns. The factories were destroyed in World War II, but afterward several of the top managers set about reorganizing the company. Operations were first started to replace furniture destroyed by the war. Later piano manufacturing was resumed, with many older craftsmen returning to their former occupation.

In 1991, Zimmermann was acquired by Bechstein and incorporated into the Bechstein Gruppe-Berlin. The Zimmermann factory was renovated to meet the higher standards of production now employed, and the instruments were extensively redesigned by Bechstein. The new models are not being marketed in the United States at this time.

Until acquired by Bechstein, Zimmermann produced only a 43" console, a 46" studio, and a 4'9" grand, all in a variety of styles and finishes, some with beautiful cabinets, highlighted panels, and carved mouldings. Upon first arrival in North America in the early 1980s, these pianos had a lot of problems, among them humidity-related action problems, sometimes severe, and glue joints that would come apart in dry weather. The workmanship was just not up to the standards normally expected here from European instruments. The company was very responsive to calls for improvements, however, and by the mid to late 1980s, most of these problems were reduced to the normal ones encountered by other manufacturers, such as tight key bushings, occasional tight action centers, damping problems, and buzzing noises from hardware.

All these pianos were quite lightly constructed both in case parts and in the action and were suitable only for lighter musical tastes and casual use in the home. The 4'9" grand was too small to be seriously recommended by piano technicians, but the scale design was not bad for a piano of its size. Given that the piano performed satisfactorily, had handsome furniture, and was priced affordably, it was probably acceptable for the amateur pianist who primarily desired a nice piece of furniture, as well as a small, inexpensive musical instrument in the home. (A similar small grand piano is now being imported under the name "Niendorf" by another maker. See under that name.)

ELECTRONIC PLAYER PIANO SYSTEMS AND HYBRID ACOUSTIC/DIGITAL PIANOS

As I mentioned earlier in this chapter, player pianos have once again become extremely popular, but this time in electronic form. According to *The Music Trades*, pianos outfitted with electronic player piano systems accounted for over nine percent of all new piano sales in 1999, and more than twenty percent of grand piano sales. And that doesn't even take into account the thousands of *used* pianos into which these systems were retrofitted.

Who are buying the systems? According to dealers, many are folks who would not otherwise have thought of buying a piano, don't play, and have no intention of playing, but who find attractive the idea of a grand piano as the focus of a home entertainment system. Of course, real musicians are

buying the systems, too, often as tools for recording and teaching. And, then, many who were going to buy a piano anyway, especially for a beginner, feel they might as well enjoy some real music from the piano while they're waiting for Junior to grow up and entertain them.

The Playback feature of these systems all work essentially the same way: A row of solenoids, one for each note, is inserted into a slot cut into the keybed of the piano toward the rear ends of the keys. The slot is about two inches from front to back running most of the width of the piano. Each solenoid contains a plunger that makes contact with the back end of a key. Upon receiving an electronic signal, the plunger pushes up on the key, causing the corresponding hammer to strike the strings. Other solenoids operate the pedals via their trapwork. A rapid series of these digital messages causes the piano to play by itself, as if an invisible player were seated at the piano. The electronic signals that operate these systems are in MIDI (Musical Instrument Digital Interface) format, a computer language used throughout the music industry for the electronic transmission of music, and are generated from floppy disks, CDs and other media.

Most systems also include, or offer as options, two other important features: Accompaniment and Record. Sometimes called "Symphony" or "Orchestration," the Accompaniment feature provides accompaniment to the piano through a sound card that produces synthesized or sampled instrumental sounds, or from an actual CD audio track. The Record feature consists of a row of optical or electronic switches beneath the keys that sense any key movement from your playing and translate the movement into MIDI signals, which are sent to a recording medium for storage. One use of this feature is to allow you to record yourself playing the piano, for later playback. A second use is to turn the piano into a MIDI controller. By combining the Record feature with the sound card from the Accompaniment feature (or other tone generator), your manual piano playing can be output as synthesized or sampled piano or instrumental sounds in addition to the acoustic piano sound. Because this "MIDI Controller" combination can be used without the Playback feature, most manufacturers of these systems make it available as a separate option you can buy without Playback if desired. Add headphones and a device for mechanically silencing the acoustic piano, and you essentially have a digital piano you can play late at night without disturbing anyone. Such names as "MIDIPiano," "QuietTime," and "Practice Session" describe this separate option. These MIDI Controller features are not, technically speaking, "player piano" features, but they are so closely connected with the player piano products that I am including them here.

Please note that there are also hybrid acoustic/digital pianos on the market that do not contain a complete acoustic piano. That is, they have something like a real piano action, but they do not have strings and a soundboard for playing acoustically. They are essentially digital pianos with the action of an acoustic piano. Those models are not included in this review and are beyond the scope of this book.

Five companies manufacture electronic player piano systems. The systems vary, among other things, in the degree to which they are tied to a particular piano manufacturer's

For explanation of survey and review procedures, model listings, and price ranges, please see pages 76–81.

products, and in the extent to which they can be customized to your needs. **Yamaha** makes the **Disklavier**, which is installed only in new Yamaha pianos. Because it's installed only at the factory, it comes pretty much as a package with all the features included, though the particular package will vary depending on the piano model. Other than choosing the piano model desired, there are no "options" to choose or figure out, but also no flexibility to configure a system to your specific needs. **Baldwin** makes the **ConcertMaster**. The full-featured ConcertMaster model is installed only in new Baldwin products (Baldwin, Wurlitzer, Chickering), either in the factory or by a local dealer. A model with fewer features can be retrofitted by a technician associated with a Baldwin dealer into any piano, new or used, of your choosing. Although most ConcertMaster features are configured as a package, there is some flexibility with regard to some options. **Young Chang** makes the **Kurzweil Player System**. It comes as a package will all the features included, so it can't be customized. It is installed only in new Young Chang pianos at a factory location.

PianoDisc is designed to be retrofitted into any piano, new or used. Several manufacturers offer PianoDisc as an option in their new pianos. The system, therefore, may be installed at a piano factory, by a dealer, or at an intermediate location such as a warehouse or distribution point. PianoDisc is highly modular and is offered in a couple of packages with a variety of options. **QRS Pianomation MIDI** is also a retrofit system designed to be installed into any piano, new or used. It may be installed at a piano factory, by a dealer, at an intermediate distribution point, or by an independent piano technician. It is probably the most modular of the systems, with several packages and options to choose from. Each of the five companies offers a wide selection of prerecorded floppy disks and CDs with music of every genre to play on its system.

If your intended use of these systems is casual and primarily for the playback of prerecorded music, you probably don't need to read or investigate too much further. All the systems work very well and they are quite competitive with one another in terms of features offered. Your choice of system is likely to depend on which piano you decide to buy and which system your dealer supports. When installed by an authorized dealer or technician according to the manufacturer's instructions, none of these systems will harm the piano, and all are compatible with most piano manufacturers' warranties.

If, however, you plan to use the many features of these systems more intensively or esoterically, want to play music intended for one system on another, or are just plain curious about things technical, I've provided a little more information for you. A general description of each company's system follows this introduction. My commentary on, and comparison of, the systems is at the end of this section. No attempt has been made to cover every feature. In fact, all the systems have many more features than I've described. My aim, as usual, is to point out the differences and issues with which I think you are most likely to be interested, or should be concerned.

Finally, remember that this is modern technology. Specifications and features are subject to change and, in fact, almost guaranteed to change by the time you read this. You can keep in touch with these changes through the *Annual Supplement to The Piano Book*, the manufacturers' web sites, or your dealer.

YAMAHA DISKLAVIER

Yamaha Corporation of America
P.O. Box 6600
Buena Park, California 90622

714-522-9011
800-854-1569
infostation@yamaha.com
www.yamaha.com

The Yamaha Disklavier system is available only in new Yamaha pianos and is installed only in one of the Yamaha factories. No installations are done at dealer locations or in the field. The system is not modular; that is, you cannot choose which options you would like installed in your piano. However, the particular features Yamaha includes in the system vary tremendously from one piano model to another. In fact, the less-expensive Disklavier models bare little resemblance to the high-end ones. So if the Disklavier, rather than the piano, is your focus, you can choose your "options" to some extent through your choice of piano model.

For purposes of assigning Disklavier or Disklavier-related features among its acoustic piano models, Yamaha has divided the models into ten groups, as follows (both the Disklavier model number, and the model number of the regular piano from which it is derived, are given):

Verticals
Console and studio Disklaviers:
    44" MX500 (from M500)
    44" MX112 (from M112)
    45" MX22 (from P22)
    45" MX116 (from T116)

Upright Disklavier: 48" MX1Z (from U1).

Vertical MIDIPianos:
    44" MP500 (from M500)
    45" MP22 (from P22)
    48" MP1Z (from U1)

Technically, MIDIPianos are not Disklaviers because they do not have playback capabilities. They are included here because they are closely related products that have similar features. Sensors underneath the keys and connected to the pedals produce MIDI signals that can be output through the digital piano sound chip to headphones. The acoustic piano can be mechanically silenced, a feature known as "Silent Mode." Thus, these models are MIDI controllers and hybrid acoustic/digital pianos. They do not have disk drives for recording the MIDI data. If it is desired to add recording capabilities to these instruments, Yamaha has an add-on unit called DSR-1, which includes a floppy disk drive, an XG tone generator, and audio terminals for connecting to speakers.

Upright Disklavier with Silent Feature: 48" MPX1Z (from U1)

This is a combination of the upright Disklavier MX1Z and the upright MIDIPiano MP1Z. It has all the features of both instruments.

Grands

Most of the grand models are of the new Mark III series, introduced in 2000.

Entry-level baby grand Disklavier: 4'11" DGA1 (from GA1)

Entry-level small grand Disklavier: 5'3" DGP1 (from GP1)

Mid-level and upper-level small grand Disklaviers:
5'3" DGH1BA (from GH1B)
5'3" DC1A (from C1)
5'8" DC2A (from C2)

Large grand Disklaviers:
6'1" DC3A (from C3)
6'7" DC5A (from C5)
6'11" DC6A (from C6)
7'6" DC7A (from C7)

Disklavier Pro Series:
6'1" DC3PRO (from C3)
6'3" DS4PRO (from S4)
6'7" DC5PRO (from C5
6'11" DC6PRO (from C6)
6'11" DS6PRO (from S6)
7'6" DC7PRO (from C7)
9' DCFIIISPRO (from CFIIIS)

Disklavier Pro series grands are intended for use by recording studios and others with sophisticated recording requirements. The playback solenoid system on the Pro line contains a servo mechanism that continuously monitors performance. Most importantly, the unit can record and playback the release of notes as well as their attack, resulting in a musical rendition much more faithful to the original. At the time of this writing, the Pro line had not yet been upgraded to the Mark III specifications, and so did not yet include a CD drive, extra flash memory, or built-in speakers.

Grand MIDIPianos:
5'3" MPC1 (from C1)
5'8" MPC2 (from C2)
6'1" MPC3 (from C3)
6'11" MPC6 (from C6)
7'6" MPC7 (from C7)

Technically, MIDIPianos are not Disklaviers. See earlier explanatory note for console, studio, and upright MIDIPianos.

In 2000, Yamaha released the 7'6" Disklavier PRO 2000 in honor of its 100th anniversary of piano-making. This extravaganza of a model, costing in the neighborhood of $300,000, contains all of the Disklavier Pro features plus a built-in Pentium III computer with DVD, and a thin-panel touchscreen monitor with which a multi-media performance can be cued. It is beyond the scope of this article to analyze the features of this model.

Here is a list and explanation of the features that differ from one model group to another. A feature comparison chart that shows which features are included in each model group appears on page 163.

Data Storage

Floppy disk drive: 3.5" 1.44 MB; can read both double-density and high-density disks. Reads PianoSoft (Disklavier) software, PianoSoft Plus (with XG sounds), and Standard MIDI format types 0 and 1. Used to play solo piano disks or disks with piano and synthesized instrumentation (with tone generator), and to record piano playing if system is recording-enabled.

CD drive: Can play Pianomation, ConcertMaster, and PianoDisc CDs, as well as Disklavier's PianoSoft Plus Audio CDs. One channel contains MIDI information in analog form to drive the piano playback; the other channel contains actual audio accompaniment that plays over your speakers.

Flash Memory: Re-writeable memory on a chip that does not disappear when the system is turned off. Music can be recorded in flash memory from a floppy disk drive, or from the piano if system is recording-enabled.

Accompaniment

XG Tone Generator: 676 voices (480 accessible from the front panel), including the 128-voice General MIDI (GM) sound set; 32-note polyphony. All models except MIDIPianos can play the XG sounds. MIDIPianos use the digital piano sound chip, below. Note that the DGA1 and DGP1 grand models do not have access to the XG sounds from the control panel, but like the other grands, they can play the XG sounds when accessed from a floppy disk.

Digital Piano Sound Chip: Most sound cards have very little memory devoted to each individual instrument, so the quality of sound is limited. Piano sound is extremely complex, and given the importance of good digital piano sound to a piano, some manufacturers have a special sound chip devoted to it. 64-note polyphony except as noted.

Built-in Speakers: All the grand Disklaviers now have built-in speakers except the Disklavier Pro series, which has not yet been upgraded.

Drive Unit

Pedals: Most Disklavier models can operate both sustain and soft pedals (shift or una corda pedal on a grand) during playback. (MIDIPianos, of course, do not have playback capabilities.) Pedal playback is either *on/off* or *incremental* (also known as continuous or proportional). Incremental playback allows for half-pedaling and other subtle pedaling technique, which is critical for accurate playback of serious music. Disklavier is the only system that provides for this feature. Note that the sostenuto pedal records on a number of grand models, but does not play back. Playback of the sostenuto pedal is simulated by extending the duration of the selectively sustained notes.

Sensor Unit

Keys: All Disklavier models with recording capabilities have key sensors. Key sensors come in three types: *On/off* sensors simply sense whether or not a note is being played. Models with this type of key sensor rely on hammer sensors to measure hammer velocity, which is then translated into key velocity. *Speed-sensing* key sensors determine key velocity by interrupting two beams of light as the key is depressed. The most advanced key sensor is the *continuous* type. It keeps a continuous measurement of key position, including key release.

Hammers: On models with hammer sensors, little flags on the hammer shanks break a beam of light to determine velocity. Models that don't record, or that use only key sen-

DISKLAVIER and MIDIPIANO FEATURES BY MODEL

FEATURES	Console and Studio Disklaviers: MX500 MX112 MX22 MX116	Upright Disklavier: MX1Z	Vertical MIDIPianos: MP500 MP22 MP1Z	Upright Disklavier with Silent Feature: MPX1Z	Entry-Level Baby Grand Disklavier: DGA1	Entry-Level Small Grand Disklavier: DGP1	Mid-Level and Upper-Level Small Grand Disklaviers: DGH1BA DC1A DC2A	Large Grand Disklaviers: DC3A DC5A DC6A DC7A	Disklavier Pro Series: DC3PRO DC4PRO DC5PRO DC6PRO DC7PRO DCFIIISPRO	Grand MIDIPianos: MPC1 MPC2 MPC3 MPC6 MPC7
Floppy Disk Drive	YES	YES	NO	YES	YES	YES	YES	YES	YES	NO
CD Drive	NO	NO	NO	NO	NO	NO	YES	YES	NO	NO
Flash Memory	1 MB	1 MB	NO	1 MB	16 MB	16 MB	16 MB	16 MB	1 MB	NO
Tone Generator	XG, GM	XG, GM	Digital Piano only	XG, GM	XG, GM	XG, GM	XG, GM	XG, GM	XG, GM	Digital Piano only
Digital Piano Sound Chip	NO	NO	16 MB	16 MB	NO	16 MB	16 MB	16 MB	30 MB	30 MB / 32-note polyphony
Built-In Speakers	NO	NO	NO	NO	YES	YES	YES	YES	NO	NO
Sustain Pedal Playback	On/Off	Incremental	NO	Incremental	Incremental	Incremental	Incremental	Incremental	Incremental	NO
Soft Pedal Playback	NO	Incremental	NO	Incremental	Incremental	Incremental	Incremental	Incremental	Incremental	NO
Key Sensors	On/Off	On/Off	Speed-Sensing	On/Off	NO	NO	Continuous	Continuous	Continuous	Continuous
Hammer Sensors	YES	YES	NO	YES	NO	NO	NO	YES	YES	YES
Sustain Pedal Sensor	On/Off	Incremental	Incremental	Incremental	Incremental	NO	Incremental	Incremental	Incremental	Incremental
Sostento Pedal Sensor	NO	NO	NO	NO	NO	NO	YES	YES	YES	YES
Soft Pedal Sensor	NO	Incremental	On/Off	Incremental	NO	NO	Incremental	Incremental	Incremental	Incremental
16-Track Recording	YES	YES	NO	YES	NO	NO	YES	YES	YES	NO
Silent Mode	NO	NO	YES	YES	NO	YES	YES	YES	YES	YES
Quiet Mode	NO	NO	NO	YES	NO	YES	YES	YES	YES	NO
Quick Escape Action	NO	NO	NO	YES	NO	NO	YES	YES	YES	YES
Headphones / Jacks	NO	NO	1 Set 2 Jacks	1 Set 2 Jacks	NO	2 Jacks	2 Jacks	2 Jacks	1 Set 2 Jacks	1 Set 2 Jacks
SmartKey / CueTime	NO	NO	NO	NO	NO	NO	YES	YES	NO	NO

sors to determine velocity, don't have hammer sensors. As mentioned above, Disklaviers with the on/off type of key sensors use hammer sensors to create velocity sensitivity. The most advanced Disklaviers use information from the hammer sensors to supplement the information from their continuous key sensors for greatest accuracy.

Pedals: Most Disklavier and MIDIPianos, except those that don't record, have pedal sensors for the sustain and soft pedals (shift or una corda in a grand). Pedal sensing is either *on/off* or *incremental* (see explanation under "Drive Unit," above). All the grands with pedal sensors also sense sostenuto pedal movement, but only as on or off (this pedal is not usually played in an incremental manner). The sostenuto pedal is recorded, but is not played back, except by extending the duration of individual notes.

Recording

16-Track Recording: Most Disklaviers have 16-track recording capabilities. MIDI Pianos do not have recording capabilities, though it can be added by connecting Yamaha's DSR-1 unit, consisting of an XG tone generator, a floppy disk drive, and an audio connection to speakers.

Silent Mode Features

Silent Mode: In Silent Mode, the acoustic piano is mechanically silenced by means of a rail that prevents the hammer shanks from advancing far enough for the hammers to strike the strings. The rail is operated by the middle pedal on verticals and by a lever under the keybed on grands. When the piano is silenced, the digital piano sound is turned on and directed to the headphone jacks.

Quiet Mode: Whereas in Silent Mode the digital piano sound is directed to the headphone jacks, in Quiet Mode it is directed to the built-in (or other) speakers. The idea is that it is possible to turn the speakers down to a much lower volume than the piano could be turned down to. All piano models that have Silent Mode also have Quiet Mode, except the MIDI Pianos.

Quick Escape Action: When Silent or Quiet Mode is invoked and the hammers are prevented from striking the strings, the normal action regulation is disturbed somewhat. Quick Escape Action is a Yamaha feature that restores the normal action regulation when playing in these modes. Most models with Silent Mode have the Quick Escape Action.

Headphones: All models with Silent Mode have two headphone jacks. All MIDI Pianos and the upright Disklavier with Silent Feature (model MPX1Z) also come with one set of headphones.

Teaching Software

SmartKey: SmartKey helps the beginning player learn music quickly by indicating with a slight wiggle of the key the next note to be played as it approaches, and by adding riffs here and there to make the music more interesting. SmartKey requires advanced Disklavier technology and is only available at this time on the mid-priced and larger grand models.

CueTIME: CueTIME is a smart accompaniment feature that slows down and waits for a student to catch up before proceeding. Certain notes in the music are denoted as "cue notes" and are, in effect, instructions to the synthesized ac-

companiment to go no further until the student reaches that point. CueTIME also requires advanced Disklavier technology and is only available at this time on the mid-priced and larger Disklavier models.

BALDWIN CONCERTMASTER

Baldwin Piano & Organ Co.
4680 Parkway Drive
Mason, Ohio 45040

513-754-4500
800-876-2976
www.baldwinpiano.com

Baldwin's ConcertMaster electronic player piano system was introduced in 1997. ConcertMaster can be installed by Baldwin or one of its dealers into new Baldwin, Wurlitzer, and Chickering pianos. ConcertMaster CD, a new product in 2000, can be installed into any brand of piano, new or used, by a Baldwin dealer.

ConcertMaster utilizes under license some of the technology of QRS (see the review of QRS Pianomation MIDI). It is customized for Baldwin products, including a low-profile solenoid rail design on factory-installed systems. Like QRS, Baldwin uses an eighty-note solenoid rail, not eighty-eight, to make installation easier and avoid cutting into the piano legs, but at the risk of occasionally not being able to play a note at the extremes of the piano. Unlike QRS, Baldwin offers hardware pedal solenoid control for the sustain pedal as a standard feature on all grand piano installations, but does use QRS' "Magic Pedal" technology on verticals. Baldwin also uses QRS' analog MIDI interface (AMI) technology, which allows it to read MIDI information in analog form from a CD, video CD, DVD, or VHS tape. It also enables wireless transmission of MIDI data to ConcertMaster from a computer or other external playback devices. The disadvantage of the analog to MIDI conversion is that the 128 levels of MIDI information are compressed to sixteen levels, spread over the same range as the original 128. At least theoretically, this means there could be a small loss of expression in the music; many people, however, may not be able to notice the difference. This compression does not occur when playing from floppy disks or other digital MIDI source.

ConcertMaster comes in two system packages: the fully-featured one and ConcertMaster CD. In addition, a Performance Option, available only on the fully-featured system, adds recording capabilities and turns the piano into a MIDI controller.

ConcertMaster is available only on new Baldwin, Wurlitzer, and Chickering pianos, both grand and vertical. Sometimes it is installed at the Baldwin factory, sometimes by a local dealer. Although the "back end" of the system comes from QRS, the "front end," or user interface, is Baldwin's own. The system comes with a floppy disk drive, a compact disc (CD) drive, and a 1.2-gigabyte hard drive—a three-playback-source design exclusive to Baldwin—preloaded with twenty hours of music. Baldwin says the floppy disk drive can read just about any type of General MIDI music software on the market, including such software made

For explanation of survey and review procedures, model listings, and price ranges, please see pages 76–81.

for other systems, and the CD drive can read the QRS CDs containing analog audio accompaniment. The hard drive has a capacity of at least 50,000 songs, which can be input from any MIDI source, including computer disks, the internet, and so forth, and organized into as many as 500 different libraries containing 99 songs each. ConcertMaster can read video discs, too, allowing you to view on your television set multi-media software performances of Baldwin artists performing "live" while your piano plays every note the artist does. ConcertMaster was named the "Best New Product Technology" in 1998 by the Custom Electronic Design and Installation Association for its ability to be integrated into whole-house audio and video systems.

ConcertMaster comes with a 128-voice General MIDI sound card and two amplified speakers. The operating system is software upgradeable, allowing new features to be added without purchasing new hardware. The system is operated via a stationary controller attached under the front or side of the piano or by a 900 MHz hand-held RF (radio-frequency) remote control with a built-in LCD window, included. The remote has 100-plus channels to choose from so you can be sure you won't interfere with any other radio-controlled devices in your immediate area.

A **Performance Option** adds recording capabilities and features found on many digital keyboards, including velocity sensitivity, assignable split point, and others. The Option includes a record strip with mechanical shutters that interrupt light beams to determine key velocity, made by Gulbransen. There is also an optional stop rail to silence the piano and let you to listen via headphones to the instrumental sounds from the sound card, a nice feature when using the onboard 64-track sequencer.

ConcertMaster CD, new in 2000, includes a CD drive, but not a floppy drive, hard drive, or sound card. It is intended as a simpler, less expensive unit for those who just want to play their piano with audio accompaniment from CDs. It has MIDI-in and -out connectors, however, so external controllers and sound modules can be added if desired. It comes with an IR (infrared) remote control, not as fancy as the RF remote that comes with ConcertMaster. Baldwin allows its dealers to retrofit ConcertMaster CD into any brand of piano.

The ConcertMaster music library includes the entire QRS music library of historic piano rolls and modern arrangements transferred to CD and floppy disk, plus those of a number of independent producers. At the time of this edition, Baldwin has over 4,000 song titles available in its catalog.

YOUNG CHANG / KURZWEIL PLAYER SYSTEM

Young Chang America, Inc.
9501 Lakewood Drive, S.W. #D
P.O. Box 99995
Lakewood, Washington 98499-0995

253-589-3200
www.youngchang.com

As this is being written, Young Chang has just entered the electronic player piano market with its Kurzweil Player System (KPS). The KPS is built for Young Chang by QRS and, except for the tone generator, is almost identical to the Pianomation system. The tone generator is a 128-voice General MIDI sound card from Kurzweil, the well-known subsidiary of Young Chang that manufacturers digital and electronic musical instruments. Young Chang says it has also revised some of the menus in the control box.

At the present time, the KPS is offered only in the top-of-the-line QRS system configuration, with Analog MIDI Controller, floppy disk drive, and CD drive, plus the Practice Session features of LiteSwitch for recording and the mute rail for silencing the acoustic piano (see "QRS Pianomation MIDI" for details). Like the QRS system, the KPS uses only eighty solenoids; however, unlike QRS, the sustain pedal solenoid and the sostenuto pedal cable are standard. The KPS is being installed in a limited number of Young Chang grand piano models at the Story & Clark piano factory in Seneca, Pennsylvania. Story & Clark is a subsidiary of QRS.

PIANODISC

PianoDisc
4111-A North Freeway Blvd.
Sacramento, California 95834

800-566-3472
916-567-9999
www.pianodisc.com

In 1979, Gary Burgett, a music teacher in Sacramento, California, and his brother Kirk, a machinist and piano rebuilder, opened a piano store together in Nevada City, California. In 1984, Burgett Pianos secured the Pianocorder franchise (see "Marantz/Pianocorder" elsewhere in this chapter) and ran a very successful piano business for a number of years. Unfortunately for the Burgetts, however, Yamaha acquired Pianocorder in 1987 and closed it down. Almost immediately, the brothers decided to design and manufacture their own electronic player piano system, and in 1988 the Burgetts produced the first PianoDisc model.

PianoDisc can be installed into virtually any piano, new or used. A number of manufacturers endorse PianoDisc and install it at one of their manufacturing or distribution points or at a dealer location. PianoDisc imports several brands of piano from Asia and installs PianoDisc systems in them at their Sacramento headquarters (see listings for "Knabe" and "Geo. Steck" elsewhere in this chapter). The same company also manufactures the Mason & Hamlin piano in Massachusetts (see "Mason & Hamlin"). All requests for PianoDisc installation originating with a customer on a new or used piano must go through a piano dealer. Independent technicians not associated with a dealer are usually not licensed to perform the installation. In addition to being associated with a dealer, a technician must go through an extensive training session before being approved.

The flagship PianoDisc system is called the PDS 128 Plus. It includes an 88-note solenoid rail and processor unit installed in the piano, and a slim control box with a built-in floppy disk drive and an optional built-in CD drive. The control box, which mounts under the keybed or sits on or near the piano, can be purchased without the CD drive if desired. It has terminals for connecting your own CD player, as well as for other MIDI and audio devices. An IR (infrared) remote control, revised to be more user-friendly, is also included. The system is software upgradeable. When playing Piano-Disc's specialized PianoCD software, the right channel contains the MIDI signal that drives the piano solenoids. It is encoded in a proprietary analog format that retains all 128 expression levels in the MIDI language. The left channel is an actual audio instrumental or vocal accompaniment that plays through your stereo system or through optional amplified speakers.

The PDS 128 Plus is a highly modular system and there are several important options available. **SymphonyPro** is a sound card with a 128-voice General MIDI sound set. It will accompany the piano with sampled-sound orchestration when driven by encoded floppy disks. **Music Expansion (MX)** utilizes 32 megabytes of flash memory to store hours of music. In fact, it comes loaded with 25 hours worth, 430 songs. Flash memory is re-writable memory, stored on a chip, that does not disappear when the system is turned off. With MX you could play back a thousand songs without ever having to change a disk. You can load new music into MX memory from floppy disks or from any other MIDI source. **TFT MIDI Record** ("TFT" stands for Touch Film Technology) lets you record your playing by turning your piano keyboard into a MIDI controller. A strip of eighty-eight sensors mounted beneath the keys generates MIDI signals as you play. This code can be recorded on a floppy disk or in flash memory, and later played back through the playback function of the PDS 128 Plus, so you can hear what your playing sounds like to others. When combined with Symphony-Pro, you can create orchestrated accompaniment from the keyboard and record the sounds to floppy disk or MX memory, or output it to speakers or headphones. If you prefer to send the actual acoustic piano sound to speakers, rather than a sampled piano sound, **PianoAmp** will pick up the piano from the piano's soundboard. Combine it with sampled-sound orchestration from SymphonyPro and send both through the house audio system. **ProControl** is a wireless remote control with an LCD display that operates on RF (radio frequency) technology so you can control the system from another part of the house (expected release date: early 2001).

PianoCD is PianoDisc's entry-level, easy-to-use player piano system. It plays only CDs—both the PianoCD software and regular audio CDs—and has far fewer features than the PDS 128 Plus. The only options that can be connected to it are the amplified speakers and the PianoAmp.

Although the SymphonyPro sound card and the TFT MIDI Record sensor strip are optional add-ons to the PDS 128 Plus system, they are also part of PianoDisc's **PianoDigital with QuietTime** system. This system turns the piano into a MIDI controller and hybrid acoustic/digital piano, but without the PDS 128 Plus playback features and disk drives. In regular mode, the piano plays just like an ordinary piano. If desired, the system will provide orchestrated accompaniment through optional amplified speakers. When the QuietTime feature is activated by moving a small lever underneath the keyboard, a mute rail prevents the hammers from hitting the strings, silencing the piano. At the same time, the digital piano and other sounds are turned on and can be accessed using the supplied headphones (perfect for late-night playing). QuietTime can be installed in any piano, independent of the player piano systems, or it can be combined with PDS 128 Plus and other options to create the most fully-featured system PianoDisc offers.

QuietTime comes in two varieties: Model GT-360 supplies 128 General MIDI sounds (like SymphonyPro), 16 megabytes of memory, 64-note polyphony, MIDI-In, Out & Thru, 16 MIDI channels with reverb and other effects, key range settings, and the ability to create and save up to 75 of your own custom sound-combination presets. The less expensive model GT-90 has 16 instrumental selections that are factory pre-set, and the ability to make 40 possible sound combinations. The emphasis on this model is simplicity of operation, as most functions can be accessed by pushing one or two buttons.

PianoDisc maintains a large and growing music library of floppies and CDs for use on its systems, including solo piano with famous artists, piano with orchestrated accompaniment (some "live"), and piano and vocal. PianoDisc says its system will also play any Standard MIDI file (type 0 format), much of the PianoSoft (Yamaha Disklavier) library, and disks of independent producers.

QRS PIANOMATION MIDI

QRS Music Technologies, Inc.
2011 Seward Avenue
Naples, Florida 34109
941-597-5888
www.qrsmusic.com

QRS is the world's oldest and largest manufacturer of player piano rolls. The company was founded in 1900 by Melville Clark, who developed the standard format for piano rolls eventually adopted by the music industry. The company survived the Depression and a generation with little interest in the player piano, then enjoyed the revival of interest that came in the 1960s, '70s, and '80s. In 1986, Richard Dolan, a player-piano enthusiast, purchased QRS. For a number of years, QRS had sold Pianocorder Reproducing Systems, but after Yamaha purchased and then discontinued that system in 1987 (see "Marantz/Pianocorder" elsewhere in this chapter), QRS set about designing its own system. Thus was born Pianomation MIDI. QRS became a public company (now called QRS Music Technologies, Inc.) in 1998, trading under the symbol QRSM.

QRS Pianomation MIDI is an electronic player piano system that can be installed into virtually any piano, new or used. It is highly modular, so it can be configured to suit a wide variety of applications.

The QRS system differs from some other systems in several respects. The standard QRS solenoid rail contains eighty solenoids, not eighty-eight; the other eight solenoids are optional. This means that without the optional solenoids, the system will not be able to play back the top and bottom four notes on the keyboard. These notes are occasionally used in the piano literature and on prerecorded discs, but not often.

QRS says that by using eighty solenoids, installation is made much easier. Using the full eighty-eight, it says, might necessitate cutting into the legs to accommodate the wider rail.

Whereas most systems actually operate the sustain (damper) pedal via its trapwork, the standard Pianomation operating system simulates pedal operation through software control of note duration, a feature QRS calls "Magic Pedal." This simulation is not as realistic as actually controlling the damper pedal, but is acceptable for simpler applications. QRS says that Magic Pedal avoids the complicated and sometimes noisy hardware pedal hookup and duplicates the sustain event duration more accurately than a pedal, but at the expense of losing the sympathetic string vibrations that occur when the real sustain pedal is used. Hardware control of the damper pedal with a pedal solenoid is offered as an option.

Depending on the particular Pianomation system and options chosen, Pianomation can be run from special compact discs, floppy disks, or any other medium that contains MIDI or QRS' patented analog MIDI information. Floppy disks usually contain the MIDI information in digital format, which can be sent to the Pianomation system by any MIDI controller, MIDI file player, or PC. As for QRS compact discs, the left CD channel carries an analog version of the MIDI signal which is compressed by QRS' patented AMI (analog MIDI interface) technology, and then uncompressed and translated back into a digital MIDI format as it is sent to the piano for playback. In the compression from digital to analog, however, the 128 expression levels carried in the MIDI signal are reduced to sixteen (spread over the same range as the original 128). QRS says this compression process offers greater reliability with analog recording and transmission without sacrificing any other MIDI channels or data events. Sixteen volume levels is probably as many as most listeners can discriminate without very careful listening, but playback of material originally recorded on modern (MIDI) equipment may not be quite as true to the original as it would be if played back with the full MIDI palette. Those who wish to avoid this possible limitation should play their Pianomation system from floppy disks. The right CD channel carries an actual audio signal, such as a live instrumental or vocal recording, that plays simultaneously on a stereo system or optionally-available amplified speaker.

Being able to translate the MIDI signal into analog form allows it to be recorded on the audio track of a standard VHS videotape so that video entertainment (such as lyrics or images of a pianist's hands) can be shown in synch with the piano playback. The analog signal can also be transmitted to the piano by radio waves using the optional wireless transmitter and receiver, which could be handy for use in commercial establishments or when you don't want to run wires from the CD player to the piano.

QRS has two different Record systems available: LiteSwitch and OptiScan. LiteSwitch is a strip of eighty-eight mechanical switches that interrupt two beams of light. The amount of time it takes each switch to go from the first beam to the second when a key is played is used to measure key velocity, which, just like on a regular piano, determines loudness of sound (this is known as "velocity sensitivity"). OptiScan, the more expensive option, contains no moving parts to touch the keys. Instead, light beams are bounced off the key bottoms to determine their velocity. With OptiScan, the "velocity curve," or degree of velocity sensitivity, can be calibrated by the user to match their playing style or listening preference.

QRS has pre-configured Pianomation MIDI into several player systems with popular features, to which many optional accessories can be added. The packages, and some of the suggested options, are as follows:

The **QRS Base Pianomation system** is simply the Pianomation playback engine. It consists of an eighty-note solenoid rail, and a box with the processor electronics, a MIDI-in terminal, and an On/Off switch. It also has an input for one of QRS' optional user interfaces (described later) and for technical test equipment. Installed without a user interface or other options, this base system is basically just a MIDI receiver. It only accepts a regular, digital MIDI signal and so will not run from a CD. It does not come with any controllers (CD drives, floppy disk drives, etc.). This base system is all you need if you want only to use a MIDI signal from a computer, for example, or other straight MIDI source to play the piano. There is no MIDI-out terminal, however, for connecting to an outside sound module or other MIDI receiver, and it does not have recording capabilities. Obviously, this base system is very limited and so is usually purchased as part of one of the systems described below.

The **QRS 2000C system** includes the Pianomation playback engine described above, the 2000C user control interface with basic piano and audio controls, and an infrared (IR) remote control. This system is for those who don't want a control box on their piano, but who want a well-featured system to use with their own CD player. It will recognize whether you are playing a QRS CD or a regular audio CD and automatically make the appropriate internal adjustments so you can listen to both through your stereo system. It has a MIDI-out terminal for connecting to an external sound module or other MIDI receiver, a MIDI-in terminal for using a computer or external floppy disk drive to play the piano, a MIDI-thru terminal to connect other MIDI devices, AMI-in and -out terminals to connect devices with analog MIDI tracks (CD players and VCRs), and audio-out terminals for connecting to your stereo system or amplified speakers. The 2000C user interface does not have recording capabilities.

The **QRS 1000CD system** includes the Pianomation playback engine plus a built-in CD player with user interface. The user interface has few controls, however; you must use the IR remote control, included, to access most of the system's features. The 1000CD is considered a barebones system for those who are looking for a simple, low-cost, plug-and-play, player piano solution. It will provide playback of the piano from the left channel of the CD and audio accompaniment from the right channel. The audio channel can be connected through the audio-out terminal on the user interface to your own stereo amplifier and speakers or to an optional, amplified speaker placed inside or near the piano. The CD player will also play regular audio CDs, but only in mono through the speakers or in stereo through the headphone port (headphones not included). The user box also has a

MIDI-in terminal for connecting your own floppy disk drive or computer, if desired. There is no MIDI-out terminal, however, for connecting to an outside sound module or other MIDI receiver, but you could connect such a receiver between the MIDI-out of the floppy drive and the MIDI-in of the Pianomation system to provide accompaniment. The 1000CD user interface does not have recording capabilities.

The **QRS 2000CD system** is essentially the same as the 2000C system, above, except that it also includes a built-in CD player with appropriate controls. This simple and self-contained player system typically comes with a speaker mounted inside the piano.

The **QRS Analog MIDI Controller (AMC)** player system is QRS' top-of-the-line system. It comes in three varieties: a stand-alone unit for use with your own CD player and stereo system, or silent practice; a unit that includes a floppy disk drive; and a unit that includes both a floppy disk drive and a CD player. All variations of the AMC system include the Pianomation playback engine (solenoids, processor). The AMC user interface contains a built-in Ensoniq effects processor and sequencer with a 128-voice General MIDI sound set. The AMC includes all the terminals described above for the 2000 systems. In addition, the MIDI-in terminal can support the optional Record function, and the audio-out terminals support both mixed and unmixed output. The unmixed output sends only the accompaniment music to optional speakers in the same room as the piano, whereas the mixed output sends both the piano sound and the accompaniment to your stereo speakers throughout the house or establishment. The piano sound included in the mixed output can be either synthesized piano from the sound module or real acoustic piano sound from a microphone attached to the piano soundboard. The AMC also hosts many other features, controls, presets, silent practice, and customizations too numerous to mention here.

Playola is a portable Pianomation system that sits atop the keys, like the "Vorsetzer" of the player piano's halcyon days, and plays all eighty-eight keys with little rubber fingers, either alone or with accompaniment. Playola uses the Magic Pedal feature in place of the sustain pedal, but the optional pedal solenoid can be added at any time (installation required). Playola itself is essentially a Pianomation playback engine, so it is usually sold configured like a 2000C, 2000CD, or AMC system (i.e., with a user interface, remote control, and with or without a built-in CD player and speaker), depending on the user's needs. Playola does not require professional installation by a technician.

Practice Session. Although the LiteSwitch and OptiScan record strips can be ordered alone, QRS has a package called Practice Session that includes the record strip of your choice; an AMC user interface (with or without floppy-drive and CD player) with built-in effects processor and sequencer containing 128 General MIDI sounds, split points, and effects; a mute rail for silencing the acoustic piano; and headphones. This is essentially the AMC system described earlier plus the record strip, mute rail and headphones, but *without* the Piano-

mation playback engine. Practice Session turns your piano into a MIDI controller and recording system, but without the player piano feature. If you want to add Practice Session to the AMC system in order to retain the player piano feature, you would just buy the optional record strip, mute rail, and headphones, since the AMC system already includes the rest.

Some of the Pianomation options and accessories available include: extra key solenoids and a sustain pedal solenoid, mentioned earlier; the record strips and other Practice Session hardware, mentioned above; self-powered speakers for placement under or near the piano; wireless transmitters and receivers for sending music from a remote CD player or MIDI controller to the piano; an analog MIDI interface (AMI) for use with the wireless transmitters and receivers when transmitting MIDI wirelessly from a computer; a remote IR sensor for extending the range of the remote control; and a piano microphone for picking up the piano sound off the soundboard.

The Pianomation catalog contains the following types of music on CD or floppy disk: solo piano from historic player piano music rolls; solo piano from full-expression, live piano performances; live concert piano performances accompanied by major orchestras; and piano plus background music and vocals with well-known artists of the past and present. There are also sing-along videos with lyrics that scroll down the TV screen while the piano plays.

COMMENTARY and COMPARISONS

My original plan was to simplify the presentation of the five systems by use of a feature comparison chart. But as I delved more deeply into the subject, it became apparent that the huge number of features, combined with the large number of possible component configurations and options, would result in a chart whose size and complexity would completely defeat its own purpose (not to mention giving me an ulcer in the process). Furthermore, most of the systems have features essentially similar to those of their competitors, though the features may be approached in different ways and presented in different combinations. Having already described, in their respective reviews, the various system packages and options offered by each manufacturer, I decided to just lay out, in plain language, the advantages and disadvantages, as I see them, of each manufacturer's offerings.

Please understand that I do not consider myself to be an expert on the subject of electronic player piano systems. But, like a very conscientious consumer, I spent several weeks studying product literature and owner's manuals and speaking with manufacturer's representatives and installers, and I have come to some conclusions.

First and foremost, all of these systems are terrific, and the vast majority of people who buy them will be thrilled with them, regardless of which manufacturer's system they purchase. Although each of the companies has gone through periods of technical difficulty early in its history, there are relatively few persistent problems now. For the home entertainment use that most people will make of them, there is hardly enough difference between the competing systems worth mentioning. That having been said, for the small percentage of buyers who care, either because of their own conscientious nature or because of the more technical or professional use they plan to make of these systems, there are some differences and issues worth discussing.

PianoDisc vs. Pianomation

Since Baldwin's, Yamaha's, and Young Chang's systems are, for the most part, reserved for their own instruments, the fiercest competition is between QRS Pianomation and PianoDisc, both of which can be installed into any piano, new or used. Some of the differences over which their marketing departments duke it out are as follows:

- The standard Pianomation system plays only eighty notes (up to eighty-eight optional); PianoDisc has eighty-eight as standard. QRS says that to install eighty-eight solenoids requires cutting into the piano legs, which could reduce their stability or be unsightly.

- Pianomation does not supply a sustain pedal solenoid as standard equipment; it's optional. Instead it relies on its "Magic Pedal" technology, which simply sustains some notes longer to mimic use of the pedal. The sustain pedal solenoid is standard on PianoDisc installations.

- The standard Pianomation system installation does not reconnect the sostenuto (middle) pedal on a grand for manual use; a linkage for that purpose is optional. On PianoDisc, it's standard.

- Finally, the number of levels of MIDI expression on the piano track of QRS compact discs is reduced from 128 to sixteen by the technology it uses. PianoDisc retains all 128.

Here's what I found out: Most buyers don't care that the four notes at each end of the keyboard don't play back on standard Pianomation systems. Hardly anyone ever asks for the optional additional solenoids. However, if you are using the system for professional applications such as recording, I would suggest having all eighty-eight notes available for playback, since all eighty-eight record. PianoDisc's cutting into the legs a little to fit the full eighty-eight-note solenoid rail in the piano doesn't show (it's on the inside surface of the legs) and does not make the piano less stable. Even Steinway authorizes it, and they're pretty conservative about such things.

The QRS "Magic Pedal" is okay, but a bit hokey. If you buy the QRS system, you'll get noticeably better musical results if you order it with the sustain pedal solenoid installed. After all, you went to all that expense to buy a grand piano; you might as well make use of one of its most important features. (Sometimes salespeople fail to tell the customer about this, causing customer relations problems later on.) Ditto for the sostenuto pedal linkage; you may not use this pedal, but a visitor may wonder why it doesn't work. (Installers say this linkage needs to be redesigned, but you should get it anyway.) Finally, studies show that most people can't consciously discriminate sixteen levels of volume between the

softest and loudest passages in a piece of music, much less 128. But that doesn't mean it isn't perceptible on some level. Most of the installers I spoke with told me they felt that PianoDisc software had slightly better expression than QRS software, but they didn't know why. Perhaps it has something to do with the number of MIDI levels expressed—I don't know for sure.

Pianomation is a great player piano system. The few shortcuts QRS takes and the many options it offers are eminently practical and probably reduce the cost a bit while still satisfying the majority of buyers. The PianoDisc system, however, seems just a little more thoughtfully packaged and presented. Its standard features contain fewer compromises and there are fewer choices to make that might tax the intelligence of the buyer. This may be more a matter of marketing than engineering, but as someone trying to navigate through strange territory, it made an impression on me. I would imagine that new-piano dealers who sell Pianomation probably compensate for this by pre-configuring the systems they install on their pianos so that their customers don't have to make so many choices. In any case, as I said before, most customers will be very happy with either system.

Installing any of these systems is very complicated. The piano must be moved to a shop for anywhere from a few days to a week or so; it cannot be done in your home. So if you are buying a piano and thinking of getting a player piano system one day, you should strongly consider doing it now. It will save you extra moving expenses and wear and tear on the piano.

Installation is complicated for a couple of reasons. First, a slot for the solenoid rail must be cut in the keybed. While this is not itself difficult, it must be done precisely and there is no second chance. Second, installation often requires major surgery on the grand piano pedal lyre and trapwork. In addition to hooking up the sustain pedal solenoid, the manual use of the pedals must be restored as closely as possible to their original feel and function. Because every piano model has a slightly different trapwork arrangement, accomplishing this requires a lot of experience and ingenuity on the part of the installer, and there is no guarantee the pedals will end up feeling like they did before the installation. If you are concerned about this, ask to play a piano of the same model that already has a system installed in it.

According to my installer sources, installing a PianoDisc system is a little easier than installing a Pianomation, and results in a neater installation. Pianomation more often requires actually repositioning the pedal lyre on a grand piano. This is not for the faint of heart. Repositioning the lyre means also moving the trapwork, the una corda (soft) pedal shift lever, and the place on the keyframe the shift lever contacts, which could affect how well the soft pedal works. The Pianomation installation sometimes requires removing more material from the back rail of the keyframe than does the PianoDisc, which may entail moving the back rail cloth. This disturbs the keyboard regulation, so the action must be re-regulated and may not feel the same. Don't get me wrong: An experienced installer can install any of these systems well; it's those who do only an occasional installation I would worry about, especially for Pianomation. When shopping for a system, then, be sure to inquire as to the experience level of the installer. The best ones are probably those who do at least several installations a month and who have done them on the piano model you own or are buying.

Pianomation may potentially be a little less expensive than PianoDisc, at least in part because Pianomation can be installed by any technician who buys an installation kit, thereby allowing a shopper to bypass a piano dealer's markup by contracting directly with an installer. PianoDisc is only available through piano dealers whose technician/installer has completed a training course. (QRS also offers a training course, and strongly encourages its installers to attend, but it isn't required.) There are many competent installers of each system; in fact, in some areas, the same technician installs and services all kinds of systems. But if you are contracting directly with a technician for installation of a Pianomation system, make sure he or she has attended the company's training course.

By the way, most of my discussion has been about grand piano installations because the vast majority of systems are installed in grands. Installation in verticals is more difficult than in grands. The cast-iron plate and the keybed supports may get in the way of the solenoid rail and have to be modified. The keyframe back rail usually has to be moved, too. Installing the sustain pedal solenoid can be challenging (here's one place where QRS' Magic Pedal may be preferable). Basically, I would suggest not installing any of these systems in a vertical piano. The extra work and difficulty, potential problems, and questionable musical value make it, in my opinion, not worthwhile.

Baldwin ConcertMaster

The Baldwin ConcertMaster uses the QRS technology for much of its system, and so will share some of its advantages and disadvantages, including some of those related to installation. Some ConcertMaster installations are performed at the Baldwin factory, some by dealers. Baldwin's user interface, however, is a big leap forward. Its three-playback-source design and its library system for storing songs are very intelligent. Baldwin's RF remote control with a built-in LCD display is one of the most attractive and user-friendly interfaces I've seen.

Young Chang / Kurzweil Player System

The Young Chang KPS also uses QRS technology, even more than Baldwin does, so it should be expected to install and function like Pianomation in most ways. Since the first models are just being shipped as I write this (Spring 2000), it is too soon to have any feedback or criticism from installers and others.

Yamaha Disklavier

Yamaha's Disklavier marketing department may think Disklavier is in competition with the other systems, but for most technicians I've spoken with, there's no contest: the Disklavier is far superior. For one thing, Disklaviers are installed only at the Yamaha factory, so there is no monkeying with pedal lyres and trapwork, trying to get them to feel and work right, or worrying about the competence of the installer. Combined with Yamaha's reputation for attention to detail and serviceability, this means that Disklaviers work nearly flawlessly. For another, Yamaha is the only player piano manufacturer whose pedals record and play back incrementally, rather than in on/off mode. This allows for more precise and subtle recording of the pedaling. Disklavier also supports recording and playback of the soft pedal, the only system to do so. These and other aspects of Yamaha's technology translate into a greater range of expression in both recording and playback. As a result, Disklavier is the best choice for professional applications. Technicians also like Disklavier's self-diagnostic abilities.

Yamaha's reputation, however, derives chiefly from its mid-level and upper-level pianos. The features included in each Disklavier model vary from model to model, and the entry-level models are not that impressive. The two least expensive grands, for example, are playback-only models and have no CD drive. Use the chart on page 163 to help you compare a specific Disklavier model to other systems.

The principal drawback to the Disklavier system, however, is that it is only available in Yamaha pianos. It is also not modular; you have to take the whole package even if all you want to do is play back CDs on your piano. Actually, if you want all the bells and whistles, the Disklavier is not much more expensive than one of the other systems with all the comparable options. But if you don't, the Disklavier becomes a very expensive purchase, which is why some who buy a Yamaha piano end up installing one of the other, more modular, systems in it.

Warranty

None of the systems have major warranty problems at this point, although they all have had some at one time or another (which their competitors will be quick to point out). One technician called Pianomation "bomb proof," and each of the other systems received praises, too. Any of the systems can suffer an occasional bad electronic part, but most of these show up during the installation process or soon after. PianoDisc and Disklavier offer five-year parts warranties, Baldwin and QRS, two years. The labor warranty on the Baldwin, QRS, and Disklavier systems is one year. PianoDisc automatically gives a labor warranty of 90 days, but relies on the dealer or installer to supply the remainder of the labor warranty. I would suggest asking for at least a year. On systems PianoDisc installs at its own facility (for example, in Knabe and Steck pianos), the company gives a one-year labor warranty.

Wireless

A word about wireless transmission of audio and MIDI data and RF remote control: QRS actively promotes wireless transmission, perhaps because its analog MIDI interface technology is especially well suited to performing this feat, but all the manufacturers told me their systems are capable of transmitting wirelessly with off-the-shelf (but sometimes expensive) equipment. For the most part, wireless works well, but not flawlessly. Background interference may cause occasional dropping of data and missed notes on the piano. RF remote control may also malfunction once in a while. Conditions can vary depending on the location.

Compatibility

The library of music software available for each of these systems is immense, so I'm not sure why you'd want to seek out another company's disc or diskette to play on your system. But if you do, you should know that the issue of compatibility is an unsettled one. Most of the manufacturers told me that at any point in time they are not quite sure which software will play on which system. Playing floppy disks is generally less of a problem than playing CDs because many floppies are recorded in standard MIDI format and all the systems can read that. But the piano track of the CD is usually recorded in a proprietary format. It is up to each manu-facturer to reverse-engineer their competitors' formats and then redesign their own equipment to accept or translate that format if they choose to.

There is also software on the market that can translate each company's format into standard MIDI format, from which it can then be played or translated into another company's format. For more information on this translation software, contact: Giebler Enterprises, 26 Crestview Drive, Phoenixville, Pennsylvania 19460; (610) 933-0332; **www.giebler.com**.

Downloading Music From the Internet

There are many web sites on the internet that contain standard MIDI files you can download and play on your player piano system. A listing of some of these sites can found at **www.ptg.org**. Click on "MIDI."

For more information, I recommend the article "MIDI Files on the Internet" by George F. Litterst, in *Piano & Keyboard* magazine, November/December 1998. See the end of Chapter 7 for magazine contact information.

CHAPTER FIVE

Buying a Used Piano

IF YOU READ NO FURTHER IN THIS CHAPTER than just this first paragraph, remember this: the most important thing you should know about buying a used piano is that you should have it inspected by a piano technician before putting your money down. Each year countless people, thinking that the piano in question "just needs tuning," throw away hundreds or even thousands of dollars on "instruments" that would be better put to use as firewood and baling wire. This is not to say that the seller necessarily tries to defraud the buyer. Usually the seller is as ignorant of the piano's condition as the buyer. But this experience does tend to lead to "fraud," as the buyer, on being informed by the technician that the piano is untunable or unrepairable, often tries to get his or her money back by selling the piano to another unwary buyer, sometimes seeking the technician's help in doing so. The "hot potato" thus passes from hand to hand until someone finally either accepts the loss and junks the piano or shells out the money to have it repaired properly. These people could have saved themselves a lot of grief and money if they had only consulted a technician before buying.

Of course, it's impractical and too expensive to take a technician along to inspect *every* piano you check out. You want to inspect most of them yourself as best you can, and then hire a technician to look at the one or two most likely candidates for purchase. This chapter is largely about how to inspect a piano yourself—to avoid the worst catastrophes, to anticipate future problems, and to estimate repair costs. However, de-

pending on the pianos you encounter and your ability to use the material presented here to inspect them, you may find it necessary to hire the services of a technician several times before you settle on a satisfactory instrument, so you should budget enough money to cover that possibility. Most technicians charge a fee similar to their tuning fee to inspect a piano.*

One important note: Both extreme dryness and extreme dampness can seriously damage a piano, particularly in regions where the weather annually swings from one extreme to the other and back again. Such regions include most of the United States and Canada. Usually the most severe problems will show up during the dry season, in the form of cracked wooden parts, broken glue joints, and loose tuning pins that won't hold the piano in tune. These problems may be absent or disguised during the damp season, and may be especially severe when pianos previously stored in damp places or humid climates have been moved to drier places or climates. I would therefore advise you to do your piano shopping at the driest time of the year. This way you can see the piano at its worst before purchase and avoid unpleasant surprises later on.

WHAT'S OUT THERE

Before you go out into the "cruel world" of used pianos, you might want me to tell you something about what

*See page 16.

172

you're going to find out there. The best way I can do this is to give you a *very* brief, and *very* selective, history of the piano.

The piano was invented about 1700 by an Italian harpsichord maker named Bartolomeo Cristofori of Padua. Cristofori replaced the plucking quill action of a harpsichord, which could pluck only with unvarying force and hence unvarying volume of sound, with a newly designed striking hammer action, whose force and volume could be precisely controlled by the player. Thus was born the *Gravicembalo col piano e forte* or "keyboard instrument with soft and loud." This later got reduced to *pianoforte*, then *fortepiano*, and finally just *piano*. (Considering some of the harsh-sounding instruments today, perhaps it's time to change the name to *forte*.) During the 1700s the new instrument, made mostly by craftsmen in their shops, spread quietly through upper-class Europe. A number of different forms of piano action and structure were invented, such as the "Viennese action," the "English action," the "square piano," and so on. (Replicas of early fortepianos are now popular among certain musicians who prefer to play music of that period on the original instruments for which the music was written.)

During the 1800s, the piano spread more quickly through the middle classes and across the ocean to North America. Riding along with the Industrial Revolution, piano making became an industry, as opposed to a craft. Many important changes took place during the century. The upright piano was invented; the modern grand piano action was invented, incorporating the best aspects of the previous rival actions; the cast-iron plate was invented, vastly strengthening the structure and allowing for the strings to be stretched at a higher tension, increasing their power and volume of sound; the range of the instrument was extended from about five octaves to the present seven-plus octaves; cross-stringing was invented, improving the bass tone; and, toward the end of the century, the square piano died out, leaving just grands of various sizes and the full-size upright. By 1880, most of these changes were in place, and the pianos made today are not very different from those of a hundred years ago.

In your searching for a piano, you're unlikely to run across instruments made before 1880. There are two possible exceptions that I want to warn you about. One of them is the **square piano**, or square grand, as it is sometimes called—really a rectangular box—which was so popular as a home piano during the nineteenth century (Figure 5-1). Stories about these pianos are stock-in-trade among technicians. A typical story goes something like this: A person shopping for a used piano stops into an antique store where a square piano is on display, and, charmed by the ornate legs and un-

usually shaped case—highly polished for the occasion—the shopper plunks down her money and drags the beast home. How lovely it will look with the pseudo-Victorian furniture! Then begin the phone calls to piano technicians to get the charming antique "tuned up." Well, the first five technicians called politely decline the work. They don't know anything about square pianos, they say, or they find them too much trouble to work on. The sixth technician needs the work badly, and so agrees to do the best he can to patch up the musical innards using a hodgepodge assortment of antique and modern parts he manages to scrounge up. After several months of futile tinkering, the piano still does not work right, and phone calls to the technician are no longer being returned, so a seventh technician is called. This one, a wise and compassionate soul, assesses the damage and calmly tells the owner the sad truth. This piano, she says, like most other squares, has little or no historical, artistic, or financial value, would cost thousands of dollars to repair correctly, and even then would be unsuitable to practice on, even for a beginner. Indeed, especially for a beginner—unless that beginner is to lose all interest in music!

Another kind of piano to avoid is a type of upright made primarily in Europe from the middle to the end of the nineteenth century. The dampers on this piano are positioned *above* the hammers and are actuated by wires in *front* of the action, unlike in a modern upright, in which the damper system is entirely behind and beneath the hammers. This "over-damper" system has been nicknamed the "birdcage action," and you can see why in Figure 5-2. Besides being very difficult to tune and service through the "bird cage," these pianos are usually so worn out that they will not hold a tuning longer than about ten seconds, and their action works erratically at best. Many of these pianos were cheaply made to begin with, but they often have fancy features, such as candlesticks, that make them attractive to antique collectors. In recent years, hundreds of

FIGURE 5-1. The square piano—or square grand, as it is sometimes called—should be left to antique collectors. It is not suitable for practice purposes, even for beginners, and may be next to impossible to repair properly.

How Long Does a Piano Last?

You might as well ask how long a human being lasts—it can vary almost that much. Given the need for a brief answer to the latter question, we might answer "seventy-five or eighty years," even though we know that some people die in infancy or childhood and others live to over one hundred. Similarly, one often hears that pianos last "forty or fifty years," but this is just a brief answer to a very complicated question.

There are at least four factors that determine the life span of a piano: original quality, environmental stability, use and abuse, and maintenance. A piano that was well made, for which the woods were carefully selected, dried, machined, and joined, for example, will last much longer than one that received little thought or attention to these details. A piano located in an environment in which the humidity wildly swings seasonally from one extreme to the other without amelioration by humidity control equipment will perish much sooner than one in a more temperate climate or climate-controlled situation. A piano banged on sixteen hours a day in a school practice room, or into which drinks are spilled and cigarettes are allowed to burn, will live a shorter time than one that enjoys a pampered life in a livingroom and a family in which nobody plays much.

Finally, a technician who regularly services a piano, catching and correcting small problems before they become big ones, may be able to extend the useful life of a piano beyond what it would otherwise enjoy.

What makes the question about the piano more complicated than its counterpart about human beings, however, is the difficulty of defining the "death" of a piano. Most pianos receive repair piecemeal and slowly wither away over time. A piano may finally be considered "dead" and be discarded when the space it takes up is needed for other things, when a student outgrows the piano's ability to adequately play more advanced music, or when the resources to buy a better instrument suddenly become available. Until that time, the piano may have been deemed very much "alive" by its owner. Even upon being "discarded," however, a piano that is no longer considered usable by one person may be considered just right for its intended purpose or the available budget by another. And unlike people, pianos can be resurrected, i.e., restored, and enjoy an entirely new life all over again.

But most people don't want to hear such a lengthy answer to what seems like a simple question, so when the customer asks "How long does a piano last?", we just answer "forty or fifty years"—and then return to our work tuning the customer's beautiful, unrestored 1925 upright.

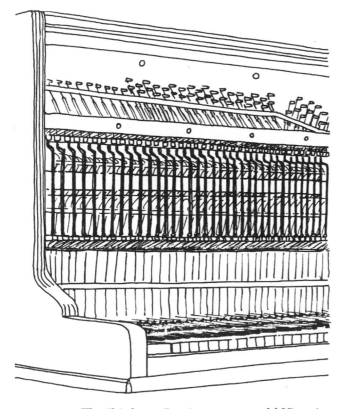

FIGURE 5-2. The "bird cage" action on some old Victorian uprights makes servicing very difficult. Also, these pianos are usually too worn out to be usable.

these and other useless antique pianos have been dumped on uninformed buyers in the United States and Canada, often at extravagant prices. (Note: Serious collectors of antique musical instruments and musicians with specialized performance needs requiring those instruments should use the services of a technician who specializes in them. These technicians are a rare breed, but can generally be located through museums and universities with antique instrument collections.)

The years from 1880 to about 1900 were a transitional period, as some old styles were slow to fade. But some pianos from this period maybe suitable for you. A piano with only eighty-five notes instead of eighty-eight may be perfectly satisfactory if you don't anticipate ever needing the highest three notes. The resale value of such a piano may be slightly lower than its more modern equivalent, but so should be the price you pay for it. A piano with an old-style cast-iron plate that, while extending the full length of the piano, leaves the pinblock exposed to view is, for all practical purposes, just as structurally sound as one in which the plate covers the pinblock. In fact, some European manufacturers still make instruments in this style today. Avoid, however, the so-called "three-quarter plate" piano, with a plate that ends just short of the pinblock. These pianos have a high rate of structural failure. Pianos with actions that are only very slight

Brief Notes on a Few Old Piano Brands

Steinway. Steinway grands built since about 1880 are almost always worth buying and restoring, both because a conscientious restoration job will usually result in a superior instrument and because the market value of the restored piano will justify the cost of the restoration. Old Steinway uprights, on the other hand, are worth buying and restoring only if the action is in good condition. Although good replacement action parts are available for old Steinway uprights, due to a lack of standardization these parts will not always precisely fit. The extra labor required to make them fit can render this job impractical. When in good condition, these uprights are great instruments.

Mason & Hamlin. Old Mason & Hamlin grands are often considered the equals of old Steinways. Especially prized are the smaller models, such as the model A (5'8"). For a couple of decades around the turn of the century, Mason & Hamlin also made pianos known as "screw stringers." These had an unusual tuning mechanism using machine screws instead of tuning pins. Although this mechanism required different tuning tools and techniques, it worked extremely well. Many of these old screwstringers, both grands and uprights, are still around, some in good condition. The only drawback to buying a screwstringer is that the parts for the tuning mechanism are obsolete and hard to obtain, and some of the parts, if broken, may be difficult even for a machinist to duplicate.

Chickering. Chickering was an illustrious and innovative piano maker who liked to experiment. Sometimes it seems as if each Chickering was a one-of-a-kind instrument. The grands were known for their terrific bass tone . . . and for their lackluster treble. Chickerings have a lot of charm and history and a very loyal following, especially in New England. But the unusual technical features in some of them, especially the earlier ones, make them a pain in the neck to rebuild, and in the end many a rebuilder has wondered whether it was, musically speaking, worth all the trouble. Later ones were usually more conventional.

Steinert. Steinert was a Steinway dealer who, until 1932, also manufactured his own pianos. Steinert grands were basically "budget" copies of Steinways. Steinert also made pianos under the names Jewett and Hume. All are considered good pianos and are frequently rebuilt. They are rarely found, however, outside the Northeast.

---

variations on modern actions are fine as long as the parts are not obsolete and absolutely unobtainable. Most pianos this old will need a considerable amount of repair and restoration to be fully usable, so the best candidates from this period will be those instruments that justify the expense involved, such as Steinway, Mason & Hamlin, Bechstein, and Blüthner grands, or in rare instances a more ordinary brand that has been exceptionally well preserved. With occasional exceptions, the vast majority of uprights and cheaper grands left from this period are not worth repairing, unless for historical or sentimental reasons.

The period from about 1900 to 1930 was the heyday of piano manufacturing. Thousands of small firms turned out millions of pianos during this time; in fact, far more pianos were made per annum then than are made today. If you are shopping for a used full-size upright or a grand, probably many of the pianos you see will be from this period. Smaller pianos were not introduced until later on.

You may wonder whether it's advisable to buy a piano that is seventy to one hundred years old. What you must remember is that pianos age more as people do than as present-day automobiles and appliances. With proper care and some replacement of parts, a piano well made seventy years ago may have many years of use left in it. Of course, a good deal of junk is left over from this period too, but the average level of quality is surprisingly high, and your chances of finding an instrument in satisfactory condition or worth putting in shape are quite good.

People in the market for used pianos often ask me to recommend specific brands. This is a problem, because the present condition of the piano, the kind of use you will be giving it, and the cost of the piano and repairs are far more important factors than the brand when considering the purchase of an old piano. Even a piano of the best brand, if poorly maintained or badly repaired, can be an unwise purchase. Time and wear are great levelers, and a piano of only average quality that has not been used much may be a much better buy. Nevertheless, since this answer never satisfies anyone, I offer the following list of some of the brand names of the period which were most highly regarded. Please note that this list, which is by no means complete—or universally agreed upon—applies only to pianos made before about 1930, since in many cases the same names were later applied to completely different pianos made to entirely different (usually lower) quality standards.

Steinway	Baldwin	Mason & Hamlin
Knabe	Chickering	Bechstein
Bösendorfer	Blüthner	Sohmer
Ivers & Pond	Henry F. Miller	McPhail
Steinert	Jewett	Hume

Emerson	Vose	Chas. Stieff
Apollo	A.B. Chase	Packard
Weber	Wing	Haines Bros.
Krakauer	Hallet & Davis	Lester
Everett	Hamilton	Kimball
Ibach	Heintzman	

The piano industry was full of mergers and acquisitions during the early 1900s. During the Great Depression many piano makers, both good and bad, went bankrupt, and their names were bought up by the surviving companies. In some cases, the defunct company's design continued to be used, but most of the time, as I've said, only the name lived on.

To revive the depressed piano market in the late thirties, piano makers came up with a new gimmick— the small piano. Despite the fact that small pianos, both vertical and grand, are inferior in almost every way to larger pianos, marketing experts managed to convince the public that spinets and consoles were to be preferred to larger pianos because they would look better in the smaller homes and apartments of the day. This involved a major change in the perception of the piano from a musical instrument to a piece of furniture, a view that lasts to this day. Because of their perceived value as furniture, used spinets and consoles will usually cost more than used full-size uprights of comparable condition. (An exact comparison is not really possible because when the manufacture of spinets and consoles started, the manufacture of full-size uprights almost entirely ceased.) Please see page 44 for the technical differences between vertical pianos of different size.

Should I Buy A Used, "Gray Market" Yamaha or Kawai Piano?

One of the most controversial topics in the piano business is whether it is advisable to purchase a used Yamaha or Kawai piano originally made for the Japanese market. Sometimes called "gray market" pianos, these are instruments that were originally sold to families and schools in Japan and then, some years later, discarded in favor of new instruments. There being little market for these pianos in Japan—the Japanese are said to have a cultural bias against buying used goods—enterprising businesspeople buy up these used pianos and export them to the United States and other countries, where they are sold by dealers of used pianos at a fraction of the price of a new Yamaha or Kawai. Naturally, Yamaha and Kawai and their authorized dealers are not exactly pleased at the competition.

Yamaha has taken a public stand warning against the purchase of these pianos. According to the company, the wood used in Yamaha pianos is seasoned for destination: the highest moisture content for Japan, which is relatively humid; the lowest for the U.S., which has areas that are extremely dry; and in between for Europe. According to Yamaha, gray market Yamahas, having been manufactured for a humid climate, may develop loose tuning pins, cracked soundboards, glue joint failure, and other serious problems when relocated to the United States. Yamaha also points out that there is no Yamaha warranty on the gray market pianos, and that it cannot provide technical support or sell parts for these pianos because the models are often different from those sold in the U.S. The many dealers who sell these used Japanese pianos, however, insist that they do not experience the problems Yamaha warns about, and they question whether Yamaha is telling the truth about seasoning for destination.

I have always found the people I know at Yamaha to be honest, so it seems unlikely they would all lie about the issue of seasoning for destination. I do believe, however, that while there is definitely a basis for their concerns, their dire warnings are exaggerated. For one thing, Yamaha's pronouncements fail to differentiate between different regions of this country, some of which are just as humid as Japan, even when winter heating is factored in. Large areas of the South and West require little or no heating in the winter, whereas some parts of Japan get quite cold. Nor do they consider the benefits of climate control systems that might be used to offset the alleged problems. Finally, they do not take into account the wide variation in age, quality, and condition of the gray market pianos entering this country. Yamaha pianos are well built and it's hard to imagine that they would all be so temperamental as to fall apart with a moderate change in humidity.

Over the years I have had the opportunity to speak to many technicians who have serviced made-for-Japan pianos. For this edition, I specifically contacted technicians who live and work in the driest parts of this country, such as the desert southwest, and northern states with bitterly cold winters, where heated homes in the winter show humidity readings in the single digits. Some of these technicians do report that they have had problems with gray market Japanese pianos. The problems reported range from serious ones like cracked soundboards and loose tuning pins to the more mundane, such as the need for an unusual amount of action regulating. However, technicians in these areas also say that any piano, especially ones that relocate there from more humid climates (regardless of country), can exhibit problems if the owner doesn't heed advice to monitor and, if necessary, supplement the humidity. Problems are most likely to occur with pianos that show significant signs of having been exposed to excessive humidity in Japan, such as heavy rusting of metal parts, although they can affect normal-looking pianos, too. But, the technicians say, when humidity control is in place, there do not seem to be more problems with gray market Japanese pianos than with any others. In my experience, technicians in milder or more humid climates rarely report problems at all. While it is reasonable to assume that pianos seasoned for a humid destination might, statistically, have a somewhat higher risk of trouble in severely dry areas, my research has simply not turned up, in the country as a whole, a problem as severe as Yamaha warns of.

As for Yamaha's other statements, I would remind them that *no* used Yamaha carries a manufacturer's warranty (the warranty is not transferable to future owners), regardless of origin, and that technicians can order commonly replaced parts from third-party suppliers. It's true, however, that some less commonly requested Yamaha parts can only be ordered from the company, so there is some risk of difficulty later on in securing parts.

Kawai has made no public pronouncements about the risks of purchasing gray market Kawais. In private, however, Kawai representatives say that for some years now, the wood for all Kawai pianos has been seasoned for the dry areas of the U.S., regardless of destination. There is no manufacturer's warranty in the U.S. on Kawai pianos originally sold in Japan, but the company says it will provide technical information and parts if it is able to. Parts for pianos not originally sold in the U.S., however, may require a special order from Japan, with a long wait time. Kawai America also says it occasionally imports used Kawais itself. The pianos come from its music schools in Japan and are sold primarily to authorized Kawai dealers in Canada, to help them compete with other dealers of these pianos.

Most importers grade gray market Japanese pianos (A, B, C, etc.) according to condition. However, this grading system is not standardized and is, to some extent, arbitrary. Some technicians suggest that pianos made in the sixties and seventies may be a little more susceptible to humidity-related problems, so to be safest, stick to the higher-grade pianos made since the mid-eighties. As with any used piano, have it inspected by an independent technician and, by all means, get a warranty from the dealer. Technicians say that any problems that are going to happen generally do so within the first three years in this country, so the warranty should be for at least that long, preferably longer. If you live in a dry area or one that becomes dry for part of the year, understand the risks involved and humidify the environment of the piano accordingly (see Chapter 7 for information on humidity and climate control systems).

Determining visually whether a Yamaha or Kawai was made for Japan or the U.S. is not always easy. Yamahas made for Japan prior to the mid-1980s, and Kawais prior to the early 1960s, generally have two pedals; later ones have three. However, many brokers add a third pedal to the gray market pianos, if needed, before the pianos leave Japan. Yamaha grands made for Japan have a small brass plate containing the piano's serial number on the underside of the front lid, and a plastic holder for warranty documents on the inside of the spine (straight side) of the piano, but, of course, these could be removed by the dealer. In any case, the dealer should tell you the background of the piano and warn you of the possible risks involved. Occasionally a dealer will fraudulently pass a used gray market piano off as a new one. In addition, Yamaha says that some *actual* new Yamaha pianos are now being imported on the gray market through non-authorized dealers. You should know that these pianos, though new, do not come with a manufacturer's warranty. If in doubt, call Yamaha or Kawai with the serial number of the piano. You can also look up a Yamaha serial number on **www.yamaha.com** to see whether it is gray market or not.

Whether you decide to buy a gray market Japanese piano will ultimately depend on how much money you can save, where you live, and how much risk you are willing to take. Those who live in more humid areas of the U.S. or areas with mild winters probably assume little risk. Those who live in drier or colder areas assume greater risk, but this can be largely offset by careful choosing and inspection of the piano, proper climate control, and a good warranty from a reliable dealer. It would appear from the companies' statements that there may be greater risk with a gray market Yamaha than with a Kawai.

[Note: Yamaha was provided with a pre-publication copy of this article on gray market pianos and chose to respond. A company spokesman said that he felt the risk of problems from these pianos to be much greater than my assessment suggests. He reminds my readers that indoor humidity can be low even in some so-called mild climates (the humid ones) due to air conditioning, which dries the air in order to cool it, and that in general, indoor humidity is lower in North American households, regardless of climate, than in households in other parts of the world due to the types of heating and cooling systems employed. Yamaha learned this the hard way when it first entered the U.S. market in the early 1960s with pianos seasoned much like the gray market pianos are today. He did say, however, that the reported problems have been most severe and numerous in the Midwest and Northeast.

The spokesman also said that my input from technicians appeared to be inconclusive and anecdotal in nature, whereas Yamaha's service department gets many calls reporting problems with the gray market pianos. I can only respond by saying that although my survey was anecdotal, it was not seeking a particular outcome and has no stake in one. I concede that Yamaha may have a larger sample of responses to draw upon in forming an opinion on the subject. However, there are thousands of satisfied owners of these pianos who have no reason to call Yamaha, which may skew Yamaha's perspective.

The Yamaha spokesman concluded by saying, ". . . we're selling all the pianos that we can make. Used gray market pianos are not really taking away a lot of business. Long-term, however, they threaten to damage a reputation that was carefully, responsibly and arduously built over four decades. This is the real issue. We will do everything we can to prevent this."]

Piano making in the 1930s, though reduced in quantity from earlier years, was of a similar high quality in most cases. During World War II many piano factories were commandeered to make airplane wings and other wartime products, and what piano making there was fell in quality because of a lack of good raw materials and skilled labor. Things changed for the better in the fifties, and then reversed again in the sixties as some companies came under management that sought to expand the industry at the expense of quality.

Also in the sixties, the Japanese began exporting pianos to the United States in large numbers. Although at first they had some difficulties building pianos to the demands of our climate, by the mid-seventies their quality was so high and their price so low that they threatened to put all the domestic makers out of business. The international takeover of the U.S. market accelerated in the eighties as the Koreans began to export here, and by 1985 all but a few U.S. piano makers had gone out of business.

Please see page 87 for more information about the piano market today.

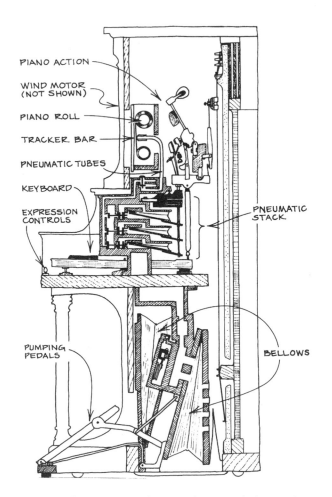

FIGURE 5-3. Cross-sectional view of a typical player piano.

Purchase of a used piano made within the past few decades can often be a very good deal, as these pianos may still show very few signs of age and wear but may be priced far below a new piano. In some cases a warranty may still be in effect. General information on piano quality that will be of use to you if you are buying a used piano made within the past couple of decades can be found in Chapter 3, "Buying a New Piano." Chapter 4, "A Consumer Guide to New and Recently Made Pianos," may be useful if you want to look up a particular brand and model made since the early 1980s (or, in some cases, even earlier).

Though in each decade both good and bad pianos have been produced, and each piano must be judged on its own merits, this brief historical overview may give you some idea of what to expect to see as you shop for a used piano. You can determine the age of a piano by finding its serial number and looking it up in a book called the *Pierce Piano Atlas*. (See page 200 for where to find the serial number of a piano.) Most piano technicians and many libraries have copies of this invaluable reference book, which lists serial numbers, dates, and other historical information for thousands of piano brands. Your technician will probably be happy to look up information for you without charge. To purchase the book, contact: Pierce Piano Atlas, P.O. Box 20520, Albuquerque, New Mexico 87154; phone (505) 296-5499; **www.pinon.com/atlas/**.

Old Player and Reproducing Pianos

The success of the piano industry in the early part of this century was partly due to the popularity of the **player piano**. The player piano (Figure 5-3) is a regular piano, usually an upright, with a slightly deeper cabinet into which is installed a player mechanism that enables the piano to play by itself. This mechanism is operated by reduced air pressure (vacuum) created by a foot-operated bellows or an electric pump. Figure 5-4 shows how this works. All player pianos can also be manually played just like a regular piano, if desired.

Most player pianos were made between 1910 and 1925, when their popularity was so intense that more than half of all pianos made in the United States were players—over 2.5 million in all. After 1925 the player piano declined in popularity, due first to the rise of the radio and phonograph as the dominant forms of entertainment, and then to the Depression. In the decades that followed, many people removed their piano's player mechanism as it fell into disrepair, or to make the rest of the piano easier to service. Since the 1960s player pianos have become quite the fad again, and many an unwary buyer purchases an old player, com-

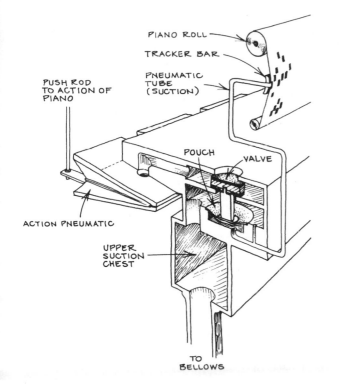

PIANO ROLL

TRACKER BAR

PNEUMATIC
TUBE
(SUCTION)

PUSH ROD
TO ACTION OF
PIANO

POUCH   VALVE

ACTION PNEUMATIC

UPPER
SUCTION
CHEST

TO
BELLOWS

FIGURE 5-4. How each note in a player piano works. Suction created by the foot-operated pumping bellows normally pulls the valve downward, causing it to close off the lower opening, as shown in the drawing. When a punched hole in the paper piano roll passes over a corresponding hole in the tracker bar, normal atmospheric pressure is allowed to enter the pneumatic tube for that note. The pouch, a flexible diaphragm, still under the influence of suction from above but no longer from below, rises. The valve, attached to a valve stem that sits on the pouch, also rises, uncovering the lower opening and closing the upper one. This allows the suction from the bellows to enter the action pneumatic, which collapses, causing a push rod to push up on the corresponding note of the piano action. When the hole in the piano roll moves away from the tracker bar, the opening is again sealed, restoring suction underneath the pouch, which allows the valve to again be pulled downward. Air enters the upper opening and rushes into the action pneumatic, which opens, and the push rod returns to its normal position. A wind motor, using the very same vacuum pressure, winds and rewinds the piano roll. Expression controls allow the user to manually vary the tempo and dynamics as the roll plays.

plete with music rolls, with the intention of making it work again.

There are a number of things you should think about before investing in an old player piano. A player piano is, in a sense, two pianos in one—a regular piano, with its thousands of parts and their potential problems, and a player action, with *its* thousands of parts and *their* potential problems. It's vital that the regular piano be in good condition, or worth putting in good condition, before you even consider restoring the player action. Beware of any player piano advertised as "partially restored" or just needing a little work. Restoring a player piano that has been poorly or partially repaired is sometimes more expensive than restoring one that has never been touched at all, so if you don't know for certain that the piano has been completely restored, consider it completely unrestored. Also, don't waste your money on a former player piano that is now missing the player action in the hope that you will be able to find one that fits. You may wait forever.

Very few piano technicians know or care anything about player pianos. In fact, many won't even consent to tune them because the player mechanism is in the way and makes tuning difficult. (Actually, a knowledgeable technician can often remove the parts that are in the way quite quickly, but most aren't that knowledgeable.) Restoring the player mechanism is probably not something you should attempt yourself, so you will have to locate someone fully qualified to do the job. The restoration will be very time consuming and expensive, possibly exceeding the value of the regular piano itself. Because of these considerations, I would advise that you locate the qualified technician before shopping, then use his or her advice to secure a piano. Buying a fully restored player piano from such a technician might be the safest route to take.

Though some kinds of folds and tears are repairable, old music rolls with torn and brittle edges can be hazardous to your player piano. They won't track properly, and small bits of paper can get sucked into the mechanism, clogging it up hopelessly. Many fine old piano rolls are still in excellent condition, however, and thousands of tunes unavailable on new rolls can be found on these old ones. For a list of sources of both new and old piano rolls, see the Mechanical Music Digest web page at: **www.mmd.foxtail.com**. The sources are listed under "Gallery/Sources."

The player mechanism in a player piano imparts the same amount of force to every note, so every note sounds at the same volume. This is, of course, different from the way (most) people play. The constant volume is part of what gives a player piano that machine-like sound that lets you know it's a player piano and not a real person, even without looking. During the same period that player pianos were being made, another, much more sophisticated mechanism was being installed in high-quality grand pianos. These instruments, called **reproducing pianos**, were capable of copying every nuance of an artist's playing, and many of the greatest pianists of the late nineteenth and early twentieth century recorded music rolls for them.

The most famous brands of reproducing piano were Ampico, Duo-Art, and Welte, which were installed in many top-name grand pianos, such as Steinway and Mason & Hamlin. Some of these pianos were made several inches longer to accommodate the mechanism; others housed the mechanism in a drawer. Usually slots or holes were cut through the keybed to connect the portion of the player action below with the piano action inside. Witnessing one of these marvels in action is an experience you'll not soon forget. Unfortunately, reproducing pianos in good working condition are very rare. And if you think it's hard to find a competent player piano technician, just try to find someone to service or rebuild a reproducing piano! Music rolls for reproducing pianos were never standardized, but rolls for a few makes are again being commercially made.

If you are seriously thinking of buying an old player or reproducing piano, you should definitely read *Player Piano Servicing & Rebuilding* by Arthur Reblitz (The Vestal Press Ltd.). This well-written, thorough, fully illustrated book will tell you in more detail how player and reproducing pianos work, how to inspect one—restored or unrestored—before buying, and how a serious hobbyist or professional should restore them.

For information on modern electronic player piano systems, please see Chapter 4, page 160.

HOW TO FIND A USED PIANO

Here are some of your options—you may be able to think of others:

- Contacting piano technicians and rebuilding shops
- Visiting new piano dealers (who sometimes have used pianos for sale as well)
- Visiting used piano dealers
- Answering ads or notices offering pianos for sale
- Hunting up a piano by placing an ad yourself or by contacting places that might have pianos they would like to get rid of
- Shopping on the internet
- Buying a piano from friends or relatives or accepting one as a gift

Let's discuss these options one at a time:

Contacting technicians and rebuilding shops. The first thing to do as you start looking for a used piano is to call your piano technician (or the technician you plan to use when you find a piano). He or she may know of, or have, used pianos for sale, or may be able to refer you to someone who does. He or she can also inform you about local market conditions and prices, what stores to patronize or avoid, and so on. Most technicians are glad to give you this advice over the phone without charge or obligation.

If at all possible you should visit a technician's shop and look at pianos that are being, or have been, repaired, reconditioned, or rebuilt. Ask exactly what has been done to the pianos and why. Ask what you should be looking for in a used piano. This is an invaluable opportunity to supplement the technical information contained in this chapter so that you'll feel confident in using it to inspect a piano on your own if necessary. You'll also meet some fascinating people and see a slice of life in your community you might not otherwise encounter. There's more to this piano business than meets the eye.

If you decide to buy a piano from a technician, you will probably pay quite a bit more than you would for an equivalent piano from a private owner. The advantages are that the piano has (presumably) been carefully checked over and repaired, a warranty is given (see "Warranty," page 202), and you may save yourself the hassle of shopping in the private market, where you might or might not find an "equivalent" piano. You will also have the satisfaction of patronizing a local craftsperson.

Even if you buy from a technician you trust, it's not a bad idea to have the piano inspected first by another, independent technician. This may be a little awkward for everyone concerned, but even the best technicians can differ in their opinions. Also, a technician who has a considerable amount of money and time invested in an instrument must sell it even if it hasn't turned out so hot, which happens often and unpredictably, and it makes good sense to protect yourself. Make sure the technician you hire determines that the repair or rebuilding work claimed to have been performed has actually been done. If a technician balks at having you bring in another technician to appraise a piano, shop elsewhere.

When considering buying a rebuilt piano from a piano technician, the amount of experience the technician has had should count heavily in your decision. The complete rebuilding of a piano requires many dissimilar skills. That is, the skills required for installing a soundboard, for example, are very different from those required for installing a new set of hammers or for regulating the action. Mastering all these skills can take a very long time. In a sense, you should be shopping for the rebuilder as much as for the piano.

It may occur to you that you could save a lot of money by buying an unrestored piano—a "wreck"—and having a technician completely restore it, rather than buying the completely restored piano direct from

Repair, Reconditioning, and Rebuilding

Three terms are often used when discussing restoration work on pianos: repair, reconditioning, and rebuilding. There are no precise definitions of these terms, and any particular job may contain elements of more than one of them. It's therefore vital, when having work done on your piano or when buying a piano that has been worked on, that you find out exactly what jobs have been, or will be, carried out. "This piano has been reconditioned" or" I'll rebuild this piano" are not sufficient answers. One person's rebuilding may be another's reconditioning.

Generally speaking, a *repair* job involves fixing isolated broken parts, such as a broken hammer, a missing string, or an improperly working pedal. That is, it does not necessarily involve upgrading the condition of the instrument as a whole, but attends only to specific broken parts.

Reconditioning always involves a general upgrading of the whole piano, but with as little actual replacement of parts as possible. For instance, the reconditioning of an old upright piano might include resurfacing the hammers (instead of replacing them) and twisting the bass strings to improve their tone (instead of replacing them), as well as cleaning the whole instrument and regulating the action. If parts are broken or missing, of course, they must also be repaired or replaced, so this particular reconditioning job might also include replacing a set of bridle straps and other relatively minor parts, if needed.

Rebuilding is the most complete of the three levels of restoration. Rebuilding involves restringing the piano and usually, replacing the pinblock in a grand and repairing or replacing the soundboard. In the action, rebuilding would include replacing the hammer heads, damper felts, and key bushings, and possibly replacing or completely overhauling other sets of parts as well. Refinishing the piano case may also be done as part of a rebuilding job. Ideally, rebuilding means putting the piano into "factory-new" condition. In practice, however, it may involve much less, depending on the needs and the value of the particular instrument, the amount of money available, and the scrupulousness of the rebuilder. The bottom line is the restringing. If a piano has not been restrung, it really cannot qualify as a rebuilt instrument. Indeed, many technicians would assert that a piano has been rebuilt only if the pinblock has been replaced.

Due to the varied and sometimes unwarranted use of the word *rebuilding*, some rebuilders have come up with a new term—*remanufacturing*—to indicate the most complete restoration job possible, with special emphasis on the fact that the soundboard has been replaced, which may not be included in a regular rebuilding job. In my opinion, this new word only confuses the issue and, in time, it too will become tarnished. There is no substitute for requesting an itemization of the work performed.

the technician. This is often true. But as I said, the results of restoration jobs are unpredictable. If a lot of money is involved and you are particular in your tastes for tone and action, you would be better off letting the technician make the profit—and take the risks. If you're interested in a particular piano, a technician might be willing to buy it and restore it and give you the first chance at it when it's done. If you do go ahead and buy the "wreck," by all means make sure a technician inspects it first and ascertains that it's worth restoring. Sometimes the price of the "wreck" plus the cost of the restoration far exceeds the value of the restored piano. (Hint: If the technician won't buy the piano, that may be why.) At the time this is being written, a complete rebuilding of a grand piano could cost from ten to twenty thousand dollars.

Visiting new piano dealers. Dealers of new pianos sometimes rebuild pianos too, or at least recondition used pianos that they take in on trade. Because these pianos take up valuable floor space and compete with new pianos for the customer's attention, their prices are usually rather high. But visiting one of these dealers is a convenient way to shop for a used piano, espe-cially if you are not sure whether you will be buying new or used. An independent technician you hire to inspect a used piano here may be able to tell you whether you are getting good value. Sometimes these used pianos are just bait to get you into the store, and may be vastly overpriced compared to what you would pay to a private owner, or even to an independent rebuilding shop. Be sure the technician you hire is unconnected with, and owes no favors to, the dealer.

Visiting used piano dealers. There are many honorable used piano dealers, but here I want to warn you about dealers who are basically entrepreneurs without technical skills or knowledge, out to make a buck. Even if they have a few tuners working for them, their instructions are generally just to "make all the keys work." My first job was for a place like this. It was a small storefront that sold used pianos and refrigerators. Each time a piano was delivered to a customer, I was sent out to tune it and to fix anything that the customer wasn't happy with. Considering the pitiful state of some of these pianos, it was often difficult to satisfy the customer, especially since I was paid only a flat fee for each piano I serviced. And when I would suggest to

Grand Piano Rebuilding Checklist

The following is a list of tasks that might comprise a fairly complete grand piano rebuilding job. Any particular job may be either more or less extensive than shown here, depending on the needs and value of the instrument and other factors, but this list can serve as a guide. See also page 207 for information on specific rebuilding issues pertaining to Steinway and Mason & Hamlin pianos.

Notice that the restoration can be divided into three main parts: the soundbox or resonating unit, the action, and the cabinet. The *soundbox* includes the soundboard, ribs, bridges, strings, pinblock, tuning pins, the plate, and the structural parts of the case; the *action* includes the keyframe and action frame, keys and keytops, hammers, dampers and trapwork, and all other moving action parts; the *cabinet* includes cosmetic repair and refinishing of the case and of the non-structural cabinet parts and hardware. Note that the damper parts that contact the strings are restored with the soundbox, whereas the damper underlever action is treated with the rest of the action.

There is very little overlap between the three types of work, so if technical conditions permit or financial considerations require it, each of the three parts could be performed alone or at different times. In a typical complete job, restoration of the soundbox might comprise forty-five percent of the cost, the action thirty percent, and the cabinet twenty-five percent, though these percentages will vary according to the particulars of the job.

Soundbox or resonating unit:
  Replace soundboard, finish, install new soundboard decal
    (If not replacing soundboard: shim soundboard cracks, reglue ribs as necessary, refinish, install new soundboard decal)
  Replace pinblock
  Replace bridge caps
  Replace or ream agraffes, restore capo bar bearing surface
  Refinish plate, paint lettering, replace understring felts
  Replace strings and tuning pins
  Replace damper felts, refinish damper heads, regulate dampers

Action:
  Replace hammers, shanks, and flanges
  Replace or overhaul wippen/repetition assemblies
  Replace backchecks
  Replace front rail key bushings
  Replace balance rail key bushings or key buttons
  Replace or clean keytops
  Replace key-end felts
  Clean keys
  Clean and refelt keyframe
  Replace let-off felts or buttons
  Clean and, if necessary, repair action frame
  Regulate action
  Overhaul or replace damper underlever action and damper guide rail
  Overhaul pedal lyre and trapwork, regulate

Cabinet:
  Repair music desk, legs, and other cabinet parts, if necessary
  Repair loose or missing veneer
  Strip and refinish exterior
  Buff solid brass hardware, replate plated hardware

---

the manager, who didn't know a hammer from a bridle strap, that a piano might need more than fifteen dollars' worth of repair, he would accuse me of wanting "to rebuild the damn thing." I lasted only a month there.

Places like this are often well disguised. They may appear quite respectable and advertise widely in the media. In some cases they may have extensive repair facilities, but do very sloppy work. The best way to tell is to ask some reputable technicians which places to avoid—they will tell you. Interestingly, once in a while these stores will have a few pianos of high value selling for very low prices simply because the owners are unaware of what they have, or they need the cash. But do you really want to patronize a place like this?

Furniture stores and antique dealers sometimes take in pianos on consignment. These establishments tend to be ignorant about what they're selling—or are selling the instrument for its antique or furniture value—rather than dishonest. Their pianos are, at best, overpriced, or, at worst, defective and overpriced.

Answering ads. This is probably the most common way to buy a used piano. Classified ads for pianos can be found in big city daily and Sunday papers, local weekly papers, and in the "alternative press." Especially useful are the little booklets of want ads that appear weekly or biweekly, usually found at supermarket checkout counters and newsstands, published under such names as *Want Advertiser, Bargain Hunter, Buy Lines,* and *Pennysaver.* You'll also find ads or notices posted anywhere people congregate—laundromats, churches, synagogues, community centers, food co-ops, and so on. Most of the people who place these ads will be private individuals selling the piano from their home. A few, though, will be dealers and technicians who advertise a couple of their pianos this way and then invite you to come see the rest of their wares when you call. (Some may be trucking companies; see the cautionary note on page 64 about buying a "repossessed" piano from the back of a truck.)

Most ads say very little. When you call, you'll want to find out some more, such as: What brand is it? What size is the piano? Is it a spinet? When was it made? What condition is it in? When was it last tuned or otherwise serviced? What additional work needs to be done on it? You may be shocked to find out how little people know about their piano. Often they don't even know the brand name without looking, though they can tell you the location of every scratch on the case. Nevertheless, using what scanty information you have, as well as your hunches, you must decide which ones are worth your while to visit.

Hunting up a piano. This is the more aggressive approach. Place a "piano wanted" ad in the classifieds or post a note to that effect on a bulletin board. Someone who never got around to doing something about that old piano that's been sittin' around unplayed for years just might give you a call.

Another approach that falls into this category is to call around to all the churches and private schools in your area to see if they have any pianos they want to get rid of. But you must be very careful here. Pianos in institutions suffer incredible abuse, either from constant pounding by players (especially in "gospel" churches), from vandalism, from neglect by administrators charged with their care, or from the ravages of winter dryness and overheating in cold climates. By the time institutions are ready to get rid of their pianos, they are usually ready for the junk pile. You will therefore want to check them very carefully. An exception may be once wealthy churches and schools that are now in need of funds and may still have some healthy pianos.

Movers and storage warehouses are another potential source of pianos. These places sometimes get stuck with pianos that won't fit through the door or up the stairs and which for these or other reasons their customers abandon. Conditions for inspecting these pianos may be less than ideal.

Another audacious approach is to go to an auction where a piano is up for bid. The problem here is that you may not have enough time beforehand to inspect the piano and have a technician inspect it, and if yours is the winning bid, you have to pay for it, like it or not. Also, if the piano is one of much value, you're likely to be competing with piano technicians for it. Don't get carried away and end up paying more than the piano's worth.

One last idea—I've never tried it, but it might work if you're in no hurry—is to leave your card with lawyers and others who handle the disposition of estates, letting them know you're in the market for a piano. If one comes by their desk, they might give you first crack at it just to save themselves the trouble of having to advertise it.

Shopping on the internet. Recently, via e-mail, I helped a woman in China who was negotiating the purchase of a rebuilt piano over the internet from an American rebuilder. Not only was she buying the piano sight unseen from a stranger in a foreign land with whom she had never spoken, but she was buying it for a friend who was temporarily out of the country, not for herself. Think of all the trust issues involved in that transaction!

When buying a used piano, the issue of trust looms large, much larger than when buying a new one: Are there hidden defects in the piano? Is there a warranty, and if not, what do I do if there are problems? Is the rebuilder any good? Buying over the internet, at least at the time this is being written, also involves significant trust issues: Is this a scam? Will they actually deliver the goods? Will my credit card information be misused? So buying a used piano over the internet has two areas of concern working against it, not to mention the difficulties in examining the merchandise beforehand. In fact, my research suggests that, perhaps for these reasons, there is a lot more used-piano advertising than selling going on over the internet, and most of the buying and selling is between established companies and individuals, rather than between two individuals. For example, I recently answered a couple of dozen internet classifieds for used Steinway grands and found to my surprise that many of the advertisers had received fewer than three calls in a six-month period. The callers—and ultimate buyers—tended to be rebuilders looking for pianos to rebuild for resale. Naturally, they snatched up the lower-priced instruments. The higher-priced (usually rebuilt) pianos were usually being sold by rebuilders or by brokers for rebuilders.

Some of the major piano classified ad sites on the internet are **www.pianomart.com**, **www.pianoworld.com**, and **www.pianobroker.com**. Sellers advertise on these sites either for a flat monthly charge or for a three percent commission, depending on the site. Unfortunately, some of the listings on these sites are stale, as sellers frequently forget to inform the site host when their pianos have been sold or taken off the market. There are many other sites with piano ads, however. Usually the pianos on those sites are owned or being brokered by the site host, rather than just being listed. You can find a good listing of these and other sites where pianos may be for sale on The Piano Page (**www.ptg.org**), hosted by the Piano Technicians Guild. As usual with the internet, you will also find additional sites by following links or querying search engines, but the above references will get you started.

You will also find pianos listed on internet auction sites, especially eBay. Search on a variety of keywords (piano, pianos, Steinway [or other brand name], etc.), as each keyword will bring up a different group of pianos for sale. Many of the bids are frivolous (i.e., one hundred dollars for a Steinway grand) and do not result in a sale, so if you are a serious buyer with cash to spend, you have a decent chance of placing the winning bid. The bidding process generally provides a window of time during which you can contact the seller for more information, see the piano, and have it inspected before placing a bid. This is definitely not a good way to buy a piano unless you have the opportunity to try out the piano and have it inspected first.

The best way to use the internet to shop for a used piano is to look for sellers within driving distance of your home. That way, you can more easily try out the piano, develop a face-to-face relationship with the seller, and get a better sense whether you want to do business with him or her. If you travel frequently, however, you should check out sellers in other cities, too. In the case of commercial sellers, before making a long trip, I suggest you contact technicians in the seller's area to inquire about the seller's reputation for quality and honesty. Be aware, however, that technicians have their biases and allegiances, so be sure to check with a number of technicians, not just one. In addition, as with any other used piano purchase, you should have the piano inspected by an independent piano technician. A list of Registered Piano Technicians by state and province can be found at **www.ptg.org**, or call the Piano Technicians Guild at 816-753-7747. Also check the *Piano Book* web site (**www.pianobook.com**), which from time to time may have resources to help piano buyers like yourself find dealers and technicians in their area. If you buy from a piano technician or rebuilder, it's possible he or she will move the piano or be able to make arrangements for moving. Otherwise, see Chapter 6 for the names of some movers that specialize in long-distance piano moving. Be sure you have a firm understanding with a commercial seller of how warranty issues will be handled.

Obtaining a piano from friends and relatives. It's nice when pianos remain in the family. I got my piano this way. But pianos purchased from friends and relatives or received as gifts are as likely as any others to have expensive problems you should know about. It's very hard to refuse a gift, and perhaps embarrassing to hire a piano technician to inspect it before you accept it, but for your own protection you should insist on doing so. Otherwise you may spend a lot of money to move a "gift" you could have done without.

Which of these routes you end up following will depend on your situation and what you are looking for. If you have a lot of time and transportation is no problem, you may get the best deal by shopping around among private owners or in out-of-the-way places. If you are busy or without a car, but have money to spend, it may be more convenient to shop among piano technicians, who may be able to show you several pianos at the same time and spare you from worrying about future repair costs and problems. The best route also depends on where you live, as some communities may have a brisk trade in used pianos among private owners but few rebuilding shops, or vice versa, or have an abundance of old uprights but few grands.

CHECKING OUT THE PIANO

Unless you're very rich and can afford to keep a piano technician on retainer full time, chances are that at some point in your searching for a used piano you're going to have to go it alone. Knowing that you'd rather not stare dumbly at the piano, I've prepared a little inspection routine for you here. A thorough inspection of a piano must really be a joint effort with a technician, because some crucial parts of the piano, such as the pinblock, can be tested only by feel or with special tools, and an overall judgment of the condition of the piano requires some experience. At the very least, though, this inspection will teach you a lot about the piano, enable you to talk intelligently with your technician, and make you feel a useful and involved participant instead of a passive bystander. And while in many cases a decision about purchase involves a balancing of pros and cons rather than a clear yea or nay, this routine may help you to weed out those occasional catastrophes that do not deserve your, or your technician's, further attention.

In addition, I've tried to give some idea of the relative significance of each part as I cover it, and, in very general terms, of the probable cost of repairing it, if necessary. As such, I've used the terms "cheap" and "inexpensive" to refer to repairs that are likely to cost less than $100, "moderate" to mean $100 to $500, and "expensive," over $500. This value system is more likely to apply to inexpensive uprights than to other pianos, but you can make the translation as needed.

Much of the information you need can be found in previous chapters. Basic descriptions of piano parts and how they work are in Chapter 1, which you may want to review now. Page references are given to sections of Chapter 3, "Buying A New Piano," and other chapters that contain more helpful technical material. The information on how pianos differ in quality and features, also in Chapter 3, applies to used pianos too, especially those made since about 1960.

The tools you should bring with you are: a flashlight; a soft brush, such as a paint brush, for brushing away dust; a small screwdriver (with about a 1/8-inch tip) and a large screwdriver(with about a 5/16-inch tip), for removing outer case parts, if needed; a tuning fork or pitch pipe, obtainable from a music store, to determine if the piano is up to standard pitch; paper and pencil for taking notes; this book; and someone to play the piano, if you don't, and to lend moral support.

Looks, styling, and finish. Look the piano over. Imagine it in your home. Could you live with it? If not, you might as well not go any further. A grand can be partially restyled by changing the legs and music desk, and any piano can be refinished, but both of these are expensive (refinishing a grand piano can easily cost more than three thousand dollars.)

If you're thinking of refinishing the piano yourself, let me warn you: stripping and refinishing a piano is much more work than refinishing other furniture, and most do-it-yourselfers give up long before this job is done. Some take short cuts, and end up sealing the piano shut or painting the strings. But if you're prepared for the long haul, hire a technician first to remove all the outer case parts and the action and to cover the strings; then get a good book on furniture refinishing.

Also check for loose veneer and other signs of water damage along the bottom edge of verticals. In general, loose veneer is found on pianos that have undergone extremes of both dryness and dampness. If you're going to refinish the piano, of course, the veneer will first have to be reglued; otherwise, it's up to you.

Beware of old uprights that have been restyled in nonstandard ways, such as by cutting down the height of the upper panel, installing mirrors, and so on. Sometimes this work is done by people who haven't thought of the consequences and who turn out pianos that are henceforth difficult or impossible to service. If the work has been done by an experienced piano technician, though, it's probably all right.

Finally, check for missing or broken cabinet parts and hardware, especially the music desk and its hinges, and to see if there is a matching bench in good condition or if you will have to buy one.

Play the piano a bit to get some sense of what this instrument is all about and to relax a little before the next step. Make mental or written notes about anything you think needs looking into.

Open up the piano. First ask the owners to remove anything (other than music) that's on the piano. Let

them break their knickknacks, not *you*. If they look askance as you start to take their piano apart, remind them that they wouldn't buy a used car without first looking under the hood, would they? Following Figures 5-5 through 5-13, for a grand, very carefully open the lid (after checking to make sure that the hinges and hinge pins are in place) and prop it up, and remove the music desk. You might also want to remove the fallboard, which may require removing the keyslip and keyblocks too. On a vertical, open the lid; remove the upper panel, music shelf, and music desk (depending on the style); and remove the bottom door. (Note: Removal of these parts is usually not difficult and is mandatory if you expect to do any reasonable inspection of a piano, so don't be shy.) No need to remove other parts at this time.

Pitch and tuning. Does the piano sound more or less in tune? When was it last tuned? If the piano is so far out of tune that some individual notes sound like chords—that is, the two or three strings of a single note (p. 7) are at radically different pitches from each other—then nine times out of ten that spells trouble. Even pianos left untuned for many years rarely go out of tune in that manner unless the tuning pins are loose (more about this shortly).

Now take out your pitch pipe or tuning fork (Figure 5-14). Tuning forks usually sound A or C; pitch pipes usually have a choice of notes to sound. Whatever note you choose, play the same note on the piano and see if they match. Play the same letter-name note at different octave intervals up and down the piano to see if they all sound pretty much in tune with each other and with the fork or pipe. If they are mostly within about a quarter step of being on pitch, fine. If a substantial portion of the piano is a semitone or more flat, this may or may not mean trouble—we don't know yet—but it *will* mean extra tuning work to bring it up to pitch—if it *can* be brought up to pitch. Make an ominous note in your notebook.

The pinblock. The condition of this crucial part of the piano's structure determines whether or not the piano will stay in tune (p. 31). Unfortunately, it's the part of the piano you can tell the least about yourself, as the experience and tools of a professional are needed to determine if the tuning pins are tight enough to hold the strings at their proper tension. Nevertheless, you can read a few clues. Look at the tuning pins. Do they look uniform in appearance, or do some appear to have been replaced? When tuning pins get loose, they are often replaced with ones slightly larger in diameter, so some new pins may suggest an aging or defective pinblock. Now look at the coils around the tuning

Opening the Piano for Inspection

Removing the cabinet parts of a piano is seldom difficult and will usually follow the directions outlined below. However, sometimes you will have to play detective to find an elusive screw or latch. If you understand the general principles involved in these instructions, you will probably be able to handle the exceptions.

When removing screws, be sure to identify them and return them to the same holes from which they were taken. Even screws that look alike can sometimes make slightly different holes in the wood. One method piano technicians sometimes use to keep screws organized is to punch them through a piece of cardboard and write on the cardboard the name of the cabinet part from which they were taken and their position.

Take special care not to scratch or otherwise damage the cabinet parts, especially if the piano doesn't belong to you. These parts can sometimes be unwieldy to handle, so I suggest that these procedures always be followed by two persons working together.

Grand

Open and prop up the lid (Figure 5-5). Fold the front part of the lid back onto the main lid. Then prop the lid open with the longer of the two propsticks. *Caution:* Before opening the lid, be sure the lid hinges are attached and the hinge pins are in place or your lid may fly away like the one shown in the inset.

Remove the music desk (Figure 5-6). Try sliding the music desk out as shown in 5-6a. If it won't slide all the way out,

then it's possible that a tab on the bottom of the desk must be lined up with a space in the sliderail, after which the desk can be lifted out, as in 5-6b. Some music desks are held in place by screws or hinge pins instead.

Remove the fallboard (Figure 5-7). (Note: Removing the fallboard from a grand piano can be tricky, and has the highest potential for scratching the case of all the operations described in this section. What you can see with the fallboard removed is helpful, but not essential, to your inspection of the piano.) There are two kinds of fallboard: One kind can be removed by itself, as shown in 5-7a. The other kind is attached to the keyblocks in such a way that the fallboard and keyblocks must be removed together as a unit, as in 5-7b.

Tilt the fallboard toward you at about a 45-degree angle, and, with both hands, try lifting the fallboard up and out of the piano. If there are set screws at the pivot points of the fallboard, as shown in the inset of (a), unscrew them several turns, then try lifting the fallboard up and out. If this doesn't work, try unscrewing the set screws another turn or two, but don't remove them entirely. Some fallboard pivot systems are very visible, as in (a); some are more hidden or of a slightly different design.

If there are no set screws, and the fallboard cannot be removed by just lifting, then it is probably type (b). You will need to skip ahead to "Remove the keyslip (Figure 5-8)" to complete that operation; then return here.

Look at the underside of the keybed, directly under the center of each keyblock, for a large screw that holds the

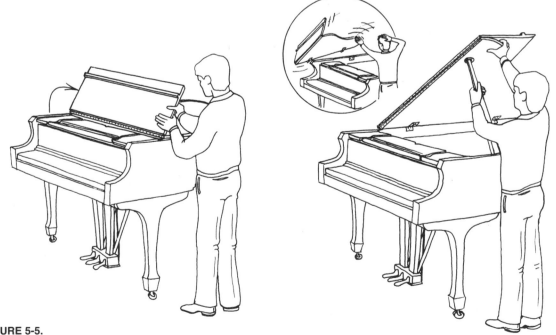

FIGURE 5-5.

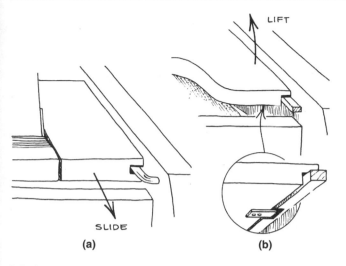

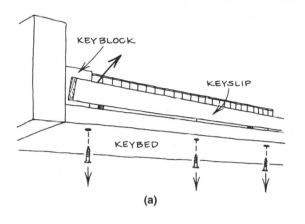

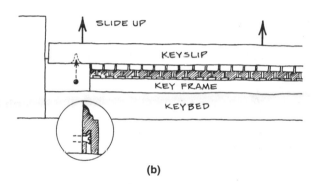

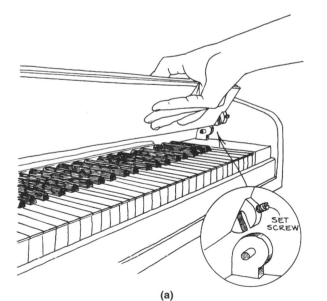

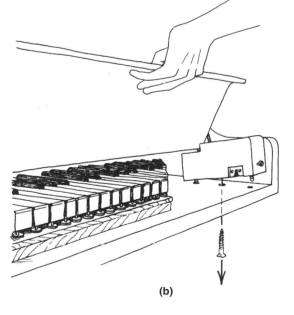

FIGURE 5-6.

keyblock down. Remove the two screws (one for each key-block). Then lift up on the front of each keyblock to disengage its dowels (if any) from their holes in the keybed. Tilt the fallboard toward you and lift up on the whole fallboard-keyblock system. If it feels entirely loose and ready to be lifted out, do it. If not, check to see what's holding it in place (usually the dowels on the bottom of the keyblocks will still be stuck in their holes in the keybed). Lift the system out and place it on the floor. (Note that the keyblocks may not be fastened to the type (b) fallboard and may fall off once clear of the case, possibly landing on the floor or scratching the case. Be prepared to catch them or remove them before they fall.)

FIGURE 5-8.

FIGURE 5-7.

Opening the Piano for Inspection (*continued*)

To return the fallboard to the piano when the inspection is finished: If the fallboard is type (a), be sure to notice how the pin in the case side (or in a metal bracket attached to the keyblock) lines up with the slot in the fallboard (or vice versa, depending on the particular piano). Sometimes this is tricky to do. Tighten the set screws, if any. If the fallboard is type (b), when you removed it from the piano and set it down on the floor it's possible that the keyblocks fell off. Not to worry. Set the fallboard in place on the keyboard, then, one at a time, reattach each keyblock to the metal stub at the end of the fallboard. Push each keyblock down so its dowels are firmly seated in their holes in the keybed. Then screw the keyblocks down with their large screws. Replace the keyslip (see Figure 5-8).

Remove the keyslip (Figure 5-8). (For the purpose of this inspection, you need only remove the keyslip if you are removing a type (b) fallboard, as previously described.) Most keyslips are removed as in 5-8a, by taking out three to six screws located under the keybed. On Steinway and Mason & Hamlin grands (and occasionally others), the keyslip is held in place by the *heads* of two screws, one projecting from the front of each keyblock, that fit into slots in the back of the keyslip (5-8b). Slide the keyslip up to disengage it; sometimes the fit is tight. When removing a keyslip, be sure to save any cardboard shims you find between the keyslip and the key frame and return them to the same position later.

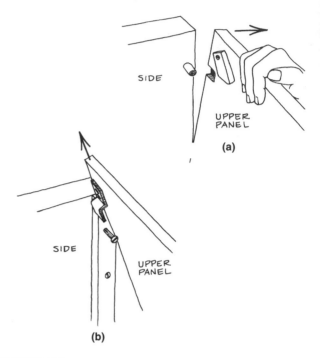

FIGURE 5-10.

Vertical

Open the lid (Figure 5-9). Most lids open one of the three ways shown in the drawing. The example on the right is a "grand style" lid, hinged on the left side, found on some contemporary verticals. To inspect the piano, remove the hinge pins on the grand style lid and take the lid off. (Note: Some studio pianos, such as the Baldwin Hamilton, open differently; see Figure 5-12.)

Remove the upper panel (Figure 5-10). If the piano is an upright, first close the fallboard down over the keys. This is done because on some uprights the fallboard mechanically interlocks with the upper panel, or leans against the upper panel, and makes disassembly difficult when open. The upper panel either is secured by a latch on each end, a common type of which is shown in 5-10a, or swings on screws or stout pins sticking out from the cabinet sides, as in 5-10b.

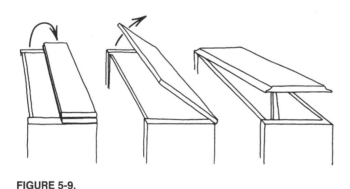

FIGURE 5-9.

pins (Figure 5-15). When the piano is new, the pins are set so the coil of wire around each pin is about 3/16 inch above the plate. If pins get loose, they can be driven further in to tighten them—if necessary, until the coils are almost touching the plate. That 3/16 inch acts as a safety margin: even if the tuning pins on the piano you are inspecting turn out to be loose, the piano may still be worth buying if there is still sufficient space left between the coils and the plate to drive the pins in further to tighten them. (However, this repair doesn't always work, and repinning the piano with larger tuning pins is preferred when economically feasible.) Conversely, if the piano is dreadfully out of tune and far below standard pitch *and* the tuning pins have already been driven in as far as they can go, the chances are fairly good that that piano would require extensive rebuilding to bring it

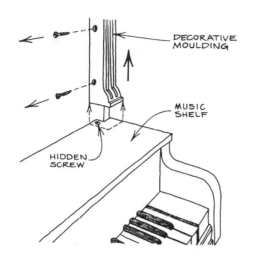

FIGURE 5-11.

Sometimes these methods may be combined, in which case you should proceed as for the first type. On some spinets and consoles, the upper panel-music shelf assembly is attached to the cabinet sides with screws. After removing the upper panel, try opening the fallboard. On some pianos the fallboard, when open, hits the action when the upper panel is not in place. Usually this kind of fallboard assem-

bly can be removed by simply lifting it straight up and out of the piano. Otherwise, it's generally not necessary to remove the fallboard to inspect the vertical piano.

Remove the music shelf (Figure 5-11). Some old uprights have a separate music shelf, which must be removed. Sometimes the music shelf just slides out, or slides and then lifts, and sometimes it is held in by screws. The screws may be hidden under decorative moldings that must first be removed by unscrewing them from the cabinet sides.

How to open some studio pianos (Figure 5-12). On some studio pianos, especially the Baldwin Hamilton, the lid, upper panel, and music shelf are all contained in one bulky piece. A propstick swings down to support this assembly on the cabinet side.

Remove the lower panel (Figure 5-13). The lower panel is usually held in place by a leaf spring or two. Simply press the spring(s) up toward the keybed and pull the panel out. Sometimes a rotating wooden latch is used instead. When replacing the lower panel, be sure the bottom edge of the panel is lined up correctly with the bottom rail on which it sits.

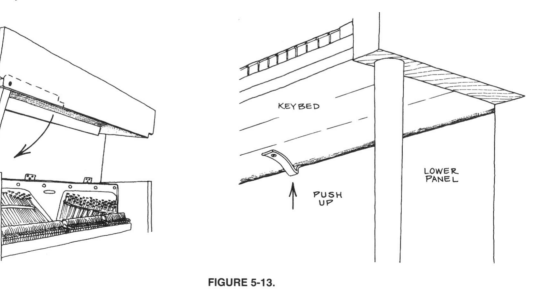

FIGURE 5-12.

FIGURE 5-13.

back to life. A new set of larger tuning pins could cost at least several hundred dollars, and a new pinblock, if necessary, could cost a few thousand by the time all the work necessitated by it was completed. These are just clues; a final judgment on the matter must await the technician.

Also look around the tuning pins and on nearby areas of the plate for ugly, dark brown, gummy-looking stains that indicate the pinblock has been doped

with chemicals to tighten the pins. On a grand, also look on the underside of the pinblock for the stains and for signs of cracking (Figure 5-16). Don't confuse dirt and rust with the chemical stains. Unless the piano is otherwise in very good condition, the price is right, or you plan to replace the pinblock anyway (a major rebuilding job), you would probably do best to steer away from a piano that has been doped.

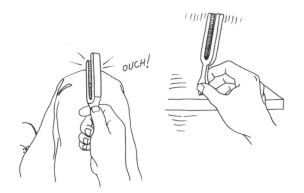

FIGURE 5-14. Hold the tuning fork by the stem and hit one of the tines on your knee good and hard (ouch!), *not* on the piano. Then touch the stem to a wooden part of the piano. The wood will amplify the sound of the fork. The note that the fork sounds, usually A or C, is printed on the side. Compare the fork to the same letter-name notes up and down the piano keyboard to see if the piano is up to standard pitch.

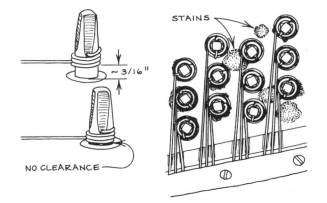

FIGURE 5-15. The distance between the plate and the coil of wire around each tuning pin gives a clue about the condition of the pinblock. When the piano is new, the tuning pins are set so the coils are about 3/16 inch above the plate. If the coils are close to the plate, this means that the tuning pins were once loose and were hammered in further to tighten them, and that if they should still be loose or should get loose again in the future, there will be no room to hammer them in again. Also look around the tuning pin area, and around the wooden plate bushings surrounding the tuning pins, for ugly, dark brown, oily-looking stains that indicate the pinblock has been chemically treated.

Strings. How rusty are the strings? Some tarnish or a very light coating of rust is normal for an old piano. What you want to avoid is heavy, encrusted rust on the strings and pressure bar that will make the tone bad and cause the strings to break during tuning (although strings sometimes break even if they aren't rusty). Has

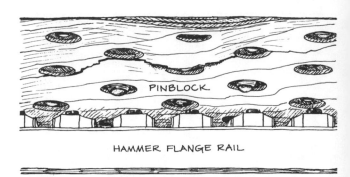

FIGURE 5-16. On a grand piano, with the fallboard off, look at the underside of the pinblock for chemical stains or signs of cracking. The pinblock shown here is in extremely poor condition. Notice especially that the bottom lamination is separating from the rest of the pinblock. Most ruined pinblocks are not this obvious, but you might as well recognize the ones that are. Also: if the tuning pins are sticking out the bottom of the holes, beware. This usually means someone installed the wrong size pins; if they should require hammering in, it will be impossible to do so. The protruding ends of the tuning pins may interfere with the action if there is not much clearance between them.

this piano had a string breakage problem? Look carefully at the strings, which are arranged in sets of one, two, or three called *unisons* (p. 7), to see if any are missing (Figure 5-17a). Are there many new-looking, untarnished strings on the piano? Some new strings—how nice, right? Wrong. Those new strings were installed to replace ones that broke, so their presence amidst the rusty ones indicates a possible string breakage problem, especially if several strings are missing too. Occasional string replacement (an inexpensive item) can be tolerated, but the expense and nuisance add up if strings break often. The presence of spliced bass strings, an alternative to replacement of broken bass strings, can also indicate a possible string breakage problem (Figure 5-17b).

Now play some bass notes. Do they "resound"? Or do they sound like they're underwater or being struck through a heavy blanket (thud . . . thud)? The copper or iron windings (p. 33, 38) on these strings loosen with time and also become clogged with dirt, which diminishes their flexibility. Replacing an entire set of bass strings, a moderate expense, is generally worth doing if the piano is otherwise in reasonable condition. Twisting and cleaning the old bass strings to make them sound better costs about half as much, but doesn't always work satisfactorily, and can make marginally tight tuning pins too loose to hold the strings in tune. If the bass strings need replacing and the piano is one of some value, you should consider restringing the entire piano at one time.

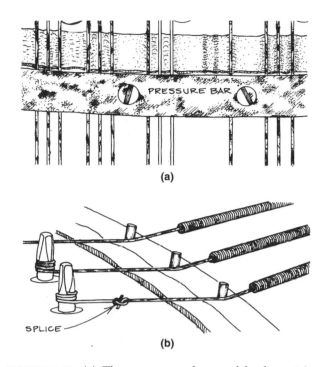

FIGURE 5-17. (a) The presence of several broken strings and several new, untarnished strings (meaning that some broken ones were recently replaced) among otherwise rusty or tarnished strings may indicate the piano has a string breakage problem. (Remember that in the treble section of most pianos each length of wire forms two strings, as shown in Figure 1-13.) (b) Broken and replacement bass strings may also indicate a string breakage problem. Sometimes a new piece of wire is spliced to the remains of a broken bass string as an alternative to replacing it.

The bridges. The treble and bass bridges transfer the vibration of the strings to the soundboard (p. 39). Of special interest to us here is the bass bridge, which has a strong tendency to form cracks around the bridge pins due to the side pressure of the strings against them. Follow the bass strings toward their far end (on a vertical, to their bottom end) to find the bass bridge. As you look for cracks around the bridge pins you may need your flashlight to chase away the shadows and your brush to chase away the dust. Now, you may see some tiny hairline cracks around some—maybe even all—the bridge pins. This is very common and usually not a problem. The problem begins when the cracks get big enough so the bridge pins are actually pushed aside. This can cause a severe deterioration or loss of tone in the affected notes. Then the problem worsens when the cracks around adjacent pins run together, resulting in a perforated bridge ready to fall apart (Figure 5-18). If the pitch of the piano must be raised much to get it up to standard pitch, the resulting increase in string tension may exacerbate this condition.

A loose bass bridge will also cause a loss of tone. If one end of the bass has a much weaker tone than the other end, you might try pushing that end of the bridge down toward the soundboard while someone else plays the keys. If the tone noticeably improves, then the bridge is coming loose from the soundboard.

The treble bridge can also develop cracks, usually in the highest octave. On a vertical piano these can be hard to see because the action is in the way. Try peering down behind the action with your flashlight. If the bridge appears to be badly cracked, check the tone of these notes by plucking individual strings with your fingers. Do they give off a tone of a definite pitch, or is the pitch indistinct? The treble bridge on a grand piano can easily be viewed throughout.

Bridge repairs, unless very minor, tend to be moderately to very expensive, and are usually unjustified for the cheaper pianos, although it is not uncommon for a good upright to be fitted with a new bass bridge cap (p. 39). If the damage is not too severe, sometimes a less expensive repair can be made to a cracked bridge by removing bridge pins, filling cracks with epoxy, and then reinstalling the pins. A loose bass bridge can often be reattached by stuffing glue under the loose part and securing with a screw from the back of the soundboard.

One more bridge-related concern should be mentioned. On some pianos, both verticals and grands, made in the early part of this century (or earlier), the upper bearing point (the end of the vibrating portion

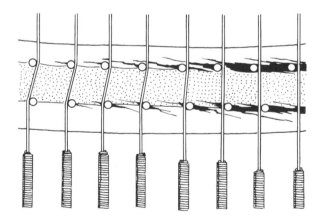

FIGURE 5-18. The strings exert sidebearing pressure against the bridge pins—pressure that is necessary for good tone, but that may eventually cause cracks in the bridge. This is especially a concern with the bass bridge. The bass bridge shown here is worse toward the right, where the hairline cracks are larger and have merged, allowing the bridge pins to be pushed out of line until there is no more sidebearing. A bridge like this would probably have to be replaced.

of the string that is closer to the tuning pins) for the bass strings is made of wood instead of being an integral part of the cast-iron plate. This wooden "upper bridge" tends to have the same cracking problems that the lower bridge does, sometimes worse. Be especially cautious about buying a piano with serious cracks in this area.

Structural integrity. This refers to the condition of the cast-iron plate (p. 30) and the supporting wooden case, posts, and beams (p. 28). Once in a great while, a crack will develop in one of these parts, most often the plate, usually rendering the piano useless (and usually unrepairable). In a grand, the plate can be seen in its entirety from above, and the rest of the supporting structure from below. In a vertical, much of the plate is hidden from view; the wooden structure, though, can easily be examined by moving the piano away from the wall and looking at the back. (Note: When pulling a vertical piano away from the wall, watch for wooden blocks under the back if the casters are missing.) In a vertical, look especially at the back of the top horizontal beam, and, if exposed, the top of the piano back (under the lid), for anything other than minor surface cracking. Also make sure the case sides are not coming unglued from the vertical back structure. In a grand, check the bottom edge of the rim for delamination. To be honest, I'm including these items only for the sake of completeness; your chance of finding a major structural problem of this sort is probably very tiny. (An important exception is when a piano has been moved from a humid climate to a very dry one. In this situation it is more common to find wooden structural parts coming unglued.) An indication that a structural problem should be looked for might be, for example, that a piano only recently tuned has gone quickly and drastically out of tune for no apparent reason (although there are certainly lots of other reasons why this could happen). Major structural problems, especially a cracked plate, are very risky to try to repair. The risk should be left to a rebuilder, not you.

Another, more likely, structural problem—this one unrelated to tuning—is the condition of the legs. The front legs of spinets and consoles very frequently crack or become loose (p. 26).Usually they can be repaired or replaced at not too great a cost. Check also for visible (or invisible) cracks in the legs of grands. Push on the piano gently both forward and sideways to see if it rocks unduly. Installing a new set of grand legs or leg plates (which hold the legs on) is a bit costly, but usually worth doing if the piano is otherwise worth buying. Last, check for cracks in the lid of a grand, or loose lid hinges. A cracked lid could necessitate an expensive lid replacement, but only for aesthetic reasons. Damaged lid hinges should be repaired or replaced for safety.

Soundboard and ribs. While you're underneath the grand piano or behind the vertical looking at its structural components, you should also check out the soundboard and ribs (p. 39). Cracks in the soundboard, while unattractive, are not necessarily important, as long as the tone has not suffered. (This runs contrary to popular thought on the subject, I realize.) Very extensive cracking, however, can be taken as an indication that the piano has suffered great dryness or climatic extremes, and that its life expectancy may be short. (The more expensive the piano, the more important is the consideration of life expectancy.) Usually in such a case, the symptoms of dryness will be evident elsewhere in the piano as well. If the cracks are fitted with wooden shims, this means the piano was rebuilt at some time in the past (Figure 5-19a). Also check around the perimeter of the soundboard to make sure it isn't coming unglued from the piano.

The ribs run perpendicular to the grain of the soundboard, and therefore perpendicular to any cracks. Check each point where a rib crosses a crack to see if the ribs are still firmly glued to the soundboard or if they have separated (Figure 5-19b). Rib separations are potential sources of buzzing noises. Again, how important this is to you depends on the severity of the problem, whether buzzing sounds are currently present, and how expensive the piano is. In any case, this is rarely a fatal problem, and often (though not always) ribs can be reattached to the soundboard with glue and screws at reasonable cost without "rebuilding" the piano.

When manufactured, the soundboard has a curvature or *crown* built into it to help resist the downbearing pressure of the strings on the bridges and to enhance the tone (p. 39, 41). Over time, principally because of the drying out of the wood, the soundboard loses some or all of its crown. In theory, a soundboard with no crown shouldn't sound good, but actually many fine-sounding pianos have no measurable crown. This is one of those grey areas of piano technology, where every technician has a different opinion on the role that soundboard crown plays in determining the quality of tone.

My sense is that a measurement of soundboard crown can be useful in conjunction with other data. For instance, if the tone in the treble lacks sufficient sustain (p. 42), there is no measurable downbearing of the strings on the bridges (p. 39) (to be measured by the technician), and the soundboard has no crown, then the tonal problem may be due to a worn-out soundboard that needs replacing. But if the soundboard has

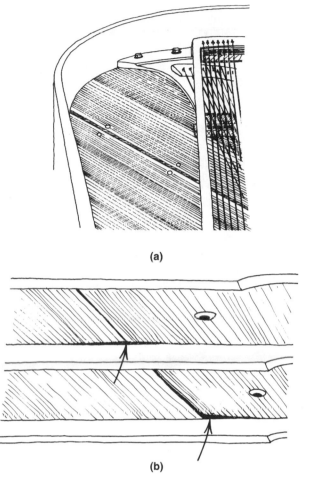

(a)

(b)

FIGURE 5-19. (a) When a piano is rebuilt without replacing the soundboard, the soundboard cracks are fitted with shims of wood, mostly for aesthetic reasons. In this drawing, the circles on either side of the shimmed crack are wooden plugs that cover the heads of screws used to reattach loose ribs. (b) Ribs often come unglued where they cross cracks in the soundboard (and sometimes elsewhere as well), causing buzzing sounds. They can usually be reattached with glue and screws.

plenty of crown, we might look elsewhere for the cause of the problem.

To test whether the treble has sufficient sustain, try the Pluck Test. Slowly depress a key in the octave that begins an octave above middle C. This area is the critical "melody range." While holding the key down (to lift its damper), pluck one of the three strings of the note you've chosen. The sound should swell slightly immediately after the pluck and then get softer as the string vibrates. The tone should be clearly audible for at least five seconds. If the sound is less than three seconds in duration, the soundboard may not be functioning properly or the scale may be poorly designed. We pluck the string rather than strike it with a hammer

in order to separate out the hammer's effect on the tone from the soundboard's effect.

To measure soundboard crown, hold a long piece of thread, *pulled taut*, against the back of the soundboard parallel to the longest ribs (Figure 5-20). See if there is a space between the thread and the soundboard created by the soundboard crown. How much space? *Any* amount is considered sufficient. An eighth of an inch would be excellent.

Again, measuring crown, although much talked about, is of uncertain value. It's probably worth paying attention to when inspecting high-quality grands, but don't bother on verticals.

The action. Read about the action in Chapter 1 and also in Chapter 3 (pp. 44–47); there's plenty to know about it. We won't be removing the action. It may be okay to do that (with proper instruction) when inspecting your own or perhaps a friend's piano, but *not* when examining a piano you are considering buying from a stranger—it's too easy to break parts. (You may legitimately ask to look under the hood of a used car before buying, but unless you're a trained mechanic, the owner may justifiably complain when you start to remove the transmission.) Fortunately, in most cases you can inspect a vertical piano action very thoroughly without removing it. If you're inspecting a grand piano, though, you'll have to be content with

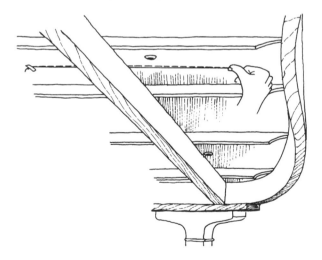

FIGURE 5-20. To measure soundboard curvature or *crown*, stretch a thread against the back of the soundboard parallel to the longest ribs. You can either tape one end of the thread to the soundboard, get someone else to hold it there, or try to hold both ends yourself. You may have to pass the thread over one of the case beams. Look for a space between the thread and the soundboard indicating that the soundboard is curved. A flashlight might be handy for this operation. Theoretically, crown is necessary for good tone, but actually many fine-sounding pianos have no measurable soundboard crown.

what you can see looking down through the strings or in through the front with the fallboard removed. If you're seriously interested in the piano, your technician can do a more complete inspection of the action later.

Do a general inspection of the action. Do the action parts look evenly spaced and uniform in appearance? Does every note work? Do any keys stick or do any dampers not damp properly? Are the hammers, dampers, and other felt parts badly moth-eaten? Check the condition of the bridle straps (vertical pianos only). If they are old and brittle or show signs of deteriorating (Figure 5-21), they need to be replaced. This is a relatively inexpensive repair that is important and very common.

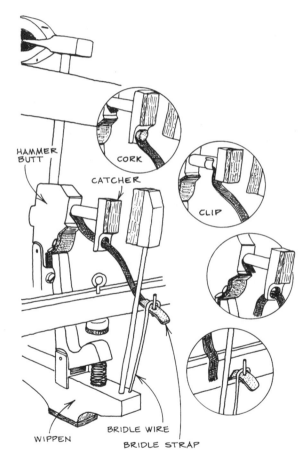

FIGURE 5-21. Bridle straps are cloth tapes with leather or vinyl tips that connect the wippen assembly to the hammer assembly on vertical pianos. There are eighty-eight of them. They are among the first parts in a piano to become worn out and may be replaced several times in the life of a piano. They are always worth replacing if the piano is worth keeping. The bottom two insets show how bridle straps may break at the end attached to the bridle wire or closer to the end attached to the hammer butt. The top two insets show two common types of replacement bridle straps: one with a cork that fits into the hole in the catcher, and one with a spring clip that clips to the catcher shank when the catcher is a type with no hole.

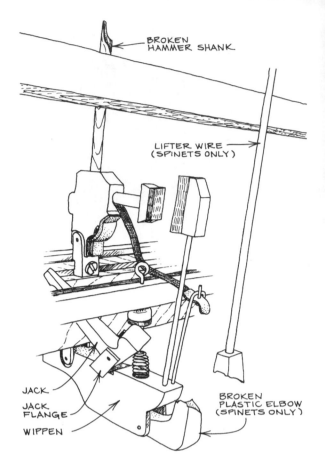

FIGURE 5-22. This drawing shows three of the most common action problems that would cause a note on a vertical piano to not play at all: (a) The jack flange has come unglued from its slot in the wippen and has fallen over, so the jack can no longer push against the hammer butt. This is especially common in old uprights during the dry season. The repair is simple—clean out the old glue joint and reglue. (b) The hammer shank has broken and the hammer head has fallen into the piano somewhere. If it can be found, it may be possible to splice the shank back together. If the break was jagged or occurred too close to the top or bottom of the shank, the remains will have to be drilled out and the shank replaced. An inexpensive repair. (c) On spinets made during the 1940s and 1950s, the plastic elbows that connect the lifter wires to the wippens deteriorate and break. Once one or two break, the rest will soon follow, so it's most economical to replace the whole set at once with elbows made of wood or durable modern plastic. This is a moderate expense.

There are thousands of parts in an action and *zillions* of things that can go wrong. I wish I could go into all of them here, but obviously that's not possible. If you enjoy playing detective, trace down the cause of malfunctions by comparing notes that work properly with ones that don't. The action diagrams and explanations in Chapter 1 should help you. Also make an inventory of any broken parts and strange noises (Figure 5-22).

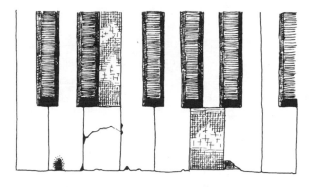

FIGURE 5-23. Missing, broken, and cigarette-burned ivory and plastic keytops can be unsightly, and jagged edges can be dangerous to the fingers. Replacing a few keytops is inexpensive, but if many are missing or broken, it's best to have the whole set recovered with plastic, a moderate expense.

Buyers of used pianos are often scared away from instruments with one or more notes that don't play. Actually, broken or missing action parts are usually among the easiest and cheapest repairs to make. Unless the action is utterly worn out or there has been wholesale destruction of parts, problems in this area of the piano are usually much less cause for alarm than some of the other, less obvious problems previously discussed. However, if a lot of wooden parts are broken or loose or appear to have been repaired, and the breakage occurred through normal use, this may indicate that the wood is overly dry and brittle and that future breakage may occur. Such a piano should be avoided by pianists who plan to make heavy demands on the instrument, but it may still be suitable for others, as long as it's humidified during the dry season. (Note: If a vertical piano was made before 1960 and some of the action parts are made of plastic, don't buy the piano. The old plastic breaks easily and the piano is likely to require wholesale replacement of parts.)

Keys (p. 47). Look at the keytops. Are they ivory or plastic (p. 51)? Ivory usually has an irregular, natural-looking grain; plastic has no grain or a simulated grain of straight lines. Are any keytops missing or chipped or cigarette-burned (Figure 5-23)? Don't let a bad-looking keyboard scare you away. A few missing keytops can be replaced inexpensively and a new set of plastic keytops is available at moderate cost.

Do the keys rattle? Press a key down at the front and wiggle it left and right (Figure 5-24). Does it move a lot and make noise? The keys pivot on a key frame with metal guide pins underneath the front and sticking through the balance point of each key. Pieces of cloth called **key bushings** buffer the key wood from the guide pins. The key bushings in the most-used cen-

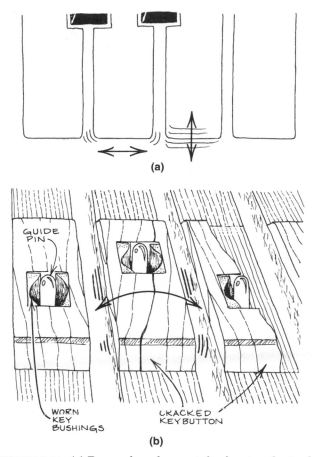

FIGURE 5-24. (a) Press a key down at the front and wiggle it left and right. There should be a very small amount of side play. If the key moves a lot and makes noise, it's time to get the front key bushings replaced. Also grab at the front of a key and try moving it forward and backward. Any play at all here is too much; it indicates abnormal wear of the balance hole at the bottom of the key at its balance point. (b) At the top of the keys at the balance point on most pianos are key buttons, inside of which are another set of key bushings. Like the key bushings at the front, these wear too, allowing the keys to wobble too much and make noise. Also check for cracked key buttons. Replacing an individual cracked key button or repairing an occasional worn balance hole is an inexpensive job.

ter area of the keyboard get the most wear. A new set of key bushings is another moderate-cost repair, but one that returns great value in the form of a quieter, smoother-feeling action. Also check the balance point of the key for excessive side-play in those bushings and for cracked key buttons.

Hammers (p. 51). Of all the parts in the action, the hammers are the most important for you to inspect. In them, too, can be read some of the history of the piano. First look at the string-cut grooves on the striking point of the hammer. Unless the hammer heads have been replaced at some point in the life of the piano, or

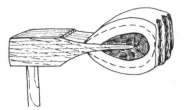

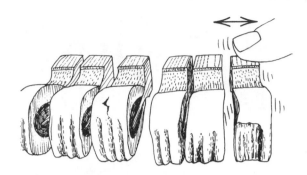

FIGURE 5-25. When hammers are flattened and deeply grooved, for best tone they should be reshaped by sanding off a layer of felt. But too little felt on the hammer—both at the striking point and on the shoulders—can make the tone ugly and hard. Imagine restoring the hammer to its rounded-point shape (indicated by the dotted line). Would there still be a reasonable amount of felt left? Not on this hammer.

FIGURE 5-26. Unless the piano is brand new or the hammers have recently been reshaped, they will probably have some grooves in them. The grooves should be well defined and approximately centered on the hammers. In this drawing, the fourth hammer from the left has moved so it is hitting only two of its three strings (the third string appears to have worn away the very edge of the hammer). The right-most hammer has only a broad worn spot indicating, as does the finger test, that the hammer is wobbly. Realigning or repairing misaligned or wobbly hammers is not in itself a big job, but the realignment or repair could be temporary unless hammers are resurfaced or, in some cases, replaced.

the hammer felt resurfaced to its original shape by filing off a layer of felt (which would eliminate the grooves), the depth of the grooves will tell you something about how much use the piano has gotten over the years. More importantly, the deeper the grooves or the flatter the striking face of the hammer, the sooner you will need to have the hammers resurfaced, a low to moderate expense. But if there isn't enough felt left for resurfacing, the hammer heads will have to be replaced. This is expensive (at least a few hundred dollars, possibly much more) but worth doing on most grands, but a questionable investment for some of the cheaper verticals. Look especially at the hammers in the mid-treble section. These tend to experience the greatest wear in comparison to the amount of felt on them. Imagine these hammers restored to their original rounded-point shape by filing felt off the shoulders and the striking point. Is there enough felt left on the hammers of the top notes to do this without just about reaching wood (Figure 5-25)?

The presence of deep grooves adversely affects the tone of a piano. Of course, on many pianos, particularly cheaper ones that won't be getting serious or fussy artistic use, the presence of grooves on the hammers—even deep ones—isn't of great importance. But it becomes more important in conjunction with certain other hammer problems. Look at the grooves again. Does each of the hammers that are supposed to strike three strings have three well-defined grooves approximately centered on the hammer? Or have some of the hammers moved over a bit, now striking only two of the three strings (Figure 5-26)? You can also check the alignment of vertical piano hammers by pushing hammers toward the strings with your hand (see Figure 3-32 on page 53). On a grand, pressing down keys will lift hammers closer to the strings for viewing from above. Moving a hammer over a bit to realign it with the strings is usually a simple matter, but if the ham-

mer has become grooved in the misaligned position, the misaligned grooves will constantly "seek" the strings, attempting to move the hammer back into the wrong position every time you play the note. Eventually this will weaken or break the hammer at its pivot point. This problem can be avoided by resurfacing the hammers to eliminate the grooves, but, as I said, if there isn't enough felt left to resurface, the hammer heads will have to be replaced. Thus, in appraising the condition of the hammers, the presence of deep grooves becomes critical if many hammers are misaligned with the strings.

Look at the grooves one last time. Do any of the hammers have poorly defined grooves—just a broad flat spot at the striking point? This indicates that the hammer has been wobbly from side to side, striking the strings at a slightly different point with each stroke. You can also check for wobbly hammers by running your fingers lightly over the tops of the hammers, wiggling them slightly from left to right as you go. Each hammer should be fairly rigid at its pivot point, snapping back quickly to its central position as you let go of it. The wobbly hammers will stand out quite easily. (*Caution:* Don't try to move a non-wobbly hammer to the left or right more than about 1/16 of an inch, or you may damage the action center [pivot point].) Wobbly hammers are caused by either loose hammer flange screws (the screws that attach the hammer assemblies to the action rail) or by loose or defective action centers. Tightening loose screws is a simple, inexpensive, and normal maintenance procedure (p.

229). Repinning or repairing action centers is also relatively simple and inexpensive if only a few need to be done, but can turn into a major expense if a large number of hammers are involved. Whether the problem is due to loose screws or defective action centers (or both) will be hard for you to determine by yourself. But regardless of which it turns out to be, the result is usually badly misshapen hammers which, if you're lucky, will need only to be resurfaced, and at worst, will need to be replaced.

The action centers on which the hammers pivot are sometimes too *tight*. On a vertical, push groups of five or six hammers at a time toward the strings with your hand, release them, and watch for any slow returners. You won't be able to do this on a grand until the action is removed, but you can watch the hammers through the strings as you play several keys at a time. A few sluggish action parts are usually not a major problem. If many hammers, or even a whole set of hammers, are sluggish, repair can be moderately expensive, but sometimes not out of the question, even for an old upright. The advisability of doing this will depend on the cause and severity of the problem and whether wholesale replacement of parts is necessary or if simpler remedies will suffice.

One last hammer problem and we'll move on to something else. Hammer *heads* sometimes become loose on their shanks due to drying and cracking of the glue joint, and will make a slight clicking sound at the moment the hammer hits the string. Test for this by wiggling the hammer heads up and down (in relation to the shank). If they wiggle at all, they're loose (Figure 5-27).Regluing loose hammer heads is about the same size job as repairing loose or tight action centers.

Dampers. Dampers are the felt pads and wedges that rest against the strings to keep them from vibrating

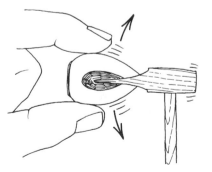

FIGURE 5-27. A loose hammer head will make a slight clicking sound at the moment it hits the strings. Test for this by gently trying to move it up and down. Any looseness is too much. A loose hammer head can be removed and reglued inexpensively.

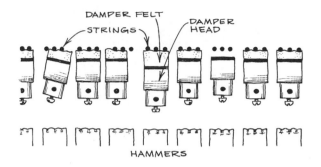

FIGURE 5-28. A row of vertical piano dampers resting against their strings, as seen from above. Notice that the felt on the damper in the center of the drawing has been replaced, and that the other damper felts, in contrast, appear to be quite worn. Some of the dampers are also misaligned and may not be damping all of their strings. One damper felt is missing.

when they're not supposed to (Figure 5-28). Are they doing their job? Play each note and release it, making sure that it stops ringing promptly. (Note: The strings in the top couple of octaves don't have dampers and are supposed to keep ringing.) Do many of the dampers buzz when they come back down on the strings? It may be time for a new set of damper felts if they do, usually a moderate-cost repair. Press the right-hand pedal slowly and see if all the dampers rise off the strings at precisely the same moment. If not, they may need regulating. Damper problems are sometimes difficult to solve, but not usually so expensive or severe that they should prevent you from buying a piano that has them.

Pedals. Do all the pedals work? If not, investigate to see why not (see page 53 and Figure 3-33 for a description of how the pedals and trapwork operate). In a vertical, often a dowel will be missing or out of place or the pedal will need minor adjustment. The vertical piano's pedal system is very simple, and usually inexpensive to fix or adjust. The grand's pedal system is a lot more complicated, and since some of it is located behind the action, you may need a technician to inspect it. One thing you *can* check on a grand is whether the pedal lyre is coming apart at the joints, or falling off the piano (Figure 5-29). Both conditions can be fixed at moderate expense. Loose and noisy pedals are usually relatively minor problems on both grands and verticals. However, on verticals, do check to make sure that the board to which the pedals are attached isn't cracking, bending, or falling off the bottom of the piano (this, too, can be fixed at low to moderate expense).

Is there a middle pedal? What does it do? If you are buying a grand and are a serious player of classical

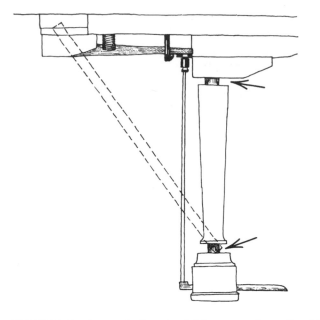

FIGURE 5-29. A grand piano pedal lyre seen from the side. The arrows point to where it's coming apart at the joints. Lyres on old pianos, particularly ones that have been moved many times, are often missing their diagonal lyre braces, shown here by dotted lines. These braces help the lyre to withstand the constant pressure of the feet on the pedals. They can be replaced inexpensively.

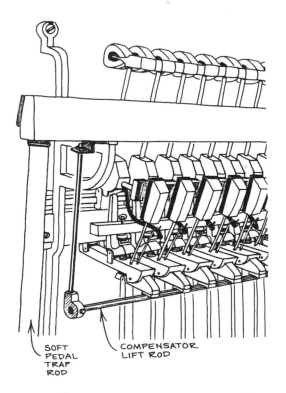

SOFT PEDAL TRAP ROD

COMPENSATOR LIFT ROD

FIGURE 5-30. A lost motion compensator in an old upright piano. This mechanism took up the slack, or "lost motion," in the action that was created when the hammers were pushed closer to the strings.

music, you may desire a true sostenuto pedal. You probably won't need it often, but when you do, there is no substitute for it. Some cheaper grands have a middle pedal that just lifts the bass dampers—a fairly useless feature. This feature is standard for many verticals. Some verticals don't have a middle pedal, or have one that never worked or no longer works—no great loss!

As discussed on page 54, the left pedal of a vertical piano makes the sound quieter by pushing the hammers closer to the strings, but in doing so it puts the action out of adjustment. Some old uprights were outfitted with a "lost motion compensator" mechanism (Figure 5-30) that allowed the action to remain in proper adjustment when this pedal was used. Vertical pianos with a lost motion compensator or a true sostenuto mechanism, or both, were usually among the best old uprights made and are often still in good condition.

Regulation. *Regulating* is the process of making technical adjustments to the piano action to compensate for the effects of wear and atmospheric changes on the wood and cloth parts that have occurred over the months and years of use, and to restore the functioning of the action as close as possible to the original factory specifications. The cost can vary from very cheap for minor amounts of regulating to moderate (three to four hundred dollars) for a complete vertical piano regulation to expensive (four to seven hundred dollars) for a complete grand action regulation. A full technical discussion of regulating would be too lengthy to be included here, but to give you an idea of what regulating involves, a few examples are included in Figure 5-31.

In addition, here are two tests you can do now: First, check repetition on several keys by playing a key rapidly with alternating hands while depressing the right pedal. (Depressing the pedal removes the assistance of the dampers in returning the keys to rest and thus reveals any excessive friction in the action.) Second, play a number of keys as softly as possible. If the action fails to play reliably (i.e., skips or misses) at reasonably soft dynamic levels, the action probably needs regulating.

Your technician can more fully evaluate the piano's regulation needs later. How much importance you should place on proper action regulation depends on how fine an instrument you're buying and on your level of technical skill. However, playing on a piano that is grossly out of regulation can be very frustrating, and possibly harmful to the piano.

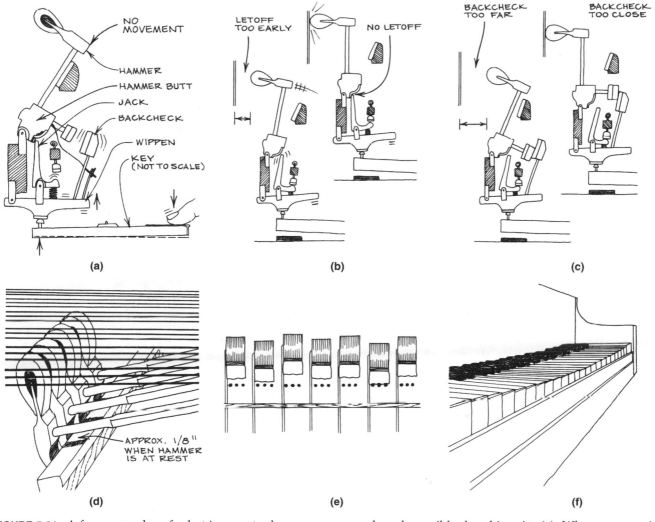

FIGURE 5-31. A few examples of what is meant when an action is said to be "out of regulation." See Chapter 1 for details of action operation. (a) When you just begin to press a key down on a vertical piano, the hammer should respond immediately. Sometimes the wippen and attached parts (such as the backcheck), will move a lot before the hammer will respond. This is due to a space between the top of the jack and the hammer butt, which causes slack in the action known as *lost motion*. This wasted motion can cause the action to malfunction. (b) The jack, which imparts power to the hammer, should disengage when the hammer is about 1/8 inch from the string (sometimes a little more on spinets and consoles and a little less on concert grands). This allows the hammer to go the rest of the way to the string on its own momentum and then freely rebound. You can test for this disengagement by pressing a key down very slowly and watching a hammer. (If you press slowly enough, the hammer won't even reach the string because of a lack of momentum.) The point of disengagement is known as *escapement* or *letoff*. When letoff occurs too early (that is, when the hammer is too far from the string), the hammer won't have enough momentum to reach the string when a key is played softly and will "miss." If letoff occurs too late (when the hammer is too close to the string), there is a risk it won't occur at all and the hammer will jam against the string, damping its sound and possibly breaking it. (c) When a note is played normally, the backcheck should catch the hammer on the rebound roughly 5/8 inch from the string. If the hammer is caught too far from the string, the ability to repeat notes may be affected. If the hammer is caught too close, the hammer may jam against the string. If the backcheck doesn't catch the hammer at all, repetition may be affected, the hammer may double-strike the string, and the touch may feel strange. (d) Hammers seen through the strings of a grand piano. When grand piano hammers are at rest, the hammer shanks should be suspended about 1/8 inch (sometimes a little more) above the hammer rest rail or rest cushions. If the shanks are actually resting on the rail or cushions, the action may not function correctly. This applies to a grand piano action only. (e) When the sustain pedal, grand or vertical, is pressed, all the dampers should rise simultaneously as if made of one piece of wood and felt. Press the pedal very slowly to test for this. The drawing shows grand dampers rising at different times to different heights. (f) The keyboard should be perfectly level from one end to the other (although some are regulated slightly higher in the center in anticipation of settling). Over time, the well-used center area settles due to compacting of the key frame cloth under the keys. The drawing, slightly exaggerated, shows what this might look like as you sight down the keyboard from one end.

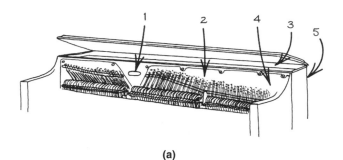

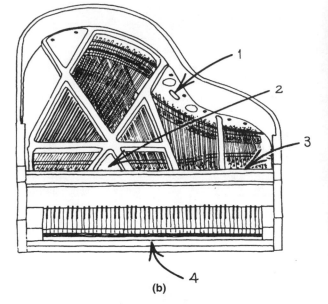

(a)   **(b)**

FIGURE 5-32. (a) The serial number of a vertical piano can usually be found in position 1, either stamped on the plate or engraved in the pinblock and showing through a cut-away portion of the plate. Positions 2 and 4, also on the plate, are other possibilities. On newer pianos, the serial number is sometimes on the top of the piano back (position 3) or stamped on the back of the piano (position 5). (b) The serial number of a grand piano is usually in position 2, stamped on the plate or engraved in the pinblock; elsewhere on the plate or soundboard (such as positions 1 and 3); or stamped on the front of the key frame (position 4). Access to the key frame is gained by removing the keyslip (for directions, see Figure 5-8).

Serial number. Find the serial number of the piano so you can look up its year of manufacture in the *Pierce Piano Atlas* (p. 178). Usually four to eight digits, the serial number is most often located near the tuning pins, either printed directly on the plate or engraved in the wooden pinblock and showing through a cut-away portion of the plate. Or the number may be printed somewhere else on the plate or soundboard, printed or engraved on the top or back of a vertical piano back, or printed or engraved on the front edge of a grand piano key frame (Figure 5-32). (Sometimes a three- or four-digit number used in the manufacturing process also appears on various case parts; don't confuse this with the serial number.) When no serial number can be found or if the year of manufacture isn't listed in *Pierce*, sometimes a technician can estimate the age within about ten years just by looking at the case styling or technical details.

Close the piano now, reversing the instructions in Figures 5-5 through 5-13. Play the piano again and listen to the tone. Is there a smooth transition in tone from one end of the keyboard to the other, or are some sections completely different in character from the others? Do the bass strings sound full and alive, or dead and muffled? Do the few lowest and highest notes have a definite pitch and pleasing sound, or are they indistinct and essentially useless? Are you pleased with the tonal quality, brightness, and volume? Remember that: (1) room acoustics have a significant effect on tonal quality; (2) if the piano is out of tune, you may not be able to make an informed judgment about the tone; and(3) to some extent, tone can be altered by a technician through a process known as *voicing* or *tone regulating*. Read about all this in Chapter 3 (p. 41) and in Chapter 7 (p. 229).

This concludes the portion of the inspection that you can do yourself. If you later have a technician look at the piano, he or she will go over much the same ground you did, in addition checking the tightness of the tuning pins with a tuning hammer or a torque wrench, removing and inspecting the action of a grand piano, evaluating the state of the action regulation, and possibly measuring the downbearing of the strings against the bridge to check for possible soundboard and tone problems. Some technicians prefer to check out a piano alone, later issuing a written or oral report, whereas others wouldn't mind your presence and might be happy to answer your questions as they work.

Used-Piano Checklist

Here is a checklist you can copy and take with you when checking out a used piano. The list is a brief summary of the section "Checking Out the Piano." I assume you have read the section and know how to remove the outer case parts of a piano to look inside. If you decide to proceed further with a piano after examining it with this list, you will need to hire the services of a professional piano technician to check some things you could not, such as the tightness (torque) of the tuning pins, and to render an experienced judgment about the piano as a whole.

Looks, styling and finish
- ☐ Can you live with it?
- ☐ Does it need refinishing?
- ☐ Has it been restyled in an unusual way?
- ☐ Does it have any missing or broken cabinet parts or hardware (music desk, hinges, etc.)?
- ☐ Check for loose veneer and other signs of water damage.
- ☐ Does a matching bench in good condition come with the piano?

Pinblock and tuning
- ☐ Is the piano up to standard pitch? Is it in reasonable tune?
- ☐ Badly out-of-tune unisons may be a sign of loose tuning pins, especially if the piano has been tuned recently or if the mistuning of the unisons is gross. The tuning pins should be checked by a technician.
- ☐ Are tuning pins uniform in appearance, or are there some obvious replacements? The latter could indicate the pinblock is going bad.
- ☐ Look for at least 1/8" clearance between tuning pins coils and the pinblock or plate.
- ☐ Look for ugly, dark brown, gummy stains which indicate the pinblock has been doped with chemicals to temporarily tighten tuning pins.
- ☐ On a grand, if you are able to remove the fallboard, look at the underside of the pinblock for signs of cracking and delaminating.

Strings
- ☐ How rusty? Light rust or tarnish is okay, but excessive rust, especially on coils or at bearing points, is a problem, and could lead to breakage.
- ☐ Are any strings missing?
- ☐ Too many new-looking strings among the older ones indicates a breakage problem; too many splices, as well.
- ☐ Do bass notes sound clear and resonant, or short and tubby?

Bridges
- ☐ Primary problem area is the bass bridge.
- ☐ Some hairline cracks around bridge pins are customary.
- ☐ Excessive cracks that cause dislocation of bridge pins, especially on bass bridge, are a big problem and indicate the need for a new bridge or bridge cap.
- ☐ A piano with a loose bass bridge will have much weaker tone on one end of the bass section than the other.
- ☐ Also check the treble bridge for serious cracking.
- ☐ If piano is very old, check wooden upper bearing point for cracks.

Structural integrity
- ☐ Look for cracks in the plate, both in the struts and in the tuning pin area. Repairing a cracked plate is costly and usually not guaranteed. Cracked plates are very rare.
- ☐ Look for separations or delaminations in the bottom edge of the rim of a grand piano, or for a large crack in the back of the top horizontal beam of a vertical piano.
- ☐ Check legs for cracks or for an undue amount of rocking of the piano.
- ☐ Check vertical piano for missing casters.
- ☐ Before lifting the lid, check it for cracks and missing hinges.

Soundboard and ribs
- ☐ Play all the keys from one end to the other, listening for evenness of tone across the keyboard. Note any buzzing or rattling sounds.
- ☐ Look for excessive soundboard cracking. More than a few unrepaired cracks in the soundboard may be cause for concern.
- ☐ Wooden shims in cracks indicate that the piano was rebuilt at some point in the past. Make sure there are no new cracks alongside the shims.
- ☐ Check to ensure soundboard is glued around the perimeter.
- ☐ Where ribs cross cracks, check to ensure they are still firmly glued.
- ☐ Soundboard crown: any measurable crown is good. Some good-sounding pianos have no measurable crown.
- ☐ Pluck Test: Slowly depress a key in the octave that begins an octave above middle C. This area is the critical "melody range." While holding the key down (to lift its damper), pluck one of the three strings of the note you've chosen. The sound should swell slightly immediately after the pluck and then get softer as the string vibrates. The tone should be clearly audible for at least five seconds. If the sound is less than three seconds in duration, the soundboard may not be functioning properly or the scale may be poorly designed.

Action, Keys, Hammers, Dampers & Regulation
- ☐ Verify that all keys play. If not, try to determine why. Are some parts missing, broken, or unglued?
- ☐ Check visually inside, looking for consistent spacing and alignment of action parts.
- ☐ If made before 1960 and some action parts are plastic, do not buy the piano unless the plastic parts are post-1960 replacement parts (ask your technician).
- ☐ Visually check condition of hammers, dampers, and other felt parts for moth damage.
- ☐ Check that all bridle straps (verticals only) are in place and look okay.
- ☐ Note any sticking or sluggish keys.
- ☐ Check visually for even spacing and squaring of keys.
- ☐ Are keytops ivory or plastic? Are any keytops missing, chipped, or damaged?
- ☐ Check keys for minimal wiggle, rattle, or excessive left-right movement. Are new key bushings needed?
- ☐ Check hammers for depth of grooves, amount of remaining felt, correct number of string dents, possible wobbly hammers (string dents are misplaced or unclear), loose hammer heads (clicking noise or up/down movement of hammer head).
- ☐ Play all notes staccato, except those with no dampers (upper 15-20 notes). Do all notes cut off cleanly? If some buzz or continue ringing, dampers may need regulating or replacing.
- ☐ Make sure dampers move together when right pedal is depressed.
- ☐ Check condition of action regulation, using visual examples on page 199.
- ☐ Check repetition on several keys by playing a key rapidly with alternating hands while depressing the right pedal.
- ☐ Play a number of keys as softly as possible. If the action fails to play reliably (i.e., skips or misses) at reasonably soft dynamic levels, the action probably needs regulating.

Pedals
- ☐ Right pedal: see dampers, above.
- ☐ Middle pedal: If the middle pedal activates a true sostenuto mechanism on a vertical piano, the piano is probably a higher-quality instrument. If the middle pedal does *not* activate a sostenuto mechanism on a grand piano, the piano may be a lower-quality instrument. To test the sostenuto: Depress right pedal to lift dampers, then depress middle pedal and keep depressed while releasing right pedal. Dampers should remain raised.
- ☐ Left pedal: moves hammers closer to strings to quiet the piano (verticals), or shifts keyboard (grands). If left pedal on grand just operates bass dampers, it is often a sign of a lower-quality instrument.
- ☐ Lost motion compensator (verticals): keeps action in adjustment when soft pedal is used. Usually indicates a better-quality older piano.
- ☐ Is grand pedal lyre coming apart at the glue joints? Are lyre braces in place and lyre feels secure when pedals are used?

Other
- ☐ Find serial number of piano for later determination of age.
- ☐ Ask owner about piano's history (but don't take it all as the gospel truth).

HOW MUCH IS IT WORTH?

Ultimately, something is worth only as much as someone will pay for it. There is no reliable "Blue Book" for used pianos, and their prices vary capriciously depending on the locale and the particular situation.

The value of a piano also depends very much on how knowledgeable the seller and potential buyers are. For every piano, there is what I would call an "informed value" and an "ignorant value." The informed value takes into account the technical quality and condition of the piano, whereas the ignorant value does not, being based primarily on how the piano case looks (if even that). Unfortunately, the ignorant value is more often than not what the piano actually sells for.

For example, I was recently called to inspect an old upright piano that the prospective buyer, my client, said had a beautiful case, seemed to need only tuning, and was "about fifty years old." The asking price was $700. As soon as I took off the upper panel, I knew that only the part about the "beautiful case" was accurate. The piano, in fact, was ninety-five years old and had almost every problem a piano could have and still play. The sellers were clearly as surprised as we were about the age and condition (don't ask me how they arrived at the asking price) and as we were leaving asked me how much I thought it was worth. I thought a moment and then said, "To a private buyer, I couldn't recommend it at any price, so it's worth nothing. But it's possible that a rebuilder would give you $50 or $100 for it." Then I added, somewhat reluctantly, "If you hold out awhile, though, you'll probably get $700 for it from someone who doesn't bring a technician along to inspect it." And with that, I left them to ponder the ethical dilemma of whether to continue asking $700 for the piano.

So how much was that piano actually "worth"? The value I assigned to it was an artificial one, based on my moral and technical sense and expertise. The seller's value was based (at least theoretically) on an observation of market conditions. The piano was clearly worth something very different to each party. In practice, when a piano is worth buying but the informed value and the market value differ substantially (such as with spinets), I will usually suggest some sort of compromise value. When the transaction is between friends, or where the seller isn't interested in making money, my figure is usually accepted. But if there is competition for the piano, the buyer may have to pay more.

My experience is that, in most private transactions, the seller hasn't the foggiest notion of what the piano is worth, and the asking price is vastly overinflated, often based on such considerations as that "Uncle Joe liked this piano, and he played all his life, so it must be a fine instrument." I'm not exaggerating! In these cases, there's plenty of room for negotiating. If the piano needs considerable repair, encourage the technician to tell you this in front of the seller, as it will better your bargaining position. Even where the seller knows the informed value of the instrument, the asking price is usually set high in the expectation of bargaining, and you can generally expect to agree at a price of from 10 to 30 percent less.

For typical market values of used pianos, please see the chart on pages 204-205.

Depreciation. The "fair market value" method of appraising pianos, presented above, is actually only one of three methods commonly used by professional appraisers. A second is the "depreciation" method, especially useful for appraising pianos of recent make when the models are still in production.

A third appraisal method is the "idealized value minus cost of restoration" method. If a rebuilt piano of the same or comparable model costs $15,000, and it would cost $10,000 to restore your piano to like-new condition, then according to this method your piano is currently worth $5,000.

These three methods of appraising will typically yield three very different values. Which you choose to use will depend to some extent on your reason for having the piano appraised (buying, selling, insurance appraisal, etc.). Professional appraisers will sometimes use all three methods and then take an average to obtain a final value.

AFTER THE SALE

Moving. If you buy from a private owner, moving costs are your responsibility unless the seller agrees otherwise. If you buy from a technician, rebuilder, or dealer, moving charges may be included in the price of the piano or may not be; you should inquire. See Chapter 6 for more information about moving.

Warranty. You receive no warranty, of course, when you buy from a private owner. All other sellers should provide at least a one-year warranty covering parts and labor for all repair work other than that needed to correct normal changes in tuning, regulation, and voicing. Be sure to get the warranty in writing. If the seller doesn't have enough confidence in the piano to guarantee it for at least one year, don't buy it. Pianos that have had extensive reconditioning or rebuilding work are customarily guaranteed for longer periods. It's not unusual for a completely rebuilt piano to be guaranteed for five years. A technician's warranty, however, is only good as long as he or she is in business. One rule of thumb might be that every two years a technician has

Depreciation Schedule for Pianos

There is no universally agreed-upon depreciation schedule for pianos, but one such schedule is provided below. The percentages given represent what the unrestored, used piano is worth relative to the *actual selling price today* of a new piano *comparable in quality* to the used one in question. The values computed are meant to reflect what the piano would sell for between private, non-commercial parties. We suggest adding twenty to thirty percent to the computed value when the piano is for sale by a dealer, unrestored, but with a warranty given. These figures are intended only as guidelines, reflecting our general observations of the market. "Worse," "Average," and "Better" refer to the condition of the used piano for its age. A separate chart is given for Steinway pianos. Other fine pianos, such as Mason & Hamlin, may command prices somewhere in between the regular and Steinway figures.

Age in Years	Percent of New Value		
	Worse	*Average*	*Better*
1	82	85	88
2	79	82	85
3	77	80	83
5	71	74	77
10	59	62	65
15	49	52	55
20	40	43	46
25	31	34	37
Verticals only			
30	24	27	30
35 to 70	17	20	23
Grands only			
30 to 70	25	30	33
Steinways			
1	82	85	88
2	79	82	85
3	77	80	83
5	71	74	77
10	62	65	68
15	52	55	58
20	43	46	49
25	36	39	42
Verticals only			
30	30	33	36
35 to 70	27	30	33
Grands only			
30 to 70	30	35	40

Depreciation schedule courtesy of Stephen H. Brady, RPT, Seattle, Washington

been in business gives value to one year of warranty. Be sure to follow the terms of the warranty as to proper maintenance and climate control or you may void it.

If you have bought a piano from a commercial source (such as a technician or dealer), did not receive an adequate warranty, and are having problems with the piano that are not being solved to your satisfaction by the seller, you may still have legal recourse. Some states have *implied warranty laws* on the books that protect you even though you were not given a warranty in writing.

In Massachusetts, for instance, there are implied warranties of "merchantability" and "fitness for a particular purpose." Under the implied warranty of merchantability, a piano that will not hold its tune due to a defective pinblock is not merchantable (salable). Under the implied warranty of fitness for a particular purpose, the consumer relies on the seller's skill or judgment to select goods that are suitable. An antique square piano sold as a practice instrument would probably be judged as unfit for its particular purpose. These warranties come automatically with every sale and the seller cannot disclaim them by saying they don't apply in your case. Check with your state office of consumer affairs or a similar state agency for details.

Tuning. Most dealers and technicians include one home tuning in the sale price. This tuning should be done no sooner than two weeks after delivery, as it takes at least that long for the piano to adjust to the new conditions. Note also that if you are buying a piano that has recently been restrung, it may need more frequent tuning during the first year.

SELLING YOUR PIANO

Much of the information in this chapter about buying a piano is equally applicable to selling one. Use it to determine where, how, and for how much to advertise your piano. But one more piece of advice remains: tune your piano before you advertise it. You are probably thinking that since the buyer will have to have the piano tuned after moving it anyway, you might as well save money by not having it tuned now. But most prospective buyers know so little about the piano that when an instrument they encounter is out of tune or has some keys that don't work quite right, they have no way of knowing whether the problem is major or minor, or how the piano would sound after being tuned. Buyers will often reject out of hand a perfectly good piano because of relatively insignificant problems. By having the piano tuned and minor repairs made before selling it, you will eliminate any problems that would distract or confuse a prospective buyer. In my experience, piano owners who do this sell their pianos much faster and at a higher price than those who don't, easily recovering their expenses several-fold.

Prices of Used Pianos

The valuation of used pianos is difficult. Prices of used pianos vary wildly depending on local economies, supply and demand, and the cosmetics and playing condition—including both the amount and the quality of any reconditioning or rebuilding work—of the instrument at hand. As if this weren't enough, it's almost a certainty that no two piano technicians or piano salespeople would return exactly the same verdict on any given piano's value. Art being what it is, beauty is in the eye of the potential purchaser, and values are very much subjective.

These disclaimers aside, we've tried to assemble some used-piano values as general guidelines for shoppers. We asked a number of knowledgeable technicians and dealers across the country, including the online service **Piano-mart.com**, to give their opinions on prices for used pianos in each of our categories, then reconciled their varied responses to produce a price range for each category. The chart is organized by categories of vertical and grand pianos broken down by age (pre-1940 and 1940 to 1970), quality (highest, better, and average), and condition (worse, average, better, reconditioned, and rebuilt). For prices for pianos made since 1970, we refer you to the depreciation schedule on page 203 and the *Annual Supplement to The Piano Book*.

The price ranges given reflect the wide possibilities a buyer faces in the used-piano market. At the low end of each range is a price one might find in a poor economy or in a "buyers market," where supply exceeds demand. On the high end, the prices are consistent with both a better economy and a higher demand for the type of instrument indicated. In some categories, the prices we received from our sources varied all over the map, and we had to use a considerable amount of editorial discretion to produce price ranges that were not so large as to be useless as guidelines, and to retain at least a modicum of internal consistency in the chart. For that reason, you should expect to find some markets or situations in which prices higher or lower than those given here are normal or appropriate.

The prices given here for un-reconditioned or un-rebuilt pianos (worse, average, and better) are the price ranges one might expect to find when buying pianos *from private owners*. The "reconditioned" and "rebuilt" categories represent prices one might encounter when shopping for such pianos *at piano stores or from piano technicians*, with a warranty given. In some cases we have omitted the "rebuilt" price because we would not expect pianos of a given general age and type to be candidates for rebuilding. In every case, prices assume the least expensive style and finish; prices for pianos with fancier cabinets, exotic veneers, inlays, and so forth, could be much higher.

About the Categories

Quality
- "Highest quality" includes brands such as Steinway, Mason & Hamlin, and the very best European makes such as Bechstein, Blüthner, and Bösendorfer.
- "Better brand" includes well-regarded older names such as Knabe, Chickering, Baldwin, and among newer pianos, Ya-

maha, Kawai, Schimmel, and many other European makers.
- "Average brand" refers to pretty much everything else.

Condition
- "Average" means that the piano shows a normal amount of wear, tear, and deterioration for its age. For pianos made before 1940, this usually means that a noticeable amount of wear is present but the piano should be very playable and serviceable. It may well need some work to bring it into optimum condition. Newer instruments will, of course, be generally somewhat less worn than older ones.
- "Worse," for a pre-1940 piano, means the instrument is quite worn. It should be playable and serviceable, however. Older pianos in this category will have well-worn actions, obvious cosmetic deficiencies, and the possibility of some pinblock or soundboard problems. Newer pianos in this category will, of course, have fewer structural and cosmetic problems than the older ones, but will not perform as well as newer pianos in the "Average" or "Better" categories.
- "Better" means that the instrument has had less-than-average use, or perhaps has lived in a milder climate than usual, resulting in less age-related deterioration.
- "Rebuilt" is probably the most widely abused and misunderstood term in the piano business. Technically, a rebuilt piano has been restored by the replacement of as many parts-both moving and structural-as necessary to bring the instrument into a condition of like-new appearance, performance, and life expectancy. Be aware, though, that what constitutes a complete rebuild on a high-quality grand piano will probably be different than what passes for a "completely rebuilt" vertical or cheaper grand. The rebuilding of fine grands almost always includes replacement of the pinblock, for instance, and often the soundboard, whereas in lesser grands, soundboard and pinblock replacement is less common, and in verticals, is very rare. In pianos built since 1940, pinblock and soundboard replacements are not always necessary to get another 20 to 40 years of service from the piano, even in high-quality grands. Thus, for less expensive pianos and younger pianos of all quality levels, "rebuilding" may often consist only of restringing and replacement of hammers, damper felts, and key bushings. But any rebuild including less than everything the piano needs to make it just like new should properly be referred to as a "partial rebuild."

Unfortunately, many rebuilders and resellers fail to make that distinction when representing pianos that have been only partially rebuilt. For these and other reasons, the line between "reconditioned" and "rebuilt" is frequently blurred.
- A "reconditioned" piano, for our purposes, is one that has been restored by such work as cleaning, lubricating, polishing, repinning and regulating, and/or by replacement of some minor parts such as bridle straps or key bushings. Bear in mind that the terms "rebuilt" and "reconditioned" are used interchangeably by many people, and there may be some overlap in the price ranges of these two categories.

	Worse	(Private) Average	Better	(Dealer) Recond.	Rebuilt
Vertical, pre-1940, average brand	50–300	400–750	600–1,000	1,000–1,500	2,500–3,500
Vertical, pre-1940, better brand (i.e., Knabe, Chickering; see list on pages 175–176 for guidance)	150–500	500–1,000	700–1,500	1,200–2,000	3,500–5,500
Vertical, pre-1940, Steinway and others of highest quality	500–900	1,000–2,000	2,000–3,000	3,500–6,000	10,000–17,000
Vertical, 1940-1970, average brand	300–600	500–1,000	1,000–1,500	1,200–2,500	—
Vertical, 1940-1970, better brand (i.e., Baldwin, Sohmer, Everett)	400–800	700–1,500	1,000–2,000	1,800–3,000	—
Vertical, 1940-1970, Steinway and others of highest quality (Note: Steinway did not make a tall upright during this period.)	700–1,200	1,200–2,000	2,000–3,000	2,800–5,000	6,000–9,000
Vertical piano, 1970–	Use *Annual Supplement to The Piano Book* and Depreciation Schedule, page 203				
Grand, pre-1940, average brand					
5′	600–1,000	1,000–1,500	1,500–2,500	3,500–4,500	7,000–8,500
6′	800–1,200	1,500–2,000	1,800–2,800	4,500–5,500	8,500–9,500
7′	500–1,500	1,600–2,500	2,000–4,000	5,000–8,000	9,000–12,000
Grand, pre-1940, better brand (i.e., Knabe, Chickering; see list on pages 175–176 for guidance)					
5′	800–2,000	2,000–3,500	2,500–5,500	5,500–9,500	12,000–15,000
6′	1,000–2,200	2,200–4,500	3,500–6,500	6,000–10,000	13,000–16,000
7′	1,500–3,000	3,000–6,500	4,000–8,000	6,500–15,000	14,000–20,000
Grand, pre-1940, Steinway, Mason & Hamlin, and other grands of highest quality					
5′	4,000–6,000	6,000–8,000	8,000–13,000	16,000–21,000	19,000–26,000
6′	4,500–6,500	7,000–10,000	10,000–14,000	18,000–26,000	26,000–35,000
7′	5,000–10,000	8,000–12,000	12,000–18,000	20,000–30,000	30,000–45,000
Grand, 1940–1970, average brand					
5′	700–1,200	1,500–2,500	2,000–5,000	4,000–6,000	6,000–12,000
6′	800–1,800	1,500–3,000	2,500–6,000	4,000–8,000	8,000–13,000
7′	1,000–2,500	2,000–3,500	3,000–7,000	5,000–10,000	10,000–14,000
Grand, 1940–1970, better brand					
5′	1,400–2,300	2,300–3,500	2,800–6,000	5,000–8,500	10,500–14,000
6′	2,000–3,000	2,500–4,000	3,000–7,000	6,500–10,000	12,500–18,000
7′	2,200–5,000	3,000–7,000	4,000–8,500	7,000–15,000	14,000–20,000
Grand, 1940–1970, Steinway, Mason & Hamlin, and other grands of highest quality					
5′	4,000–6,000	6,000–8,000	8,000–14,000	16,000–21,000	19,000–26,000
6′	5,000–8,000	7,000–14,000	12,000–18,000	18,000–26,000	26,000–35,000
7′	7,000–10,000	10,000–16,000	14,000–20,000	20,000–30,000	30,000–45,000
Grand, 1970–	Use *Annual Supplement to The Piano Book* and Depreciation Schedule, page 203				

ADDENDUM: BUYING A USED STEINWAY OR MASON & HAMLIN

It seems everyone today is talking about buying a "vintage" piano, by which is usually meant a Steinway or Mason & Hamlin made between about 1880 and World War II. Sometimes the term is also applied to Baldwin, Knabe, Chickering, and other great American pianos built during the heyday of American piano manufacturing. (Like any popular term, of course, it can also be misused, such as the time I heard it applied to a piano from 1964.) The demand for these pianos—and consequently their prices—has mushroomed over the last five to ten years due to a strong economy, increased entrepreneurial activity on the part of rebuilders and brokers, allegations by rebuilders and others that today's new pianos are not as well made as the older ones were, and the purchase of many older Steinways by Steinway & Sons itself for rebuilding in its factory. The Mason & Hamlin company is back in business building fine pianos, but only at the rate of fewer than two dozen instruments per month, so the supply of that brand is not being adequately replenished.

Just what makes these vintage pianos so alluring? There are a sizable number of musicians and technicians who believe that these pianos, when rebuilt, sound better than new pianos. However, nobody knows for sure why this should be so, since most of the components in the piano are replaced during rebuilding. Some point to the fact that Steinway operated its own plate foundry until about 1930, stockpiling enough plates at the end to last (as it turned out, because of the Depression and World War II) until well into the 1940s. Since then, Steinway plates have been made by an outside commercial foundry, which Steinway recently purchased. Because this radical change in the manufacture of such an important component roughly corresponds with the end of the vintage era, and because the plate is one of the few original parts to survive the rebuilding process, some speculate that it holds the key to the difference. Others say it has to do with changes in the quality of wood available to the company. Still others say it wasn't any one thing, but rather a combination of many fortuitous factors, including extremely skilled and talented craftsmen, that enabled the company to make such special pianos during that period, but allegedly not afterward (though that doesn't explain why the rebuilt ones from that period should be better).

[Steinway & Sons disputes the entire idea that older Steinways are better, and says it is just a romantic notion spread by purveyors of those pianos in their own financial interest. The company says it has done extensive testing of both plates and woods, and the idea that the older plates and woods were better has no scientific basis. It says it has also had the opportunity to carefully inspect hundreds of older Steinways at its factory rebuilding facility, which is the largest Steinway rebuilding facility in the world, and finds no evidence that the older pianos were built better than today's instruments—in fact, it believes just the opposite is true. Steinway acknowledges that some pianists may prefer the sound of specific older pianos for subjective artistic reasons, but says that those considering the purchase of a restored, older instrument should do so to save money, not to seek better quality.]

For Mason & Hamlin, the story and timeline are a little different. Mason & Hamlins were made in Boston until about 1932, and during that period they were considered the equal of Steinways. After the merger of several piano companies at the beginning of the Depression, their manufacture was consolidated in East Rochester, New York with Knabe and Chickering. The East Rochester pianos were considered good instruments, but not quite as good as those from Boston. From the early 1960s to the mid-1980s, new owners cheapened the pianos, especially the actions. See "Mason & Hamlin" in Chapter 4 for more recent history.

I am frequently asked whether it is preferable to buy a new Steinway or Mason & Hamlin, or a used one. Or, put another way, whether a fully rebuilt instrument is better than a new one. These questions are important because a rebuilt Steinway or Mason & Hamlin usually costs from twenty to forty percent less than a new one, and an older, used instrument in playing condition, but not rebuilt, often sells for half the price of a rebuilt one.

There are no clear answers to these questions. Naturally, technicians who are primarily rebuilders will point you in one direction and those who primarily sell or service new pianos will point you in the other. But technicians who both rebuild old pianos *and* sell or service new ones are torn between the two options, and say that it really depends on the particular new and rebuilt pianos being compared, and on the use the piano will be getting. As I said earlier, a piano considered by one technician to be rebuilt might be considered by another technician to be only reconditioned, and the technical competence of rebuilders varies considerably. So does the condition of new pianos.

A rebuilt piano is not the exact equivalent of a new one. Even a fully and competently rebuilt piano will still retain the original case, cast-iron plate, keys, key frame, and action frame, and possibly the soundboard and some of the action parts, too. These original parts will probably not give any trouble for the next twenty or thirty years if the piano was properly rebuilt and is well maintained, but it's hard to say for sure, especially about the soundboard and action parts, if not replaced, and about the keys, which may get brittle.

If you're considering the purchase of a Steinway or Mason & Hamlin grand for professional or institutional use, and an older piano to which a new one is being compared was manufactured before about 1900, my sense is that the age of the older piano and the heavy use it will be getting would tip the balance in favor of buying the new one. But if you're buying a piano for casual use in the home, or the older piano is of more recent vintage, the purchase of a used or rebuilt instrument would be a very reasonable way to save money, and, if you buy wisely, it's unlikely you would ever regret having made the purchase.

There are several issues that frequently arise with respect to used and rebuilt pianos and, in particular, to Steinways and Mason & Hamlins. These are: whether to replace the soundboard, pinblock, and action parts; what replacement action parts and hammers to use; the question of rebuilders who make radical design changes to the pianos; and with Steinways, the issues of Teflon bushings and verdigris. See also pages 180–182 for general information on piano restoration, and pages 202–205 for price and depreciation information.

Soundboard. One of the principal decisions a rebuilder must make is whether to replace the soundboard. Through repeated seasonal expansion and contraction, soundboards eventually dry out, shrink, crack, and lose their crown. Crown, as you may recall from page 192, is the slight arching of the soundboard necessary for good sound transmission. Soundboards subjected to constant seasonal humidity changes may deteriorate in a matter of a few decades, whereas those in areas of more stable humidity sometimes last a lifetime. Some rebuilders, feeling that it's no longer possible to obtain wood of the same high quality, will do just about anything to save the old soundboard, including shimming the cracks, reattaching loose ribs, and attempting to restore the crown. (Until fairly recent times, the knowledge and equipment needed to replace a piano soundboard were virtually nonexistent outside the factory, and many rebuilders still do not have the facilities to do this job in-house. This may also explain some of the conservatism about replacing soundboards.) Others, not wanting to have to rebuild the piano again if the old soundboard should fail within a short time, nearly always install a new soundboard. They also claim that pianos with new soundboards generally sound better. Although I know excellent rebuilders on each side of this argument, personally, I usually prefer the sound of rebuilt pianos with new soundboards, and would generally

advise taking that route if the piano is more than fifty years old.

Pinblock. Old Steinway pinblocks were amazingly well made, and some rebuilders like to keep the old one when they don't think it possible to replace it with a better one. When the old pinblock is in good condition, the tuning pins can be replaced with oversized ones at least once, and sometimes twice, before the pinblock must be replaced. As with the soundboard issue, other rebuilders prefer to replace everything, lest they be caught by surprise a few years down the line and have to rebuild the piano again. For reconditioning or partial rebuilding, using the old pinblock is fine; to qualify as a complete rebuilding, in my opinion, the pinblock should be replaced.

Action Parts. As with soundboards and pinblocks, some technicians routinely replace action parts and some overhaul the old ones. Overhauling old action parts is extremely labor intensive and usually cannot be justified today either on grounds of cost or quality. The practice probably stems from a time when quality replacement action parts were simply not available, which is no longer the case for Steinways and Mason & Hamlins.

If the action parts are to be replaced in rebuilding a Steinway, whose parts do we use—Steinway's or those of third-party suppliers? Steinway advertising suggests that it's not a "genuine" Steinway piano unless all the parts are genuine Steinway parts. But what is a "genuine" Steinway part—one purchased from Steinway, or one that enables the piano to play as it did originally?

The reason I ask these questions is that Steinway has experimented with many different action specifications over the years. Such dimensions as the size of the knuckle, its distance from the center pin, the angle and position of the capstan screw, and the weight of hammers and shanks have all varied. Variations can even be found between pianos with adjacent serial numbers because some things have traditionally been left to the judgment of the action installer. (There was also an intense period of experimentation, change, and some just plain faulty action making from about 1960 to 1990, but that's a subject for another story.* See also "Teflon bushings," below.) To accommodate all these variations, rebuilders need a variety of parts with different specifications so they can experiment and find

---

*For a thorough explanation of these changes and the problem of Steinway replacement parts, see "Replacing Steinway Parts," by Robert Cloutier (*Piano & Keyboard*, Jan./Feb. 2000). See the end of Chapter 7 for magazine contact information.

the combination that works best for a specific piano. Only for the last five to ten years has such a choice been available. Even overhauling and using the old parts is no panacea, for today's hammers are heavier than those of a century ago, requiring parts with greater leverage if the action is not to feel too heavy. For decades, rebuilders have struggled with this situation of varying specifications and heavy hammers, with the less capable among them helplessly turning out pianos that didn't play correctly.

Steinway now makes several different sets of replacement parts for rebuilders, which the company feels should accommodate just about every situation. Some of these parts are made in Steinway's New York factory and some are made to its specifications by Renner, the German action maker that supplies parts for Steinway's branch factory in Hamburg, Germany, as well as for most other makers of fine pianos. Some rebuilders use these Steinway replacement parts successfully, even exclusively. Many others, though, find that the parts from Steinway do not solve their problems and have turned to Renner's U.S. distributor and other third-party suppliers for parts made specifically for older Steinways. These parts are being used very successfully by many of the top rebuilders in the country.

Returning to my original question—what makes a Steinway part "genuine"—my feeling is that if a part is faithful to the original intentions of the manufacturer, that is, if it enables the piano to sound and feel as originally intended, then the part should be considered "genuine" for all intents and purposes whether or not purchased from Steinway. I have never known a Steinway piano to lose value as a result of the use of quality parts purchased from third-party suppliers, provided that the result was correct. (I realize there are times when it is appropriate to preserve and restore the original parts for the historical record, such as when restoring some antique pianos and museum pieces. The discussion above is not meant to apply to those situations.)

Hammers. Hammers from several different makers are commonly used when rebuilding Steinways, including from Steinway itself, from Renner, and from Abel, another German hammer maker, among others. Steinway hammers typically come from the factory very soft and must be extensively shaped and hardened with chemicals. Hammers from the other makers generally do not require the use of chemical hardeners, and are voiced using other techniques. Although the Steinway hammers require more work, some feel that ultimately they come closest to producing the fabled "Steinway sound." Typically, a rebuilder becomes

adept at working with a particular brand of hammer and therefore favors it, but excellent results can be had from any of these brands.

Design Changes. A few rebuilders make changes—sometimes radical ones—to the scale design of Steinway pianos, changes they claim will improve the sound of the piano. Steinway designs are classic. Any piano can be improved, but the number of real design improvements possible on a piano like a Steinway is probably quite small. Of course, each such claim would have to be evaluated on its own merits. Whatever the merits, however, such design changes should be disclosed to the customer and, where the piano belongs to the customer, the customer's permission obtained. Customers should be told that changes that would be obvious to another buyer or their technician might impair the value of the piano.

Teflon bushings. All moving piano action parts pivot on small metal pins, called **center pins**, that rotate in tiny holes in the wooden parts. Traditionally, these holes have always been lined, or *bushed*, with wool cloth. These cloth **flange bushings** (flanges are the hinges to which action parts are attached) are amazingly durable and resilient, and it is not unusual for a hundred-year-old piano to have flange bushings that are almost as good as new. The only problem with them is that, like the wood around them, they respond to humidity changes, swelling up in damp weather and shrinking in dry weather, causing the attached moving parts to become alternately sluggish or loose.

To minimize the servicing that its pianos needed from one season or climate to another, Steinway in 1962 introduced its "Permafree" action, in which all the cloth bushings were replaced with Teflon bushings. Teflon, created by DuPont, is a very slippery inert plastic, immune to temperature and humidity changes. The bushings were tiny, hollow cylinders of Teflon; the center pins would rotate in these instead of in cloth (Figure 5-33). Switching to Teflon bushings involved changing more than just the bushings themselves, though. To accommodate the new bushings required manufacturing the wooden parts differently, making a new kind of center pin, supplying new tools and supplies, and teaching new techniques to technicians who had to service these actions.

Several unforeseen problems with these bushings eventually caused their downfall. First, although they themselves did not respond to humidity changes, the wood around them continued to expand and contract with the seasons. This had the unexpected effect of causing some of the bushings to become loose in their

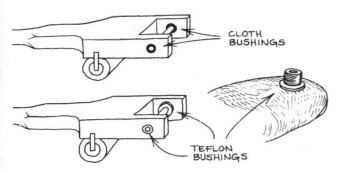

FIGURE 5-33. A cloth-bushed and a Teflon-bushed grand hammer shank with center pin inserted. The flanges that the center pins attach to the shanks are not shown (see Figure 4-5). A Teflon bushing is shown actual size on a finger.

wooden parts during the humid season (the opposite of what one might guess), resulting in a clicking sound whenever those particular notes were played. The remedy was to replace the offending bushings—not particularly difficult, but with approximately a thousand bushings in a piano action, there were plenty of potential trouble spots. The wood could also squeeze the bushings in the dry season, causing the action parts to become sluggish, which completely defeated the purpose of the Teflon bushing. A second problem—annoying but not as serious—was that Teflon, unlike cloth, was an "unforgiving" material: when dented it did not bounce back, but remained dented. This meant that the slightest mishandling of an action part might cause the center pin to dent and ruin a bushing. The technical problems of Teflon bushings were magnified by bad press and the conservatism of piano technicians, and Steinway finally gave up and began a return to cloth bushings in 1981.

If you are buying a used Steinway made between 1962 and 1981, you may not need to be as concerned with the presence of the Teflon bushings as the previous discussion might suggest, especially if your piano will be receiving only average use in the home. According to technicians with extensive experience servicing these pianos, there are usually few problems with these bushings after those that give trouble during the first few seasons are replaced. But the bushings (or, rather, the wooden action parts into which the bushings are inserted) are very sensitive to humidity changes, and the technician, when servicing these bushings, must be very careful to take into account the humidity conditions at the time of servicing. Because

of the bushings' sensitivity, and the fussy service they require, pianos under heavy use or in adverse conditions, such as in some schools and concert halls, will probably benefit by changing to cloth-bushed action parts. Also, if a piano with Teflon bushings is in the shop for rebuilding, it would make sense to rebuild the action with cloth-bushed parts. Note that it is not possible to replace the Teflon bushings with cloth bushings without replacing all the action parts as well.

Verdigris (*pronounced VER-di-gree*). Verdigris is a green-colored substance produced by a chemical reaction between the metal center pins and chemicals in the bushing cloth or in lubricants applied to the cloth. The effect of this green "gunk" is to make the action parts move sluggishly or, in the worst cases, to prevent their movement altogether. Although certainly not unique to Steinways, the verdigris problem is frequently found in Steinways from the 1920s and to a lesser extent in pianos made during the several decades before and after that period. If you encounter an older Steinway with an extremely heavy touch or one in which the keys and hammers appear not to return to their rest position quickly, there is a good chance the piano has a verdigris problem.

Technicians have attempted many solutions to this problem, using chemical, mechanical, heat, and electrical methods, and some of these methods appear to provide at least temporary relief when the problem is not severe. But because verdigris may penetrate the wood as well as the cloth, the only really permanent solution, especially in severe cases, seems to be replacement of all the action parts affected. This makes verdigris an expensive problem to correct, so be aware of it when inspecting a used Steinway prior to purchase. (Note: A chemical treatment called Protek appears to be effective in solving the verdigris problem in many, though not all, cases.)

Rebuilding Quality. From the craftsperson's point of view, it's sad to see a piano like a Steinway or Mason & Hamlin poorly rebuilt. The owner has too much invested in it to rebuild it again, so the opportunity for producing a fine work of art is permanently lost. Don't make the mistake of thinking that a rebuilding job is a rebuilding job, regardless of who does it. Rebuilding involves many different skills, including skills and knowledge that are particular to each brand, and takes the better part of a lifetime to perfect. Get recommendations from people you trust and ask to see examples of the rebuilder's finished work, preferably in the homes of satisfied customers.

List of Steinway Models

As an aid to those buying a used Steinway, I have listed below all models of Steinway pianos made in New York City since the firm's inception in 1853.* Since this list has never before been published, I have, for the record, given a much more complete list than most piano buyers will ever need. Hopefully, piano technicians and historians will also find the list useful. (Square pianos and other pianos made before about 1880 are listed for academic purposes only; see pages 173–174 for information on buying square and antique pianos.)

Note that entries in the list refer to models in regular stock manufacture only, as they appeared in catalogs and price lists. There are no listings here of the different furniture styles available in each model, or of custom cases or experimental variations that were made from time to time. During the formative years of Steinway & Sons, an immense amount of experimentation and development was in progress. Hence, some details are elusive, especially concerning pianos built during the first twenty-five years of manufacture. This list is based on the best available information to date, but should not be considered infallible.

The keyboard compass (range) began at seven octaves (eighty-five notes, AAA to a'''', unless otherwise indicated) and was gradually expanded to seven and a quarter octaves (eighty-eight notes, AAA to c'''''). Because most of the dates listed here are from catalogs, whereas the serial numbers are from production records, dates and serial numbers may not match each other exactly, and dates may differ by a year or more from other versions of this list in circulation. Also, a given model may have been manufactured or sold in limited quantities after the time it was officially discontinued.

Steinway & Sons piano manufacture officially began on March 5, 1853, but the first illustrated catalog did not appear until 1865. Until 1859 piano styles were identified by name (plain, fancy, double round, middle round, prime, and so on). In that year Steinway began to assign style numbers to some of their pianos and by 1866 each piano was designated in this way. These early style numbers, however, referred to both differences in scale design and differences in furniture styling. Furthermore, the style to which each number referred changed from year to year, and so the numbers cannot be relied upon for identification. An 1878 catalog lists pianos by style *letter* as well as style number for the first time, and letters and numbers appeared together in the catalogs through 1896, after which letters were used exclusively. During the nineteenth century some letters, like the numbers, were used to designate more than one scale design or style, but in the twentieth century a given letter has been applied to only one scale design regardless of the case styling. In 1932 the term *style* was replaced by *model* in price lists and catalogs. In the list below, to avoid confusion, only the word *model* is used and, as I said, furniture style variations are omitted.

---

*I gratefully acknowledge Mr. Roy Kehl, piano technician, of Evanston, Illinois for generously sharing with me the results of his research into the history of Steinway scale designs, from which this list was largely developed.

Steinway (New York) Models—1853 to Present

	Compass	Size	Dates	Serial No.
SQUARE PIANOS				
Early scales				
[20-note bass]	7 (CC to c'''')	6'6¾"	1853–1856	(First) 483
[19-note bass]	6¾ (CC to g'''')	6'5"	1854–1856	(First) 499
[15-note bass]	6⅓ (FF to a'''')	6'1⅛"	1854–1860	(First) 587
[19-note bass]	6¾ (CC to a'''')	6'6"	1855–1865	(First) 687
Bichord treble scale	7	6'8"	1856–1881	
[21-note bass]	7¼	6'8½"	c. 1856–1874	
	7¼	6'8"	1881–1886	
Trichord treble scale: Square Grand [23-note bass]	7¼	6'11½"	1857–1889	(Last) 62,872
GRAND PIANOS				
Model D Concert Grand	7 (straight-strung)	c. 8'3"	1856–1864	(First) 791
(and ancestors)	7 (overstrung)	8'4"	1858–1865	(First) 2,522
	7¼	8'5"	1863–1878	(First) 7,894
	7¼ (Centennial D)	8'9"	1875–1883	(First) 33,449

The model D pianos above have a 17-note bass section; those below have a 20-note bass section.

	Compass	Size	Dates	Serial No.
	7¼	8'10"	1884–1914	
	7¼	8'11¼"	1914–1965	
	7¼	8'11¾"	1965–	

	Compass	Size	Dates	Serial No.
Model C Parlor Concert Grand (and ancestors)	7 (straight-strung)	7'2"	1859–1862	(First) 2,485
	7 (overstrung)	7'1"	1862–1869	(First) 5,127
	7	7'2"	1869–1884	
	7	7'3½"	1884–1886	

The model C pianos above have a 21-note bass section;
that below has a 20-note bass section.

	Compass	Size	Dates	Serial No.
	7¼	7'5"	1886–1936	(First) 58,952
				(Last) 285,748

Model C was listed in the catalog and price list through 1905 and said to be discontinued in 1913, but was made and sold on special order as late as 1936 in New York. This model is still made in Steinway's factory in Hamburg, Germany.

Model B Music-Room Grand (and ancestors) [20-note bass]	7	6'8"	1872–1884	(First) 25,006
	7	6'10½"	1884–1892	(Last) 75,473
	7¼	6'10½"	1891–1914	(First) 73,212
	7¼	6'11½"	1914–1917	
	7¼	6'11"	1917–1967	
	7¼	6'10½"	1967–	

Model A Drawing-Room Grand [20-note bass]	7 (Model A I)	6'	1878–1893	(First) 38,726
	7¼ (Model A I)	6'	1892–1897	(First) 74,766

The model A pianos listed above have 57 wound strings, including two two-string unisons and seven three-string unisons strung over a return bridge in the low tenor. The pianos listed below have 42 wound strings, including five two-string unisons in the tenor on the long bridge. The pianos above have round tails, those below have square tails. The squared-off tail allows for more soundboard vibrating area near the bass bridge. The piano listed below as 6'1", officially given in catalogs as 6', usually measures between 6'1" and 6'2". This is the model A currently made at Steinway's factory in Hamburg, Germany as 6'2". The versions of model A below are considered to be of a superior scale design to those listed above.

	7¼ (Model A II)	6'1"	1896–1914	(First) 85,985
	7¼ (Model A III)	6'4½"	1913–1945	(First) 161,865
				(Last) 321,289

Model O and Model L Living-Room Grand [26-note bass]	7¼	5'10" (O)	1900–1924	(First) 96,766
				(Last) 227,471

Some early pianos have two-string wound unisons on the two lowest tenor notes; later ones have all steel wire three-string unisons in the tenor. Early pianos have a straight bass bridge; later ones, above number 110,000, have a curved bass bridge.

The model O, above, has a round tail. The model L, below, has a square tail. The squared-off tail allows for more soundboard vibrating area near the bass bridge. This is the only difference between the model O and model L. The model O is still made in Steinway's factory in Hamburg, Germany.

	7¼	5'10½" (L)	1923–	(First) 217,995

Model M Medium Grand [26-note bass]	7¼	5'6"	1911–1914	(First) 149,500
	7¼	5'6¾"	1914–1917	
	7¼	5'7"	1917–	

Model S Baby Grand [26-note bass]	7¼	5'1"	1935–	(First) 280,900

UPRIGHT PIANOS—NINETEENTH CENTURY

Small scales:

Model E, EE (and ancestors)	7	45"	1865–1866	
[26-note bass]	7	48"	1866–1872	
	7	46"	1872–1884	
	7	48"	1884–1890	
	7	50"	1890–1892	
	7¼ (Model E)	50"	1891–1899	(First) 73,333
	7¼ (Model EE)	50"	1897–1900	(First) 87,401

Medium scales:

Model F (and ancestors and successors)	7	52½"	1862–1866	(First) 5,451
	7	52"	1866–1874	
[26-note bass except for	7	52¼"	1878–1882	
7-octave F (24 notes, 1878–1881)]	7	53¾"	1880–1882	
	7¼	53¾"	1881–1884	
	7¼	53½"	1884–1908	

Other letter-named case variations on medium scales include N, O, L, R, T, X, H, R (again), S, and FF.

Large scales:

Model G (and ancestors and successors	7¼	56"	1872–1884	
	7¼	56¾"	1884–1902	
[20-note bass (1872–1884)]				
[26-note bass (1884–1902)]				

Other letter-named case variations on large scales include M, P, Q, S, K, T, and O.

UPRIGHT PIANOS—TWENTIETH CENTURY

Model I	7¼	54¼"	1898–1914	(First) 91,702
[26-note bass]	7¼	54"	1914–1923	(Last) 216,280
Model N	7¼	52"	1900–1907	(First) 95,105
[26-note bass]	7¼	53"	1907–1917	(Last) 183,939
Models K and K-52	7¼	52"	1903–1914	(First) 107,181
[26-note bass]	7¼	51½"	1914–1930	(Last) 269,581
	7¼	52" (K-52)	1981–	(First) 472,970
Model V	7¼	49"	1913–1933	(First) 163,340
[26-note bass]				(Last) 279,249

Earliest examples of model V have 52 wound strings, the highest ten strung over a return bridge in the low tenor. Later ones have 46 wound strings, the highest four on the long bridge. Model V is currently made in Steinway's factory in Hamburg, Germany.

STUDIO AND CONSOLE PIANOS (1938 TO THE PRESENT)

Studio pianos:

Models P and 45	7¼	45½" (P)	1938–1962	(First) 291,575
[26-note bass]	7¼	46½" (45, Sk. 1098)	1950–	(First) 338,018
	7¼	45" (45, Sk. 45-10)	1958–	(First) 358,233

Console pianos:

Models 40, 100, and F				
[32-note bass (40)]	7¼	40" (40)	1939–1953	(First) 297,092
[32-note bass (100)]	7¼	40" (100)	1953–1971	
[28-note bass (F)]	7¼	40" (F)	1967–1989	(Last) 503,556

REPRODUCING (PLAYER) PIANOS

Steinway made grands and uprights with extended cases for the Aeolian Co., who installed the Duo-Art reproducing mechanism. (In Hamburg, reproducing mechanisms were installed by both Aeolian and Welte.) The suffix "Y" was used instead of "R" on those pianos (1930–1931) made with normal-size cases for the Concertola (remote control with player mechanisms in separate cabinet). As a consequence of the Great Depression, some of these latter were sold without installation of player components and were identified as YM, YL, and YA.

Model XR and XY	6′1¾″ or 6′2″	1914–1931

The model XR used the model M scale.

Model OR and OY	6′5″	1910–1931

The model OR used the model O and, later, model L scales.

Model AR and AY	6′8½″	1911–1917
	6′11¼″ or 6′11½″	1918–1931

The first model AR listed above used the model AII scale; the second used the model AIII scale.

Model B	6′11″

One piano on special order (1931). Likely normal-size case for Concertola.

Model D	9′5¾″

The model D used the model D scale.
Ten of these were made on special order (1920–1923, 1925, 1930).

Model I	55¼″	1909–1914
Model K	53″	1909–1916
Model V (K scale)	53″	1914 1929

Steinway Pianos—Dates and Serial Numbers

Researchers studying the historical Steinway serial number books have found them to be a nest of inconsistencies. First, with the exception of the years 1898–1903 and 1916–1931, pianos were not always shipped in the order in which they were manufactured. Second, the point in the manufacturing process at which the serial numbers are assigned has changed over the years. Research suggests that, at times, serial numbers may even have been assigned at the time of shipping, rather than at the time of manufacture. For these reasons, pianos with consecutive serial numbers may differ by as much as two years in the time they were made. When combined with the fact that it takes months to build a Steinway, it becomes almost impossible to say precisely when any particular Steinway was "manufactured."

The table of dates and serial numbers supplied by Steinway & Sons, although certainly adequate for most purposes, is very approximate and does not deal with issues of manufacturing vs. shipping, nor does it specify whether the serial numbers are those from the beginning of the year or the end of the year given (in fact, it varies).

The following table, developed by researcher Joel Honig of New York City, is more specific. The dates represent approximate beginning-of-year shipments to the dealers or, in some of the earliest years, directly to the customers. (Accuracy is uncertain for years since 1990.)

483	1853	37,000	1878	105,500	1903	253,620	1928	340,460	1953	455,300	1978
500	1854	38,700	1879	108,300	1904	261,260	1929	343,200	1954	460,400	1979
570	1855	41,000	1880	112,900	1905	268,300	1930	346,340	1955	465,700	1980
690	1856	44,000	1881	118,300	1906	271,500	1931	349,560	1956	470,900	1981
920	1857	46,000	1882	123,600	1907	273,850	1932	353,600	1957	476,300	1982
1,300	1858	48,000	1883	129,300	1908	275,100	1933	357,600	1958	480,800	1983
2,000	1859	50,500	1884	133,800	1909	277,700	1934	360,490	1959	485,900	1984
2,850	1860	54,000	1885	139,100	1910	279,020	1935	364,700	1960	490,700	1985
4,160	1861	56,600	1886	144,300	1911	280,900	1936	368,900	1961	495,100	1986
5,000	1862	58,400	1887	150,200	1912	286,140	1937	373,180	1962	498,920	1987
6,200	1863	61,000	1888	157,000	1913	290,530	1938	376,900	1963	503,600	1988
8,000	1864	64,000	1889	164,600	1914	294,120	1939	382,600	1964	508,500	1989
9,500	1865	66,000	1890	168,000	1915	300,000	1940	387,860	1965	512,500	1990
11,000	1866	70,000	1891	173,600	1916	305,430	1941	392,700	1966	516,700	1991
13,100	1867	73,000	1892	180,860	1917	312,170	1942	398,500	1967	520,500	1992
15,000	1868	75,000	1893	186,600	1918	314,480	1943	403,450	1968	524,200	1993
17,000	1869	78,600	1894	191,450	1919	315,400	1944	409,400	1969	528,500	1994
19,300	1870	81,600	1895	196,260	1920	317,000	1945	414,100	1970	530,000	1995
21,000	1871	84,000	1896	203,000	1921	318,570	1946	418,600	1971	533,300	1996
24,000	1872	86,500	1897	207,870	1922	320,480	1947	424,080	1972	536,500	1997
26,300	1873	88,700	1898	214,000	1923	324,000	1948	429,500	1973	541,000	1998
28,000	1874	92,540	1899	221,370	1924	327,830	1949	434,450	1974	546,000	1999
30,600	1875	94,970	1900	228,800	1925	330,450	1950	439,650	1975	549,600	2000
33,000	1876	98,160	1901	236,740	1926	333,540	1951	445,300	1976		
35,000	1877	101,700	1902	246,120	1927	336,800	1952	450,300	1977		

CHAPTER SIX
Piano Moving and Storage

Why *Not* to Move a Piano Yourself

Movers like to tell stories like this one:

> A young woman asked her father to help her move a
> piano from one place to another in her house. Her father
> got a couple of his friends to come along and they
> brought a dolly. While they were lifting the piano—a full-
> size vertical—it tipped back too far and got away from
> them. While it was falling, its upper corner dug down
> through the wall. The trench it made was deep enough to
> sever an electric conduit, which shorted and began to
> burn. The "movers" were unable to stop the fire, which
> also spread to the floor below, another person's apart-
> ment. After the fire department was done, there was little
> left of the two apartments and the piano.

Obviously, this is an extreme example of the damage that can be inflicted when moving a piano in do-it-
yourself fashion. But even if you don't burn down
your house, there is a substantial risk of personal injury, not to mention damage to the piano.

Pianos are very heavy. The average spinet or console weighs in at from three hundred to five hundred
pounds, full-size uprights at about seven hundred, but
sometimes as much as a thousand. Grands vary from
about five hundred to a thousand pounds, though a
concert grand may weigh close to a ton. If it were simply a matter of weight, though, all it would take would
be enough strong people to do the job. Unfortunately,
along with the weight come problems of balance and
inertia, knowledge of which can make all the difference in doing a moving job safely and efficiently.

Piano moving may conjure up images of men with
monstrous arms and huge torsos, but actually two or
three people of average build can do most piano moving jobs—even grands—if they have some brains, experience, the right equipment, and a knowledge of just
when and where to apply a little force.

How Pianos Are Moved

Anyone with even a little bit of curiosity inevitably
wonders how pianos get moved. How do you fit a
grand piano through a door? How do you get a piano
up to the fifth floor?

Unless the piano is very small and light, it is almost
always placed on a special skid called a piano board.
The piano is covered with blankets and strapped to
the board. If the piano is to be moved over a level surface for any distance, the piano board is put on a
dolly—a small platform on wheels—and rolled to its
destination, such as a truck or a stairway. At the stairway, the dolly is removed and the piano board is slid
in a very slow and controlled manner up or down the
stairs.

As shown in Figure 6-1, a grand piano is moved on
its side, straight side down. First the lid and the pedal
lyre are removed. Then the leg at the straight side of
the piano is removed and the piano is carefully lowered down to the piano board. (Some movers unscrew
and remove the lid hinges because they overhang the
case side and would otherwise cause damage to the
case when the piano is put on its side. Others prefer to

214

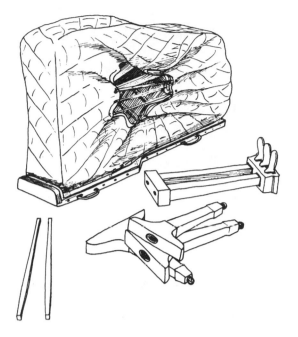

FIGURE 6-1. Grand pianos are moved on their side, with legs and lyre removed.

position the piano so the hinges overhang the edge of the piano board.) After the remaining two legs are removed, the piano is covered with blankets and strapped to the board. Stripped down in this manner, a grand piano is quite thin and will actually fit through a door or other opening very easily.

When a piano must be moved to or from a floor other than the first, many movers prefer to hoist or rig it (Figure 6-2) rather than move it up or down stairs. Believe it or not, moving a piano by stairs is actually more dangerous, both to the piano and to the movers, than hoisting it through an upper-story window with a crane. Most movers will consent to moving by stairs when only one flight is involved, or when no other alternative is possible. Of course, if the building has a freight elevator that can support the piano, that method is preferred over all others.

Basically, it is the customer's responsibility to make sure the piano will fit in its new location. This means not expecting a piano to be hoisted in a window that's too small or carried down a stairway with too low an

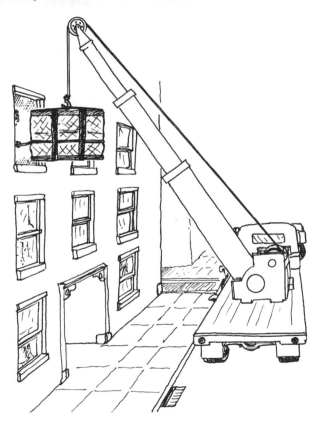

HOISTING

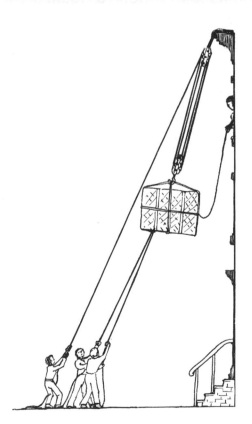

RIGGING

FIGURE 6-2. Hoisting is done with a crane. When the house is set too far back from a road or driveway or for some other reason the window isn't accessible to a crane, the piano can be rigged. Rigging involves using a block and tackle, supported from the window above or from the roof, to lift the piano.

overhang or moved around a corner that's too tight. Figure 6-3 shows how the dimensions of the piano relate to some common moving situations. Corners are the hardest to judge because they can't be easily measured. An experienced mover can usually judge these situations pretty accurately by eye and may prefer to visit the moving sites prior to moving day if there is any question about the difficulty of the job. This probably won't be possible if the move is a long-distance one. If the piano won't fit in its intended location, the customer will have to pay for its delivery back to its point of departure, to an alternate destination, or to storage.

Note that some movers like to "keyboard" a vertical piano—that is, remove the front part (keybed, keys, action)—to get the piano around a tight corner when there is no other alternative. You should know that this is not recommended, as it can sometimes result in permanent damage to the piano and make it difficult or impossible to get the piano working properly again.

Moving a Piano Around a Room

It's understandable that you might not want to hire a mover just to move a piano around a room, but these small moves can be surprisingly dangerous. With both grands and verticals, it's primarily the legs you want to watch out for. Breaking a leg on a vertical may just be an inconvenience, but on a grand it can be disastrous. I was once called twice in a single month to repair a grand piano that had been dragged across a floor. Both times a leg had gotten caught in the grate of a heating duct, causing the piano to crash to the floor. Of course, the pedal lyre broke too. Dragging a grand piano across carpeting can also be too much for the legs to handle. If you insist on moving the grand yourself, three to five strong people should gather around its circumference and lift while moving. Don't actually try to lift it off the floor; just relieve the strain on the legs.

At least two people should always move a vertical piano. Spinets and consoles with free-standing legs should have their legs protected by lifting or tilting the piano back ever so slightly while moving. But remember that most of the weight of the piano is in its back, so be sure you have a firm grip on it and don't tilt so far that the piano is in danger of falling over. Larger verticals and smaller ones without legs can simply be rolled, although this may be hard to do on carpeting. Piano casters can sometimes get stuck unexpectedly, so move slowly with one person on each end of the piano. When making turns, keep the back of the piano on the *inside* of the turn. And be careful not to push a stubborn vertical piano over your helper's foot!

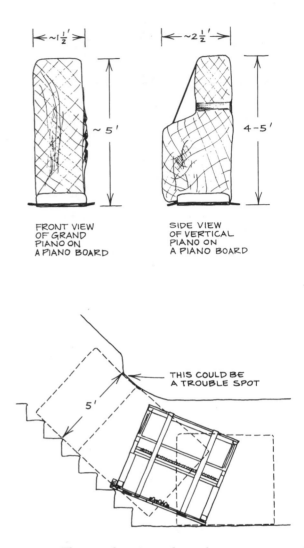

FIGURE 6-3. The top drawings show the approximate dimensions of pianos on skids, which you might want to know if moving a piano through a window or a door. These dimensions vary by a few inches from piano to piano. Note that a grand piano on a skid is almost always very close to 60 inches tall, regardless of the length of the piano (remember, this is the keyboard end of the piano standing up). A standard-size window is also about 60 inches tall, so you will have to measure carefully here to avoid disappointment. Movers routinely remove window sashes, window frames, storm window frames, and just about anything else they have to get a piano through a window. However, pianos will not usually fit through garret or attic windows or windows with sashes that can't be removed. The bottom drawing shows a problem that can occur when moving a piano up or down a stairway. The important measurement is the *minimum* clearance between the edge of the steps and the ceiling, measured *perpendicular to the plane of the stairs*. The fact that people can walk down the stairs without hitting their head does not necessarily mean the piano will fit, because people do not walk perpendicular to the plane of the stairs! Grands and large verticals will not fit down cellar bulkhead stairways, except, sometimes, when the bulkhead stairs themselves are removable.

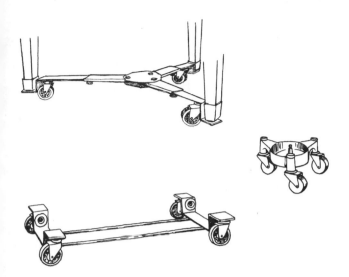

FIGURE 6-4. Grand pianos that are going to be moved around a lot can be mounted on a truck or carriage like the one shown at top. These are a bit ugly, though classier ones than that shown are available. The three-wheeled caster at right is less obtrusive. One of these casters under each grand piano leg will support the piano quite well. The truck shown at bottom is for vertical pianos.

Casters and trucks. If you're going to be moving a piano around a room or stage, or from room to room, often, be sure the piano is properly equipped. Grand pianos should be mounted on a piano truck or fitted with special casters. Small verticals are best not moved around much, but there are special piano trucks for them, too. (See Figure 6-4.) Larger verticals often come with heavy-duty casters, but casters that are too small or old cast-iron casters can be replaced by your piano technician with double rubber-wheel ones that move easily and don't mar the floor. (Note: These replacement casters may sometimes lift your piano an inch further off the floor, making the pedals hard to reach. A piece of thick carpeting or wood placed in front of the pedals for the heel of your foot to rest on will remedy this problem.)

Hiring a Piano Mover for a Local Move

Finding a piano mover. As with most other services, the best way to find a piano mover is by word-of-mouth referral from another piano owner or from your piano technician. A piano dealer can also recommend a mover. Some movers move pianos only, some move all kinds of household goods but specialize in piano moving, and some otherwise competent general movers don't know the first thing about piano moving. Since piano moving requires some specialized knowledge and equipment to do properly, always have the piano moved by a specialist.

Licensing and insurance. Most states require that anyone offering to move household goods for hire be licensed by the state department of public utilities or similar state regulatory agency. To get a license in those states that require one, a moving company must show that there is a need for its services, that it has the proper equipment, and that it has at least the minimum amount of cargo insurance required by state law. In addition, the mover's rates must be approved by the regulatory agency. We've all seen ads of the "two men and a truck—$40/hr." variety, but in regulated states these ads are illegal unless the firm is licensed, and newspapers are not supposed to carry ads for unlicensed firms. Ads for licensed firms will usually be accompanied by their license number. Since the deregulation of the interstate trucking industry in 1980, there has been an increasing tendency on the part of the states to deregulate, too. You should therefore check with your state regulatory agency about the current status of moving regulation in your state.

Most regulated states require that movers carry around five or ten thousand dollars worth of cargo insurance, the amount varying from state to state. But this is simply an upper limit or aggregate amount. It does *not* mean that each item moved is insured for that much. A careful reading of the moving contract will reveal that your piano (for instance) is insured for only so much per pound, the amount again varying from state to state, but usually somewhere between fifty cents and one dollar. This may be fine for your funky old upright, which is very heavy but not worth much, but won't help much if your expensive Baldwin grand is dropped from a third-story window.

To protect yourself against the latter kind of loss, you can buy extra insurance either from your insurance company or from the mover. The cost can run from as little as five cents to more than a dollar per $100 of declared value, depending on whether the piano is insured for replacement value minus depreciation or full replacement value with no deduction for depreciation, and on what deductible is chosen, if any. In some cases, your homeowner's insurance may provide the coverage you need. Even if your instrument is insured for less than its full value, you still may be able to sue the mover for the unreimbursed part of the damage.

Some states may not require it, but you should also be sure that your mover carries personal liability and worker's compensation insurance. The former will protect you in case, for instance, your walls are damaged. Without the latter you may be responsible for hospital bills if a mover is hurt on your property. Don't just accept the mover's word that he's "fully insured;" ask to see his insurance certificate.

Prices. Some movers charge by the job. Others charge by time and mileage and are willing to give only a rough estimate of the total charge, if that. At least you should assume it's an estimate unless otherwise told. It's definitely worth getting several estimates for a piano moving job because prices often vary enormously, even among equally reputable movers in the same locality. However, be sure you are dealing with a skilled piano mover; the lowest estimate is not necessarily the best choice. Also, when comparing estimates, be sure you factor in insurance charges, as some movers include generous insurance coverage in their base price, whereas others include only the state-mandated coverage and charge extra for additional coverage.

The price of a moving job will depend on the type and size of piano and the complexity of the job, because the larger pianos and more complex jobs require more workers. A first-floor-to-first-floor move of a small vertical or small grand usually requires only two people. Moving a full-size vertical or a smaller grand piano up or down stairs requires three, and moving a large grand may require more than three.

Typical prices for first-floor-to-first-floor local moves are as follows: small vertical, $150–300; upright or small grand, $200–350; medium grand, $250–400. Each staircase could add from thirty to seventy-five dollars to the cost. Hoisting and rigging might cost from one to three hundred dollars additional plus, in some jurisdictions, the cost of permits and police detail. These are intended only as approximate figures and obviously don't include unusual situations and complications. (I've heard of hoisting charges over $1,000 in some cities.) Be aware that what to you may seem only "a few steps up" to the front door may be significant to a mover and could result in an extra charge. Also, some movers may have minimum charges.

Damage. Before the piano is moved, both you and the mover should inspect it carefully and note any pre-existing damage, such as scratches, dents, and loose veneer, on the bill of lading. Then, after the piano is moved to its destination, inspect it again and note any new damage on the bill of lading. Most damage to pianos in local moves is quite small and is repaired or touched up by the mover or by a piano technician or refinisher hired by the mover. Only in rare cases, or with some large interstate movers, will you need to file an insurance claim, but if you do, the mover is required to furnish you with the claim forms and process them for you (unless you obtained your insurance coverage independently).

Although damage to pianos from moving certainly does occur, piano owners also tend to imagine or suspect a lot of damage that doesn't exist. One reason is they probably examine their piano far more carefully after a move than at any other time in its life, and so discover scratches and marks that have been there for years unnoticed. This is why it's so important to agree on pre-existing damage before the move. Another reason for the suspicion is simply a lack of knowledge about the technical and maintenance needs of pianos. When I tune a piano after a move, and in the process notice the need for some additional maintenance, I'm invariably asked if the need for the extra work wasn't, after all, caused by the movers and therefore subject to reimbursement by them. In most cases the maintenance was needed before the move, too, but was never mentioned or not noticed by previous technicians. Usually, a piano has to be handled quite roughly for internal damage to occur.

Interstate, Long-Distance, and Household Moves

Interstate movers must be licensed by the Interstate Commerce Commission (ICC) and registered with the Department of Transportation (DOT), regulatory agencies of the U.S. government. As with the regulated states, applicants for an ICC license must have the proper equipment for the job, a minimum of $10,000 worth of cargo insurance, and $750,000 worth of liability insurance.

When you dial the phone number listed for a major van line, you're actually calling its local agent. The agents book the moves and own a fleet of trailers. They hire drivers, called owner-operators, who own tractors to pull those trailers. It's an owner-operator who actually hauls your goods. (Sometimes the agents own the tractors, too, and just hire drivers.) Since the partial deregulation of the trucking industry in 1980, thousands of additional owner-operators have received ICC licenses.

The price of moving a piano alone a long distance is prohibitively expensive. For instance, several movers quoted prices of $1,500 to $2,000 for moving a 1,000-pound piano (such as a large, crated grand) from New York to California. The price is computed from both the weight and the distance, but the higher the weight, the lower the price per pound. This means that a piano moved with a typical 8,000-pound load of household furniture might cost from less than one-third to one-half as much as when moved alone. Also, most long-distance movers have a minimum charge, usually based on a weight of 1,000 pounds, but the minimums could range from 500 to 2,500 pounds. If a piano being moved alone weighs less than the minimum, it will be charged at the rate for the minimum weight. If you live in New York and are considering sending your old upright piano to your child in California, you might be better off selling it locally instead and sending your child the money to buy one in his or her area.

In addition to the rate quoted you for moving your piano long distance—with or without other household goods—there may be other hidden costs that you should inquire about. Because a piano requires special packing, a handling charge is usually added on to the bill. In some cases the moving price includes only the trucking of the piano and not the cost of moving it in and out of the house. This may be so when the long-distance mover is equipped to haul pianos but not to handle them and must hire local piano movers on both ends of the trip. You may be required to pay the piano movers directly, which could add several hundred dollars to the moving cost if you thought all this was included in the bill.

Many people contemplating a major move automatically call a major van line whose name is a household word. But in most localities there are also smaller moving companies, sometimes with many years of experience, that specialize in moves to certain regions of the country. For instance, in Boston there are companies that specialize in moves within the New York-New England area and others that specialize in moves to Florida, where many New Englanders spend the winter. These smaller firms sometimes offer more personal service, more flexible scheduling, and lower prices.

There are now several movers that specialize in cross-country piano moving. They are listed here for your convenience, but the listing should not be considered an endorsement or guarantee of satisfaction. Remember, when using their services, that you need to be flexible about pickup and arrival times. Call as far in advance as possible so the company can coordinate your move with that of others. Expect that the time from pickup to delivery can range from a couple of weeks to a couple of months.

Keyboard Carriage (809 South Park Rd., Elizabethtown, Kentucky 42701; 270-737-5797; contact: Rick Dawson) warehouses and delivers pianos to dealers for most of the piano manufacturers who do business in the U.S. The company has a large fleet of trucks constantly on the move around the country. Space permitting, Keyboard Carriage will also move pianos for consumers at reasonable rates. However, they will only move to and from a dealer or bona fide moving company; they will not move the piano into or out of a home. When using their services, therefore, it will be necessary to arrange for local moving services on both ends of the trip. Keyboard Carriage is a logical choice when buying a piano from a far-off dealer.

Modern Piano Moving (992 Hwy. D, Sullivan, Missouri 63080; 800-737-5600; www.modernpiano.com) has been moving pianos since 1935, cross-country moving since 1985. It has offices in Missouri, California, and Virginia. A company representative estimated normal cross-country moving costs of $450 to $1,000 for a vertical piano and $600 to $1,500 for a grand, depending on size, weight, distance, and difficulty. Their services include not only the cross-country hauling, but also the move into and out of the home or other location. They move only pianos.

Schafer Brothers Piano Movers (1981 E.213th St., P.O. Box 6278, Carson, California 90749; 310-835-7231, 800-222-2888; www.pianomove.com)

If you are moving your household goods long distance yourself in a rented truck, the safest and most economical way to move the piano is to hire local piano movers at both ends to load and unload the piano.

International Moving

Who does it? International moving is one of the services that many regular movers provide. The actual overseas shipping is done by a "freight forwarder," who consolidates the goods from a number of different customers or movers into containers (large metal boxes that are hauled by trucks and ships) and deals with the steamship line. Freight forwarders require a license from the Freight-Maritime Commission to do this. Your mover may or may not be a freight forwarder, but if not, it will have a relationship with one. The mover will pick up your piano and deliver it to them; you don't have to deal directly with the freight forwarder unless you prefer to. The mover or freight forwarder will tell you (or you should ask) what steamship line your goods will take, what port they will leave from, the container number, dates of departure and arrival, and ports of call on the way. Your mover does not need to have an ICC license to provide this service for you unless it will be moving your goods interstate in the process.

Some foreign manufacturers wrap their pianos in airtight plastic when shipping overseas to avoid having the pianos exposed to excess humidity. You should inquire of the mover whether airtight shipment would be possible for your instrument.

Shipping costs. International moving is priced either by weight or by volume. Pianos are heavy and so should be priced by volume. My sources quoted from six hundred to thirteen hundred dollars to move most pianos overseas, depending on the size of the shipment and the destination port. However, crating, pickup, and brokerage charges could double the cost.

Import duties. While the shipping costs described above are considerable, higher still can be the import duties and taxes assessed by the foreign governments once the shipment has arrived. These duties vary from as little as a few percent to as much as 200 percent of the instrument's value. With these duties, governments seek to prevent the import of pianos for resale, presumably to protect their own local piano industry. Some countries have exclusions from duties for professionals in the music field, and some require proof of ownership of six months to two years to avoid duties. A call to any international mover will provide country-specific information on duties.

Insurance. Movers are not required to provide insurance coverage, but generally make it available. Insurance is always on the replacement value at the destination. One price quoted was $6 per $1,000 of value, with a minimum value of $1,000. A special point mentioned by my sources was that the insurance should be an "all-risk marine policy," which includes what is known as a "general average clause." This will insure against any extra costs the shipper might otherwise have to pay if damage is sustained to the ship en route and the cargo is impounded in a port other than one that is scheduled. These extra costs can be huge.

Shipping times. Shipments to Europe and the Middle East are made from the East Coast, and to Australia and the Far East from the West Coast. Shipping charges from your locality will include "land bridge service" to one coast or the other as appropriate. "All-water" service may also be available, which allows goods to be shipped by sea anywhere in the world from either coast via the Panama Canal. Door-to-door shipping of a piano from the East Coast will usually take about fifteen days to Europe, a month or so to most other parts of the world. Shipping times from the West Coast will differ from those from the East Coast accordingly. Shipping to Canada and Mexico is usually by land, although reaching certain coastal cities may sometimes be cheaper by sea. Overland shipping for pianos should be by air-ride vans; rail flat car shipping can be hard on pianos.

Arrival. The customer or the customer's designee will be notified by the shipper's agent when the piano has arrived at the destination port and he or she must go to the agent's office to file the necessary paperwork. Various forms are needed to establish the value of the piano, including the insurance company's valuation, so that any duty may be paid. (Shipping fees and insurance premiums are paid in advance at the point of origin; only duties are due on arrival.) The duty must be paid before the agent can complete the delivery to the house. If the customer is not at the destination when the piano arrives, it will have to be stored, which is expensive. It's better to delay shipping the piano than to have it wait at the destination port.

Damage claims. If there is damage, the customer should file a claim form, available from the mover's claims personnel at either end of the move. The customer must also arrange to have the insurance agent inspect the damage, usually after delivery to the new residence, obtain an estimate for repairs from any qualified technician, and submit it to the claims personnel of either the mover or the insurer, depending on the usual procedure used by the mover. If the customer doesn't have any idea of who to call for repair estimates, which could be the case in a foreign country, the names of local businesses are usually available from the insurance company or the mover.

Ivory Ban. If the piano being moved internationally has real ivory keytops, as many older pianos do, you may be in for trouble when the piano goes through customs. As a result of the international ban on ivory production and sale, many nations, including the United States, will rip the ivories off the piano as a condition of letting it pass through customs in the misguided notion that this will somehow save the lives of elephants. If the piano is over one hundred years old, you may be able to obtain documentation from the U.S. Fish and Wildlife Service (or the equivalent agency in the foreign country) that will allow the piano to pass through unscathed. Allow at least ninety days to get these papers. If the piano is less than a hundred years old, however, you're out of luck; plan to get the keytops recovered in plastic or don't move the piano. If having the keytops recovered, have it done before you move. The customs officials might damage the keys in the process of removing the old ivories.

Storage

The best advice about storing a piano is not to do it if you can help it, or to store it with a friend who will use it and take good care of it. Storing a piano involves extra moving and an uncertain environment and certainly doesn't improve the instrument, to say the least. Still, there are times when storing a piano is unavoidable, such as when you have to move out of your house before the movers are scheduled for the long-distance haul (in which case they will pick up and store your goods for you) or when you arrive in a new city before you've found a permanent place to live.

Most cities and towns now have self-storage places that offer cubicles of various sizes for rent by the month. When choosing one, it's preferable that it be at least minimally heated, though an unheated space is by far better than one that is overheated. The smallest-size cubicle in which you can store the piano will probably be determined by the size of the door, rather than by the size of the cubicle. Typical cubicle sizes might be $8 \times 8 \times 6$ feet or $5 \times 10 \times 8$ feet. Smaller sizes may not have a big enough door. Also be sure that the cubicle you're given is not upstairs and does not have an overhead entrance requiring a ladder, movable stairs, or forklift.

Monthly rates for the sizes mentioned above vary enormously. Phone calls around the country revealed rates as low as thirty dollars a month in some rural Midwestern towns and as high as a hundred dollars or more a month in the larger cities.

Storage in an unheated space. Many people keep pianos in summer homes and wonder how to protect the piano in the winter when the place is unheated. The conventional wisdom is that pianos should never be allowed to freeze, but any technician will tell you that pianos left unheated year after year are often in better condition than those in well-heated houses, the latter usually suffering from the effects of overdryness. Some experts advise stuffing the piano with rolled-up newspaper to absorb the dampness that often accompanies low temperatures. But my sources in the Maine woods tell me that, more often than not, those newspapers just end up as nests for mice, and the torn up, soggy newsprint is hard to extricate from the piano come spring. Their advice? Place some mothballs in the piano (but don't let them touch the finish), close up the piano, and leave it as is. (Alternatively, says the Maine woodsman, put some chewing tobacco in a cheesecloth sack and hang it inside the piano.)

The Effects of Moving and Storage

Tuning. The piano is hoisted out of a third-story window, trucked across the state, and later that day hoisted into a fifth-floor apartment. After the movers leave, the pianist sits down to play, and is surprised to find the piano in very good tune. Two weeks later, the piano sounds terrible. This common scenario occurs because it is not generally the physical moving of the piano that puts it out of tune—it is the change in humidity from one location to another, and this change takes anywhere from a few days to a few weeks to show its effect. For this reason, you should wait at least two weeks after moving before having the piano tuned. Only with some of the cheaper spinets and consoles will the actual physical moving affect the tuning directly.

Pedals. Grand piano pedals are frequently out of kilter after a move. Shims of leather or cardboard used to take up slack in the trapwork often fall out when the lyre is removed. Also, less careful movers sometimes mix up the order of the pedal rods that rise from the back of the pedals. These rods are not always equal in length and so may not be interchangeable. Pedal dowels in verticals also sometimes fall out of place. It is a fairly simple matter for your piano technician to correct these problems when he or she comes to tune the piano. *Special note:* If your grand piano has lyre braces (which it should), be sure the movers remember to put them back on. Movers often forget and leave them in the truck, never to be seen again (see Figure 5-29, page 198).

Other effects. The effects of moving, except those mentioned above, are very unpredictable, especially if there is a large difference in humidity between the old and new locations. *Warning:* A piano that has been in a damp or unheated place for many years should never be moved to a dry or well-heated location. Such pianos are known to self-destruct in a short time.

One additional item to check on a grand piano before moving: Because a grand is placed on its side to be moved, a narrow wooden rail called a **key stop rail** is mounted on top of the keys, behind the fallboard, to prevent the keys from falling off the key frame during moving. If the key stop rail is missing or not securely installed, as sometimes happens, the keys will be in terrible disarray and completely unplayable after moving. A technician can fix this, but it may take awhile even to extricate the action from the piano. If you know you're going to be moving, have your technician check for the key stop rail before the move. Otherwise, see Chapter 5 for instructions on removing the grand fallboard to look inside. Although less common, a similar problem can occur in a vertical if it has to be upended to get it around a tight corner.

CHAPTER SEVEN
A Beginner's Guide to Piano Care

SINCE THIS BOOK MAY BE ALL YOU WILL EVER read about the technical aspects of pianos, it would be a mistake to let you go without giving you some basic information about the kind of service your piano will need in the months and years after you buy it. If you have read this far, you probably appreciate by now that, as sturdy as a piano may look, it actually contains some ten thousand parts, many of them quite delicate, and needs much more servicing than most people realize. To maintain your piano in top condition, you should attend to its servicing with the same kind of diligence and thoroughness that you would with any other major purchase, such as an automobile. And as with an automobile, if you can't afford to service your piano, you really can't afford to buy it.

TUNING

Tuning is the most basic kind of piano maintenance there is, yet it is perennially misunderstood. What is tuning? Why do pianos go out of tune? How often and when should my piano be tuned? How can I minimize its going out of tune? These are some of the questions I and every other piano technician get asked constantly, and which I'll take up in this chapter.

What Is Tuning?

As explained elsewhere in this book, the more than two hundred strings in a piano are stretched at high tension across a cast-iron frame, one end of each string being attached to a hitch pin and the other end coiled around a tuning pin. The pitch of each string when vibrating depends, among other things, on the tension at which it's stretched. By turning the tuning pin, the tension can be tightened or slackened, and thus the pitch altered, according to the wishes of the tuner, who performs this operation with a special kind of socket wrench confusingly called a "tuning hammer." Tuning, then, means adjusting the tension of each of the piano strings, using a tuning hammer to turn the tuning pins, so that the pitch of each string sounds pleasingly in harmony with every other string according to certain known acoustical laws and aesthetic rules and customs. Note that whereas most tuners are also capable of providing other kinds of piano maintenance, tuning, properly speaking, is only the operation defined above, and does not include repairs and adjustments, fixing squeaky pedals, cleaning, and so on, as is often thought to be the case.

Why Do Pianos Go Out of Tune?

By far, the most important factor causing pianos to go out of tune is the change in humidity from season to season that occurs in most temperate climates, affecting all pianos, good and bad, new and old, played and unplayed. The soundboard, glued down around its perimeter and bellied like a diaphragm in the center, swells up with moisture in the humid season and pushes up on the strings via the bridges on which the strings rest. This causes the strings to be stretched at a higher tension, raising their pitch. In the dry season, the opposite happens. The soundboard releases its moisture to the air and subsides, releasing the pressure on the strings, which then fall in pitch. Unfortunately, the strings don't rise and fall in pitch by exactly the same amount at the same time. The process is more random than that, with the result that the strings no longer sound in harmony with one another and need retuning.

To make matters worse, the change in pitch tends to be most pronounced in the tenor and low treble areas of the piano, whose bridges are located on the flexible center area of the soundboard (Figure 7-1). It's not at all unusual to find that the high treble and low bass, whose bridges are located near the more stable perimeter of the soundboard, have remained virtually unchanged in pitch despite a huge change in the center. Any octaves or chords that, for example, span the bass and tenor at these times will sound especially out of tune.

If the piano has been properly tuned, moderate playing will not, by itself, have a large effect on the tuning. Rather, its effect is to accelerate whatever changes in tuning are happening due to humidity fluctuations. A vibrating string more easily slides over its friction points than a stationary one, and thus is more apt to go randomly out of tune when its tension is being altered by the movement of the soundboard. Obviously, the harder and more frequently the piano is played, the

faster this process will happen. But an unplayed piano will still go out of tune with the seasons.

Although all pianos go out of tune, some do so more than others. Some pianos, including some very well-made ones, have soundboards that are very responsive to humidity changes and go through large seasonal variations in pitch. Other pianos, particularly some of the cheaper spinets and consoles, have weak structures that actually twist slightly from season to season or even while the pianos are being tuned, making stable tunings all but impossible. These pianos go out of tune chaotically, in addition to showing large seasonal variations in pitch.

How Often and When Should I Have My Piano Tuned?

When to tune your piano obviously depends on your local climate and how responsive your piano is to humidity changes. But, in general, you should avoid times of rapid humidity change and seek times when the humidity will be stable for a reasonable length of time. Turning the heat on in the house in the fall and winter, and then off again in the spring, both cause major indoor humidity changes, and in each case it may take several months before the piano soundboard fully stabilizes again at the new humidity level.

In Boston, the tuning cycle goes something like this for most pianos (Figure 7-2): A piano tuned in April or May when the heat is turned off in the house will probably be out of tune by late June. If it is tuned in late June or July, it may well hold its tune until October or later, depending on when the heat is turned on for the winter (although sometimes extreme humidity in August will do it in). If you have the piano tuned right after the heat is turned on, say in October or November, the piano will almost certainly be out of tune by

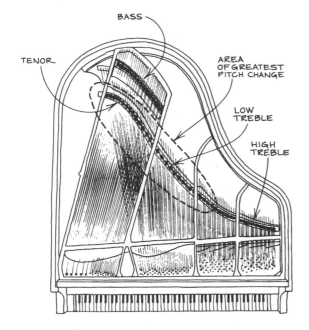

FIGURE 7-1. The area of greatest pitch change from season to season is in the tenor and low treble sections of the piano.

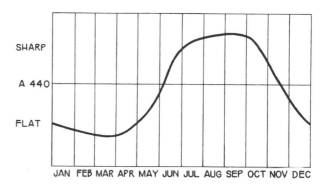

FIGURE 7-2. The pitch of the piano in the tenor and low treble range closely follows the annual indoor humidity cycle. The diagram shows how a typical piano in Boston might behave. Most areas of the country that have cold winters will show a similar pattern.

Christmas. But if you wait until after the holidays (and of course, everyone wants it tuned *for* the holidays), it will probably hold pretty well until April or even May. In my experience, most accusations of tuner incompetence occur in November or December, and then to a lesser degree in June, and are caused not by the tuner at all, but by poor timing of the tuning with the seasonal changes.

If you have the piano tuned four or more times a year, you don't have to worry too much about the "right" time to tune it. Any seasonal tuning changes will be corrected soon enough. It's those who tune their pianos twice a year who have a problem. For these people, there will be at least two times per year when the piano is noticeably out of tune but when it will not yet be the right time to tune it. If you are in this group, you will have to decide then whether to go ahead and have it tuned—knowing it may go out of tune within a month or so—or to suffer until the "right" time. At those times of year, I try to inform customers who call for a tuning about the consequences of having the piano tuned then, and let them decide how badly they want it done.

There is an additional problem for the twice-a-year people. The times of rapid humidity change—spring and fall—are also the times of most moderate indoor humidity levels, while the times of stable humidity—summer and winter—are the times of most extreme humidity levels. As shown in Figure 7-2, the pitch of the middle range of the piano follows the humidity changes and is therefore most sharp and flat at the "recommended" tuning times. Pianos tuned at these times may have to undergo large pitch changes to bring them back to standard pitch. As any tuner can tell you, large pitch changes are the bane of stable tuning, as structural forces within the piano tend to make a piano tuning creep back in the direction from which it was moved. Pianos showing large seasonal pitch variations may require extra tuning work, at greater expense, and may not stay in tune as well. Thus, ironically, the tuning times recommended in response to climatic factors are the least recommended times in relation to structural stability, and vice versa. Unfortunately, there is no solution to this problem except to have the piano tuned more often.

If you tune the piano only once a year, you should do it at the same time each year so the tuner will not have to make much pitch adjustment. Some pianos actually go back into almost perfect tune each year around the anniversary of their tuning (but don't count on this happening).

How often you have the piano tuned will depend not only on the piano and the humidity inside your house, but also on your ear (how much out-of-tune-

ness you notice and can tolerate) and on your budget. Four times a year is ideal, but impractical for most folks. The "official line" is twice a year. Where the piano is rarely used, once a year may suffice, but less than that is not recommended. The average cost of a piano tuning is currently from seventy-five to one hundred twenty-five dollars, depending on where you live. The cost could be higher if a "double tuning" (a rough tuning followed by a fine tuning) is required to compensate for large seasonal variations in pitch, or if for some other reason the piano was not at standard pitch. In some areas of the country, a double tuning is required almost every time a piano is tuned. Also, as mentioned in Chapter 3, new pianos (or pianos that have been restrung) may need to be tuned more frequently the first year or so as the new strings continue to stretch.

You may legitimately ask how important it is to have a piano tuned; that is, will harm be done to the instrument if it isn't tuned? This is a subject piano technicians don't discuss much. When they do, they offer a variety of pseudoscientific explanations to convince their customers (or themselves) of the necessity for tuning. The truth, as I see it, is that in most cases no harm will be done to the piano. The harm is mostly to one's aesthetics—an out-of-tune piano can be painful to listen to. It can also be discouraging and distracting to a student. It may be impossible to play along with other instruments or with recordings, and the piano's tonal quality may be impaired. In the extreme case where a piano is being tuned after, say, twenty years of neglect, raising the pitch of the piano back to standard pitch will entail a good deal of extra work and could result in some broken strings or split bridges, but I'm not convinced that these problems wouldn't have occurred anyway, and possibly sooner, if the piano had been maintained. Raising the pitch of a piano can also alter the positions of the strings in relation to their bearing points, introducing tonal irregularities (false beats) and buzzing strings, but this can often be corrected, and in any case is not what I would call "harmful." Suggestions that the piano will be structurally harmed if it is not precisely at standard pitch and in tune are, in my opinion, spurious. Having the piano serviced at regular intervals, however, may allow the technician to catch and correct small, non-tuning-related problems before they become big, expensive ones.

HUMIDITY AND PIANOS

When you consider that a piano is made largely of wood, it's not surprising that the subject of humidity plays such an important role in piano technology.

Relative Humidity

Relative humidity is a measurement, expressed as a percentage, of the amount of water vapor in the air compared to the maximum amount the air could possibly hold at a given temperature. The relative humidity of the outdoor air depends on the nature of the air mass—that is, how moist or dry it is—and on the temperature, because the ability of the air to hold moisture increases with increasing temperature. So if we take a "parcel" of air with a certain amount of moisture in it and we heat it up, the relative humidity will decrease, because the amount of moisture in the air will have decreased *in comparison* to the amount the air is now capable of holding. Alternatively, if we cool that air, again without adding or subtracting moisture, the relative humidity will increase, because the capacity of the air to hold moisture will have diminished.

The relative humidity of the outdoor air can be high or low from day to day, regardless of the season. The reason such a fuss is made about low winter humidity is that in climates that have cold winters, the *indoor* relative humidity is artificially lowered by heating the air with a furnace system without supplying any additional moisture. If, for example, the outdoor temperature is 32 degrees Fahrenheit and the outdoor humidity is 100 percent (an extreme example), by the time the air is heated to 68 degrees indoors, the indoor relative humidity will have dropped (theoretically) to only 28 percent (the actual amount may be a little higher due to human respiration, plants, and other factors).

A continuous exchange of moisture goes on between the air and the wooden piano parts and other porous objects around the house, as the moisture level attempts to reach a state of equilibrium. Since the air is usually a much greater reservoir of moisture than the objects, it tends to dictate the terms of this interchange. When the relative humidity is low, the air sucks up moisture from the piano, causing the pitch to fall, tuning pins to loosen, and parts to rattle (not to mention causing plants to wither, furniture joints to loosen, skin to crack, and throats to get sore).

Piano manufacturers suggest that the ideal humidity level for pianos is about 40 to 50 percent, whereas studies show that for people, 50 to 60 percent is best. Actually, as far as pianos are concerned, the particular humidity level is not nearly as important as the change in humidity through the seasons. In most cases, a piano can be adjusted to exist quite well at any reasonable level of humidity as long as it doesn't change much. But when, as happens in most of North America, the indoor humidity goes from very high to very low and back again, year after year, the alternate expansion and contraction has the net effect of shrinking, cracking, and warping even wood that has been well seasoned prior to manufacturing. One of the most important parts of good piano maintenance is keeping the humidity as constant as possible.

Where to Place the Piano

There are several ways you can protect your piano from extremes and fluctuations of humidity. The most important of these is putting the piano in the right place. *NEVER* put a piano near or against a working radiator, next to or over a hot-air vent, or under a ceiling vent. If you can't observe this one simple rule, there's no point to even buying a piano. You'll be throwing your money away. A concert pianist who is a customer of mine insisted, over my objections, on situating her fifteen-thousand-dollar grand over a large heating vent in her living room. "It doesn't look good any place else," she said. Her piano is now almost untunable. Priorities, please!

Some tuners advise their customers not to place a piano near a window or a door because of possible drafts, or against an outside wall that may get cold. This is undoubtedly good advice, but following it may severely restrict your ability to have a piano at all. Use your judgment. My experience is that these factors are often not too significant unless the conditions are extreme (Figure 7-3). If in doubt, and an inside wall is not available, move your piano six inches away from an outside wall to provide an insulating air space, or try putting a sheet of styrofoam insulation behind the piano. Remember, too, not to place your piano in an unusually damp place, such as a damp basement.

Direct sunlight on a piano should be diffused with curtains or venetian blinds. Besides damaging the finish of a piano, sunlight can wreak havoc on the tuning. I remember the time I was called by a grand piano owner who claimed his piano seemed to go out of tune at certain times of the day and back in tune at other

FIGURE 7-3. Where *not* to put your piano. (Illustration by Rick Eberly, © 1986 GPI Publications, Cupertino, CA. Reprinted by permission.)

times. "Sure," I thought skeptically, but agreed to check it out. Not finding anything obviously wrong, I proceeded to tune the piano. Halfway through the tuning, I discovered, to my dismay, that the piano was already going out of tune. Then I noticed that while I had been tuning, the sun had shifted its position in the sky and was now shining directly on the soundboard. I quickly got up and closed the blinds. After five minutes, to my relief and amazement, the piano was back in almost perfect tune.

Temperature

Another way you can keep the humidity up in the wintertime is to keep the temperature at a moderate level. Temperature alone does not affect a piano very much unless extreme, but it decidedly affects relative humidity. A temperature difference of just 5 degrees can make the difference between a house that is hazardously dry and one that is moderate and comfortable. Some of the best-preserved pianos I have seen have been in rooms that were relatively poorly or indirectly heated. Some of the worst have been in houses heated to over 70 degrees. Some piano manufacturers state that the ideal temperature for a piano is 72 to 75 degrees. In my opinion, this is ridiculous. Not only would this be a waste of expensive energy resources, but it can be nearly impossible to keep an adequate humidity level when a house is heated to such temperatures in the wintertime. Studies have shown that the best temperature for most physically active people is around 64 degrees, although there is, of course, a certain amount of variation from one person to another (for instance, people who are elderly or ill usually need a much higher temperature to avoid hypothermia). Obviously you need to strike a balance between your health and comfort needs and the requirements of your piano. Fortunately, this balance is usually not hard to find if you are willing to be flexible and wear a sweater indoors from time to time.

Humidifiers and Climate Control Systems

Recognizing the importance of an adequate humidity level to their health and possessions, including their piano, households in increasing numbers are artificially raising the humidity during the dry months by using humidifiers. These come in three kinds: a central humidifier directly connected to your forced hot-air heating system (if you have this kind of system), a portable unit that can humidify one or several rooms, and a miniature climate control system installed right in your piano.

If you do heat with forced hot air, connecting a central humidifier is by far the best route. A heating and cooling contractor can install one for four or five hundred dollars. This may cost more than the smaller portable models, but it will take care of the entire house with no additional noise or clutter of extra appliances. Central humidifiers are usually designed to refill themselves with water automatically, but you must clean them often to remove mineral deposits, especially in hard-water areas, and to prevent the growth of bacteria.

If you heat by other means than forced hot air, you should consider buying a portable humidifier, usually priced from one hundred to two hundred dollars. These, however, require a lot of maintenance. Like the central kind, they must be cleaned often (weekly, or at least monthly) to avoid the growth and spread of airborne diseases. They must also be filled with water quite often (on the average, daily), the frequency depending on the capacity and output of the humidifier, the temperature of the house, and how well the house is insulated. If you go away for a few days and the humidifier runs out of water, the house could get dry and the piano could go out of tune. Also, these appliances

Buying Tips: Shopping for a Humidifier

When shopping for a portable console humidifier, be prepared to see big, ugly plastic boxes in fake Mediterranean styling. You may have to pay more to be offended less. Be sure to ask the following questions: How many gallons does it hold? (The more it holds, the longer between fillings.) How many square feet is it rated to cover in the average house? (If your ceilings are very high, adjust this figure downward accordingly.) Does it have a water-level indicator? A low-water warning light? Automatic shutoff when it runs out of water? An automatic humidistat? (If it doesn't have an automatic humidistat, it will keep running until the house becomes a tropical rain forest.) Check how accessible the tank is for cleaning and filling, as these tasks will occupy most of the time you spend on maintenance. Does the tank lift out of the cabinet for easier cleaning? Are there casters so you can roll it to the sink? Is a hose provided? Check how much noise the fan makes; the larger models, and models with more than one fan speed, sometimes make less noise.

The new ultrasonic humidifiers work on a different principle than the evaporative type and don't require as much in the way of cleaning. Ease of filling and cleaning aren't problems because the units are so small, but their capacity and output are limited, so they won't cover as large an area. Also—very important—if you live in a hard-water area, ultrasonic humidifiers may spread a fine white dust over all the surfaces in your house.

tend to make a lot of noise, something to which a musician is likely to be sensitive. Last, when the temperature is very low outside, indoor humidity must also be kept low—often lower than is acceptable for your piano—to prevent water vapor from condensing on windows and other cold surfaces. In fact, too much humidification can result in moisture seeping into the walls and, over time, causing structural damage to the house. If you would like to avoid this risk, would be bothered by the motor noise of a console humidifier, want to avoid the nuisance of frequent cleaning and filling, go away for long periods of time, live in an area that is too *damp* all the time, or just want to give extra special attention to protecting your piano, the best route is to have a climate control system installed right inside your piano (Figure 7-4). These systems can be ordered and installed by your piano technician. The system consists of a humidifier (a tank of water with a heating element and fabric wicks), a dehumidifier (a long heating element that raises the temperature and thus lowers the relative humidity), a humidistat

(senses the humidity level and turns on and off the humidifier and dehumidifier as needed), a low-water warning light mounted under the keybed, and an easy-fill tube so you can refill the humidifier without having to open up the piano. In a vertical piano, the system is installed right inside the lower panel, near the pedals. Optionally available are components that provide protection at the back of the piano, too. In a grand, it fits under the soundboard. The cost for the system and installation is about $300 to $400 in a vertical and $400 to $500 in a grand.

The advantages of this system are that it makes no noise at all, requires filling (extremely easy) only every one to four weeks, depending on conditions, and needs cleaning and changing of the humidifier wicks only once a year, which your technician can do. Since the system covers only a small area, it can control the humidity in that area very closely. The drawback is that it can't reach the entire piano, only the inside of the vertical (unless optional components are installed) and the underneath of the grand. In both cases, it will

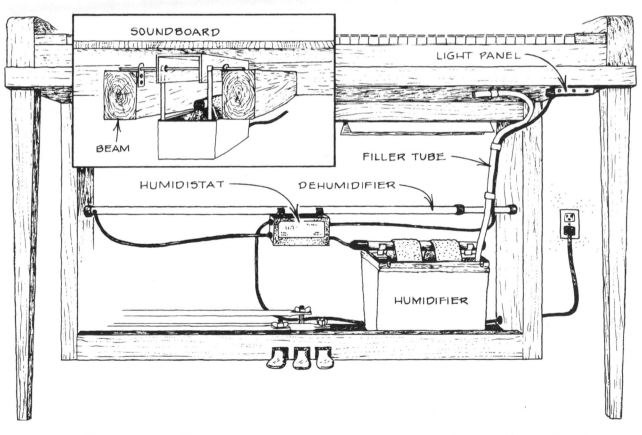

FIGURE 7-4. The Dampp-Chaser climate control system includes a humidifier (tank in lower right corner), a dehumidifier (long heating rod), a humidistat (box hanging from dehumidifier), and a low-water warning light and filling tube mounted under the keybed. The inset shows how the system is mounted under the soundboard of a grand piano, supported by the wooden braces. In areas that are always damp, such as Florida, only the dehumidifier part of the system is required, but it must always be used with the system humidistat to prevent overdrying the piano.

help to stabilize the tuning, and in the vertical it will protect the action as well, but in a very dry room, it may not provide the kind of total protection that the room humidifier can. I highly recommend these systems for both vertical and grand pianos, but sometimes suggest that they be supplemented by a room humidifier, especially for grands, if the piano owner doesn't mind the inconvenience.

OTHER KINDS OF PIANO SERVICE

Cleaning and Polishing

Polishing the case. Most piano manufacturers recommend *against* the use of furniture polish. The best way to clean dust and finger marks off the piano, they say, is with a soft, clean, lintless cloth (such as cheesecloth) slightly dampened with water and wrung out. Fold the cloth into a pad and rub in the direction of the grain of the wood, using long straight strokes. Then repeat with a dry cloth pad to remove any remaining water droplets. If you insist on using furniture polish, make sure it contains no silicone. Some piano supply companies sell polish especially made for piano finishes, available from your technician.

Cleaning the keys. Use the same kind of soft, clean cloth to clean the keys. Dampen the cloth slightly with water or with a mild white soap solution. Don't let water run down the sides of the keys. If your keytops are made of ivory, be sure to rub each key with a dry cloth right after cleaning it. Don't let the water stand on the ivory for any length of time. Since ivory absorbs water, the keytops will curl up and fall off if water is allowed to collect on them. Use a separate cloth to clean the black keys, in case any black stain comes off. Never use chemical solvents, furniture polish, or cleaning fluids on the keys.

Cleaning the interior of the piano. Dust inevitably collects inside a piano no matter how good a housekeeper you are. When the technician removes the outer case parts during regular servicing it's a good time to dust some of their less accessible spots. In a vertical, you can also vacuum behind the lower panel, where the pedals and trapwork are. In a grand, the area around the tuning pins and the inside perimeter of the case can be vacuumed out. The tops of the dampers in a grand can be cleaned very gently with a clean, dry cloth (no water here, please).

The big question is how to clean the grand piano soundboard under the strings. Piano technicians clean this area with specialized tools that are inserted between the strings. Thoroughly cleaning the soundboard

in this manner can take a long time. A simpler way that will suffice for most piano owners is to attach the vacuum cleaner hose to the exhaust end of the appliance (you can't do this with all vacuum cleaners, however) and to blow the dust toward the tail end and straight side of the piano, where it can then be vacuumed up. An air compressor will do the job even better. (Hanging a damp sheet from the lid at the tail of the piano will prevent the blown dust from spreading about the room.) This method won't get the soundboard spanking clean, but it will put off the day when the more thorough cleaning will be necessary. Cleaning the piano action and under the keys on both verticals and grands should be left to a piano technician. In most cases, once every few years will be often enough.

Mothproofing. Moths love the wool cloths and felts in pianos, especially the hammers, dampers, and under the keys. The wool is mothproofed in the factory, but this is only a temporary treatment, good for a few years. In most situations, a periodic, thorough cleaning of the piano action, as described above, will keep the moth problem under control. In more severe cases, the technician can provide mothproofing agents that are safe to put inside the piano.

Action Regulating

Action parts need periodic adjustment to compensate for wear, compacting and settling of cloth and felt, and changes in wooden parts due to atmospheric conditions. Making these adjustments is called *regulating*. Regulating is also discussed in Chapter 3, page 56; some examples of regulating adjustments are shown in Chapter 5, page 199. Most new and rebuilt pianos will need to be regulated to some extent within six months to a year of purchase because of initial settling of cloth parts. Thereafter, frequency of regulation will depend on the amount of use. A piano in the home played an hour a day might need a full regulation only once every five to ten years, whereas one played all day by a professional might benefit by a full regulation every year. Small amounts of regulating done as necessary at each tuning will put off the day when a full regulation is needed. A full regulation of a vertical piano action in good basic condition usually costs between $300 and $400; a grand regulation between $400 and $700. The price spread partially reflects the lack of agreement about what particular procedures regulation should include. Some adjustments, such as hammer filing, may not be included in a standard list of regulating procedures, but are often performed in conjunction with regulating nonetheless.

Although letting your piano go out of tune may not harm it, letting it go badly out of regulation may. For instance, hammers that block against the strings instead of releasing could break, or cause strings to break. Excess space or "lost motion" between two contacting parts could make one part punch the other instead of pushing, causing unnecessary wear.

Two other operations I would like to call your attention to are screw tightening and hammer spacing. The hinges, called **flanges**, on which all the action parts move, are screwed to the action frame. These screws— some two to three hundred of them—loosen with time due to vibration and wood shrinkage. When they get loose, the parts get noisy and move out of alignment. Have your technician check the tightness of these flange screws once a year, preferably during the dry season when they're loosest.

When flange screws get loose, or when wooden parts warp, hammers and other parts may go out of proper alignment. Figure 3-32, on page 53, and Figure 5-26, on page 196, show what misspaced hammers look like. As explained in Chapter 5, once hammers are left misspaced for a length of time, spacing them correctly can be more involved, requiring reshaping or replacement. A little time spent at each tuning checking and adjusting hammer spacing can lengthen the life of the hammers considerably and can also provide benefits in evenness of tone.

Voicing

Voicing, or tone regulating, is the adjustment of the tone of the piano, mostly by changing the density or hardness of the hammer felt. To put it simply, hardening the felt will make the tone brighter, softening it will make the tone mellower. Sometimes other, more complex, changes in tone can be accomplished, too. Voicing techniques include proper alignment of the hammers with the strings, filing or sanding a layer of felt off to reshape the hammer and eliminate grooves, ironing the hammer felt or treating it with chemicals to harden it, and pricking it with needles to soften it. To eliminate any other variables that could affect the tone, a piano must be in perfect tune and regulation before it can be voiced.

New and rebuilt pianos may sound quite bright after six months or a year of use and may need some voicing to compensate for the packing down of the hammer felt. After that, frequency of voicing should depend on how much you use the piano and on how often you think the tonal quality is no longer optimum.

A hint: I find that 90 percent of complaints about tonal quality disappear after the piano is tuned.

ROOM ACOUSTICS

Room acoustics affect the tone of a piano far more than is often realized. Sometimes adjusting the room acoustics is the easiest and most effective way of "voicing" a piano to a particular loudness level or balance between treble and bass, after which hammer voicing can take care of the fine adjustment from note to note.

My own piano is a good example. When I was in high school, my parents bought what was supposed to be a very fine grand piano, but at the time, I was convinced it was a lemon. The sound was very muffled and I had to bang on the piano to get what I wanted out of it. I was told, of course, that it would get louder in time, but years went by and it never did, despite the strenuous workout I gave it.

When I was in my late twenties, I inherited the piano and moved it to my apartment in Boston, expecting to do some major work on it to improve the tone (I had, by that time, become a piano technician). To my surprise, the piano came alive without a stitch of work on my part. The hardwood floor and the relative lack of furniture in the room did the work for me. Whereas my parents' living room had been heavily carpeted and draped and filled with upholstered chairs and sofas, my apartment was filled with sound-reflecting surfaces and few sound absorbers.

The sound we hear, especially indoors, comes in part in the form of direct sound and in larger part from reverberant sound—sound reflected from walls, floor, ceiling, windows, and so forth. Acousticians have studied the phenomenon of reverberant sound for many years in relation to the design of auditoriums and concert halls, but relatively little work has been done on the acoustical design of small rooms—practice rooms, living rooms, and rehearsal studios.

In the study of auditorium acoustics, great emphasis is placed on the reverberation time—the amount of time it takes for a burst of sound to decay by sixty decibels (to one-millionth of its original intensity). The larger the volume of the room and the more reflective the surfaces, the longer the reverberation time. But too long a reverberation time will create a "muddy" sound, as one sound runs into the next. By placing more sound-absorbent surfaces in the room, the reverberation time can be decreased, but this will also decrease the intensity of the sound because sound will not be able to "build up." Too short a reverberation time will thus create a "dry" sound, and the performer may have to work too hard to be heard. Acousticians have found that concert halls sound best when reverberation time is between 1.5 and 2.0 seconds. The slightly higher reverberation times work best for Romantic orchestral music, lower for Classical orchestral music, and lower still for chamber music.

In a small room, such as a living room or music room, the reverberation time will usually be much shorter. Efforts to make a small room sound like a concert hall by increasing the amount of reflective surface until reverberation time reaches concert-hall levels usually won't work because in a reverberant small room certain individual resonant frequencies become prominent, producing a "shower room" type of reverberation. Anyway, it has been found through listening tests that piano music in small rooms sounds best to most people at a reverberation time of about 1.1 seconds, though individual tastes will vary. Although it's not practical, of course, for a homeowner to measure reverberation time, it is possible, when designing a small room, to adjust it to some extent to one's taste, and to balance the treble and bass. The key is in the balance between absorbent and reflective surfaces, and in the diffusion or "scattering" of sound so it is evenly dispersed.

Each kind of building and decorating material absorbs sound differently, and the ability to absorb sound varies with the frequency, too. A smooth concrete floor, for example, is an excellent reflector of sound of all frequencies—too good, in fact. A thin carpet on concrete will continue to reflect low frequencies, but will absorb most sounds of high frequency. Putting a pad under the carpet will significantly increase its ability to absorb sound at all frequencies.

A wooden floor is also a good reflector, though a little less so at low frequencies. A carpet on the floor, especially right under the piano, may help to create a better balance if the treble is too brilliant. Because the piano case also vibrates—particularly a grand piano case—it makes sense to put the rug under the legs of the piano, too, or to replace metal casters with rubber-wheeled ones so that the wooden floor doesn't become another soundboard.

Window glass and plywood paneling reflect high frequencies while somewhat absorbing lower ones. Some of the large window or paneled areas can be covered with a drapery, which will do just the opposite. Large multi-purpose rehearsal rooms that may have a band rehearsal one day and a chamber music rehearsal the next may benefit by hanging a drapery along one wall that can be extended or drawn into a corner as needed to provide the correct amount of sound absorption. This technique can also be used for teaching studios that must accommodate the tastes of several different teachers. Upholstered furniture, of course, is always useful as a sound absorber. One can also experiment with different kinds of window shades and draperies, wall textures and wall hangings, open vs. closed doors, and the placement of art objects and other things about the room, all of which will absorb, reflect, or scatter sound.

A living room or music room with a reverberation time of 1.1 seconds, mentioned above, is a fairly "live" room, one with more reflective surfaces than absorbent ones. One acoustical engineer consulted suggested that for best results the room should be at least twice as long as the (grand) piano. Ceilings shouldn't exceed around twelve feet or reverberation time may increase to the point where the sound becomes muddy. If there are two acoustically different ends to the room, the piano should be placed at the "live" end so the sound can develop and diffuse before being absorbed by the objects at the other end. Others I spoke with thought that a little shorter reverberation time, and more absorbent surfaces, yielded better results.

Small practice rooms should be sound-insulated between rooms, and should have acoustic tile ceilings. One problem that may develop in these small rooms is "flutter echo," where flat, reflective, parallel-sided walls cause the sound to bounce back and forth annoyingly. Orienting the piano differently in relation to the walls or putting it in a corner may help, but putting sound absorbing material on the walls or using large sound-absorbing panels is the best remedy. When designing small practice rooms, try to avoid having two sets of parallel walls; one or two walls should be at an angle to avoid echos. Larger practice rooms are preferable acoustically, but may not be economical.

Making a room sound more "live"—increasing the sound reflection—is generally more difficult than deadening it because people are usually more reluctant to remove carpets, drapes, and furniture than they are to add them but, unfortunately, that is exactly what is required.

THE PIANO TECHNICIAN

Throughout this book I've used the term *piano technician* rather than the better-known *piano tuner*. Technically speaking, a tuner is one who only tunes, and perhaps is capable of a few minor repairs, whereas a technician—sometimes called a tuner-technician—both tunes and does most kinds of on-site repair and regulating. It's much better to hire the latter, even if you believe your piano doesn't need any repair at a given time. One very pleasant fellow who tunes in another part of the state confessed to me that he always avoided raising the pitch of pianos that were flat for fear he might break a string—he didn't know how to replace strings. If you hire people like this, they may have to cover up for their ignorance, and you may have to hire someone else to undo the damage. Even an experienced technician, though, may sometimes subcontract out work or refer you elsewhere for certain complicated or specialized jobs, such as key recovering, rebuilding, or refinishing.

The best way to find a piano technician is to ask for a referral from someone whose needs are similar to your own. If you are a piano teacher with a high-quality instrument, ask another teacher or professional musician who seems to take good care of his or her instrument, or inquire as to who tunes for the local symphony. If you own a spinet, the person who tunes for the symphony may decline the job, so you should ask someone else who owns a home piano, or ask your teacher (if you have one) for an appropriate referral. Of course, since very few pianists know much about their instrument, there's no guarantee that the referral will get you someone who will do a good job, but at the very least it will get you the peace of mind that comes with not having to deal with a total stranger.

The worst way to find a technician is through the *Yellow Pages*. One doesn't have to have any certification to hang out a shingle as a piano technician, and all it takes to advertise in the *Yellow Pages* is the money to buy the business phone service. Some of the best technicians don't advertise because they don't want to pay for business service and because they prefer the rapport with customers who were referred to them by word of mouth. They also don't want to be bothered by people who call around just to find the lowest price. The better technicians usually don't charge the least, although they may not charge the most, either.

If in a total quandary about whom to hire, you might check to see if there is a chapter of the Piano Technicians Guild in your area. The Guild is an international organization of piano technicians devoted to promoting a high level of skill and business ethics among its members. To that end it sponsors regular technical meetings and seminars and produces a technical magazine. Extensive testing of tuning and repair skills and theoretical knowledge is required to attain the Guild's rating of Registered Piano Technician (RPT). The Guild is not a labor union and does not set rates. To find out if there are Guild members in your area, look in the *Yellow Pages* (here's one way the *Yellow Pages* can be helpful), which may have a list of Guild members, write to the Piano Technicians Guild at 3930 Washington, Kansas City, Missouri 64111; call (816) 753-7747; or see their web site at **www.ptg.org**. (Also see **www.pianobook.com** for names of Registered technicians in your area.) The Guild advises that you should allow someone to service your piano only if he or she can show a current, paid-up Guild membership card at the door. This is, in my opinion, a bit overzeal-

ous. For a variety of reasons, only about half the qualified technicians in the country choose to belong to the Guild. It would therefore be foolish to turn away someone who came otherwise well recommended.

Here are some specific pointers to help your piano service go smoothly:

Calling a technician. When you call a piano technician for the first time, be prepared to give the following information: who referred you or where you heard about his or her service; whether your piano is a grand or a vertical, and, if a vertical, whether or not it is a spinet; the brand name and age of the piano, if known; when it was last tuned; if the piano has been moved from a radically different climate since the last tuning; and any special service requirements or needed repairs that you are aware of (be as specific as possible). Having this information will make it easier for the technician to bring along the proper tools and supplies and to budget an adequate amount of time for the job. Although binding price estimates can never be given over the phone because of the many variables involved, having information about the condition of the piano may allow the technician to give you in advance some rough idea of the kind of expense that may be involved.

Making an appointment. Technicians vary in their willingness to work at odd hours to suit their customers' schedules. It may be necessary for you to leave a key with a neighbor or make other arrangements to let the technician in. This is very commonly done, and if you have chosen someone reputable to service your piano, you need have no fear about doing this. I usually prefer that my customers be present at the first appointment so we can meet each other, talk about any special problems the piano may have, and agree on what work is to be done. Thereafter, the presence of the customer is not necessary, although, of course, it is often pleasant. If you won't be there, try to leave a number where you can be reached, in case there is a problem.

Unless the technician specifically agrees otherwise, assume that the time agreed upon for the appointment is very approximate. The pianos being serviced before yours may require extra tuning work or unexpected repairs, and traffic conditions are highly variable.

Payment. So as not to be caught short, find out in advance whether the technician will be sending a bill or wants to be paid at the time the work is done, and whether cash or check is preferred.

Remember that if no work can be performed, through no fault of the technician (such as if the piano turns out to be untunable or unrepairable), you will be expected to pay a minimum service fee, usually a little less than the regular tuning fee. Also, if you live outside the technician's regular area, an additional travel charge may apply.

Cancellations. Without a doubt, the most exasperating situation technicians encounter is when a customer fails to be home at the appointed time or cancels the appointment with less than twenty-four hours' notice. Some people can be incredibly rude, or seem not to realize that we do this for a living, not as a hobby. Once I drove forty miles to do a full day of repair, only to find the customer gone, the door locked, and no note of explanation. My phone calls to him were never returned. It's nearly impossible to fill holes in one's schedule at such short notice, so I spent the day twiddling my thumbs, with no income, and paying for gas besides. You should expect to pay the technician's minimum service fee for appointments missed or cancelled at short notice, even if you had to cancel for a good reason.

Working conditions. Noise and poor lighting are technicians' two biggest enemies on the job, the first much more than the second. Remember that when we tune, we are not just listening to the notes being played, but also to very faint vibrations related to those notes' higher harmonics, sounds which you are probably unaware of. Noises that bother us are those with high-pitched vibrations, such as electric fans, vacuum cleaners, garbage disposals, egg beaters, and running water; sounds that capture our attention, such as talking, music, and television; and general clatter, such as setting up chairs in an auditorium or stage set-up before a concert. Your walking around the room also gets in our way, not because of the noise (tiptoeing doesn't help), but rather because sound waves reflecting off a moving object cause irregularities in the vibrations we listen to.

Poor lighting is more of a problem when doing repair work than when tuning. Clubs and bars are the very worst places for both noise and lighting. If you're the manager of such an establishment, do your very best to minimize these distractions when having your piano serviced.

Be sure the technician has enough time to do a thorough job. Teachers should have their pianos tuned on days when their teaching schedule is less crowded or more flexible. Concert producers should give the technician enough time, when possible, to complete the work before the musicians start to set up, not just before the audience arrives.

If you store the Harvard University library, museum, and arboretum on your piano, please clear them off before the technician arrives. You know best where

to put them and how to handle them to avoid breakage, and it only wastes our time to have to deal with them. (You wouldn't believe how much stuff some people pile on their pianos!)

Blind technicians, of whom there are many, should be warned about hazards, such as standing lamps and stage microphones.

Complaints. Complaints should be registered first with the person who can do something about it—this means with the technician, not with friends, relatives, and future technicians. (However, we don't mind an occasional word of praise, which you are welcome to spread everywhere.)

The Long-Range Outlook

As the piano gets on in years, it will need more extensive service, such as replacement of hammer heads, key bushings, dampers, and occasional broken strings or action parts. Read about some of these items in Chapter 5, "Buying A Used Piano." Ultimately, there will come a time when the piano will either have to be completely rebuilt or (sniffle, sniffle) disposed of. Since pianos do not usually abruptly die, it's hard to say just what their lifetime is, but a figure of forty or fifty years is often given. Strings are said to lose their resiliency and thus their potential for good tone after about twenty-five years, though certainly many pianos and their owners have not yet figured this out and are quite happy with their forty-, sixty-, or eighty-year-old strings. Suffice it to say that if you choose your piano carefully, give it good care, and use the services of a competent piano technician, your piano will enjoy a long life and enrich yours as well.

ADDITIONAL RESOURCES

Quiet Keys™
Piano owners often ask for a way to quiet down their pianos so they can play late at night without disturbing others. Many old uprights and some new vertical piano models have a mute ("practice") pedal. One can also spend thousands of dollars to convert one's piano into a MIDI (hybrid acoustic/digital) piano, which can be played silently and listened to through headphones (see "Electronic Player Pianos", Chapter 4). Less complicated and certainly less expensive is Quiet Keys™, the universal mute for vertical pianos, which can be installed into just about any vertical. Until recently, most retrofit mute mechanisms have been difficult to install and even more difficult to remove to allow the piano

to be serviced. Quiet Keys™, however, installs by slipping right over the tuning pins, which are, of course, standardized from piano to piano. Removal and installation take a matter of seconds, and the unit adjusts to fit any vertical piano. A cable connects to an on/off lever placed beneath the keybed. When "on," a piece of acrylic felt is lowered between hammers and strings for nearly eighty percent reduction in sound volume. The cost, including installation by a technician, should be around a hundred dollars, though the pictorial instructions are written for the do-it-yourselfer. Scissors, screwdriver, and wire cutters are the only tools needed. Quiet Keys, Rt. 3 Box 179, Austin, MN 55912; (800) 777-5397; **www.pppkeys.com**.

The Stanwood Precision TouchDesign™ System

Pianists agree that piano actions vary widely in their characteristic feel and in the way they respond. Of course, regulation of the action and tone of the instrument have a significant effect on what the pianist experiences. But there exist more basic underlying elements in piano action design that no amount of regulation or voicing can change. This fact becomes most evident when attempting to correct the feel of a piano with unusually heavy action that "plays like a truck."

Research and study of piano actions carried out by David C. Stanwood has shed a whole new light on the subject of piano action design and has led to the development of Stanwood Precision TouchDesign™ for the grand piano action. Stanwood's system is known to improve even the finest pianos, so if your piano plays like a truck, the transformation is likely to be miraculous.

The Stanwood Precision TouchDesign™ system is installed in the piano by modifying the piano's action parts. Each touch design is a special recipe that specifies for each note the exact proportions of hammer weight, hammer leverage, key balancing weight, and frictional resistance. Once calibrated to these rigid specifications, the piano takes on the expected characteristic feel, with an extremely consistent response from note to note. Touch designs are chosen based on quantitative computer analysis of your action combined with your own qualitative assessment. A Precision TouchDesign is then designed to fit your specific need.

Stanwood says that the advantages of his touch designs include improved dynamic range, control, and repetition for "best possible" performance pianos; reducing, or in some cases stopping, repetitive stress injury due to inordinate physical stress; increasing the value of the piano; facilitating the purchase and sale of pianos; and generally improving pianistic ability and expression. Stanwood is currently licensing and training technicians worldwide to install his touch designs, which have received strong endorsements from concert artists and technicians. Stanwood Piano Innovations, P.O. Box 1499, West Tisbury, MA 02575; (508) 693-1583; **www.stanwoodpiano.com**.

Magnetic Balanced Action

The Magnetic Balanced Action, invented by Evert Snel and Hans Velo from the Netherlands, is a system that uses magnets, instead of key leads, to create the keyboard's touchweight. A pair of attracting magnets is active in front of the fulcrum and a pair of repelling magnets in back. The gap between the magnets in each pair, and therefore the attracting or repelling force, can be set by means of a screw adjustment in each key. In addition, there are several screws that can be used to make global adjustments for whole sections of the keyboard at once.

When the Magnetic Balanced Action is installed in a piano, any pianist can adjust the touchweight to his or her personal preference in a matter of seconds. Also, when maintenance is performed that alters the touchweight, such as filing or replacing hammers, the optimal touchweight can be easily restored. Besides the ability to adjust the touchweight, however, are the advantages that come from the reduced inertia due to the lack of key leads: better control for soft playing, faster return of the key, and less strain on the pianist's hands.

The only manufacturer currently making the Magnetic Balanced Action available as an option in new pianos is Fazioli. However, the Fazioli distributor in the United States is coordinating efforts to make the system available as a retrofit for existing pianos. The approximate installed price is $8,500. International Brokers, Inc., 5827A Crystal Hill Rd., N. Little Rock, Arkansas 72118; (501) 753-8616; **piano@ipa.net**, **www.internationalbrokersinc.com**.

Reduced-Size Keyboard For Small Hands

Pianists with small hands can experience great difficulty in playing the standard piano repertoire, and sometimes suffer injury from the physical stress involved. There is now a solution to their problem. A $7/8$-size keyboard—one in which the width of each key, and therefore the width of the entire keyboard, is $7/8$ that of a standard keyboard—is being offered by American manufacturer David Steinbuhler. No piano manufacturer yet has this as a factory-supplied option in new pianos, but the "D.S. Standard" keyboard (as it is called) can be retrofitted into existing pianos. Steinbuhler is also exploring the possibility of manufacturing other sizes of keyboard and says he can custom-make keyboards to fit any hand. He maintains a showroom with facilities for overnight visitors for pianists who would like to try out instruments outfitted with various sizes of keyboard.

To have a grand piano retrofitted with the new keyboard, the old keyframe, keyboard, and action are shipped to Steinbuhler's shop, where the old keyframe's size is precisely duplicated, and the new keyframe is fitted with the new keyboard. The action, new keyframe, and new keyboard are returned to the customer, where a local technician slides them back into the piano and regulates everything. The cost of having a 7/8-size keyboard retrofitted into a grand piano is approximately $7,800, and so is most appropriate for serious pianists with high-quality instruments. Steinbuhler and Co., 11810 North Perry Rd., Titusville, PA 16354; (814) 827-0296; **www.dskeyboards.com**.

Mail-Order Sources For Piano Accessories

There are several good mail-order catalogs that sell accessories such as piano benches and bench cushions, piano lamps, music stands, sheet music cabinets, metronomes, soundboard cleaning tools, caster cups, piano covers, piano polishes, piano trucks and dollies, books, videos, and software. Both of the companies listed below are owned and operated by experienced piano technicians.

Perfectly Grand Piano Accessories
P.O. Box 444
Highland Mills, NY 10930
(800) 792-4457
www.perfectlygrand.com

Three Rivers Music Products
Grand Workshoppe Piano Co.
1720 Burrstone Rd.
New Hartford, NY 13413
(800) 331-2438
www.threeriversmusic.com

Two internet-only sources for piano accessories are **www.pianoworld.com** and **www.pianomart.com**.

Piano & Keyboard Magazine

There are several references in this book to the excellent magazine *Piano & Keyboard*. To subscribe, contact:

Piano & Keyboard
P.O. Box 2626
San Anselmo, California 94979-2626
(415) 458-8672
Piano@sparrowhawkpress.com
www.pianoandkeyboard.com

Glossary/Index

See also Index to Trade Names, pages 90–91.

See also Index to Trade Names, pages 90–91.

Keys, 4, 6, 9–11, 47–51. *Wooden levers, covered with plastic, wood, or ivory at their playing ends, that the player presses to activate the action parts and hammers.*
    and accelerated action, 145
    angle of, 48–49
    black (sharps), 48, 50, 51
    cleaning, 228
    covering on. *See* Keytops
    grain of wood in, 49–50
    inspection of, in used piano, 194, 195
    length of, 45, 47–48
    quality of, 50
    recovering, 195
    regulation of, 50, 198, 199
    sluggish or sticking, 48–50, 194
    for small hands, 233–234
    warped, 50
    weighting of, 49–50, 233
    white (naturals), 48, 51
    width of, 233–234
Keyslip, 8. *The decorative wooden strip that runs the width of the piano, right in front of the keys.*
    removing, 187–188
Key stop rail, 221. *A thin wooden strip, above the keys and behind the fallboard in a grand piano, to prevent the keys from falling off the key frame when the piano is put on its side for moving.*
Keytops. *The plastic, ivory, or wooden coverings on the playing surfaces of the keys.*
    cleaning, 228
    length of, 48
    material used for, 51
    missing or broken, inspection of, in a used piano, 195
Kilns, wood drying, 23
Knuckle, 9–11. *A small cylinder of wood, cloth, and leather attached to a grand hammer shank, against which the jack pushes.*
Korean pianos, 60, 65, 85–86, 89–90

Lacquer finish, 25, 26, 28
Laminated soundboard, 40, 57. *A soundboard made of three layers of wood glued together with grain running at right angles, like plywood.*
Lamps, piano, 234
Langer action, 45. *A Schwander-type action made by Langer, a British company. See also* Schwander *and* Herrburger Brooks
Leg plates, 192. *Metal plates used to fasten grand piano legs to the bottom of the piano.*
Legs, piano, 8
    breakage of, in moving, 216
    inspection of, on used piano, for cracks, 192
    styles of, in vertical piano, 23, 25–26, 28
Letoff, 9–10, 199. *Disengagement of the force pushing on the hammer, just before the hammer strikes the strings. Also known as escapement.*
Letoff button, 9–10. *An action part that causes the jack to escape from under the hammer assembly at letoff. See* Letoff.
Licensing, of movers, 217, 218
Lid, 8. *The cabinet part that covers the top of the piano.*
    grand piano, 26; inspection of, on used piano, 192; opening, 185–186; particle board in, 21; removal of, for moving, 214–215; and tonal quality, 43
    grand-style vertical, 25–26, 188
    vertical piano, opening, 188
Lid hinges, 8
    loose or missing, 185–186, 192
    removal of, for moving, 214–215
Lid prop. *See* Propstick
Lifetime of piano, 174, 232
Liner, soundboard, 40–41. *A simple wooden frame attached to the front of a vertical piano back, to which the soundboard is glued.*
Locks, for school pianos, 75
Loop stringing, 7. *A system of stringing, found on most pianos, in which a single length of wire serves as two strings.*
Loss leader, 18, 65–66. *See also* Promotional pianos

Lost motion, 199, 229. *Slack in the action or trap work, resulting in part of the motion of keys or pedals being wasted in taking up this slack.*
Lost motion compensator, 198. *A mechanism in some old uprights that compensated for the lost motion created when the soft pedal was used. See also* Lost motion
Lower panel, 8. *The large rectangular cabinet part on a vertical piano located above the pedals, near the player's legs.*
    removing, 189
Lumber, 22–24. *Wood that has been cut into boards. See also* Wood; Plain-sawn lumber; Quarter-sawn lumber
Lumber-banding, 21–22. *The framing of a particle-board panel with solid lumber or plywood to increase its strength and to camouflage it.*
Lyre, 8. *The grand piano part that descends from the case bottom and holds the pedals.*
    attachment of, 27
    inspection of, in used piano, 27, 197–198
Lyre braces, 8, 27, 198, 221. *Diagonal braces of wood or metal that help prevent the pedal lyre from being pushed backward under the pressure of the feet on the pedals.*

Magnetic Balanced Action, 233. *A system that uses magnets, instead of key leads, to create the keyboard touch weight, which can be adjusted by the pianist.*
Magnuson-Moss Warranty Act, 58. *A law that set federal standards for warranties on consumer purchases.*
Mahogany
    finish, 25
    in grand piano rims, 23
    in soundboards, 40
Mail-order sources for piano accessories, 234
Maintenance. *See also* Tuning; Regulating; Voicing; Servicing
    cost of, 13
    of school and institutional pianos, 13, 74–75
Maple
    in action parts, 47
    in Steinway action rails, 145
    in grand piano rims, 23
    in hammer shanks, 53
    in pin blocks, 32
Marketing, of new pianos, 17–19
Mason & Hamlin
    rebuilt and reconditioned, 206–209
    removal of keyslip from, 188
    reproducers installed in, 180
    tension resonator, 123–124
    used, 175, 206–209
Materials, synthetic versus traditional, 19
MDF. *See* Medium density fiberboard
Medium-density fiberboard, 22. *A high-quality type of particle board frequently used in piano cabinets. See also* Particle board
Merchandising, of new pianos, 64–68
MIDI (Musical Instrument Digital Interface), 160. *An electronics standard that allows instruments made by different manufacturers to be compatible with each other and with computers and acoustic instruments equipped with it.*
Mirrors, restyling a piano with, 185
Modern Piano Moving, 219. *Interstate mover of pianos for consumers.*
Moisture. *See* Humidity
Moisture barrier, 33
Molded flanges, 145. *Steinway action flanges molded in a special shape that matches the shape of their action rails.*
Molding, hammer. *See* Hammer molding
Money. *See also* Prices; Cost
    as purchase consideration, 13
    saving, on new piano, 68–70
Moth damage and mothproofing, 194, 221, 228
Movers, licensing and insurance required for, 217, 218
Moving
    damage to pianos in, 218, 220
    effect on pianos of, 192, 221
    industry, deregulation of, 217, 218
    international, 219–220

See also Index to Trade Names, pages 90–91.

See also Index to Trade Names, pages 90–91.

Scale design, 33–38, 43, 208. *The entire tonal design of a piano, including technical specifications for all tone-related parts; sometimes refers only to the stringing scale. See also* Stringing scale

Schafer Brothers Piano Movers, 219. *An interstate mover of pianos for consumers.*

School and institutional pianos
   locks and casters for, 75
   maintenance of, 13, 74
   new, 74–75
   room acoustics for, 229–230
   sales to the public of, 67–68
   used, 183
   warranty on, 58, 75

School and institutional style. *See* Institutional style

Schwander or Schwander-type action, 46. *One of the action designs made by the English company Langer, or an action of a similar design. In a vertical, an action with hammer return springs individually attached to the hammer butts.*

Screws, action flange, tightening of, 196–197, 229

Screws, cabinet, removing, 186

Screwstringer, 175. *A type of piano made by Mason & Hamlin early in this century that had an unusual tuning mechanism, using machine screws instead of tuning pins.*

Seasoning, of wood, 23, 176

"Seconds," 66. *Pianos with slight cosmetic defects being sold at a discount.*

Selling a piano, 203

Serial number
   checking, of new piano, 63
   locating, 200
   looking up in *Pierce Piano Atlas*, 178, 200
   of Steinways, 210–213

Serviceability, 57
   effect of cabinet design on, 26
   of spinet, 45

Service fee, minimum, 231–232

Servicing. *See also* Tuning; Regulating; Voicing
   by dealer in store, 46, 56–57, 62–64, 68, 70–71, 73
   of new piano after purchase, 59–60, 63, 70–71, 73–74, 224, 228–229
   pointers for successful, 231–232
   of school and institutional pianos, 13, 74
   of Steinways, 207–209

Sharps, 48, 50, 51. *The black keys.*

Shims, in soundboard, 182, 192–193, 207. *Narrow pieces of spruce fitted and glued into soundboard cracks when a soundboard is repaired, mostly for aesthetic reasons.*

Shipping. *See* Moving

Shoe, 50. *A piece of hardwood on the bottom of a high-quality key to protect the balance hole from wear and to strengthen the key.*

Shopping for a new piano, 60–75

Sidebearing, 39, 191. *The side pressure of the strings against the bridge pins, necessary for good tonal transmission .*

Size, of piano, 12–15
   and key length, 48
   and moving, 216
   and tonal quality, 14, 33–34, 43

Soft pedal, 54–55, 198. *Left-hand pedal on a vertical piano; moves the hammers closer to the strings. The reduced striking distance results in a softer sound.*

Softwood. *A botanical term referring to wood from conifer trees.*
   in grand piano rims, 29–30

Sostenuto pedal, 54–55, 197–198. *The middle pedal on most grand, and a few vertical, pianos; sustains only those notes being played at the moment the pedal is pressed.*

Sound. *See also* Room acoustics, Tonal quality
   reflection and absorption of, 229–230.
   reducing volume of, 160, 232–233

Soundboard, 3, 6. *A large, thin wooden diaphragm that changes the strings' vibrating energy into sounds that we can hear.*
   cleaning, 228
   construction of, 39–41
   cracked, 40, 192–193
   crown, 39–41, 192–193

   effect of humidity on, 40, 222–223
   inspection of, in used piano, 192–193
   laminated, 40, 57
   liner, 41
   replacing, 181, 182, 207
   ribs, 6, 40–41, 182, 192–193
   shims in, 182, 192–193, 207
   spruce used in, 23, 39–40
   and tonal quality, 39–41, 192–193
   and tuning stability, 222–223
   warranty on, 40, 57

Space, floor, 12–13, 14, 15

Speaking length, 6, 7, 36–38. *The part of each string that actually vibrates; doesn't include the waste ends, usually muted, near the tuning pin and near the hitch pin.*

Spine, 8. *The long, straight side (left side as seen from the keyboard) of a grand piano.*

Spinet. *A small vertical piano, usually 36 to 39 inches tall, with an indirect-blow action. See also* Vertical piano
   action, 14–15, 44–45
   broken plastic elbows in, 194
   height of, 14
   keys in, 45, 48
   legs, 26
   reasons not to buy, 15, 45

Splicing, of string, 190–191. *Repairing a broken bass string by attaching a length of new wire to the remains of the old when the break occurs near the tuning pin.*

Spoon, 9. *A small metal part of a vertical piano action, attached to the wippen, that causes a damper to lift off the strings when a key is pressed.*

Spruce
   in Bösendorfer rim, 30, 87
   in keys, 50
   in soundboards, 23, 39–40
   in structural parts, 23, 29–30

Square pianos, 173, 210. *Rectangular pianos, also called square grands, popular during the nineteenth century.*

Stanwood Precision TouchDesign™, 49, 233. *A system for customizing grand piano touch.*

Steinert, 175

Steinway pianos
   accelerated action in, 145
   action parts for, 207–208
   bridges in, 39
   Hamburg, 146, 211, 212
   hammers in, 52, 208
   keyslip removal on, 187–188
   list of models, of 1853 to present, 210–213
   pinblock in, 32, 207
   prices of used, 13, 203, 204–205
   rebuilt and reconditioned, 206–209
   reproducing mechanism installed in, 180, 212–213
   serial numbers and dates of manufacture of, 200, 210–213
   servicing by technicians of, 207–209
   Teflon bushings in, 208–209
   tonal quality of, 43
   used, 175, 203, 204–205, 206–213
   verdigris in, 209
   warranty on, 58

Stencil pianos, 92. *Pianos bearing a name of a dealer or distributor, or a name owned by one, rather than the name of a manufacturer. Also known as "private-label brands" or "house brands."*

Step-up feature, 18. *A technical feature whose purpose is to get the consumer to buy a higher-priced piano.*

Sticker, 9, 45. *An action part in a full-size upright that connects the keys to the rest of the action.*

Storage of pianos, 220–221

Straight side, 8. *The left side of a grand piano, as seen from the keyboard. Also known as the "spine."*

Strike-point adjuster, 41. *A mechanism in most grand pianos that adjusts the position of the action in relation to the strings, and thus the strike point of the hammers on the strings.*

See also Index to Trade Names, pages 90–91.

See also Index to Trade Names, pages 90–91.

See also Index to Trade Names, pages 90–91.